THE SOURCE BOOK OF THE R·A·F

THE
SOURCE
BOOK
OF THE
R·A·F

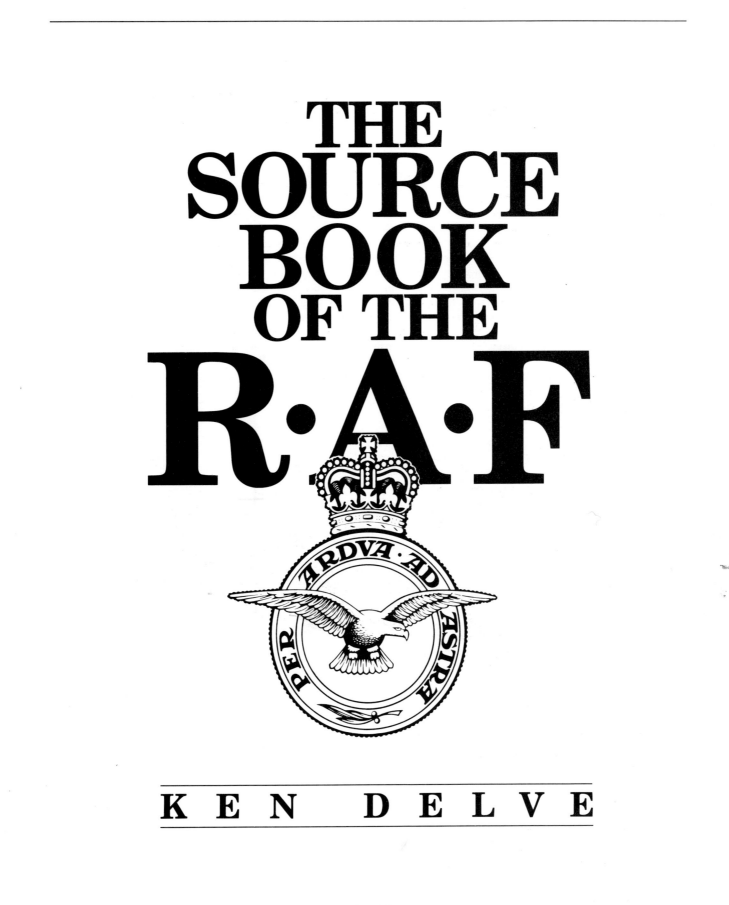

KEN DELVE

Airlife

England

ACKNOWLEDGEMENTS

THIS BOOK HAS been in preparation for almost 20 years and during that time countless individuals have provided information and photographs, all of which has proved invaluable in building up a picture of the RAF since April 1918. I owe you all a debt of thanks and apologize for not being able to list all your names here.

The majority of the primary research has been conducted at the Air Historical Branch, London and to the staff of that organisation I am most grateful for hours of patient advice and assistance. In these days of financial stringency the AHB has more than once been looked at as a cost-saving measure — it has survived and continues its work of both storing and recording RAF history.

On a more individual basis, thanks to Peter Jacobs for providing the basis of the section of Honours and Awards and to Peter Green for the enormous amount of help with photographs and proof-reading. Finally, to Andrew and Benjamin for helping with the research, and Mike for the maps.

358.4/DEL

Copyright © 1994 by Ken Delve

First published in the UK in 1994
by Airlife Publishing Ltd

British Library Cataloguing in Publication Data
A catalogue record for this book
is available from the British Library

ISBN 1 85310 451 5

Printed by Livesey Ltd., Shrewsbury.

Airlife Publishing Ltd.

101 Longden Road, Shrewsbury SY3 9EB, England

CONTENTS

INTRODUCTION

"THE DAY may not be far off when aerial operations with their devastation of enemy lands and destruction of industrial and populous centres on a vast scale may become the principle operations of war" — General Smuts, 1917.

"The outstanding lesson of the late war [World War Two] was that air superiority is the pre-requisite to all war-winning operations, whether at sea, on land or in the air. Air warfare cannot be separated into little packets, it knows no boundaries on land or sea .. it is a unity and demands unity of command." — Lord Tedder, 1947.

"The only real security upon which sound military principles will rely is that you should be master of your own air; an air force must keep its doctrines ahead of its equipment and its vision into the future" — RAF Doctrine.

To all intents and purposes, air power has been in existence for a mere eight decades; in that short period it has come to represent the major influence on the outcome of virtually all armed conflict. This is not, of course, to claim that air power, despite its dominance, is an independent 'war winner'; that claim, made by many in the aftermath of the Gulf War, is way off the mark. It is, however, valid to claim a pre-eminent position for air power within the combined military operations of MOST scenarios. The Royal Air Force, and its Royal Flying Corps predecessor, has been at the forefront of air power development — despite the frequent limitations imposed by political constraints.

April 1st, 1993 saw the RAF celebrate its 75th anniversary, a most significant date and one deserving of recognition. With the 1917 decision to form an independent third service the air arm was given the freedom to develop its own doctrine without being tied to the requirements of either the Army or the Navy. The part played by the RFC in developing the basic precepts and concepts of air power, often in the face of bitter experience, was of course vital and provided a sound platform upon which the RAF could build.

This book is not intended as a history of the Royal Air Force from 1918 to 1993, there will no doubt be many other titles claiming that honour. It is, however, a reference book of RAF history, bringing together, for the first time, a wealth of facts and figures — which in themselves are the material from which RAF history is constructed. As a reference book it is largely constructed from primary sources, although much secondary, i.e published, material has also been used and is duly credited in each section. To cover every aspect of the RAF in detail would be impossible under the constraints of commercial publishing. Large slices of RAF history have been left out; for example, there are few references to the RAF Regiment or the Airfield Contruction Branch, the latter having played a vital part in World War Two, this does not imply that they are seen as unimportant but simply that space precludes a great deal that the author would otherwise have hoped to include. There are so many fascinating aspects to RAF history, all of which deserve to be recorded!

It became apparent during the research that many published works have simply repeated previous errors, errors that have been repeated so many times that they are now accepted as 'fact'! An introduction to each section gives details of the type of source material used, areas of error, and if required, a 'user friendly' guide of how to make best use of that particular section. There are, inevitably, gaps in the reference material, as there are inevitable errors, and I would be delighted to hear from anyone who can help correct these failings — aviation history is very much an on-going subject!

A NOTE ON SOURCES:
One of the primary research tools for any element of RAF history is the Operational Record Book (Form 540/541). This monthly return is compiled by every unit and it is the ONLY document more or less guaranteed to survive into the historical record (a copy is always sent to the Air Historical Branch). There are, unfortunately, a number of problems with the ORB! Firstly, it does not always survive — squadrons based overseas during World War Two often have gaps in their ORBs, in the case of units in the Far East virtually all records and documents fell into the hands of the Japanese in 1942. Invariably the ORB was not compiled by a historian but rather by a 'volunteer' on the unit who was, usually, inclined to write no more than the bare minumum — hence the quality of the document (to the researcher) varies with the quality of its compilation. As a monthly return it refered to the previous month's activities and was often compiled in a hurry (in a tent in the desert as Rommels forces were advancing once more?) using whatever information was to hand. It was, for obvious reasons, not always the most important item on the agenda! Typing errors abound — was that meant to be LW or LV for the aircraft serial? All of these problems and a host of others, face the unwary user of the ORB. Nevertheless, it remains a primary source of contemporary information and is invaluable if treated with a certain circumspection. Loose documents and files form the next major batch of source material. The former are excellent value in that many cover a specific topic in the form of an expert report, an example being the AHB narratives written just after World War Two and compiled using primary sources, some of which no longer exist. The files tend to be hard going, a great deal to sift through before the gem of information appears. A wealth of other weekly/monthly/annual official documents provides great detail on every aspect of RAF life and organisation, although often in a

confusing and contradictory manner, where a long and detailed diatribe on a particular topic, say, aircraft camouflage, may be cancelled a few months later by a curt one-line entry.

These few comments are not intended as a user guide to primary sources, that in itself would require a lengthy exposé, but rather an introduction to some of the problems which occur and which can lead to errors. Any historian who claims his material is without error should think again.

Here's to the next 75 years of RAF history.

Ken Delve
October 1993   RAF Marham

CHRONOLOGY OF
ROYAL AIR FORCE HISTORY

THE AIM OF this chronology is to provide an easy to use guide to the major events/incidents which involved the Royal Air Force between April 1918 and 1993 (delivery of this book to the printers!). It has, of course, been essential to keep the entries selective (and short). Not all Command and Group changes are included, for details of these see the appropriate sections. Date variation for such events is usually caused by the disbandment taking effect at midnight and the reforming/renaming taking effect the following day.

Many of the events are also covered in other parts of this book. A wide range of primary sources provides material for the chronology, amongst the most useful are:

1. Air Ministry Orders.
2. Air Ministry Confidential Orders.
3. Defence Council Instructions.
4. RAF List.
5. RAF Confidential List.
6. Secret Organisational Memoranda.
7. AHB narratives.
8. Bomber/Coastal Command Quarterly Reviews.
9. Files, various.
10. Operational Record Books.
11. Assorted loose memoranda.
12. RAF News.

As with so much else of RAF history, there are many areas of confusion over dates — a day here, a month there — it is often very tricky to determine the true date for an event. Over the years many incorrect dates have appeared and by repetition have joined the historical record as 'fact'. There will no doubt be errors in the material contained here, although where possible primary sources have been used, any remaining areas of confusion are highlighted at the relevant entry.

1918:

1 Apr	Formation of the Royal Air Force and WRAF. Portsmouth Group, RNAS becomes No 10 Group.
9-29 Apr	Battle of the Lys, heavy air support employed.
14 Apr	Sir Hugh Trenchard resigns as CAS, replaced by Maj-Gen Sir Frederick Sykes.
8 May	Nomenclature change for Home Commands: No 1 Area renamed South-Eastern Area No 2 Area renamed South-Western Area No 3 Area renamed Midland Area No 4 Area renamed North-Eastern Area No 5 Area renamed North-Western Area

The members of the WRAF played a crucial role in two World Wars.

31 May	UC.49 sunk first definite sinking involving an aircraft.
3 Jun	Institution of air awards DFC, DFM, AFC, AFM.

5 Jun	Formation of the Independent Force, the first air force organisation not subordinate to Army or Navy requirements.
Jun	RAF operations commence in Russia (Murmansk and Archangel).
Jun	RAF Nursing Service formed.
Jun	Entry to service of DH.9A, No 110 Sqn.
Aug	RAF Ireland renamed No 11 (Irish) Group.
4 Aug	Last airship raid on Britain.
8 Aug	VC to Capt F West/8 Sqn (gazette: 8.11.18) Start of Battle of Amiens.
16 Aug	First massed low level attack by RAF, 65 aircraft attack Haubourdin aerodrome.
21 Aug	Start of Second Battle of the Somme.
Aug	British forces occupy Archangel during anti-Bolshevik ops.
21 Sep	Aircraft destroy Turkish forces at Wadi el Far'a, first decisive 'solo' victory for air power.
30 Sep	Hindenburg Line breached, using heavy air support.
3 Oct	RAF drop supplies to French and Belgian troops First major use of air supply.
8 Oct	VC to Capt B Proctor/84 Sqn. (gazette: 30.11.18)
26 Oct	Inter-Allied Independent Air Force now under command of Major-General Sir Hugh Trenchard.
27 Oct	VC to Major W Barker/201 Sqn. (gazette: 30.11.18)
11 Nov	Armistice, end of WWI. RAF strength of 22 647 aircraft.
Dec	Ops in S.Russia in support of 'White' Russians (end Mar 20).
12 Dec	Chaplain Branch established.
13-30 Dec	First flight England to India (Major A.S.C. MacLaren in HP V/1500).

1919:

1 Jan	North-Eastern area absorbed into North-Western Area.
11 Jan	Major-General Sir Hugh Trenchard returns as CAS.
Jan	Creation by Air Ministry of Department of Civil Aviation.
Mar	Commence RAF air-mail service from Hendon to Army of Occupation in Germany. (service terminated Aug 1919.)
Mar	Titles Secretary of State for Air and Under-Secretary of State for Air introduced.
May	Third Afghan War (end 8 Aug).
May	Revolt of Sheik Mahmud, Mesopotamia.
Jun	North-Western Area renamed Northern Area.
14-15 Jun	First non-stop air crossing of Atlantic (Capt J Alcock and Lt A Whitten Brown).
28 Jun	Versailles Peace Treaty signed.
2-6 Jul	First Atlantic Crossing by airship (R-34), S/L G H Scott.
18 Jul	VC to Major E Mannock/85 Sqn (gazette: 18.7.19)
Jul	Entry to service of Vimy, No 58 Sqn.
27 Aug	New RAF rank and appointment titles adopted.
15 Sep	Formation of Coastal Area.
20 Sep	South-Eastern Area renamed Southern Area. South-Western Area becomes No 7 Group within Southern Area.
18 Oct	Midland Area absorbed into Northern Area.
23 Oct	Foundation of RAF Benevolent Fund.

11 Nov	'Z' Force arrives Berbera for ops against Mad Mullah.
11 Dec	Presentation to Parliament of peace-time plan for RAF organisation.

1920:

Jan	RAF Halton to Command status.
Jan	RAF operations against 'Mad Mullah' in Somaliland.
5 Feb	RAF College Cranwell open, Command status.
1 Apr	Southern and Northern Areas combine to form Inland Area.
	RAF Central Band formed. WRAF disbanded.
26 Apr	Announcement of Apprentice Scheme.
5 Jul	First RAF Tournament at Hendon.

Close formation flying for air displays was hazardous – as proved by this D.H.9A.

1921:

Mar	Cairo Conference agreed 'air control policy' to give RAF overall control of Mesopotamia.
24 Mar	RAF Ensign instituted.
23 Jun	Start of weekly RAF air-mail service Cairo to Baghdad.(continued until 1927 when taken over by Imperial Airways.)
24 Aug	Airship R-38 broke up over Hull.

1922:

1 Feb	RAF Iraq formed, under command of AVM Sir John Salmond. Palestine Command formed.
17 Feb	RAF Ireland reformed.
1 Apr	RAF Staff College Andover open.
1 Oct	RAF assumes control in Iraq, Iraq Command formed.
Oct	Ops by Constantinople Wing commence (end Aug 1923).

1923:

—	RAF Ireland disbanded.
9 Feb	Reserve of Air Officers formed.
Feb	Ops against Sheik Mahmud, Mesopotamia (end 1931).
May	Air Minister given seat in Cabinet.
1 Apr	Re-organisation of squadrons serving with FAA on a Flight basis for HMS Argus, Hermes, Eagle, Illustrious. (AO/1526)
Jun	RAF Nursing Service renamed Princess Mary's RAF Nursing Service.

20 Jun	Interim report of Salisbury Committee (on National and Imperial Defence), proposes Home Defence force of 52 Squadrons.

1924:

3 Jan	RAF Short Service Commission Scheme 400 officers for flying duty.
20 Mar	Aeroplane and Armament Experimental Establishment formed at Martlesham.
27 Mar	Role to be included in Sqn title.
1 Apr	Palestine Command formed.
	Marine Aircraft Experimental Establishment formed at Felixstowe.
	Fleet Air Arm formed.
	Formation of Imperial Airways to develop air transport.
Jul-Oct	'Pink's War', Waziristan, India.
Aug	Ops against Wahabi tribesmen, Palestine.
16 Oct	Locarno Pact signed by Britain, Belgium, France, Germany and Italy.
1 Dec	Egypt Group disbanded.

1925:

1 Jan	Formation of ADGB, comprising Bombing Area, Fighting Area, Special Reserve, Auxiliary Air Force.
May	Entry to service of Woodcock, 3 Sqn.
15 Jul	Basrah Group disbanded.
12 Sep	First Auxiliary Air Force Sqn formed No 602 (City of Glasgow), at Renfrew.
1 Oct	Cambridge University Air Squadron formed the first such unit.
14 Oct	Two Auxiliary Air Force units formed 600 (City of London) and 601 (County of London).
22 Oct	No 1 Apprentice Wing formed at Halton.
29 Oct	Observer Corps formed.
Oct	First independent use of air action Waziristan NWFP, India.

1926:

1 Mar	Cairo to Cape flight by four Fairey IIIDs, returned 27 May.

1927:

1 Jan	Lord Trenchard as first Marshal of the Royal Air Force.
	Imperial Defence College opened.
Mar	Siskin IIIA enters service, first all-metal fighter.
Apr	RAF operations in China, Shanghai Defence Force.
26 Sep	Victory in Schneider Trophy at Venice by Supermarine S.5 (F/L S N Webster, 281.49 mph).
17 Oct	Far East flight by four Southamptons departs Plymouth for cruise to Egypt, India, Australia, Japan, to Singapore (arrive 10 Dec 1928.)
Oct	Entry to service of Atlas, 26 Sqn First purpose-designed Army Co-operation aircraft.

1928:

Feb	Aden Command formed to take control of Aden area.
21 Feb	Formation of Trans-Jordan and Palestine Group.
Apr	High Speed Flight formed at Felixstowe.
23 Dec	Start air evacuation of British Legation at Kabul (end 25 Feb 1929).

1929:

1 Jan	Control of Observer Corps transfered to RAF. Coastal Recce Flights given squadron status and renumbered.
Apr	Non-stop flight Cranwell to Karachi 4130 miles in 50 hours 48 minutes by Fairey Long-Range monoplane (S/L A G Jones-Williams and F/L N H Jenkins).
Sep	Victory in Schneider Trophy by RAF High-Speed Flight SupermarineS.6 (F/O H R D Waghorn 328.63 mph).

1930:

1 Jan	Far East Command formed.
5 Oct	Airship R101 crashed near Beauvais, amongst dead is Lord Thomson, the Air Minister.

1931:

13 Sep	RAF High-Speed Flight wins Schneider Trophy outright with Supermarine S.6B (340.08 mph by F/L J N Boothman.)
Dec	Commence air survey of British Somaliland (ended Mar 1933), to cover 3000 square miles.

1932:

2 Feb	Geneva Disarmament Conference.
25 Apr	Use of airborne loudspeakers (later called 'Skyshouting'), plus leaflet dropping in Iraq.
Nov	Entry to service of Vildebeest, 100 Sqn.

1933:

1 Jan	Rank of Sgt Major abolished in RAF and replaced by Warrant Officer.
Apr	Introduction of squadron numbering into FAA to replace Flights.
3 Apr	First flight over Mt Everest (Westland Wallace).
14 Oct	Germany leaves Disarmament Conference and League of Nations.

1934:

Mar	Prime Minister (Baldwin) seeks Disarmament Conference, but at same time states that if this failed then Britain would expand its air force to that of its 'rivals' (the 'One Power Standard').
24 May	First Empire Air Days RAF stations open to the public.
Jul	Expansion Programme announced for increase to 75 squadrons in Home Defence.
Dec	Rota autogiro to School of Army Co-operation at Old Sarum, first rotary-wing aircraft.

1935:

Feb	Entry to service of Vincent, 8 Sqn.
	Entry to service of Valentia, 216 Sqn.
9 Mar	Germany announces formation of an air force.
Apr	Entry to service of Singapore III, 230 Sqn.
May	Entry to service of Gauntlet, 19 Sqn.
	Entry to service of Scapa, 202 Sqn.
31 May	Quetta earthquake, RAF base destroyed.
6 Jul	Royal Review by King George V at Mildenhall and Duxford.
Oct	Italian invasion of Abyssinia.
18 Nov	Reinforcements sent to Middle East because of Italian invasion of Abyssinia.
Dec	Entry to service of Hind, 21 Sqn.

1936:

6 Mar	Entry to service of Anson, 48 Sqn first operational monoplane.
7 Mar	German forces re-occupy Rhineland.
1 May	Coastal Area renamed Coastal Command. Inland Area renamed Training Command. First RAF unit badges approved by the King. Formation of No 1 Gp.
13 Jul	ADGB disbanded.
14 Jul	Formation of Bomber Command. Formation of Fighter Command. Formation of Coastal Command. Formation of Training Command.
18 Jul	Start of Spanish Civil War.
30 Jul	Formation of RAF Volunteer Reserve.
Aug	HSL100, the first such launch, in service at Manston.
Oct	Entry to service of London, 204 Sqn.
Nov	Balloon Barrage Scheme announced.

Singapore III of 209 Squadron, 1937.

1937:

Jan	Entry to service of Blenheim, 114 Sqn.
Jan	Entry to service of Gladiator last bi-plane fighter.
1 Mar	Formation of Air Registration Board.
12 Apr	Whittle ground tests his first gas-turbine engine (U-type).
30 Jul	Government announce that FAA to revert to Admiralty control.
Sep	Deployment to Arzeu on anti-submarine patrol.
Nov	Entry to service of Oxford, CFS.
Dec	Entry to service of Hurricane, 111 Sqn first eight-gun fighter.

1938:

30 Jan	AM announce end of RAF Display at Hendon, airfield too small for the latest types of aircraft.
11 Mar	German forces move into Austria.
31 Mar	Formation of Maintenance Command.
20 Apr	RAF Purchasing Mission to USA.
21 Apr	Shadow aircraft factory scheme announced.
May	Entry to service of Lysander, 16 Sqn.
Jun	Entry to service of Spitfire, 19 Sqn.
9 Jun	First major order for American aircraft200 Hudson and 200 Harvard.
7-8 Jul	Wellesleys of LRDF return flight to Persian Gulf, 4300 miles in 32 hours.
23 Jul	Formation of Civil Air Guard.
Sep	Munich Crisis, Chamberlain announces "Peace in our Time."
Oct	Entry to service of Hampden, 49 Sqn.
1 Nov	Formation of Balloon Command.

1939:

17 Jan	Formation of RAF Reserve.
Jan	Entry to service of Wellington, 9 Sqn.
	Entry to service of Harvard, 12 FTS.
1 Feb	Formation of Reserve Command.
20 Apr	Creation of Ministry of Supply.
20 May	Last Empire Air Days.
May	Entry to service of Hudson, 224 Sqn.
24 May	FAA to Admiralty control.
26 Jun	Announcement that RAF would impress civil aircraft for transport duties.
28 Jun	WAAF formed, Miss J Trefusis Forbes as first Senior Controller.
4 Aug	Imperial Airways and British Airways amalgamate.
24 Aug	General mobilisation of RAF.
25 Aug	Russo-German non-aggression Pact signed in Moscow.
	Anglo-Polish Treaty of Alliance signed.
1 Sep	RAF Reserve and VR called to permanent service, Auxiliary Air Force embodied into RAF. German forces invade Poland. Formation of ATA under Gerard d'Erlanger.
2 Sep	Squadrons of AASF to France.
3 Sep	Declaration of war with Germany. 139 Sqn Blenheim recce of Schillig Roads, the first operational sortie. 51 and 58 Sqn Whitleys drop leaflets over Germany.
4 Sep	Attacks on shipping in Schillig Roads and Kiel Canal. First RAF attack on enemy aircraft, 224 Sqn Hudson against a Do.18 over North Sea.
5 Sep	First attack on a U-boat (Anson of No 500 Squadron). South Africa enters the war.
6 Sep	First WAAF Substitution officers employed on Signals duties. First enemy aircraft sorties over England.

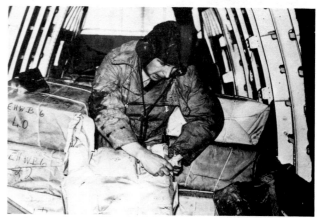

Leaflet-dropping over Germany was a major task in the early months of the war.

9 Sep	Hurricanes of Air Component and AASF to France.
10 Sep	Canada declares war on Germany.
15 Sep	HQ Air Component operational in France.
21 Sep	Formation of No 43 Gp (AMO B9/39).
25 Sep	Formation of No 200 Gp (but see below).
1/2 Oct	First BC sorties to Berlin leaflet dropping.
10 Oct	First DFCs of war announced F/O McPherson and F/O Doran for the 4 Sep sortie against shipping.
11 Oct	Empire Air Training Scheme announced.

12 Oct	Move of RAF Air Component to France completed. Formation of No 54 Gp (AMO B33/39)
16 Oct	First German air raid on Britain Firth of Forth.
19 Oct	Renaming of Groups in ME/MED: Med GR Gp becomes No 200 Gp ME GR Gp becomes No 201 Gp (Cadre 18.9.39) Egyptian Gp becomes No 202 Gp (Cadre 18.4.39) (AMO B44/39)
Oct	Entry to service of Beaufort, 22 Sqn.
28 Oct	First German aircraft to be brought down on British soil, He.111 near Dalkeith.
1 Nov	First CHL station operational (Fifeness).
18 Nov	Start of German magnetic mine campaign off British coast.
30 Nov	Formation of No 20 Gp. (AMO B96/39)
12 Dec	BC attack on seaplane base on Sylt only cleared to attack aircraft on sea or after take-off NOT on land or installations.
14 Dec	99 Sqn lose 6 of 12 Wellingtons attacking German capital ships.
17 Dec	EATS agreement signed in Ottowa by UK, Canada, Australia, New Zealand.
18 Dec	50% losses on shipping attacks in Schillig Roads.
21 Dec	First 'Gift' sqn donated by the Nizam of Hyderabad, No 152 Sqn renamed No 152 (Hyderabad) Sqn.
26 Dec	First RAAF Sqn established in UK with Coastal Command (No 10 RAAF).(NB. Not part of the RAF numbering sequence.)
Dec	Entry to service of Defiant, 264 Sqn

Time to relax — roller skating at Finningley, with Lysander as back-drop.

1940:

1 Jan	Introduction of IFF codes.
4 Jan	Commence formation of Coastal Patrol Flights. (AMO B7/40).
8 Jan	First special-fit Wellington on sweeps for magnetic mines.
20 Jan	Formation of No 14 Gp.
31 Jan	First Coastal Command aircraft fitted with ASV. (150cm ASV Mk1)
31 Jan	U-55 sunk by 228 Sqn Sunderland first 'kill' by Coastal Command.
12 Feb	Formation of No 26 Gp (or 11.4.40).
16 Feb	Hudson of CC locates 'prison ship' ALTMARK off Norway. 14 or 25 Feb First RCAF Sqn arrives in England (No 110 Sqn)

7 Mar	No 34 Gp formed (AMO B59/40).
11 Mar	First U-boat sunk by RAF Blenheim of No 82 Sqn.
12 Mar	Russo-Finnish war ended.
16 Mar	British civilians killed in bombing near Scapa Flow.
19/20 Mar	Sylt attacked in retaliation first attack on a land target.
23 Mar	Formation of No 60 Gp.
8 Apr	Formation of Civilian Repair Organisation.
9 Apr	Germans invade Denmark and Norway.
11 Apr	First RAF bombing raid on mainland Europe Stavangar airfield. Formation of No 26 Gp (AMO B100/40).
13/14 Apr	First minelaying ('Gardening') sortie, BC Hampdens off coast of Denmark.
15-18 Apr	Op 'SICKLE' British forces land in Norway (Aandalsnes and Molde)
19 Apr	First EATS course assembles.
23 Apr	Gladiators of 263 Sqn operational in Norway off frozen lake at Lesjeskogen. (16 destroyed by German air raid on 25th)
29 Apr	EATS commences in Canada, Australia and New Zealand.
2 May	British forces evacuate Norway from Narvik.
7 May	First 2000lb bomb dropped, by 22 Sqn Beaufort.
10 May	German offensive in West launched. British forces land in Iceland.
10/11 May	First bombing attacks of German mainland.
11 May	New Coalition Govt with Churchill as Prime Minister.
11/12 May	First raid on German town, Monchengladbach.
12 May	First VCs — F/O D E Garland and Sgt T Gray/ 12 Sqn, bridge near Maastricht. (gazette 11.6.40)
14 May	Ministry of Aircraft Production established.
15/16 May	War Cabinet authority for bombing attacks east of Rhine. 99 bombers attack industrial targets in Hamburg and Ruhr. First strategic bombing mission
17 May	Formation of Ministry of Aircraft Production under Lord Beaverbrook.
22 May	Second RAF expedition to Norway. 263 Sqn to Bardufoss.
24 May	First FTS in Rhodesia.
26 May	Evacuation from Dunkirk commences.
27 May	Formation of Flying Training Command and Technical Training Command by division of Training Command. Reserve Command disbanded. (AMO B156/40)
28 May	Belgians capitulate.
29 May	Defiants of 264 Sqn claim 35 E/A for no loss. First fighter ops using VHF R/T.
1 Jun	Norway evacuated (again).
4 Jun	Operation DYNAMO evacuation of Dunkirk completed. (316 663 troops evacuated)
10 Jun	Italy declares war on Britain.
11/12 Jun	First BC raid on Italy, Genoa and Turin.
11 Jun	First air raid on Malta.
Jun	First Hurricane reinforcements to Malta.
14 Jun	Germans enter Paris.
15 Jun	Formation of No 10 Gp.
16 Jun	Birth of RCM organisation with decision to form a ground intercept network plus use of associated specialist aircraft.
17 Jun	Last RAF squadronns leave France.

20 Jun	Decision to use reinforcement route to ME via Takoradi.
22 Jun	France signs Armistice.
25 Jun	Central Landing Establishment formed.
28 Jun	First Hurricane sorties from Malta.
30 Jun	German forces occupy Guernsey, Channel Islands.
6 Jul	First operational use of depth-charges against U-boats.
	Formation of RAF Northern Ireland. (AMO B285/40)
10 Jul	Opening phase of Battle of Britain German attacks on coastal convoys. First Czech sqn within RAF formed. (310 Sqn).
Jul	Formation of ATFERO.
16 Jul	Hitler Directive for Op 'SEALION', the invasion of Britain.
22/23 Jul	First destruction of aircraft by AI, Blenheim of FIU destroys Do.17.
Jul-Oct	Battle of Britain anti-invasion campaign.
8 Aug	First true phase of Battle of Britain, attacks on shipping and coastal towns.
	Air Training Scheme announced in South Africa, Formation of No 7 Gp (AMO B285/40).
9 Aug	Formation of No 9 Gp.
12/13 Aug	First BC VC to F/L Learoyd/49 Sqn Dortmund-Ems.(gazette: 20.8.40)
	HQ British Air Forces France disbanded.

Radar gave Fighter Command an edge during the Battle of Britain.

15 Aug	Eagle Day RAF claim 182 'kills' (actual approx. 76)
	True opening of Battle of Atlantic as U-boats use surface attack against convoys.
16 Aug	VC to F/L J Nicolson/249 Sqn Battle of Britain. The only Fighter Command VC. (gazette: 15.11.40)
19 Aug	Second phase of Battle of Britain attacks on airfields.
20 Aug	Churchill speech containing "Never in the field of human conflict was so much owed by so many to so few."
	First Special Duties Flight formed.
24 Aug	Luftwaffe bomb London.
25/26 Aug	First bombs on Berlin, retaliation for attack on London.
29 Aug	Formation of No 14 Gp (AMO B16/40) (or 1.8.40).
2/3 Sep	First raid on U-boat bases Lorient.

3 Sep	Signing of 'Lend-Lease' agreement.
5 Sep	First consignment of aircraft arrive at Takoradi for ME.
7 Sep	Third phase of Battle of Britain London.
8 Sep	Invasion Alert No 1 in force.
9 Sep	AI-equipped Beaufighters enter service with No 29 Sqn.
15 Sep	Peak day of Battle of Britain, the tide turns.
15/16 Sep	VC to Sgt J Hannah/83 Sqn Antwerp. (gazette: 1.10.40)
16 Sep	Italians occupy Sidi Barrani, Egypt high point of their offensive.
19 Sep	Formation of first Eagle sqn of American volunteers (No 71 Sqn).
22 Sep	Royal Warrant authorizes award of DFC. AFC, DFM, AFM to members of any Air Force raised in the UK, Dominions, Colonies and British Protectorates. George Cross and George Medal instituted.
23 Sep	Op MENACE, Combined ops against Dakar.
23/24 Sep	First true 'Main Force' attack, Berlin.
27 Sep	Germany, Italy and Japan sign Tripartite Pact.
6 Oct	Fourth phase of Battle of Britain — night attacks.
7 Oct	First RCM unit formed, No 80 Wing.
8 Oct	First 'Eagle' sqn of American volunteers formed.
11 Oct	First Beaufighter night-fighter squadron operational/29 Sqn.
15/16 Oct	Last operational use of Fairey Battle by BC.
28 Oct	Italy invades Greece.
Nov	Entry to service of Halifax, 35 Sqn.
5 Nov	Start of RAF detachment to Greece.
10-11 Nov	First air delivery of landplanes over Atlantic, seven Hudsons from Canada to Aldergrove.
16 Nov	Hamburg attacked with incendiaries used to 'mark' target.
28 Nov	Formation of No 33 Gp (AMO A429/40)
1 Dec	Army Co-operation Command formed. (AMO B25/41).
9 Dec	First British offensive in Western Desert.
16 Dec	Offensive in Italian East Africa.
16/17 Dec	First 'area attack' (Mannheim), retaliation for attack on Coventry on 14/15 Nov.
17 Dec	First 'air' George Cross, S/L E L Moxey for bomb disposal work at Biggin Hill.
20 Dec	First 'RHUBARB' offensive sweep, two Spitfires of 66 Sqn to Le Touquet.
21/22 Dec	First 'INTRUDER' patrols, by 23 Sqn.
26 Dec	Blind Approach equipment enters operational service.

1941:

3 Jan	Luftwaffe units transferred to Mediterranean theatre.
10 Jan	First GCI station (Durrington) handed over by TRE.
	First 'CIRCUS' operation nine Blenheims of 114 Sqn with fighter escort to Foret de Guines.
	Start of first Blitz of Malta.
5 Feb	Air Training Corps established by Royal Warrant.
5 Feb	Formation of No 19 Gp.
6 Feb	Directorate of Sea Rescue (ASR) established in CC.
10/11 Feb	Stirling first operation (No 7 Sqn) to Rotterdam, also first four-engined bomber operation.

10 Feb	Op COLOSSUS first use of paratroopers, Commando raid in Italy.
13 Feb	Formation of University Air Squadrons. (AMO B52/41).
19 Feb	Air reninforcements arrive at Singapore.
24/25 Feb	Manchester first op (No 207 Sqn) to Brest.
6 Mar	Churchill directive that Battle of Atlantic has priority.
	Change in Flight numbering, addition of 1000 to each e.g 431 Flight becomes 1431 Flight.
10/11 Mar	Halifax first op (No 35 Sqn) to Le Havre.
11 Mar	'Lease-Lend' bill signed by President Roosevelt.
30 Mar	German offensive in North Africa.
31 Mar/ 1 Apr	First use of 4000lb bomb, Emden.
6 Apr	VC to F/O K Campbell/22 Sqn. (gazette: 13.3.42)
	German invasion of Yugoslavia and Greece.
7/8 Apr	First night 'INTRUDER' by Havocs over airfields in France.
8 Apr	No 4 SFTS at Habbaniya forms five 'operational' sqns in preparation for Iraqi attack.
10 Apr	WAAF incorporated as element of Armed Forces of the Crown.
15 Apr	Admiralty assumes Operational Control of CC.
21 Apr	Greeks request withdrawal of Allied forces.
22 Apr	Op DEMON, evacuation from Greece commences.
30 Apr	Iraqi forces attack Habbaniya. (siege from 2-6 May).
1 May	Lt-Col Moore-Brabazon takes over as Minister of Aircraft Production.
	First attacks by Malta-based Blenheims on Axis convoys en-route to North Africa.
8 May	Observer Corps becomes Royal Observer Corps.
10 May	Rudolf Hess parachutes into Scotland.
15 May	First British jet aircraft flight E28/39 from Cranwell.
19 May	RAF withdraw from Crete.
26 May	Formation of No 27 Gp.
31 May	Armistice with Iraq.
1 Jun	Main RAF delegation arrives in Washington.
13 Jun	Torpedo attack by Beauforts on pocket-battleship 'Lutzow'.
16 Jun	CAM ships introduced to service.
22 Jun	Germans attack Russia, Op BARBAROSSA.
	First 'Gee' chain completed (three stations at Daventry, Ventnor and Stenigot)
24 Jun	First air delivery of aircraft to West Africa via the South Atlantic Route.
4 Jul	VC to W/C H Edwards/105 Sqn Bremen. (gazette: 22.7.41)
7/8 Jul	VC to Sgt J Ward/75 Sqn Munster. (gazette: 5.8.41)
8 Jul	RAF B-17 first op (No 90 Sqn), Wilhelmshaven.
12 Jul	Anglo-Russian Agreement signed in Moscow.
Jun/Jul	Cherwell Commission on bombing accuracy.
20 Jul	Formation of Ferry Command, taking over from ATFERO.
3 Aug	MSFU Hurricane scores first success.
9-12 Aug	'RIVERIA' conference. 'ATLANTIC CHARTER' signed after meeting between Churchill and Roosevelt. Defined war aims.
11/12 Aug	First op trial of GEE, Munchen-Gladbach. (115 Sqn)
15 Aug	Formation of No 44 Gp.

25/26 Aug	Last RAF BC raid by B-17, Emden.
27 Aug	U-boat surrenders to Hudson of 269 Sqn.
29/30 Aug	First op by Australian sqn 455 Sqn to Frankfurt.
29/30 Aug	First ops in support of Resistance.
31 Aug	First convoy from Britain arrives at Archangel, Russia.
1 Sep	No 151 Wing to Murmansk, Russia. (operational 11 Sep).
22 Sep	British mission to Russia, led by Lord Beaverbrook.
9 Oct	Formation of Western Desert Air Force.
28 Oct	AHQ West Africa formed. (AMO A291/41).
7/8 Nov	BC loses 37 aircraft from 400 on various ops, conservation policy introduced.
14 Nov	Russian forces repel attack on Moscow, the turn of the tide.
18 Nov	Op CRUSADER, offensive in Western Desert.
29 Nov	First confirmed ASV kill U-boat by Whitley of 502 Sqn.
	No 151 Wing departs Russia.
Dec	First operational use of OBOE, Stirlings to Brest.
6 Dec	Britain declares war on Finland, Hungary and Roumania (all Axis clients).
7 Dec	Japan attacks Pearl Harbour.
8 Dec	VC to F/L A Scarf/62 Sqn. (gazette: 21.6.46)
	Britain and United States declare war on Japan.
9 Dec	China declares war on Germany, Italy and Japan.
10 Dec	Russian offensive along whole of Eastern Front.
22 Dec	German air assault on Malta opens.
22 Dec (-14 Jan)	ARCADIA Conference in Washington, Churchill, Roosevelt, and Combined Chiefs-of-Staff. Outline Grand Strategy and 'Germany First' policy.
27 Dec	Op ARCHERY, Combined op to Vaagso and Maaloy, Norway.

An important role was played by the WRAF in the World Wars.

1942:

2 Jan	UN anti-Axis Pact signed by 26 nations.
	Formation of ABDACOM to co-ordinate Far Eastern theatre.
16 Jan	Formation of Combined Chiefs-of-Staff committee in Washington.
19 Jan	Japanese attack Burma.
21 Jan	Counter-attack by Rommel in Western Desert as CRUSADER stalls.
11/12 Feb	Channel Dash by German warships Scharnhorst, Gneisenau, Prinz Eugen.
12 Feb	Formation of RAF Regiment.
15 Feb	Surrender of Singapore.

22 Feb	Advanced element of US 8th AF arrives in England.
23 Feb	Harris takes over as C-in-C BC.
25 Feb	ABDACOM disbanded with loss of Far East to Japan.
14 Feb	Directive No 22 BC maximum effort, area targets against morale.
27/28 Feb	Op BITING, the Bruneval raid on German radar station.
3/4 Mar	Successful precision attack on Renault factory Billancourt.
3/4 Mar	First Lancaster op (44 Sqn) minelaying..
7 Mar	First Spitfires to Malta, from HMS Eagle.
8/9 Mar	First use of SHAKER technique (GEE) , Essen.
10/11 Mar	First Lancaster bombing op (No 44 Sqn), Essen.
12 Mar	Formation of ECFS at Hullavington.
27/28 Mar	Op CHARIOT, Combined operation raid on St Nazaire.
28/29 Mar	Trial incendiary attack tactic on Lubeck.
6 Apr	First Japanese air attack on India.
7/8 Apr	Peak of air attacks on Malta.
9-14 Apr	'Marshall Plan' discussed in London.
10/11 Apr	First 8000 lb bomb dropped, Essen.
14 Apr	AHQ renamed HQ British Forces, Aden. (AMO A60/42).
16 Apr	Singleton Enquiry into accuracy of strategic bombing campaign.
	George Cross awarded to island of Malta.
17 Apr	Daylight raid on Augsburg by Lancasters.
	VC to S/L J Nettleton/44 Sqn. (gazette 28.2.42)
20 Apr	Introduction of air bomber as aircrew member.
23/24 Apr	First German 'Baedeker' raid. (Exeter).
29/30 Apr	Last Whitley op (except OTU).
30 Apr	British forces withdraw across Irrawaddy.
4 May	Op IRONCLAD, British forces land in Madagascar.
19 May	Training conference opens in Ottowa.
20 May	Allied forces evacuation from Burma complete.
25 May	First operational use of Baltimore.
26 May	Anglo-Soviet Treaty signed in London to run for 20 years.
	German offensive at Gazala the Battle for Egypt.
26-30 May	BOLERO Conference, London, for United Nations Air Forces.
30/31 May	First 1000 bomber op (1050 ac), Cologne.
	First use of OTU on bomb raid. VC to F/O L Manser/50 Sqn. (gazette: 20.10.42)
31 May	Mosquito first op with BC (No 105 Sqn), Cologne.
1/2 Jun	1000 bomber op (956 ac), Essen.
3/4 Jun	First attack using Leigh Light Wellington of 172 Sqn.
4/7 Jun	Battle of Midway turning point in Pacific War.
5 Jun	EATS extended.
11/12 Jun	First USAAF bombing op in ME, Liberators attack Ploesti oil fields.
18-26 Jun	White House Conference, Churchill and Roosevelt discuss options for 1942/43. Decide to invade Tunisia Op TORCH.
18 Jun	Policy statement concerning 'Gift' squadrons. (AMO A611/42).
22 Jun	CFS becomes ECFS.
25/26 Jun	1000 bomber op (1006 ac), Bremen.
	Last op by Manchester and Whitley (except mine-laying).

1 Jul	Formation of No 29 Gp.
	German offensive in Egypt halted at El Alamein.
	CC deploys Catalinas to Russia.
12 Aug	Churchill in Moswcow to 'sell' idea of TORCH to Stalin.
15 Aug	Pathfinder Force formed.
17 Aug	First attack over Europe by US 8th Air Force (VIII Bomber Command)
17/18 Aug	Last Blenheim op by BC 18 Sqn.
18/19 Aug	First Pathfinder op, Flensburg.
19 Aug	Op JUBILEE, the Dieppe Raid.
8 Sep	Anglo-US directive for fighter escort with day bombing.
14/15 Sep	Last BC Hampden op (No 408 Sqn), Wilhelmshaven.
19 Sep	First BC daylight raid on Berlin.
25 Sep	Mosquito pinpoint attack on Gestapo HQ, Oslo, Norway.
11-19 Oct	Final air Blitz on Malta.
17 Oct	BC daylight attack on Le Creusot.
19 Oct	Start of El Alamein offensive.
24 Oct	First BC daylight attack on Italy (Milan).
25 Oct	Formation of No 6 (RCAF) Gp.
28 Oct	First operational use of Marauder 14 Sqn.
1 Nov	Formation of No 28 Gp.
3 Nov	First Ventura op (21 Sqn) Hengelo.
8 Nov	Op TORCH, landings in North Africa.
28/29 Nov	First use of 8000lb bomb, Turin.
28/29 Nov	VC to F/S R Middleton/149 Sqn Turin. (gazette: 13.1.43)
4 Dec	VC to W/C H Malcolm/18 Sqn. (gazette: 27.4.43)
20/21 Dec	First op use of OBOE, Lutterade.
31 Dec	Chief of Staff memo on allied bombing policy, plan for force of 3000 heavy bombers.

1943:

3/4 Jan	Operational debut by 6 Group Essen.
7 Jan	AHQ Iraq becomes AHQ Iraq and Persia. (AMO A2/43)
14-24 Jan	SYMBOL Conference at Casablanca, Churchill and Roosevelt. Main points Combined Bomber Offensive, Invasion of Europe for 1944.
14 Jan	RAF contingent in Algeria and Tunisia becomes Eastern Air Command. (AMO A4/43)
16/17 Jan	First use by BC of 250lb TIs Berlin.
21 Jan	Casablanca Directive issued.
22 Jan	First op by BC Mitchells.
25 Jan	No 8 (PFF) Group formed.
30/31 Jan	First op use of H2S, Hamburg.
2 Feb	Formation of Mediterranean Air Command.
6 Feb	Establishment of North African Theatre of Operations.
26 Feb	Formation of NWAAF.
Feb	First Chindit raids, Burma.
5/6 Mar	Battle of Ruhr starts, Essen.
18 Mar	VC to Newton/22 Sqn. (gazette: 19.10.43)
25 Mar	Formation of Transport Command, absorbed Ferry Command (AMO A48/43).
30 Mar	Height of Battle of Atlantic record shipping losses.
1 Apr	Introduction of Squadron Standards to mark 25th anniversary of RAF.
	Formation of No 83 Gp.
5 Apr	First flight of Gloster Meteor, first production jet fighter.

11 Apr	Formation of No 45 Gp, supercedes Ferry Command.
12 Apr	Eaker Plan for combined offensive.
18 Apr	First successful CC Strike Wing operation.
3 May	VC to S/L L Trent/487 Sqn, Amsterdam. (gazette: 1.3.46)
12-27 May	TRIDENT Conference, Washington Churchill and Roosevelt.
12 May	German surrender in North Africa.
16/17 May	Op Chastise, the Dams raid. VC to W/C G Gibson/617 Sqn. (gazette: 28.5.43)
21 May	First American-built airbase in UK opens.
28 May	First U-boat sunk by RPs, from 608 Sqn Hudson (FAA Swordfish had made similar kill 5 days before.)
31 May	Last ops by No 2 Gp as part of BC. Start of the Battle of the Bay of Biscay.
1 Jun	No 2 Group transfered to AEAF. Army Co-operation Command disbanded. Formation of 2nd Tactical Air Force.
10 Jun	Directive for POINTBLANK, German industry and aircraft.
11 Jun	End of Op CORKSCREW, air offensive against island of Pantelleria.
14/15 Jun	First use of SERRATE. Oberhausen raid.
15 Jun	First autogiro squadron formed 529 Sqn at Halton (was 1448 Flt)
18 Jun	Adoption of term RADAR in place of RDF.
19/20 Jun	First operational use of MONICA.
20 Jun	First use of Master Bomber technique by No 5 Group.
20/21 Jun	First 'SHUTTLE' op, 60 Lancasters attack Friedrichshafen then onto N.Africa.
4 Jul	First glider towed across Atlantic.
9/10 Jul	End of Battle of Ruhr, Gelsenkirchen. Op HUSKY, airborne assault on Sicily.
15 Jul	Formation of No 84 Gp.
17 Jul	First landing on runway cleared of fog by FIDO.
24 Jul-3 Aug	Battle of Hamburg. Op GOMORRAH.
24/25 Jul	First op use of WINDOW, BC over Hamburg.
25 Jul	Resignation of Mussolini.
1 Aug	Formation of No 22 Gp.
11 Aug	VC to F/O L Trigg/200 Sqn. (gazette: 2.11.43)
12/13 Aug	VC to F/Sgt A Aaron/218 Sqn. (gazette: 3.11.43)
14-24 Aug	QUADRANT Conference, Quebec. Churchill and Roosevelt to discuss cross-Channel invasion of Europe.
16/17 Aug	Last attack on Italy, Turin.
17/18 Aug	Attack research centre at Peenemunde. Op HYDRA.
Aug	Formation of SEAC.
1 Sep	Formation of No 38 Gp (or 11.10.43).
2 Sep	Conference in Washington, Churchill and Roosevelt.
3 Sep	Armistice with Italy (not declared until 8 Sep).
9 Sep	Op AVALANCHE, seaborne assault on Salerno.
14 Sep	Op BRIMSTONE, landings in Sardinia.
15 Sep	Mussolini back in power.
15/16 Sep	First use of 12 000lb TALLBOY, Dortmund-Ems canal.
22/23 Sep	First use of 'spoof' target technique. Main target Hanover, 'spoof' target Oldenburg.
23 Sep	Allied forces land in Greece.
4 Oct	CC sink their 100th U-boat.
7/8 Oct	First op use of GEE-H, Aachen. First op use of ABC, Stuttgart.
8 Oct	Op ALCRITY, establish air base in Azores.
8/9 Oct	Last BC bombing op with Wellington, Hannover.
13 Oct	Italy declares war on Germany.
22/23 Oct	First op use of CORONA, Kassel.
23 Oct	Formation of MASAF.
3/4 Nov	VC to F/L W Reid/61 Sqn Dusseldorf. (gazette: 14.12.43)
7 Nov	Mosquito of 248 Sqn makes first anti U-boat attack using 6-pdr gun.
8 Nov	No 100 (Special Duties) Group formed.
15 Nov	ADGB reformed by renaming Fighter Command. Formation of AEAF.
16 Nov	Formation of ACSEA.
18/19 Nov	Battle of Berlin starts.
22-26 Nov	SEXTANT Conference, Cairo. Churchill, Roosevelt and Chiang Kai-Shek.
28 Nov	EUREKA Conference, Teheran. Churchill, Roosevelt and Stalin. Details of invasion of Europe (OVERLORD and ANVIL)
30/1 Dec	First op by No 100 (Special Duties) Group, 192 Sqn.
4 Dec	CAIRO Conference Churchill, Roosevelt and President Inonu (of Turkey).
10 Dec	Formation of MAAF.
15 Dec	Formation of Eastern Air Command at Delhi.
16/17 Dec	First Serrate op 141 Sqn.
17 Dec	Formation of No 85 Gp.
20 Dec	CROSSBOW, First attack on Flying-bomb site.
23 Dec	Eisenhower appointed Supreme Allied Commander of Expeditionary Forces in UK
1944:	
1 Jan	Start Second Arakan campaign, Burma.
4 Jan	Air attacks on rail comms in support of Op SHINGLE, landings at Anzio-Nettuno.
17 Jan	Formation of No 46 Gp.
21/22 Jan	Renewed Luftwaffe offensive on London (the 'Baby Blitz').
23/24 Jan	Start of 'Big Week', offensive against German aircraft manufacturing.
1 Feb	'Allied' added to Mediterranean Command titles.
15 Feb	First major bombing of Monte Cassino.
18 Feb	Pinpoint attack by Mosquito on Amiens Prison, France.
5 Mar	Op THURSDAY, Chindit glider assault.
6/7 Mar	Start pre-invasion bombing campaign, Trappes rail yards.
24/25 Mar	Battle of Berlin ends.
25 Mar	Transportation Plan accepted for OVERLORD support.
30/31 Mar	Last POINTBLANK op, Nuremburg. Heaviest losses for one attack. VC to P/O C Barton/578 Sqn. (gazette: 27.6.44)
31 Mar	Start of siege of Imphal re-supply by air.
3 Apr	First Allied air attack on Hungary.
5 Apr	Start of campaign against Ploesti oil fields (end 19 Aug).
9/10 Apr	First attacks on coastal batteries in France.
14 Apr	Operational control of BC passed to SHAEF.
17 Apr	Supreme Commander co-directive prime aim to destroy German air combat strength.
26/27 Apr	VC to Sgt N Jackson/106 Sqn Schweinfurt. (gazette:26.10.45)

1 May	Term 'H'-hour replaces 'Z'-hour as operational timing reference (AMO A67/44).
11/12 May	Op DIADEM, Air attack on Gustav Line, Italy.
12/13 May	First sea mining by Mosquito, Kiel Canal.
23 May	Breakout from Salerno beach-head.
4 Jun	5th Army enters Rome.
6 Jun	D-Day, landings in Normandy.
8 Jun	First use of 12 000lb 'Tallboy', Saumur railway tunnel.
12/13 Jun	VC to P/O A Mynarski/419 Sqn Cambrai. (gazette: 11.10.46)

267 Squadron Dakotas on field re-supply in Greece.

13/14 Jun	First Flying Bombs land on England.
14 Jun	Daylight bombing raids by BC resume.
	First flying-bomb shot down, Mosquito of 605 Sqn.
16/17 Jun	First BC op against V-weapon sites. (NOBALL)
19 Jun	Formation of Balkan Air Force (or 1st Jun?)
24 Jun	VC to F/L D Hornell/162 Sqn. (gazette: 28.7.44)
7 Jul	Heavy bombers used to area bomb troops near Caen, 2300 tons of bombs in 38 minutes. (11 days later BC dropped a further 5600 tons around Caen.)
12 Jul	First allied jet squadron operational, 616 Sqn, Meteor.
17 Jul	VC to F/L J Cruickshank/210 Sqn. (gazette: 1.9.44)
18 Jul	First true operational use of CAS using "cab-rank" and R/T control by FAC on ground.
20 Jul	Assassination attempt against Hitler.
1 Aug	Start of Warsaw Rising by Polish partisan army. (ended 3 Oct).
4 Aug	VC to S/L I Bazalgette/635 Sqn. (gazette: 17.8.45)
15 Aug	Op DRAGOON, landings in Southern France.
21 Aug	Start of Dumbarton Oaks discussions, Washington led to post-war establishment of United Nations. (provisional charter issued 7 Oct.)
23 Aug	Liberation of Paris.
27 Aug	First major daylight raid on Germany, Homberg.
29 Aug	Op BLOCKADE, against road and rail comms in Northern Italy.
30 Aug	Ploesti taken by Russian forces.
3 Sep	Liberation of Brussels.
4/5 Sep	German use of air-launched flying bombs.
8 Sep	Last bombing op by Stirling, Le Havre.
	First V2 lands on London.
11-16 Sep	OCTAGON Conference, Quebec, Churchill and Roosevelt to discuss Pacific theatre, and Zones of Occupation in Europe.
15 Sep	Operational Control of BC reverts to Air Staff.
17 Sep	Op MARKET, the airborne assault element of MARKET-GARDEN, assault to cross the Rhine.

19 Sep	VC to F/L D Lord/271 Sqn. (gazette: 13.11.45)
23/24 Sep	Dortmund-Ems canal breached by 12 000lb bombs.
Sep	VC to W/C L Cheshire.
1 Oct	Formation of BAFSEA.
14 Oct	Liberation of Athens.
14/15 Oct	Largest raid by BC, 1576 aircraft dropped 5453 tons.
15 Oct	Fighter Command reforms by renaming ADGB. AEAF disbanded.
18 Oct	Formation of Combat Cargo Task Force.
1 Nov	Op INFATUATE, amhibious assault on Walcheren.
12 Nov	Tirpitz destroyed by No 9 Sqn and No 617 Sqn.
3 Dec	Civil unrest in Greece, ELAS (Communist) revolt.
14 Dec	German Ardennes offensive starts.
23 Dec	VC to S/L R Palmer/109 Sqn Cologne. (gazette: 23.3.45)

1945:

1 Jan	VC to F/S G Thompson/9 Sqn Dortmund-Ems. (gazette: 20.2.45)
	Luftwaffe attack Allied airfields in Belgium destroying 150 aircraft. Formation of No 47 Gp.
Jan	Helicopter Training School formed at Andover.
4 Feb	ARGONAUT Conference, Yalta Churchill, Roosevelt and Stalin to discuss Poland, Zones of Occupation, division of Germany.
13/14 Feb	Attack on Dresden, part of Op THUNDERCLAP.
22/23 Feb	Op CLARION, intensive attacks on rail comms.
23/24 Feb	VC to Capt E Swales/582 Sqn Pforzheim. (gazette: 24.4.45)
24 Feb	Formation of 'Tiger Force' for ops in Far East.
7 Mar	American forces cross Rhine at Remagen.
14 Mar	First op use of 22 000lb GRAND SLAM, Bielefeld viaduct.
20 Mar	Recapture of Mandalay.
24 Mar	Op VARSITY, airborne support of main Rhine crossing.
27 Mar	Last V2 falls on England.
31 Mar	Announcement of end of EATS.
12 Apr	Death of President Roosevelt.
16 Apr	Directive, Area Bombing halted.
20 Apr	Last air attack on Berlin.
25 Apr	United Nations Conference, San Franciso.
	Last mining op by BC.
26 Apr	Start of Op EXODUS, repatriation of POWs.
29 Apr	Start of Op MANNA food dropping in Holland.
2/3 May	Last BC op, naval targets in Kiel area.
2 May	Berlin captured by Russians.
	Op DRACULA, assault on Rangoon.
7 May	Last U-boat sunk, by Catalina of 210 Sqn.
8 May	Victory Europe (VE) Day.
	ROC reverts to peace-time basis.
23 May	Churchill resigned, but formed 'Caretaker' Government pending elections.
26 May	Lancaster 'Aries' returns after North Pole flight.
31 May	Eastern Air Command disbanded.
4 Jun	Last anti-submarine patrol by CC.
15 Jun	Balloon Command disbanded.
	2nd TAF renamed BAFO.
26 Jun	Charter of United Nations signed by 50 Nations at San Franciso.
6 Jul	MATAF disbanded.

15 Jul	2TAF becomes BAFO.
	SHAEF disbanded. BAF disbanded.
1 Aug	MAAF disbanded. Formation of MEDME.
	RAF Northern Ireland becomes part of Coastal Command.
6 Aug	First Atomic bomb dropped on Hiroshima.
9 Aug	Second Atomic bomb dropped on Nagasaki.
14 Aug	Victory Japan Day.
25 Aug	Lend-Lease agreements ceased.
26-30 Aug	Medical teams and supplies dropped to POW locations in Burma and Siam. (Op BIRDCAGE and Op MASTIFF).
2 Sep	Japanese official surrender on board USS Missouri.
8 Sep	Advance party to Saigon, involvement in Indo-China.
9 Sep	Re-occupation of Malaya.
10 Sep	Re-occupation of Singapore.
15 Sep	Start of ops in Netherlands East Indies (end Nov 46).
1 Oct	Formation of No 48 Gp.
19 Oct	MACAF becomes AHQ RAF Italy.
25 Oct	First operational flights in Netherlands East Indies.
31 Oct	Tiger Force disbands.
	Jewish revolt in Palestine.
15 Dec	Disbandment of No 5 Gp and No 8 Gp.

1946:

15 Jan	Op SUNBEAM commenced. Sea recce for Jewish immigrants off Palestine.
28 Mar	As part of re-organisation, transport squadrons transferred to overseas Commands.
Apr	ECFS becomes EFS.
Apr	Entry to service of Vampire, 247 Sqn.
1 May	Reserve Command reformed.
7 May	CFS reformed.
20 May	Disbandment of No 13 Gp.
2 Jun	Auxiliary Air Force reformed.
10 Jul	Announced that RAF Ragiment to remain part of RAF.
12 Jul	RAF High-Speed Flight formed at Tangmere.
30 Nov	ACSEA renamed ACFE.

1947:

3 Jan	King's Flight reconstituted at Benson.
6 Jan	RAF/USAF exchange post scheme announced.
10 Jul	Dedication of Battle of Britain Memorial in Westminster Abbey.
14 Aug	India Independence.
1 Sep	Ops in connection with partition of India.
16 Dec	Auxiliary Air Force renamed Royal Auxiliary Air Force. (?15.1.48 in AMO 35/48).

1948:

2 Feb	Disbandment of No 4 Gp.
17 Mar	Western Union, Brussels Treaty, agreed.
15 May	End of British Mandate in Palestine.
24 Jun	Berlin Airlift. Operation 'PLAINFARE'.
16 Jun	Operations against CT in Malaya commence Operation 'FIREDOG'
6 Jul	First air strike in Malaya, by Spitfires of 60 Sqn.
12-14 Jul	First Atlantic crossing by jet aircraft six Vampires of 54 Sqn.
15 Oct	Formation of CALTF for Berlin Airlift.

1949:

7 Jan	RAF aircraft shot down by Israeli fighters.

27 Jan	Policy of linking squadron numbers e.g 57/104 Sqn. (AMO A86/49).
1 Feb	Creation of WRAF, by renaming WAAF.
4 Apr	Formation of NATO.
20 Apr	HMS Amethyst attacked on Yangtse, China. Sunderlands as part of relief force.
11 May	Blockade of Berlin officially raised. RAF had made 49 733 flights and moved 281 727 tons of supplies in to Berlin.
1 Jun	MEDME renamed MEAF.
	ACFE renamed FEAF.
	Formation of RAF Flying College at Manby.
6 Jul	Colour of the RAF College, Cranwell, presented.
8 Sep	Introduction of Preliminary Flying Badge. (AMO A631/49).
6 Oct	Berlin Airlift ends.

1950:

1 Apr	Casualty Evacuation Flight formed at Seletar first operational helicopter unit.
26 Jun	Korean War (end 27 Jul 53).
28 Jun	British troops join UN forces in Korea.
1 Aug	Reserve Command renamed Home Command.
Aug	Entry to service of B-29 Washington, 115 Sqn.
	Start of Mau Mau troubles, Kenya (end Aug 56).
23 Nov	Change of aircrew titles to Officer (Aircrew) and Airmen (Aircrew). (AMO A721/50)
7 Dec	Reserve of Air Force Officers retitled RAF Reserve of Officers (AMO A751/50).

1951:

Jan	Announcement of expansion plans and re-armament, including call-up of Reservists.
1 Feb	Change of terminology in CC Maritime Reconnaissance (MR) replaces General Reconnaissance (GR). (AMO A74/51)
Feb	Entry to service of Shackleton, 236 OCU.
May	Canberra operational with 101 Sqn, Binbrook, first jet bomber.
26 May	Presentation of first RAF Royal Colour, by Princess Elizabeth. Colour of the RAF in the United Kingdom.
Jun	Persian Crisis.
Jun	Entry to service of Varsity, 201 AFS.
1 Sep	BAFO renamed 2nd Tactical Air Force.
16 Oct	Egypt abrogates the 1936 Anglo-Egyptian Treaty.

1952:

19 Feb	First British-designed helicopter (Sycamore) delivered.
25 Jul	Colour of No 1 SoTT, RAF Halton, presented.
Aug	Ops around Buraimi Oasis, Oman.
3 Oct	Atom bomb tests at Monte Bello islands.

1953:

1 Feb	Formation of 194 Sqn, first helicopter squadron.
Mar	Entry to service of Sabre, 67 Sqn, first transonic fighter.
12 Mar	Lincoln shot down by MiGs in Berlin Corridor.
17 Mar	Colour of the RAF Regiment presented.
Apr	Major operations against Mau Mau, Kenya.
15 Jul	Royal Review at Odiham.
27 Jul	Korean War ends.
Aug	Entry to service of Pioneer, 267 Sqn.

1 Sep	BC reinforcment plan for Malayan Emergency first det by Lincolns of 83 Sqn to Tengah.
Oct	Commence Op SUNRAY. BC detachments to Canal Zone, Egypt.
8-10 Oct	London to New Zealand Air Race won by RAF Canberra (PR.3 WE139).

1954:

Feb	First swept-wing fighter in RAF service, Swift, 56 Sqn.
1 Apr	Last operational flight by RAF Spitfire, Malaya.
31 Jul	Entry to service of Hunter, 43 Sqn.
Sep	Entry to service of Pembroke, 267 Sqn.
1 Oct	Canberra 'Aries IV' makes flight over North Pole.
Oct	Operations by BC against Mau Mau in Kenya.
11 Nov	Tudor crown replaced by St Edward's crown on official RAF badges. (AMO A274/54).

1955:

Jan	First V-bomber enters service (Valiant) with 138 Sqn, Gaydon.
Feb	Formation of SEATO.
17 Feb	Announcement that Britain would develop H-bomb.
Feb	Entry to service of Whirlwind, 22 Sqn.
1 Apr	First EOKA terrorist bomb, Cyprus.
4 Apr	Formation of Baghdad Pact.
7 Jul	New organisation in MEAF HQ Cyprus, with Northern Group (AHQ Levant) and Southern Group (British Forces Aden)
Aug	First (experimental) 'all-jet' training scheme introduced.
27 Nov	State of Emergency declared in Cyprus (end Dec 59).

1956:

10 Feb	Death of MRAF Lord Trenchard.
24 Feb	Entry to service of Javelin, 46 Sqn, first all-weather fighter interceptor.
14 May	Last RAF base in Egypt, Abu Sueir, handed over.
May	Entry to service of Vulcan, 230 OCU.
Jun	Entry to service of Comet, 216 Sqn first jet transport.
26 Jul	Nationalisation of Suez Canal. (casus belli for Suez War)
11 Oct	First British air-dropped atomic bomb, Maralinga.
20 Oct	First operational flight over Egypt, PR sortie.
29 Oct-7 Nov	Suez War.
31 Oct	First bombing sorties of Suez War.
Nov	Entry to service of Hunter, 43 Sqn.
6 Nov	Last bombing sorties of Suez War.

1957:

9 Jan	Introduction of AEO brevet. (AMO A18/57).
Mar	Termination of Anglo-Jordanian Treaty.
Mar	Disbandment of ALL RAuxAF squadrons.
4 Apr	Defence White Paper proposes sweeping changes to RAF structure and strength.
15 May	First British air-dropped hydrogen bomb, Christmas Island.
31 Aug	Malaya independent.
Nov	Entry to service of Victor, 232 OCU.

1958:

13 Feb	Defence White Paper outlines plan for acquisition of American Thor IRBMs.
Feb	Nuclear capability for V-bombers and Canberras. Trans-Antarctic flight by Austers.
Jul	Bloodhound SAM enters service with 264 Sqn at North Coates.
17 Jul	Reinforcements flown to Jordan.
Aug	First Thor IRBM site formed at Feltwell.
Sep	Entry to service of Thor, 77 Sqn.
Oct	First AAM (Firestreak) enters service with Javelins.
3 Nov	Formation of Signals Command.
15 Nov	Disbandment of No 2 Gp.

1959:

1 Jan	2nd TAF renamed RAFG.
19 Feb	End of EOKA hostilities, Cyprus.
4 Mar	Badge of RAF Regiment approved. (AMO A54/59).
1 Apr	Home Command disbanded.
16 Apr	First THOR launch by RAF crew, at Vandenburg AFB.
15 May	Last operational flight by flying boat, Sunderland of 205 Sqn.
Jun	Entry to service of Britannia, 99 Sqn.
22 Jul	'Daily Mail' Paris to London (Arc to Arch) air race won by RAF team in 40 min 44 sec.
20 Aug	Formation of CENTO to replace Baghdad Pact.
Sep	First jet ab initio pilot training course established at Syerston (although trials held earlier).
1 Oct	Formation of British Forces Arabian Peninsula (BFAP).
1 Nov	First Maritime HQ unit, RAuxAF formed at Edinburgh.

1960:

1 Jan	No 38 Gp reformed as specialist tactical Group in Transport Command.
Mar	Force of Thor IRBMs complete.
Apr	Cancellation of Blue Streak (follow-on ICBM).
Jun	Entry to service of Lightning, 74 Sqn, first supersonic fighter.
Jul	Operations in support of UN intervention in Congo.
31 Jul	End of Malayan Emergency.
16 Aug	Cyprus becomes a Republic, formation of Sovereign Base Areas.
13 Oct	Entry to service of Belvedere, BTU.

1961:

1 Mar	BFAP renamed AFME (Aden). Formation of MEC. Formation of NEC and NEAF.
Apr-May	Air-drop food and supplies to famine areas in Kenya.
1 May	Fighter Command assigned as part of SACEUR air defence system for NATO.
1 Jul	Op VANTAGE, deployment to Kuwait during 'Kuwait Crisis'.
1 Oct	Commence Operation 'TANA FLOOD', food drops in Kenya and, later, Somalia. (end Jan 1962.)
Oct	First RAF participation in US national defence exercise.

2 Nov	Commence Operation 'SKY HELP', supplies to Belize after destruction by hurricane 'Hattie'.
15 Nov	Re-organisation into unified Command structure: Near East Command controls NEAF, Middle East Command controls AFME. (AMO A313/61).

Javelin F(AW)4 XA636 in company with Hunter F.6 XF440.

1962:

31 Jan	Purchase of AS.30 announced, to be RAF's first true air-to-ground guided missile.
Feb	Entry to service of Gnat, CFS.
26 Apr	Belvedere places 80 ft spire on Coventry cathedral.
May	Near East Command disbanded.
16 May	Introduction of QM brevet. (AMO A117/62).
5 Aug	UK signs Nuclear Test-Ban Treaty.
Oct	Javelins to India on ADEX, threat of invasion by China.
Nov	Last Mosquito, of CAACU, leaves RAF service.
28 Nov	Re-organisation into unified Commands: Far East Command controls FEAF. (AMO A299/62).
Dec	Operations in Brunei commence.
Dec	SKYBOLT cancelled, BLUE STEEL enters service.

1963:

1 Jan	Formation of FEC.
31 Mar	11 Gp and 12 Gp disband replaced by Sector system.
1 Apr	AM Directorate-General of Works becomes part of Ministry of Public Buildings and Works.
8 May	Last Mosquito 'retires'.
15 Aug	Last of the Thor sites closed down, end of RAF participation in strategic ground-based missiles.
Dec	Rioting in Nicosia, Cyprus. Start of Emergency in Aden.

1964:

Jan	BMEWS site at Fylingdales operational.
Jan	Entry to service of Wessex, 18 Sqn.
1 Apr	Unified Ministry of Defence formed, Air Ministry becomes Air Force Department, Air Council becomes Air Force Board.
Aug	Whirlwinds of No 1310 Flight, British Guiana, revive names 'Faith', 'Hope', 'Charity'.
28 Sep	First flight of TSR.2, planned as the key element of the RAF in the 1970s.
Sep	RAF takes over IS ops in British Guiana.
Oct	Technician and Craft Apprentice Scheme replaced the Aircraft (Apprentice) and Boy Entrants.
15 Oct	Kestrel Evaluation Flight formed UK/US/West Germany at West Raynham.
Dec	Valiant leaves service after major structural problems.

1965:

2 Feb	Cancellation of P1154 in favour of Phantom. Cancellation of HS.681 in favour of Hercules.
6 Apr	Cancellation of TSR.2
Oct	Entry to service of Dominie, 1 ANS.
Nov	Declaration of independence (UDI) by Rhodesia.
Dec	Deployment to Zambia, Rhodesian UDI.

1966:

10 Jan	Entry to service of Belfast strategic transport, 53 Sqn.
22 Feb	Announcement of 50-aircraft buy of F-111.
1 Apr	Airfield Construction Branch disbanded.
7 Apr	Entry to service of VC.10, 10 Sqn.
Oct	Technical Branch renamed Engineer Branch.
30 Nov	AHQ Gibraltar disbanded.
Nov	Entry to service of Andover, 46 Sqn.

1967:

28-31 Mar	Hunters attempt to break up the stricken oil tanker 'Torry Canyon'.
3 May	Commence evacuation of families from Aden.
May	Spain imposes a prohibited air zone near Gibraltar, RAF deploys Hunters to the rock.
Jul	Hercules enters service, 36 Sqn.
Jul	Major redundancy scheme announced in White Paper.
1 Aug	Transport Command renamed Air Support Command.
1 Nov	Disbandment of No 3 Gp.
Nov	Withdrawal from Aden.

1968:

16 Jan	F-111 purchase cancelled as part of sweeping defence cuts and withdrawal from overseas.
1 Apr	50th anniversary of RAF, held at Odiham.
30 Apr	Bomber Command and Fighter Command merge to form Strike Command.
1 Jun	Flying Training Command and Technical Training Command merge to form Training Command.
20 Jun	AHQ Malta disbanded.
28 Jun	Last Anson leaves service.
1 Aug	WRAF adopts RAF ranks.
Aug	Soviet invasion of Czechoslovakia, NATO on alert.
11 Oct	VC.10 transports given names of RAF VC winners.

1969:

1 Jan	Signals Command renamed as No 90 (Signals) Gp.
19 Mar	Reinforcements to Anguilla and Antigua after local unrest.
4-11 May	'Daily Mail' Transatlantic race, Harrier flew London to New York, using AAR, in 6 hr 11 min 57.15 sec.
7 May	Entry to service of Phantom, 6 Sqn.
Jul	End of Blue Steel nuclear role, strategic nuclear deterrent role passed to RN 'Polaris' submarines.
15-21 Aug	Reinforcements to Northern Ireland.
1 Sep	Coup in Libya. Withdrawal of RAF forces starts.
1 Oct	Entry to service of Harrier, 1 Sqn.
2 Oct	Entry to service of Nimrod, MOTU, first jet MPA.
2 Nov	Launching of 'Skynet' military communications satellite.
28 Nov	Coastal Command absorbed into Strike Command.

1970:

26 Mar	GEE chain closed.
4 Apr	Last RAF DC-3 'retires' (but BBMF acquires one in 1993!).
Aug	RAF take over Canadian share of NATO training range at Decimomanu, Sardinia.
30 Sep	Terrorist Leila Khaled flown by Comet to Beirut on hostage swop.
Nov	Op BURLAP, flood relief in Pakistan.

1971:

Jan	Entry to service of Buccaneer, 15 Sqn. Entry to service of Puma, ATS.
1 Nov	FEAF disbanded.
10-12 Dec	Evacuation of civilians from West Pakistan.
21 Dec	Last RAF units withdrawn from Arabian Gulf except for Staging Post at Masirah.

1972:

Jan	First AEW aircraft Shackleton, enters service, 8 Sqn.
1 May	No 90 Gp transferred to MC.
1 Jul	No 38 Gp transferred to STC.
1 Sep	ASC absorbed into STC. Formation of No 46 Gp.
Sep	Start of 'Cod War' with Iceland (end Oct 73).
14-28 Sep	Ex 'Strong Express', largest NATO exercise to date.

1973:

Mar	Op 'KHANA CASCADE' airlift supplies to villages in Nepal.
Jul	Op 'SAHIL CASCADE' mercy flights in Mali.
31 Aug	Maintenance Command disbanded.
1 Sep	Formation of Support Command.
13 Sep	Entry to service of Jaguar, 226 OCU.

1974:

Apr	Wessex detachment ops in Oman.
20 Jul	Turkish invasion of Cyprus. British forces on alert, airlift of civilians.
Oct	Programme of HAS building and tone-down at stations in RAFG.

1975:

Jan	Airlift Turkish Cypriot refugees to Turkey.
10 Mar	Hercules used for evacuation at Phnom Penh, Cambodia.
Oct	Evacuation missions in Angola.
Nov	Reinforcements to Belize, threat of Guatemalan invasion.
24 Nov	First Nimrod patrol into 200 mile zone claimed by Iceland, Third 'Cod War'.

1976:

29 Mar	Handover of Gan to civilian authorities.
31 Mar	Disbandment of NEAF, replaced by AHQ Cyprus.

1977:

Feb	Commence Op TAPESTRY, surveillance of oil rigs.
13 Jun	Training Command and Support Command merge to form Support Command.
30 Jun	SEATO disbanded.
Jul	Reinforcement of Belize, invasion threat.
29 Jul	Silver Jubilee review of RAF at Finningley.
6 Aug	First RAF participation in Ex RED FLAG

1978:

Oct	Last squadron leaves Malta, No 13 Sqn.

1979:

31 Mar	Final departure from Malta, Luqa handed over.
Dec	Support of Commonwealth Monitoring Force, Rhodesia.

1982:

2 Apr	Argentina invades Falkland Islands.
1 May	Vulcan attack on Port Stanley airfield.
14 Jun	Argentinian surrender.
Jun	Entry to service of Tornado, 9 Sqn.

1986:

8 Jan	Disbandment of Marine Branch.
14 Feb	First flight of Shorts Tucano.
24 Mar	IOC of Tristar tanker/216 Sqn.
Aug	Terrorist attack on Akrotiri, Cyprus.
18 Dec	Announcement that E-3 selected for AWAC requirement after failure of Nimrod AEW.

1987:

Jan	During Op SWIFT SWORD, Oman, first AAR of a passenger aircraft.
24 Sep	First un-refuelled Atlantic crossing by British fighter, Tornado F.3, 2200 nms in 4 hours 45 minutes.

1988:

Jan	Re-organisation at A&AEE into Fixed Wing Test Sqn and Rotary Wing Test Sqn.
Feb	First Air Combat Simulator (ACS) taken into RAF service.
30 Apr	Lightning retires from service.
1 May	Royal Aircraft Establishment renamed Royal Aerospace Establishment.
Jun	Policy announced of removing Spitfire gate guardians and replacing them with replicas.

Jul	Massive SAR operation following PIPER ALPHA rig explosion.
Aug	Tornado F.3s to Far East on Ex GOLDEN EAGLE.

1989:

3 Feb	RAF Cranwell BFTS retitled as 3 FTS.
18 Mar	Last Hercules 'Airbridge' flight to Falklands. Task taken over by Tristars of 216 Sqn.
13 May	Canberra celebrates 40 years since first flight.
20 Jul	Announcement that RAF to recruit female aircrew (first student navigator arrived at Finningley in Sep.)
Sep	Hercules mercy flights from Belize to Antigua and Monserrat after Hurricane HUGO.
Dec	First Tucano course assembled at 7FTS, Church Fenton.

1990:

5 Jan	First flight of E-3D Sentry (ZH101).
Feb	RAF helicopters from Valley assist in flood relief at Towyn.
Mar	RAF Hercules fleet reached its one millionth flying hour!
May	First AT (Airborne Technicians) awarded brevets.
10 May	First female pilots go solo at Linton-on-Ouse.
Jun	Red Arrows on tour of Russia.
Jul	Chipmunk celebrates 40 years of service.
Jul	Secretary of State for Defence, Tom King, announces 'Options for Change' force reductions.
2 Aug	Iraq invades Kuwait.
Aug	RAF aircraft deploy to Saudi Arabia and Gulf area under Op GRANBY.

1991:

17 Jan	First air strikes by Coalition Forces against Iraq.
17 Jan	First RAF operational loss in Gulf War, Tornado (ZD791).
26 Jan	First Buccaneers arrive in theatre (first op 1/2 Feb).
Jan-Mar	Gulf War (ceasefire 3 Mar).
24 Feb	Ground offensive launched.
8 Apr	First Hercules supply drop on Op PROVIDE COMFORT.
	Jaguars deploy to Turkey on Op WARDEN.
1 Jul	Commence final rundown of Bloodhound SAM system.
10 Jul	ROC disbanded.
2 Oct	Final Phantom scramble (as farewell gesture) in RAFG.

1992:

Jun	Wings awarded to first female pilot (Julie Gibson).
Aug	Tornado deployment to Gulf for Southern Watch.
1 Nov	No 38 Gp reforms

1993:

23 Jan	Wessex rescue sick Palestinians from 'DMZ' between Israel and Lebanon.
23 Mar	Farewell flight by Vulcan XH558.
1 Apr	RAFG becomes No. 2 Gp.
	RAF 75th Anniversary celebrations at RAF Marham.
23 Apr	231 (Canberra) OCU disbands — longest existence with single aircraft type of any OCU.
30 Jul	Upavon closed (handed back to Army — the oldest RFC/RAF airfield.
1 Oct	No. 55 Sqn disbands — end of the Victor.

AAR was essential to ops in the Gulf region — VC10 to Tornado.

ABBREVIATIONS

ALMOST EVERY ASPECT of Service life, especially within the RAF, is a seeming mass of abbreviations (acronyms) and mnemonics, and this has held true since 1918. The list given here brings together, for the first time, the vast majority of the commonest abbreviations to be found in RAF documents. It would, of course, be impossible to record every single abbreviation to be found in every technical manual — the Tornado list alone is a wonder to behold!

There are many problems when it comes to a consideration of abbreviations, not least of which is the sheer quantity; however, the major problem is that of inconsistency, whereby different references give different decodes for the same series of letters, often through local variation. There are also many instances of an abbreviation being peculiar to a single unit (of even an individual!). Also, different units often use different abbreviations for the same function or institution — a good example being the outfit which looks after visiting aircraft, which attracts such varying titles as VASF (Visiting Aircraft Servicing Flight), TASF (Transit Aircraft Servicing Flight), plus any combination of leaving out the word 'Servicing' or changing the 'Flight' into 'Section' or 'Squadron'.

With a basic knowledge of the 'system' of abbreviations, i.e an insight into the mentality behind the use of such abbreviations, it is always possible to make an educated guess at the decode — based on the context; this is particularly valid when it comes to considering combinations of abbreviations; for example, HQ is always Headquarters and so an abbreviation of HQ ... must be Headquarters ...! As an extension of this argument, many abbreviations assume the presence of others to clarify their meaning; for example HQ STC is Headquarters Strike Command, but the full meaning is Headquarters Royal Air Force Strike Command — the RAF element (as in HQ RAF STC) is almost always left out. To take a look at the educated guess concept ... TF most commonly stands for Training Flight, so to come across an abbreviation LTF would almost certainly imply L Training Flight, the question is what does the L stand for. Now comes the guesswork based on the general context; if we are looking at a unit in the 1980s and talking about aircraft then try Lightning Training Flight, if we are back in 1944 then how about Lancaster Training Flight. Whilst most of the commonest such abbreviations are included in the following list there is still plenty of room for the educated guess! However, for the general reader of aviation books, where so often the author does not give decodes of abbreviations, and for the researcher looking at official documents such as the F540, this list will prove invaluable.

Certain elements, such as 'And' (as A as in SARTU — Search and Rescue Training Unit) or 'Of' (as o in SoTT — School of Technical Training) may or may not be present and should in many instances simply be assumed.

You will notice that in some instances there is more than one decode for a particular entry, in most cases the context in which you find the abbreviation in your source material will make it obvious which is the appropriate decode.

Following the general precept adopted in this book, elements pre the formation of the RAF are not included — except where they occur in post-formation records.

(A)	Accountant Branch officer
A	Army Co-Operation (ac role)
AA	Anti-Aircraft
AA	Air Attache
AAA	Anti-Aircraft Artillery
AAAM	Advanced Air to Air Missile
AAAW	Advanced Anti-armour Weapon
AAC	Army Air Corps
AAC	Anti-aircraft Co-operation
AACC	Army Air Corps Centre
AACF/U	Anti-Aircraft Co-operation Flight/Unit
AADC	Anti-Aircraft Defence Commander
A&AEE	Aeroplane and Armament Experimental Establishment
AAF	Auxiliary Air Force
AAFCE	Allied Air Forces Central Europe
AAFGL	Auxiliary Air Force General List
AAFRO	Auxiliary Air Force Reserve of Officers
AAGS	Air Armament and Gas School

AAM	Air to Air Missile
AAOR	Anti-Aircraft Operations Room
AAP	Aircraft Acceptance Park
AAP	Air Ammunition Park
AAPC	Anti-Aircraft Practice Camp
AAR	Air to Air Refuelling
AARI	Air to Air Refuelling Instructor
AAS	Air Armament School
AASCU	Army Air Support Control Unit
AASF	Advanced Air Striking Force
AATO	Army-Air-Transport Organisation
AATT	Anti-Aircraft and Target Towing (Flight)
AAU	Anti-aircraft Unit
AAU	Air Ambulance Unit
AAU	Aircraft Acceptance/Assembly Unit
AAW	Anti-Aircraft Warfare
A/B	Airborne
ABC	Airborne Cigar
ABC	Air Booking Centre

ABDACOM	American, British, Dutch, Australian Command.	ADF	Automatic Direction Finding
ABDRF	Aircraft Battle Damage Repair Flight	ADF	Aircraft Delivery Flight
ABF	Airborne Forces	ADF/U	Air Defence Flight/Unit
ABGS(ME)	Air Bombing and Gunnery School (Middle East)	ADGB	Air Defence of Great Britain
Abm	Abeam	ADGE	Air Defence Ground Environment
ABM	Anti Ballistic Missile	ADI	Attitude director indicator
ABR	Amphibian Boat Reconnaissance (ac role)	ADLS	Air Despatch Letter Service
ac	Aircraft	ADNC	Air Defence Notification Centre
AC	Air Commodore	ADOA	Air Defence Operations Area
AC	Aircraftman	ADIZ	Air Defence Identification Zone
AC	Alternating current	ADOC	Air Defence Operations Centre
AC	Army Co-Operation (ac role)	ADP	Automatic Data Processing
ACAS	Assistant Chief of Air Staff	ADR	Airfield Damage Repair
ACC	Army Co-operation Command	ADR	Accident Data Recorder
ACC	Allied Control Commission	ADR	Air Defence Region
ACC	Area Control Centre	ADRU	Aircraft Delivery and Reception Unit
ACCCF	Army Co-Operation Command Comms Flight	ADS	Advanced Dressing Station
ACCS	Air(borne) Command and Control System	AdSR	Advanced Ship Reconnaissance
ACDC	Aircrew Despatch Centre	ADU	Aircraft Delivery Unit
A/Cdr	Air Commodore	ADUME	Aircraft Delivery Unit, Middle East
ACDU	Army Co-operation Development Unit	ADV	Air Defence Variant
ACDU(ME)	ACDU (Middle East)	ADW	Air Disbandment Wing
ACE	Allied Command Europe	AE	Aircraft Establishment
ACFE	Air Command Far East	AEAES	Air Electronics and Air Engineer School
acft	Aircraft	AEAF	Allied Expeditionary Air Forces
ACFT	Air Commodore Flying Training	AECF	Army Experimental Communications Flight
Ach	Aircrafthand	AED	Aircraft Equipment Depot
ACHU	Aircrew Holding Unit	AEF	Air Experience Flight
ACI	Airborne controlled intercepts/airborne control of interception	AEF	Armament Engineering Flight
		AEM	Air Engineering Mechanic
ACM	Air Combat Manoeuvres	AE	Air Engineer
ACM	Air Chief Marshal	AEOB	Alternate Escort Operating Base
ACM	Advanced Cruise Missile	AEOD	Airfield Explosive Odnance Disposal
ACMI	Air Combat Manouevres Installation	AES	Air Electronics School
ACN	Air Classification Number	AES	Aerial Erectors School
ACP	Air Crew Pool	AES	Aeromedical Evacuation Squadron
ACR	Air Control Radar	AES	Armament Engineering Squadron
ACRC	Air Control and Reporting Centre	AES	Airship Experimental Station
ACRS	Air Crew Refresher School	AESS	Aircraft Electrical Servicing Section
ACS	Air Construction Service/Station	AESS	Acoustic Experimental Sub-station
ACS	Airship Constructional Station	AEU	Aircrew Educational Unit
ACS	Aircrew School	AEU	Aircrew Examing Unit
ACS	Airfield Construction Squadron	AEW	Airborne Early Warning
ACS	Armoured-Car Section	A/F	After Flight
ACS	Air Combat Simulator	AFA	Air Force Area
ACSEA	Air Command South East Asia	AFAP	Air Forces Arabian Peninsula
ACSTRS	Air Crew Synthetic Trainer Refresher School	AFB	Air Force Base
A Ct	Air Commandant	AFB	Air Force Board
ACT	Air Contact/Control Team	AFC	Air Force Cross
ACT	Active Control Technology	AFCENT	Air Forces Central (Europe)
ACT	Air Combat Training	AFCO	Airborne Forces Control Officer
ACW	Airfield Construction Wing	AFDC/S	Autopilot and flight director computer/system
ACW	Air Component Wing	AFDS	Air Fighting Development Squadron
AD	Air Depot	AFDS	Air Fighter Development Squadron
ADA	Air Defence Area	AFDS	Autopilot and Flight Director System
ADA	Aircraft Dispersal Area	AFDU	Air Fighting Development Unit
ADAA	Air Defence Action Area	AFEE	Airborne Forces Experimental Establishment
ADACA(BE)	Air Division, Allied Commission Austria (British Element)	AFG	Air Forces Gulf
		AF(I)	After Flight (Inspection)
ADC	Aide-de-Camp	AFI	Annual Formal Inspection
ADC	Aircraft Disposal Company	AFLO	Airborne Forces Liaison Officer
ADC	Air Data Computer	AFM	Air Force Medal
ADCC	Air Defence Control Centre	AFME	Air Forces Middle East
ADEX	Air Defence Exercise	AFNORTH	Air Forces Northern (Europe)

AFP	Automatic flight plan	AMDP	Air Member for Development and Production
AFRU	Advanced Flying and Refresher Unit	AMDU	Air Movements Development Unit
AFS	Advanced Flying School	AMES	Air Ministry Experimental Station
AFS	Air Formation Signals	AMF	ACE Mobile Force
AFS(ME)	Air Fighting School (Middle East)	AMFS	Air Ministry Fire Service
AFS	Auxiliary Fighter Squadron	AMG	Advanced Maintenance Group
AFSDS	Air Fighter Support Development Unit	AMI	Air Mileage Indicator
AFSOUTH	Air Forces Southern (Europe)	AMIR	Air Mission Intelligence Report
AFTDU	Airborne Forces Tactical Development Unit	AMMRU	Air Ministry Manpower Research Unit
AF(T)S	Advanced Flying (Training) School	AMO	Air Ministry Order
AF(T)U	Advanced Flying (Training) Unit	AMP	Air Member for Personnel
AFTU	Air Fighting Training Unit	AMRAAM	Advanced Medium Range Air to Air Missile
AFU	Advanced Flying Unit	AMSDU	Air Ministry Servicing Development Unit
AFW	Airship Fabric Works	AMSL	Above Mean Sea Level
AFWE	Air Forces Western Europe	AMSO	Air Member for Supply and Organisation
AG	Air Gunner	AMT	Air Member for Training
AGC	Automatic Gain Control	AMTC	Aviation Medicine Training Centre
AGFFS	Anti-Gas Fire Fighting School	AMTLS	Air Ministry Target Liaison Section
AGITS	Air Gunner Initial Training School	AMU	Aircraft Modification Unit
AGL/agl	Above Ground Level	AMU	Air Mileage Unit
AGLT	Automatic Gun Laying Turret	AMU	Anti-Mosquito Unit
AGM	Air to ground missile	AMU/S/F	Air Mobile Unit/Squadron/Flight
AGM	Annual General Meeting	AMWD	Air Ministry Works Department
AGME	Aircraft Gun Mounting Establishment	AMWO	Air Ministry Weekly Order
AGRS	Air and Ground Radio School	AMX	Amatol explosive
A&GS	Armament and Gunnery School	ANBS	Air Navigation and Bombing School
AGS	Air Gunnery School	ANE	Automatic numbering equipment
AGS	Aircrew Grading School	ANI	Air Navigation Instructor
AGS(ME/I)	AGS (Middle East/India)	ANS	Air Navigation School
A/H	Alter Heading	AO	Air Organisation
AH	Army Helicopter (ac role)	AO	Administrative Order
AHB	Air Historical Branch	AOA	Air Officer Administration
AHQ	Air Headquarters	AOA	Amphibious Operations Area
AHRS	Attitude and Heading Reference System	AOA	Angle of attack
AI	Aircraft Interception	AOC	Air Officer Commanding
AI	Air Interdiction	AOCS	Altitude and Orbit Control System
AID	Accident Investigation Department	AOCU	Andover Operational conversion unit
AID	Aeronautical Inspection Department	AOG	Aircraft on Ground
AIDS	Airborne Integrated Data System	AONS	Air Observer and Navigator School
AIDU	Aeronautical Information Documents Unit	AOP	Air Observation Post
A&IEU	Armament and Instrument Experimental Unit	AOP(S)	Air Observation Post (School)
AIL	Advanced Information Leaflet	AORG	Army Operations Research Group
AIM	Air Interceptor Missile	AOS	Air Observers School
Air Cdre	Air Commodore	AOTS	Aircrew Officers Training School
AIS	Air Interception School	A/P	Aiming Point
AIU	Accident Investigation Unit	AP	Accounting Period
AIU	Air Information Unit	AP	Armour Piercing
AL	Army Liaison (ac role)	AP	Air Publication
ALARM	Air Launched Anti-Radiation Missile	AP	Aircraft Park
ALBM	Air Launched Ballistic Missile	APC	Armament Practice Camp
ALCM	Air Launched Cruise Missile	APC	Armoured Personnel Carrier
ALDP	Airborne Laser Designator Pod	APC	Air Priorities Committee
ALG	Advanced Landing Ground	APC&SS	Aden Protectorate Control and Support Squadron
ALO	Air Liaison Officer	APCS	Aden Protectorate Comms Squadron
ALS	Air Landing School	APDU	Air Photographic Development Unit
AM	Air Ministry	APFC	Air Portable Fuel Cell
AM	Air Marshal	API	Attitude Position Indicator
AM	Albert Medal	API	Air Position Indicator
AM	Air Mechanic	API	Armour-piercing incendiary
AMBT	Air Ministry Bombing Trainer	APIS	Army Photographic Interpretation Section
AMBS	Aeronautical Marker Beacon Station	APL	Aden Protectorate Levies
AMC	Aircraft Manufacturing Company (later Airco)	APO	Acting Pilot Officer
AMC	Air Monitoring Centre		
AMCU	Anti-malarial Control Unit		

APS/U	Air Pilotage School/Unit
APS	Armament Practice Station
APSF	Aden Protectorate Station/Support Flight
APU	Auxiliary Power Unit
AQ	Air Quartermaster
ARB	Attack release button
ARB	Aircraft Repair Base
ARB	Angle rate bombsight
ARC	Aeronautical Research Council
ARD	Aircraft Repair Depot
ARD	Advance Repair Depot
ARDRP	Aircraft Repair Depot Reserve Pool
ARF	Aircraft Repair Flight
ARI	Air Radio Installation
ARIC	Air Reconnaissance Intelligence Centre
ARM	Anti-Radiation Missile
ARP	Air Raid Precautions
ARR	Air Radio Relay
ARS	Aerospace Research Squadron
ARS	Aircraft Repair Station
ARTF	Alkali Removable Temporary Finish
ARU	Aircraft/Advanced Repair Unit
ARWF	Advanced Rotary Wing Flight
ARWS	Advanced Rotary Wing Squadron
AS	Air Staff
A-S	Armstrong-Siddeley
ASC	Air Support (Service) Command
ASC	Advanced Staff Course
ASC	Air Safety Centre
ASCC	Allied Standards Co-ordinating Committee
ASDS	Air Support Development Section
ASE	Admiralty Signals Establishment
ASF	Aircraft Servicing Flight
ASI	Air Speed Indicator
ASM	Air to Surface Missile
ASM	Anti-Submarine Missile
ASO	Assistant Section Officer
ASO	Anti-Submarine Observer
ASO	Armament Staff Officer
ASP	Aircraft Servicing Pan/Platform
ASP	Air Stores Park
ASR	Air Sea Rescue
ASRF/U	Air Sea Rescue Flight/Unit
ASR	Air Staff Requirement
ASRAAM	Advanced Short Range Air to Air Missile
A/SRS	Air Sea Rescue Service
ASRTU	Air-Sea Rescue Training Unit
AS&RU	Aircraft Salvage and Repair Unit
ASS	Air Signals/Signallers School
AST	Air Service Training Ltd
AST	Air Staff Target
ASU	Aircraft Storage Unit
ASUW	Anti-Surface Warfare (Maritime)
ASV	Air to Surface Vessel
ASW	Anti-Submarine Warfare
ASWDU	Air-Sea (anti-submarine) Warfare Development Unit
ASWORG	Anti Submarine Warfare Operational Research Group
AT	Anti-tank
ATA	Air Transport Auxiliary
ATAF	Allied Tactical Air Force
ATAIU	Allied Technical Air Intelligence Unit
ATC	Air Training Corps

ATC	Air Traffic Control
ATC	Armament Training Camp
ATD	Air Transient Depot
AT&DF	Air Test and Delivery Flight
ATDU	Air Torpedo Development Unit
ATDU	Air Transport Development Unit
ATF	Autogiro Training Flight
ATF	Andover Training Flight
ATFERO	Atlantic Ferry Organisation
ATGW	Anti-Tank Guided Weapon
ATLWS	Air Transportable Light Warning Set
ATM	Air Tasking Message
ATM	Anti-tank Missile
ATOC	Allied Tactical Operations Centre
ATP	Advanced Training Pool
ATREL	Air Transportable Reconnaissance Exploitation Laboratory
ATRF	Airframe Training and Repair Flight
ATRI	Air Transportable Radio Installation
ATS	Apprentices Training School
ATS	Armament Training School/Station
ATS	Air Training Squadron
ATTC	Air Traffic Control Centre
ATTDU	Air/Army Transport Tactical/Testing Development Unit
ATU	Aircrew Training Unit
ATU	Armament Training Unit
ATW	Apprentice Training Wing
ATW	Airship Training Wing
AUAS	Aberdeen University Air Squadron
AUDS	Anti U-boat Devices School
auw	All up weight
AVM	Air Vice Marshal
AW	Armstrong Whitworth
AWA	Armstrong Whitworth Aircraft Ltd
AWACS	Airborne Warning and Control System
AWAS	Air Warfare Analysis Section
AWC	Advance Warning Centre
AWDS	All-Weather Development Squadron
AWF	All-Weather Fighter
AWFCS	All-Weather Fighter Combat/Conversion Squadron
AWG	All-Weather interceptor (ac role)
AWI	Air Warfare Instructor
AWI	Air Weapons Installation
AWJRU	All Weather Jet Refresher Unit
AWOCU	All Weather Operational Conversion Unit
AWR	Air Weapons Range
AWRE	Atomic Weapons Research Establishment
AWSS	Amphibious Warfare Signals School
AWX	All-Weather Fighter (ac role)
(B)	Balloon Branch officer
B	Bomber (ac role)
BABS	Blind Approach Beacon System
BAC	British Aircraft Corporation
BAC	British Air Commission
BAC	Berlin Air Command
BAC	Bristol Aircraft Company
BAC Flt	Beam Approach Calibration Flight
BADU	Beam/Blind Approach Development Unit
BAe	British Aerospace
BAF	Balkan Air Force
BAFF	British Air Forces in France

BAFO(G)	British Air Forces of Occupation (Germany)
BAFSEA	British/Base Air Forces South-East Asia
BAI	Battlefield Air Interdiction
BALO	Brigade Air Liaison Officer
BANS	Basic Air Navigation School
BAOR	British Army of the Rhine
BAPC	British Aircraft Preservation Council
BARU	British Airways Repair Unit
BAS	Beam Approach School
BAS/U	Bombing Analysis School/Unit
BAT	British Aerial Transport Company
BAT	Beam Approach Training
BATDU	Blind Approach Training and Development Unit
BATF	Beam/Blind Approach Training Flight
BBBLEE	Bomb Ballistics & Blind Landing Experimental Establishment
BBMF	Battle of Britain Memorial Flight
BBOC	Brought back on charge
BBRM	British Bombing Research Mission
BBSU	British Bombing Survey Unit
BBU	Bomb Ballistics Unit
BCAHU	Bomber Command Aircraft Holding Unit
BCAR	British Civil Airworthiness Requirement
BCAS	Bomber Command Analysis School
BCATP	British Commonwealth Air Training Plan
BCBRU	Bomber Command Bombing Research Unit
BCBS	Bomber Command Bombing School
BCCF	Bomber Command Comms Flight
BCCS	Bomber Command Comms Squadron
BCD	Barrack and Clothing Depot
BCDU	Bomber Command Development Unit
BC Flt	Bengal Communications Flight
BCFU	Bomber Command Film Unit
BCIS	Bomber Command Instructors School
BCOF(J)	British Commonwealth Occupation Forces (Japan)
BCRS	Bomber Command Radar School
BCSMS	Bomber Command Strategic Missile School
BCU	Bird Control Unit
BD	Bomb Disposal
BDE	Balloon Development Establishment
Bde	Brigade
BDF/S/U	Bomb Disposal Flight/Squadron/Unit
BDR	Battle Damage Repair
BDT	Bomber Defence Training
BDTF	Bomber Defence Training Flight
BDU	Bomber Development Unit
BDU	Balloon Development Unit
BEA(C)	British European Airways (Corporation)
BEF	British Expeditionary Force
BEM	British Empire Medal
BF	Blast Fragmentation
B/F	Before Flight
BFAP	British Forces Arabian Peninsula
BFBS	British Forces Broadcasting Service
BFT	Basic Fitness Training/Test
BFTS	Basic Flying Training School
BFTS	British Flying Training School
BG	Bombardment Group (USAAF)
(B)G	(Bomber) Gunnery
BGS	Bombing and Gunnery School
bhp	Brake horse power
B(I)	Bomber (Interdictor)
BIB	Baby Incendiary Bomb

BIO	Brigade Intelligence Officer
BIS	British Instructional Staff
BIT(E)	Built-In Test (Equipment)
BJTF	British Joint Trials Force
B(K)	Bomber (Tanker) (ac role)
BLEU	Blind Landing Experimental Unit
BLG	Base Landing Ground
BLO	Brigade Liaison Officer
BLU	Bomb Live Unit
BMEWS	Ballistic Missile Early Warning System
BMMF	Buccaneer Major Maintenance Flight
BMSMS	Bloodhound Missile System Maintenace School
Bn	Battalion
BOAC	British Overseas Airways Corporation
BoB	Battle of Britain
BOTU	Bomber OTU
BP	Boulton Paul
BPC	British Purchasing Commission
BPD	Base Personnel Depot
BPR	Bypass Ratio
B(PR)	Bomber (Photo Reconnaissance) (ac role)
BPSO	Base Personnel Staff Officer
BPU	Base Postal Unit
BRSL	Bomb release safety lock
BSC	Basic Staff Course
BSDU	Bomber Support Development Unit
BSE	Bristol-Siddeley Engines
BSF	Base Supply Flight
BSF	Bomber Support Flight
BSS	Base Salvage Section
BSTF	Bloodhound Standards and Training Flight
BSTU	Bomber Support Training Unit
BSU	Base Signals Unit
BT	Bomber Transport
BTB	Balloon Training Base
BTD	Balloon Training Depot
BTS/F/U	Base Training Squadron/Flight/Unit
BTS/W/D	Bys Training Squadron/Wing/Depot
BTO	Bombing Through Overcast
BTU	Bomber Training Unit
BTU	Belvedere Trials Unit
BTW	Balloon Training Wing
BU	Broken up
BUAS	Bristol University Air Squadron
BUCO	Build-up Control Organisation
BVR	Beyond Visual Range
BW	Bandwidth
BWM	British War Medal
C	Cargo/Transport (ac role)
C	Command — as in:
C2	Command and Control
C3	Command, Control and Communications
C Arm O	Command Armament Officer
C ATCO	Command Air Traffic Control Officer
C Cat O	Command Catering Officer
C Comp O	Command Computer Officer
C Fire O	Command Fire Officer
C Met O	Command Meteorological Officer
C Mov O	Command Movements Officer
C PEd O	Command Physical Education Officer
C PSY O	Command Provost and Security Officer
C Res O	Command Research Officer
C Stat O	Command Statistics Officer

C Tp O	Command Transport Officer
CA	Controller, Aircraft
CA	Coastal Area
CAA	Civil Aviation Authority
CAACU	Civilian Anti-aircraft Co-operation Unit
CAAD	Coastal Area Aircraft Depot
CACF	Coast Artillery Co-operation Flight
CACU	Coast Artillery Co-operation Unit
CAEU	Casualty Air Evacuation Unit
CAG	Civil Air Guard
CAI	Command Administrative Instruction
Cal	Calibration
CALTF	Combined Airlift Task Force
CAM	Catapult Aircraft Merchant (ship)
CANS	Civil Air Navigation School
CAP	Combat Air Patrol
CAP	Command Air Publications
Capt	Captain
CAR	Civil Airworthiness Requirement
CARP	Calculated Air Release Point
CAS	Close Air Support
CAS	Chief of the Air Staff
CAS	Calibrated airspeed
CASEVAC	Casualty Evacuation
CAT/Cat	Category or categorisation
CAT	Clear Air Turbulence
CATCS	Central Air Traffic Control School
CATOR	Combined Air Transport Operations Room
CATS	Communications Analysis Training School
CATS	Combined Air Targets Section
CAVU/S	Casualty Air Evacuation Unit/Section
CAW	College of Air Warfare
CB	Companion of the Order of the Bath
CBE	Commander of the Order of the British Empire
CBE	Central Bomber Establishment
CBFAP	Commander British Forces Arabian Peninsula
CBFC	Commander British Forces Cyprus
CBLS	Carrier bomb light store
CBS	Command Bombing School
CBT	Computer Based Training
CBU	Cluster Bomb Unit
CC	Cargo and Communication (ac role)
CC	Coastal Command
CCCF	Coastal Command Comms Flight
CCCS	Coastal Command Comms Squadron
CCDU	Coastal Command Development Unit
CCF	Check and Conversion Flight
CCF	Combined Cadet Force
CCF/S	Command Communications Flight/Squadron
CCGS	Coastal Command Gunnery School
CCIL/P	Continuously computed impact line/point
CC(F)IS	Coastal Command (Flying) Instructors School
CCLPP	Coastal Command Landplane Pilots Pool
CCP	Coastal Command Pool
CCS	Communications Control System
CCS	Casualty Clearing Station
CCTDU	Coastal Command Tactical Development Unit
CCTF	Combat Cargo Task Force
CCU	Check and Conversion Unit
CD	Coast Defence
CDCF	Coast Defence Co-operation Flight
CDCN	Controller Defence Communications Network
CDDF/U	Coast Defence Development Flight/Unit
CD Flt	(Indian) Coastal Defence Flight

CDPP	Central Despatch Pool of Pilots
Cdr	Commander
CDRE	Central Defect Recording Establishment
CDT	Coast Defence Training
CDT	Course Design Team
CDTBF	Coast Defence Torpedo Bomber Flight
CEF	Casualty Evacuation Flight
CEFTS	Chinese EFTS
CENTO	Central Treaty Organisation
CEP	Circular Error of Probability
CEPE	Canadian Experimental Proving Establishment
CF	Conversion Flight
CF	Communications Flight
CFCS	Central Fighter Control School
CFE	Central Fighter Establishment
CFE	Conventional Forces Europe
CFE	Central Flights Establishment
CFI	Chief Flying Instructor
CFPC	Central Filter Plotting Centre
CFRP	Carbon Fibre Reinforced Plastics
CFS	Central Flying School
CFWD	Comms Flight Western Desert
CG	Command Guidance
CGI	Chief Ground Instructor
CGIS	Central Gliding Instructors School
CGM	Conspicuous Gallantry Medal
CGS	Central Gunnery School
CGS	Central Gliding School
CH	Chain Home
(Ch)	Chaplain
CHB	Chain Home Beamed
CHEL	Chain Home Extra Low
ChinDet	Chinook Detachment
CHL	Chain Home Low
C3I	Command, Control, Communications and Intelligence
CI	Chief Instructor
CI	Counter Intelligence
CIC	Combined Intelligence Centre
C-in-C	Commander in Chief
CINCENT	Commander-in-Chief Central Europe
CINCHAN	Commander-in-Chief Channel
CINCNORTH	Commander-in-Chief Northern Europe
CINCSOUTH	Commander-in-Chief Southern Europe
CINCUKAIR	Commander-in-Chief UK Air Forces
CIO	Careers Information Office
CIS	Communications Information Systems
CIU	Central Interpretation Unit
CIWS	Close-In Weapons System
CLE	Central Landing Establishment
CLO	Civil Liaison Officer
CLOS	Command to Line of Sight
CLS	Central Landing School
CLTS	Central Link Trainer School
C&M	Care and Maintenance
CMC	Chairman of the Mess Committee
CMC	Command Modification Centre
CME	Central Medical Establishment
CMH	Centimetric Height Finding
CMP	Central maintenance panel
CMSU	Central Management Services Unit
C/n	Constructor's number
CNCS	Central Navigation and Control School
CNS	Central Navigation School

CofA	Certificate of Airworthiness		CSW	Conventional Stand-off Weapon
COD	Carrier Onboard Delivery (ac role)		C/T	Chief Technician
C of E	Church of England		CTA	Control Area
CO	Commanding Officer		CTF	Command Training Flight
COC	Combat Operations Centre		CTOL	Conventional Take-Off and Landing
CODF	Combined Operations Development Flight		CTP	Chief Test Pilot
COI	Central Office of Information		CTS	Command Training School
COIN	Counter Insurgency		CTTB	Central Trade Test Board
COL	Chain Overseas Low		CTTO	Central Trials and Tactics Organisation
COM	Command Organisational Memorandum		CTTS	Communications and Target-Towing Squadron
COMAIR	Commander Air (Forces) as in e.g. COMAIRNON — Commander Air Northern Norway		CTTS	Civilian Technical Training School
			CTU	Conversion Training Unit
COO	Command Organisational Order		CTU	Combat Training Unit
COS	Chiefs of Staff		CTZ	Control Zone
COTU	Coastal OTU		CU	Conversion Unit
Coy	Company		CU	Communications Unit
CP	Critical Point		CUAS	Cambridge University Air Squadron
CP	Control Point		CVARIS	Central Visual Aircraft Recognition Instructors School
CPE	Central Photographic Establishment			
CPF	Coastal Patrol Flight		CVO	Commander, Royal Victorian Order
Cpl	Corporal		CVR	Cockpit Voice Recorder
CP/RA	Concrete Piercing/Rocket Assisted (bomb)		CW	Chemical Warfare
CPSU	Carrier Pigeon Service Unit		CW	Cold Weather
CPU	Central Processing Unit		CW	Continuous Wave
CPX	Command Post/Paper Exercise		CW	Communications Wing
CR	Coastal Reconnaissance (ac role)		CWS	Central Wireless School
CRAFT	Controller of RAF Communications		CWS	Chemical Warfare School
CRAM	Clearance range ahead monitor		CWS/P	Central warning system/panel
CRBF	Coastal Reconnaissance Beaufighter Flight			
CRC	Control and Reporting Centre		D	Deputy, as in, for example, D Ops O — Deputy Operations Officer
CRD	Controller of Research and Development			
CRDF	Cathode Ray Detection Finding		D	Drone (ac role)
CRE	Central Reconnaissance Establishment		(D)	Dental Branch Officer
CRO	Civilian Repair Organisation		DA	Danger Area
CRO	Community Relations Officer		DA	Direct Action (bomb)
CRO	Civilian Repair Organisation		DAAC	Director of Allied Co-operation
CRP	Control and Reporting Post		DAC	Dangerous Air Cargo
CRPMD	Combined Radar and Projected Map Display		DACT	Dissimilar Air Combat Training
CRS	Control and Reporting School		DAF	Desert Air Force
CRT	Cathode ray tube		DAFL	Director of Allied Air Co-operation and Foreign Liaison
CRU	Chemical Research Unit			
CS	Communications Squadron		DAO	Duty Aircrew Officer
CS(A)	Controller of Supplies (Air)		DAIS	Department of Administration Information Systems
CSAR	Central School of Aircraft Recognition			
CSAS	Command and stability augmentation system		DArmD	Directorate of Armament Development
CSBS	Course Setting Bomb Sight		DAS	Defensive Aids Suite
CSCE	Conference on Security and Co-operation in Europe		DAU	Directly Administered Unit
			DAW	Department of Air Warfare
CSDE	Central Servicing Development Establishment		DB	Dive Bomber (ac role)
CSE	Central Signals Establishment		DBE	Dame Commander (of the Order of the British) Empire
CSF	Canberra Servicing Flight			
CSF	Central Servicing Flight		DBF	Destroyed by Fire
CSF	Component Servicing Flight		DB ops	Director of Bomber Operations
CSFC	Church of Scotland and Free Churches		DBR	Damaged Beyond Repair
CSF/S/U	Communications and Support Flight/Squadron/Unit		DC	District Commissioner
			DC	Direct current
CSI	Companion, Order of the Star of India		DCA	Defensive Counter Air
CSI	Combined speed indicator		DCAS	Deputy Chief of the Air Staff
CSSAD	Committee for the Scientific Survey of Air Defence		DCFI	Deputy Chief Flying Instructor
			DCGI	Deputy Chief Ground Instructor
CSSAO	Committee for the Scientific Survey of Air Offence		DCM	District Court Martial
			DCM	Distinguished Conduct Medal
CSTC	Combined Strategic Targeting Committee		DEC	Defence Environment Committee

DEFA	Direction des Etudesn et Fabrications d'Armament
DES	Director of Educational Services
Det	Detachment
DetCo	Detachment Commander
Dev	Development
DEW	Directed Energy Weapon
D/F	Direction Finding
DF	Development Flight
DF	Defensive Fighter (ac role)
DF	Day Fighter (ac role)
DFC	Distinguished Flying Cross
DFCS	Day Fighter Combat School
DF/GA	Day Fighter/Ground Attack
DFLS	Day Fighter Leaders School
DFM	Distinguished Flying Medal
DF ops	Director of Fighter Operations
DFT	Director of Flying Training
DGAS	Director General of Aircraft Safety
DGCA	Director General of Civil Aviation
DGD	Director General of Ground Defence
DGE	Director General of Equipment
DGMS	Director General of Medical Services
DGO	Director General of Organisationan
DGAS	Director General of Aircraft Safety
DGRD	Director General of Research and Development
DGS	Director General of Signals
DGW	Director General of Works
DH	de Havilland
DIOT	Department of Initial Officer Training
DMC	Director of Military Co-operation
DME	Distance Measuring Equipment
DMH	Decimetre Height Finding
DMO	Director of the Meteorological Office
DMS	Director of RAF Medical Service
DNO	Director of Operations (Naval Co-operation)
Do	Dornier
D of A	Director of Accounts
D of C(AM)	Director of Contracts (Air Ministry)
D of I(O)	Director of Intelligence (Operations)
D of I(S)	Director of Intelligence (Signals)
D of M	Director of Manning
D of O	Director of Organisation
D of O (Home)	Director of Operations (Home)
D of Plans	Director of Plans
D of P	Director of Postings
D of R	Director of Radio
D of S	Director of Signals
D of Tels	Director of Telecommunications
D of W	Director of Works
DOAS	Defence Operational Analysis Section
DoD	Department of Defense
DOE	Department of the Environment
DOE	Directorate of Equipment
DO(M)	Director of Operations (Malaya)
DONC	Director of Operations (Naval Co-operation)
DOO	Director of Operations (Overseas)
DOR	Director of Operational Requirements
DOT	Director of Training
D&P	Development and Production
DP	Director of Postings
DPET	Director of Pre Entry Training
DPM	Disrupted Pattern Material
DPR	Director of Public Relations
DPS	Director of Personal Services
DPS	Detachment Provost Service
DR	De-Rated
DR	Dead Reckoning
DRA	Defence Research Agency
DRLS	Despatch Rider Letter Service
DRS	Director of Repair and Service
DS	Director of Signals
DS	Directing Staff
DSA	Defence Support Agency
DSC	Digital scan converter
DSC	Distinguished Service Cross
DSF	Domestic Supply Flight
DSGT	Department of Specialist Ground Training
DSM	Distinguished Service Medal
DSM	Director of Servicing and Maintenance
DSO	Distinguished Service Order
DSvy	Director of Survey
DTD	Director of Technical Development
DTF	Director of Flying Training
DTG	Date Time Group
DTM	District Target Map
DTO	Director of Operational Training
DTT	Director of Technical Training
DU	Display unit
DUAS	Durham University Air Squadron
DUS	Deputy Under-Secretary of State
DW	Mine-exploding (ac role)
DWAAF	Director of WAAF
DWRAF	Director of WRAF
DWI	Directional Wireless Installation
DWO	Director of War Organisation
DZ	Drop Zone
E	Experimental (ac role)
E	Electronic (ac role)
(E)	Equipment Branch Officer
EA	East Africa
E/A	Enemy Aircraft
EAAS	Empire Air Armament School
EAC	Eastern Air Command
EAC	Enemy Air Circus
EACF	East African Communications Flight
EAP	Experimental Aircraft Programme
EAS	Equivalent Air Speed
EASSU	Enemy Aircraft Storage and Servicing Unit
EANS	Empire Air Navigation School
EATS	Empire Air Training Scheme
EBTS	Elementary and Basic Training School
ECAS	Empire Central Armament School
ECDU	Electronic Countermeasures Development (Demonstration) Unit
ECDU	Engine Control Demonstration Unit
ECM	Electronic Counter Measures
ECCM	Electronic Counter-counter measures
ECFS	Empire Central Flying School
ECPF	Engineering Co-ordinations and Plans Flight
ECU	Engine Change Unit
ECU	Electronic Countersmeasures Unit
ECU	Experimental Co-operation Unit
EE(C)	English Electric (Co)
EES	Electrical Engineering Squadron
EFA	European Fighter Aircraft
EFIS	Electronic Flight Instrument System

EFS	Empire Flying School
EFTS	Elementary Flying Training School
EGM	Empire Gallantry Medal
EGS	Elementary Gliding School
EGTP	External ground test programme
EIS	Entry Into Service
EJ	Emergency jettison
ELG	Emergency Landing Ground
ELINT	Electronic Intelligence
ELUAS	East Lowlands University Air Squadron
EMUAS	East Midlands University Air Squadron
EN&AGS	Elementary Navigation and Air Gunnery School
ENSA	Entertainments National Service Association
EMP	Electromagnetic Pulse
EMS	Experimental Meteorological Station
Eng	Engineering
EO	Electro-Optical
EO	Education Officer
EOD	Explosive Ordnance Disposal
EPF	Exhibition Production Flight
EPIP	European Personnel Indian Pattern (tent)
ERB	Executive Responsibility Budget
ERFTS	Elementary and Reserve Flying Training School
ERG	Experimental and Research Group
ERS	Empire Radio School
ERU	Ejector release unit
ESA	Explosives Storage Area
ESA	European Space Agency
ESG	Electronic Stores Group
ESM	Electronic Support Measures
ESOJ	Electronic Stand-Off Jamming
ESS	Engineering Support Squadron
ETA	Estimated Time of Arrival
ETO	European Theatre of Operations
ETPS	Empire Test Pilots School
ETR	Electronic Training Range
E&TS	Education and Training Squadron
EU	Examining Unit
EU	Electronics unit
EU	Embarkation Unit
EUAS	Edinburgh University Air Squadron
EW	Electronic Warfare
EWAU	Electronic Warfare Avionics Unit
EWETU	Electronic Warfare Experimental and Training Unit
EWOSE	Electronic Warfare Operational Support Establishment
EWS	Electrical and Wireless School
EWTR	Electronic Warfare Training Range
Ex	Exercise
F	Fighter (ac role)
FA	Financial Adviser
FA	Fighting Area
FAA	Fleet Air Arm
FAAA	First Allied Airborne Army
FAC	Forward Air Controller
FADS	Forward Ammunition Depot Scheme
FAL	Field Aircraft Ltd
FAMO	Forward Air Maintenance Organisation
FARELF	Far East Land Forces
FASO	Forward Airfield Supply Organisation
F/AT	Fighter/Anti-tank (ac role)
FATU	Fighter Affiliation Training Unit
F(AW)	Fighter (All Weather)
FB	Fighter Bomber
FBD	Fighter Bomber Dual (ac role)
FBDF	Flying Boat Development Flight
FBFTS	Franco-Belgian Flying Training School
FBS	Fighter Bomber Strike (ac role)
FBSA	Fighter Bomber Strike Attack (ac role)
FBSU	Flying Boat Servicing Unit
FBTS	Flying Boat Training Squadron
FBW	Fly By Wire
FBX	Fighter Bomber All-weather
FC	Ferry Control
FC	Fighter Command
FCCF	Fighter Command Communications Flight
FCCHU	Fighter Command Central Holding Unit
FCCRS	Fighter Command Control and Reporting School
FCCS	Fighter Command Communications Squadron
FCIRS/F	Fighter Command Instrument Rating Squadron/Flight
FCP	Forward Control Post
FCPU	Ferry Command Preparation Unit
FCS	Fighter Combat School
FCS	Flying Control Section
FCS	Fighter Control School
FCS	Facility Checking Squadron
FCTS	Fighter Controllers Training School
FCTU	Fighter Command Trials Unit
FCU/F	Fighter Control Unit/Flight
FD	Flight Director
FD	Fighter Direction
FDF	Fighter Defence Flight
FDP	Forward Director Post
FDT	Fighter Direction Tender
FE	Far East
FEAF	Far East Air Force
FEBA	Forward Edge of the Battle Area
FEC	Far East Command
FECAEF	Far East Casualty Air Evacuation Flight
FECF/S	Far East Communications Flight/Squadron
FECT	Further Education and Continuation Training
FEE	Fighter Experimental Establishment
FETDU	Far East Tactical Development Unit
FETS	Far East Training Squadron
FETW	Far East Transport Wing
FEU	Forward Equipment Unit
ff	First Flight
FF	Fleet Fighter (ac role)
FF	Fighter Flight/Ferry Flight
FFAF	Free French Air Force
FFAR	Folding-Fin Air(craft) Rocket
FFCU	Forward Fighter Control Unit
FFR	Forecast Flying Rate
FFS	Fire-Fighting School
FFU	Ferranti Flying Unit
FFU	Film Flight Unit
FG	Fighter Group
FG	Fighter Ground Attack (ac role)
FG	Fighter Gunnery (Flight)
FGA	Fighter Ground Attack (ac role)
FGF	Fighter Gunnery Flight
FGRI	Fixed Ground Radio Installation
FHU	Field Hygiene Unit
FIDS	Fighter Interception Development Squadron (School)

FIU	Fighter Interception Unit		FT	Flying Training
F/O	Flying Officer		FTB	Fleet Torpedo Bomber (ac role)
Fg Off	Flying Officer		FTC	Flying Training Command
FGR	Fighter Ground Attack Reconnaissance		FTCCS	Flying Training Command Communications
FIDO	Fog Investigation and Dispersal Operations			Squadron
	Fog Intensive Dispersal of		FTF/U	Ferry Training Flight/Unit
FIPZ	Falkland Islands Protection Zone		FTS	Fixed Telecommunications System
FIR	Front-line Immediate Replacement		FTS	Flying Training School
FIR	Flight Information Region		FTSC	Flying Training Support Cell
FIS	Flying Instructors School		FTSF	Firedog Transport Support Force
FIS	Flight Information Service		FTU	Ferry Training Unit
FJ	Fast Jet		FTU	Floatplane Training Unit
FLAPS	Front-Line Armament Practice School		FU	Ferry Unit
FLG	Fuelling Landing Ground		FVCP	Forward Visual Control Post
FLIR	Forward Looking Infra Red		F/W	Fair Weather
FLM	Flight Line Mechanic		FW	Focke-Wulf
FLOSY	Front for the Liberation of South Yemen		FWS	Fighter Weapons School
FLOT	Forward Line of Own Troops		FWSU	Fighter Wing Servicing Unit
FLS	Fighter Leaders School		FWTS	Fixed Wing Test Squadron
Flt	Flight		FY	Financial Year
Flt Cdr	Flight Commander			
F/L	Flight Lieutenant		G	General Purpose (ac role)
F/Lt	Flight Lieutenant		(G)	Air Gunner Officer
Flt Lt	Flight Lieutenant		GA	Ground Attack
Fl O	Flight Officer		GAC	Gloster Aircraft Ltd
FM	Frequency Modulated		GAF	German Air Force
FMCW	Frequency Modulated Continuous Wave		GAF	Ground-Attack Fighter
FN	Frazer Nash		GAI	Group Administrative Instruction
FNSF	Fast Night Striking Force		GAL	General Aircraft Limited
FOB	Forward Operating Base		GAS	Ground Armament School
FOD	Foreign Object Damage		GATU	Ground Attack Training Unit
FOL	Forward Operating Location		GBU	Glider Bomb Unit
FONA	Fleet Officer Naval Aviation		GC	George Cross
FP	Ferry Pool		GC	Gliding Centre
FPDU	Field Punishment and Detention Unit		GC.	Groupe de Chasse
fpm	feet per minute		GCA(U)	Ground Controlled Approach (Unit)
FPP(U)	Ferry Pilots Pool (Unit)		GCB	Knight Grand Cross of the Order of the Bath
FPT	Ferry Pilot Training		GCC	Group Control Centre
FPU	Ferry Preparation Unit		GCF	Gunnery Co-operation Flight
FPU	Film Production Unit		GCF	Ground Control of Flying
FR	Fighter Reconnaissance		GCF	Group Communications Flight
FRA	First Run Attack		GCI	Ground Controlled Interception
FRA	Federal Regular Army		GCIE	Knight Grand Commander of the Indian Empire
FRADU	Fleet Requirements and Air Direction Unit		GCMG	Knight Grand Cross of St Michael and St George
FRD	Forward Repair Depot		GCSI	Knight Grand Commander of the Star of India
FRF	Farnborough Research Flight		GCT	Ground Combat Training
FRL	Flight Refuelling Ltd		GCTO	Ground Combat Training Officer
FRS	Flying Refresher School		GCVO	Knight Grand Cross of the Royal Victorian
FRS	Fighter Reconnaissance Strike (ac role)			Order
FRU	Fleet Requirements Unit		GD	General Duties
FRU	Field (Forward) Repair Unit		GD	Ground Defence
FS	Float Seaplane		GDA	Anti-aircraft Gun Defended Area
FS	Fleet Spotting (ac role)		GDC	Group Disbandment Centre
F/S	Flight Sergeant		GDCC	Ground Defence Control Centre
FSCL	Fire Support Co-ordination Line		GDGS	Ground Defence Gunnery School
FSD	Full Scale Development		GDOC	Ground Defence Operations Centre
F/Sgt	Flight Sergeant		GE	Ground Environment
FSCTE	Fire Service Central Training Establishment		GED	Ground Equipment Depot
FSF	Forward Supply Flight		GEF	General Engineering Flight
FSI	Flight Sub-Imprest		GEU	Gyro electronics unit
FSR	Fleet Spotter Reconnaissance (ac role)		GGS	Ground Gunners School
FSS	Flying Selection School		GGS	gyro gunsight
FSS	Ferry Support Squadron		GH	General Handling
FSW	Forward Swept Wing		GH	General Hospital

GHQ	General Headquarters		HAST	Harrier Avionic System Trainer
GI	Ground Instructional		HB	Heavy Bomber
GIF	Glider Instructors Flight		HC	Helicopter Cargo (ac role)
GIS	Glider Instructors School		HC	High Capacity (bomb)
GM	George Medal		HC	Home Command
GMR	Ground mapping radar		HCB	Heavy Conversion Base
GMSG	Guided Missile Support Group		HCCS	Home Command Communications Squadron
GMT	Greenwich Mean Time		HCEU	Home Command Examining Unit
GOC	General Officer Commanding		HCGC	Home Command Gliding Centre
GOI	Group Operational Instruction		HCS	Hercules Conversion Squadron
GOM	Group Operational Memorandum		HCT	Harrier Conversion Team
GOO	Group Operational Order		HCU	Heavy Conversion Unit
GOR	General Operational Requirement		HD	Home Defence
GOTU	Glider Operational Training Unit		HDD	Head-down display
Gp	Group		HDF	Halifax Development Flight
GP	General Purpose		HDF	Helicopter Development Flight
G/C	Group Captain		HDDR	Head-down display recorder
Gp Capt	Group Captain		HDU	Hose Drum Unit
GPEU	Glider Pilots Exercise Unit		HDU	Helicopter Development Unit
GPI	Ground Position Indicator		He	Heinkel
GPLU	Ground programme loading unit		HE	High Explosive
GPMG	General Purpose Machine Gun		HEAT	High Explosive Anti Tank
GPR	Glider Pilot Regiment		HEI	High explosive incendiary
GPS	Global Positioning System		HES	Hardened Equipment Shelter
GPU	Ground Power Unit		HF	High Altitude Fighter (ac role)
GR	Ground Attack Reconnaissance		HF	High frequency
GR	General Reconnaissance (ac role)		HFU	Home Ferry Unit
GR&ANS	General Reconnaissance and Air Navigation School		HGCU	Heavy Glider Conversion Unit
			HGSU	Heavy Glider Servicing Unit
GRFB	General Reconnaissance Flying Boat		HGTU	Heavy Glider Training Unit
GRF	Ground Radio Flight		HLB	Higher Level Budget
GRP	Glass Fibre Reinforced Plastics		HMG	His/Her Majesty's Government
GRSS	Ground Radio Servicing Section		HML	Hadrami Bedouin Legionnaires
GRU	General Reconnaissance Unit		HMMF	Hawk Major Maintenance Flight
GRU	Gunnery Research Unit		HMS	His/Her Majesty's Ship
GRU/F	Gunnery Research Unit/Flight		HMT	His/Her Majecty's Troopship
GS	Gliding School		HOCF	Helicopter Operational Conversion Flight
GS	Grading School		HOJ	Home-on-Jam
GSE	Ground Support Equipment		HOT	Haut Subsonique Optiquement Teleguide tire d'un tube
GSEU	Glider Storage and Erection Unit			
GSI	Group Signals Instruction		HP	Handley Page
GSM	General Service Medal		hp	Horse power
GSTS	General Service Training School		HPOX	High Pressure Oxygen
GSU	Group/Ground Support Unit		HPS	Hardened Personnel Shelter
GSU	Group Standardisation Unit		HQ	Headquarters
GT	Glider Tug (ac role)		HR	Helicopter Rescue (ac role)
GTF	Gunnery Training Flight		HRN	Hurricane Repair Network
GTF	Ground test facility		HS	Hawker Siddeley
GTS	Glider Training School		HSF	High-Speed Flight
GTS	Glider Training Squadron		HSI	Horizontal situation indicator
GU	Grading Unit		HSL	High Speed Launch
GUAS	Glasgow University Air Squadron		HSP	Heavy Stressed Platform
GWDS	Guided Weapons Development Squadron		HT	Helicopter Training (ac role)
GWTS	Guided Weapons Training Squadron		HTF	Heavy Transport Flight
			HTF	Helicopter Training Flight
HAA	Heavy Anti-aircraft		HTS	Hercules Training Squadron
HAD	Home Aircraft Depot		HT(S)CU	Heavy Transport (Support) Conversion Unit
HAECO	Hong Kong Aircraft Engineering Company		HU	Helicopter Utility (ac role)
HAL	Hawker Aircraft Ltd		HUAS	Hull University Air Squadron
HAR	Helicopter Air Rescue (ac role)		HUD	Head-Up Display
HarDet	Harrier Detachment		HVAR	High Velocity Aircraft Rocket
HARM	High-Speed Anti-Radiation Missile		HVM	Hyper-Velocity Missile
HAS	Hardened Aircraft Shelter		HxCF	Halifax Conversion Flight
HAS	Helicopter Anti-Submarine (ac role)			

(I)	Intelligence Officer
IA	Inland Area
IADS	Integrated Air Defence System
IAF	Indian Air Force
IANS	Initial Air Navigation School
IATA	International Air Transport Association
iaw	in accordance with
ILF	Independent Liaison Flight
IAM	Institute of Aviation Medicine
IAS	Indicated Air Speed
IAS	Immediate air support
IAS	Indirect air support
IB	Incendiary Bomb
i/c	In charge
I/C	Inter-comm
ICAO	International Civil Aviation Organisation
ICBM	Inter-Continental Ballistic Missile
ICO	Idle Cut-off switch
ICO	Instinctive Cut-Out
ICOM	Institute of Community and Occupational Medicine
ICW	Intermittent continuous wave
IDF	Interceptor Day Fighter (ac role)
IDHT	Insitute of Dental Health and Training
IDS	Interdictor Strike (ac role)
IE	Initial (Immediate) Establishment (Equipment)
IF	Instrument Flying
IF	Intermediate frequency
IF	Independent Force
IF(D)F	Intensive Flying (Development) Flight
IFF	Identification Friend and Foe
IFR	In-Flight Refuelling
IFR	Instrument Flight Rules
IFS	Inspector(ate) of Flight Safety
IFTU	Intensive Flying Trials Unit
IFU	Interface unit
IIR	Imaging Infra Red
ILS	Instrument Landing System
IMC	Instrument Meteorological Conditions
IMP	Instantaneous-fuzed Magnum
IN	Inertial Navigation
INAS	Inertial Navigation-Attack System
INCDU	Inertial Navigation Control and Display Unit
INF	Intermediate Range Nuclear Forces
INS	Inertial Navigation System
INU	Inertial Navigation Unit
IO	Intelligence Officer
IOC	Initial Operational Capability
IOGROPS	Indian Ocean General Reconnaissance Operations
IOR	Inspectorate of Recruiting
IPS	Intelligence Planning Squadron
IPS	Into Productive Service
IPTM	Institute of Pathology and Tropical Medicine
IR	Infra Red
IR	Immediate Reserve
IRBM	Intermediate Range Ballistic Missile
IRCM	Infra-Red Counter Measures
IRCCM	Infra-Red Counter-Counter Measures
IRD	Infra Red Decoy
IRE	Instrument Rating Examiner
IRF	Independent Reconnaissance Flight
IRLS	Infra Red Line Scan
IRR	Immediate Readiness Reserve

IRS	Inertial Reference System
IRS	Instrument Rating Squadron
IRT	Instrument Rating Test
ISA	International Standard Atmosphere
ISF	Internal Security Flight
ISO	International Standards Organisation
ISO	Companion of the Imperial Service Order
ISS	Individual Staff Studies
IT	Information Technology
ITF/S	Instrument Training Flight/Squadron
ITP	Instruction To Proceed
ITS	Initial Training School
ITT	Into Training Target
ITW	Initial Training Wing
J	Junior, as in J Eng O — Junior Engineering Officer
JABC	Joint Air Booking Centre
JACIG	Joint Arms Control Implementation Group
JAG	Judge Advocate General
JAPIC	Joint Air Photograhic Intelligence Centre
JARIC	Joint Air Reconnaissance Intelligence Centre
JASS	Joint Anti-Submarine School
JATE	Joint Air Transport Establishment
JCC	Joint Concealment Centre
JCSS	Junior Command and Staff School
JCU	Javelin Conversion Unit
JCU	Joint Conversion Unit
JEFTS	Joint Elementary Flying Training School
JEHU	Joint Experimental Helicopter Unit
JFACTSU	Joint Forward Air Controller Training and Standardisation Unit
JHU	Joint Helicopter Unit
JHSU	Joint Helicopter Support Unit
JIC	Joint Intelligence Centre
JIRS/F	Javelin Instrument Rating Squadron/Flight
JMC	Joint Maritime Course
JMF	Jaguar Maintenance Flight
JMTU	Javelin Mobile Training Unit
JMU	Joint Maintenance Unit
JOC	Joint Operations Centre
JOCU	Jaguar Operational Conversion Unit
JP	Jet Provost
JPT	Jet Pipe Temperature
JSATC	Joint Services Air Trooping Centre
JSAWC	Joint Services Amphibious Warfare Centre
JSBDS	Joint Service Bomb Disposal School
JSNCGD	Joint School of Nuclear and Chemical Ground Defence
JSP	Joint Service Publications
JSPI	Joint School of Photographic Interpretation
JSPU	Joint Services Port Unit
JSSC	Joint Service Staff College
JSTARS	Joint Surveillance Target Attack Radar
JSTU	Joint Services Trials Unit
JSU	Joint Supply Unit
JTF	Jet Training Flight
JTIDS	Joint Tactical Information Distribution System
JTMU	Joint Transport and Movement Unit
JTRU	Jungle Target Research Unit
JSSC	Joint Services Staff College
Ju	Junkers
JWE	Joint Warfare Establishment

K	Tanker (ac role)		L Lt	Leigh Light
KAF	Kenya Air Force		LLR	Low Level Route
KAR	King's African Rifles		LLTV	Low Light Television
KB	Kite Balloon		LNSF	Light Night Strike Force
KBE	Knight Commander of the Order of the British		LOAL	Lock-On After Launch
	Empire		LOBL	Lock-On Before Launch
KCAS	Knots calibrated airspeed		LORAN	Long Range Aid to Navigation
KCB	Knight Commander of the Order of the Bath		LOS	Line Of Sight
KCIE	Knight Commander of the Indian Empire		LOX	Liquid Oxygen
KCSI	Knight Commander of the Star of India		LP	Low Pressure
KCVO	Knight Commander of the Royal Victorian		LPD	Last Point of Diversion
	Order		LPO	Local Purchase Order
KE	Kinetic Energy		LR	Long Range
KF	King's Flight		LRDU	Long Range Development Unit
KF	Kalman Filter		LRMR	Long Range Maritime Reconnaissance (ac role)
KG	Knight of the Garter		LRMTS	Laser Ranger and Marked Target Seeker
KGMG	Knight Commander of St Michael and St George		LRPTE	Long Range Pilot Training Element
KIA	Killed in Action		LRU	Line Replacable Unit
KP	Knight of St Patrick		LRWE	Long Range Weapons Establishment
KP	Key Point		LS	Long Stroke
KR's	King's Regulations		LSGM	Long Service and Good Conduct Medal
KT	Knight of the Thistle		LSP	Light Stressed Platform
kT	Kiloton		LST	Landing Ship Tank
kt	knot		LSU	Lancaster Servicing Unit
KUAS	Kent University Air Squadron		L/T	Line Telegraphy
KVa	Kilovolt Amperes		LTC	Long Term Costing
			LTF	Lightning Training Flight
(L)	Legal Branch Officer		LTW	Lyneham Transport Wing
L/A	Land/Air		LUE	Local Unit Establishment
LAA	Light Anti-aircraft		LVO	Lieutenant, Royal Victorian Order
LABS	Low Altitude Bombing System		LWU	Light Warning Unit
LAC	Leading Aircraftman		LZ	Landing Zone
LACW	Leading Aircraftwoman			
LADA	London Air Defence Area		M.	Mach number
LAIS	Low Attack Instructors School		M	Torpedo Bomber (ac role)
LAL	Launch-And-Leave		m	Metre
LANTIRN	Low Altitude Navigation Targeting Infra Red		(M)	Medical Officer
	Night		MAAF	Malayan Auxiliary Air Force
LAPG	London Aircraft Production Group		MAAF	Mediterranean Allied Air Force
LAS	Light Aircraft School		MABS	Magnetic Airborne Bombsight
LASU	Local Air Supply Unit		MAC	Mediterranean Air Command
LB	Light Bomber		MAC	Military Airlift Command (USAF)
LBR	line of bomb release		MACA	Military Aid to the Civil Authority
LBTI	Long Burning Target Indicator		MACAF	Mediterranean Allied Coastal Air Forces
LCF	Lancaster Conversion Flight		MAD	Magnetic Anomaly Detector
LCF	Lightning Conversion Flight		MAD	Marine Acceptance Depot
LCF	Lincoln Conversion Flight		MADGE	Microwave Aircraft Digital Guidance Equipment
LCF	Levant Communications Flight		MAE	mean area of effectiveness
LCN	Load Classification Number		MAEE	Marine Aircraft/Armament Experimental
LCS	Lightning Conversion Squadron			Establishment
LCT	Landing Craft tank		MAEOp	Master Air Electronics Operator
LDV	Local Defence Volunteers		MAFL	Manual of Air Force Law
LE	Logistics Establishment		MALM	Master Air Loadmaster
LERX	Leading Edge Root Extension		MAMS	Mobile Air Movements Squadron
LF	Low Frequency		MAOT	Mobile Air Operations Team
LF	Low Altitude Fighter (ac role)		MAP	Ministry of Aircraft Production
LFA	Low Flying Area		MAP	Mutual Aid Pact
LFS	Lancaster Finishing School		MAPR	Mediterranean PR (wing)
LG	Landing Ground		MAREL	Mobile Air Reconnaissance Exploitation
LGB	Laser-Guided Bomb			Laboratory
LID	Lift Improvement Device		MARTSU	Mobile Aircraft Repair, Transport and Salvage
LL	Light Liaison (ac role)			Unit
LL	Leigh Light		MARU	Mobile Air Reporting Unit
LL	Low Level		MAS	Malayan Auxiliary Squadron

MASAF	Mediterranean Allied Strategical Air Force	mg	machine gun
MASB	Motor Anti-Submarine Boats	mg	milligrammes
MASS	Master armament safety switch	MGRI	Mobile Ground Radio Installation
MATAF	Mediterranean Allied Tactical Air Forces	MHz	Megaherz
MATO	Military Air Traffic Operations	MIA	Missing in action
MB	Motor Boat	mic/tel	Microphone/telephone
mb	millibar	MiD	Mentioned in Despatches
MBE	Member (of the order of the) British Empire	mm	millimetre
MBF	Mobile Balloon Flight	MMU	Mobile Meteorological Unit
MBFR	Mutual Balanced Force Reduction	Mk	Mark number
MBT	Main Battle Tank	Mintech	Ministry of Technology
(Mc)	Marine Craft Officer	MIS	Monthly Intelligence Summary
MC	Military Cross	MLO	Military Landing Officer
MC	Medium Capacity (bomb)	MLU	Mid-Life Update
MC	Main Computer	MNC	Major NATO Commander
MCA	Ministry of Civil Aviation	MOA	Ministry of Aviation
MCC&FF	Maintenance Command Communications and Ferry Flight	MOB	Main Operating Base
		MOD	Ministry of Defence
MCCS/F	Maintenance Command Communications Squadron/Flight	MOD(PE)	Ministry of Defence (Procurement Executive)
		mods	Modifications
MCF	Mechanical Components Flight	MOP	Mission Operating Procedures
MCRS	Marine Craft Repair Section	MORU	Mobile Operations Room Unit
MCS	Metropolitan Communications Squadron	MOS	Ministry of Supply
MCSU	Mobile Catering Support Unit	MOTU	Marine Operational Training Unit
MCSU	Marine Craft Storage Unit	MOU	Memorandum of Understanding
MCTC	Military Corrective Training Centre	Mov O	Movements Officer
MCTS	Marine Craft Training School	MPA	Maritime Patrol Aircraft (ac role)
MCS/U	Marine Craft Section/Unit	MPBU	Mobile Pilot Balloon Unit
MCU	Mosquito Conversion Unit	mph	miles per hour
MDA	Master Diversion Aerodrome	mpi	Mean Point of Impact
MDAP	Mutual Defence Air/Assistance (Aids) Pact (Programme)	MPP	Most Probable Position
		MQ	Married Quarter
MDC	Miniature Detonating Cord	MR	Maritime Reconnaissance (ac role)
MDS	Main Dressing Station	M/R	Medium Range
Me	Messerchmitt	MRA	Multi-role aircraft
ME	Middle East	MRAF	Marshal of the Royal Air Force
MEAF	Middle East Air Force	MRCA	Multi-Role Combat Aircraft
MEAS	Mechanical Engineering Air Squadron	MRCP	Mapping radar control panel
MEAS	Middle East Armament School	MRCP	Mobile Radar Control Post
MEC	Middle East Command	MRR	Maritime Radar Reconnaissance
MECCS/U	Middle East Check and Conversion Squadron/Unit	MRR	Medium Range Reconnaissance
		MRS	Marine Reconnaissance School
MECF/S	Middle East Communications Flight/Squadron	MRS	Medical Receiving Station
MECGS	Middle East Central Gunnery School	MRT	Mountain Rescue Team
MEDA	Military Emergency Diversion Aerodrome	MRTT	Medium Range Tactical Transport
MEDME	Mediterranean and Middle East	MRU	Missile Range Unit
MEFC	Middle East Ferry Control	MRU	Mobile Radio Unit
MEGS	Mechanical Engineering Ground Squadron	MS	Medium Supercharged
MEP	Mobile Equipment Park	MSC	Major Subordinate Commander
MERF	Middle East Rescue Flight	MSFU	Merchant Ship Fighter Unit
MET (Met)	Meteorological	MSH	Maritime Support Helicopter (ac role)
METAR	Meteorological Actual Report	MSOW	Modular Stand-Off Weapon
METS	Middle East Torpedo (Training) School	MSP	Medium Stressed Platform
METS	Multi-Engine Training Squadron	MSSU	Mobile Signals Servicing Unit
MEW	Ministry of Economic Warfare	MSU	Major/Mobile Servicing Unit
MEXO	Multi-Engine Cross-over	MSU(T)	Mobile Servicing Unit (Torpedo)
MF	Medium Frequency	MSU	Mobile Surgical Unit
MFA	Malta Facilities Agreement	MSW	Mission Support Wing
MFC/U	Meterological Forecast Centre/Unit	MT	Mechanical (Motor) Transport
MFH	Mobile Field Hospital	MT	Megaton (One million tons of TNT equivalent)
MFK	Multi-function keyboard	MTBF	Mean Time Between Failures
MFPU	Mobile Field Processing/Photographic Unit	MTI	Moving Target Indicator
MFS	Marshall's Flying School	MTLRU	Mechanical Transport Light Repair Unit
MFU	Metropolitan Forecast Unit	MTMS	Mechanical Transport Maintenance Section

MTR	Marked target receiver		NWATC	North West Africa Training Command
MTRD	Mechanical Transport Reception Depot		NWATCC	North West Africa Troop Carrier Command
MTU	Mobile Torpedo Unit		NWASAF	North West African Strategic Air Force
MTU	Mosquito Training Unit		NWATAF	North West African Tactical Air Force
MTU	Mechanical Transport Unit		NWFP	North West Frontier Province
MU	Maintenance Unit		NYK	Not Yet Known
MUAS	Manchester University Air Squadron			
MV	Merchant Vessel		O	Observation (ac role)
MVO	Member of the Royal Victorian Order		(O)	Observer Officer
MWDP	Mutual Weapons Defense Programme		OAC	Overseas Aircraft Control
			OADF/U	Overseas Aircraft Delivery Flight/Unit
N	Naval (ac role)		(O)AFU	(Observer) Advanced Flying Unit
(N)	Navigation Instruction Officer		OAFU	Overseas Aircraft Ferry Unit
NA	North Africa		OAMC	Overseas Aircraft Movement Control
N/A	Not Applicable		OAPU	Overseas Aircraft Preparation Unit
NAAF	Northwest African Air Forces		OASC	Officer and Aircrew Selection Centre
NACAF	Northwest African Coastal Air Force		OATS	Officers Advanced Training School
NADA	Northern Air Defence Area		OBE	Officer (of the Order of the) British Empire
NADGE	NATO Air Defence Ground Environment		OC	Officer Commanding
NARO	Nuclear Accident Reporting Organisation		OCA	Offensive Counter-Air
NASAF	Northwest African Strategic Air Forces		OCC	Observer Corps Centre
NATAF	Northwest African Tactical Air Forces		OCC	Officers Command Course
NATO	North Atlantic Treaty Organisation		OCL	Obstacle Clearance Limit
NATS	National Air Traffic Services		OCTU	Officer Cadet Training Unit
Navex	Navigation Exercise		OCU	Operational Conversion Unit
NAVHARS	Navigation, Heading and Attitude Reference System		ODM	Operating Data Manual
			OEU	Operational Evaluation Unit
NBS	Naval Bombardment Spotting		(O)FIS	(Operational) Flying Instructors School
NBTS	Night Bomber Tactical School		OFP	Operational flight plan
NCO	Non-Commissioned Officer		OFU	Overseas Ferry Unit
NCS	Northern Communication Squadron		O/H	Overhead
NDT	Non-destructive Testing		OLG	Operational Landing Ground
NEC	Near East Command		OM	Order of Merit
NEAF	Near East Air Force		OOA	Out Of Area
NECS	Near East (Air Force) Communications Squadron		OOP	Out Of Phase
			Op	Operation
NF	Night Fighter		OPCON	Operational Control
NFF	Night Flying Flight		OPTU	Oxygen Production Training Unit
nff	no fault found		OPTW	Operations and Pilot Training Wing
NFLS	Night Fighter Leaders School		OR	Operational Requirement
NGTE	National Gas Turbine Establishment		ORB	Operational Record Book
NHC	Navigator's hand controller		ORBAT	Order of Battle
NJG	Nachtjagdgeschwader		ORP	Operational Readiness Platform
NLF	National Liberation Front		ORS	Operational Research Section
nm	Nautical Mile		ORTU	Operational Refresher Training Unit
NMCP	Navigation Mode control panel		OS	Offensive Support
NMMU	Nimrod Major Maintenance Unit		OSC	Overseas Staff College
NMS	New Management Strategy		OSS	Operational Support Squadron
NREF	North Russian Expeditionary Force		OTF	On-top fix
NS	National Service		OTF	Overseas Training Flight
NST	Nimrod Software Team		OTF	Observer Training Flight
NTO	Naval Transport Officer		OTH	Over the Horizon
NTS	Navigation Training Squadron		OTR	Operational Turn Round
(N)TS	(Night) Training Squadron		OTS	Officers Training School/Squadron
NTU	Navigation Training Unit		OTU	Operational Training Unit
NUAS	Northumbrian Universities Air Squadron		OUAS	Oxford University Air Squadron
NV	Normal Vetting			
NVG	Night Vision Goggles		P	Principal, as in P MO — Principal Medical Officer
NVTIC	Night Vision Training Instructors Course			
NVTS	Night Vision Training School		PA	Personal Assistant
NWA	North West Africa		PAC	Parachute and Cable
NWAAF	North West African Air Force		PACT	Preliminary Air Crew Training
NWAASC	North West Africa Air Service Command		PAF	Polish Air Force
NWACAF	North West African Coastal Air Force		(P)AFU	(Pilot) Advanced Flying Unit

PAF BTS	Polish Air Force Boys Training School		PP	Present Position
PAI	Pilot Armament Instructor		PPI	Plan Position Indicator
PAP	Pilots and Aircrew Pool		PPP	Pupil Pilots Pool
PAR	Precision Approach Radar		PR	Photographic Reconnaissance (ac role)
PAS/U	Pilotless Aircraft Section/Unit		PR	Public Relations
PAS	Pre-planned air support		PRC	Personnel Reception Centre
PATP	Packed Aircraft Transit Pool		PRDU/E	Photographic Reconnaissance Development Unit/Establishment
PB	Pusher Biplane		PRF	Pulse Repetition Frequency
pb	practice bomb		PRFU/S	Pilot Refresher Flying Unit/School
PBF	Pilot/Personnel Briefing Facility		PRO	Public Record Office
PC	Privy Councillor		PRO	Public Relations Officer
PC	Permanent Commission		PRRP	Pilots Reserve and Reinforcement Pool
PCB	Plenum Chamber Burning		PRU	Photographic Reconnaissance Unit
PCF	Pioneer Conversion Flight		P&SS	Provost and Security Services
PCSS	Protectorate Communication and Support Squadron		psa	Graduate of RAF Staff College
PD	Pulse Doppler		PSA	Property Services Agency
PD	Precision Device		PSC	Principal Subordinate Commander
PDC	Personnel Despatch Centre		PSF	Personnel Services Flight
P Det	Port Detachment		psi	Per square inch
P DO	Principal Dental Officer		PSO	Personal/Principal Staff Officer
PDS	Post Design Services		PSP	Pierced Steel Planking
PDU	Photographic Development Unit		(PT)	Physical Training Officer
PDU	Pilot's display unit		PTC	Personnel Transit Centre
PDU	Pylon decoder unit		PTF	Phantom Training Flight
PE	Procurement Executive		P&TJ	Palestine and Trans Jordan
PEC	Personal Equipment Connector		PTS	Parachute Training School
PEC	Photographic Experimental Station		PTU	Parachute Test Unit
PEE	Proof and Experimental Establishment		PTURP	Pilots Training Unit and Reinforcement Pool
PFA	Popular Flying Association		PUS	Permanent Under Secretary of State
PFB	Preliminary Flying Badge		PV	Private Venture
PFCU	Powered Flying Control Unit		PV	Positive Vetting
PFF	Pathfinder Force		PW	Prisoner of War
PFFNTU	Pathfinder Force Navigational Training Unit		PW	Psychological Warfare
PFS	Parachute Flying Section			
PFTS	Polish Flying Training School			
PFU	Parachute Flying Unit			
PFU	Practice Flying Unit			
PGI	Pilot Gunnery Instructor			
PGTS	Parachute and Glider Training School			
(Ph)	Photographic Officer			
PHC	Pilot's hand controller			
PIO	Pilot Induced Oscillation			
PIT	Permit Identity Tag			
PIU	Power interface unit			
Plt Off	Pilot Officer			
(PM)	Provost Marshal Duties Officer			
PMC	Personnel Management Centre			
PMD	Projected map display			
PMO	Principal Medical Officer			
PMP	Provost Marshal Prohibited (Area)			
PMR	Provost Marshal Restricted (Area)			
PMRAFNS	Princess Mary's Royal Air Force Nursing Service			
PMS	Personnel Managament Squadron			
PNB	Pilot Navigator Bomber			
PNR	Point of No Return			
P/O	Pilot Officer			
POC	Point of Contact			
POI	Point of Interest			
POL	Petrol, Oil, Lubricants			
POR	Personnel Occurrance Records			
POTU	Polish Operational Training Unit			
PoW	Prisoner of War			

Q Code — The code was used as a convenient way of reducing RT conversation when requesting a standard item of information, it was also used to a limited extent in signals and other correspondence.Each subject area, e.g meteorology, flying control, was given a series of codes, the letters for which bore no relationship to the information they gave. Over the years the system has reduced in importance and the vast majority of terms have now vanished from general use. However, a number of the met terms are still common.

Q	Target Tug (ac role)
QB	Queen Bee
QCS	Queens Colour Squadron
QCVSA	Queen's Commendation for Valuable Service in the Air
QF	Queen's Flight
QF	Quick Firing
QGM	Queen's Gallantry Medal
QFI	Qualified Flying Instructor
QGH	Radar-controlled descent
QMG	Quartermaster General
QHI	Qualified Helicopter Instructor
QNI	Qualified Navigation Instructor
QR's	Queen's Regulations
QRA	Quick Reaction Alert
Qr M	Quartermaster
QUAS	Queen's University Air Squadron
R	Reconnaissance

RA	Royal Artillery		Res	Reserve
R&D	Research and Development		Ret/Retd	Retired
R&D	Receipt and Despatch		REU	Radio Engineering/Experimental Unit
RAAF	Royal Australian Air Force		RF	Radio Frequency
RACP	Reserve Air Crew Pool		RFC	Royal Flying Corps
RAD	Reserve Ammunition Depot		RFP	Request For Proposals
RADAR	Radio Direction And Ranging		RFS	Reserve Flying School
RAE	Royal Aircraft Establishment		RFTS	Refresher Flying Training School
RAeC	Royal Aero Club		RFU	Refresher Flying Unit
RAeS	Royal Aeronautical Society		RHAF	Royal Hellenic Air Force
RAF	Royal Air Force		R&I	Repair and Inspection
RAF	Royal Aircraft Factory		R&R	Refuel and Re-arm
RAFC	Royal Air Force College		R&R	Rest and Recreation
RAF FC	Royal Air Force Flying College		RIAF	Royal Indian Air Force
RAFG	Royal Air Force Germany		RIMU	Radio Installation and Maintenance Unit
RAFGSA	Royal Air Force Gliding and Soaring Association		RIU	Radio Introduction Unit
			RIU	Recruit Instructors Unit
RAFLO	Royal Air Force Liaison Officer		RIW	Repair in Works
RAFM	Royal Air Force Mission		RLC	Rest and Leave Camp
RAFO	Reserve of Air Force Officers		RLG	Relief Landing Ground
RAFVR	Royal Air Force Volunteer Reserve		RM	Royal Marines
RAI	Reconnaissance/attack interface		RMAF	Royal Malaysian Air Force
RAM	Radar Absorbent Material		RML	Rescue Motor Launch
RAFNI	Royal Air Force Northern Ireland		RMU	Radio Maintenance Unit
RAFRS	Royal Air Force Regiment School		RN	Royal Navy
RAFTC	Royal Air Force Technical College		RNAS	Royal Naval Air Service
RAM	Radar Asborbent Material		RNAY	Royal Navavy Air Yard
RAMO	Rear Air Maintenance Organisation		RNEFTS	Royal Navy Elementary Flying Training School
RAP	Regimental Aid Post		RNFS	Royal Navy Fighter Squadron
RAS	Reserve Aeroplane Squadron		RNethAF	Royal Netherlands Air Force
RAS	Rectified Air Speed		RNFS	Royal Naval Fighter Squadron
RASC	Royal Army Service Corps		RNoAF	Royal Norwegian Air Force
RASO	Rear Airfield Supply Organisation		RNR	Royal Naval Reserve
RATF	Radio Aids Training Flight		RNZAF	Royal New Zealand Air Force
RATG/W	Rhodesia Air Training Group/Wing		ROA	Restricted Operations Area
RATO(G)	rocket assisted take-off (gear)		ROC	Royal Observer Corps
RAuxAF	Royal Auxiliary Air Force		ROC	Required Operational Capability
R/B	Range and Bearing		ROE	Rules of Engagement
RBS	Radar Bombsight		ROL	Read-out line
RC	Receiving Centre		RP	Rocket Projectile
RC	Reserve Command		RPAF	Royal Pakistan Air Force
RCAF	Royal Canadian Air Force		RPM	Revolutions per minute
RCC	Rescue Co-ordination Centre		RPMD	Repeater projected map display
RCCS/F	Reserve Command Communications Squadron/Flight		RPTF	Rocket Projectile Training Flight
			RPV	Remotely-Piloted Vehicle
RCDI	Rate of Climb and Descent Indicator		R-R	Rolls Royce
RCITF	Reserve Command Instructor Training Flight		RRAF	Royal Rhodesian Air Force
RCL	Recoilless gun		RRDE	Radar Research and Development Establishment
RCM	Radio Counter-Measures		RRE	Royal Radar Establishment
RCS	Radar Cross Section		RRF/U	Radar Reconnaissance Flight/Unit
RCS	Radar Conversion School		RRFU	Radar Reconnaissance Flying Unit
RCW	Reception and Classification Wing		RRP	Reinforcement and Reserve Pool
RD	Royal Naval Reserve Officers Decoration		RRP	Refuelling and Re-arming Party
RDAF	Royal Danish Air Force		RS	Radio School
RDE	Rapid data entry		RS	Reserve Squadron
RDF	Radio Direction Finding		R&S	Repair and Salvage
RDFS	Radio Direction Finding School		RS&RE	Royal Signals and Radar Establishment
RDP	Recruits Disposal Pool		RSU/S	Repair and Servicing Unit/Section
RDU	(Aircraft) Receipt and Despatch Unit		RSU	Repair and Salvage Unit
RDX	Research Department Explosive		RTP	Recruit Training Pool
RE	Royal Engineers		RTU	Rapier Training Unit
RE	Research and Experiments (Department)		rtu	return to unit
REAF	Royal Egyptian Air Force		RU	Repair Unit
REC	Release Embarkation Centre		RVC	Radio/Radar Visual Corridor

RVR	Runway Visual Range
RW	Receiving Wing
RWE	Radar Warfare Establishment
RWE	Radar Warning Equipment
RWR	Radar Warning Receiver
RWTS	Rotary Wing Test Squadron
Rx	Receiver
S	Senior, as in S Ed O — Senior Education Officer
S	Strike (ac role)
S	Supercharged
S/A	Strike/Attack
SAA	small arms ammunition
SAAF	South African Air Force
SABS	Stabilised Automatic Bombsight
SAC	Strategic Air Command
SAC	Senior Aircraftman
SofAC	School of Army Co-operation
SACEUR	Supreme Allied Commander Europe
SACLANT	Supreme Allied Commander Atlantic
SACLOC	Semi-Automatic Command to Line of Sight
SACSEA	Supreme Allied Command South East Asia
SACW	Senior Aircraftwoman
SAEE	Small Arms Experimental Establishment
SAEU	Strike Attack Evaluation Unit
SAFO	Senior Air Force Officer
SAFU	Safety arming and functioning unit
SAHR	Secondary attitude and heading reference
SAM	Surface to Air Missile
SAMIOTS	Surface to Air Missile Operational Training School
SAN	School of Air Navigation
SAOEU	Strike Attack Operational Evaluation Unit
SAP	Semi Armour Piercing
SAP	School of Air Pilotage
SAP	Simulated Attack Profile
SAPI	Semi armour piercing incendiary
SAR	Search and Rescue
SARAH	Search and Rescue Aircraft Homing
SARBE	Search and Rescue Beacon Equipment
SARH	Semi-Active Radar Homing
SARTU/S	Search and Rescue Training Unit/Squadron
SAS	Special Air Service
SAS	Singapore Auxiliary Squadron
SAS	Stability Augmentation System
SofAS	School of Air Support
SofAT	School of Air Transport
SASO	Senior Air Staff Officer
SATC	School of Air Traffic Control
SATCOM	Satellite Communications System
SATNAV	Satellite Navigation System
SBA	Standard Beam Approach
SBA	Sovereign Base Area
SBAC	Society of British Aircraft Constructors
SBC	Small Bomb Carrier
SBC	Services Booking Centre
SBX	Slow-burning explosive
SofC	School of Catering
SC	Strike Command
SC	Support Command
SCAF	Supply Control and Accounting Flight
SCBS	Strike Command Bombing School
SCCS	Strike Command Communications Squadron
SCF	Sabre Conversion Flight

SCF	Signals Co-operation Flight
SCGDS	Support Command Ground Defence School
SCI	smoke curtain installation
SofCSR	School of Combat Survival and Rescue
SCR	Signal Corps Radar
SCS	Southern Communications Squadron
SCS	Special Communications Squadron
SCSR	School of Combat Survival and Rescue
SCTS	Synthetic Crew Training Scheme
SCU	Servicing Commando Unit
SD	Special Duties
SDF	Special Duties Flight
SDF	Special Defence Flight
SDU	Signals Development Unit
SE	Single engine
SEAAC	South East Asia Air Command
SEAC	South East Asia Command
SEACOS	South East Asia Chiefs of Staff
SEAD	Suppression of Enemy Air Defences
SEATO	South East Asia Treaty Organisation
SEB	Single-engined Bomber
SEDB	Single-engined day bomber
SEE	Signals Engineering Establishment
SENB	Single-engined Night Bomber
SEP	Special Erection Party
SEP	Static Equipment Park
SEPECAT	Societe Europeenne de Production de l'Avion Ecole de Combat et Appui Tactique
SES	Safety Equipment Section
SF	Station Flight
SF	Special Forces
SofFC	School of Fighter Control
SFC	School of Flying Control
S&FCS	Squadron and Flight Commanders School
SFF	Service Ferry Flight
SFPP	Service Ferry Pilots Pool
SFSO	Station Flight Safety Officer
SFTS	Service Flying Training School
SFU	Signals Flying Unit
SGR	School of General Reconnaissance
SGR&AN	School of General Reconnaissance and Air Navigation
Sgt	Sergeant
S/H	Set Heading
SHAEF	Supreme Headquarters Allied Expeditionary Force
SHAPE	Supreme Headquarters Allied Powers Europe
SHF	Support Helicopter Force
SHORAD	Short Range Air Defence
shp	Shaft horse power
SHQ	Station Headquarters
SIO	Senior Intelligence Officer
SIS	Special Intelligence Service
SITF	Station Instrument Training Flight
SITREP	Situation Report
SIU	Signals Intelligence Unit
SIU	Special Installation Unit
SJ	Selective jettison
SKTU	Sea King Training Unit
S/L	Squadron leader
SLAIS	Specialised Low Attack Instructors School
SLAPS	Second-Line Armament Practice Camp
SLAR	Sideways-Looking Airborne Radar

SLAW	School of Land-Air Warfare
SLC	Searchlight Control
S/Ldr	Squadron Leader
SLG	Satellite Landing Ground
SLJ	'Silly little job'
SLU	Special Liaison Unit
S&M	Supply and Movements
SMF	Station/Scheduled Maintenance Flight
SMO	Senior Medical Officer
SMR	School of Maritime Reconnaissance
SMS	Stores management system
SMT	Square Meshed Track
SNC	School of Naval Co-operation
SNCO	Senior Non-commissioned Officer
SNTDU	Synthetic Navigation Training Development Unit
S O	Section Officer
SOM	Secret Organisational Memoranda
SOP	Standard Operational Procedure

Schools — The nomenclature for schools is somewhat variable, many appearing as 'S of ...', others simply as 'So ..'. The following list uses the S of format, although the reader may find instances of these schools using the alternative format.

S of A	School of Administration
S of AC	School of Airfield Construction
S of AC	School of Army Co-operation
S of AE	School of Aeronautical Engineering
S of AFTT	School of Air Force Technical Training
S of AG	School of Air Gunnery
S of AN	School of Air Navigation
S of AP	School of Air Pilotage
S of AS	School of Air Support
S of ASR	School of Air Sea Rescue
S of AT	School of Air Transport
S of ATC	School of Air Traffic Control
S of C	School of Catering
S of CSR	School of Combat Survival and Rescue
S of FC	School of Fighter Control
S of FC	School of Ferry Control
S of GR	School of General Reconniassance
S of JSPT	School of Jungle Self Preservation Training
S of LAW	School of Land/Air Warfare
S of MR	School of Maritime Reconnaissance
S of N&BN	School of Navigation and Bomb Dropping
S of NC	School of Naval Co-operation
S of P	School of Photography
S of RF	School of Refresher Flying
S of RT	School of Recruit Training
S of SF	School of Special Flying
SO	Staff Officer
SOAF	Sultan of Omans Air Force
SOC	Struck off Charge
SOC	Sector Operations Centre
SOE	Special Operations Executive
SOETS	School of Education and Training Support
SOJ	Stand-Off Jamming
SOM ·	School of Music
SofP	School of Photography
SoRF	School of Refresher Training
SoTT	School of Technical Training
(SP)	Special Duties Officer
SP	Staging Post
SP	Service Police

Spec	Specification
SPFS	Station Publications and Forms Store
SPF&AGS	Seaplane Pilot's Finishing and Aerial Gunnery School
SPTU	Staff Pilot Training Unit
Sqn	Squadron
Sqdn	Squadron
Sqn Ldr	Squadron leader
Sq O	Squadron Officer
SR	Strategic Reconnaissance
SR	Short Range
SRAAM	Short Range Air to Air Missile
SRAF	Southern Rhodesian Air Force
SRAFO	Senior RAF Officer
SRAM	Short Range Attack Missile
SRAF	Southern Rhodesian Air Force
SRCU	Short Range Conversion Unit
SRF	Sea Rescue Flight
SRF	School of Refresher Flying
SRIM	Service Radio Instrument Modification
SRO	Station Routine Orders
SRMP	Short Range Maritime Patrol
SRP	Supply Refuelling Point
SRR	Sortie Raid Report
SRS	Seaplane Refuelling Station
SRSAR	Short Range Search and Rescue (ac role)
SRT	Short Range Transport (ac role)
SRTU	Survival and Rescue Training Unit
SRU	Self Recording Unit
SRU	Strategic Reconnaissance Unit
SS	Submarine Scout
SS	Single Seat
SS	Steam Ship
SS	Signals School
SSA	Supplementary Storage Area
SSB	Single Sideband Transmission
SSM	Surface to Surface Missile
SSO	Special Service Officer
SSP	Stressed Supply Platform
SSS	Station Services Squadron
SSU	Special Signals Unit
SSU	Special Servicing Unit
SSVAF	Straits Settlements Volunteer Air Force
SSVC	Services Sound and Vision Corporation
ST	Standard Transport
STC	Strike Command
S&T	Supply and Transport (Column)
STC	Supply and Transport Column
STCAAME	Strike Command Air to Air Missile Establishment
STCASMSU	Strike Command Air to Surface Missile Support Unit
STCVMS	Strike Command Victor Maintenance School
STDU	Synthetic Training Development Flight
STOL	Short Take-off and Landing
STS	Support Training Squadron
STS	Seaplane Training Squadron
STT	School of Technical Training
STT	Special Tactical Transport
S&TT	Station and Target Towing
STW	Sentry Training Wing
SU	Signals Unit
SU	Support Unit
SUP	Statement of Unit Policy
SupO	Supply Officer
SWO	Station Warrant Officer

SWPA	South West Pacific Area	TFOA	Temporary Full Operational Airfield
SWS	Special Weapons System	TFPP	Temporary Ferry Pilots Pool
SWUAS	South Wales University Air Squadron	TFP	Training Ferry Pool
Sy	Security	TFR	Terrain Following Radar
		TFS/U/F	Target Facilities Squadron/Unit/Flight
(T) (a)	Armament Officer	TFU	Telecommunications Flying Unit
(T) (e)	Engineer officer	TG	Trade Group
(T) (s)	Signals Officer	TGRI	Transportable Ground Radio Installation
T	Trainer (ac role)	THUM	Temperature and Humidity
TA	Terrain avoidance	TI	Texas Instruments
TA	Territorial Army	TI	Target Indicator
TAC	Tactical Air Command (USAF)	TI	Trial Installation
TAC	Transatlantic Air Control	TIALD	Thermal Imaging and Laser Designation
TACAN	Tactical Air Navigator	TIB	Target Indicator Bomb
TAD	Tactical Air Depot	TISSMT	Tornado In Service Software Maintenance Team
TAF	Tactical Air Force	TM	Tractor Monoplane
TAF	Terminal Airfield Forecast	TMB	Tactical Medium Bomber (Ac role)
TAFC	Training Area Flying Control	TMOA	Temporary Minimum Operational Airfield
TAFSU	Tactical Air Force Support Unit	TMS	Tornado Maintenance School
TAMU	Transport Aircraft Maintenance (Modification) Unit	TMSG	Technical and Mobility Supply Group
TANS	Tactical Air Navigation System	TMTS	Trade Management Training School
TAP	Terminal Approach Plate	T/O	Take-off
TAS	True Air Speed	TOC	Taken on charge
TAS	Tactical Air Support	TOCU	Tornado Operational Conversion Unit
TASF	Transit Aircraft Servicing Flight	TOEU	Tornado Operational Evaluation Unit
TASMO	Tactical Air Support of Maritime Operations	TOO	Target of opportunity
TASS	Transit Aircraft Servicing Section	TOR	Terms of Reference
TB	Tractor Biplane	TOS	Target Operating Squadron
TB	Torpedo Bomber (ac role)	TP	Test Pilot
TBC	To be confirmed	TPF	Tornado Propulsion Flight
TBD	To be decided	Tpt	Transport
TBF	Tactical Bomber Force	TR	Tactical Reconnaissance
TCA	Terminal Control Area	T/R	Turn Round (servicing)
TC	Transport Command	TRE	Telecommunications Research Establishment
TC	Training Command	Trg	Training
TC	Tactical Control	TRI	Tactical Reconnaissance Intelligence
TCASF	Transport Command Air Support Flight	TRRU	Tornado Radar Repair Unit
TCB	Twin Cable Bomb	TRS	Torpedo Refresher School
TCC	Transport/Cargo Carrier (ac role)	TRU	Transportable Radio Unit
TCCS/F	Transport Command Communications Squadron/Flight	TRW/S	Tactical Reconnaissance Wing/Squadron
		TS	Training Squadron
TCDU	Transport Command Development Unit	TSC	Twin store carrier
TCEU	Transport Command Examining Unit	TSCU	Transport Support Conversion Unit
TCG/W	Troop Carrier Group/Wing	TSF	Transport Supply Flight
TCU	Transport Conversion Unit	TSF	Technical Supply Flight
TCW	Tactical Communications Wing	TSR	Torpedo Spotter Reconnaissance (ac role)
TCZ	Terminal Control Zone	TSTU	Transport Support Training Unit
TD	Territorial Decoration	TSU	Tornado Standardisation Unit
TDP	Target Director Post	TSW	Tactical Support/Supply Wing
TDS	Training Depot Station	TT	Technical Training Depot
TDS	Trade Defence Squadron	TT	Target Tow(ing)
TDU/F	Torpedo Development Unit/Flight	TTC	Temporary Training Camp
TDU	Tactical Development Unit	TTC	Technical Training Command
TDY	Temporary Duty	TTCCF	Technical Training Command Communications Flight
TEA	Temporary Emergency Airfield		
TEB	Twin-engined Bomber	TTF	Target Towing Flight
TEDB	Twin-engined Day Bomber	TTF	Tactics and Trials Flight
TENB	Twin-engined Night Bomber	TTF	Tanker Training Flight
TES	Tripartite Evaluation Squadron	TTGF	Target Towing and Gunnery Flight
TEU	Tactical Exercise/Evaluation Unit	TTTE	Tri-national Tornado Training Establishment
TEU	Tropical Experimental Unit	TTTF	Typhoon Tropical Trials Flight
TEW	Test Equipement Wing	TTU	Torpedo Training Unit
TEZ	Total Exclusion Zone	TTW	Transition to War
TF	Torpedo Fighter (ac role)	TURP	Training Unit Reserve Pool
TF	Training Flight	TVC	Thrust Vector Control
		TVM	Television (guided) missile

TV/TAB	Television Tab
TWCU	Tornado Weapons Conversion Unit
TWDU	Tactical Weapons Development Unit
TWS	Track While Scan
TWU	Tactical Weapons Unit
TX	Training Glider (ac role)
Tx	Transmitter
U	Unmanned (ac role)
U	Utility (ac role)
UAS	University Air Squadron
UBAS	University of Birmingham Air Squadron
u/c	Undercarriage
UDI	Unilateral Declaration of Independence
UED	Universal Equipment Depot
UET	Unit Equipment Table
ufn	until further notice
UHF	Ultra High Frequency
UK	United Kingdom
UKADGE	United Kingdom Air Defence Ground Environment
UKADR	United Kingdom Air Defence Region
UKALM	United Kingdom Air Lisison Mission
ULAS	University of London Air Squadron
UN	United Nations
UNAF	United Nations Air Forces
UNEF	United Nations Emergency Force
UNFICYP	United Nations Force In Cyprus
u/s	Unserviceable
USAAF	United States Army Air Force
USAEB	United States Air Evaluation Board
USAF	United States Air Force
USAFE	United States Air Force Europe
USMC	United States Marine Corps
USN	United States Navy
USSTAF	United States Strategic Air Forces
U/T	Under Training
UTC	Universal Time Clock
UTM	Universal Tranverse Mercator
UTP	Unit Test Pilot
UV	Ultra-Violet
UXB	Unexploded Bomb
V-A	Vickers Armstrong
VA	Vulnerable area
VAC	Vocational Advice Centre
VAD	Voluntary Aid Detachment
VASF/S	Visiting Aircraft Servicing Flight/Section
VC	Victoria Cross
VCAS	Vice Chief of Air Staff
VCP	Visual/Vehicle Control Post
VE	Victory in Europe
VEB	Variable Elevation Beam
VGS	Volunteer Gliding School
VHF	Very High Frequency
VIP	Very Important Person
VISTRE	Visual Inter-Service Training and Research Establishment
VJ	Victory in Japan
VLBTI	Very Long Burning Target Indicator
VLF	Very Low Frequency
VM	Victory Medal
VMMU	Victor Major Maintenance Unit
Vne	Maximum Speed, never exceed
Vno	Maximum Speed, normal operating

VOR	Very High Frequency Omni-directional Range
VP	Vulnerable point
VR	Visual Reconnaissance
VR	Volunteer Reserve
VSF	Victor Servicing Flight
VSG	Variable speed gear
VTF	Victor Training Flight
V/STOL	Vertical/Short take-off and Landing
VV	Vertical velocity
W	Weather (ac role)
WA	West Africa
WA	Western Air (Plans)
WA	Western (bombing) Area
WAAC	Womens Army Auxiliary Corps
WAAF	Women's Auxiliary Air Force
WAMS	Weapon aiming mode selectors
WAP	Western Aden Protectorate
WATU	Western Approaches Tactical Unit
WCF	Wessex Conversion Flight
WCP	Weapon control panel
WCS	Western Communications Squadron
WCU	Washington Conversion Unit
WDCF/U	Western Desert Communications Flight/Unit
WDU	Wireless Development Unit
WEE	Wireless Experimental Establishment
WEE	Winterisation Experimental Establishment
wef	With immediate effect
W/C	Wing Commander
WETF	Winter Experimental and Training Flight
Wg Cdr	Wing Commander
Wg O	Wing Officer
WI	Wireless Intercept(ion)
WIDU	Wireless Intelligence Development Unit
wie	with immediate effect
WIU	Wireless Intelligence Unit
W/O	Warrant Officer
WO	Warrant Officer
WO2	Warrant Officer 2nd Class
WOP	Wireless Operator
WOP/AG	Wireless Operator/Air Gunner
WOU	Wireless Observer Unit
WPU	Weapon programming unit
WRAF	Women's Royal Air Force
WRB	Weapon release button
WRD	Works Repair Depot
WS	Working store
WSAO	Weekly Summary of Air Operations
WSF	Weapons Storage Flight
WST	Weapons Standardisation Team
WSU	Wing Signals Unit
WSU	Wing Support Unit
W/T	Wireless Telegraphy
WTF	Wessex Training Flight
WTU	Warwick Training Unit
WUDO	Western Union Defence Organisation
W/V	Wind Velocity
Wx	Weather
X	Glider (ac role)
Y/S 'Y'	Service (Special Duties signals)
YTF	Yugoslav Training Flight
YUAS	Yorkshire University Air Squadron
ZCL	Zero command line
ZFW	Zero Fuel Weight

ROYAL AIR FORCE ORDER OF BATTLE

THE FOLLOWING TABLES give details of the ORBAT for all flying units — squadrons, flights, flying training and specialist units — for certain years. The list starts with April 1918, the formation of the RAF, and then moves to April 1922, significant as the start of the, albeit minor, expansion period after the post-war low. List 3 is for 10 years later, April 1932, and although the RAF is a little larger the basic aircraft types, at least as performance and role is concerned, have changed little. There is a marked difference in the list for 1939 — expansion has taken place and the number of types has increased. The World War Two period contains annual listings to show the development of RAF air power to the massive striking potential of late 1944/early 1945 — and the huge training machine needed to support it. Post-war the lists return to an 10-yearly basis (roughly), ending with the ORBAT for October 1993.

This is the first time that details such as these have been published, although squadron locations have been provided in a number of published works. Primary sources have been used in the compilation of the data presented here — the two most important sources being the SD. 161 (Location of RAF Units) and the Royal Air Force List. As with all research material there are a number of problems involved! These problems really only manifest themselves in the records covering World War Two when units, or rather, squadrons, moved around at frequent intervals and records were not as well kept, for obvious reasons, as might be otherwise desirable. The net result of this tends to be a time lag between the unit having moved and that move being recorded in the SD.161. Consulting the squadron ORB can help in sorting out this dilemma — although the ORB is also not always an unambiguous source. 1944 proved to be a particular difficult year as the records adopted a new format with home-based units being listed under their main base location even if they were in fact operating from a satellite airfield. A further complication comes from the frequent use of detached elements operating from a variety of locations — which one is listed in the official record? (in general terms the answer is that the HQ element is recorded — even if they have no aircraft!)

The list has been restricted to giving details of ONLY flying units, except for reference to non-flying Groups and Wings, along with the basic details of their function and composition. The source material gives details of every unit — from the Mobile Dental Surgeries to the Anti-Maleria Units — far too much material to be covered in this format. The listings of training units and assorted Flights should provide an excellent starting point for additional research into this ill-published area of RAF history.

The lists are presented in the format, i.e running order, in which they appear in the source material — they also, therefore, detail the organisation of each Command and Group.

Although a selection of Squadron ORBs was examined it was not possible to refer to every unit entry, for the purpose of cross-checking squadron location where required (e.g 1944) the secondary source of 'RAF Squadrons', (by Jeff Jefford and published by Airlife) was used. As mentioned above, there is always an element of date discrepancy due to paperwork transfers and moves not agreeing with actuality; some moves were cancelled and yet not changed in the written record. At other times a unit may be called upon to make many moves, possibly as detachments, over a short period of time — an example being four moves by No 140 Squadron Mosquitoes in July 1945. In these cases it is usually the HQ location which is recorded by officialdom. Similar problems exist with a consideration of the aircraft being operated by a particular unit, the authorised equipment often varied from that actually held by the unit. A typical example of this situation was No 7 BATF at Finningley which was allocated Blenheims as its primary type; however, the unit also acquired a number of Ansons and Oxfords, albeit on a temporary basis, due to the unsuitability of the Blenheims. The vast majority of units, including squadrons, also managed to acquire a range of 'hacks' for general flying and communications; the standard types were Masters, Tiger Moths, and such like, but some units had more spectacular additions — No 39 Sqn operated a Ju87!

In the ORBATS the stations listed under a Command/Group do not necessarily belong to that Command/Group, rather, it is the unit listed which is under command — hence the reader will observe that some stations occur more than once in the same ORBAT.

Spelling of locations varied (e.g. Spitalgate or Spittlegate) and, in most cases, the common-use spelling has been used.

Additional notes are provided with each list as required.

Following the standard principle for this reference work, Allied squadrons of other air forces have been left out unless they were part of the RAF numbering sequence as an integrated element of the RAF. Thus ORBATS for certain theatres, especially the Middle East, may appear a little 'thin' due to the absence of SAAF, RHAF, REAF etc. units.

Location	Flying Sqn	Other Flying Unit	Ac Type

April 1918

TRAINING DIVISION: HQ — ST JAMES, LONDON
NORTHERN TRAINING BRIGADE: HQ — FOSSGATE, YORK
8th WING: HQ — YORK

Location	Flying Sqn	Other Flying Unit	Ac Type
Tadcaster	—	68, 14 TS	
Doncaster	—	41, 49 TS	
Beverly	—	72 TS	

19th WING: HQ — NEWCASTLE-ON-TYNE

Catterick	—	46, 52, 115, 118, 127 TS	
Cramlington	—	75, 120 TS	

23rd WING: HQ — SOUTH CARLTON, LINCOLN

Scampton	—	11, 60 TS	
South Carlton	—	39, 45, 61 TS	
Scampton	81	—	Camel

24th WING: HQ — HILL HOUSE, GRANTHAM

Spittlegate	—	15, 37, 50 TS	
Harlaxton	—	20, 58, 64 TS	

27th WING: HQ — WADDINGTON

Hucknall	117	—	DH4/RE8
Hucknall	130	—	DH9
Waddington	—	44, 47, 48, 51 TS	
Hucknall	135	—	nil?

30th WING: HQ — MONTROSE

Montrose	—	6, 18, 36 TS	

SOUTHERN TRAINING BRIGADE: HQ — SALISBURY
4th WING: HQ — NETHERAVON

Netheravon	—	7, 97, 116 TS	

17th WING: HQ — BEAULIEU

Beaulieu	—	1, 70, 73 TS	

28th WING: HQ — YATESBURY

Yatesbury	—	13, 16, 17, 66 TS	

33rd WING: HQ — DRUIDS LODGE, LAKEDOWN

Old Sarum	99, 103	—	DH9
Lake Down	107, 108, 109, 136	—	DH9
Lake Down	136	—	nil?

34th WING: HQ — STOCKBRIDGE

Chattis Hill	—	34, 43 TS	

36th WING: HQ — THRUXTON

Andover	104	—	DH9
Andover	105, 106	—	RE8

EASTERN TRAINING BRIGADE: HQ — ST JAMES, LONDON
6th WING: HQ — MAIDSTONE

Croydon	—	40 TS	
Dover	—	62, 65 TS	
Joyce Green	—	63 TS	
Wye	—	42 TS	

7th WING: HQ — KING'S LYNN

Sedgeford	—	9 TS	
Narborough	—	26, 69 TS	
Narborough	121	—	DH9
Sedgeford	110	—	DH4/DH9
Sedgeford	122	—	DH9

18th WING: ST JAMES, LONDON

Curragh	—	19 TS	
London Colney	—	27, 56 TS	
Northolt	—	2, 4 TS	
Shoreham	—	3 TS	
Hounslow	85	—	SE5A
Hounslow	87	—	Dolphin
Northolt	86	—	nil?
Tangmere	91	—	various inc. RE8

Tangmere	92, 93	—	SE5A
Ford Junction	148, 149	—	FE2b/FE2d

26th WING: ST MARY'S, ELY

Wyton	—	31, 5 TS	
Thetford	—	12, 25 TS	
Duxford	119	—	(various)
Duxford	123, 129	—	DH9
Fowlmere	124, 125	—	DH4/DH9
Fowlmere	126	—	DH9
Thetford	128	—	DH9

39th WING: BRANDON

Harling Road	88	—	F2b
Harling Road	89	—	(various)
Harling Road	94	—	Camel

WESTERN GROUP COMMAND: HQ — EDGBASTON, BIRMINGHAM
21st WING: CIRENCESTER

Witney	—	8, 24 TS	
Oxford	—	35, 71 TS	
Rendecombe	—	38, 59 TS	

35th WING: CASTLE BROMWICH

Castle Bromwich	—	28, 54 TS	
Castle Bromwich	—	74 TS	
Lilbourne	—	55 TS	

29th WING: SHAWBURY

Shawbury	—	10 TS	
Shawbury	131	—	(various)
Shawbury	137	—	DH9
Tern Hill	132	—	(various)
Tern Hill	133	—	FE2b
Tern Hill	134	—	HP 0/400

37th WING:

Shotwick	—	67 TS	
Shotwick	90, 95	—	(various)
Shotwick	66	—	Camel

1ST TRAINING WING AFC: HQ — TETBURY
(not included)
Units under direct Divisional Control

Upavon	—	CFS	(various)
	—	S of SF	
	—	S of AG	
	—	1 S of AF	
	—	2 S of AF	
	—	1 (0) S of AG	
	—	2 (Aux) S of AG	
	—	4 (Aux) S of AG	

6TH BRIGADE: HQ — HORSE GUARDS PARADE, LONDON
46th WG: HQ — YORK

Jesmond	36 (HQ)	—	Pup/F2b
Hylton	36 (A Flt)	—	Pup/F2b
Ashington	36 (B Flt)	—	Pup/F2b
Seaton Carew	36 (C Flt)	—	Pup/F2b
Ripon	76 (HQ)	—	BE12b
Copmanthorpe	76 (A Flt)	—	BE12b
Helpenby	76 (B Flt)	—	BE12b
Catterick	76 (C Flt)	—	BE12b
Edinburgh	77 (HQ)	—	—
Whitburn	77 (A Flt)	—	BE12b
Penston	77 (B and C Flt)	—	BE12b

47th WING: HQ — CAMBRIDGE

Melton Mowbray	38 (HQ)	—	
Stanford	38 (A Flt)	—	FE2b
Buckminster	38 (B Flt)	—	FE2b
Leadenham	38 (C Flt)	—	FE2b
Marham	51 (A Flt and HQ)	—	BE12b
Tydd St Mary	51 (A Flt)	—	BE12b
Mattishall	51 (C Flt)	—	BE12b
Newmarket	—	190/191 TS	(various)

Location	Flying Sqn	Other Flying Unit	Ac Type
Marham	—	192 TS	(various)
48th WING: HQ — GAINSBOROUGH			
Gainsborough	33 (HQ)	—	—
Brattleby	33 (A Flt)	—	FE2d
Kirton Lindsey	33 (B Flt)	—	FE2d
Elsham	33 (C Flt)	—	FE2d
East Retford	—	187, 188, 199, 200 TS	(various)
Suttons Farm	—	189 (N) TS	(various)
49th WING: HQ — UPMINSTER			
North Weald Bassett	39	—	F2b
Hainault Farm	44	—	Camel
Hornchurch	78	—	Camel
Westerham (Biggin Hill)	141	—	F2b
50th WING: HQ — CHELMSFORD			
Stow Maries	37 (A and B Flt)	—	(various)
Goldhanger	37 (C Flt)	—	(various)
Rochford	61	—	SE5A
Elmswell	75 (HQ and B Flt)	—	BE12b
Harling Road	75 (A Flt)	—	BE12b
Hadleigh	75 (C Flt)	—	BE12b
Rochford	—	198 (N) TS	(various)
53rd WING: HQ — MAIDSTONE			
Bekesbourne	50	—	BE12b
Throwley	112	—	Camel
Throwley	—	186 (N) TS	Avro 504J, 504K
Detling	143	—	SE5A
Plus No 2 Wireless School, and five Schools of Aeronautics			

Under Air Ministry Control

Wide range of storage parks, repair depots, schools, balloon units, etc.

Wireless experimental establishment

Armament experimental establishment

Aeroplane experimental establishment

RAF IN THE FIELD

1ST BRIGADE
Ist (Corps) WG

Location	Flying Sqn	Other Flying Unit	Ac Type
Hesdigneul	2	—	FK8
Chocques	4, 42	—	RE8
Acq (and dets)	5	—	RE8
Camblain-l'-Abbé	16	—	RE8
10th (ARMY) WING:			
Treizennes	18	—	DH4
Treizennes	203	—	Camel
Bruay	40	—	SE5A

2ND BRIGADE
2nd (CORPS) WING:

Location	Flying Sqn	Other Flying Unit	Ac Type
Proven	7, 9	—	RE8
Droglandt	10	—	FK8
La Lovie	21	—	RE8
Boisdinghem	53	—	RE8
11th (ARMY) WING:			
Ste-Marie-Cappel	1	—	SE5A
Savy	19	—	Dolphin
Boisdingham	20	—	F2b
La Lovie	29	—	SE5A
Le Quesnoy	57	—	DH4

3RD BRIGADE
12th (CORPS) WING:

Location	Flying Sqn	Other Flying Unit	Ac Type
Vert Galand	8	—	FK8
Vert Galand	59	—	RE8/F2b
Soncamp	12	—	F2b
Le Hameau	13	—	RE8
Fienvillers	15	—	RE8
13th (ARMY) WING:			
Fienvillers	60	—	SE5A
Fienvillers	11	—	F2b

Location	Flying Sqn	Other Flying Unit	Ac Type
Fienvillers	70	—	Camel
Vert Galand	22	—	F2b
Alquines	41	—	SE5A
Avesnes-le-Comte	43	—	Camel
Filescamp Farm	46	—	Camel
Petite Synthe	49	—	DH4/DH9
Valheureux	56	—	SE5A
?	61	—	SE5A

5TH BRIGADE
15th (CORPS) WING:

Location	Flying Sqn	Other Flying Unit	Ac Type
Abbeville	35	—	F2b
Abbeville	35	—	F2b
Agenvillers	82	—	FK8
Bois-de-Roche	205	—	DH4
22nd (ARMY) WING:			
Bertangles	23	—	Dolphin
Bertangles	48	—	F2b
Bertangles	54	—	Camel
Bertangles	84	—	SE5A
Conteville	24	—	SE5A
Conteville	65	—	Camel

8TH BRIGADE
41st WING:

Location	Flying Sqn	Other Flying Unit	Ac Type
Tantonville	55	—	DH4
Tantonville	100	—	FE2C
Villesneux (and dets)	216	—	HP0/400

9TH (GHQ) BRIGADE
9th (GHQ) WING:

Location	Flying Sqn	Other Flying Unit	Ac Type
Ruisseauville	25, 27	—	DH4
Beauvois	32	—	SE5A
Beauvois	73	—	Camel
Planques	62	—	F2b
Beauvois	79	—	Dolphin
Belleville Farm	80	—	Camel
54th (GHQ) WING:			
?	68	—	SE5A
Auchel	83	—	FE2b
Haute Vissée	101	—	FE2b
Le Hameau	102	—	FE2b

7TH BRIGADE
51st (CORPS) WING:

Location	Flying Sqn	Other Flying Unit	Ac Type
Le Crotoy (and dets)	6	—	RE8
St Omer	74	—	SE5A
St Omer	98	—	DH9
La Gorgue	208	—	Camel

MIDDLE EAST
TRAINING BRIGADE: HQ — HELIOPOLIS
20th (TRAINING) WING: HQ — ABOUKIR

Location	Flying Sqn	Other Flying Unit	Ac Type
Aboukir	—	22, 23 TS	
Amriya	—	193, 194 TS	

32nd (TRAINING) WING: HQ — ISMAILIA

Location	Flying Sqn	Other Flying Unit	Ac Type
Ismalia	—	21 TS	
Suez	—	58 TS	
Abu Sueir	—	57, 195 TS	

38th (TRAINING) WING: HQ — HELIOPOLIS

Location	Flying Sqn	Other Flying Unit	Ac Type
Heliopolis	—	S of Aerial Flying	
Heliopolis	—	AOS	
Heliopolis	—	S of AG	

PALESTINE
5th (CORPS) WING:

Location	Flying Sqn	Other Flying Unit	Ac Type
Junction Station (and dets)	14	—	RE8/Nieuport 17
Sarona (and dets)	113	—	RE8/Nieuport 17, 23, 24
40th (ARMY) WING:			
Ramleh (and det)	111	—	SE5A/Nieuport

Location	Flying Sqn	Other Flying Unit	Ac Type
Ramleh (and det)	142	—	BE12A/ Martinsyde G.102

SALONIKA
16th (CORPS) WING:

Location	Flying Sqn	Other Flying Unit	Ac Type
Lahana (and dets)	17	—	BE2C/BE12A/FK8
Yanesh (and dets)	47	—	FK3/FK8/ Bristol M1C
Kirec (and dets)	150	—	Bristol M1C/SE5A

MESOPOTAMIA
31st (GHQ) WING:

Location	Flying Sqn	Other Flying Unit	Ac Type
Baquba (and dets)	30	—	RE8/Spad S.VII
Samarra (and dets)	63	—	BE2e/DH4
Baghdad (and dets)	72	—	DH4/SE5A/S S.VII/Bristol M1C

INDIA
52nd (CORPS) WING:

Location	Flying Sqn	Other Flying Unit	Ac Type
Risalpur (and dets)	31	—	BE2c/BE2e
Quetta	114	—	BE2c/BE2e
(and 1/2 Flt at Aden)			

EAST AFRICA

Location	Flying Sqn	Other Flying Unit	Ac Type
Dar-es-Salaam	26 (HQ)	—	Henry Farman
with mobile column	26 (A Flt)	—	Henry Farman
Nahunga	26 (B and C Flts)	—	Henry Farman

ITALY
14th (ARMY) WING:

Location	Flying Sqn	Other Flying Unit	Ac Type
Grossa	28, 45	—	Camel
Villaverla	34	—	RE8/F2b
San-Pietro-in-Gu	66	—	Camel

CANADA: HQ — TORONTO
42nd WING: HQ — CAMP EVERYMAN, TEXAS

Location	Flying Sqn	Other Flying Unit	Ac Type
Camp Everyman	—	78, 79, 80, 82, 87 TS	
Camp Everyman	—	S of AG	

43rd WING: HQ — CAMP BENBROOK, TEXAS

Location	Flying Sqn	Other Flying Unit	Ac Type
Camp Benbrook	—	81, 83, 84, 85, 86 TS	

44th WING: HQ — CAMP LEASIDE, NORTH TORONTO

Location	Flying Sqn	Other Flying Unit	Ac Type
Camp Armour Heights	—	88, 92 TS	
Camp Leaside	—	89, 90, 91 TS	

45th WING: (FORMING)

Location	Flying Sqn	Other Flying Unit	Ac Type
?	—	93, 94, 95, 96, 97 TS	

APRIL 1922

INLAND AREA: HQ — HILLINGDON HOUSE, UXBRIDGE
No. 11 WING: HQ— SPITTLEGATE

Location	Flying Sqn	Other Flying Unit	Ac Type
Spittlegate	39	—	DH9A
Spittlegate	100	—	Vimy
Digby	2	—	F2b
Digby	—	3FTS	
Bircham Newton	207	—	DH9A

No 1 GP: HQ — KENLEY

Location	Flying Sqn	Other Flying Unit	Ac Type
Kenley	24	—	DH9A
Eastchurch	—	A&GS	
Biggin Hill	—	SCF	
Manston	—	6FTS	
Hawkinge	25	—	Snipe

No 7 GP: HQ — ANDOVER

Location	Flying Sqn	Other Flying Unit	Ac Type
South Farnborough	—	S of P	
South Farnborough	—	RAE	
South Farnborough	4	—	F2b
Netheravon	—	1FTS	
Old Sarum	—	S of AC	
Upavon	—	CFS	

Location	Flying Sqn	Other Flying Unit	Ac Type
Shotwick	—	5FTS	
Andover	—	APS	

RAF IRELAND: HQ — BALDONNELL
COASTAL AREA: HQ — TAVISTOCK PLACE, LONDON

Location	Flying Sqn	Other Flying Unit	Ac Type
Felixstowe	230	—	Felixstowe F.5
Isle of Grain	—	MAEF	

No 10 GP: HQ — LEE ON SOLENT

Location	Flying Sqn	Other Flying Unit	Ac Type
Calshot	—	S of NC	
Lee on Solent	—	STS	
Gosport	210	—	Cuckoo
Gosport	—	OTF	
Gosport	—	Dev. Flt	
Cattewater	238	—	Felixstowe F.3

No 29 GP: HQ — DONIBRISTLE

Location	Flying Sqn	Other Flying Unit	Ac Type
Leuchars	3	—	Walrus
Leuchars	203	—	Camel
Leuchars	205	—	Panther
Plus air elements HMS *Argus*, HMS *Furious*, HMS *Ark Royal*			

RAF CRANWELL

Location	Flying Sqn	Other Flying Unit	Ac Type
Cranwell		College Flying Wing	

RAF HALTON

RAF RHINE

Location	Flying Sqn	Other Flying Unit	Ac Type
Bickendorf	12	—	F2b

MIDDLE EAST AREA: HQ — CAIRO

Location	Flying Sqn	Other Flying Unit	Ac Type
Aden		Aden Flt	

EGYPTIAN GP: HQ — HELIOPOLIS

Location	Flying Sqn	Other Flying Unit	Ac Type
Heliopolis	216	—	DH10
Almaza	45	—	Vernon
Helwan	47	—	DH9A
Aboukir	56	—	Snipe

PALESTINE GP: HQ — ISMAILIA

Location	Flying Sqn	Other Flying Unit	Ac Type
Ismailia/Moascar	208	—	F2b
Ramleh	14	—	F2b
Amman	14 det	—	F2b
Abu Sueir	—	4FTS	

IRAQ GP: HQ BAGHDAD

Location	Flying Sqn	Other Flying Unit	Ac Type
Hinaidi	1	—	Snipe
Hinaidi	8	—	DH9A
Hinaidi	70	—	Vimy
Baghdad West	6	—	F2b
Baghdad West	30	—	DH9A
Mosul	55	—	DH9A
Shaibah	84	—	DH9A

INDIAN GP: HQ — AMBALA
No 1 WING: HQ — PESHAWAR

Location	Flying Sqn	Other Flying Unit	Ac Type
Kohat	28	—	F2b
Peshawar	31	—	F2b

No 2 WING: HQ — AMBALA

Location	Flying Sqn	Other Flying Unit	Ac Type
Ambala	20	—	F2b

No 3 WING: HQ — QUETTA

Location	Flying Sqn	Other Flying Unit	Ac Type
Quetta	5	—	F2b

No 4 WING: HQ — RISALPUR

Location	Flying Sqn	Other Flying Unit	Ac Type
Risalpur	27	—	DH9A
Risalpur	60	—	Dh10

MEDITERRANEAN GP: HQ — VALETTA

Location	Flying Sqn	Other Flying Unit	Ac Type
Calafrana	267	—	Fairey III D
Plus air element on HMS *Pegasus*			

Location	Flying Sqn	Other Flying Unit	Ac Type

April 1932
AIR DEFENCE OF GREAT BRITAIN: HQ — UXBRIDGE
WESSEX BOMBING AREA: HQ — ANDOVER

Location	Flying Sqn	Other Flying Unit	Ac Type
Andover	12	—	Hart
Andover	101	—	Sidestrand
Andover	—	SF	
Bicester	33	—	Hart
Bircham Newton	35	—	Gordon
Bircham Newton	207	—	Fairey III F
Boscombe Down	9	—	Virginia
Boscombe Down	10	—	Hinaidi
Netheravon	57	—	Hart
Upper Heyford	18	—	Hart
Upper Heyford	40	—	Gordon
Upper Heyford	99	—	Hinaidi
Upper Heyford	—	SF	
Worthy Down	7	—	Virginia
Worthy Down	58	—	Virginia
Oxford	—	UAS	

Royal visit to Wittering, an airfield in the middle of the expansion programme, late 1930s.

FIGHTING AREA: HQ — UXBRIDGE

Location	Flying Sqn	Other Flying Unit	Ac Type
Biggin Hill	—	AACF	
Duxford	2	—	Atlas
Duxford	19	—	Bulldog
Hawkinge	25	—	Fury
Homchurch	54, 111	—	Bulldog
Northolt	24	—	Tutor
Northolt	41	—	Bulldog
Tangmere	1, 43	—	Fury
Upavon	3, 17	—	Bulldog
Cambridge	—	UAS	

NO 1 (AD) GP: HQ — TAVISTOCK PLACE, LONDON

Location	Flying Sqn	Other Flying Unit	Ac Type
Manston	500	—	Virginia
Filton	501	—	Wapiti
Aldergrove	502	—	Virginia
Waddington	503	—	Hyderabad
Hucknall	504	—	Horsley
Hendon	600, 601, 604	—	Wapiti
Renfrew	602	—	Wapiti
Turnhouse	603	—	Wapiti
Castle Bromwich	605	—	Wapiti
Usworth	607	—	Wapiti
Thornaby	608	—	Wapiti

INLAND AREA: HQ — BENTLEY PRIORY

Location	Flying Sqn	Other Flying Unit	Ac Type
Catfoss	—	1 ATC	
North Coates	—	2 ATC	
Sutton Bridge	—	3 ATC	
Hendon	-	Home CF	

NO 21 GP: HQ — WEST DRAYTON

Location	Flying Sqn	Other Flying Unit	Ac Type
Martlesham	15, 22	—	Horsley
Martlesham	—	A and AEE	

No 22 GP: HQ — SOUTH FARNBOROUGH

Location	Flying Sqn	Other Flying Unit	Ac Type
South Farnborough	—	S of P	
South Farnborough	—	RAE	
South Farnborough	4	—	Audax
Old Sarum	16	—	Atlas
Old Sarum	—	S of AC	
Netheravon	13	—	Audax
Catterick	26	—	Atlas
Eastchurch	—	CDCF	

No 23 GP: HQ — GRANTHAM

Location	Flying Sqn	Other Flying Unit	Ac Type
Digby	—	2 FTS	
Grantham	—	3 FTS	
Sealand	—	5 FTS	
Wittering	—	CFS	

COASTAL AREA: HQ — LEE ON SOLENT

Location	Flying Sqn	Other Flying Unit	Ac Type
Calshot	201	—	Southampton
Calshot	—	TS, New School	
Donibristle	100	—	Horsley
Felixstowe	—	FBDF	
Gosport	—	BTS	
Lee on Solent	—	S of NC	
Leuchars	—	TS	
Mount Batten	204	—	Southampton
Mount Batten	209	—	Saro
Pembroke Dock	210	—	Southampton

Plus air elements on HMS *Furious* and HMS *Courageous*

RAF CRANWELL

RAF HALTON

MIDDLE EAST: HQ — VILLA VICTORIA, CAIRO

Location	Flying Sqn	Other Flying Unit	Ac Type
Abu Sueir	—	4 FTS	
Heliopolis	208	—	Atlas
Heliopolis	216	—	Victoria
Helwan	45	—	Fairey III F
Ismailia	6	—	Gordon
Khartoum	47	—	Fairey III F

TRANS-JORDAN AND PALESTINE: HQ — JERUSALEM

Location	Flying Sqn	Other Flying Unit	Ac Type
Amman	14	—	Fairey III F
Ramleh	6 (1 Flt)	—	Gordon

IRAQ COMMAND: HQ — HINAIDI

Location	Flying Sqn	Other Flying Unit	Ac Type
Mosul	30	—	Wapiti
Hinaidi	55	—	Wapiti
Hinaidi	70	—	Victoria
Shaibah	84	—	Wapiti
Basrah	203	—	Rangoon

Risalpur NWFP, India — an important airfield for the colonial policing policy.

Location	Flying Sqn	Other Flying Unit	Ac Type
RAF INDIA; HQ — NEW DELHI			
Ambala	28	—	Wapiti
No 1 (1) GP: HQ — PESHAWAR			
Kohat (No 1 (1) Wing)	27, 60	—	Wapiti
Risalpur (No 2 (1) Wing)	11, 39	—	Wapiti
RAF MEDITERRANEAN: HQ — VALETTA			
Calafrana	202	—	Fairey III F
Halfar	—	SF	
Plus air element on HMS *Glorious*			
ADEN COMMAND; HQ — STEAMER POINT			
Khormaksar	8	—	Fairey III F
FAR EAST COMMAND: HQ — SINGAPORE			
Singapore	36	—	Horsley
Singapore	205	—	Southampton
Plus air element on HMS *Hermes*			

November 1939

(Note: some squadrons not established until early December

ADVANCED AIR STRIKING FORCE
(Nos 71, 72, 74, 75, 67 WINGS)

Location	Flying Sqn	Other Flying Unit	Ac Type
Bétheniville	139	—	Blenheim
Reims	226	—	Battle
Plivot	103	—	Battle
Aubierives-sur-Suippes	218	—	Battle
Berry-au-Bac	12, 142	—	Battle
Condé	114	—	Blenheim
Villeneuve	105	—	Battle
Mourmelun-le-Grande	88	—	Battle
Vassincourt	1	—	Hurricane
Ecury-sur-Coole	150	—	Battle
Wittening	23	—	Blenheim

RAF COMPONENT FIELD FORCE

Location	Flying Sqn	Other Flying Unit	Ac Type
Monchy-Lagache (No 50 Wing)	4	—	Lysander
Mons-en-Chaussée (No 50 Wing)	13	—	Lysander
Abbeville (No 51 Wing)	2, 26	—	Lysander
Poix (No 52 Wing)	53, 59	—	Blenheim
Lille (No 60 Wing)	85, 87	—	Hurricane
Rosières-en-Santerre (No 70 Wing)	18, 57	—	Blenheim
Merville	607, 615	—	Gladiator

BOMBER COMMAND
No 2 GP: HQ — HUNTINGDON

Location	Flying Sqn	Other Flying Unit	Ac Type
Wattisham (No 83 Wing)	107, 110	—	Blenheim
Watton (No 79 Wing)	21, 82	—	Blenheim
West Raynham	101	—	Blenheim
Wyton (No 82 Wing)	15, 40	—	Blenheim

No 3 GP: HQ — MILDENHALL

Location	Flying Sqn	Other Flying Unit	Ac Type
Feltwell	37, 214	—	Wellington
Honington	9	—	Wellington
Marham	38, 115	—	Wellington
Mildenhall	99, 149	—	Wellington

No 4 GP: HQ — LINTON-ON-OUSE

Location	Flying Sqn	Other Flying Unit	Ac Type
Boscombe Down	58	—	Whitley
Dishforth	10, 51	—	Whitley
Driffield	77, 102	—	Whitley
Linton-on-Ouse	78	—	Whitley

No 5 GP: HQ — GRANTHAM

Location	Flying Sqn	Other Flying Unit	Ac Type
Finningley	106	—	Hampden
Hemswell	61, 144	—	Hampden
Scampton	49, 83	—	Hampden
Waddington	44, 50	—	Hampden

No 6 GP: HQ — ABINGDON

Location	Flying Sqn	Other Flying Unit	Ac Type
Abingdon	97, 166	—	Whitley
Bassingbourn	215	—	Wellington

Whitley K7244 at Finningley.

Location	Flying Sqn	Other Flying Unit	Ac Type
Bassingbourn	35	—	Blenheim
Benson	52, 63	—	Battle
Bicester	104, 108	—	Blenheim
Cranfield	35	—	Blenheim/Battle
Cranfield	207	—	Anson
Cranfield	—	New Zealand Flt	
Hucknall	98	—	Battle
Upper Heyford	7	—	Hampden
Upper Heyford	76	—	Anson
Upwood	90	—	Blenheim
Cottesmore	185	—	Hampden

FIGHTER COMMAND
No 11 GP: HQ — UXBRIDGE

Location	Flying Sqn	Other Flying Unit	Ac Type
Biggin Hill	601	—	Blenheim
Biggin Hill	32	—	Hurricane
Croyden	3	—	Hurricane
Croyden	145	—	Blenheim
Filton	263	—	Gladiator
Hendon	248	—	Blenheim
Hendon	24	—	(various)
Hornchurch	54, 74	—	Spitfire
Hornchurch	600	—	Battle
Manston	235, 253	—	Battle
Manston	79	—	Hurricane
Martlesham Heath	56	—	Hurricane
Martlesham Heath	236	—	Blenheim
Martlesham Heath	264	—	Defiant
Northolt	65	—	Spitfire
Northolt	25	—	Blenheim
North Weald	604	—	Blenheim
North Weald	151	—	Hurricane
Tangmere	501, 605	—	Hurricane
Tangmere	92	—	Blenheim
St Athan	—	Gp Pool	Hurricane/Mentor

No 12 GP: HQ — HUCKNALL

Location	Flying Sqn	Other Flying Unit	Ac Type
Debden	17, 504	—	Hurricane
Debden	29	—	Blenheim
Digby	29	—	Blenheim
Digby	46	—	Hurricane
Digby	611	—	Spitfire
Duxford	19, 66	—	Spitfire
Duxford	222	—	Blenheim
Sutton Bridge	266	—	Battle
Sutton Bridge	254	—	Defiant
Wittering	610	—	Spitfire
Wittering	213	—	Hurricane
Wittering	23	—	Blenheim
Aston Down	—	Gp Pool	Hurricane/Spitfire/Blenheim

Location	Flying Sqn	Other Flying Unit	Ac Type
No 13 GP: HQ — NEWCASTLE-ON-TYNE			
Acklington	43, 111	—	Hurricane
Acklington	152	—	Gladiator
Catterick	41	—	Spitfire
Catterick	219	—	Blenheim
Church Fenton	64, 242	—	Blenheim
Drem	72, 602, 609	—	Spitfire
Grangemouth	141	—	Blenheim
Leconfield	234, 245	—	Blenheim
Leconfield	616	—	Spitfire
Turnhouse	603	—	Spitfire
No 22 GP: HQ — FARNBOROUGH			
Odiham	613	—	Hector
Odiham	225, 614	—	Lysander
Old Sarum	16	—	Lysander
COASTAL COMMAND			
No 15 GP: HQ — PLYMOUTH			
Aldergrove	502	—	Anson
Carew Chilton	217 (Flt)	—	Anson
Carew Cheriton	—	CPF	Moth
Hooton Park	502 (det)	—	Anson
Hooton Park	—	CPF	Moth
Mount Batten	204	—	Sunderland
Mount Batten	—	2 AACU (C Flt)	
Pembroke Dock	210, 228	—	Sunderland
St Eval	217	—	Anson
No 16 GP: HQ — CHATHAM			
Bircham Newton	206	—	Anson/Hudson
Bircham Newton	42	—	Vildebeest/Botha
Detling	500	1 CACU (det)	Anson
Thorney Island	48	—	Anson
Thorney Island	22	—	Vildebeest/Botha
Thorney Island	—	1 CACU	Anson
No 17 GP: HQ — GOSPORT			
Calshot	—	STS	(various)
Gosport	—	TTU/TDU	
Gosport	—	2 AACU	
Silloth	—	S of GR	Anson
Silloth	—	CC Pool	(various)
No 18 GP: HQ — PITREAVIE CASTLE			
Abbotsinch	—	CPF	Moth
Dyce	612	—	Anson
Dyce	—	CPF	Moth
Helensburgh	—	MAEE	(various)
Invergordon	201	—	London
Leuchars	224	—	Hudson
Leuchars	233	—	Hudson/Blenheim
Leuchars	612 (Flt)	—	Anson
Shetlands	240	—	London
(SS *Manela*)	—	Fighter Flt	Gladiator
Oban	209	—	Stranraer
Thornaby	220	—	Hudson
Thornaby	608	—	Anson
Wick	269	—	Anson
TRAINING COMMAND			
No 21 GP: HQ — CRANWELL			
Cranwell	—	RAF College	
Montrose	—	8 FTS	
Grantham	—	12 FTS	
Kinloss	—	14 FTS	
Lossiemouth	—	15 FTS	
Yatesbury	—	RDF School (forming)	
No 23 GP: HQ — SOUTH CERNEY			
Upavon	—	CFS	
Netheravon	—	1 FTS	
Brize Norton	—	2 FTS	
South Cerney	—	3 FTS	

Location	Flying Sqn	Other Flying Unit	Ac Type
Sealand	—	5 FTS	
Little Rissington	—	6 FTS	
Peterborough	—	7 FTS	
Hullavington	—	9 FTS	
Ternhill	—	10 FTS	
Shawbury	—	11 FTS	
St Athan	—	S of AN	
Ternhill	—	SF	
No 24 GP: HQ — HALTON			
Various recruit centres and SoTTs			
Boscombe Down	—	A & AEE	(various)
St Athan	—	SD Flt	
No 25 GP: HQ — BRIZE NORTON			
Manby	—	1 AAS	
Pembrey	—	2 AAS	
Aldergrove	—	3 AOS	
West Freugh	—	4 AOS	
Jurby	—	5 AOS	
Porthcawl	—	7 AOS	
Evanton	—	8 AOS	
Penrhos	—	9 AOS	
Warmwell	—	10 AOS	
MAINTENANCE COMMAND			
No 40 GP: HQ — ABINGDON			
MUs: 1, 3, 4, 7, 14, 16, 25, 35, A, B, C, D, E, F, G, H, L, K			
No 41 GP: HQ — ANDOVER			
MUs: 5, 6, 8, 9, 10, 12, 19, 20, 22, 24, 27, 36			
No 42 GP: HQ — READING			
MUs: 2, 11, 21, 28, 91, 92, 93, 94, 95			
No 43 GP: HQ — ANDOVER			
MUs: 13, 26, 30, 32, 49, 50, 54, 58, 60, 63			
No 30 GP: HQ — LONDON			
10 Sqns			
No 31 GP: HQ — BIRMINGHAM			
17 Sqns			
No 32 GP: HQ — PORTSMOUTH			
8 sqns			
No 33 GP: HQ — NEWCASTLE			
14 sqns			
RESERVE COMMAND			
No 50 GP: HQ — BRISTOL			
Fairoaks	—	18 EFTS	
Filton	—	2 EFTS	
Staverton	—	6 AONS	
Hamble	—	3 EFTS	
Hamble	—	11 AONS	
Hanworth	—	5 EFTS	
Hatfield	—	1 EFTS	
Reading	—	8 EFTS	
Redhill	—	15 EFTS	
Weston-super-Mare	—	5 AONS	
White Waltham	—	13 EFTS	
Yatesbury	—	10 EFTS	
Yatesbury	—	2 AONS	
No 51 GP: HQ — LEEDS			
Ansty	—	9 EFTS	
Ansty	—	4 AONS	
Belfast Harbour	—	24 EFTS	
Blackpool	—	9 AONS	
Brough	—	4 EFTS	
Cambridge	—	22 EFTS	
Carlisle	—	3 AONS	
Derby	—	30 EFTS	
Desford	—	7 EFTS	

Location	Flying Sqn	Other Flying Unit	Ac Type
Elmdon	—	14 EFTS	
Perth	—	11 EFTS	
Perth	—	7 AONS	
Prestwick	—	12 EFTS	
Prestwick	—	1 AONS	
Sywell	—	6 EFTS	

No 54 GP: HQ — READING
Various ITWs

MEDITERRANEAN COMMAND
VALETTA, AHQ MALTA

Location	Flying Sqn	Other Flying Unit	Ac Type
Hal Far, Malta	—	3 AACU	
Hal Far, Malta	—	SF	
Alexandria, (No 201 GP)			
Gibraltar, (No 200 GP)	202	—	London
(No 86 Wing, SS Dumana)			

MIDDLE EAST COMMAND
EGYPT: HQ — CAIRO

Location	Flying Sqn	Other Flying Unit	Ac Type
Heliopolis (No 202 GP)	113	—	Blenheim
Heliopolis (No 251 Wing)	216	—	Bombay
Heliopolis	—	CF	
Ismalia (No 250 Wing)	30, 55	—	Blenheim
Ismalia	14	—	Wellesley
Helwan	112	—	Gladiator
Helwan	70	—	Valentia
Shafrakana (No 252 Wing)	—	—	
Maaten Bagush (No 253 Wing)	—	—	
Fuka	45	—	Blenheim
Daba	211	—	
Qasaba	14 (Flt)	—	Wellesley
Qasaba	208	—	Lysander
Mersa Matruh	33	—	Gladiator
Amriya	80	—	
Plus Nos 101, 102, 103 MUs			
Khartoum, Sudan (No 254 Wing)	47	—	Wellesley
Summit, Sudan	223	—	Wellesley
Ramleh, Palestine and T-J	6	—	Lysander

IRAQ

Location	Flying Sqn	Other Flying Unit	Ac Type
Habbaniya	—	4 FTS	Vincent, Audax
Shaibah	84	—	Blenheim

INDIA: HQ — NEW DELHI

Location	Flying Sqn	Other Flying Unit	Ac Type
Risalpur	27	—	Hart
Ambala	60	—	Blenheim
Fort Sandeman	5	—	Wapiti
Fort Sandeman (No 1 (1) Gp)	20	—	Audax
Kohat	28	—	Audax
Lahore	31	—	Valentia

FAR EAST

Location	Flying Sqn	Other Flying Unit	Ac Type
Seletar	36, 100	—	Vildebeeste
Seletar	230	—	Sunderland
Seletar	205	—	Singapore
Seletar	—	4 AACU	
Tengah	34, 62	—	Blenheim
Kallang (No 2 (1) Wing)	11, 39	—	Blenheim
Kallang	—	CF	
China Bay	273	—	Vildebeeste
China Bay	—	SF	
Kai Tak	—	SF	

May 1941

BOMBER COMMAND: HQ — HIGH WYCOMBE
No 1 GP: HQ — Hucknall

Location	Flying Sqn	Other Flying Unit	Ac Type
Binbrook	12, 142	—	Wellington
Newton	103, 150	—	Wellington
Swinderby	300, 301	—	Wellington
Syerston	304, 305	—	Wellington

No 2 GP: HQ — HUNTINGDON

Location	Flying Sqn	Other Flying Unit	Ac Type
Horsham	18, 39	8 BATF	Blenheim
Swanton Morley	105	—	Blenheim
Wattisham	110	—	Blenheim
Watton	21, 82	—	Blenheim
West Raynham	101	—	Wellington

No 3 GP: HQ — EXNING

Location	Flying Sqn	Other Flying Unit	Ac Type
Feltwell	57, 75	—	Wellington
Honington	9, 311	—	Wellington
Honington	—	5 BATF	
Marham	115, 218	—	Wellington
Mildenhall	149	3 BATF	Wellington
Mildenhall	—	1401 Met	Gladiator
Oakington	7	—	Stirling
Oakington	—	3 PRU	Spitfire/ Wellington
Stadishall	214	3 GTF	Wellington
Stadishall	—	1419	(various)
Wyton	15	—	Wellington/ Stirling
Wyton	40	4 BATF	Wellington
Waterbeach	99	—	Wellington

No 4 GP: HQ — YORK

Location	Flying Sqn	Other Flying Unit	Ac Type
Dishforth	51	—	Whitley
Driffield	104, 405	–	Wellington
Linton-on-Ouse	35	—	Halifax
Linton-on-Ouse	58	2 BATF	Whitley
Leeming	10	—	Whitley
Leeming	76	—	Halifax
Middleton St George	78	—	Whitley
Topcliffe	77, 102		

Course photo of 25 OTU — the role of the OTUs was of vital importance.

Location	Flying Sqn	Other Flying Unit	Ac Type
No 5 GP: HQ — GRANTHAM			
Coningsby	106	5 GTF	Hampden
Coningsby	97	—	Manchester
Doncaster	271	—	(various)
Lindholme	50	—	Hampden
Hemswell	61	—	Manchester
Hemswell	144	—	Hampden
Scampton	49, 83	—	Hampden
Waddington	44	—	Hampden
Waddington	207	—	Manchester
Waddington	—	6 BATF	Blenheim
No 6 GP: HQ — ABINGDON			
Abingdon	10 OTU	1 BATF	Whitley
Bassingbourn	11 OTU	—	Wellington
Benson	12 OTU	—	Wellington
Bramcote	18 OTU	—	Wellington
Harwell	15 OTU	—	Wellington
Kinlos	19 OTU	—	Whitley
Lossiemouth	20 OTU	—	Wellington
Moreton-in-Marsh	21 OTU	—	Wellington
Pershore	23 OTU	—	Wellington
No 7 GP: HQ — BRAMPTON			
Bicester	13 OTU	—	Blenheim
Cottesmore	14 OTU	—	Hampden
Finningley	25 OTU	—	Hampden
Finningley	—	7 BATF	Blenheim
Upper Heyford	16 OTU	—	Hampden
Upwood	17 OTU	—	Blenheim
FIGHTER COMMAND: HQ — STANMORE			
No 9 GP: HQ — BARTON HALL			
Baginton	308	—	Hurricane
Baginton	403	—	Tomahawk
High Ercall	68	—	Blenheim
Jurby	258	—	Hurricane
Speke	229, 315	—	Hurricane
Squires Gate	96, 256	—	Defiant
Ternhill	608	—	Hurricane
Valley	312	—	Hurricane
No 10 GP: HQ — RUDLOE MANOR			
Carew Cheriton	238 (Flt)	—	Hurricane
Colerne	87, 501, 504	—	Hurricane
Colerne	307	—	Defiant
Exeter	504	—	Hurricane
Exeter	66	—	Spitfire
Filton	263	—	Whirlwind
Ibsley	32	—	Hurricane
Middle Wallop	604	—	Beaufighter
Middle Wallop	93	—	Boston/ Wellington
Middle Wallop	—	FEE	(various)
Pembrey	79, 238, 316	—	Hurricane
Portreath	152	—	Spitfire
Roborough	247	—	Hurricane
Warmwell	118, 234	—	Spitfire
No 11 GP: HQ — UXBRIDGE			
Biggin Hill	74, 92, 60	—	Spitfire
Debden	85	—	Defiant
Ford	23	—	Havoc
Ford	—	FIU	Blenheim
Gravesend	141	—	Defiant
Hatfield	116	—	Lysander
Hawkinge	91	—	Spitfire
Hendon	24	1 Cam unit	(various)
Hornchurch	64, 611	—	Spitfire
Kenley	1, 615	—	Hurricane
Martlesham	3, 71	—	Hurricane
Northolt	303	—	Spitfire
Northolt	306, 601	—	Hurricane
North Weald	56, 249	—	Hurricane
Southend	54	—	Spitfire

Location	Flying Sqn	Other Flying Unit	Ac Type
Stapleford Tawney	242	—	Hurricane
Tangmere	302, 610, 616	—	Hurricane
Tangmere	145	—	Spitfire
Tangmere	219	—	Blenheim/ Beaufighter
No 12 GP: HQ — WATNALL			
Coltishall	222	—	Spitfire
Coltishall	257	—	Hurricane
Digby	46, 401, 402	—	Hurricane
Digby	29	—	Beaufighter
Driffield	485	—	Spitfire
Duxford	19	—	Spitfire
Duxford	310	—	Hurricane
Duxford	—	AFDU AGME	(various)
Kirton in Lindsey	65, 452	—	Spitfire
Kirton in Lindsey	255	—	Defiant
Wittening	151	—	Defiant
Wittening	25	—	Beaufighter
Wittening	266	—	Spitfire
No 13 GP: HQ — NEWCASTLE			
Acklington	72	—	Spitfire
Ackington	317	—	Hurricane
Aldergrove	245	—	Hurricane
Catterick	41	—	Spitfire
Catterick	600	—	Blenheim/ Beaufighter
Drem	43, 607	—	Hurricane
Prestwick	602	—	Spitfire
Turnhouse	603	—	Spitfire
No 14 GP: HQ — INVERNESS			
Castletown	17, 213	—	Hurricane
Dyce	111 (Flt)	—	Hurricane
Elgin	232	—	Hurricane
Montrose	111 (Flt)	—	Hurricane
Skaebrae	253	—	Hurricane
Skilten	260	—	Hurricane
Sumburgh	213 (Flt)	—	Hurricane
No 81 GP: HQ — WORCESTER			
Church Fenton	54 OTU	—	Blenheim/ Defiant/ Beaufighter
Crosby	59 OTU	—	Hurricane
Debden	52 OTU	—	Hurricane
Grangemouth	58 OTU	—	Spitfire
Hawarden	57 OTU	—	Spitfire
Heston	53 OTU	—	Spitfire
Leconfield	60 OTU	—	Blenheim/ Defiant/ Beaufighter
Sutton Bridge	56 OTU	—	Hurricane
Usworth	55 OTU	—	Hurricane
No 60 GP: HQ — LEIGHTON BUZZARD			
Nos: 70, 71, 72, 73, 74, 75, 76, 77, 78 Signals Wings			
COASTAL COMMAND			
No 15 GP: HQ — LIVERPOOL			
Aldergrove	233	—	Hudson
Aldergrove	252	—	Beaufighter
Hooton Park	48 (Flt)	—	Anson
Hooton Park	—	GCF	
Islay/Bowmore	119	—	
Port Ellen	48 (Flt)	—	Anson
Limavady	221	—	Wellington
Limavady	502	—	Whitley
Lough Erne	209	—	Catalina/Lerwick
Lough Erne	240	—	Catalina/ Stranraer
Oban	210	—	Catalina/ Sunderland

Location	Flying Sqn	Other Flying Unit	Ac Type
No 16 GP: HQ — GILLINGHAM			
Bircham Newton	206	—	Hudson
Bircham Newton	235	1403 Met	Blenheim
Bircham Newton	500 (Flt)	—	Anson
Detling	500 (Flt)	—	Anson/Blenheim
North Gates	22	—	Beaufighter
Rochester	—	GCF	(various)
Thorney Island	59	—	Blenheim
Wattisham	86	—	Blenheim
No 17 GP: HQ — GOSPORT			
Abbotsinch	—	TTU	Beaufort
Catfoss	2 OTU	—	Blenheim/Anson
Chivenor	3 OTU	—	(various)
Detling	—	I CACU	Blenheim
Gosport	—	TDU, 2 AACU	(various)
Greenock	—	FB MM U	
Silloth	1 OTU	—	(various)
Squires Gate	—	3 SoGR	Botha
Stranraer	4 OTU	—	(various)
No 18 GP: HQ — PITREAVIE CASTLE			
Dyce	248	—	Blenheim
Dyce	608 (Flt)	—	Anson
Helensburgh	—	MAEE	(various)
Kaldadarnes	98	—	Battle
Kaldadarnes	269 (Flt)	—	Hudson
Leuchars	234, 320	—	Hudson
Leuchars	107	—	Blenheim
Leuchars	—	10 BATF	Wellington
Leuchars	—	GCF	(various)
Reykjavik (No 30 Wing)	204	—	Sunderland
(No 100 Wing on SS *Manela*)			
Stornaway	48 (Flt)	—	Anson
Sullom Voe	201	—	Sunderland
Sumburgh	254	—	Blenheim
Thornaby	220	—	Hudson
Thornaby	608	—	Anson/Blenheim
Thornaby	114	—	Blenheim
Thornaby	—	9 BATF	Wellington
Wick	269	—	Hudson
Wick	248	—	Blenheim
Wick	612	—	Whitley
Wick	—	PRU (C Flt)	Spitfire/ Blenheim
No 19 GP: HQ — PLYMOUTH			
Carew Cheriton	236	—	Blenheim
Carew Cheriton	—	CCOU	Beaufighter/ Hudson
Roborough	—	GCF	(various)
St Eval	217	—	Beaufort
St Eval	53	1404 Met	Blenheim
St Eval	—	PRU (B Flt)	Spitfire/ Blenheim
No 200 GP: HQ — GIBRALTAR			
Gibraltar	202	—	London/Catalina
UNDER HQ COATAL COMMAND			
Benson	—	1 PRU	(various)
Freetown, W. Africa	95	—	Sunderland
ARMY CO-OPERATION COMMAND			
No 70 GP: HQ — SOUTH FARNBOROUGH			
Andover	—	2 S of AC	Anson/Blenheim
Cardiff	—	8 AACU	(various)
Castle Bromwich	—	7 AACU	(various)
Christchurch	—	1 AACU (H Flt)	
Christchurch	—	SD Flt	
Farnborough	—	1 AACU (HQ)	
Farnborough	—	RAE	
Larkhill	—	1 AACU (D Flt)	
Old Sarum	—	1 S of AC	Hector/Lysander
Ringway (No 110 Wing)	—	6 AACU	(various)

Location	Flying Sqn	Other Flying Unit	Ac Type
Ringway	—	CLE	Whitley
St Athan	—	PAU	
Penrhos	—	1 AACU (C Flt)	
Weston Zoyland	—	1 AACU (A Flt)	
Carew Cheriton	—	1 AACU (B Flt)	

1 AACU also operated flights at Cleave (D, G, O, V, Flts), West Freugh (E Flt), Squires Gate (F Flt), Aberffraw (J, Z Flts), Bircham Newton (K, M Flts), Aberporth (L, X Flts), Morfa Towyn (U Flt), Weybourne (T Flt), Kidsdale (W Flt), Manorbier (Y Flt)

Location	Flying Sqn	Other Flying Unit	Ac Type
No 71 GP: HQ — SUNNINGDALE			
Bury St Edmunds	241	—	Lysander
Firbeck	613	—	Lysander
Gatwick	26, 239	—	Lysander
Hendon	—	1416 Recce	Spitfire
Hooton Park	13	—	Lysander
Inverness	614 (Flt)	—	Lysander
Macmerry	614	—	Lysander
Odiham	400	—	Lysander
Renfrew	309	—	Lysander
Sawbridgeworth	2	—	Lysander
Snailwell	268	—	Lysander
Tilshead	225	—	Lysander
Weston Zoyland	16	—	Lysander
York	4	—	Lysander
RAF N. IRELAND: HQ — BELFAST			
Aldergrove	—	1402 Met	Gladiator
Aldergrove	—	1405 Met	Blenheim
Newtonards	231	—	Lysander
Sydenham (No 31 Wing)	88, 226	—	Battle
Sydenham	—	GCF	
No 21 GP: HQ — CRANWELL			
Cranage	—	2 S of AN	
Cranwell	—	RAF Coll. FTS	
Cranwell	—	2 CFS	
Grantham	—	12 SFTS	
Hucknall	—	1 (Polish) SFTS	
Montrose	—	8 SFTS	
Shawbury	—	11 SFTS	
Ternhill	—	5 SFTS	
No 23 GP: HQ — SOUTH CERNEY			
Boscombe Down	—	A and AEE	(various)
Boscombe Down	—	Handling Flt CFS	(various)
Brize Norton	—	2 SFTS	
Cranfield	—	14 SFTS	
Hullavington	—	9 SFTS	
Kidlington	—	15 SFTS	
Little Rissington	—	6 SFTS	
Netheravon	—	1 SFTS	
South Cerney	—	3 SFTS	
Upavon	—	CFS	
No 25 GP: HQ — MARKET DRAYTON			
Dumfries	—	10 BGS	
Evanton	—	8 BGS	
Exeter	—	GRU	
Exeter	—	RAE (det)	
Jurby	—	5 BGS	
Manby	—	1 AAS	
Millom	—	2 BGS	
Penrhos	—	9 BGS	
Stormy Down	—	7 BGS	
Warmwell	—	CGS	
West Freugh	—	4 BGS	
No 50 GP: HQ — READING			
Cambridge	—	22 EFTS	
Cambridge	—	4 (Supp) FIS	
Elstree	—	CLTS	
Fair Oaks	—	18 EFTS	
Hatfield	—	1 EFTS	

Location	Flying Sqn	Other Flying Unit	Ac Type
Luton	—	24 EFTS	
Odiham	—	Franco-Belgian Air Training School	
Peterborough	—	13 EFTS	
Reading	—	8 EFTS	
Staverton	—	2 EFTS	
Staverton	—	6 AONS	
Sywell	—	6 EFTS	
Watchfield	—	3 EFTS	
Watchfield	—	11 AONS	
Watchfield	—	BAS	
Weston-super-Mare	—	10 EFTS	

No 51 GP: HQ — LEEDS

Location	Flying Sqn	Other Flying Unit	Ac Type
Ansty	—	9 EFTS	
Ansty	—	4 AONS	
Bobbington	—	3 AONS	
Brough	—	4 EFTS	
Carlisle	—	15 EFTS	
Derby	—	16 EFTS	
Desford	—	7 EFTS	
Elmdon	—	14 EFTS	
Meir	—	5 EFTS	
North Luffenham	—	17 EFTS	
Perth	—	11 EFTS	
Pertdh	—	5 (Supp) FIS	
Prestwick	—	1 AONS	
Sealand	—	19 EFTS	
Yeadon	—	20 EFTS	

No 54 GP: HQ — TORQUAY

Location	Flying Sqn	Other Flying Unit	Ac Type
Aberdeen	—	UAS	
Aberystwyth	—	UAS	
Belfast	—	UAS	
Bristol	—	UAS	
Cambridge	—	UAS	
Cardiff	—	UAS	
Edinburgh	—	UAS	
Glasgow	—	UAS	
Leeds	—	UAS	
Liverpool	—	UAS	
London	—	UAS	
Manchester	—	UAS	
Newcastle	—	UAS	
Oxford	—	UAS	
Reading	—	UAS	
St Andrews	—	UAS	
Sheffield	—	UAS	
Southampton	—	UAS	
Swansea	—	UAS	

RAF Schools in Canada and South Africa
CANADA (ADMIN BY RCAF):

Location	Flying Sqn	Other Flying Unit	Ac Type
Kingston	—	31 SFTS	
Moose Jaw	—	32 SFTS	
Carberry	—	33 SFTS	
Medicine Hat	—	34 SFTS	
Pt Albert	—	31 ANS	
Debest, Nova Scotia	—	31 GRS	
Picton	—	31 BGS	

SOUTH AFRICA (ADMIN BY SAAF):

Location	Flying Sqn	Other Flying Unit	Ac Type
Oudsthoorn	—	5 AONS	
Queenstown	—	7 AONS	
George, Cape Province	—	1 GRS	

TECHNICAL TRAINING COMMAND
No 20 GP: HQ — MARKET DRAYTON
Various Recruit Centres etc

No 24 GP: HQ — HINDLIP HALL
Various SoTTs, other schools and hospitals

No 26 GP: HQ — LANGLEY

Location	Flying Sqn	Other Flying Unit	Ac Type
Boscombe Down	109		
Cranwell	—	1 RS	
Prestwick	—	3 RS	

RADLETT (No 80 WING)

Location	Flying Sqn	Other Flying Unit	Ac Type
Yatesbury	—	2 RS	

MAINTENANCE COMMAND
No 53 WING

No 40 GP: HQ — ANDOVER
MUs: 5, 6, 8, 9, 10, 12, 15, 18, 19, 20, 22, 23, 24, 27, 29, 33, 37, 38, 39, 44, 45, 46, 47, 48, 51, 52, — ASUs and Packing Depôts

Location	Flying Sqn	Other Flying Unit	Ac Type
Hamble	—	15 FPP	
Hatfield	—	5 FPP	
Hawarden	—	3 FPP	
Hullavington	—	8 FPP	
Kemble	—	OA DF	
Prestwick	—	4 FPP	
Ratcliffe	—	6 FPP	
Ringway	—	14 FPP	
Whitchurch	—	2 FPP	
White Waltham	—	1 FPP	

No 42 GP: HQ — BURGHFIELD COMMON
MUs: 2, 11, 21, 28, 36, 53, 91, 92, 93, 94, 95, 98 — Ammunition Depôts plus aviation fuel and oil depôts

No 43 GP: HQ — OXFORD
MUs: 1, 4, 13, 26, 30, 32, 34, 49, 50, 54, 56, 60, 63, 65, 67, 71, 75, 83, 86, 90 — Salvage centres and repair depôts

BALLOON COMMAND
No 30 GP: HQ — LONDON
15 Sqns

No 31 GP: HQ — BIRMINGHAM
13 Sqns

No 32 GP: HQ — ROMSEY
12 Sqns

No 33 GP: HQ — SHEFFIELD
12 sqns

No 34 GP: HQ — EDINBURGH
11 Sqns

MALTA COMMAND: HQ — VALLETTA

Location	Flying Sqn	Other Flying Unit	Ac Type
Hal Far	—	SF	Magister, Gauntlet, Swordfish, Seal
Luqa	69	—	Maryland, Beaufort
Takali	261	—	Hurricane

MIDDLE EAST COMMAND: HQ — CAIRO

Location	Flying Sqn	Other Flying Unit	Ac Type
Heliopolis (HQ No 202 GP)	267	—	(various)
Heliopolis	216	—	Bombay
Heliopolis	208	—	Lysander, Hurricane
Heliopolis	—	2 PRU	Maryland
Amriya	274, 89, 450	—	Hurricane
Ismailia (HQ 250 Wing)	70 OTU	—	(various)
Abu Sueir	—	102 MU	Anson, Gordon
Alexandria (HQ 201 GP)	228, 230	—	Sunderland
Alexandria (HQ 101 Wing)			
Shafrakana (HQ 252 Wing)	—	—	—
Kabrit	70, 148	—	Wellington
Shallufa (HQ 257 Wing)	37, 38	—	Wellington
Shandur	39	—	Blenheim
Maaten Bagush (HQ 253 Wing)	45, 55	—	Blenheim
Sollum	—	1 GRU	Wellington
Fuka	38, 70, 148 det	—	Wellington
Aboukir	230 det	—	Sunderland
Qasaba	6	—	Hurricane, Lysander
Sidi Haneish	73	—	Hurricane

MUs: 101, 103, 107

Location	Flying Sqn	Other Flying Unit	Ac Type
GREECE			
Suda Bay	113	—	Blenheim
Maleme	30	—	Blenheim
Maleme	33	—	Hurricane
Argos	11	—	Blenheim
SUDAN			
Khartoum (HQ 203 Gp)	117	—	(various)
Gordon's Tree	251	—	Gauntlet
Carthago	47	—	Wellesley
Erhoweit (No 254 Wing)	—	—	—
Summit	223	—	Wellesley
Port Sudan	14	—	Blenheim
Fowl	—	1430	Vincent
Umritsa	237	—	Lysander, Hardy
No 104 MU			
EAST AFRICA: HQ — NAIROBI			
(All SAAF Sqns)			
No 105 MU			
WEST AFRICA			
Bunee River	95	—	Sunderland
PALESTINE: HQ — JERUSALEM			
Lydda	211	—	Blenheim
Lydda	—	SF	Proctor, Magister
Aqir	6 det	—	Lysander
Aqir	80	—	Gladiator
Aqir	84	—	Blenheim
Aqir	250	—	Tomahawk
ADEN COMMAND: HQ — STEAMER POINT			
Sheikh Othman	—	CTF	Blenheim, Moth, Vincent
Khormaksar	—	SF	Vincent
Khormaksar	8, 203	—	Blenheim
IRAQ COMMAND: HQ — HABBANIYA			
Habbaniya	—	CCF	Gordon, Valentia, Oxford, Moth
Habbaniya	70 det	—	Valentia
Habbaniya	—	4 FTS	Moth, Audax, Hart, Oxford, Gordon
Shaibah	244	—	Vincent
INDIA COMMAND: HQ — DELHI			
Delhi	—	CCF	Envoy
Lahore (HQ 2(1) Gp)	31	—	Valentia
Risalpur	5	—	Hart
Peshawar (HQ 1(1) Gp)			
Kohat	28	—	Audax
Miranshah	20, 28	—	Audax
Madras	20 det	—	Audax
Bombay	20 det	—	Audax
Begumpet	—	1 EFTS	
(plus IAF units)			
FAR EAST COMMAND: HQ — BUKIT TIMAT			
Seletar	36, 100	—	Vildebeest
Seletar	205	—	Singapore
Tengah	34	—	Blenheim
Tengah	—	4 AACU	Shark, Queen Bee, Swordfish
Alor Star	62	—	Blenheim
Kallang	—	CF	Moth, Walrus
Kallang	67, 243	—	Buffalo
Kallang	27	—	Blenheim
CEYLON, HONG KONG, BURMA			
China Bay	273	—	Vildebeest
China Bay	—	SF	Seal
Kai Tak	—	SF	Vildebeest, Tutor, Walrus
Rangoon	60	—	Blenheim

Location	Flying Sqn	Other Flying Unit	Ac Type
April 1942			
BOMBER COMMAND: HQ — HIGH WYCOMBE			
No 1 GP: HQ — BAWTRY			
Binbrook	12, 142	—	Wellington
Binbrook	—	1481 TTGF	Lysander
Elsham Wolds	103	—	Wellington
Hemswell	300, 301	—	Wellington
Holme	460	1520 BATF	Wellington
Lindholme	304, 305	—	Wellington
Snaith	150	—	Wellington/ Liberator
No 2 GP: HQ — HUNTINGDON			
Horsham St Faith	105	1508 BATF	Blenheim
Horsham St Faith	—	1428, 1444	Hudson
Swanton Morley	88, 226	—	Boston/Blenheim
Swanton Morley	—	1515 BATF	Oxford
Wattisham	18, 1	1517 BATF	Blenheim
Watton	21	—	Blenheim
West Raynham	107, 114	—	Blenheim
West Raynham	—	1482	Lysander
No 3 GP: HQ — EXNING			
Feltwell	57, 75	—	Wellington
Feltwell	—	1519 BATF	Oxford
Honington	9, 311	1505 BATF	Wellington
Honington	—	1513 BATF	Wellington
Honington	—	1429 (Czech)	Wellington
Marham	115	—	Wellington
Marham	218	—	Wellington/ Stirling
Mildenhall	149	—	Wellington/ Stirling
Mildenhall	419	1503 BATF	Wellington
Oakington	7	—	Stirling
Oakington	101	—	Wellington
Stradishall	214	—	Wellington/ Stirling
Stradishall	109	—	Wellington
Stradishall	—	1521 BATF	Oxford
Tempsford	138	—	
Tempsford	—	1418	Wellington
Waterbeach	—	1651 CU	Stirling
Wyton	15	—	Stirling
Wyton	156	1504 BATF	Wellington
No 4 GP: HQ — YORK			
Dishforth	51	—	Whitley
Dishforth	—	1512 BATF	Oxford
Driffield	158	—	Wellington
Driffield	—	1502 BATF	Whitley
Driffield	—	1484 TTGF	Whitley/Defiant
Leeming	10	—	Whitley/Halifax
Leeming	77	—	Whitley
Linton-on-Ouse	35	—	Halifax
Linton-on-Ouse	58	—	Whitley
Marston Moor	—	1652 CU	Halifax
Middleton St George	76	—	Halifax
Middleton St George	78	—	Whitley
Middleton St George	—	1516 BATF	Oxford
Pocklington	405	—	Wellington
Topcliffe	102	—	Whitley/Halifax
No 5 GP: HQ — GRANTHAM			
Bottesford	207	—	Manchester/ Lancaster
Bottesford	—	1524 BATF	Oxford
Coningsby	106	—	Hampden/ Manchester
Coningsby	97	—	Manchester/ Lancaster
Coningsby	—	1514 BATF	Oxford
North Luffenham	61	—	Manchester/ Lancaster
North Luffenham	144	—	Hampden

Location	Flying Sqn	Other Flying Unit	Ac Type
Scampton	49	—	Hampden
Scampton	83	—	Manchester
Scampton	—	1485 TTGF	Lysander
Scampton	—	1518 BATF	Oxford
Swinderby	50	—	Hampden/ Manchester
Swinderby	455	—	Hampden
Syerston	408	—	Hampden
Waddington	44	—	Hampden/ Lancaster
Waddington	420	—	Hampden
Waddington	—	1506 BATF	Oxford

No 6 GP: HQ — ABINGDON

Location	Flying Sqn	Other Flying Unit	Ac Type
Abingdon	10 OTU	1501 BATF	Whitley
Bassingbourn	11 OTU	—	Wellington
Bassingbourn	—	1446 FTF	Wellington/ Anson
Bramcote	18 OTU	—	Wellington
Chipping Warden	12 OTU	—	Wellington
Harwell	15 OTU	—	Wellington
Harwell	—	1443	
Kinloss	19 OTU	—	Whitley
Lichfield	27 OTU	—	Wellington
Lossiemouth	20 OTU	—	Wellington
Moreton-in-the-Marsh	21 OTU	—	Wellington
Pershore	23 OTU	—	Wellington
Wellesbourne Mountford	22 OTU	—	Wellington

No 7 GP: HQ — WINSLOW

Location	Flying Sqn	Other Flying Unit	Ac Type
Bicester	13 OTU	—	Blenheim
Bicester	—	1442 FTF	
Cottesmore	14 OTU	—	Hampden
Finningley	25 OTU	—	Hampden/ Wellington/ Manchester
Finingley	—	1507 BATE	Oxford
Upper Heyford	16 OTU	—	Wellington
Upwood	17 OTU	—	Wellington
Upwood	—	1511 BATF	Oxford
Wing	26 OTU	—	Wellington

(note: ALL OTUs also have Ansons on UE)

No 8 GP: HQ — BRAMPTON GRANGE

Location	Flying Sqn	Other Flying Unit	Ac Type
Polebrook	—	1653 CU	Liberator

No 26 GP: HQ — LANGLEY HALL, SLOUGH
Controls 83 W/T stations in No 80 and No 81 Wings

FIGHTER COMMAND: HQ — STANMORE
No 9 GP: HQ — BARTON HALL

Location	Flying Sqn	Other Flying Unit	Ac Type
Andreas	452	—	Spitfire
Baginton	79	—	Hurricane
High Ercall	255	—	Beaufighter
Honiley	257	—	Hurricane
Honiley	—	1456	Havoc
Speke	—	MSFU	Hurricane
Squires Gate	256	—	Defiant
Valley	456	—	Beaufighter
Valley	275	—	Lysander/Walrus
Valley	131	—	Spitfire
Valley	—	1486 TTF	Lysander
Woodvale	315	—	Spitfire
Wrexham	285	—	Hudson/Defiant
Wrexham	96	—	Defiant

No 10 GP: HQ — RUDLOE MANOR

Location	Flying Sqn	Other Flying Unit	Ac Type
Angle	312	—	Spitfire
Charmy Down	87	—	Hurricane
Charmy Down	—	1454	Havoc
church Stanton	306	—	Spitfire
Colerne	125	—	Beaufighter
Colerne	286	—	Oxford/ Hurricane/ Defiant

Location	Flying Sqn	Other Flying Unit	Ac Type
Exeter	307	—	Beaufighter
Exeter	308	—	Spitfire
Fairwood Common	615	—	Hurricane
Fairwood Common	402	—	Spitfire
Fairwood Common	263	—	Whirlwind
Harrowbeer	267	—	Lysander/Walrus
Harrowbeer	302	—	Spitfire
Hurn	—	TFU	(various)
Ibsley	118, 234, 501	—	Spitfire
Middle Wallop	604	—	Beaufighter
Middle Wallop	245	—	Hurricane
Middle Wallop	—	1458	Havoc
Perranporth	310, 130	—	Spitfire
Portreath	66	—	Spitfire
Predannack	600	—	Beaufighter
Predannack	247	—	Hurricane
Predannack	—	1457	Havoc
St Mary's	—	1449	Hurricane
Warmwell	175	—	Hurricane
Warmwell	—	1487 TTF	Lysander

No 11 GP: HQ — UXBRIDGE

Location	Flying Sqn	Other Flying Unit	Ac Type
Biggin Hill	72, 124	—	Spitfire
Bradwell Bay	418	—	Boston
Castle Camps	157	—	Mosquito
Croydon	287	—	Oxford/ Hurricane/ Defiant
Debden	65, 111, 350	—	Spitfire
Ford	—	FIU	Beaufighter
Gravesend	401	—	Spitfire
Hawkinge	91	—	Spitfire
Hendon	116	—	Lysander/ Hurricane
Hendon	24	1 CAMU	(various)
Heston	—	1422	Havoc
Hornchurch	122, 313	—	spitfire
Hunsdon	85	1451	Havoc
Hunsdon	3	—	Hurricane
Kenley	485, 602	—	Spitfire
Manston	32, 174, 607	—	Hurricane
Manston	23 (1 Flt)	—	Havoc
Martlesham	71	—	Spitfire
Merston	340	—	Spitfire
Northolt	303, 316, 317	—	Spitfire
North Weald	121, 222, 403	—	Spitfire
Redhill	457	—	Spitfire
Southend	64	—	spitfire
Southend	—	1488 TTF	Lysander
Stapleford	277	—	Lysander/Walrus
Tangmere	1	—	Hurricane
Tangmere	219	—	Beaufighter
Tangmere	23 (1 Flt)	1455	Havoc
West Malling	264	—	Defiant
West Malling	29	—	Beaufighter
West Malling	—	1452	Havoc
Westhampnett	41, 129	—	Spitfire

No 12 GP: HQ — WATNALL

Location	Flying Sqn	Other Flying Unit	Ac Type
Church Fenton	(885 FAA)	—	Hurricane
Coltishall	68	—	Beaufighter
Coltishall	278	—	Lysander/Walrus
Coltishall	154 (1 Flt)	—	Spitfire
Coltishall	—	1489 TTF	Lysander
Digby	288	—	Oxford/ Hurricane/ Defiant
Digby	409	—	Beaufighter
Digby	412, 411, 609	—	Spitfire
Duxford	266	—	Typhoon
Duxford	609	—	Spitfire
Duxford	—	AFDU 1426	(varous)
Fowlmere	154 (1 Flt)	—	Spitfire
Hibaldstowe	253	—	Hurricane
Hibaldstowe	—	1459	Havoc

Location	Flying Sqn	Other Flying Unit	Ac Type
Hutton Cranswick	19	—	Spitfire
Kingscliffe	616	—	Spitfire
Kirton-in-Lindsey	133	—	Spitfire
Kirton-in-Lindsey	486	—	Hurricane
Ludham	610	—	Spitfire
Matlask	137	—	Whirlwind
Snailwell	56	—	Typhoon
Wittering	151	—	Defiant
Wittering	—	1453	Havoc
Wittering	—	1529 BATF	Master
No 13 GP: HQ — NEWCASTLE			
Acklington	43	—	Hurricane
Acklington	141	—	Beaufighter
Acklington	—	1460	Havoc
Acklington	—	1490 TTF	Lysander
Ayr	406	—	Beaufighter
Ayr	134	—	Spitfire
Catterick	332	—	Spitfire
Drem	611	—	Spitfire
Drem	410	—	Defiant
Drem	—	1528 BATF	Master
Ouston	281, 410 (1 Flt)	—	Defiant
Ouston	—	1423	Hurricane
Turnhouse	289	—	Oxford/ Hurricane/ Defiant
Turnhouse	81	—	Spitfire
Castletown	54, 123	—	Spitfire
Dyce	416 (1 Flt)	—	Spitfire
Montrose	416	—	Spitfire
Peterhead	603	—	Spitfire
Skeabrae	132, 331	—	Spitfire
Tain	417	—	Spitfire
Tain	—	1491 TTF	Lysander
No 81 GP: HQ — WORCESTER			
Annan	55 OTU	—	Hurricane
Aston Down	52 OTU	—	Hurricane
Church Fenton	54 OTU	—	Blenheim/ Defiant/ Beaufighter
Cranfield	51 OTU	—	Blenheim/ Defiant/ Beaufighter
Crosby	59 OTU	—	Hurricane
East Fortune	60 OTU	—	Defiant
Grangemouth	59 OTU	—	Spitfire
Hawarden	57 OTU	—	Spitfire
Llandow	53 OTU	—	Spitfire
Rednal	61 OTU	—	Spitfire
Tealing	56 OTU	—	Hurricane
No 82 GP: HQ — BELFAST			
Ballyhalbert	25, 153 (1 Flt)	—	Beaufighter
Eglinton	152	—	Spitfire
Kirkistown	504	—	Spitfire
Limavady	153 (1 Flt)	—	Beaufighter
Long Kesh	74	—	Spitfire
Newtonards	—	1480	Defiant
Newtonards	—	1493 TTF	Lysander
Newtonards	—	GCF	
No 60 GP: HQ — LEIGHTON BUZZARD			
Control Nos: 70, 71, 72, 73, 74, 75, 76, 77, 78, 79, Signals wings			
COASTAL COMMAND: HQ — NORTHWOOD			
No 15 GP: HQ — LIVERPOOL			
Hooton Park	—	GCF	
Aldergrove	206	—	Hudson
Aldergrove	143	—	Beaufighter
Aldergrove	—	1462	Gladiator/ Hudson/ Spitfire
Aldergrove	—	1 ATC	Lysander
Ballykelly	—	CCDU	Beaufighter/ Hudson
Limavady	224	—	Hudson
Lough Erne	240	—	Catalina
Lough Erne	201	—	Sunderland
Lough Foyle	120	—	Liberator
Nutts Corner	220	—	Fortress/Hudson
Stornoway	228	—	Sunderland
No 16 GP: HQ — GILLINGHAM			
Detling	—	GCF	
Benson	—	1 PRU	(various)
Bircham Newton	500	—	Blenheim/ Hudson
Bircham Newton	279, 407	—	Hudson
Bircham Newton	—	1401	Gladiator/ Hudson/ Spitfire
Detling	280	—	Hudson
Detling	—	1 CACF	Spitfire
North Coates	59, 53	—	Hudson
Thorney Island	415, 489	—	Hampden
Thorney Island	—	2 ATC	Lysander
Wattisham	236	—	Beaufighter/ Blenheim
No 17 GP: HQ — EDINBURGH			
Abbotsinch	—	TTU	Beaufighter
Abbotsinch	—	1441	Lysander/Anson
Catfoss	2 OTU	—	Blenheim/ Beaufighter
Chivenor	5 OTU	—	Beaufighter
Cranwell	3 OTU	—	Whitley/ Wellington
Gosport	—	TDU, 2 AACU	(various)
Invergordon	4 OTU	—	
Silloth	1 OTU	—	
Squires Gate	—	3 S of GR	Botha
Thornaby	6 OTU		
No 18 GP: HQ — PITREAVIE CASTLE			
Leuchars	—	GCF	
Dyce	248, 235	—	Beaufighter
Dyce	—	1509 BATF	Wellington
Helensburgh	—	MAEE	(various)
Leuchars	42, 217	—	Beaufighter
Leuchars	320	—	Hudson
Leuchars	—	1510 BATF	Spitfire/ Blenheim
Leuchars	—	3 ATC	Lysander
Sullom Voe	404	—	Blenheim
Sullom Voe	210	—	Catalina
Wick	48, 608	—	Hudson
Wick	86	—	Beaufighter
Wick	—	1406	Spitfire/Hudson
No 19 GP: HQ — PLYMOUTH			
Roborough	—	GCF	
Carew Cheriton	245	—	Blenheim
Carew Cheriton	—	4 ATC	Lysander
Mount Batten	(10 RAAF)	—	Sunderland
Pembroke Dock	209	—	Catalina
Pembroke Dock	—	FB MM	Lerwick/ Sunderland
St Eval	502	—	Whitley
St Eval	—	PRU (B F4)	Spitfire/ Blenheim
St Eval	233	1404	Hudson
HQ RAF ICELAND			
Kaldadarnes	269	—	Hudson
Reykjavik	330	—	Northrop
Reykjavik	612	—	Whitley
Reykjavik	—	1407	Hudson

Location	Flying Sqn	Other Flying Unit	Ac Type
HQ RAF GIBRALTAR			
Gibraltar	202	—	Catalina
Gibraltar	—	MSFU	Hurricane
ARMY CO-OPERATION COMMAND: HQ — BRACKNELL			
No 70 GP: HQ — SOUTH FARNBOROUGH			
Andover	42 OTU	—	(various)
Bodorgan	—	1 CACU, 1 AACU	Blenheim
Cardiff	—	8 AACU	
Cark	—	6 AACU	
Castle Bromwich	—	7 AACU	
Detling	—	1 AACU (det)	Spitfire
Doncaster	271	—	Albatross/ Dominie
Kidlington	101 GOTU, 102 GOTU		
Larkhill	—	1424	
Old Sarum	651	—	Taylorcraft
Old Sarum	41 OTU	—	Tomahawk/ Hector/ Lysander
Ringway	—	PTS, AFEE	(various)
St Athan	—	PAU	
No 32 Wing — SCOTTISH COMMAND — EDINBURGH			
Dunino	309	—	Lysander
Macmerry	614	—	Blenheim
No 33 Wing — NORTHERN COMMAND — YORK			
Doncaster	613	—	Tomahawk
York	4	—	Tomahawk
No 34 Wing — EASTERN COMMAND — LUTON			
Benson	140	—	Spitfire
Bottisham	241	—	Tomahawk
Sawbridgworth	2	—	Tomahawk
Snailwell	268	—	Tomahawk
No 35 Wing — SOUTHEASTERN COMMAND — REIGATE			
Croydon	414	—	Tomahawk
Gatwick	26, 239	—	Tomahawk
Odiham	400	—	Tomahawk
No 36 Wing — SOUTHEASTERN COMMAND — SALISBURY			
Odiham	13	—	Blenheim
Thruxton	225	—	Lysander
Weston Zoyland	16	—	Tomahawk
Weston Zoyland	—	1492 TTF	Lysander
No 37 Wing — WESTERN COMMAND — CHESTER			
nil			
No 38 Wing — AIRBORNE DIVISION — NETHERAVON			
Netheravon	296	—	Hart/Hector
Netheravon	297	—	Whitley
RAF NORTHERN IRELAND: HQ — BELFAST			
Belfast	—	GCF	
Long Kesh	—	1494 TTF	Lysander/ Tomahawk
Mayberry	231	—	Tomahawk
FLYING TRAINING COMMAND: HQ — READING			
No 21 GP: HQ — CRANWELL			
Cranage	—	2 S of AN	
Cranwell	—	RAFC FTS	
Grantham	—	12 (P)AFU	
Hucknall	—	25 EFTS	
Leconfield	—	15 (P)AFU	
Montrose	—	8 SFTS	
Montrose	—	2 FIS	
Newton	—	16 SFTS	
Ossington	—	14 (P)AFU	
Shawbury	—	11 (P)AFU	
Ternhill	—	5 SFTS	
Watton	—	17 (P)AFU	

Location	Flying Sqn	Other Flying Unit	Ac Type
No 23 GP: HQ — SOUTH CERNEY			
Boscombe Down	—	A and AEE	
Boscombe Down	—	1 F(D)	
Brize Norton	—	1 (P)AFU	
Brize Norton	—	1525 BATF	
Church Lawford	—	1 FIS	
Hullavington	—	ECFS	
Hullavington	—	9 (P)AFU	
Little Rissington	—	6 SFTS	
Little Rissington	—	1523 BATF	
South Cerney	—	3 (P)AFU	
Thame	—	1 GTS	
Upavon	—	7 FIS	
Weston-on-the-Green	—	2 GTS	
No 25 GP: HQ — MARKET DRAYTON			
Barrow	—	10 AGS	
Bobbington	—	3 AOS	
Chelveston	—	CGS	
Dalcross	—	2 AGS	
Dumfries	—	10 AOS	
Evanton	—	8 AGS	
Exeter	—	GRU	
Jurby	—	5 AOS	
Llandwrog	—	9 AGS	
Manby	—	1 AAS	
Millom	—	2 AOS	
Pembrey	—	1 AGS	
Penrhos	—	9 AOS	
Stormy Down	—	7 AGS	
West Freugh	—	4 AOS	
Wigtown	—	1 AOS	
No 50 GP: HQ — READING			
Booker	—	21 EFTS	
Cambridge	—	22 EFTS	
Cambridge	—	4 FIS	
Clyffe Pypard	—	29 EFTS	
Clyffe Pypard	—	2 PPP	
Fair Oaks	—	18 EFTS	
Hatfield	—	1 EFTS	
Reading	—	8 EFTS	
Shellingford	—	3 EFTS	
Staverton	—	6 FIS	
Staverton	—	6 AOS	
Stoke Orchard	—	10 EFTS	
Sywell	—	6 EFTS	
Theale	—	26 EFTS	
Watchfield	—	S of FC	
Watchfield	—	BAS, BACF	
No 51 GP: HQ — LEEDS			
Ansty	—	9 EFTS	
Brough	—	4 EFTS	
Carlisle	—	15 EFTS	
Derby	—	16 EFTS	
Desford	—	7 EFTS	
Elmdon	—	14 EFTS	
Perth	—	11 EFTS	
Perth	—	5 FIS	
Peterborough	—	17 EFTS	
Peterborough	—	1 PPP	
Sealand	—	24 EFTS	
Wolverhampton	—	3 PPP	
No 54 GP: HQ — SUNNINGDALE			
Eastbourne	—	1 EAOS	
Plus control of 15 ITWs			
CANADA: ADMINISTERED BY RCAF			
De Winton, Alberta	—	31 EFTS	
Bowden. Alberta	—	32 EFTS	
Caron, Saskatchewan	—	33 EFTS	
Assiniboia, Saskatchewan	—	34 EFTS	
Neepawa, Manitoba	—	35 EFTS	

Location	Flying Sqn	Other Flying Unit	Ac Type
Pearce, Alberta	—	36 EFTS	
Kingston, Ontario	—	31 SFTS	
Moose Jaw, Saskatchewan	—	32 SFTS	
Carberry, Manitoba	—	33 SFTS	
Medicine Hat, Manitoba	—	34 SFTS	
North Battleford, Saskatchewan	—	35 SFTS	
Penhold, Alberta	—	36 SFTS	
Calgary, Alberta	—	37 SFTS	
Swift Current, Saskatchewan	—	39 SFTS	
Weyburn, Saskatchewan	—	41 SFTS	
Port Albert, Ontario	—	31 ANS	
Charlottetown, PEI	—	32 ANS	
Hamilton, Ontario	—	33 ANS	
Charlottetown, PEI	—	31 GRS	
Picton, Ontario	—	31 B and GS	
Debert, Nova Scotia	31 (GR) OTU	—	
Patricia Bay, BC	32 (TB) OTU	—	
Clinton, Ontario	—	31 RS	

SOUTH AFRICA: ADMINISTERED BY SAAF

Location	Flying Sqn	Other Flying Unit	Ac Type
Oudtshoom, Cape	—	5 CAONBS (45 Air School)	
Queenstown, Cape	—	7 CAONBS (47 Air School)	
George, Cape	—	1 GRS (61 Air School)	

TECHNICAL TRAINING COMMAND: HQ — READING
No 20 GP: HQ — MARKET DRAYTON
Control various Recruit Centres and training establishments

No 24 GP: HQ — HINDLIP HALL, WORCESTER

No 27 GP: HQ — ROYAL AGRICULTUAL COLLEGE, CIRENCESTER

MAINTENANCE COMMAND: HQ — ANDOVER
No 53 Wing: HQ — ANDOVER
Nos: 47, 52, 76, 82, 215 MUs — all Packing Dêpots

No 40 GP: HQ — ANDOVER
Nos: 3, 7, 14, 16, 17, 25, 35, 55, 61, 62, 66, 69, 70, 72, 74, 79, 82, 201, 204, 99, 203, 217, 'A', 'B', 'E', 'F', 'L', 'R', 'S' MUs — Mainly Equipment Dêpots

No 41 GP: HQ — ANDOVER
Nos: 5, 6, 8, 9, 10, 12, 15, 18, 22, 23, 24, 19, 20, 27, 29, 33, 37, 38, 39, 45, 46, 44, 48, 51 MUs — all Aircraft Storage Units

Location	Flying Sqn	Other Flying Unit	Ac Type
Dumfries	—	11 SFF	
Hamble	—	15 FPP	
Hatfield	—	5 FPP	
Hawarden	—	3 FPP	
Hullavington	—	8 FPP	
Kington Langley	—	10 SFF	
Prestwick	—	4 FPP	
Ratcliffe	—	6 FPP	
Ringway	—	14 FPP	
Thruxton	—	1427	
Whitchurch	—	2 FPP	
White Waltham	—	1 FPP	

No 42 GP: HQ — BURGHFIELD COMMON, READING
Nos: 2, 11, 21, 31, 28, 36, 53, 59, 64, 81, 91, 92, 94, 93, 95, 96, 98, 100 MUs — All Ammunition Parks
Plus control of aviation fuel and oil reserve/distribution dêpots

No 43 GP: HQ — OXFORD
Nos: 1, 4, 13, 26, 30, 32, 34, 49, 50, 56, 58, 54, 60, 65, 67, 71, 75, 78, 83, 84, 85, 86, 90, 218 MUs — All Salvage centres/repair dêpots

FERRY COMMAND
No 44 GP: HQ — GLOUCESTER

Location	Flying Sqn	Other Flying Unit	Ac Type
Prestwick	—	1527 BATF	
Kemble	—	1 OAPU	Wellington
Kemble	—	2 OAPU	Hudson
Filton	—	3 OAPU	Blenheim

Location	Flying Sqn	Other Flying Unit	Ac Type
Filton	—	4 OAPU	Beaufighter/ Beaufort
Honeybourne	—	FTU	
Hurn	—	1425	
Lyneham	—	1445	

BALLOON COMMAND: HQ — STANMORE
No 30 GP: HQ — HOOK
Controls 17 'Sqns'

No 32 GP: HQ — BATH
Controls 13 'Sqns'

No 33 GP: HQ — SHEFFIELD
Controls 22 'Sqns'

No 34 GP: HQ — EDINBURGH
Controls 12 'Sqns'

MIDDLE EAST COMMAND
Egypt: HQ — CAIRO

Location	Flying Sqn	Other Flying Unit	Ac Type
Aboukir	230	—	Sunderland
Abu Suier	89	—	Beaufighter
Amriya	47	—	(nil)
Amriya	221	—	Wellington
Bilbeis	117	—	DC-2
Bilbeis	—	AFS	
Edcu	213	—	Hurricane
Edcu	252, 272	—	Beaufighter
El Firdan	229	—	Hurricane
Fayid	108	—	Wellington
Fayun Rd/Kilo 17	46	—	(nil)
Heliopolis	173, 267	—	(various)
Heliopolis	—	2 PRU	
Heliopolis	—	1411	Gladiator
Ismailia	—	1 GRU	Wellington
Kabrit	104, 148	—	Wellington
Kabrit	147		
(El) Khankha	216	—	Bombay/DH86
(El) Khankha	213 (1 Flt)	—	Hurricane
Mena Rd/LG 224	6	—	Wellington
Port Said	213 (1 Flt)	—	Wellington
Port Said	250	—	Tomahawk
Shallufa (HQ: No 205 GP)	38, 37/40	—	Wellington
Shallufa	220 (det)	—	Fortress
Shandur	223	—	Maryland/Boston
Shandur	73 (1 Flt)	—	Hurricane
Wadi Natrun	—	ADU	(various)

Plus Nos: 101, 102, 103, 106, 107, 108, 111, 113, MUs

WESTERN DESERT

Location	Flying Sqn	Other Flying Unit	Ac Type
Acroma	208 (det)	—	Hurricane
Amriya area	15	—	Blenheim
Amriya area	39	—	Beaufort
Burg el Arab	203	—	Blenheim
El Adem	112	—	Kittyhawk
El Adem	459	—	Hudson
El Dhaba	70	—	Wellington
El Gubbi	55 (det)	—	Blenheim
Fuka area	55	—	Blenheim
Fuka area	—	SRF	
Maaten Bagush area	14	—	Blenheim

(AHQ W. DESERT)

Location	Flying Sqn	Other Flying Unit	Ac Type
Maaten Bagush area	94, 260	—	Kittyhawk
Maaten Bagush area	40	—	Hurricane
Qasaba	216 (det)	—	Bombay
Quotafiya	335	—	Hurricane
Sidi Azeiz	208	—	Hurricane
Sidi Barrani	39 (det)	—	Beaufort
Sidi Barrani	203 (det)	—	Blenheim
Sidi Barrani	223 (det)	—	Maryland/Boston
Sidi Heneish	73, 80, 238, 274	—	Hurricane
Sidi Heneish	33, 112, 450	—	Kittyhawk

Location	Flying Sqn	Other Flying Unit	Ac Type
TOBRUK (HQ: No 211 GP)			
Plus Nos: 121, 124, Mus			
AHQ LEVANT: HQ — JERUSALEM			
Haifa	—	2 PRU (det)	
Lydda	—	CCF	
Ramleh	—	1413	Gladiator
CYPRUS			
Nicosia	451 (det)	—	Hurricane
Syria			
Beit Mery (HQ: No 213 GP)			
Rayak	451	—	Hurricane
Rayak	342	—	Blenheim
St Jean	127	—	Hurricane
SUDAN AND ERITREA			
Gordon's tree	71 OTU	—	
Khartoum (HQ: No 203 GP)	—	1412	Gladiator
Wadi Gazowza	72 OTU		
Plus Nos: 104, 109, 114, 117, 122 MUs			
EAST AFRICA COMMAND			
ABYSSINIA AND SOMALILAND			
Dar es Salaam	—	CCF (det)	
Nairobi (HQ: No 207 GP)	—	1414	
Nakura	70 OTU		
Nanyuki	72 OTU (det)		
Plus No 105 MU			
ADEN: HQ — STEAMER POINT			
Khormaksar	8	SF	Vincent
Sheikh Othman	73 OTU		
Plus No 131 MU			
IRAQ: HQ — HABBANIYA			
Habbaniya	—	GCF	
Habbaniya	52	—	Audax
Mosul	237	—	Hurricane
Kirkuk (HQ: No 214 GP)	—	—	
Shaibah	244	—	Vincent
Plus Nos: 110, 115, 118, 119, 120, 126, MUs			
9 HQ MALTA: HQ — VALLETTA			
Hal Far	185	—	Hurricane
Hal Far	—	SF	Magister/ Gauntlet/ Seal/Swordfish
Luqa	69	—	Maryland
Luqa	37 (det)	—	Wellington
Takali	126,.249	1435	Hurricane
WEST AFRICA COMMAND: HQ — FREETOWN			
Gambia			
Half Die	204	—	Sunderland
Jeswang	200	—	Hudson
Sierra Leone			
Foura Bay	95	—	Sunderland
Hastings	128	—	Hurricane
Gold Coast			
Takoradi	200 (det)	—	Hudson
Takoradi	—	FDF	Hurricane
Takoradi	—	GCF	DH89/Electra/ Hudson/ Tiger Moth
Plus Nos: 116, 176 MUs			
INDIA COMMAND: HQ — DELHI			
Dijan	146	—	Audax
Ambala	—	1 SFTS	
Begumpet	—	1 EFTS	
Delhi	—	ALS, GCF	
Drigh Rd	—	AACF	

Location	Flying Sqn	Other Flying Unit	Ac Type
Dum Dum	5	—	Mohawk
Jodhpur	—	2 EFTS	
Lahore	31	—	DC2/Valentia
Risalpur	155	—	Audax
Secunderabad	20	—	Lysander
CEYLON			
Columbo (HQ: No 222 GP)			
China Bay	—	GCF	Seal
China Bay	273	—	Vildebeest
Koggalla	205 (det)	—	Catalina
Ratmalana	11	—	Blenheim
Ratmalana	30, 261	—	Hurricane
BURMA — NORGROUP: HQ — RANGOON			
Pankham Fort	17	—	Hurricane
Dum Dum	135	—	Hurricane
Alipore	136	—	Hurricane
Asanol	45, 60, 113	—	Blenheim
Akyab	67	—	Buffalo
? Lahore	28	—	Lysander
?	—	CDF	Wapiti/Hart
Plus No 154 MU			

(NB: The primary sources of SD161 and RAF List do not give unit locations)

Location	Flying Sqn	Other Flying Unit	Ac Type
WES GROUP — NETHERLANDS EAST INDIES			
Atcham	232	—	Spitfire
Dum Dum	62	—	Hudson
Chakrata	34	—	Blenheim
Plus Nos: 151, 152, 153 MUs			

(NB: The primary sources of SD161 and RAF List do not give unit locations. The Allied collapse left a very fluid situation. The SD161 also lists the following squadrons as part of WES GROUP: 27, 36, 100, 205, 242, 243, 453, 458, 488, 605, 4 AACU, CF)

April 1943
BOMBER COMMAND: HQ — HIGH WYCOMBE
No 1 GP: GQ — BAWTRY

Location	Flying Sqn	Other Flying Unit	Ac Type
Binbrook	12	—	Wellington
Grimsby	100	—	Lancaster
Elsham Wolds	103	—	Halifax
Kirmington	166	—	Wellington
Hemswell	199, 300, 301, 305	—	Wellington
Holme	101	—	Wellington
Breighton	460	—	Wellington/ Halifax
Breighton	—	1520 BATF	Oxford
Lindholme	—	1481 BG	Lysander
Blyton	—	1503 BATF	Oxford
Blyton	—	1656 CU	Lancaster/ Manchester
Blyton	—	1662 CU	Halifax/ Manchester

No 2 GP: HQ — HUNTINGDON

Location	Flying Sqn	Other Flying Unit	Ac Type
Fettwell	21	—	Ventura
Methwold	464, 487	—	Ventura
Methwold	—	1519 BATF	Oxford
Methwold	320	—	Mitchell
Foulsham	98, 180	—	Mitchell
Horsham St Faith	—	1508 BATF	Oxford
Marham	139, 105	1655 MTU	Mosquito
Marham	—	1483 B and G	Wellington
Swanton Morley	88, 226	—	Boston
Oulton	—	1515 BATF	Oxford
West Raynham	107, 342	—	Boston
Great Massingham	—	1482 BG	Lysander/ Blenheim
Steeple Morden	17 OTU (det)	—	Blenheim

No 3 GP: HQ — EXNING

Location	Flying Sqn	Other Flying Unit	Ac Type
(various)	—	1504 BATF	Oxford
Downham Market	218	—	Stirling

Location	Flying Sqn	Other Flying Unit	Ac Type
Mildenhall	149	—	Wellington/Stirling
Mildenhall	115	—	Lancaster
Newmarket	75	—	Wellington
Oakington	7	—	Stirling
Bourn	15	—	Stirling
Stradishall	90	—	Stirling
Chedburgh	214	—	Stirling
Ridgewell	—	1657 CU	Stirling
Tempsford	138	—	(various)
Gransden Lodge	161	—	Whitley/Lysander
Gransden Lodge	192	—	Wellington/Mosquito
Gransden Lodge	—	BDW	(various)
Waterbeach	—	1651 CU	Stirling

Bomber Command stalwart, Stirling of 15 Squadron.

No 4 GP: HQ — YORK

Location	Flying Sqn	Other Flying Unit	Ac Type
Driffield	158	—	Halifax
Driffield	196	—	Wellington
Leconfield	466	—	Wellington
Lissett	—	1502 BATF	Oxford
Lissett	—	1484 BG	Whitley/Lysander
Linton-on-Ouse	76	—	Halifax
East Moor	78	—	Halifax
Tholthorpe	429	—	Wellington
Marston Moor	—	1652 CU	Halifax
Rufforth	—	1663 CU	Halifax
Pocklington	102	—	Whitley/Halifax
Melbourne	10	—	Halifax
Elvington	77	—	Whitley
Riccall	—	1658 CU	Halifax
Snaith	51	—	Whitley/Halifax
Burn	431	—	Wellington

No 5 GP: HQ — GRANTHAM

Location	Flying Sqn	Other Flying Unit	Ac Type
Bottesford	467	—	Lancaster
Langar	207	—	Lancaster
Coningsby	97	—	Lancaster
Woodhall Spa	—	1514 BATF	Oxford
Scampton	57	—	Wellington
Dunholme Lodge	49	—	Hampden/Manchester
Fiskerton	—	1518 BATF	Oxford
Swinderby	—	1654 CU	Lancaster/Halifax/Manchester
Winthorpe	—	1661 CU	Lancaster/Manchester
Wigsley	—	1660 CU	Lancaster/Manchester
Syerston	61	—	Lancaster
Balderton	106	—	Lancaster
Fulbeck	—	1485 BG	Lysander
Waddington	—	1506 BATF	Oxford
Skellingthorpe	50	—	Lancaster
Bardney	9, 44	—	Lancaster

No 6 (RCAF) GP: HQ — ALLERTON PARK, KNARLESBOROUGH

Location	Flying Sqn	Other Flying Unit	Ac Type
Leeming	405	—	Halifax
Skipton on Swale	408	—	Halifax
Middleton St George	419	—	Halifax
Croft	420, 427	—	Wellington
Croft	—	1535 BATF	Oxford
Topcliffe	—	GCF	Wicko/BA Eagle
Dishforth	424, 425, 426, 428	—	Wellington
Dishforth	—	1659 CU	Halifax
Dishforth	—	1512 BATF	Oxford

No 8 GP: HQ — WYTON

Location	Flying Sqn	Other Flying Unit	Ac Type
Wyton	35	—	Halifax
Graveley	83	—	Lancaster
Warboys	109	—	Mosquito
Warboys	156	—	Wellington
Warboys	—	1507 BATF	Oxford

No 91 GP: HQ — ABINGDON

Location	Flying Sqn	Other Flying Unit	Ac Type
Abingdon	10 OTU	—	Whitley
Stanton Harcourt	—	1501 BATF	Oxford
Harwell	15 OTU	—	Wellington
Hampstead Norris	—	1516 BATF	Oxford
Hampstead Norris	—	1443 FTF	Wellington
Honeybourne	24 OTU	—	Whitley
Kinloss	19 OTU	—	Whitley
Lossiemouth	20 OTU	—	Wellington
Moreton-in-Marsh	21 OTU	—	Wellington
Edgehill	—	1446 FTF	Wellington/Anson
Pershore	23 OTU	—	Wellington
Wellesbourne Mountford	22 OTU	—	Wellington

No 92 GP: HQ — WINSLOW

Location	Flying Sqn	Other Flying Unit	Ac Type
Bicester	13 OTU	—	Blenheim
Finmere	—	307 FTU	Blenheim
Finmere	—	1473	Wellington
Finmere	—	1551	Anson/Master
Chipping Warden	12 OTU	—	Wellington
Silverstone	—	1517 BATF	Oxford
Cottesmore	14 OTU	—	Hampden/Wellington
North Luffenham	29 OTU	—	Wellington
Upper Heyford	16 OTU	—	Wellington
Upwood	17 OTU	—	Blenheim
Upwood	—	1511 BATF	Oxford
Wing	26 OTU	—	Wellington
Little Horwood	—	GCF	
Westcott	11 OTU	—	Wellington
Oakley	—	ECDU	Wellington

No. 30 OTU Wellingtons.

Location	Flying Sqn	Other Flying Unit	Ac Type
No 93 GP: HQ — EGGINTON HALL			
Bramcote	18 OTU	—	Wellington
Nuneaton	—	1513 BATF	Oxford
Finningley	18 OTU	—	Wellington
Finningley	—	1521 BATF	Oxford
Hixon	30 OTU	—	Wellington
Lichfield	27 OTU	—	Wellington
Tatenhill	—	GCF	
Whitchurch Heath	81 OTU	—	Whitley
Wymeswold	28 OTU	—	Wellington
No 26 GP: HQ — LANGLEY HALL, SLOUGH			
Control of No's 80 and 81 Signals Wings; numerous W/T; D/F stations etc			
FIGHTER COMMAND: HQ — STANMORE			
No 9 GO: HQ — BARTON HALL, PRESTON			
High Ercall	247	—	Typhoon
High Ercall	41	—	Spitfire
High Ercall	—	3 ADF	
Honiley	255, 96	—	Beaufighter
Honiley	285	—	Defiant/Oxford
Speke	—	MSFU	Hurricane
Valley	275	—	Walrus/Anson
Valley	256, 456	—	Mosquito
Valley	—	1486 (FG)	Lysander/Master
Woodvale	195	—	Typhoon
No 10 GP: HQ — RUDLOE MANOR			
Church Stanton	312, 313	—	Spitfire
Colerne	264	—	Mosquito
Weston-super-Mare	286	—	Defiant/Oxford/Hurricane
Weston-super-Mare	184	—	Hurricane
Weston-super-Mare	—	GCF, 2ADF	
Defford	—	TFU	
Exeter	266	—	Typhoon
Bolt Head	307	—	Mosquito
Bolt Head	310	—	Spitfire
Fairwood Common	125	—	Beaufighter
Fairwood Common	412	—	Spitfire
Harrowbeer	276	—	Walrus/Spitfire/Anson
Harrowbeer	193	—	Typhoon
Ibsley	129, 504, 616	—	Spitfire
Middle Wallop	406	—	Beaufighter
Middle Wallop	164	—	Hurricane
Odiham	175	—	Typhoon
Portreath	—	1449	Hurricane
Perranporth	19, 130, 602	—	Spitfire
Predannack	141	—	Beaufighter
Warmwell	257	—	Typhoon
Warmwell	263	—	Whirlwind
Warmwell	—	1487 (FG)	Lysander/Master
No 11 GP: HQ — UXBRIDGE			
Biggin Hill	1	—	Typhoon
Biggin Hill	340, 611	—	Spitfire
Bradwell Bay	23, 157	—	Mosquito
Castle Camps	605	—	Mosquito
Croydon	287	—	Defiant/Oxford/Hurricane
Croydon	—	1 ADU	
Croydon	116	—	Oxford/Moth
Ford	418	—	Mosquito
Ford	604	—	Beaufighter
Ford	—	FIU	
Gravesend	277	—	Walrus/Spitfire
Hawkinge	91	—	Spitfire
Heston	303	—	Spitfire
Heston	515	—	Defiant
Heston	—	1422	Boston/Hurricane/Mosquito
Hornchurch	64, 122	—	Spitfire

Location	Flying Sqn	Other Flying Unit	Ac Type
Fairlop	350	—	Spitfire
Hunsdon	85	—	Mosquito
Hunsdon	3	—	Typhoon
Kenley	402, 403, 421	—	Spitfire
Manston	137	—	Whirlwind
Manston	609	—	Typhoon
Martlesham	132	—	Spitfire
Martlesham	182	—	Typhoon
Martlesham	—	1488 (FG)	Lysander/Master
Northolt	308, 315, 316	—	Spitfire
Northolt	—	GCF	
North Weald	124, 331, 332	—	Spitfire
Odiham	174	—	Typhoon
Redhill	416	—	Spitfire
Southend	453	—	Spitfire
Tangmere	129	—	Spitfire
Tangmere	486	—	Typhoon
Merston	485	—	Spitfire
Westhampnett	165, 610	—	Spitfire
West Malling	29	—	Mosquito
No 12 GP: HQ — WATNALL			
Church Fenton	183	—	Typhoon
Church Fenton	25	—	Mosquito
Coltishall	68	—	Beaufighter
Coltishall	278	—	Anson/Walrus/Moth
Coltishall	56	—	Typhoon
Coltishall	118	—	Spitfire
Matlask	—	1489 (FG)	Lysander/Master
Digby	288	—	Defiant/Hurricane/Oxford/Spitfire
Digby	410	—	Mosquito
Digby	411	—	Spitfire
Duxford	—	AFDU	
Fowlmere	—	1426 EAC	
Hutton Cranswick	306	—	Spitfire
Kirton-in-Lindsey	302, 317	—	Spitfire
Ludham	167	—	Spitfire
Snailwell	181	—	Typhoon
Wittering	151	—	Mosquito
Kingscliffe	—	1530 BATF	Oxford
Acklington	409	—	Beaufighter
Acklington	198	—	Typhoon
Ayr	488	—	Beaufighter
Ayr	222	—	Spitfire
Ayr	—	1490 (FG)	Lysander/Master
Catterick	401	—	Spitfire
Catterick	219	—	Beaufighter
Drem	65	—	Spitfire
Drem	197	—	Typhoon
Ouston	281	—	Anson/Walrus
Woolsington	—	GCF	
Turnhouse	289	—	Defiant/Oxford/Hurricane
Turnhouse	341	—	Spitfire
Turnhouse	—	4 ADF	
No 14 GP: HQ — INVERNESS			
Castletown	282	—	Anson/Walrus
Castletown	131	—	Spitfire
Inverness	—	GCF	
Peterhead	245	—	Typhoon
Peterhead	—	1479	Oxford
Skeabrae	66, 234	—	Spitfire
Skeabrae	—	1491 (FG)	Lysander/Master
No 81 GP: HQ — AVENING			
Annan	55 OTU	—	Hurricane
Aston Down	52 OTU	—	Spitfire
Charter Hall	54 OTU	—	Beaufort/Beaufighter
Cranfield	51 OTU	—	Beaufighter/Havoc/Mosquito

Location	Flying Sqn	Other Flying Unit	Ac Type
Eshott	57 OTU	—	Spitfire
Grangemouth	58 OTU	—	Spitfire
Llandow	53 OTU	—	Spitfire
Millfield	59 OTU	—	Hurricane/ Typhoon
Rednal	61 OTU	—	Spitfire
Tealing	56 OTU	—	Hurricane
Usworth	62 OTU	—	Anson

FC UNITS IN RAF IN N. IRELAND

Location	Flying Sqn	Other Flying Unit	Ac Type
Ballyhalbert	—	1493 (FG)	Lysander/Master
Kirkistown	501	—	Spitfire
Newtownards	—	1480	Oxford/ Hurricane
Newtownards	—	CF	

No 60 GP: LEIGHTON BUZZARD

Control of No's: 71, 72, 73, 74, 75, 76, 77, 78, 79 Signals Wings

COASTAL COMMAND: HQ — NORTHWOOD

Control of 63 MCUs, allocated to the various Groups

No 15 GP: HQ — LIVERPOOL

Location	Flying Sqn	Other Flying Unit	Ac Type
Aldergrove	120	—	Liberator
Aldergrove	—	1402	Hampden/ Spitfire/ Gladiator
Aldergrove	—	1 APC	
Ballykelly	280 (det)	—	Anson
Benbecula	206, 220	—	Fortress
Castle Archdale	201, 228, 423	—	Sunderland
Oban	330	—	Sunderland
Oban	422	—	Catalina
Port Ellen	246	—	Sunderland
Speke	—	GCF	

No 16 GP: HQ — GILLINGHAM

Location	Flying Sqn	Other Flying Unit	Ac Type
Benson	540	—	Mosquito
Benson	541, 542, 543	—	Spitfire
Benson	544	—	Spitfire/Anson/ Wellington
Bircham Newton	521	—	Mosquito/ Spitfire/ Hampden/ Gladiator
Bircham Newton	53, 279	—	Hudson
Bircham Newton	280	—	Anson
Bircham Newton	—	1525 BATF	Oxford
Detling	—	GCF	
Gosport	—	TDU	
North Coates	143, 236, 254	—	Beaufighter
Thorney Island	86	—	Liberator
Thorney Island	415	—	Hampden
Thorney Island	—	2 APC	Lysander

No 17 GP: HQ — EDINBURGH

Location	Flying Sqn	Other Flying Unit	Ac Type
Alness	4 OTU	—	Catalina/ Sunderland
Castle Kennedy	—	2 TTU	Beaufort/ Beaufighter
Catfoss	2 OTU	—	Blenheim/ Beaufighter
Cranwell	3 OTU	—	Whitley/ Wellington
Crosby	9 OTU	—	Beaufort/Oxford/ Beaufighter
Dyce	8 OTU	—	Mosquito
Dyce	—	1509 BATF	Wellington
East Fortune	132 OTU	—	Beaufighter
Killadeas	131 OTU	—	Catalina
Limavedy	7 OTU	—	Wellington
Long Kesh	5 OTU	—	Beaufort/ Hampden
Port Ellen	—	304 FTU	Beaufighter

Location	Flying Sqn	Other Flying Unit	Ac Type
Silloth	6 OTU	—	Hudson/Anson
Squires Gate	—	3 S of GR	Botha
Stranraer	—	302 FTU	Catalina
Templeton	—	306 FTU	Beaufort
Thornaby	1 OTU	—	Hudson/Anson/ Oxford
Turnberry	—	1 TTU	Wellington/ Hampden

No 18 GP: HQ — PITREAVIE CASTLE

Location	Flying Sqn	Other Flying Unit	Ac Type
Helensburgh	—	MAEE	
Leuchars	—	1510 BATF	
Leuchars	540 (det)	—	Spitfire/ Blenheim
Leuchars	455	—	Hampden
Leuchars	144, 235	—	Beaufighter
Leuchars	—	3 APC	Lysander
Leuchars	—	1477	Catalina
Sullom Voe	190	—	Catalina
Tain	547	—	Wellington
Wick	407	—	Hudson
Wick	489	—	Hampden
Wick	612	—	Whitley
Wick	—	1406	Spitfire/ Hampden

No 19 GP: HQ — PLYMOUTH

Location	Flying Sqn	Other Flying Unit	Ac Type
Beaulieu	224	—	Liberator
Chivenor	59	—	Fortress
Chivenor	172, 547, 179 (det)	—	Wellington
Chivenor	404	—	Beaufighter
Hamworthy	461	—	Sunderland
Holmsley South	58	—	Whitley/Halifax
Holmsley South	502	—	Halifax
Mountbatten	(10 RAAF)	—	Sunderland
Roborough	—	GCF	
Pembroke Dock	119	—	Sunderland
Pembroke Dock	210	—	Catalina
Predannock	248	—	Beaufighter
St Eval	543 (det)	—	Spitfire/ Blenheim
St Eval	10 OTU (det)	—	Whitley
St Eval	—	1404	Hudson/Ventura/ Albemarle
Talbenny	311, 304	303 FTU	Wellington

HQ — RAF ICELAND

Location	Flying Sqn	Other Flying Unit	Ac Type
Kaldadarnes	269	—	Hudson
Reykjavik	330 (det)	—	Northrop
Reykjavik	—	1407	Hampden

HQ — RAF GIBRALTAR

Location	Flying Sqn	Other Flying Unit	Ac Type
Gibraltar	48, 233	—	Hudson
Gibraltar	544 (det)		
Gibraltar	202	—	Catalina/ Sunderland
Gibraltar	179	—	Wellington
Gibraltar	210 (det)	—	Catalina
Gibraltar	—	MSFU	Hurricane
Gibraltar	—	1403	Hampden/ Gladiator

ARMY CO-OPERATION COMMAND: HQ — BRACKNELL

No 70 GP: HQ — FARNBOROUGH

Location	Flying Sqn	Other Flying Unit	Ac Type
Aberporth	—	1608, 1609, 1621	(various)
Ashbourne	42 OTU	—	Blenheim/Anson/ Whitley
Bircham Newton	—	1611, 1612	
Bodorgan	—	1606, 1620	
Cardiff	—	8 AACU	Oxford/Master
Cark	—	1614	
Castle Bromwich	—	6, 7 AACU	Oxford/Master
Cleave	—	1602, 1603 1604, 1608	

Location	Flying Sqn	Other Flying Unit	Ac Type
Detling	—	1624, 1 CACU	
Driffield	—	1613	
Farnborough	—	RAE	
Farnborough	—	GCF	
Gosport	—	1622	
Hawarden	41 OTU	—	Mustang/Harvard
Ipswich	—	1616	
Manorbier	—	PAU	Queen Bee
Netheravon	—	1526 BATF	Oxford
Newtownards	—	1617	
Old Sarum	43 OTU		
Ringway	—	PTS	Whitley/Anson
Roborough	—	1623	
Towyn	—	1605, 1613	
Weston Zoyland	—	1492 TTF	Lysander
Weston Zoyland	—	1600, 1601	

No 72 GP: HQ — FARNBOROUGH
Various units but primarily RAF Regiment

32 Wing — SCOTTISH COMMAND: HQ — EDINBURGH

Location	Flying Sqn	Other Flying Unit	Ac Type
Kirknewton	309	-	Mustang
Macmerry	63	—	Mustang
Macmerry	—	1497 TTF	Lysander

33 WING — NORTHERN COMMAND: HQ — YORK

Location	Flying Sqn	Other Flying Unit	Ac Type
Dishforth	—	1472	Hurricane
Duxford	169	-	Mustang
Ouston	613	—	Mustang
York	4	—	Mustang

34 WING — EASTERN COMMAND: HQ — LUTON

Location	Flying Sqn	Other Flying Unit	Ac Type
Bottisham	2	—	Mustang
Bottisham	654	—	Auster
Sawbridgeworth	652, 656	—	Auster
Sawbridgeworth	—	1495 TTF	Lysander
Snailwell	268, 170	—	Mustang
Westley	657	—	Auster

35 WING — SOUTH-EAST COMMAND: HQ — REIGATE

Location	Flying Sqn	Other Flying Unit	Ac Type
Detling	318	—	Hurricane
Detling	—	1 CACU	Blenheim/Spitfire
Gatwick	653	—	Auster
Gatwick	26	—	Mustang
Odiham	168	—	Mustang
Odiham	140	—	Spitfire/Ventura

36 WING — SOUTHERN COMMAND: HQ — SALISBURY

Location	Flying Sqn	Other Flying Unit	Ac Type
Andover	16	—	Mustang
Old Sarum	655	—	Auster
Stoney Cross	239	—	Mustang

37 WING — WESTERN COMMAND: HQ — CHESTER
Nil

38 WING — AIRBORNE DIVISION: HQ — NETHERAVON

Location	Flying Sqn	Other Flying Unit	Ac Type
Hurn	296	—	Whitley/Halifax
Hurn	—	1498 TTF	Lysander
Netheravon	295	—	Whitley/Halifax
Netheravon	—	GPEU	Master/Moth/Hotspur
Thruxton	297	—	Whitley/Halifax

39 (RCAF) WING — 1ST CANADIAN ARMY: LEATHERHEAD

Location	Flying Sqn	Other Flying Unit	Ac Type
Dunsfold	400	—	Mustang/Tomahawk
Dunsfold	414	—	Mustang
Dunsfold	430	—	Tomahawk

RAF NORTHERN IRELAND: HQ — STORMONT, BELFAST

Location	Flying Sqn	Other Flying Unit	Ac Type
Belfast	—	1494 TTF	Lysander
Belfast	—	CF	
Nutts Corner	23	—	Tomahawk

FLYING TRAINING COMMAND: HQ — READING
No 21 GP: HQ — CRANWELL

Location	Flying Sqn	Other Flying Unit	Ac Type
Andover	—	15 PAFU	
Cranwell	—	RAFC FTS	
Dalcross	—	19 PAFU	
Grantham	—	12 PAFU	
Hucknall	—	25 PAFU	
Montrose	—	2 FIS	
Newton	—	16 SFTS	
Newton	—	1524 BATF	
Ossington	—	14 PAFU	
Peterborough	—	7 PAFU	
Shawbury	-	11 PAFU	
Shawbury	—	1534 BATF	
Sherbum-in-Elmet	—	AFEE	
Ternhill	—	5 PAFU	
Watton	—	17 PAFU	

No 23 GP: HQ — SOUTH CERNEY

Location	Flying Sqn	Other Flying Unit	Ac Type
Boscombe Down	—	A and AEE	
Bodscombe Down	—	1 FDF	
Brize Norton	—	HGCU	
Brize Norton	—	FT CIS	
Church Lawford	—	18 PAFU	
Hullavington	—	ECFS	
Hullavington	—	3 FIS	
Hullavington	—	1532 BATF	
Kidlington	—	20 PAFU	
Kidlington	-	1538 BATF	
Little Rissington	—	6 PAFU	
Little Rissington	—	1523 BATF	
Shobdon	—	5 GTS	
Shobdon	—	GIF	
South Cerney	—	3 PAFU	
South Cerney	—	1539, 1540 BATF	
Stoke Orchard	—	3 GTS	
Upavon	—	7 FIS	
Upavon	-	1537 BATF	

No 25 GP: HQ — MARKET DRAYTON

Location	Flying Sqn	Other Flying Unit	Ac Type
Bobbington	—	3 OAFU	
Cranage	—	CNS	
Cranage	—	1531 BATF	
Exeter	—	GRU	
Manby	—	1 AAS	
Mona	—	3 AGS	
Pembrey	—	1 AGS	
Penrhos	—	9 OAFU	
Staverton	—	6 AOS	
Stormy Down	—	7 AGS	
Sutton Bridge	—	CGS	

No 29 GP: HQ — DUMFRIES

Location	Flying Sqn	Other Flying Unit	Ac Type
Barrow	—	10 AGS	
Cark	—	SPTU	
Dalcross	—	2 AGS	
Dumfries	—	10 OAFU	
Evanton	—	8 AGS	
Jurby	—	5 AOS	
Millom	—	2 OAFU	
Morpeth	—	4 AGS	
West Freugh	—	4 AOS	
Wigtown	—	1 OAFU	

No 50 GP: HQ — READING

Location	Flying Sqn	Other Flying Unit	Ac Type
Booker	—	21 EFTS	
Cambridge	—	22 EFTS	
Clyffe Pypard	—	29 EFTS	
Fairoaks	—	18 EFTS	
Holwell Hyde	—	1 EFTS	
Shellingford	—	6 EFTS	
Sywell	—	6 EFTS	
Theale	—	26 EFTS	
Watchfield	—	BAS, BADU	
Woodley	—	10 FIS	
Worcester	—	2 EFTS	

Location	Flying Sqn	Other Flying Unit	Ac Type
No 51 GP: HQ — LEEDS			
Ansty	—	9 EFTS	
Brough	—	4 EFTS	
Carlisle	—	15 EFTS	
Derby	—	16 EFTS	
Desford	—	7 EFTS	
Elmdon	—	14 EFTS	
Elmdon	—	1533 BATF	
Perth	—	11 EFTS	
Perth	—	1 PPP	
Sealand	—	24 EFTS	
Wolverhampton	—	28 EFTS	
Wolverhampton	—	3 PPP	

No 54 GP: HQ — SUNNINGDALE
Control numerous ITWs, ACDCs, etc

Location	Flying Sqn	Other Flying Unit	Ac Type
CANADA: ADMINISTERED BY RCAF			
De Winton, Alberta	—	31 EFTS	
Bowden, Alberta	—	32 EFTS	
Caron, Saskatchewan	—	33 EFTS	
Assiniboia, Saskatchewan	—	34 EFTS	
Neepawa, Manitoba	—	35 EFTS	
Kingston, Ontario	—	31 SFTS	
Moose Jaw, Saskatchewan	—	32 SFTS	
Carberry, Manitoba	—	33 SFTS	
Medicine Hat, Manitoba	—	34 SFTS	
North Battleford, Saskatchewan	—	35 SFTS	
Penhold, Alberta	-	36 SFTS	
Calgary, Alberta	—	37 SFTS	
Estevan, Saskatchewan	—	38 SFTS	
Swift, Current, Saskatchewan	—	39 SFTS	
Weyburn, Saskatchewan	—	41 SFTS	
Port Albert, Ontario	—	31 ANS	
Hamilton, Ontario	—	33 ANS	
Charlottetown, PEI	—	31 GRS	
Picton, Ontario	—	31 B and GS	
Debert, Nova Scotia	31 (GR) OTU	—	
Patricia Bay, BC	32 (TR) OTU	—	
Pennfield Ridge, New Brunswick	34 (B) OTU	—	
Greenwood, Nova Scotia	36 (GR) OTU		
Clinton, Ontario	—	31 RS	

TECHNICAL TRAINING COMMAND: HQ — READING
No 20 GP: HQ — MARKET DRAYTON
Control Reception Centres etc

No 24 GP: HQ — HINDLIP HALL, WORCESTER
Control various 'Schools', including SoTTs

No 27 GP: HQ — ROYAL AGRICULTURAL COLLEGE, CIRENCESTER
Control various training units, including Radio Schools

No 28 GP: HQ — QUEEN'S SQUARE, LONDON
Control mainly medical and administrative institutions

MAINTENANCE COMMAND: HQ — ANDOVER
No 53 WING: HQ — ANDOVER
MUs: 47, 52, 76, 82, 215, 222 — Packing Depôts

No 54 WING: HQ — LONDON
Various MT Companies

No 40 GP: HQ — ANDOVER
MUs: 3, 5, 7, 14, 16, 17, 25, 35, 55, 61, 62, 66, 68, 69, 70, 72, 73, 74, 79, 87, 89, 99, 201, 203, 204, 205, 207, 208, 210, 211, 216, 228, 229, 232, 236, A, E, H, T — all Equipment Depôts

No 41 GP: HQ — ANDOVER
MUs: 6, 8, 9, 10, 12, 15, 18, 19, 20, 22, 23, 27, 29, 33, 38, 39, 44, 45, 46, 48, 51 — all Aircraft Storage Units

Location	Flying Sqn	Other Flying Unit	Ac Type
Dumfries	—	11 SFF	
Hamble	—	15 FPP	
Hatfield	—	5 FPP	

Location	Flying Sqn	Other Flying Unit	Ac Type
Hawarden	—	3 FPP	
Hullavington	—	8 FPP	
Kington Langley	—	10 SFF	
Luton	—	5 FPP	
Marham	—	1427	
Marston Moor	—	1475	
Prestwick	—	4 FPP	
Ratcliffe	—	6 FPP	
Ringway	—	14 FPP	
Whitcurch	—	2 FPP	
White Waltham	—	1 FPP	

No 42 GP: HQ — BURGH COMMON
MUs: 2, 11, 21, 28, 31, 36, 53, 59, 64, 77, 80, 81, 91, 92, 93, 94, 95, 96, 98, 100, 202, 219, 224 — Ammunition Depôts
Plus control of aviation fuel and oil distribution depôts

No 43 GP: HQ — OXFORD
MUs: 1, 4, 13, 24, 26, 30, 32, 34, 49, 49, 50, 54, 56, 58, 60, 63, 65, 67, 71, 75, 78, 83, 84, 85, 86, 88, 97, 213, 218, 226, 235 — Salvage centres/repair depôts

FERRY COMMAND
No 44 GP: HQ — GLOUCESTER

Location	Flying Sqn	Other Flying Unit	Ac Type
Doncaster	271	—	
Filton	—	2 OAPU	Blenheim/ Beaufort/ Beaufighter
Hendon	24		
Hendon	510		
Kemble	—	1 OAPU	Wellington/ Hudson/+
Lyneham	511	—	
Lyneham	—	301 FTU	
Prestwick	—	1527 BATF	

BALLOON COMMAND: HQ — STANMORE
No 30 GP: HQ — CHESSINGTON
Controls 22 'Sqns'

52 Squadron dispersal at Bo Rizzo, December 1943.

Location	Flying Sqn	Other Flying Unit	Ac Type
No 32 GP: HQ — BATH			
Controls 12 'Sqns'			
No 33 GP: HQ — SHEFFIELD			
Controls 24 'Sqns'			
MEDITERRANEAN AIR COMMAND			
NORTH WEST AFRICA			
HQs:			
NWAAF — Maison Caree			
NWATAF — Aine Beida			
NWACAF — Algiers			
NWASAF — Constantine			
NWAASC — Algiers			
Algiers	283	—	Walrus
Blida	500, 608	—	Hudson
Blida	142, 150	-	Wellington
Canrobert	13, 18, 114	—	Bisley
Constantine	72	—	Spitfire
Jemappes	253	—	Hurricane
Le Kroub	654	—	Auster
Maison Blanche	43, 32	—	Hurricane
Maison Blanche	682	—	Spitfire
Maison Blanche	153	—	Beaufighter
Oulmeme	614	—	Bisley
Setif	255, 600	—	Beaufighter
Souk El Khemis	225, 241	—	Hurricane
Souk El Khemis	93, 111, 152, 243	—	Spitfire
(HQ: No 242 GP)			
Tingley	81, 154, 232, 242	—	Spitfire
Tahir	87	—	Hurricane
Gibraltar (det)	202, 210	—	Catalina
Gibraltar	48, 233	—	Hudson
Gibraltar	179	—	Wellington
Gibraltar	—	Met Flt	Hudson
AHQ Malta: HQ — Valletta			
Hal Far	185	—	Spitfire
Hal Far	-	CF	
Krendi	229, 249	—	Spitfire
Luqa	69	—	Baltimore/ Wellington
Luqa	39	—	Beaufort
Luqa	23	—	Mosquito
Luqa	221, 458	—	Wellington
Luqa	126, 683, 1435	—	Spitfire
Luqa	108 (det)	—	Beaufighter
Ta Kali	272	—	Beaufighter
Plus No. 143 MU			
CYRENAICA, LIBYA, TUNISIA			
Bir El Gardabia	37, 40, 70, 104	—	Wellington
Bir El Gardabia	462	—	Halifax
(HQ: No 205 GP)			
Bir El Gardabia	—	GCF	
Bu Amud	80	—	Hurricane
Berka	38	—	Wellington
Benina (HQ: No 212 GP)	—	1563	
Bersis	33	—	Hurricane
Bersis	89	—	Beaufighter
Castel Benito	417	—	Hurricane
Castel Benito	89 (det)	—	Beaufighter
Castel Verdi	—	1437	Baltimore
El Assa	112, 250, 260, 450	—	Kittyhawk
El Assa	73	—	Hurricane
Chemines	178	—	Halifax/Liberator
Hazbub	92, 145, 601	—	Spitfire
Marble Arch	117, 216, 267 (det)		
Martuba	94	—	Hurricane
Mellaha	274	—	Hurricane
Magrun	252	—	Beaufighter
Medenine (HQ: No 211 GP)			
Misurata	213	—	Hurricane
Misurata	47	—	Beaufighter
Misurata	55, 223	—	Baltimore

Location	Flying Sqn	Other Flying Unit	Ac Type
Sorman	6	—	Hurricane
Tripoli	—	1564	
Plus MUs: 113, 114, 122, 124, 136			
MIDDLE EAST COMMAND			
ALEXANDRIA (HQ: No 201 GP)			
Almaza	—	1411	Gladiator
Bilbeis	117	—	Hudson
Bilbeis	162	—	Wellington/ Blenheim
Cairo	—	1 ADU	
Cairo West	216	—	Bombay/Hudson
Cairo West	267	—	Hudson
Edku	46, 272 (det), 277, 603	—	Beaufighter
Edku	451	—	Hurricane
Gebel Hamzi	—	2 ADU	
Gianaclis	75 OTU		
Gianaclis	39 (det)	—	Beaufort
Gambut	14	—	Marauder
Gambut	459	—	Hudson
Heliopolis (HQ: No 206 GP)	173		
Ismalia	—	1 GRU	Wellington
LG 39	—	SRF	
LG 91	52	—	Baltimore
LG 91	454	—	Blenheim
LG 106	237	—	Hurricane
LG 121	134	—	Hurricane
LG 211	458 (det)	—	Wellington
LG 227	203	—	Baltimore
Mariut	—	GCF (201 GP)	
Matariya	680	—	Spitfire
Port Said	238	—	Hurricane
Mersha Matruh	235	—	Hurricane
Shallufa	221 (det)	—	Wellington
Shallufa	—	5 METS	
Shandur	—	SLF	Liberator
Plus MUs: 101, 106, 108, 109, 111, 112, 128, 132, 135, 141			
AHQ LEVANT: HQ — JERUSALEM			
PALESTINE AND TRANS-JORDAN			
Agir	74 OTU		
Lydda	—	CF	
Lydda	—	1413	Gladiator
Ramat David	127	—	Hurricane
Plus MUs: 120, 129, 142			
SYRIA			
123 MU plus various radar (AMES) stations and assorted units			
CYPRUS			
Nicosia	—	1565	
Plus various radar (AMES) stations and assorted units			
AHQ IRAQ AND PERSIA: HQ — HABBANIYA			
Abadan	123	—	Hurricane
Agsu	208	—	Hurricane
Basrah (HQ: No 215 GP)			
Habbaniya	—	CCF	
Habbaniya	—	1415	Gladiator
Jiwani	240 (det)	—	Catalina
Masirah	244 (det)	—	Blenheim
Ras E Hadd	244 (det)	—	Blenheim
Shaibah (HQ: No 218 GP)			
Sharjah	244	—	Blenheim
Teheran	74	—	Hurricane
Teheran	—	1438	Blenheim
Plus MUs: 110, 115, 119, 125, 127, 134, 138			
BRITISH FORCES ADEN: HQ — STEAMER POINT			
ADEN			
Khormaksar	8	—	Blenheim
Khormaksar	—	CF	Beechcraft
Plus No 131 MU			

Location	Flying Sqn	Other Flying Unit	Ac Type
SUDAN/ERITREA			
Carthago	71 OTU		
Carthago	—	1412 (det)	Gladiator
Khartoum (HQ: No 203 GP)	—	1412	
Khartoum	—	GCF	
Plus MUs: 104, 17			
AHQ EAST AFRICA: HQ — NAIROBI			
Dar es Salaam	230	—	Sunderland
Eastleigh	—	CF	
Eastleigh	—	1414	Gladiator
Kapivu	209, 259	—	Catalina
Kisumu	209 (det)	—	Catalina
Nakuru	70 OTU		
Nanyuki	72 OTU		
Port Reitz	—	CF (det)	
Thika	105 OTU		
Pamanxi	209 (det)	—	Catalina
Arrachart, Madagascar	—	1433	Lysander
Plus No 133 MU			
WEST AFRICA COMMAND: HQ — FREETOWN			
Gambia			
Half Die	204	—	Sunderland
Jeswang	200	—	Hudson
Plus No 176 MU			
SIERRA LEONE			
Jui	95	—	Sunderland
Jui	270	—	Catalina
GOLD COAST			
Takoradi	—	CF	
Plus No 116 MU			
NIGERIA			
Ikeja	349	—	Tomahawk
Kaduna	—	1432	Hurrsicane
WEST INDIES: HQ — BAHAMAS			
Nassau	111 OTU	—	Liberator/Mitchell
INDIA COMMAND: HQ — NEW DELHI			
Ambala	—	1 SFTS	
Alipore	67, 146	—	Hurricane
Armarda Road	177	—	Beaufighter
Angel (Calcutta)	17	—	Hurricane
Agartala	5	—	Mohawk
Agartala	27		Beaufighter
Barrackpore	—	CF	
Baroda	-	AO and AGS	
Bombay (HQ: No 227 GP)			
Begumpet	—	1 EFTS	
Baigachi	176	—	Beaufighter
Baigachi	261	—	Hurricane
Bangalore	(HQ: No 225 GP)		
Chittagong	136, 607	—	Hurricane
Charra	20	—	Lysander
CALCUTTA (HQ: No 221 GP)			
Chandina	113	—	Blenheim
Chaklala	215	—	Wellington
Chaklala	—	ALS	
Cholavaram	45	-	nil
Cholavaram	84	—	Vengeance
Dhubalia	353	-	Hudson
Digri	99	—	Wellington
Dohazari	60	—	Blenheim
Dum Dum	681	—	Spitfire/Mitchell
Fenny	615	—	Hurricane
Fenny	11	—	Blenheim
Imphal	155	—	Mohawk
Jakkar	—	CF	
Jessore	62	—	Hudson

Location	Flying Sqn	Other Flying Unit	Ac Type
Juhu (Bombay)	—	AACU	
Juhu	—	Cal Flt	
Karachi	212	—	Catalina
Madhaighanja	110, 82	—	Vengeance
Madhaighanja	135	—	Hurricane
New Delhi	—	CCU	
Palam (HQ: 226 GP)	31	—	DC2/DC3
Palam	194	—	Hudson
Peshawar	—	CF	
Peshawar	152 OTU		
Ranchi	28	—	Hurricane
Red Hills Lake	240	—	Catalina
Ramu	79, 135	—	Hurricane
Risalpur	151 OTU		
Salbani	159	—	Liberator
Silchar	34	—	Blenheim
Tanjore	36	—	Wellington
Yelahanka	42	—	Bisley
Plus Nos: 301, 302, 306, 307, 308, 312, 313, 320 MUs			
CEYLON			
Colombo	30	—	Hurricane
Colombo	—	Cal Flt	
China Bay	321	—	Catalina
China Bay	273	—	Hurricane
Dambulla	258	—	Hurricane
Kogalla	205, 413	—	Catalina
Ratmalana	160	—	Liberator
Ratmalana	—	CF	
Vavuniya	217	—	Hudson
Vavuniya	22	—	Beaufort

July 1944

(NB: The primary sources of SD161 and RAF List do not, for UK Commands, give individual airfield locations for each squadron, they are listed under the main base airfield. Squadron locations here are taken from *RAF Squadrons* by J. Jefford).

BOMBER COMMAND: HQ — HIGH WYCOMBE

No 1 GP: HQ — BAWTRY

Location	Flying Sqn	Other Flying Unit	Ac Type
Wickenby	12,626	—	Lancaster
Binbrook	460	—	Lancaster
Grimsby	100	—	Lancaster
Elsham Wolds	103, 576	—	Lancaster
Kelstem	625	—	Lancaster
Hemswell	—	1 LFS	Lancaster
Hemswell	—	1481 BGF	Wellington/Martinet
Kirmington	166	1687	Spitfire/Hurricane
Lindholme	—	1656 CU	Lancaster
Lindholme	—	1662 CU	Lancaster/Halifax
Lindholme	—	1667	Halifax
Ludford Magna	101	—	Lancaster
Ludford Magna	—	1546 BATF	Oxford
North Killingholme	550	—	Lancaster

No 3 GP: HQ — EXNING

Location	Flying Sqn	Other Flying Unit	Ac Type
Feltwell	149	—	Stirling
Feltwell	—	3 LFS	Lancaster
Feltwell	—	1519 BATF	Oxford
Mepal	75	—	Lancaster
Mildenhall	15, 622	—	Lancaster
Mildenhall	—	GCF, BDW	(various)
Mildenhall	—	1688 BDTF	Spitfire/Hurricane
Tuddenham	90	—	Lancaster
Tempsford	138	—	Stirling
Tempsford	161	—	Lysander/Hudson/Halifax
Stradishall	—	1653 CU	Stirling
Stradishall	—	1657 CU	Stirling
Stradishall	—	1651 CU	Stirling
Waterbeach	514	—	Lancaster

Location	Flying Sqn	Other Flying Unit	Ac Type
Waterbeach	—	BBU	Halifax/Mosquito
Woolfox Lodge	218	—	Stirling
Wichford	115	—	Lancaster

No 4 HP: HQ — YORK

Location	Flying Sqn	Other Flying Unit	Ac Type
Driffield	466	—	Halifax
Holme	76	—	Halifax
Holme	—	1689 BDTF	Spitfire/Hurricane
Holme	—	1520 BATF	Oxford
Marston Moor	—	1652 CU	Halifax
Marston Moor	—	1663 CU	Halifax
Marston Moor	—	1658 CU	Halifax
Pocklington	102	—	Halifax
Pocklington	—	GCF	
Lisset	158	—	Halifax
Leconfield	640	—	Halifax
Breighton	78	—	Halifax
Melbourne	10	—	Halifax
Full Sutton	77	—	Halifax
Elvington	346, 347	—	Halifax
Snaith	51	—	Halifax
Little Staughton	578	—	Halifax

No 5 GP: HQ — MORETON HALL, SWINDERBY

Location	Flying Sqn	Other Flying Unit	Ac Type
Coningsby	83, 97	—	Lancaster
Woodhall Spa	617, 627	—	Lancaster
Metheringham	106	—	Lancaster
East Kirkby	57, 630	—	Lancaster
Spilsby	207	—	Lancaster
Scampton	1514	BATF	Oxford
Dunholme	44, 619	—	Lancaster
Fiskerton	49	—	Lancaster
Swinderby	—	GCF	
Swinderby	—	1654 CU	Stirling
Swinderby	—	1660 CU	Stirling
Swinderby	—	1661 CU	Stirling
Swinderby	—	1690 BDTF	Spitfire/Hurricane
Syerston	—	5 LFS	Lancaster
Waddington	463, 467	—	Lancaster
Skellingthorpe	50, 61	—	Lancaster
Bardney	9	—	Lancaster

No 6 (RCAF) GP: HQ — ALLERTON PARK, KNARESBOROUGH

Location	Flying Sqn	Other Flying Unit	Ac Type
Leeming	427, 429	—	Halifax
Skipton on Swale	414, 433	—	Halifax
Linton on Ouse	408	—	Lancaster
Linton on Ouse	426	—	Halifax
Linton on Ouse	—	GCF	
Tholthorpe	420, 425	—	Halifax
East Moor	432	—	Halifax
Middleton St George	419, 428	—	Lancaster
Croft	431, 434	—	Halifax
Topcliffe	—	1659 CU	Halifax
Topcliffe	—	1664 CU	Halifax
Topcliffe	—	1666 CU	Halifax
Topcliffe	—	1695 BDTF	Spitfire/Hurricane

No 8 GP: HQ — HUNTINGDON

Location	Flying Sqn	Other Flying Unit	Ac Type
Bourn	105	—	Mosquito
Downham Market	635	—	Lancaster
Gransden Lodge	405	—	Lancaster
Graveley	35	—	Lancaster
Graveley	692	—	Mosquito
Graveley	—	1696 BDTF	Spitfire/Hurricane/Martinet
Little Staughton	109	—	Mosquito
Little Staughton	582	—	Lancaster
Oakington	7	—	Lancaster
Oakington	571	—	Mosquito
Upwood	139	—	Mosquito
Upwood	156	—	Lancaster

Location	Flying Sqn	Other Flying Unit	Ac Type
Warboys	—	PFF NTU	Halifax/Lancaster
Warboys	—	1655 NTTU	Mosquito/Oxford
Wyton	—	GCF	
Wyton	—	1409 Met	Mosquito

No 91 GP: HQ — ABINGDON

Location	Flying Sqn	Other Flying Unit	Ac Type
Abingdon	—	GCF	
Abingdon	10 OTU	—	Whitley
Honeybourne	24 OTU	—	Wellington
Honeybourne	—	1681 BDTF	Hurricane
Kinloss	19 OTU	—	Whitley
Lossiemouth	20 OTU	—	Wellington
Moreton-in-Marsh	21 OTU	—	Wellington
Moreton-in-Marsh	—	1682 BDTF	Hurricane
Wellesbourne Mountford	22 OTU	—	Wellington

No 92 GP: HQ — WINSLOW (NB: ALL OTUs have Anson)

Location	Flying Sqn	Other Flying Unit	Ac Type
Bruntington	29 OTU	—	Wellington
Chipping Warden	12 OTU	—	Wellington
Chipping Warden	—	1517 BATF	Oxford
Desborough	84 OTU	—	Wellington
Husbands Bosworth	85 OTU	—	Wellington
Market Harborough	14 OTU	—	Wellington
Market Harborough	—	1683 BDTF	Hurricane
Silverstone	17 OTU	—	Wellington
Upper Heyford	16 OTU	—	Wellington
Wing	26 OTU	—	Wellington
Wing	—	GCF	
Wing	—	1684 BDTF	Hurricane
Westcott	11 OTU	—	Wellington
Westcott	—	ECDU	Wellington

No 93 HP: HQ — EGGINGTON

Location	Flying Sqn	Other Flying Unit	Ac Type
Finningley	18 OTU	—	Wellington
Finningley	—	GCF	
Finningley	86 OTU	—	Wellington
Finningley	30 OTU	—	Wellington
Finningley	—	1686 BDTF	Hurricane
Lichfield	27 OTU	—	Wellington
Lichfield	—	GCF (det)	
Ossington	82 OTU	—	Wellington
Ossington	—	1685 BDTF	Tomahawk
Peplow	83 OTU	—	Wellington
Wymeswold	28 OTU	—	Wellington
Wymeswold	—	1521 BATF	Oxford

No 100 GP: HQ — BYLAUGH HALL, EAST DERHAM

Location	Flying Sqn	Other Flying Unit	Ac Type
Foulsham	192	—	Halifax/Wellington/Mosquito/Anson/Tiger Moth
Great Massingham	—	1694 TTF	Martinet
Great Massingham	—	1692 BSF	Beaufighter
Great Massingham	169	—	Mosquito
Little Snoring	515	—	Mosquito
North Creake	199	—	Stirling
Oulton	214	1699	Fortress

No 80 WING

Location	Flying Sqn	Other Flying Unit	Ac Type
Swannington	—	BSDU	
West Malling	85, 157	—	Mosquito
West Raynham	141, 239	—	Mosquito
Swanton Morley	—	GCF	

No 26 GP: HQ — LANGLEY HALL

ALLIED EXPEDITIONARY AIR FORCE: HQ — STANMORE

No 38 GP: HQ — NETHERAVON

Location	Flying Sqn	Other Flying Unit	Ac Type
Ashbourne	296	—	Albemarle
Ashbourne	42 OTU	—	Blenheim/Anson/Whitley

Location	Flying Sqn	Other Flying Unit	Ac Type
Fairford	190, 620	—	Stirling
Harwell	295, 570	—	Albemarle
Hampstead Norris	—	ORTU	Albemarle/Horsa/ Tiger Moth
Hampstead Norris	—	1526 BATF	
Keevil	196, 299	—	Stirling
Netheravon	—	GCF	
Netheravon	—	1677 TTF	Martinet
Netheravon	—	1 HGSU	Horsa/Hamilcar
Ringway	—	PTS	
Tarrant Rushton	298, 644	—	Halifax
Tilstock	81 OTU	—	Whitley
Tilstock	—	1665 HCU	Stirling

No 85 GP: HQ — UXBRIDGE

Location	Flying Sqn	Other Flying Unit	Ac Type
Newchurch	3, 5, 486	—	Tempest
Hunsdon	29, 409	—	Mosquito
Deanland	91	—	Spitfire
Bradwell Bay	124	—	Spitfire
Hartford Bridge	264	—	Mosquito
West Malling	322	—	Spitfire
Zeals	410, 488	—	Mosquito
Hurn	604	—	Mosquito
West Malling	—	GCF	

Nos: 141, 142, 147, 148, 149, 150 Wings

AEAF — 2ND TACTICAL AIR FORCE: HQ — UXBRIDGE AND BRACKNELL
No 2 GP: HQ — WALLINGFORD

Location	Flying Sqn	Other Flying Unit	Ac Type
Thorney Island	21, 464, 487	—	Mosquito
Hartford Bridge	88, 226, 342	—	Boston
Dunsfold	98, 180, 320	—	Mitchell
Lasham	107, 305, 613	—	Mosquito

Nos: 137, 138, 139, 140, Wings

A classic pair of light-medium bombers — Mitchell and Boston.

Location	Flying Sqn	Other Flying Unit	Ac Type
No 34 WG: HQ — NORTHOLT			
Northolt	—	CF	
Northolt	16	—	Spitfire
Northolt	69	—	Wellington
Northolt	140	—	Mosquito
No 83 GP: HQ — PURBROOK HEATH AND HINTON DAUBNEY			
Coningsby	—	GCS	
B12/Ellon	19, 65, 122	—	Mustang
B11/Longues	132, 441, 453, 602	—	Spitfire
B8/Sommerview	168, 480	—	Mustang
B8/Sommerview	400	—	Spitfire
B5/Camilly	174, 175, 184, 245	—	Typhoon
B6/Colombs	181, 182	—	Typhoon
B30/Crehon	247	—	Typhoon
B2/Bazenville	403, 416, 421, 443	—	Spitfire
B4/Beny-sur-Mer	401, 411, 412, 442	—	Spitfire
Odiham	414	—	Spitfire
B9/Lantheuil	438, 439, 440	—	Typhoon
Réviers	652	—	Auster
Bretteville	653	—	Auster
Secqueville-en-Bessin	658	—	Auster
Basly	659	—	Auster
Bayeux	662	—	Auster

Nos: 39, 121, 122, 124, 125, 126, 127, 129, 143, 144 Wings

No 84 GP: HQ — GOODWOOD PARK			
Samungli	—	GCF	
B10/Plumetot	2	—	Mustang
B10/Plumetot	198, 609	—	Typhoon
Odiham	4	—	Spitfire
Odiham	268	—	Typhoon
Tangmere	66, 331, 332	—	Spitfire
Brenzett	129, 306, 315	—	Mustang
B8/Sommerview	164	—	Typhoon
Hurn	183, 193, 197, 257	—	Typhoon
Funtington	222, 349, 485	—	Spitfire
Eastchurch	266	—	Typhoon
Ford	302, 308, 317	—	Spitfire
Lympne	310, 312, 313	—	Spitfire
Selsey	329, 340, 341	—	Spitfire
Pierrepoint	660	—	Auster
Penshurst	661	—	Auster

Nos: 35, 123, 131, 132, 133, 134, 135, 136, 145, 146 Wings

AEAF — ADGB: HQ — STANMORE			
No 9 GP: HQ — BARTON HALL, PRESTON			
Salmesbury	—	GCF	
Annan	—	3 TEU	Hurricane
Bicester	13 OTU	—	(various)
Charter Hall	54 OTU	—	Beaufighter/ Beaufort
Cranfield	51 OTU	—	Beaufighter/ Havoc/ Mosquito
Cranfield	—	A1 CF	Beaufighter
Eshott	57 OTU	—	Spitfire
Grangemouth	—	2 TEU	Spitfire
Hawarden	41 OTU	—	Mustang/Harvard
High Ercall	60 OTU	—	Mosquito
Kirton-in-Lindsey	53 OTU	—	Spitfire
Milfield	—	FLS	Hurricane/ Typhoon/ Spitfire
Ouston	62 OTU	—	Anson
Rednal	61 OTU	—	Spitfire
Tealing	—	1 TEU	

No 10 GP: HQ — RUDLOE MANOR			
Colerne	—	GCF	
Defford	—	TFU	
Culmhead	126, 131, 616	—	Spitfire
Bolt Head	263	—	Typhoon
Friston	41, 610	—	Spitfire

Prestwick.

Bramcote.

Kemble.

Melton Mowbray.

Talbenny.

Hurn.

Valley.

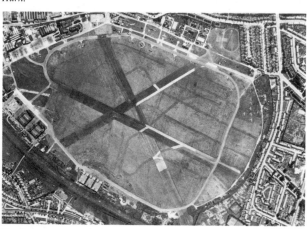

Hendon.

Location	Flying Sqn	Other Flying Unit	Ac Type
Winkleigh	406	—	Beaufighter
Castle Camps	68	—	Mosquito
Fairwood Common	—	11 APC	Lysander/Master/Martinet
Portreath	276	—	Warwick
Predannack	151	—	Mosquito
Lympne	1, 165	—	Spitfire
Predannack	—	1449	Hurricane

No 11 GP: HQ — UXBRIDGE

Location	Flying Sqn	Other Flying Unit	Ac Type
Croydon	116	—	Oxford
West Malling	274, 80	—	Spitfire
Coltishall	229	—	Spitfire
Friston	350, 501	—	Spitfire
Lympne	33, 74, 127	—	Spitfire
Ford	96, 456	—	Mosquito
Holmsley South	418	—	Mosquito
Hurn	125	—	Beaufighter
Warmwell	275	—	Spitfire/Walrus
Bradwell Bay	219	—	Mosquito
Bradwell Bay	278	—	Spitfire/Walrus
Manston	137	—	Typhoon
Manston	605	—	Mosquito
Manston	—	1401 Met	Spitfire
Southend	—	17 APC	Master/Martinet/Lysander
Shoreham	345	—	Spitfire
Shoreham	277	—	Spitfire/Walrus
Lee-0n-Solent	26, 63	—	Spitfire
Harrowbeer	64, 611	—	Spitfire
Predannack	234	—	Spitfire
Merston	130, 303, 402	—	Spitfire

No 12 GP: HQ — WATNALL

Location	Flying Sqn	Other Flying Unit	Ac Type
Church Fenton	307	—	Mosquito
Coltishall	25	—	Mosquito
Coltishall	316	—	Mustang
Digby	504	—	Spitfire
Wittering	—	1530 BATF	Oxford
Wittering	—	AFDU, FIU, NFDU	(various
Collyweston	—	GRU	
Hucknall	—	GCF	

No 13 GP: HQ — INVERNESS

Location	Flying Sqn	Other Flying Unit	Ac Type
Skeabrae	118	—	Spitfire
Drem	309	—	Hurricane
Inverness	—	GCF	

No 70 GP: HQ — FARNBOROUGH

Location	Flying Sqn	Other Flying Unit	Ac Type
Aberporth	595	—	Hurricane
Bircham Newton	695	—	Hurricane
Bodorgan	—	1606 AAC	
Cark	650	—	Hurricane
Castle Bromwich	577	—	Hurricane/Oxford
Cleave	639	—	Henley
Colerne	286	—	Oxford/Hurricane
Croydon	287	—	Hurricane
Culmhead	587	—	Hurricane
Detling	567	—	(various)
Farnborough	—	GCF	
Gosport	667	—	(various)
Hutton Cranswick	291	—	Hurricane
Long Kesh	290	—	Oxford/Hurricane
Manorbier	—	PAU	Queen Bee
Peterhead	598	—	Oxford
Rob orough	691	—	(various)
Towyn	631	—	Henley/Hurricane
Turnhouse	289	—	Oxford/Defiant/Martinet
Woodvale	285	—	Oxford/Hurricane

No 60 GP: HQ — LEIGHTON BUZZARD
Nos: 70, 73, 75, 78, 84 Wings

COASTAL COMMAND: HQ — NORTHWOOD
No 15 GP: HQ — LIVERPOOL

Location	Flying Sqn	Other Flying Unit	Ac Type
Aldergrove	—	1490 Met	Gladiator/Spitfire
Aldergrove	—	1 APC	Lysander/Martinet
Bally Kelly	59, 120	—	Liberator
Lough Erne	423	—	Sunderland
Castle Archdale	422	—	Sunderland
Speke	—	GCF	
Tiree	518	—	Halifax
Tiree	281	—	Warwick

No 16 GP: HQ — GILLINGHAM

Location	Flying Sqn	Other Flying Unit	Ac Type
Bircham Newton	415	—	Wellington/Albacore
Bircham Newton	521	—	Hudson/Gladiator
Bircham Newton	279	—	Hudson
Bircham Newton	—	1525 BATF	Oxford
Calshot	—	6 FBSU	(various)
Detling	—	GCF	
Gosport	—	ATDU	
Hawkinge (No 157 Wing)	—	—	—
Langham	—	1 APC	Lysander/Martinet
Langham	455, 489	—	Beaufighter
Manston (No 155 Wing)	143	—	Beaufighter
North Coates	236, 254	—	Beaufighter
Strubby (No 154 Wing)	280	—	Warwick

No 17 GP: HQ — EDINBURGH

Location	Flying Sqn	Other Flying Unit	Ac Type
Aldergrove	—	1674 HCU	Liberator
Aldergrove	4 OTU	—	Sunderland
Crosby	9 OTU	—	Beaufighter/Beaufort
Crosby	—	1674 HCU (det)	Halifax
East Fortune	132 OTU	—	Beaufighter/Beaufort/Mosquito
Haverfordwest	—	4 RFU	Wellington
Killadeas	131 OTU	—	Catalina
Killadeas	—	12 (O) FIS	Wellington/Beaufort/Mosquito
Oban	—	302 FTU	Catalina/Sunderland
Silloth	6 OTU	—	Wellington
Silloth	281 (det)	—	Warwick
Squires Gate	—	3 S of GR	Anson
Turnberry	5 OTU	—	Warwick/Ventura/Beaufighter/Hudson
Turnhouse	—	GCF	

No 18 GP: HQ — PITREAVIE CASTLE

Location	Flying Sqn	Other Flying Unit	Ac Type
Helensburgh	—	MAEE	
Leuchars	544 (det)	—	Mosquito
Leuchars	—	GCF	
Leuchars	—	3 APC	Lysander
Leuchars	333	—	Catalina/Mosquito
Leuchars	—	ATDU (det)	
Leuchars	281 (det)	—	Warwick
Sullom Voe	210	—	Catalina
Sullom Voe	330	—	Sunderland
Skitten	519	—	Hudson/Spitfire
Skitten	618	—	Mosquito
Skitten	—	1693	Anson
Tiree	281 (det)	—	Warwick

Location	Flying Sqn	Other Flying Unit	Ac Type
No 19 GP: HQ — PLYMOUTH			
Chivenor	172, 304, 407, 612	—	Wellington
Davidstow Moor	282	—	Warwick
Strubby	144, 402	—	Beaufighter
Docking	524	—	Wellington
Mount Batten	—	GCF	
Pembroke dock	201, 228, 461	—	Sunderland
Pembroke Dock	—	CCDU	
Harrowbeer (No 156 Wing)	—	—	—
Portreath (No 153 Wing)	235	—	Beaufighter
Portreath	248	—	Mosquito
Predannack (No 152 Wing)	179	—	Wellington
Predannack	311	—	Liberator
Brawdy	517	—	Halifax
St Davids	58, 502	—	Halifax
St Eval	53, 206, 224	—	Liberator
St Eval	541 (det)	—	Spitfire
St Eval	547	—	Wellington
Talbenny	—	4 APC	Lysander
No 106 GP: HQ — BENSON			
Benson	541, 542	—	Spitfire
Benson	540	—	Mosquito
Benson	544	—	Mosquito/Spitfire
Drem	—	309 FT ADU	Master
Dyce	8 OTU	—	Mosquito/Spitfire
No 247 GP: HQ — AZORES			
Azores	172 (det)	—	Wellington
Lagens	220	—	Fortress
Lagens	269	—	Spitfire/Hudson/ Martinet
HQ RAF ICELAND			
Reykjavik	86	—	Liberator
Reykjavik	—	1407 met	Hudson
Reykjavik	279 (det)	—	Hudson

Gibraltar pictured from 10,000 feet on 15 March 1944.

HQ RAF GIBRALTAR

Location	Flying Sqn	Other Flying Unit	Ac Type
Gibraltar	—	1500 TTF	Martinet
Gibraltar	541 (det)	—	Anson
Gibraltar	202	—	Catalina/ Sunderland
Gibraltar	520	—	Halifax/ Hurricane

FLYING TRAINING COMMAND: HQ — READING
No 21 GP: HQ CRANWELL

Location	Flying Sqn	Other Flying Unit	Ac Type
Banff	—	14 PAFU	
Banff	—	1511, 1542 BATF	
Calveley	—	11 PAFU	
Cranwell	—	17 SFTS	

Location	Flying Sqn	Other Flying Unit	Ac Type
Erroll	—	9 PAFU	
Hucknall	—	25 EFTS	
Montrose	—	2 FIS	
Montrose	—	1518, 1541 BATF	
Newton	—	16 SFTS	
Newton	—	1524 BATF	
Shawbury	—	CNS	
Shawbury	—	1534 BATF	
Sherbum-in-Elmet	—	AFEE	
Spitalgate	—	12 PAFU	
Spitalgate	—	1544, 1536 BATF	
Ternhill	—	5 PAFU	
Wheaton Aston	—	21 PAFU	
Bridleway Gate	—	1511 BATF	
No 23 GP: HQ — SOUTH CERNEY			
Babdown Farm	—	15 PAFU	
Babdown Farm	—	1532 BATF	
Boscombe Down	—	A and AEE	
Boscombe Down	—	IFDF, AGME, TPS	
Church Lawford	—	18 PAFU	
Church Lawford	—	1533 BATF	
Hullavington	—	ECFS	
Kidlington	—	20 PAFU	
Kidlington	—	1538 BATF	
Little Rissington	—	6 PAFU	
Little Rissington	—	1523 BATF	
Lulsgate Bottom	—	3 FIS	
Lulsgate Bottom	—	1540 BATF	
North Luffenham	—	HGCU	
North Luffenham	—	CIS	
South Cerney	—	3 PAFU	
South Cerney	—	1539 BATF	
Stoke Orchard	—	3 GTS	
Upavon	—	7 FIS	
Upavon	—	1537 BATF	
No 25 GP: HQ — MARKET DRAYTON			
Barrow	—	10 AGS	
Blackpool	—	S of ASR	
Cark	—	SPTU	
Catfoss	—	CGS	
Halfpenny Green	—	3 OAFU	
Halfpenny Green	—	1545 BATF	
Manby	—	1 AAS	
Millom	—	2 OAFU	
Mona	—	8 OAFU	
Pembrey	—	8 OAFU	
Pembrey	—	1 AGS	
Penrhos	—	9 OAFU	
Staverton	—	6 OAFU	
Stormy Down	—	7 AGS	
No 29 GP: HQ — DUMFRIES			
Andreas	—	11 AGS	
Bishops Court	—	7 OAFU	
Bishops Court	—	12 AGS	
Castle Kennedy	—	3 AGS	
Dalcross	—	2 AGS	
Dumfries	—	10 OAFU	
Evanton	—	8 AGS	
Evanton	—	EANS	
Morpeth	—	4 AGS	
West Freugh	—	4 OAFU	
Wigtown	—	1 OAFU	
No 50 GP: HQ — READING			
Booker	—	21 EFTS	
Cambridge	—	22 EFTS	
Clyffe Pypard	—	29 EFTS	
Elstree	—	CLTS	
Fair Oaks	—	18 EFTS	
Panshangar	—	1 EFTS	
Panshangar	—	CLTS (det)	

Location	Flying Sqn	Other Flying Unit	Ac Type
Shellingford	—	3 EFTS	
Sywell	—	6 EFTS	
Theale	—	26 EFTS	
Watchfield	—	S of FC	
Woodley	—	10 FIS	
Worcester	—	2 EFTS	

No 51 GP: HQ — LEEDS

Location	Flying Sqn	Other Flying Unit	Ac Type
Brough	—	4 EFTS	
Carlisle	—	15 EFTS	
Derby	—	16 EFTS	
Desford	—	7 EFTS	
Elmdon	—	14 EFTS	
Perth	—	11 EFTS	
Sealand	—	24 EFTS	
Wolverhampton	—	28 EFTS	
Wolverhampton	—	PPP	

No 54 GP: HQ — SUNNINGDALE

Control numerous ITWS, Reception Wings, ITSs, etc

CANADA: ADMINISTERED BY RCAF

Location	Flying Sqn	Other Flying Unit	Ac Type
De Winton, Alberta	—	31 EFTS	
Bowden, Atlanta	—	32 EFTS	
Kingston, Ontario	—	31 SFTS	
Carberry, Manitoba	—	33 SFTS	
Medicine Hat, Manitoba	—	34 SFTS	
Penhold, Alberta	—	36 SFTS	
Port Albert, Ontario	—	31 ANS	
Hamilton, Ontario	—	33 ANS	
Picton, Ontario	—	31 BGS	
Debert, Nova Scotia	—	31OTU	
Pennfield Ridge, New Brunswick	—	34 OTU	
Greenwood, Nova Scotia	—	36 OTU	

TECHNICAL TRAINING COMMAND: HQ — READING
No 22 GP: HQ — MARKET DRAYTON

Control Recruit Centres, RAF Regiment AA Camps, etc

No 24 GP: HQ — HINDLIP HALL, WORCESTER
Control various 'Schools', including SoTTs

Location	Flying Sqn	Other Flying Unit	Ac Type
Halton	—	BC CF	

No 27 GP: ROYAL AGRICULTURAL COLLEGE, CIRENCESTER
Control various training units including Radio Schools

Location	Flying Sqn	Other Flying Unit	Ac Type
Blackpool	—	13 RS	
Bolton	—	6 RS	
Carew Chilton	—	10 RS	
Compton Bassett	—	3 RS	
Cranwell	—	1, 8 RS	
Hooton Park	—	11 RS	
Madley	—	4 RS	
Oxford	—	5 RS	
St Athan	—	12 RS	
Yatesbury	—	9 RS	

No 28 GP: HQ — ANDOVER

Control various schools, institutes and hospitals

MAINTENANCE COMMAND: HQ ANDOVER
No 53 WING: HQ — ANDOVER
MUs: 47, 52, 76, 82, 215, 222 — Pacing Depôts

No 54 WING: HQ — LONDON
Various MT companies

No 40 GP: HQ — ANDOVER
MUs: 3, 7, 14, 16, 17, 25, 35, 61, 62, 66, 68, 69, 70, 72, 73, 74, 79, 87, 89, 99, 203, 204, 205, 207, 208, 209, 210, 211, 212, 214, 216, 217, 220, 221, 225, 227, 230, 232, 236, 238, 239, 240, 241

No 41 GP: HQ — ANDOVER
MUs: 5, 6, 8, 9, 10, 12, 15, 18, 19, 20, 22, 23, 27, 29, 33, 38, 39, 44, 45, 48, 51, 57 — all Aircraft Storage Units

Location	Flying Sqn	Other Flying Unit	Ac Type
Hamble	—	15 FPP	
Hawarden	—	3 FPP	
Prestwick	—	4 FPP	
Ratcliffe	—	6 FPP	
Ringway	—	14 FPP	
Sydenham	—	8 FPP	
Thame	—	5 FPP	
Whitchurch	—	2 FPP	
White Waltham	—	1 FPP	

No 42 GP: HQ — BURGH COMMON
MUs: 2, 11, 21, 28, 31, 36, 53, 59, 64, 77, 80, 81, 91, 92, 93, 94, 95, 96, 98, 100, 202, 219, 231, 233, 224, 243, 244 — all Ammunition Parks
Plus control of all aviation fuel and oil distribution depôts

No 43 GP: HQ — OXFORD
MUs:

TRANSPORT COMMAND: HQ — HARROW
No 44 GP: HQ — GLOUCESTER

Location	Flying Sqn	Other Flying Unit	Ac Type
Bramcote	105 OTU	—	Wellington
Bramcote	—	1513 BATF	
Filton	—	2 OAPU	
Filton	—	Centaurus test flt	
Hendon	24		
Hendon	510		
Hurn	—	3 OADU	
Kemble	—	1 OAPU	
Llandow	—	3 OAPU	
Llandow	—	CNVTS	
Lyneham	511, 525	—	
Melton Mowbray	—	4 OAPU	
Melton Mowbrazy	—	304 FTU	
Pershore	—	1 FU	
Pershore	—	1516 BATF	
Portreath	—	1 OADU	
Prestwick	—	1680 CF	
Prestwick	—	1527 BATF	
Prestwick	—	Liberator Flt	Liberator
St Mawgan	—	2 OADU	
Talbenny	—	303 FTU	

No 45 GP: HQ — DORVAL, CANADA

Location	Flying Sqn	Other Flying Unit	Ac Type
Dorval — No 112 Wing	—	2 FCP	
Nassau — No 113 Wing	—	3 FCP	

No 46 GP: HQ — HARROW WEALD

Location	Flying Sqn	Other Flying Unit	Ac Type
Blakehill Farm	233	—	Dakota
Broadwell	512, 575	—	Dakota
Down Ampney	48, 271	—	Dakota
Hendon	—	1697 ADLS	
Netheravon	—	ATTDU	

No 114 Wing — ACCRA, W. AFRICA
No 216 GP: Heliopolis
Algier — No 284 Wing
Bari — No 249 Wing
Cairo — No 282 Wing
Habbaniya — No 119 Wing
Wadi Seidna — No 115 Wing

No 229 GP: DELHI
Delhi — No 177 Wing

MAAF: HQ — CASERTA AND ALGIERS

Location	Flying Sqn	Other Flying Unit	Ac Type
Anzio (No 324 Wing)	—	—	—
Piombino	43, 93, 111, 72	—	Spitfire
Follonica	225	—	Spitfire
Follonica	600	—	Beaufighter
Pescara	223	—	Baltimore
Perugia	145	—	Spitfire

Location	Flying Sqn	Other Flying Unit	Ac Type
Cecina	18, 114	—	Boston
Recanati	651	—	Auster
Pignataro	654	—	Auster
Calenzana	154, 232, 242, 243	—	Spitfire
Poretta (No 323 Wing)	—	—	—
Giovanni	655	—	Auster
Creti	657	—	Auster
Creti	112, 250, 450	—	Kittyhawk
Creti	260	—	Mustang
San Angelo (No 239 Wing)	—	—	—
San Severo (Med Allied PR Wing)	—	—	—
Calvi	237, 238, 451	—	Spitfire
Serragia (No 251 Wing)	—	—	—
Sinello (No 285)	—	—	—
Fermo	241, 318	—	Spitfire
Vasto (HQ DAF)	—	—	—
Venafro	92, 208, 417, 601	—	Spitfire
Volturno		DAF CF	

AHQ 'G' FORCE: — Bari

Borgo	6 (det)	—	Hurricane
Brindisi (No 334 Wing)	148	—	Halifax
Brindisi	—	1586	Halifax/Liberator
Marcianise (No 232 Wing)	—	—	—
Grottaglie	6	—	Hurricane
Lete	352	—	Hurricane
Regina (No 232 Wing)	13, 55	—	Baltimore

MATAF: HQ — CASERTA

Capodichino	—	CF	

MACAF: HQ — ALGIERS

Alghero (No 328 Wing)	39, 272	—	Beaufighter
Alghero	14	—	Marauder
Alghero	284	—	Warwick
Bone	458	—	Wellington
Bone	153 (det)	—	Beaufighter
Borgo	284 (det)	—	Warwick/Walrus
Cutella	293 (det)	—	Warwick
Djidjelli (No 332 Wing)	—	—	—
Foggia	32	—	Spitfire
Foggia	243 (det)	—	Warwick
Gibraltar	500 (det)	—	Ventura
Grottaglie	14 (det)	—	Marauder
La Senia (No 337 Wing)	500	—	Ventura
La Senia	256	—	Mosquito
Pomigliano	293	—	Warwick/Walrus
Reghaia (No 338 Wing)	153	—	Beaufighter
Reghaia	256 (det)	—	Mosquito
Reghaia	—	CF	
Reghaia	—	1578 cal	
Sinello	293 (det)	—	Warwick/Walrus
Sidi Amor (No 287 Wing)	—	—	—

AHQ MALTA: HQ — VALLETTA

Alghero	108 (det)	—	Mosquito
Catania (No 335 Wing)	87	—	Spitfire
Catania	108 (det)	—	Mosquito
Hal Far	283	—	Warwick
Hal Far	185	—	Spitfire
Hal Far	—	CF	
Luga		SF	Mosquito
Palermo	185 (det)	—	Spitfire
Valletta (No 248 Wing)	—	—	—
MUs: 118, 137, 143			

No 205 GP: HQ — FOGGIA

amendola (No 330 Wing)	142, 150	—	Wellington
Celone (No 240 Wing)	178	—	Liberator
Foggia (No 236 Wing)	40, 104	—	Wellington
Stornara	614	—	Halifax
Tortorella (No 231 Wing)	37, 70	—	Wellington
Tortorella	—	GCF	

No 214 GP: HQ — NAPLES

Alghero	682 (B Flt)	—	Spitfire
Blida	624	—	Halifax/Lysander
San Severo (No 336 Wing)	682	—	Spitfire
San Severo	683	—	Mosquito
Vasto	683 (det)	—	Mosquito
Capodichino	—	CF	
Maison Blanche	—	MED/ME CF	
MUs: 110, 113, 117, 124, 141, 159			

No 218 GP: HQ —

MUs: 125, 144, 145, 156, 164, 163, 351			

No 242 GP: HQ — TARANTO

Borgo	6 (det)	—	Hurricane
Bo Rizzo	608 (det)	—	Baltimore
Brindisi	1435		Spitfire
Foggia (No 232 Wing)	72, 253	—	Spitfire
Foggia	255	—	Beaufighter
Grottaglie (No 286 Wing)	255 (det)	—	Beaufighter
Grottaglie	221	—	Wellington
Luga	221 (det)	—	Wellington
Monte Corvino (No 325 Wing)	608	—	Hudson
San Vito	—	GCF	

MIDDLE EAST COMMAND
RAF MIDDLE EAST: HQ — CAIRO

El Genina	—	1567 met	
Khartoum	—	1412 met	
Khartoum (No 283 Wing)	—	CF	

AHQ EASTERN MEDITERRANEAN: HQ — ALEXANDRIA

Alexandria (HQ No 219 GP)	—	—	—
Benina (No 212 GP)	—	1563 met	
Bersis	335	—	Spitfire
Berka	227	—	Beaufighter
Berka	294	—	Warwick/Walrus
Berka	454	—	Baltimore
Berka	38	—	Wellington
Bu Amud	94	—	Spitfire
Castel Benito	—	1564 met	
Edcu	46	—	Beaufighter
Edcu	294 (det)	—	Warwick/Walrus
Edcu	162	—	Wellington/ Baltimore
Edcu	213	—	Mosquito
El Firdan	—	26 AACU (det)	Spitfire
El Adem	—	26 AACU (det)	
Gambut	46, 663	—	Beaufighter
Gambut	294 (det)	—	Warwick/Walrus
Gambut	38 (det)	—	Wellington
Lakatamia	294 (det)	—	Warwick/Walrus
Mariut	—	26 AACU	
Mariut	—	CF	
Mersa Matruh	336	—	Spitfire
Marsa Matruh	252	—	Beaufighter
Ramat David	—	26 AACU (det)	
St Jean	459	—	Ventura
St Jean	294 (det)	—	Warwick/Walrus
St Jean	46	—	Beaufighter
Tocra	46 (det)	—	Beaufighter

AHQ Levant: HQ — JERUSALEM

La Katamia	—	1565 met	
Lydda	—	1413 met	
Lydda	—	CF	
MUs: 104, 120, 142, 160			

AHQ IRAQ AND PERSIA: HQ — HABBANIYA

Habbaniya	—	CF	
Habbaniya	—	1415 met	
MUs: 115, 119, 127, 138			

Location	Flying Sqn	Other Flying Unit	Ac Type
AHQ EAST AFRICA: HQ — NAIROBI			
Congella	262	—	Catalina
Dar-es-Salaam	259	—	Catalina
Diego Suarez (No 258 Wing)	265	—	Catalina
Diego Suarez	—	1568 met	
Eastleigh	—	1414 met	
Kipevu	209	—	Catalina
Plaisance	—	1569 met	
MUs: 105, 133, 165			
HQ BF ADEN: HQ — STEAMER POINT			
Aden	—	Ogaden Flt	
Hiswa	—	1566 met	
Khormaksar	8	—	Wellington
Khormaksar	621	—	Wellington
Khormaksar	—	Catalina Flt	Catalina
Khormaksar	—	CF	
Masirah	244	—	Wellington
No 203 GP: HQ — HELIOPOLIS			
Abu Sueir	73 OTU		
Agir	76 OTU		
Ballah	—	13 AGS	
Ballah	—	ME CGS	
Ein shemer	78 OTU		
Gianaclis	75 OTU		
Ismailia	71 OTU		
Nicosia	79 OTU		
Lydda	—	1675 MCU	
Petah Tiqua	74 OTU		
Qastina	77 OTU		
Shallufa	—	11 FIS	
Shallufa	—	MEAS	
Shallufa	—	5 METS	
No 206 GP: HQ — HELIOPOLIS			
Aboukir	—	23 AACU	
Heliopolis	—	GCS	
Lakatamia	680 (det)	—	Mosquito
Matariya	680	—	Mosquito
Tocra	680 (det)	—	Mosquito
MUs: 101, 102, 103, 106, 107, 109, 111, 112, 126, 128, 132, 135, 140, 168			
No 216 GP: HQ — HELIOPOLIS			
Algiers (No 284 Wing)	—	—	—
Bari	267	—	Dakota
Bilbeis	—	1 CCU	
Cairo West	216	—	Dakota
Caserta (GP adv HQ)	—	—	
Catania	—	4 ADU	
Gebel Hamzi	—	2 ADU	
Habbaniya (No 151 Wing)	—	—	—
Heliopolis (No 282 Wing)	—	—	—
Heliopolis	—	1 ADU	
Naples (No 249 Wing)	—	—	—
Oujda	—	3 ADU	
Wadi Seidna (No 115 Wing)	—	—	—
WEST AFRICA COMMAND			
Dakar (No 295 Wing)	343	—	Sunderland
Dakar	344	—	Wellington
GAMBIA			
Bathurst	95	—	Sunderland
Port Etienne	95 (det)	—	Sunderland
Port Etienne	343 (det)	—	Sunderland
SIERRA LEONE			
Jui	490	—	Sunderland
Jui	204	—	Sunderland
Waterloo	—	1562 met	
Waterloo	—	CF	
No 176 MU			
Gold Coast			

Location	Flying Sqn	Other Flying Unit	Ac Type
Takoradi	—	CF	
Takoradi	—	21 AACU	
NIGERIA			
Apapu	270	—	Sunderland
Ikeja	—	1561 met	
Lagos (No 298 Wing)	—	—	—
Maiduguri	—	1560 met	
LIBERIA			
Fishlake	490 (det)	—	Catalina
Fishlake	204 (det)	—	Sunderland
IVORY COAST			
Abidjan	490 (det)	—	Catalina
Abidjan	270	—	Catalina
Adidjan	204 (det)	—	Sunderland
FRENCH EQUATORIAL AFRICA			
Libreville	270 (Det)	—	Catalina
BELGIAN CONGO			
Bunand	270 (det)	—	Catalina
UNDER TRANSPORT COMMAND			
Accra (No 114 Wing)			
WEST INDIES			
Nassau	111 OTU	—	Liberator/ Mitchell
AIR COMMAND SOUTH-EAST ASIA: HQ — NEW DELHI			
Kalyan	110	—	Baltimore
plus No's 164 (Signals) Wing			
No 222 GP: HQ — COLUMBO			
China Bay	321	—	Catalina
Koggala	205, 413	—	Catalina
Koggala	230	—	Sunderland
Koggala	—	GR/ANS	
Minneriya	17	—	Spitfire
Minneriya	135	—	Thunderbolt
Minneriya	89	—	Beaufighter
Ratmalana	273	—	Spitfire
Ratmalana	—	GCF	
Ratmalana	—	SEAC CF	
Sigiriya	160	—	Liberator
Sigiriya	292 (C Flt)	—	Warwick/Walrus
Sigiriya	—	1579 cal	
Sigiriya	—	1303 met	
Sigiriya	—	20 APC	
Vavuniya	22, 217	—	Beaufighter
plus No 338 MU			
No 223 GP: HQ — PESHAWAR			
Peshawar	151 OTU	—	
Peshawar	—	1 SFTS	
Peshawar	—	GCF	
Walton	—	Chinese EFTS	
Plus No 316 MU			
No 225 GP: HQ — BANGALORE			
Arkonam	134, 258	—	Thunderbolt
Cholavaram	27, 47	—	Beaufighter
Cuttack (No 173 Wing)	354		Liberator
Kolar	82		Mosquito
Kolar	—	1673 MCU	
Korangi Creek	191, 212	—	Catalina
Red Hills Lake	240, 628	—	Catalina
Santa Cruz	203	—	Wellington
St Thomas Mount (No 172 Wing)	123, 146	—	Thunderbolt
St Thomas Mount	200		Liberator
St Thomas Mount	—	1302 met	
Yelahanka	30, 79, 261	—	Thunderbolt

Location	Flying Sqn	Other Flying Unit	Ac Type
Yelahanka	—	21 APC	
Yelahanka	—	GCF	
Yelahanka	—	1580 cal	
Yelahanka	—	1672 MCU	

MUs: 301, 305, 306, 303, 309, 312, 314, 318, 319, 307, 320, 322, 328, 330, 331, 315, 336, 337, 341, 344, 346

No 226 GP: HQ — PALAM

Location	Flying Sqn	Other Flying Unit	Ac Type
Bangalore (No 188 Wing)	—	—	—
Cawnpore	—	1577	Halifax
Delhi	—	1301 met	
Palam	—	GCF	
Peshawar (No 187 Wing)	—	—	—

No 227 GP: HQ — BOMBAY

Location	Flying Sqn	Other Flying Unit	Ac Type
Andheri	—	1 Signals School	
Bairagarh	—	1 AGS	
Begumpet	—	1 EFTS	
Jodhpur	—	2 EFTS	
Poona	—	3 RFU	
Santa Cruz	292 (D Flt)	—	Warwick/Walrus

No 229 GP: HQ — NEW DELHI

Location	Flying Sqn	Other Flying Unit	Ac Type
Agartala	216 (det)	—	Dakota
Chaklala	—	3 PTS	
Dum Dum	353 (det)	—	Dakota
Mauripur	—	C and C Flt	
Palam	—	GCF	
Palam	353	—	Dakota

No 230 GP: HQ — BARRACKPORE

MUs: 302, 304, 313, 321, 325, 327, 329, 353, 335, 340, 342, 345

No 231 GP: HQ — CALCUTTA

Location	Flying Sqn	Other Flying Unit	Ac Type
Alipore	681	—	Spitfire
Alipore	684	—	Mosquito
Amarda Road	—	22 APC	
Amarda Road	—	AFTU	
Bally (No 171 Wing)	—	—	—
Baigachi	—	1581 cal	
Calcutta (No 180 Wing)	—	—	—
Dalbhumgarh	45	—	Mosquito
Digri (No 185 Wing)	357, 159	—	Liberator
Jessore (No 175 Wing)	215	—	Liberator
Jessore	99	—	Wellington
Jessore	292 (A and B Flts)	—	Warwick/Walrus
Ranchi	177	—	Beaufighter
Ranchi	—	LA 1S	
Salbani (184 Wing)	355, 356	—	Liberator
Salbani	—	23 APC	

3rd TACTICAL AIR FORCE: HQ COMILLA

Location	Flying Sqn	Other Flying Unit	Ac Type
Baigachi	67, 155	—	Spitfire
Baigachi	176	—	Beaufighter
Baigachi	—	1300 met	
Baigachi	—	Beau CF	Beaufighter
Calcutta (No 293 Wing)	—	—	—
Sylhet	117	—	Dakota

No 221 GP: HQ — IMPHAL

Location	Flying Sqn	Other Flying Unit	Ac Type
Dergaon	34, 60	—	Hurricane
Dimapur	656 (C Flt)	—	Auster
Derga	5	—	Hurricane
Imphal (No 170 Wing)	607	—	Spitfire
Imphal (No 181 Wing)	—	—	—
Imphal	11	—	Hurricane
Imphal	656 (D Flt)	—	Auster
Jorhat (No 243 Wing)	28	—	Hurricane
Kangla	42	—	Hurricane
Kumbhirgram (No 168 Wing)	84, 110	—	Vengeance
Kumbhirgram	81	—	Spitfire
Mromigyaung	656 (APH)	—	Auster
Palel	113	—	Hurricane
Palel	615	—	Spitfire
Silchar (No 189 Wing)	—	—	—
St Thomas Mount	123	—	Thunderbolt

No 224 GP: HQ — CHITTAGONG

Location	Flying Sqn	Other Flying Unit	Ac Type
Agartala	31, 194	—	Dakota
Chiringa	20	—	Hurricane
Chittagong (No 166 Wing)	292 (E Flt)	—	Warwick/Walrus
Chittagong	—	3rd TAF CF	
Chittagong	136	—	Spitfire
Chittagong	—	1583 cal	
Chittagong (No 182 Wing)	—	—	—
Comilla (No 165 Wing)	—	—	—
Comilla (No 177 Wing)	62	—	Dakota
Comilla	—	CF (det)	
Fenny (No 169 Wing)	211	—	Beaufighter
Imphal	—	CF (det)	
Palel	152	—	Spitfire
Ramu (No 167 Wing)	—	—	—

AHQ INDIA: HQ — NEW DELHI

Location	Flying Sqn	Other Flying Unit	Ac Type
Alipore	—	22 AACU (det) (B Flt)	
Katni	—	22 AACU (det) (D Flt)	
Karachi	—	22 AACU (det) (A Flt)	
Peshawar (NWFP Wing)	—	—	—
Poona	—	22 AACU (det)	
St Thomas Mount	—	22 AACU (det) (C Flt)	
Vizagapatum	—	22 AACU (det)	

July 1945
BOMBER COMMAND: HQ — HIGH WYCOMBE
No 1 GP: HQ — BAWTRY

Location	Flying Sqn	Other Flying Unit	Ac Type
Binbrook	460	—	Lancaster
Bircotes	—	GCF	
Elsham Wolds	100, 103	—	Lancaster
Kirmington	166	—	Lancaster
North Killingholme	550	—	Lancaster
Ludford Magna	101	—	Lancaster
Wickenby	12, 626	—	Lancaster
Faldingworth	300	—	Lancaster
Scampton	153, 625	—	Lancaster
Fiskerton	576	—	Lancaster
Hemswell	150, 170	—	Lancaster
Hemswell	—	1687 BDTF	Spitfire/ Hurricane
Stargate	50, 61	—	Lancaster

No 3 GP: HQ — EXNING

Location	Flying Sqn	Other Flying Unit	Ac Type
Feltwell	—	BDU	
Feltwell	—	1688 BDTF	Spitfire/ Hurricane
Snailwell	—	GCF	
Woodbridge	—	BBU	
Mildenhall	15, 622	—	Lancaster
Methwold	149	—	Lancaster
Tuddenham	90, 138	—	Lancaster
Stradishall	186	—	Lancaster
Chedburgh	218	—	Lancaster
Wratling Common	195	—	Lancaster
Waterbeach	514	—	Lancaster
Mepal	75	—	Lancaster
Witchford	115	—	Lancaster

No 5 GP: HQ — MORTON HALL, SWINDERBY

Location	Flying Sqn	Other Flying Unit	Ac Type
Swinderby	—	GCF	
Coningsby	83, 97	—	Lancaster
Woodhall Spa	627	—	Lancaster
Metheringham	104, 467	—	Lancaster
East Kirkby	57, 630	—	Lancaster
Spilsby	44, 207	—	Lancaster
Strubby	619	—	Lancaster
Syerston	49	—	Lancaster
Syerston	—	FFU	Lancaster/ Mosquito
Syerston	—	1690 BDTF	
Waddington	463	—	Lancaster
Waddington	617	—	Mosquito
Bardney	9, 189	—	Lancaster

Location	Flying Sqn	Other Flying Unit	Ac Type
No 6 GP: HQ — ALLERTON PARK, KNARESBOROUGH			
Leeming	427, 429	—	Lancaster
Dishforth	—	GCF	
Dishforth	—	1695 BDTF	Spitfire/ Beaufighter
Skipton on Swale	424, 433	—	Lancaster
Linton on Ouse	405, 408	—	Lancaster
Tholthorpe	420, 425	—	Lancaster
Tholthorpe	—	12 ACMU	
No 7 GP: HQ — ST VINCENTS, GRANTHAM			
Blyton	—	7 ACHU	
Burn	—	10 ACHU	
Spittlegate	—	GCF	
Lindholme	—	1056 CU	Lancaster
Finningley	—	BCIS ECDU	(various)
Rufforth	—	8 ACHU	
Sandtoft	—	1667 CU	Lancaster
Alcaster Malbis	—	4 ACS	
North Luffenham	—	1653 CU	Lancaster/ Beaufighter
Bottesford	—	1668 CU	Lancaster/ Beaufighter
Woolfox Lodge	—	1051 CU	Lancaster/ Beaufighter
Swinderby	—	1660 CU	Lancaster
Wigsley	—	1654 CU	Lancaster
Winthorpe	—	1661 CU	Lancaster
Topcliffe	—	1659 CU	Lancaster
Dalton	—	6 ACS	
Wombleton	—	1666 CU	Lancaster
No 8 GP: HQ — HUNTINGDON			
Bourn	105, 162	—	Mosquito
Bourn	—	1696 BDTF	Hurricane
Downham Market	608	—	Mosquito
Downham Market	635	—	Lancaster
Gransden Lodge	142, 692	—	Mosquito
Graveley	35, 227	—	Lancaster
Little Staughton	109	—	Mosquito
Little Staughton	582	—	Lancaster
Oakington	7	—	Lancaster
Oakington	571	—	Mosquito
Upwood	139	—	Mosquito
Upwood	156	—	Lancaster
Warboys	—	1696 BDTF	Martinet
Warboys	—	1323	Lancaster
Wyton	128, 163	—	Mosquito
Wyton	—	GCF	
Wyton	—	1409 met	Mosquito
No 91 GP: HQ — ABINGDON			
Gamston	—	9 ACHU	
Abingdon	—	GCF	
Abingdon	10 OTU	—	Wellington
Honeybourne	24 OTU	—	Wellington
Lossiemouth	20 OTU	—	Wellington
Moreton-in-Marsh	21 OTU	—	Wellington
Silverstone	17 OTU	—	Wellington
Upper Heyford	16 OTU	—	Mosquito
Wellesbourne Mountford	22 OTU	—	Wellington
Wescott	11 OTU	—	Wellington
Little Horwood	—	GCF (det)	
No 92 GP: HQ — WINSLOW			
Bruntingthorpe	—	11 ACHU	
No 100 GP: HP — EAST DEREHAM			
Foulsham	192	—	Halifax/ Mosquito/ Anson/ Tiger Moth
Foulsham	462	—	Halifax
Great Massingham	—	1694 BDTF	Martinet
Great Massingham	169	—	Mosquito

Location	Flying Sqn	Other Flying Unit	Ac Type
Little Snoring	23	—	Mosquito
North Creake	171, 199	—	Halifax
Oulton	214, 223	—	Fortress
Swannington	85, 157	—	Mosquito
West Raynham	141	—	Mosquito
Swanton Morely	—	GCF	
Swanton Morely	—	BSDU	
Plus No 80 (Signals) Wing			
No 26 GP: HQ — LANGLEY HALL, SLOUGH			
control of No 81 (Signals) Wing; numerous W/T, D/F etc stations			
2ND TACTICAL AIR FORCE			
No 2 GP			
Nos: 136, 137, 138, 140 Wings			
B58/Melsbroek	21, 98, 107, 464, 487	—	Mosquito
B110/Achmer	180, 320	—	Mitchell
B77/Gilze-Rijen	226, 342	—	Mitchell
B80/Volkel	305, 418, 605	—	Mosquito
A75/Cambrai	613	—	Mosquito
?	—	GCS	
Plus 13 OTU			
No 34 WING			
B78/Eindhoven	16	—	Spitfire
B78/Eindhoven	69	—	Wellington
B78/Eindhoven	140	—	Mosquito
No 83 GP			
Nos: 39, 121, 122, 124, 125, 126, 143 Wings			
B156/Luneburg	3	—	Tempest
B156/Luneburg	400, 414, 430	—	Spitfire
B172/Husum	41, 350	—	Spitfire
B172/Husum	137	—	Typhoon
B160/Kastrup	56, 80, 486	—	Tempest
B164/Schleswig	175, 184, 245	—	Typhoon
B158/Lubeck	181, 182, 247	—	Typhoon
B152/Fassberg	411, 412, 416, 443	—	Spitfire
B158/Lubeck	616	—	Meteor
B166/Flensburg	438, 439, 440	—	Typhoon
Hoya	653	—	Auster
Hakimpet	658	—	Auster
Lympne	659	—	Auster
Colerne (+ det)	504	—	Meteor
?	—	GCS	
No 84 GP			
Nos: 35, 123, 131, 135, 145, 146, 148 Wings			
Warmell	2	—	Spitfire
Turnhouse	164	—	Spitfire
Turnhouse	193	—	Typhoon
B118/Celle	4	—	Typhoon
B109/Quackenbrook	33	—	Tempest
Hildesheim	197, 263, 266	—	Typhoon
B116/Wunstorf	198, 609	—	Typhoon
B116/Wunstorf	322, 349	—	Spitfire
B106/Twenthe	219, 264	—	Mosquito
B155/Dedelsdorf	222	—	Tempest
B155/Dedelsdorf	274, 302, 308	—	Spitfire
B150/Hustedt	268	—	Spitfire
B113/Varrelsbusch	317	—	Spitfire
B105/Drope	340, 341, 345, 485	—	Spitfire
Lasham	451, 453	—	Spitfire
Deilinghofen	652	—	Auster
Goslar	657	—	Auster
Kiel	660	—	Auster
Apeldoorn	661, 665	—	Auster
Neheim	662, 664	—	Auster
?	—	GCS	
No 85 GP			
Nos: 69, 142, 339 Wings			
B83/Knockle le Zout	290	—	Spitfire

Location	Flying Sqn	Other Flying Unit	Ac Type
Grossachsenheim	326, 328	—	Spitfire
Sersheim	327	—	Spitfire
?	—	GCS	
FIGHTER COMMAND: HQ — STANMORE			
130 WING			
No 11 GP: HQ — UXBRIDGE			
Manston	29	—	Mosquito
Manston	310, 312, 313	—	Spitfire
Manston	—	584 TU	
Chilbolton	183	—	Spitfire
Colerne	74	—	Meteor
Fairwood Common	—	11 ARC, 18 APC	Master/Lysander/ Martinet
Harrowbeer	329	—	Spitfire
Harrowbeer	275	—	Spitfire/Walrus/ Sea Otter
Harrowbeer	691	—	Martinet/ Vengeance/ Hurricane/ Oxford
Predannack	151, 406	—	Mosquito
Warmwell	—	14 APC, 17 APC	Master/Lysander/ Martinet
Nether Wallop	—	GCF	
Nether Wallop	—	FCCS	
North Weald	—	1494 TTF	
Andrews Field	306, 309, 315	—	Mustang
Bentwaters	64, 118	—	Mustang
Bentwaters	65, 126	—	Spitfire
Castle Camps	25	—	Mosquito
No 12 GP: HQ — WATNALL			
Church Fenton	125	—	Beaufighter
Hutton Cranswick	124	—	Spitfire
Hutton Cranswick	—	4 ADF	
Coltishall	303, 316	—	Mustang
Coltishall	307	—	Mosquito
Ludham	1, 91	—	Spitfire
Digby	441, 42	—	Mustang
Hucknall	—	GCF	
Keevil	61 OTU	—	Spitfire/Mustang
Acklington	19	—	Spitfire
Charter Hall	54 OTU	—	Beaufighter/ Beaufort/ Mosquito
Chilbolton	26	—	Spitfire
Cranfield	—	A1 CF	Beaufighter
Millfield	56 OTU	—	Mosquito
Morpeth	80 OTU	—	Spitfire/Master/ Martinet/ Dominie
No 13 GP: HQ — DRUMMOSSIE, INVERNESS			
Skeabrae	603	—	Spitfire
Drem	164	—	Spitfire
Dyce	129, 165	—	Spitfire
Inverness	—	GCF	
Peterhead	122, 234, 611	—	Mustang
No 70 GP: HQ — FARNBOROUGH			
Aberporth	595	—	Martinet/Spitfire/
VENGEANCE/HURRICANE			
Andover	43 OTU	—	Auster
Bircham Newton	695	—	Martinet/ Vengeance/ Hurricane
Bradwell Bay	287	—	Oxford/ Hurricane
Castle Bromwich	577	—	Oxford/ Hurricane
Church Fenton	288	—	Oxford/ Hurricane
Farnborough	—	GCF	

Location	Flying Sqn	Other Flying Unit	Ac Type
Gosport	667		
Hawkinge	567	—	Hurricane/ Martinet/ Vengeance
Llanbedr	631	—	Vengeance
Manorbier	—	PAU	Queen Bee
Weston Zoyland	587	—	Martinet/ Vengeance/ Hurricane
No 88 GP: HQ — EDINBURGH			
Andrews Field	276	—	Walrus/Sea Otter
Banff	333	—	Catalina/ Mosquito
Dyce	130	—	Spitfire
Gardemoen (Norway)	331, 332	—	Spitfire
Turnhouse	—	GCF	
(Plus Nos: 128, 129, 130, 132 Wings)			
Woodhaven	334		Mosquito
No 60 GP: HQ — LEIGHTON BUZZARD			
Digby	527	—	Dominie
Henley	529	—	Hoverfly
Plus Nos: 70, 72, 73, 75, 78 Signals Wings (although 72 Wing attached to No 85 Gp)			
COASTAL COMMAND: HQ — NORTHWOOD			
No 15 GP: HQ — LIVERPOOL			
Aldergrove	—	1 APC	Lysander/ Martinet
Ballyhalbert	—	1402 met	Hurricane/ Spitfire
Castle Archdale	201	—	Sunderland
Limavady	—	CC AUDS	Wellington
Limavady	281	—	Warwick/ Sea Otter
Limavady	281	—	Warwick/ Sea Otter
Speke	—	GCF	
Tiree	518	—	Halifax
Tiree	281 (det)	—	Warwick/ Sea Otter
Valley	281 (det)	—	Warwick/ Sea Otter
No 16 GP: HQ — GILLINGHAM			
Beccles	280	—	Warwick/ Hurricane
Beccles	278	—	Walrus/Sea Otter
Bircham Newton	—	2 APC	Martinet
Calshot	—	S of ASR	Sea Otter
Gosport	—	ATDU	
Hawkinge	278 (det)	—	Walrus/Sea Otter
Langham	521	—	Fortress/ Hurricane
Langham	612	—	Wellington
North Coates	254	—	Beaufighter
Rochester	—	GCF	
Thorney Island	278 (det)	—	Walrus/Sea Otter
Thorney Island	—	ASWDU	
No 17 GP: HQ — EDINBURGH			
Aldergrove	—	1674 HCU	Liberator/ Halifax
Alness	4 OTU	—	Sunderland
Alness	—	302 FTU	Catalina/ Sunderland
East Fortune	132 OTU	—	Beaufighter/ Beaufort/ Mosquito
Silloth	6 OTU	—	Wellington
Squires Gate	—	3 S of GR	Anson
Squires Gate	—	1510	Anson
Turnberry	5 OTU	—	Warwick/ Hudson/ Beaufighter
Turnhouse	—	GCF	

Location	Flying Sqn	Other Flying Unit	Ac Type
No 18 GP: HQ — PITREAVIE CASTLE			
Banff	235, 248	—	Mosquito
Banff	279 (det)	—	Warwick/ Sea Otter
Dallachy	489	—	Beaufighter
Helensburgh	—	MAEE	
Leuchars	—	GCF	
Leuchars	—	3 APC	Martinet
Milltown	224	—	Liberator
Tain	311	—	Liberator
Tain	4 OTU (det)	—	Sunderland
Thornaby	279	—	Warwick/ Sea Otter
Wick	279 (det)	—	Warwick/ Sea Otter
Wick	519	—	Fortress/ Sunderland
No 19 GP: HQ — PLYMOUTH			
Chivenor	14	—	Mosquito
Exeter	282 (det)	—	Sea Otter
Mount Batten	—	GCF	
St Davids	517		Halifax
St Eval	179	—	Warwick
St Eval	282	—	Warwick/ Walrus/ Sea Otter
St Eval	304	—	Wellington
Talberry	—	4 APC	Martinet
No 106 GP: HQ — FIFIELD HOUSE, BENSON			
Benson	8 OTU	—	Spitfire
Benson	541, 544	—	Spitfire/Mustang
Benson	542	—	Spitfire
Benson	—	309 FT and ADU	Master
No 247 GP: HQ — ANGRA, AZORES			
Azores	269	—	Spitfire/ Warwick/ Martinet
HQ RAF ICELAND			
Reykjavik	251	—	Fortress
HQ RAF GIBRALTAR			
Gibraltar			

CC also controls 63 MCUs

FLYING TRAINING COMMAND: HQ — READING
No 21 GP: HQ — SPITTLEGATE

Location	Flying Sqn	Other Flying Unit	Ac Type
Cranwell	—	19 FTS	
Hucknall	—	25 EFTS	
Montrose	—	1541 BATF	
Newton	—	16 SFTS	
Peterborough	—	7 SFTS	
Spittlegate	—	17 SFTS	
Ternhill	—	5 PAFU	
Wheaton Aston	—	21 PAFU	
Wheaton Aston	—	1517 BATF	

No 23 GP: HQ — SOUTH CERNEY

Location	Flying Sqn	Other Flying Unit	Ac Type
Beaulieu	—	AFEE	
Boscombe Down	—	A and AEE	
Boscombe Down	—	IFDF, ETPS, AGME	
Brize Norton	—	21 HGCU	
Exeter	—	3 GTS	
Hullavington	-	ECFS	
Kidlington	—	1 ACHU	
Little Rissington	—	6 PAFU	
Little Rissington	—	1523 BATF	
Lulsgate Bottom	—	3 FIS	
Lulsgate Bottom	—	1540 BATF	
South Cerney	—	13 PAFU	

Location	Flying Sqn	Other Flying Unit	Ac Type
South Cerney	—	1525 BATF	
Weston Zoyland	—	1545 BATF	
Upavon	—	7 FIS	
Upavon	—	1537 BATF	
No 25 GP: HQ — MARKET DRAYTON			
Barrow	—	10 AGS	
Cark	—	SPTU	
Catfoss	—	CGS	
Halfpenny Green	—	3 OAFU	
Manby	—	EAAS	
Penrhos	—	2 ACHU	
Shawbury	—	EANS	
No 29 GP: HQ — DUMFRIES			
Andreas	—	11 AGS	
Bishops Court	—	7 ANS	
Dalcross	—	2 AGS	
Dumfries	—	10 ANS	
Jurby	—	5 ANS	
Wigtown	—	1 OAFU	
No 50 GP: HQ — READING			
Booker	—	21 EFTS	
Cambridge	—	22 EFTS	
Clyffe Pypard	—	29 EFTS	
Fairoaks	—	18 EFTS	
Panshangar	—	1 EFTS	
Shellingford	—	3 EFTS	
Sywell	—	6 EFTS	
Theale	—	26 EFTS	
Watchfield	—	1547 BATF	
Woodley	—	10 FIS	
Worcester	—	2 EFTS	
No 52 GP: HQ — LEEDS			
Brough		4 EFTS	
Carlisle	—	15 EFTS	
Derby	—	16 EFTS	
desford	—	7 EFTS	
Elmdon	—	14 EFTS	
Perth	—	11 EFTS	
Sealand	—	24 EFTS	
Wolverhampton	—	28 EFTS	
Wolverhampton	—	PPP	

No 54 GP: HQ — SUNNINGDALE
Controls various non-flying training units

S. RHODESIA (CONTROL BY RATG)

Location	Flying Sqn	Other Flying Unit	Ac Type
Guinea Fowl, Gwelo	—	26 EFTS	
Induna, Bulawayo	—	27EFTS	
Mt Hampden, Salisbury	—	28 EFTS	
Cranborne, Salisbury	—	20 SFTS	
Thornhill, Gwelo	—	22 SFTS	
Heany, Salisbury	—	CFS (Rhodesia)	

TECHNICAL TRAINING COMMAND: HQ — READING
No 22 GP: HQ — MARKET DRAYTON
Control various training units

No 24 GP: HQ — HALTON
Control various 'schools'

No 27 GP: HQ — SOUTHROP
Control Radio Schools etc

No 28 GP: HQ — QUEEN'S SQUARE, LONDON
Control mainly medical and administrative installations

MAINTENANCE COMMAND: HQ — ANDOVER
No 53 WING: HQ — ANDOVER
MUs: 47, 52, 76, 82, 215, 222 — Packing Depôts

No 54 WING: HQ — EGGINTON
Various MT companies

Location	Flying Sqn	Other Flying Unit	Ac Type

No 40 GP: HQ — Andover
MUs: 3, 7, 14, 17, 35, 62, 68, 69, 70, 73, 74, 79, 87, 205, 208, 209, 210, 211, 212, 214, 217, 220, 225, 230, 232, 238, 239, 246, 261 — Equipment, barrack stores, MT storage — No 56 Wing (North): HQ — Annan
MUs: 16, 25, 61, 66, 72, 89, 99, 203, 204, 207, 216, 221, 227, 236, 241 — Equipment, barrack stores, MT storage — No 55 Wing (Midland): HQ — Eggington

No 41 GP: HQ — ANDOVER
(Under operational control of MAP)

Hamble	—	15 FPP	
Hawarden	—	3 FPP	
Prestwick	—	4 FPP	
Ratcliffe	—	6 FPP	
Ringway	—	14 FPP	
Sydenham	—	8 FPP	
Thame	—	5 FPP	
Whitchurch	—	2 FPP	
White Waltham	—	1 FPP	

MUs: 5, 6, 8, 9, 10, 12, 15, 18, 19, 20, 22, 23, 27, 29, 33, 38, 39, 44, 45, 46, 48, 51, 57 — Aircraft Storage Units

No 42 GP: HQ — BURGH COMMON
MUs: 2, 11, 21, 28, 31, 36, 53, 59, 64, 77, 80, 81, 91, 93, 92, 94, 95, 96, 98, 100, 202, 219, 224, 231, 233, 243, 244, 249, 245 — Ammunition Depôts
Plus control of aviation fuel and oil distribution depôts

No 43 GP: HQ — STANMORE

Abingdon	—	GCF	

MUs: 1, 4, 13, 24, 26, 30, 32, 34, 49, 50, 54, 56, 58, 60, 63, 65, 67, 71, 75, 78, 83, 84, 85, 86, 88, 97, 213, 218, 226 — Repair and salvage (plus mobile Dental Surgeries)

TRANSPORT COMMAND: HQ — BUSHY PARK
No 4 GP: HQ — YORK

Bramcote	105 OTU	—	Wellington
Nuneaton	—	1513 BATF	
Crosby on eden	109 OTU	—	Dakota
Driffield	426	—	Halifax
Leconfield	51	—	Stirling
Lissett	158	—	Stirling
Full Sutton	77	—	Halifax
Holme	76	—	Halifax
Breighton	78	—	Halifax
Melbourne	10	—	Halifax
Netheravon	—	S of AS	
Odiham	—	1516 BATF	
Ossington	—	6 LFS	Lancaster
Pocklington	102	—	Halifax
Elvington	346, 347	—	Halifax
Elvington	—	GCF	
Riccall	—	1332 MCU	
Snaith	—	17 ACHU	
Valley	—	1528 BATF	
Welford	—	1336 TSCU	
Wymeswold	108 OTU	—	Dakota
Castle Donington	—	1521 BATF	

No 38 GP: HQ — MARKS HALL, EARLS COLNE

Earls Colne	296, 297	—	Halifax
Earls Colne	—	GCF	
Great Dunmow	190, 620	—	Halifax
Matching	—	ORTU	Albemarle/Horsa/Tiger Moth
Matching	—	1677 TTF	Martinet
Keevil	—	22 MCGU/ORTU	
Netheravon	—	1 HGSU	Horsa/Hamilcar
Ringway	—	1 PTS	
Rivenhill	295, 570	—	Stirling
Saltby	—	1665 MCU	Stirling/Halifax
Shepherds Grove	196, 299	—	Stirling
Shobdon	—	5 GTS	
Tarrant Rushon	298, 644	—	Halifax
Tilstock	81 OTU	—	Whitley

No 44 GP: HQ — GLOUCESTER

Llandow	—	3 APU	
Melton Mowbray	—	12 FU	
Pershore	—	1 FU	
Portreath	—	1 OADU	
St Mawgan	—	2 OADU	
Staverton	—	GCF	
Talbenny	—	11 FU	

No 45 GP: HQ — DORVAL

Bermuda	231 (det)	—	Liberator
Dorval	231	—	Liberator
(No 112, Nth Atlantic Wing)	—	6 FU	
Lindbergh Field	—	—	—
(No 280 Wing)			
Nassau	—	7 FU	
(No 113, Sth Atlantic Wing)			
North Bay	—	313 FTU	

No 46 GP: HQ — HARROW WEALD

Blackbushe	301	—	Warwick
Broadwell	512	—	Dakota
Down Ampney	48, 271	—	Warwick
Ibsley	—	1333 TSCU (GPTF)	Warwick
Leicester East	—	1333 TSCU	Warwick
Netheravon	—	ATTDU	
Northolt	—	ADLS	
Odiham	233	—	Dakota
Paris (No 107 Wing)	—	—	—
Croydon (No 110 Wing_	147	—	Dakota
Croydon (No 110 Wing)	—	1316 (Neth)	
Blackbushe (No 110 Wing)	167	—	Warwick
Brussels (No 111 Wing)	—	—	—
Brussels/Evere	575	—	Dakota
Brussels/Melsbrook	437	—	Dakota

No 47 GP: HQ — HENDON

Hendon	24	MCS	
Holmsley South	246	—	York
Lyneham	511	—	York
Lyneham	525	—	Dakota
Merryfield	187	—	Halifax
Prestwick	—	1680	
Stoney Cross	242	—	Wellington
Stoney Cross	46	—	Stirling

No 301 Wing: HQ — NETHERAVON

Ballykelly	59	—	Liberator
Castle Archdale	423	—	Sunderland
Leuchars	206	—	Liberator
Pembroke Dock	422	—	Sunderland
Tain	86	—	Liberator

No 216 GP; 229 GP; 114 Wing parts of TC — but overseas units so see later

BALLOON COMMAND: HQ — STANMORE
Most in the process of final disbandment; except for meteorological balloon units

RAF NORTHERN IRELAND: HQ — DUNMURRY

Belfast	—	CCF	

Most other stations under C and M

MEDITERRANEAN ALLIED AIR FORCES: HQ — CASERTA & ALGIERS
(Note: all the Med area air forces contained SAAF Sqns/Wings — these are not included here)

Bellaria (No 244 Wing)	92, 145, 241, 601, 417	—	Spitfire
Borgo San Lorenzo	655	—	Auster
Cecina	—	DAF CF	
Cervia (No 239 Wing)	250, 450	—	Kittyhawk
Cervia	112, 260	—	Mustang
Cesenatico (No 253 Wing)	500, 454	—	Baltimore
Cesenatico	600	—	Mosquito
Florence	208	—	Spitfire
Florence	225	—	Beaufighter

Location	Flying Sqn	Other Flying Unit	Ac Type
Forli (No 232 Wing)	318	—	Spitfire
Forli	663	—	Auster
Forli	256	—	Mosquito
Forli	55, 18, 114	—	Boston
Gaudo	—	5 RFU	
Pontedera	87, 185	—	Spitfire
Rimini (No 324 Wing)	43, 72, 93, 111	—	Spitfire
Rimini	654	—	Auster
Russi	651	—	Auster
Plus MUs: 121, 123, 126			

BALKAN AIR FORCE: HQ — BARI

Location	Flying Sqn	Other Flying Unit	Ac Type
Bari	—	CCF	
Biferno (No 254 Wing)	39	—	Marauder
Biferno	213	—	Mustang
Biferno	249	—	Spitfire
Brindisi (No 334 Wing)	148	—	Halifax
Brindisi		YTF	
Canne (No 281 Wing)	253, 73, 351	—	Spitfire
Canne	6	—	Hurricane
Isle of Vis	352, 6 (det)	—	Hurricane
Zadar	351 (det)	—	Spitfire

MATAF: HQ FLORENCE

Location	Flying Sqn	Other Flying Unit	Ac Type
Pian del Lago	—	CF	

MACAF: HQ — CASERTA

Location	Flying Sqn	Other Flying Unit	Ac Type
Aix en Provence (No 340 Wing)	—	—	—
Ancona	253 (det)		
Blida	283 (det)	—	Warwick/Walrus
Borgo	293 (det)	—	Warwick/Walrus
Castel Benito	283 (det)	—	Warwick/Walrus
Casenatico	293 (det)	—	Warwick/Walrus
Falconara (No 287 Wing)	237	—	Spitfire
Falconara	255 (det)	—	Beaufighter
Falconara	624 (det)	—	Walrus
Florence	682 (det)	—	Spitfire
Foggia (No 323 Wing)	293	—	Warwick/Walrus
Foggia	255	—	Beaufighter
Foggia	38	—	Wellington
Foggia	624	—	Walrus
Flori	683 (det)	—	Mosquito
Gando	—	5 RFU	
Gibraltar	458	—	Wellington
Hassani	294 (det)	—	Warwick/Walrus
Hassani	283 (det)	—	Warwick/Walrus
Hassani	624 (det)	—	Walrus
Istres	255 (det)	—	Beaufighter
Leghorn (No 338 Wing)	—	—	—
Marcianise	—	MED/ME CF	
Nancy	682	—	Spitfire
Pisa	293 (det)	—	Warwick/Walrus
Pomigliano (No 335 Wing)	293 (det)	—	Warwick/Walrus
Pomigliano	—	CF	
Pomigliano	—	23 AACU	
Rosignano	237 (det)	—	Spitfire
Rosignano	255 (det)	—	Beaufighter
Rosignano	624 (det)	—	Walrus
San Severo (No 336 Wing)	680 (1 Flt), 682	—	Spitfire
San Severo	683	—	Mosquito
Taranto (No 286 Wing)	—	—	—

AHQ GREECE: HQ — ATHENS

Location	Flying Sqn	Other Flying Unit	Ac Type
Hassani (No 337 Wing)	335, 336	—	Spitfire
Hassani	252	—	Beaufighter
Hassani	—	CCF	

AHQ MALTA: HQ — VALLETTA

Location	Flying Sqn	Other Flying Unit	Ac Type
Algiers (No 210 Gp)	—	—	—
Bone	284	—	Warwick/Walrus
Elmas	284 (det)	—	Warwick/Walrus
Hal Far	283	—	Warwick/Walrus
Hal Far	—	CF	
Istres	284 (det)	—	Warwick/Walrus
Pomigliano	284 (det)	—	Warwick/Walrus
Nos: 143, 137 MUs			

No 205 GP: HQ — FOGGIA

Location	Flying Sqn	Other Flying Unit	Ac Type
Amendola (No 240 Wing)	178, 614	—	Liberator
Foggia (No 236 Wing)	40, 104	—	Wellington
Foggia	—	GCF	
Tortorella (No 231 Wing)	37, 70	—	Wellington

No 214 GP: HQ — NAPLES

MUs: 110, 113, 114, 124, 141, 159, 353, 357, 360, 375, 378

Plus various non-flying units

No 218 GP: HQ ALGIERS

Various repair and salage units, etc

MIDDLE EAST COMMAND
RAF MIDDLE EAST: HQ — CAIRO

Location	Flying Sqn	Other Flying Unit	Ac Type
El Genina	—	1567 met	
Khartoum	—	1412 met	
Khartoum	—	CF	

AHQ EGYPT: HQ — CAIRO

Location	Flying Sqn	Other Flying Unit	Ac Type
Deversoir	680	—	Mosquito
San Severo	680 (det)	—	Mosquito

AHQ EASTERN MED: HQ — ALEXANDRIA

Location	Flying Sqn	Other Flying Unit	Ac Type
Abu Sueir	—	1675 HCU	
Aqir	76 OTU		
Aqir	294 (det)	—	Wellington/Walrus/Warwick
Ballah	—	ME CGS	
Ballah	—	13 AGS	
Ballah	—	1342 RPTF	
Benina (No 212 Gp)	294 (det)	—	Wellington/Walrus/Warwick
Benina	221 (det)	—	Wellington/Warwick
Castel Benito	—	1564 met	
Deversoir	—	26 AACU	
Edcu	221	—	Wellington/Warwick
Edcu	294	—	Wellington/Warwick/Walrus
Ein Shemer	78 OTU		
El Adem	294 (det)	—	Wellington/Walrus/Warwick
El Adem	221 (det)	—	Wellington/Warwick
El Adem	—	18 MFU	Walrus/Warwick
Fayid	73 OTU		
Ismailia	71 OTU		
Lakatamia	—	1565 met	
Mariut	—	CF	
Nicosia	79 OTU		
Petah Tiqva	74 OTU		
Qastina	77 OTU		
Ramat David	—	26 AACU det	
Shallufa	75 OTU		
Shallufa	—	MEAS	
Shallufa	—	11 FIS	
Shallufa	—	7 RFU	
Shallufa	—	1343 conv.	
Shandur	70 OTU		

AHQ LEVANT: HQ — JERUSALEM

Location	Flying Sqn	Other Flying Unit	Ac Type
Aqir	221 det	—	Wellington/Warwick
Lydda	—	1413 met	
Lydda	—	CF	
Ramat David	32	—	Spitfire

AHQ IRAQ AND PERSIA: HQ — HABBANIYA

Location	Flying Sqn	Other Flying Unit	Ac Type
Habbaniya	—	1415 met	
Habbaniya	-	CF	
MUs: 115, 119, 138			

Location	Flying Sqn	Other Flying Unit	Ac Type
AHQ EAST AFRICA: HQ — NAIROBI			
Diego Suarez	—	1568 met	
Eastleigh	—	CF	
Eastleigh	—	1414 met	
Eastleigh	—	25 AACU	
Kipevu	209	—	Sunderland
Plaisance	—	1569 met	
Port Reitz (No 246 Wing)	—	—	—
No 105 MU			
HQ BRITISH FORCES, ADEN: HQ — STEAMER POINT			
Hargeisa	—	CF det	
Hiswa	—	1566 met	
Khormaksar	621	—	Wellington
Khormaksar	—	CF	
Scuisciban	621 det	—	Wellington
Socotra	621 det	—	Wellington
No 131 MU			
No 206 GP: HQ — HELIOPOLIS			
Heliopolis	—	GCF	Fairchild
MUs: 101, 102, 103, 106, 107, 108, 109, 111, 112, 117, 120, 122, 128, 132, 135, 136, 142, 160, 166.			
No 216 GP: HQ — CASERTA			
(Part of Transport Command)			
Algiers (No 284 Wing)	—	—	—
Bilbeis	—	1330 CU	
Blida	—	3 FU	
Cairo West	216	—	Dakota
Capodichino	—	4 FU	
Catania	—	4 FU det	
Gebel Hamzi	—	2 FU	
Gebel Hamzi	—	1330 CU det	
Habbaniya (No 151 Wing)	—	—	—
Heliopolis (No 216 Gp/rear)	—	5 FU	
Heliopolis (No 282 Wing)	216	CF	Dakota
Lesi	—	4 FU det	
Khartoum (No 115 Wing)	216 det	—	Dakota
Maison Blanche	216 det	—	Dakota
Ruvo (No 249 Wing)	—	—	—
Setif	—	4 FU det	
Sheikh Othman	216 det	—	Dakota
AHQ WEST AFRICA: HQ — FREETOWN			
Abidjan	204, 270, 490	—	Sunderland
Apapa	270 det	—	Sunderland
Bathurst	95	—	Sunderland
Douala	344	—	Wellington
Fishlake	490 & 204 det	—	Sunderland
Ikeja	—	1561 met	
Jui	490 & 204 det	—	Sunderland
Maiduguri	—	1560 met	
Point Noire	343	—	Sunderland
Port Etienne	95, 343	—	Sunderland
Port Etienne	344 det	—	Wellington
Takoradi	—	CCF	
Waterloo	—	1562 met	
Waterloo	—	CF	
Yumdum (No 295 Wing)			
Accra (No 114 Wing)			
(part of Transport Command)			
AUSTRALIA			
Camden (No 300 Wing) det	243	—	Dakota/Anson
Camden	—	1315	
Darwin	54, 548, 549	—	Spitfire
Melbourne (No 300 Wing)	—	—	
Narromine	618	—	Mosquito
West Indies			
Nassau	111 OTU	—	Liberator/Mitchell
AIR COMMAND SOUTH EAST ASIA: HQ — KANDY (CEYLON)			
Brown	136		Spitfire
AHQ BURMA: HQ — CALCUTTA			
Alipore	681	—	Spitfire
Alipore	684	—	Mosquito
Baigachi	89, 176	—	Beaufighter
Baigachi	—	CS	
Bally	—	PR element	
Calcutta	—	3 FPU	
Camilla (No 900 Wing)			
HQ BAFSEA: HQ — NEW DELHI			
Bombay (No 233 Gp)	—	—	—
No 221 Gp: HQ — MAIKTILA			
Kumbhirgam (No 908 Wing)	45, 47, 82	—	Mosquito
Kwetnge (No 906 Wing)	607, 155	—	Spitfire
Kwetnge	34, 113	—	Hurricane
Kyaukpuyu	656 (C Flt)	—	Auster
Meiktila	656 (B Flt)	—	Auster
Meiktila	17	—	Hurricane
Meiktila	—	GCS	
Monywa	656		Auster
Monywa	20		Hurricane
Myingyan (No 910 Wing)	—	—	—
Sinthe (No 907 Wing)	11	—	Hurricane
Sinthe	152	—	Spitfire
Thabyetha	656 (A Flt)	—	Auster
Thedaw (No 909 Wing)	28, 60	—	Hurricane
Wangjing	79, 146, 261	—	Thunderbolt
No 222 GP: HQ — COLOMBO			
Akyab (No 346 Wing)	230	—	Sunderland
Akyab	—	6 & 7 ASAF	
China Bay	321	—	Catalina
Chiringa	22	—	Beaufighter
Cuttack	8	—	Liberator
Kankesanturia	203	—	Liberator
Koggala	205	—	Catalina
Korangi Creek	212	—	Catalina
Minneriya	160	—	Liberator
Ratmalana	81	—	Spitfire
Ratmalana	—	GCF	
Ratmalana	—	1303 met	
Ratmalana	—	ACSEA CS	
Ratmalana	—	ASWDU	
Ratmalana	—	20 APC	
Ratmalana	—	5 ASR FH	
Red Hills Lake	191, 240	—	Catalina
Vavuniya	217	—	Beaufighter
Vavuniya	132	—	Spitfire
Plus MUs: 332, 338, 359.			
No 223 GP: HQ — PESHAWAR			
Charra (No 905 Wing)	—	—	—
Peshawar	151	OTU	
Peshawar	—	GCF	
No 224 GP: HQ — SHALIMAR CAMP			
Akyab (advanced HQ)			
Akyab (No 903 Wing)	30, 135	—	Thunderbolt
Chiringa (No 901 Wing)	27, 177, 211	—	Beaufighter
Cox's Bazaar (No 904 Wing)	—	—	—
Dabaing	67	—	Spitfire
Joari	110	—	Mosquito
Kyaukpyu	5	—	Thunderbolt
Kyaukpyu	273	—	Spitfire
Myaukpyu (No 902 Wing)	—	—	—
Nazir	123	-	Thunderbolt
Nidania	615	—	Spitfire
Ratnap	134, 258	—	Thunderbolt
No 225 GP: HQ — BANGALORE			
Begumpet	—	1 EFTS	

Location	Flying Sqn	Other Flying Unit	Ac Type
Cannanore	—	1340 SDF	
Charra	84	—	Mosquito
Cholavaram	—	1580 Cal	
Cholavaram	—	21 APC	
Deolali	—	1587 AOP ref	
St Thomas Mount	—	1302 met	
Sambre	—	1344 SDF	
Yelahanka	—	GCF	
Yelahanka	—	1672 MCU	
Yelahanka	—	8 RFU	Thunderbolt

No 226 GP: HQ — PALAM
MUs: 301, 302, 305, 306, 308, 307, 309, 312, 313, 314, 318, 319, 320, 328, 330, 337, 341, 343, 344, 346, 352, 355, 356, 361, 374.

No 227 GP: HQ — AGRA

Location	Flying Sqn	Other Flying Unit	Ac Type
Agra	—	GCF	
Ambala	—	1 SFTS	
Bhopal	-	1 AGS	
Jodhpur	—	2 EFTS	
Kolar	—	1 AGS det	
Nagpur	—	1301 met	

No 228 GP: HQ — CALCUTTA

Location	Flying Sqn	Other Flying Unit	Ac Type
Amarda Road	131	—	Spitfire
Amarda Road	—	22 APC	
Amarda Road	—	AFTU	
Dhubalia	—	23 APC	

No 229 GP: HQ — NEW DELHI

Location	Flying Sqn	Other Flying Unit	Ac Type
Agartala	—	14 FU	
Allahabad	—	9 FU	
Balaghat	668	—	Hadrian/Tiger Moth
Bangalore (No 109 Wing)	—	—	—
Bikram (No 344 Wing)	671, 672, 673	—	Hadrian/Tiger Moth
Bilaspur	96	—	Dakota
Calcutta (No 117 Wing)	—	—	—
Chittagong	—	9 FU det	
Comilla	238	—	Dakota
Delhi (No 118 Wing)	—	—	—
Dum Dum	52	—	Dakota
Fatehjang (No 343 Wing)	669, 670	—	Hadrian/Tiger Moth
Gujrat	—	1334 TSCU	
Hathazari (No 342 Wing)	31, 117	—	Dakota
Jharsaguda (No 345 Wing)	—	—	—
Jodhpur	—	8 FU det	
Kandy (advanced HQ)	—	—	—
Karachi (No 108 Wing)	—	—	—
Lalaghat	668	—	Hadrian/Tiger Moth
Mawnubyin (No 341 Wing)	62, 194, 267, 436	—	Dakota
Nagpur	—	10 FU	
Palam	353	—	Dakota
Palam	232	—	Dakota
Palam	—	GCF	
Santa Cruz	—	10 FU det	
Singarbil	—	9 FU det	
Tulihal	435	—	Dakota
Trichinopoly	—	10 FU det	

No 230 GP: HQ — BARRACKPORE
MUs: 321, 325, 326, 327, 329, 340, 345

Location	Flying Sqn	Other Flying Unit	Ac Type
Barrackpore	—	GCF	

No 231 GP: HQ — CALCUTTA

Location	Flying Sqn	Other Flying Unit	Ac Type
Alipore	—	1300 met	
Alipore	—	GCF	
Baigachi	—	1581 Cal	
Dhubalia (No 175 Wing)	—	—	Liberator
Digri (No 185 Wing)	159	—	Liberator
Digri	—	1341 SDF	
Jessore	200, 358	—	Liberator

Mingaladon 1947.

Location	Flying Sqn	Other Flying Unit	Ac Type
Jessore	357	—	Liberator/Dakota/Lysander
Monywa	—	1582 Cal	
Salbani (No 184 Wing)	355, 356	—	Liberator

No 232 GP: HQ — COMILLA

Location	Flying Sqn	Other Flying Unit	Ac Type
Comilla	—	GCF	

AHQ INDIA: HQ — NEW DELHI

Location	Flying Sqn	Other Flying Unit	Ac Type
Katni	—	22 AACU (D Flt)	
Karachi	—	22 AACU (A Flt)	
St Thomas Mount	—	22 AACU (C Flt)	

Negombo, Ceylon 1947.

April 1953
BOMBER COMMAND: HQ — HIGH WYCOMBE

Location	Flying Sqn	Other Flying Unit	Ac Type
Booker	—	CCF	

No 1 GP: HQ — BAWTRY

Location	Flying Sqn	Other Flying Unit	Ac Type
Bassingbourn	231 OCCU	—	Meteor/Canberra
Binbrook	9, 12 50/103, 101, 617	—	Canberra
Finningley	—	GCF	
Hemswell	83/150, 97	—	Lincoln
Hemswell	109/105, 139	—	Canberra
Hemswell	199	—	Lincoln/Mosquito
Hemswell	—	JCF	Meteor/Canberra
Scampton	10	—	Canberra
Waddington	49/102, 61/44, 100	—	Lincoln

Location	Flying Sqn	Other Flying Unit	Ac Type
Coningsby	15/21, 149, 57/104	—	Washington
Coningsby	44/55	—	Canberra
Marham	35, 90, 115/218, 207	WCU	Washington
Mildenhall	—	GCF	Anson/Proctor
Upwood	7/76, 148, 214	RRF	Lincoln
Wyton	58	—	Mosquito
Wyton	82	—	Lancaster
Wyton	540	—	Canberra

FIGHTER COMMAND: HQ — STANMORE
No 11 GP: HQ — HILLINGDON
SOUTHERN SECTOR: HQ — BOX

Location	Flying Sqn	Other Flying Unit	Ac Type
Filton	501	—	Vampire
Llandow	614	—	Vampire
Odiham	54, 247	—	Meteor
Tangmere	1, 29/22	—	Meteor

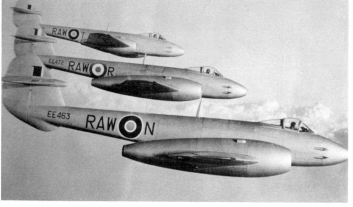

Meteor F.4s of 616 Squadron.

METROPOLITAN SECTOR: HQ — KELVEDON

Location	Flying Sqn	Other Flying Unit	Ac Type
Biggin Hill	41/253, 600, 615	—	Meteor
Duxford	64, 65	—	Meteor
North Weald	72, 601, 604	—	Meteor
Waterbeach	56, 63	—	Meteor
Wattisham	257, 263	—	Meteor
West Malling	25	—	Vampire
West Malling	85, 500	—	Meteor

No 12 GP: HQ — NEWTON

Location	Flying Sqn	Other Flying Unit	Ac Type
Newton	—	GCF	

NORTHERN SECTOR: HQ — SHIPTON

Location	Flying Sqn	Other Flying Unit	Ac Type
Church Fenton	19/152, 609	—	Meteor
Linton-on-Ouse	66, 92, 264	—	Meteor
Linton-on-Ouse	275	—	Sycamore
Ouston	607	—	Vampire
Thornaby	608	—	Vampire

EASTERN SECTOR: HQ — BAWBURGH

Location	Flying Sqn	Other Flying Unit	Ac Type
Coltishall	23	—	Vampire
Coltishall	141	—	Meteor
Finningley	616	-	Meteor
Horsham St Faith	74/34, 245	—	Meteor
Ringway	613	—	Vampire
Wymeswold	504	—	Meteor

WESTERN SECTOR: HQ — LANGLEY LANE

Location	Flying Sqn	Other Flying Unit	Ac Type
Honiley	605	—	Vampire
Hooton Park	610, 611	—	Meteor

CALEDONIAN SECTOR: HQ — BARNTON QUARRY

Location	Flying Sqn	Other Flying Unit	Ac Type
Abbotsinch	602	—	Vampire
Aldergrove	502	—	Vampire
Dyce	612	—	Vampire
Kinloss	—	Vanguard Flt	Neptune
Leuchars	43/17, 222	—	Meteor
Leuchars	151	—	Vampire
Turnhouse	603	—	Vampire

No 81 GP: HQ — PEMBREY

Location	Flying Sqn	Other Flying Unit	Ac Type
Chivenor	229 OCU	—	Vampire
Colerne	238 OCU	—	Vampire
Leeming	228 OCU	—	Meteor
Middle Wallop	233 OCU	—	Vampire
Middle Wallop	—	1906 AOP	Hoverfly
Middle Wallop	—	S of CR	Spitfire
Stradishall	226 OCU	—	Meteor

COASTAL COMMAND: HQ — NORTHWOOD

Location	Flying Sqn	Other Flying Unit	Ac Type
Bovingdon	—	CCF	

No 18 GP: HQ — PITREAVIE CASTLE

Location	Flying Sqn	Other Flying Unit	Ac Type
Aldergrove	120	—	Shackleton
Aldergrove	202	—	Hastings
Ballykelly	240/204, 269	JASS	Shackleton
Kinloss	236 OCU	—	Shackleton
Kinloss	217	—	Neptune
Leuchars	—	GCF	Anson/Proctor

No 19 GP: HQ — MOUNT BATTEN

Location	Flying Sqn	Other Flying Unit	Ac Type
Calshot	235 OCU	—	Sunderland
Pembroke Dock	201, 230	—	Sunderland
Roborough	—	GCF	Anson/Auster
St Eval	42, 206, 220	—	Shackleton
St Mawgan	—	ASWDU	Shackleton/ Sycamore/ Sunderland
St Mawgan	—	S of MR	Lancaster
Topcliffe	203/36, 210	—	Lancaster

HQ RAF GIBRALTAR

Location	Flying Sqn	Other Flying Unit	Ac Type
North Front	224	—	Shackleton

TRANSPORT COMMAND: HQ — UPAVON

Location	Flying Sqn	Other Flying Unit	Ac Type
Abingdon	—	1 PTS	Hastings
Abingdon	147	FTU	(various)
Abingdon	167	—	Valetta
Aston Down	187	1689 FPTF	(various)
Benson	30	—	Valetta
Benson	—	KF	Valetta/Viking
Hawarden	173	—	Anson/Varsity
Hendon	31	—	Anson/Proctor
Lyneham	53, 99, 511	—	Hastings
Topcliffe	47	—	Hastings
Topcliffe	24	—	Hastings/York

FLYING TRAINING COMMAND: HQ — READING

Location	Flying Sqn	Other Flying Unit	Ac Type
Woodley	—	CCF	

No 21 GP: HQ — MORTON HALL, SWINDERBY

Location	Flying Sqn	Other Flying Unit	Ac Type
Bishops Court	—	3 ANS	Anson/Valetta
Hullavington	—	1 ANS	Valetta
Shawbury	—	CNCS	Anson/Lincoln
Swinderby	—	201 AFS	Varsity
Thorney Island	—	2 ANS	Anson/Valetta
Lichfield	—	6 ANS	

No 23 GP HQ — LEIGHTON BUZZARD

Location	Flying Sqn	Other Flying Unit	Ac Type
Cranfield	—	GCF	
Cluntoe	—	2 FTS	
Cottesmore	—	7 FTS	
Dalcross	—	8 AFTS	Oxford/ Chipmunk
Feltwell	—	3 FTS	
Little Rissington	—	CFS (Advanced)	
Moreton-in-the-Marsh	—	1 FTS	
Pershore	—	10 AFTS	Oxford/ Chipmunk
South Cerney	—	CFS (Basic)	
Syerston	—	22 FTS	Harvard/Prentice
Tern Hill	—	6 FTS	
Mountford	—	9 AFTS	Oxford/ Chipmunk

Location	Flying Sqn	Other Flying Unit	Ac Type
No 24 GP: HQ — MANBY			
Driffield	—	203 AFS	Meteor/Vampire
Finningley	-	215 AFS	Meteor
Full Sutton	—	207 AFS	Meteor
Merryfield	—	208 AFS	Vampire
Middleton St George	—	205 AFS	Meteor
Oakington	—	206 AFS	Meteor
Tarrant Rushton	—	210 AFS	Meteor
Valley	—	202 AFS	Vampire
Weston Zoyland	—	209 AFS	Meteor
Worksop	—	211 AFS	Meteor

No 54 GP: HQ — BENSON
Control of various non-flying training establishments, e.g. ITS, ACS.

TECHNICAL TRAINING COMMAND: HQ — BRAMPTON GRANGE

Location	Flying Sqn	Other Flying Unit	Ac Type
Wyton	—	CCF	

No 22 GP: HQ — MARKET DRAYTON

Location	Flying Sqn	Other Flying Unit	Ac Type
Stoke Heath	—	GCF	

Controls various training establishments, e.g. Training.

No 24 GP: HQ — ASTON CLINTON
Controls SoTTs etc.

No 27 GP: HQ — COLERNE
Controls various units.

HOME COMMAND: HQ — WHITE WALTHAM

Location	Flying Sqn	Other Flying Unit	Ac Type
White Waltham	—	CCS	
White Waltham	—	EU	Anson/ Chipmunk/ Buckmaster

No 61 (EASTERN) GP: HQ — KENLEY

Location	Flying Sqn	Other Flying Unit	Ac Type
Booker	—	UAS (London)	Chipmunk
Cambridge	—	UAS (Cambridge)	Chipmunk
Cambridge	—	22 RFS	Anson/Chipmunk
Fairoaks	—	18 RFS	Anson/Chipmunk
Farnborough	—	MRF	Hastings/ Mosquito
Hendon	—	1958 AOP	Auster
Henlow	—	1959 AOP, 1961 AOP	Auster
Hornchurch	—	17 RFS	Anson/Chipmunk
Hornchurch	—	1 CAACU	
Kenley	661	1957 AOP, 1960 AOP	Auster
Little Snoring	—	2 CAACU	
Redhill	—	15 RFS	Chipmunk/Anson

No 62 (SOUTHERN) GP: HQ — PUCKLECHURCH

Location	Flying Sqn	Other Flying Unit	Ac Type
Blackbushe	622	—	Valetta
Booker	622	1 BFTS	Chipmunk
Colerne	662	1956 AOP, 1963 AOP	Auster
Exeter	662	10 RFS	Anson/Tiger Moth
Exeter	—	3 CAACU	
Filton	—	UAS (Bristol)	Chipmunk
Hamble	—	14 RFS	Chipmunk/Anson
Hamble	—	1 BANS	Anson
Kidlington	—	UAS (Oxford)	Chipmunk
Middle Wallop	—	1962 AOP	Auster
Southampton	—	UAS (Southampton)	Chipmunk

No 63 (WESTERN) GP: HQ — HAWARDEN

Location	Flying Sqn	Other Flying Unit	Ac Type
Hawarden	-	GCF	
Cardiff Airport	—	3 RFS	Chipmunk/Anson
Cardiff Airport	—	1952 AOP	Auster
Castle Bromwich	—	5 RFS	Chipmunk/Anson
Castle Bromwich	—	UAS (Birmingham)	Chipmunk
Hooton Park	663	1953 AOP, 1955 AOP	Auster
Llanbedr	—	5 CAACU	Vampire/ Beaufighter/ Spitfire
Llandow	—	4 CAACU	
Ringway	—	1951 AOP	Auster

Location	Flying Sqn	Other Flying Unit	Ac Type
Wolverhampton	—	1954 AOP	Auster
Woodvale	—	19 RFS	Chipmunk/Anson
Woodvale	—	UAS (Liverpool)	Chipmunk
Woodvale	—	UAS (Manchester)	Chipmunk

No 64 (NORTHERN) GP: HQ — RUFFORTH

Location	Flying Sqn	Other Flying Unit	Ac Type
Rufforth	-	GCF	
Derby	—	16 RFS	Prentice/Anson
Derby	—	3 BFTS	Chipmunk
Desford	—	7 RFS	Anson/ Tiger Moth
Desford	—	5 BFTS	Chipmunk
Desford	—	1969 AOP	Auster
Doncaster	—	9 RFS	Anson/ Tiger Moth
Hucknall	664	1970 AOP	Auster
Hull	—	UAS (Hull)	Chipmunk
Newton	—	UAS (Nottingham)	Chipmunk
Ouston	—	1965 AOP	Auster
Rufforth	—	1964 AOP	Auster
Sherburn-in-Elmet	—	UAS (Leeds)	Chipmunk
Sywell	—	4 BFTS	Chipmunk
Usworth	—	23 RFS	Chipmunk/Anson
Usworth	—	UAS (Durham)	Chipmunk

No 66 (SCOTTISH) GP: HQ — TURNHOUSE

Location	Flying Sqn	Other Flying Unit	Ac Type
Abbotsinch	—	1967 AOP	Auster
Dyce	—	UAS (Aberdeen)	Chipmunk
Leuchars	—	UAS (St Andrews)	Chipmunk
Perth	—	11 RFS	Anson/Chipmunk
Perth	—	UAS (Glasgow)	Chipmunk
Perth	—	1966 AOP	Auster
Turnhouse	—	UAS (Edinburgh)	Chipmunk
Turnhouse	—	1968 AOP	Auster

No 67 (NORTHERN IRELAND) GP: HQ — WHITE ABBEY

Location	Flying Sqn	Other Flying Unit	Ac Type
Aldergrove	—	GCF	
Sydenham	—	UAS (Queens)	Chipmunk

MAINTENANCE COMMANDER: HQ — ANDOVER

Location	Flying Sqn	Other Flying Unit	Ac Type
Andover	—	CCS	

No 40 GP: HQ — BICESTER
Nos: 3, 5, 7, 8, 9, 10, 12, 14, 15, 16, 19, 20, 22, 23, 25, 27, 29, 33, 35, 38, 39, 44, 45, 47, 48, 51, 61, 66, 72, 90, 99, 216, 225, 236, 248 MUs — mainly aircraft storage.
Plus the following (but under control of MoS)

Location	Flying Sqn	Other Flying Unit	Ac Type
Defford	—	TFU	
Felixstowe	—	MAEE	
Gosport	—	ATDU	
Henlow	—	PTU	
Martlesham Heath	—	AIEU	
West Freugh	—	BTU	

No 42 GP: HQ — KIDLINGTON
Nos: 2, 11, 28, 21, 31, 53, 92, 91, 93, 94, 95, 202, 243, 244, 277, 279, 280, 281, 282 MUs — mainly ammunition storage.

No 43 GP HQ — HUCKNALL

Location	Flying Sqn	Other Flying Unit	Ac Type
Hucknall	—	GCF	

Nos: 4, 30, 32, 34, 49, 54, 58, 60, 63, 238, 278 MUs — mainly repair and salvage units.

No 90 (SIGNALS) GP: HQ — MEDMENHAM

Location	Flying Sqn	Other Flying Unit	Ac Type
Watton	116	—	Anson/Lincoln
Watton	527	—	(various)
Watton	192	—	Canberra/ Washington

2nd TAF: HQ — BAD EILSEN

Location	Flying Sqn	Other Flying Unit	Ac Type
Buckeburg	—	CCF	
Buckeburg	—	1912 LL	Auster

Plus No 398 MU

No 2 GP: HQ — SUNDERN

Location	Flying Sqn	Other Flying Unit	Ac Type
Gutersloh	—	GCF	Anson/Mosquito

Location	Flying Sqn	Other Flying Unit	Ac Type
Ahlhorn	92, 256	—	Meteor
Ahlhorn	—	TDU	Canberra
Detmold	652	1901 AOP, 1904 AOP, 1905 AOP, 1909 AOP	Auster
Fassberg	14, 98, 228	—	Vampire
Gutersloh	2, 79, 541	—	Meteor
Jever	4, 93, 112	—	Vampire
Oldenburg	20, 26	—	Vampire
Oldenburg	234	—	Vampire/Meteor
Sylt	—	APC	Tempest
Wunstorf	5, 266	—	Venom/Meteor
Wunstorf	11	—	Vampire

No 83 GP: HQ — WAHN

Location	Flying Sqn	Other Flying Unit	Ac Type
Wahn	—	GCF	
Celle	16, 94, 145	—	Vampire/Meteor
Wahn	68, 87	—	Meteor
Wildenrath	3, 67, 71	—	Vampire/Meteor
Wildenrath	—	SCF	Sabre

The RAF acquired Sabres as a stop-gap pending service entry of the Hunter: 66 Squadron at Linton-on-Ouse.

MIDDLE EAST AIR FORCE: HQ — ISMAILIA/ABU SUEIR

Location	Flying Sqn	Other Flying Unit	Ac Type
Ismailia	651	1910 AOP	Auster

AHQ MALTA: HQ — VALLETTA

Location	Flying Sqn	Other Flying Unit	Ac Type
Luqa	—	CCF	
Luqa	37, 38	—	Lancaster
Takali	73	—	Vampire
Plus Nos 137, 397 MUs.			

AHQ IRAQ: HQ — HABBANIYA

Location	Flying Sqn	Other Flying Unit	Ac Type
Habbaniya	—	CCF	
Habbaniya	6	—	Vampire
Habbaniya	185	—	Vampire/Meteor
Habbaniya	683	—	Lancaster
Plus No 115 MU.			

ADEN: HQ — STEAMER POINT

Location	Flying Sqn	Other Flying Unit	Ac Type
Eastleigh	—	GCF	Anson/Valetta/Proctor
Khormaksar	8	—	Vampire/Meteor
Khormaksar	—	APSF	Anson/Auster
Plus No 114 MU.			

No 205 GP: HQ — FAYID

Location	Flying Sqn	Other Flying Unit	Ac Type
Fayid	—	GCF	Anson/Proctor
Abu Sueir	208	—	Meteor
Deversoir	32, 213, 249	—	Vampire
El Hamra	—	1908 AOP	Auster
Kabrit	13, 39, 219	—	Meteor
Nicosia	—	MEAF 1TF	Meteor
Nicosia	—	MEAF TTF	Meteor

No 206 GP: HQ — ABYAD
Nos 109, 128 MUs.

TRANSPORT WING — FAYID

Location	Flying Sqn	Other Flying Unit	Ac Type
Fayid	70, 78, 84, 114, 216	—	Valetta
Fayid	—	Special CF	

FAR EAST AIR FORCE: HQ — CHANGI, SINGAPORE
AHQ HONG KONG

Location	Flying Sqn	Other Flying Unit	Ac Type
Hong Kong	—	1900 AOP	Auster
Iwakuni, Japan	—	1903 AOP, 1913 LL	Auster
Kai Tak	28	—	Vampire
Kai Tak	80	—	Hornet

AHQ CEYLON: HQ — NEGOMBO
Controls various staging posts and signals units.

AHQ MALAYA: HQ — CHANGI

Location	Flying Sqn	Other Flying Unit	Ac Type
Butterworth	33	—	Hornet
Butterworth	—	27 ADC	Beaufighter
Changi (FE Transport Wing)	48, 523, 110	—	Valetta
Changi	—	FEAF CS	Valetta/Auster
Kuala Lipis	—	1911 LL	Auster
Kuala Lumpur	656	—	Auster
Seletar (FE FB Wing)	88, 205, 209	—	Sunderland
Sembawang	194	-	Dragonfly
Sembawang	—	1907 LL	Auster
Seremban	—	1914 AOP	Auster
Taiping	—	1902 AOP	Auster
Tengah	45	—	Hornet
Tengah	60	—	Vampire

AHQ SINGAPORE: HQ — SELETAR

Location	Flying Sqn	Other Flying Unit	Ac Type
Seletar	81	—	Mosquito
Plus No 390 MU			

RHODESIA AIR TRAINING GP: HQ — KUMALO
Under the operational control of FTC.

Location	Flying Sqn	Other Flying Unit	Ac Type
Heany, Bulawayo	—	4 FTS	Harvard/Chipmunk
Kumalo, Bulawayo	—	GCF	
Thornhill, Gwelo	—	5 FTS	Harvard/Chipmunk

Plus Nos 394, 395 MUs.

April 1962
BOMBER COMMAND: HQ — HIGH WYCOMBE

Location	Flying Sqn	Other Flying Unit	Ac Type
Booker	—	CCS	Anson/Chipmunk/Pembroke/Meteor

No 1 GP: HQ — BAWTRY

Location	Flying Sqn	Other Flying Unit	Ac Type
Finningley	—	GCF	Anson/Chipmunk
Bassingbourn	231 OCU	—	Canberra
Coningsby	9	—	Vulcan
Driffield	98	—	Thor SSM
Full Sutton	102	—	Thor SSM
Carnaby	150	—	Thor SSM
Catfoss	226	—	Thor SSM
Breighton	240	—	Thor SSM
Finningley	18	—	Valiant/Canberra
Finningley	230 OCU	—	Vulcan
Hemswell	97	—	Thor SSM
Ludford Magna	104	—	Thor SSM
Bardney	106	—	Thor SSM
Coleby Grange	142	—	Thor SSM
Caister	269	—	Thor SSM
Lindholme	—	CBS	Hastings/Varsity
Scampton	27, 83, 617	—	Vulcan
Waddington	44, 50, 101	—	Vulcan

No 3 GP: HQ — MILDENHALL

Location	Flying Sqn	Other Flying Unit	Ac Type
Mildenhall	—	GCF	Anson/Chipmunk
Cottesmore	10, 15	—	Victor

Location	Flying Sqn	Other Flying Unit	Ac Type

Thor ICBM of 107 Squadron, Feltwell.

Location	Flying Sqn	Other Flying Unit	Ac Type
Feltwell	77	—	Thor SSM
Shepherds Grove	82	—	Thor SSM
Tuddenham	107	—	Thor SSM
Mepal	113	—	Thor SSM
North Pickenham	220	—	Thor SSM
Gaydon	232 OCU	—	Valiant/Canberra
Gaydon	—	RAF	Victor
Honington	55, 57	—	Victor
Honington	90	—	Valiant
Marham	49, 148, 207, 214	—	Valiant
North Luffenham	144	—	Thor SSM
Polebrook	130	—	Thor SSM
Harrington	218	—	Thor SSM
Folkingham	223	—	Thor SSM
Melton Mowbray	254	—	Thor SSM
Wittering	7, 138	—	Valiant
Wittering	139	—	Victor
Wyton	58	—	Canberra
Wyton	543	—	Valiant

The clean aerodynamic lines of the Valiant.

FIGHTER COMMAND: HQ — STANMORE

Location	Flying Sqn	Other Flying Unit	Ac Type
Bovingdon	—	CCS	Anson/Meteor

No 11 GP: HQ — LECONFIELD

Location	Flying Sqn	Other Flying Unit	Ac Type
Leconfield	—	GCF	Anson/Meteor
Chivenor	229 OCU	—	Hunter/Vampire
Leconfield	19, 92	—	Hunter

Location	Flying Sqn	Other Flying Unit	Ac Type
Leuchars	25, 29	—	Javelin
Middleton St George	33	—	Javelin
Misson	94	—	Bloodhound SAM
Breighton	112	—	Bloodhound SAM
Carnaby	247	—	Bloodhound SAM
North Coates	264	—	Bloodhound SAM
Dunholme Lodge	141	—	Bloodhound SAM
Woodhall Spa	222	—	Bloodhound SAM

No 12 GP: HQ — HORSHAM ST FAITH

Location	Flying Sqn	Other Flying Unit	Ac Type
Horsham St Faith	—	GCF	Anson/Meteor
Coltishall	23	—	Javelin
Coltishall	74	AFDS	Lightning
Woolfox Lodge	62	—	Bloodhound SAM
Warboys	257	—	Bloodhound SAM
Old Sarum	—	S of L/AW	Anson/Vampire/ Chipmunk
Wattisham	41	—	Javelin
Wattisham	56, 111	—	Lightning
Watton	263	—	Bloodhound SAM
Marham	242	—	Bloodhound SAM
Rattlesden	266	—	Bloodhound SAM
West Raynham	85	—	Javelin
West Raynham	—	CFE	Hunter/Javelin
West Raynham	—	TFS	

COASTAL COMMAND: HQ — NORTHWOOD

Location	Flying Sqn	Other Flying Unit	Ac Type
Bovingdon	—	CCF	Anson
Londonderry	—	JASS	Shackleton
Ballykelly	—	ASWDU	Shackleton/ Sycamore

No 18 GP: HQ — PITREAVIE CASTLE

Location	Flying Sqn	Other Flying Unit	Ac Type
Turnhouse	—	GCF	Anson/Dakota
Aldergrove	202	—	Hastings
Ballykelly	203, 204, 210	—	Shackleton
Kinloss	120	—	Shackleton
Leconfield	228	—	Whirlwind

No 19 GP: HQ — MOUNT BATTEN

Location	Flying Sqn	Other Flying Unit	Ac Type
St Mawgan	22	—	Whirlwind
St Mawgan	42, 201, 206	—	Shackleton

AHQ Gibraltar: HQ — New Camp

Location	Flying Sqn	Other Flying Unit	Ac Type
North Front	224	—	Shackleton

TRAINING COMMAND: HQ — UPAVON

Location	Flying Sqn	Other Flying Unit	Ac Type
Upavon	—	CCF	Anson/Devon/ Chipmunk
Benson	114	—	Argosy
Benson	—	QF	Heron/ Chipmunk/ Whirlwind
Lyneham	99, 511	—	Britannia
Lyneham	216	—	Comet
Northolt	—	MCS	Devon/ Pembroke/ Valetta/ Sycamore
Thorney Island	242 OCU	—	Hastings/Valetta/ Beverley

No 38 GP: HQ — ODIHAM

Location	Flying Sqn	Other Flying Unit	Ac Type
Abingdon	47, 53	—	Beverley

Location	Flying Sqn	Other Flying Unit	Ac Type
Abingdon	—	1 PTS	Hastings
Aldergrove	118	—	Sycamore
Colerne	24, 36	—	Hastings
Odiham	66, 72	—	Belvedere
Odiham	225	—	Sycamore/ Whirlwind
Odiham	230	—	Pioneer
Odiham	—	SF/GCF	Anson/Devon/ Chipmunk
Waterbeach	1, 54	—	Hunter
Waterbeach	64	—	Javelin

FLYING TRAINING COMMAND: HQ — READING

Location	Flying Sqn	Other Flying Unit	Ac Type
White Waltham	—	CCS	Anson/ Pembroke/ Chipmunk
Little Rissington	—	CFS	(various)
Bicester	—	UAS (Oxford)	Chipmunk
Filton	—	UAS (British)	Chipmunk
Hamble	—	UAS (Southampton)	Chipmunk
Cranwell	—	RAF College	(various)
Manby	—	RAF FC	(various)

No 23 GP: HQ — DISHFORTH

Location	Flying Sqn	Other Flying Unit	Ac Type
Dishforth	—	GCF	Anson/Meteor/ Provost
Acklington	—	6 FTS	Provost
Dishford	—	UAS (Leeds)	Chipmunk
Linton-on-Ouse	—	1 FTS	Provost/Vampire
Newton	—	UAS (Nottingham)	Chipmunk
Oakington	—	5 FTS	Varsity
Ouston	—	UAS (Durham)	Chipmunk
Shawbury	—	8 FTS	Vampire/Meteor
Syerston	—	2 FTS	Provost
Valley	—	4 FTS	Vampire
Woodvale	—	UAS (Liverpool)	Chipmunk
Woodvale	—	UAS (Manchester)	Chipmunk
Woodvale	—	SCAACU	Meteor/Mosquito

No 25 GP: HQ — WHITE WALTHAM

Location	Flying Sqn	Other Flying Unit	Ac Type
Brough	—	UAS (Hull)	Chipmunk
Cambridge	—	UAS (Cambridge)	Chipmunk
Dyce	—	UAS (Aberdeen)	Chipmunk
Exeter	—	3/4 CAACU	Chipmunk/ Mosquito
Hullavington	—	2 ANS	Valetta/Varsity/ Vampire
Leuchars	—	UAS (St Andrews)	Chipmunk
Perth	—	UAS (Glasgow)	Chipmunk
Shawbury	—	UAS (Birmingham)	Chipmunk
Shawbury	—	CNCS	Valetta/ Chipmunk/ Provost/Varsity
South Cerney	—	1 ITS	Anson/Chipmunk
Stradishall	—	1 ANS	Valetta/Varsity/ Marathon
Sydenham	—	UAS (Queens)	Chipmunk
Topcliffe	-	AES	Varsity
Turnhouse	—	UAS (Edinburgh)	Chipmunk
White Waltham	—	UAS (London)	Chipmunk

TECHNICAL TRAINING COMMAND: HQ — BRAMPTON

Location	Flying Sqn	Other Flying Unit	Ac Type
Wyton	—	CCF	Devon/Anson/ Chipmunk
Henlow (RAF Technical College)	—	—	Chipmunk/Anson

No 22 GP: HQ — MARKET DRAYTON

Location	Flying Sqn	Other Flying Unit	Ac Type
Stoke Heath	—	GCF	Anson/Chipmunk
Jurby	—	OCTU	Ansons

Control of wide range of units, e.g. RAF Regiments, SoTTS, QCs, C10s, etc.

No 24 GP HQ —

Location	Flying Sqn	Other Flying Unit	Ac Type
Colerne	—	GCF	Anson
Cosford	—	2 SoTT	Chipmunk
Locking	—	1 RS	Varsity

MAINTENANCE COMMAND: HQ — ANDOVER

Location	Flying Sqn	Other Flying Unit	Ac Type
Andover	—	CCFS	Anson/Devon

The following units under AM control:

Location	Flying Sqn	Other Flying Unit	Ac Type
Farnborough	—	ETPS	(various)
Farnborough	—	MRF	

Nos: 2, 5, 11, 14, 15, 16, 7, 19, 21, 25, 27, 30, 32, 33, 35, 49, 60, 71, 92, 94, 99, 217, 236, 248 MUs.

SIGNALS COMMAND: HQ — MEDMENHAM

Location	Flying Sqn	Other Flying Unit	Ac Type
Tangmere	115	—	Varsity/Hastings
Tangmere	245	—	Canberra/Varsity
Watton	51	—	Canberra/Comet
Watton	151	—	Canberra/ Lincoln/ Hastings/Varsity
Watton	—	CSE	Lincoln

NEAR EAST COMMAND: HQ — EPISKOPI
NEAR EAST AIR FORCE: HQ — EPISKOPI

Location	Flying Sqn	Other Flying Unit	Ac Type
Akrotiri	6, 13, 32, 73, 249	—	Canberra
Nicosia	43	—	Hunter
Nicosia	70	—	Hastings/Valetta/ Pembroke
Nicosia	103	—	Sycamore

Plus Nos 103, 113 MUs.

AHQ MALTA: HQ — VALLETTA

Location	Flying Sqn	Other Flying Unit	Ac Type
Luqa	38	—	Shackleton
Luqa	39	—	Canberra
Takali	—	CGETTS	Devon/Meteor/ Valetta

AIR FORCES MIDDLE EAST: HQ — BAHREIN (RAF PERSIAN GULF)

Location	Flying Sqn	Other Flying Unit	Ac Type
Bahrein	152	—	Pembroke/ Twin Pioneer
Eastleigh	21	—	Twin Pioneer
Eastleigh	30	—	Beverley
Khormaksar	8, 208	—	Hunter
Khormaksar	37	—	Shackleton
Khormaksar	78	—	Twin Pioneer
Khormaksar	84	—	Beverley
Khormaksar	233	—	Valetta
Khormaksar	—	MECS	Hastings/ Camberra/ Valetta/ Dakota

Plus No 114 MU.

FAR EAST AIR FORCE: HQ — CHANGI

Location	Flying Sqn	Other Flying Unit	Ac Type
Changi	—	CCS	
Changi	48	—	Hastings
Changi	205	—	Shackleton

Plus Nos 389, 390 MUs.

AHQ HONG KONG

Location	Flying Sqn	Other Flying Unit	Ac Type
Kai Tak	28	—	Hunter

No 224 GP: HQ — SELETAR

Location	Flying Sqn	Other Flying Unit	Ac Type
Butterworth	52	—	Valetta
Butterworth	110	—	Sycamore
Seletar	34	—	Beverley
Seletar	209	—	Pioneer/ Twin Pioneer
Seletar	—	GCF	Meteor/ Pembroke
Tengah	20	—	Hunter
Tengah	45, 81	—	Canberra
Tengah	60	—	Javelin

RAF GERMANY (2nd TAF): HQ — RHEINDAHLEN

Location	Flying Sqn	Other Flying Unit	Ac Type
Wildenrath	—	CCS	Meteor/ Pembroke
Bruggen	80, 213	—	Canberra
Geilenkirchen	3	—	Canberra
Geilenkirchen	11	—	Javelin

Location	Flying Sqn	Other Flying Unit	Ac Type
Gutersloh	2, 4, 14	—	Hunter
Laarbruch	5	—	Javelin
Laarbruch	16, 31	—	Canberra
Wildenrath	17, 88	—	Canberra
Plus Nos 431, 420, MUs.			

April 1972
STRIKE COMMAND: HQ — HIGH WYCOMBE

Location	Flying Sqn	Other Flying Unit	Ac Type
Northolt	207	—	Basset/Devon/ Pembroke

No 1 GP: HQ — BAWTRY

Location	Flying Sqn	Other Flying Unit	Ac Type
Cottesmore	98, 360, 231 OCU	—	Canberra
Cottesmore	115	—	Argosy
Honington	12, 237 OCU	—	Buccaneer
Lindholme	—	STC BS	Hastings
Marham	55, 57, 214 232 OCU	—	Victor
Scampton	617	230 OCU	
Waddington	44, 50, 101	—	Vulcan
Wyton	39	—	Canberra
Wyton	51	—	Canberra/Comet
Wyton	543	—	Victor

No 11 GP: HQ —

Location	Flying Sqn	Other Flying Unit	Ac Type
Binbrook	5, 11	—	Lightning
Chivenor	229 OCU	—	Hunter
Coltishall	65, 226 OCU	—	Lightning
Kinloss	8	—	Shackleton
Leuchars	23	—	Lightning
Leuchars	43	—	Phantom
Wattisham	29, 111	—	Lightning
West Raynham	85, 100	—	Canberra

No 18 GP: HQ — NORTHWOOD

Location	Flying Sqn	Other Flying Unit	Ac Type
Honington	204	—	Shackleton
Acklington	202	—	Whirlwind
Kinloss	120, 201, 206	—	Nimrod
Leconfield	202	—	Whirlwind
St Mawgan	7	—	Canberra
St Mawgan	22	—	Whirlwind
St Mawgan	42, 236 OCU	—	Nimrod

No 90 GP: HQ — MEDMENHAM

AIR SUPPORT COMMAND: HQ — UPAVON

Location	Flying Sqn	Other Flying Unit	Ac Type
Andover	21	—	Devon/Pembroke
Benson	—	QF	Andover/ Chipmunk/ Heron/Whirlwind
Brize Norton	10	—	VC10
Brize Norton	53	—	Belfast
Brize Norton	99, 511	—	Britannia
Brize Norton	241 OCU	—	Belfast/ Britannia/VC10
Coningsby	228 OCU	—	Phantom
Lyneham	216	—	Comet
Northolt	32	—	Andover/ Dominie/ Basset/ Whirlwind
Odiham	240 OCU	—	Puma/Wessex
Thorney Island	242 OCU	—	Andover/ Hercules
Wittering	233 OCU	—	Harrier

HONG KONG

Location	Flying Sqn	Other Flying Unit	Ac Type
Kai Tak	28	—	Wessex/ Whirlwind
Tengah, Singapore	103	—	Whirlwind

No 38 GP: HQ — BENSON

Location	Flying Sqn	Other Flying Unit	Ac Type
Coningsby	6, 54	—	Phantom
Lyneham	24, 30, 36, 47, 48	—	Hercules
Odiham	33, 230	—	Puma

Location	Flying Sqn	Other Flying Unit	Ac Type
Odiham	72	—	Wessex
Thorney Island	46	—	Andover
Wittering	1	—	Harrier

TRAINING COMMAND: HQ — BRAMPTON

Location	Flying Sqn	Other Flying Unit	Ac Type
Wyton	26	—	Basset/Devon
Little Rissington	—	CFS	Chipmunk/Gnat/ Varsity/ Jet Provost
Tern Hill	—	CFS	Whirlwind/Sioux
Cranwell	—	RAF College	Chipmunk/ Jet Provost
Abotsinch	—	UAS (Glasgow & Strathclyde)	Chipmunk
Bicester	—	UAS (Oxford)	Chipmunk
Cambridge	—	UAS (Cambridge)	Chipmunk
Church Fenton	—	UAS (Yorkshire)	Chipmunk
Dyce	—	UAS (Aberdeen)	Chipmunk
Filton	—	UAS (Bristol)	Chipmunk
Hamble	—	UAS (Southampton)	Chipmunk
Newton	—	UAS (East Midlands)	Chipmunk
Ouston	—	UAS (Northumberland)	Chipmunk
St Athan	—	UAS (Wales)	Chipmunk
Shawbury	—	UAS (Birmingham)	Chipmunk
Sydenham	—	UAS (Queens)	Chipmunk
Turnhouse	—	UAS (East Lowlands)	Chipmunk
White Waltham	—	UAS (London)	Chipmunk
Woodvale	—	UAS (Liverpool/Manchester)	Chipmunk
Manby	—	CAW	Dominie/Varsity/ Jet Provost

No 23 GP: HQ — LINTON-ON-OUSE

Location	Flying Sqn	Other Flying Unit	Ac Type
Church Fenton	—	2 FTS	Chipmunk
Finningley	—	6 FTS	Dominie/Varsity/ Jet Provost
Leeming	—	3 FTS	Jet Provost
Linton-on-Ouse	—	1 FTS	Chipmunk/ Jet Provost
Oakington	—	5 FTS	Varsity
Shawbury	—	ATCS	Jet Provost
Topcliffe	—	AE & AES	Varsity
Valley	—	4 FTS	Gnat/Hunter

No 24 Gp: HQ — RUDLOE MANOR

MAINTENANCE COMMAND: HQ — ANDOVER

Location	Flying Sqn	Other Flying Unit	Ac Type
Boscombe Down	-	RAF HS	Canberra/Hunter

NEAR EAST AIR FORCE:

Location	Flying Sqn	Other Flying Unit	Ac Type
Akrotiri	9, 35	—	Vulcan
Akrotiri	13	—	Canberra
Akrotiri	56	—	Lightning
Akrotiri	70	-	Hercules
Akrotiri	84	—	Whirlwind
Sigonella, Sicily	203	—	Nimrod

RAF GERMANY:

Location	Flying Sqn	Other Flying Unit	Ac Type
Bruggen	14, 17, 31	—	Phantom
Gutersloh	18	—	Wessex
Gutersloh	19, 92	—	Lightning
Laarbruch	2	—	Phantom
Laarbruch	15	—	Buccaneer
Wildenrath	20, 3 4	—	Harrier
Wildenrath	60	—	Pembroke/Heron

January 1982
STRIKE COMMAND: HQ — HIGH WYCOMBE

Location	Flying Sqn	Other Flying Unit	Ac Type
Farnborough	—	IAM	Canberra/Hunter
Sek Kong (Hong Kong)	28	—	Wessex

No 1 GP: HQ — BAWTRY

Location	Flying Sqn	Other Flying Unit	Ac Type
Cottesmore	TTTE	—	Tornado
Honington	208, 237 OCU	—	Buccaneer
Honington	TWCU	—	Tornado
Lossiemouth	12	—	Buccaneer

Location	Flying Sqn	Other Flying Unit	Ac Type
Marham	55, 57, 232 OCU	—	Victor
Marham	231 OCU	—	Canberra
Scampton	27, 35	—	Vulcan
Waddington	9, 44, 50, 101	—	Vulcan
Wyton	39, 100, 360	—	Canberra
Wyton	51	—	Nimrod
Bawdsey	85 det	—	Bloodhound SAM

No 11 GP: HQ — BENTLEY PRIORY

Location	Flying Sqn	Other Flying Unit	Ac Type
Binbrook	5, 11	LTF	Lightning
Brawdy	ITWU	CEDIT	Hunter/Hawk
Chivenor	2 TWU	—	Hawk
Coningsby	29, 228 OCU	—	Phantom
Leuchars	43, 111	—	Phantom
Lossiemouth	8	—	Shackleton
North Coates	85 det	—	Bloodhound SAM
Wattisham	23, 56	—	Phantom
Wattisham	85 det	—	Bloodhound SAM
West Raynham	85 det	—	Bloodhound SAM

No 18 GP: HQ — NORTHWOOD

Location	Flying Sqn	Other Flying Unit	Ac Type
Finningley	22 HQ	—	Wessex/Whirlwind
Finningley	202 HQ	—	Sea King
Boulmer	202 (A Flt)	—	Sea King
Kinloss	120, 201, 206	—	Nimrod
Leconfield	22 (D Flt)	—	Wessex
Leuchars	22 (B Flt)	—	Wessex
Lossiemouth	202 (D Flt)	—	Sea King
Valley	22 (C Flt)	SARTU	Wessex
Brawdy	202 (B Flt)	—	Sea King
Chivenor	22 (A Flt)	—	Wessex
Coltishall	202 (C Flt)	—	Sea King
Manston	22 (E Flt)	—	Wessex
St Mawgan	42, 236 OCU	—	Nimrod

No 38 GP: HQ — UPAVON

Location	Flying Sqn	Other Flying Unit	Ac Type
Aldergrove	72	—	Wessex
Belize	—	1417	Harrier
Benson	—	QF	Andover/Wessex
Benson	—	WTF	Wessex
Brize Norton	10, 241 OCU	-	VC10
Brize Norton	115	—	Andover
Cottishall	6, 41, 54	—	Jaguar
Lossiemouth	226 OCU	—	Jaguar
Lyneham	24, 30, 47, 70, 242 OCU	—	Hercules
Northolt	32	—	Andover/Gazelle/HS 125/Whirlwind
Northolt	207	—	Devon
Odiham	18	—	Chinook
Odiham	33	—	Puma
Odiham	240 OCU	—	Chinook/Puma
Wittering	1, 233 OCU	—	Harrier
Church Fenton	—	7 FTS	Jet Provost
Cranwell	—	RAF College	Jet Provost
Farnborough	—	MRF	Hercules
Finningley	—	6 FTS	Dominie/Jet Provost
Finningley	—	METS	Jetstream
Kemble	—	CFS (Red Arrows)	Hawk
Leeming	—	3 FTS	Bulldog/Jet Provost
Leeming	—	CFS	Bulldog/Jet Provost/Chipmunk
Linton-on-Ouse	—	1 FTS	Jet Provost
Shawbury	—	2 FTS	Gazelle/Wessex
Shawbury	—	CFS	Gazelle
Swinderby	—	FSS	Chipmunk
Valley	—	4 FTS	Hawk

Plus 27 Air Cadet Gliding Schools and 13 Air Experience Flights.

ROYAL AIR FORCE GERMANY:

Location	Flying Sqn	Other Flying Unit	Ac Type
Bruggen	14, 17, 20, 31	—	Jaguar
Bruggen	25 det	—	Bloodhound SAM
Gatow	—	CF	Chipmunk
Gutersloh	230	—	Puma
Gutersloh	3, 4	—	Harrier
Laarbruch	2	—	Jaguar
Laarbruch	2	—	Buccaneer
Wildenrath	19, 92	—	Phantom
Wildenrath	60	—	Pembroke
Wildenrath	25 det	—	Bloodhound SAM

Tornado GR.1A of 2 Squadron outside its HAS at Laarbruch.

ROYAL AIR FORCE ORDER OF BATTLE (ORBAT) — CURRENT

At the time that this book went to press, the RAF ORBAT was as follows: (Reserve Squadrons are marked*. Training variants in use with squadrons, e.g. Jaguar T.2 are not listed).

SQUADRON	LOCATION	PRIMARY AIRCRAFT TYPE	PRIMARY ROLE(S)
1 (F)	Wittering	Harrier GR.7	CAS/BAI
II (AC)	Marham	Tornado GR.1A	TR/A
3 (AC)	Laarbruch	Harrier GR.7	CAS/BAI/TR
IV (AC)	Laarbruch	Harrier GR.7	CAS/BAI
5	Coningsby	Tornado F.3	AD
6	Coltishall	Jaguar	GA
7	Odiham	Chinook HC.1	SH
8	Waddington	Sentry E.3D	AWAC
IX	Bruggen	Tornado GR.1	SA
10	Brize Norton	VC.10 C.1/C.1K	T/AAR
11 (F)	Leeming	Tornado F.3	AD
12[3]	Lossiemouth	Buccaneer S.2B	AS
		Hunter T.7	
XIII (PR)	Honington	Tornado GR.1A	TR/A
14	Bruggen	Tornado GR.1	SA
XV*	Honington	Tornado GR.1	TR/SA
16*	Lossiemouth	Jaguar	SA/OCU
17	Bruggen	Tornado GR.1	SA
18	Laarbruch	Chinook HC.1	SH
		Puma HC.1	
19*	Chivenor	Hawk	TR
20*	Wittering	Harrier	TR/CAS/BAI OCU
22	Det Flts	Wessex HC.2	SAR
23	Leeming	Tornado F.3	AD
24	Lyneham	Hercules	T
25	Leeming	Tornado F.3	AD
27[3]*	Marham	Tornado GR.1	SA
28	Sek Kong	Wessex HC.2	SH
29	Coningsby	Tornado F.3	AD
30	Lyneham	Hercules	T
31	Bruggen	Tornado GR.1	SA
32	Northolt	BAe 125	C
		Andover	
		Gazelle	
33	Odiham	Puma HC.1	SH
39*	Wyton	Canberra PR.9	SR
41	Coltishall	Jaguar	CAS/BAI
42*	Kinloss	Nimrod MR.2P	ASW/MPA OCU
43	Leuchars	Tornado F.3	AD
45	Finningley	Jetstream	TR
47	Lyneham	Hercules	T
51	Wyton	Nimrod R.1	INT
54	Coltishall	Jaguar	CAS/BAI
55[4]*	Marham	Victor K.2	AAR
56*	Coningsby	Tornado F.3	AD OCU
57*	Lyneham	Hercules	T OCU
60	Benson	Wessex HC.2	SH
70	Lyneham	Hercules	T
72	Aldergrove	Wessex HC.2	SH
74*	Valley	Hawk	TR
78	Mount Pleasant	Chinook HC.1	SH
		Sea King HAR.3	SAR
84	Akrotiri	Wessex HC.5C	SH/SAR
92*	Chivenor	Hawk	TR
100	Wyton	Hawk	TF
101	Brize Norton	VC.10 K.2/K.3	AAR
111	Leuchars	Tornado F.3	AD
115[1]	Benson	Andover E.3	CAL
120	Kinloss	Nimrod MR.2P	ASW/MPA
201	Kinloss	Nimrod MR.2P	ASW/MPA
202	Det Flts	Sea King HAR.3	SAR
206	Kinloss	Nimrod MR.2P	ASW
208[3]	Lossiemouth	Buccaneer S.2B	AS
		Hunter T.7	
216	Brize Norton	Tristar K.1/KC.1/C.2	AAR/T
230	Aldergrove	Puma HC.1	SH
234*	Valley	Hawk	TR
360	Wyton	Canberra T.17A	EW
617[3]	Marham	Tornado GR.1	SA
1312 Flt	Mount Pleasant	Hercules	AAR/MPA/SAR
1417 Flt[2]	Belize	Harrier GR.3	CAS/R

SQUADRON	LOCATION	PRIMARY AIRCRAFT TYPE	PRIMARY ROLE(S)
1435 Flt	Mount Pleasant	Tornado F.3	AD
1563 Flt	Belize	Puma HC.1	SH/SAR
240 OCU	Odiham	Chinook HC.1	SH OCU
		Puma HC.1	
241 OCU	Brize Norton	VC.10 C.1	T OCU
SF	Berlin	Chipmunk T.10	C
TTTE	Cottesmore	Tornado GR.1	TR
SARTU	Valley	Wessex HC.2	TR
SKTF	St Mawgan	Sea King HAR.3	TR
QF	Benson	BAe 146	VIP C
		Wessex HCC.4	
SAOEU	Boscombe Down	(various)	Trials
F3 OEU	Coningsby	Tornado F.3	Trials
IAM	Farnborough	(various)	Trials
BBMF	Coningsby	(various historical)	
CFS	Scampton	Tucano/Bulldog/Hawk	TR
	Shawbury	Gazelle HT.3	TR
	Valley	Hawk	TR
	Syerston	(various gliders)	TR
EETS	Swinderby	Chipmunk T.10	TR
1 FTS	Linton-on-Ouse	Tucano/Bulldog	TR
2 FTS	Shawbury	Gazelle HT.3/Wessex HC.2	TR
3 FTS	Cranwell	Tucano T.1	TR
4 FTS	Valley	Hawk T.1/T.1A	TR
6 FTS	Finningley	Bulldog/Jet Provost/Hawk	TR
		Dominie/Jetstream	
7 FTS	Chivenor	Hawk T.1/T.1A	TR

UAS (all Bulldog T.1) —
Aberdeen, Dundee & St Andrews (Leuchars).
Birmingham (Cosford)
Bristol (Colerne).
Cambridge (Teversham).
East Lowlands (Edinburgh).
East Midlands (Newton).
Glasgow & Strathclyde (Glasgow).
Liverpool (Woodvale).
London (Benson).
Manchester (Woodvale).
Northumbria (Leeming).
Oxford (Benson).
Queens (Sydenham).
Southampton (Lee-on-Solent).
University of Wales (St Athan).
Yorkshire (Finningley).

AEF (all Chipmunk T.10) —
1 — Manston.
2 — Hurn.
3 — Colerne.
4 — Exeter.
5 — Teversham.
6 — Benson.
7 — Newton.
8 — Shawbury.
9 — Finningley.
10 — Woodvale.
11 — Leeming.
12. — Turnhouse.
13. — Sydenham.

VGS — 27 schools.

GROUP STRUCTURE. With the renaming of RAFG as No. 2 Gp, the squadron distribution was as follows:
No. 1 Gp — 1, II, 6, 7, XIII, XV, 16, 20, 27, 33, 41, 54, 60, 72, 230, 617 Sqns.
No. 2 Gp — 3, IV, IX, 14, 17, 18, 31 Sqns.
No. 11 Gp — 5, 8, 11, 23, 25, 29, 43, 56, 111 Sqns.
No. 18 Gp — 12, 22, 39, 42, 51, 100 120, 201, 202, 206, 208, 360 Sqns.
No. 38 Gp — 10, 24, 30, 32, 47, 55, 70, 101, 115, 216 Sqns.

Notes:
1 Due to disband 1.10.93.
2 Due to disband mid '93.
3 Late '93/early '94 two Tornado Sqns to move to Lossiemouth from Marham to replace Buccaneers in maritime S/A role; leave No 1 GP and join No 18 GP. No 27 Sqn will become No 12 Sqn, No 208 Sqn disbands, replaced by No 617 Sqn. No 27 Sqn numberplate to No 240 OCU.
4 Disband 15.10.93 numberplate to 241 OCU.

RAF Structure

All military organisations are, in theory, highly structured and leave no doubt as to the chain of command from the very top level down to the smallest unit. However, it is seldom as simple or obvious as that! During peacetime the ideal is usually achieved, there being plenty of time and hordes of people to sort out the paperwork. However, the wartime situation is nothing like as straightforward, often for the very simple reason that in fluid situations, such as that pertaining in the Far East in 1942, it became difficult to apply the theory. It is certainly true that most of the problems come with a consideration of the command structure in the overseas theatres.

The following sections look at each level of RAF structure from Command level down to Squadrons, with a final section providing a list of numbered Flights. There is a great deal of research crying out to be done in the area of Command, Group and Wing histories and the material presented here is very much an outline of the subject.

COMMANDS

The highest formation, under War Office/Air Minsitry/Minstry of Defence, is the Command, all other branches of the 'chain of command' spring from this. Throughout RAF history the precise nature of this chain has undergone changes, but in general terms the principles have remained the same. One of the most confusing aspects is that of subordinate Commands, whereby the structure may include two or three Command levels before moving down to lower, Group or Wing, level. These Command levels have been given various names including Supra-Command (the top of the tree), Higher Command, and Subordinate Command; such a structure was very evident in the Allied organisation in the Mediterranean and Far East areas from 1942 onwards (the organisational charts in the following pages serve to clarify this arrangement).

Also, certain lower formations may report direct to Command or even to the Air Ministry, the latter often applied to Special Duties elements in the early years of World War Two.

A typical structural tree, this one being India Command 1943, illustrates the basic principles and arrangement:

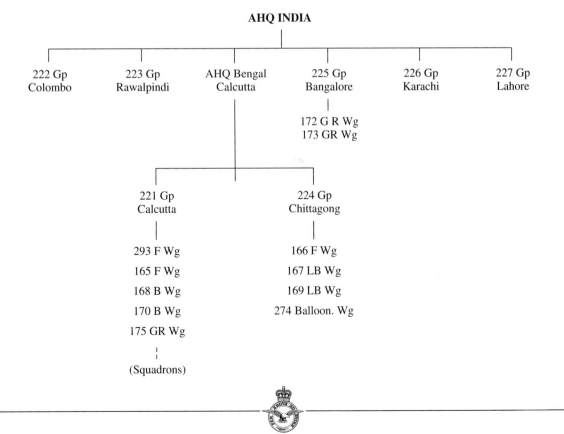

COMMAND CHRONOLOGY — Home Commands

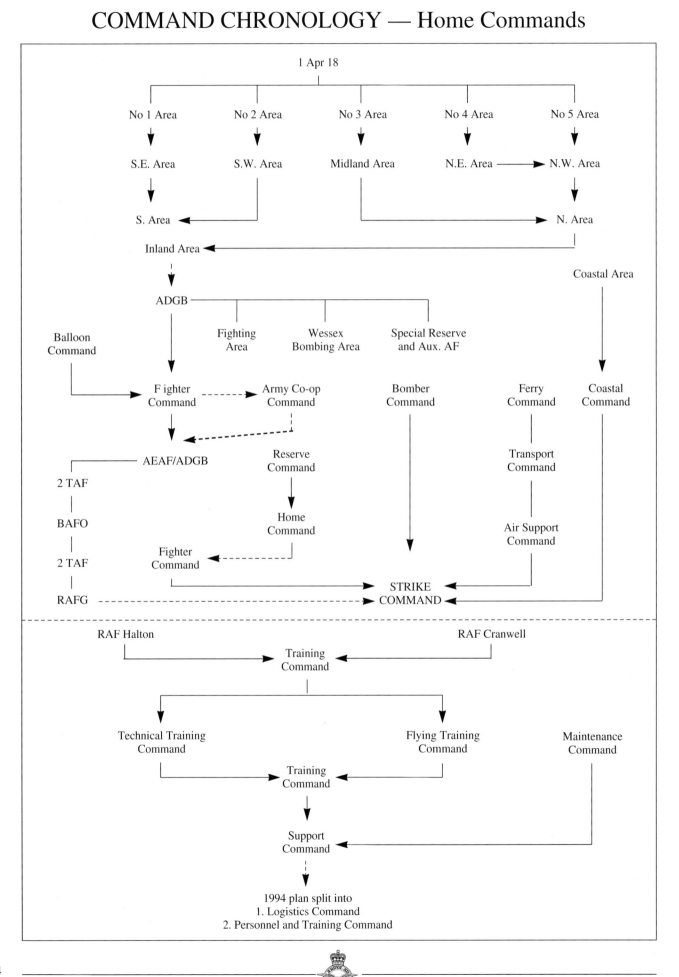

1 Apr 18

No 1 Area   No 2 Area   No 3 Area   No 4 Area   No 5 Area

S.E. Area   S.W. Area   Midland Area   N.E. Area ⟶ N.W. Area

S. Area   N. Area

Inland Area   Coastal Area

ADGB

Balloon Command   Fighting Area   Wessex Bombing Area   Special Reserve and Aux. AF

Fighter Command ⇢ Army Co-op Command   Bomber Command   Ferry Command   Coastal Command

AEAF/ADGB   Reserve Command   Transport Command

2 TAF

BAFO   Home Command   Air Support Command

2 TAF   Fighter Command

RAFG ⟶ STRIKE COMMAND

RAF Halton   RAF Cranwell

Training Command

Technical Training Command   Flying Training Command   Maintenance Command

Training Command

Support Command

1994 plan split into
1. Logistics Command
2. Personnel and Training Command

AREA COMMANDS 1918-1920

No 1 AREA
No 1 Area was formed on 1st April under Major-General F C Heath-Caldwell CB. Renamed South-Eastern Area on 8th May 1918.

SOUTH-EASTERN AREA
Formed 8th May 1918 by renaming No 1 Area. Renamed Southern Area on 20th September 1919.

No 2 AREA
No 2 Area was formed on 1st April 1918 under Major-General M E F Kerr CB MVO. Renamed South-Western Area on 8th May 1918.

SOUTH-WESTERN AREA
Formed 8th May 1918 by renaming No 2 Area. Reduced to Group status, as No 7 Group, within Southern Area on 20th September 1919.

No 3 AREA
No 3 Area was formed on 29th April 1918 under Major-General J F A Higgins DSO. Renamed Midland Area on 8th May 1918.

MIDLAND AREA
Formed 8th May 1918 by renaming No 3 Area. Absorbed into Northern Area on 18th October 1919.

No 4 AREA
No 4 Area was formed on 1st April 1918 under Major-General Hon Sir F Gordon KCB DSO. Renamed North-eastern Area on 8th May 1918.

NORTH-EASTERN AREA
Formed 8th May 1918 by renaming No 4 Area. Absorbed into North-western Area on 1st January 1919.

No 5 AREA
No 5 Area was formed on 1st April 1918 under Major-General G C Cayley CB. Renamed North-western Area on 8th May 1918.

NORTH-WESTERN AREA
Formed by renaming No 5 Area on 8th May 1918. Renamed Northern Area in June 1919.

SOUTHERN AREA
Formed by renaming South-eastern Area on 20th September 1919, at the same time absorbing, as No 7 Group, South-Western Area. As part of continued reduction and rationalisation of RAF strength Southern Area amalgamated with Northern Area on 1st April 1920 to form Inland Area.

NORTHERN AREA
Formed by renaming North-western Area in June 1919, at the same time absorbing Midland Area. As part of continued reduction and rationalisation of RAF strength Northern Area amalgamated with Southern Area on 1st April 1920 to form Inland Area.

RAF IRELAND
No 11 (Irish) Wing was raised to Command status, as RAF Ireland, on 17th February 1922, moving from Baldonnel to Island

Bridge Barracks a short while later; the first OC was Gp Capt I M Bonham-Carter OBE. The Command moved location twice more during the ensuing few months, to Templepatrick and then Aldergrove Aerodrome. The Command disbanded in early 1923.

With the outbreak of WW2 and the need to secure the Western Approaches to the British Isles, Ireland once more became a centre of operational activity. The Command was reborn, as RAF Northern Ireland (HQ RAF NI), out of No 61 Gp on 1st August 1940. The Commanding Officer was Gp Capt (acting A/Cdre) C R Carr DFC and HQ was located at Dunlambert, Fort William Park, Belfast. The region grew in importance through to 1942 as various new stations were opened; from 1943 onwards an increasing number of stations were handed to the control of USAAF VIII Composite Command.

With the re-organisation of mid 1945 the Command was reduced to Group status as part of Coastal Command.

No 5 (OPERATIONS) GROUP
During late summer 1918 No 5 (Operations) Gp was given Command status with control of units in the Kent and Dover area. It proved to be a short-lived period, in April 1919 returning to Group status within South-eastern Area.

No 29 (OPERATIONS) GROUP
No 29 Group was granted temporary Command status in late 1918 as its area of responsibility grew with an increasing number of units to control. Retitled as No 29 (Fleet) Gp in early summer 1919, still with Command status — although this was lost when the unit became part of Coastal Area on 15th September 1919.

COASTAL AREA
Coastal Area was formed on 15th September 1919, under A/Cdre A V Vyvyan CB DSO, to control all aerial units operating in Home Waters with the Royal Navy. This included naval-controlled airships. The Command controlled three Groups and had its HQ at Thurloe Place, London. During the critical period of the early 1920s, during which the Navy tried hard to re-create its own air element (and do-away with the RAF in the process), the Command controlled not only land-based units but also aircraft/seaplane flights embarked on RN ships. By April 1922 it controlled No 10 Group and No 29 Group as well as air units on Argus, Furious and Ark Royal.

With the major Command re-shuffle of 1936, Coastal Area was renamed Coastal Command with effect from 1st May.

RAF HALTON
The School of Technical Training at Halton was given Command status, as RAF Halton, originally RAF HQ Halton, in January 1920, under the command of A/Cdre F R Scarlett CB DSO. The Command also controlled a number of other training units at Halton although these varied from time to time. The 1936 major re-shuffle in RAF organisation saw RAF Halton lose its Command status, 9th July, and become part of Training Command.

RAF CRANWELL
The RAF (Cadet) College at Cranwell was given Command status on 5th February 1920 under A/Cdre C A H Longcroft CMG DSO AFC. As with Halton, the original title including the word Headquarters but this was soon dropped. RAF Cranwell controlled a number of other units, not all located at Cranwell. The 1936 major re-shuffle saw RAF Cranwell reduced to Group status as part of Training Command.

INLAND AREA

Formed by amalgamating Northern and Southern Areas on 1st April 1920 under AVM Sir John M Salmond KCB CMG CVO DSO, with HQ at Hillingdon House, Uxbridge. The original concept was for the Command to control all units not in Coastal Area, the only other Home operational Command, or RAF Halton and RAF Cranwell. By April 1922 the Command had control of No 1 Gp and No 7 Gp, No 11 Wing — a mixture of operational and training units. During the late 1920s and early 1930s this gradually changed and the Command acquired more of an adminstrative and training orientation.

The 1936 re-organisation saw Inland Area renamed, on 1st May, as Training Command.

ROLE COMMANDS 1936 -

COASTAL COMMAND (CC)

Formed by renaming Coastal Area on 1st May 1936, under AM Sir Arthur M Longmore KCB DSO, Coastal Command controlled both land-based and shipborne aircraft. The latter element was removed in July 1937 when the Admiralty resumed control of the Fleet Air Arm.

The Hudson became a major element of Coastal Command, shown here from 59 Squadron.

At the outbreak of World War Two Coastal Command was in the process of re-equipping its squadrons with specialist maritime patrol and anti-submarine warfare aircraft. In the 'panic' re-equipment of the RAF in the late 1930s, however, it came as a low priority behind Bomber and Fighter Command. By September 1939 most squadrons were using the GR Anson, an excellent aircraft but one not well suited to the roles soon to be demanded of Coastal Command. The other major operational types were the Sunderland for long-range patrol and the outdated Vildebeest for shipping attack.

The units of Coastal Command played a vital, but often unsung, part in the Second World War, and especially with the critical operations involved in the Battle of the Atlantic. Protection of coastal convoys commenced even before the outbreak of war and it soon became obvious that although the basic structure of the Command was sound, especially in regard to co-operation and liaison with the Navy, the equipment was far short of what was needed.

Amongst the roles of its maritime aircraft were anti U-boat sorties, most of which were notable for hour upon hour of uneventful flying, long-range maritime patrol and convoy escort, and air-sea rescue. However, from the first days of the war, squadrons of Coastal Command were also involved in offensive sorties, not only on anti-shipping strikes but also with attacks on land targets. In the latter years of the war the 'Strike Wings' of Beaufighters and Mosquitoes virtually cleared European waters of enemy and enemy-controlled shipping. One of the major lessons of WW2 was that air power was an essential pre-requisite for the successful application of sea power, and so Coastal Command had an assured future.

In the post-war period the maritime aspects of RAF operations remained a vital element in British defence strategy and Coastal Command maintained it expertise in anti-submarine and anti-shipping operations. The ASW role increased in importance as the Soviet Union developed a modern and efficient submarine arm. As the overseas Commands reduced in size and capabilty so the role of the UK organisations such as Coastal Command increased in importance, with more detachments and an increasing number of Exercises with various Treaty organisations.

The Command was reduced to Group status, as No 18 Gp, on 28th November 1969, becoming part of Strike Command.

TRAINING COMMAND (TC)

Formed by renaming Inland Area on 1st May 1936 under AM Sir Charles S Burnett KCB CBE DSO, with control of No 23 Gp and Armament Gp. Two months later RAF Halton and RAF Cranwell lost their Command status and joined Training Command.

The training aspect of RAF history has been given only scant attention in most histories and yet it was the foundation upon which all other operational Commands depended. The rapid expansion of the RAF during 1940, and the even greater anticipated expansion, led to Training Command being sub-divided on 27th May 1940 into Flying Training Command and Technical Training Command.

The same two Commands eventually amalgamated, as part of the 1960s re-organisation caused by a reduction in RAF strength, to re-form Training Command on 1st June 1968. Based at Brampton, the new unit had control of virtually all apsects of RAF initial and flying training, as well as looking after Air Cadet and Air Training Corps aspects. Further reductions in size brought another re-vamping in the late 1970s and Training Command was absorbed into Support Command on 13th June 1977.

AIR DEFENCE OF GREAT BRITAIN (ADGB)

The 1923 Salisbury Committee proposed a re-organisation of the RAF's structure to create a more effective and appropriate Command network. The major element of this was the forming of ADGB on 1st January 1925, under AM Sir John Salmond KCB CMG CVO DSO, to control all Home bomber and fighter squadrons not attached to Coastal Area. These units were organised into Wessex Bombing Area and Fighting Area, to control bombers and fighters respectively; also included was Air Defence Group with its, mainly cadre and auxiliary squadrons.

By 1933 the Group structure had been re-vamped and included Central Area, Western Area, Fighting Area, and No 1 (Air Defence) Gp. The Observer Corps was added to the list soon afterwards.

The 1936 re-shuffle brought a temporary end to ADGB, the organisation being renamed Fighter Command on 13th July 1936.

However, on 15th November 1943 the title was re-born, at the expense of Fighter Command, and ADGB was given the task of providing support for the Allied invasion of Europe. With the Allies safely ensconsed on the Continent, ADGB was disbanded again on 15th October 1944.

BOMBER COMMAND

Bomber Command was formed as part of the 1936 re-organisation, to control the RAF's Home bomber forces. Under the command of ACM Sir John M Steel KCB KBE CMG the Command was established on 14th July 1936. The decision had already been taken to greatly expand the bomber force, under the provisions of the various expansion plans.

By summer 1939 strength stood at almost 1000 aircraft (on paper) but just over half of these could truly be declared as operational, many of the others were in training or reserve units. The move of the ten Battle squadrons of the AASF to France in September 1939 further reduced the strength. Although these aircraft remained under notional Bomber Command control they were, from May 1940, actually employed in the tactical battle to stem the German advance. With the outbreak of war the Command tried to implement its strategic plan of daylight attacks, albeit under severe political restrictions as to what comprised an 'acceptable' target.

The might of Bomber Command rested mainly with the Lancaster, here of 90 Squadron, and Halifax squadrons.

Up until 1942 the Command faced a losing battle, the bomber offensive had to switch to night tactics to reduce aircraft losses but this also presented the problem of finding, and hitting the target. Furthermore, the pre-war bomber types were found to be sadly lacking both in their defensive capabilities and their weapon load. What could not be denied was the courage of the crews who faced the enemy defences night after night. Although the Blenheims contributed to the strategic campaign most of their effort was expended on daylight raids against shipping and land targets, losses were heavy but there were some spectacular successes.

The crunch point came in 1942, Bomber Command was at last starting to receive new aircraft, the introduction of the four-engined 'heavies' adding a new dimension to the Command's capabilities, as well as new equipment and tactics to help overcome the problems of targeting and navigation. However, many voices cried for the resources being expended on this 'ineffective' campaign to be switched to other more critical areas. The arrival in February 1942 of Sir Arthur Harris gave the Command the boost it needed and by his sheer strength of character (or dogmatism) he took Bomber Command through its low point and built it into a mighty weapon. By Spring 1944 the Lancaster and Halifax squadrons were wreaking dreadful destruction on German cities and causing the enemy to expend an enormous effort on countering this threat to his nerve centre.

The argument as to the effectiveness and relevance, even the morality, of the strategic bombing offensive by Bomber Command and the USAAF has often been debated. This is not the place to go over these complex arguments again (for that see 'The Six Year Offensive, by Ken Delve and Peter Jacobs, Arms and Armour Press, 1992), suffice it to say that for many years Bomber Command was the ONLY Allied force capable of taking the war to the enemy. In the post-war analysis the bomber was seen as a decisive weapon, especially taking into account the advent of air-delivered atomic weapons, a weapon around which future strategy would be based.

Athough the numbers of squadrons was greatly reduced in the post-war run-down, the basic concept of a powerful bomber force was maintained. 1951 saw the introduction of the Canberra, the RAF's first jet bomber, — a change of tactics, this unarmed (i.e no defensive guns) aircraft relying on height and speed. The 'heavy' jets of the V-bomber trio were intoduced shortly afterwards, and with the successful testing of a British atomic weapon, Bomber Command acquired even greater offensive potential. Bomber Command aircraft were employed in a number of active operations during the decade or so following the war, with conventional bombing missions being flown in Malaya and Egypt (Suez).

The late 1950s saw the introduction of the Thor IRBM, an American missile, and the RAF entered the missile age. It was a period when many experts were predicting the end of the manned aircraft. A follow-on missile, Blue Streak, was cancelled and by 1963 the Thor sites had been shut down, thus ending this short-lived venture into the world of strategic missiles. At around the same time the Vulcans and Victors were provided with a stand-off missile, Blue Steel, and with this weapon provided one keystone of the strategic nuclear deterrent. This was maintained until 1969 at which point strategic deterrence passed to the Royal Navy with their Polaris submarines. Two years before this, 1st November 1967, the Command had been reduced to a single Group, No 1 Group, and it was obvious that its status was no longer justified. On 1st May 1968 Fighter Command and Bomber Command amalgamated to form Strike Command.

FIGHTER COMMAND

Fighter Command was formed on 14th July 1936 following the disbandment of ADGB. With its HQ at Bentley Priory, and under the command of AM Sir Hugh C T Dowding, the new Command was given responsibility for the air defence of the British Isles. The aircraft types which it took over would not have been out of place in the 1920s, slow, under armed bi-planes. However, expansion plans had been laid and two new fighters were about to make their appearances with the squadrons.

The remaining few years of peace were put to good use with the build-up of Hurricane and Spitfire squadrons, although out-dated tactical concepts would dog the Command into the early years of the war. More importantly, and under Fighter Command control, was the network of radar stations springing up around the English coast, these were to be critical assets in countering the German offensive of 1940. The Command also controlled the Observer Corps, who proved of great value in the reporting system, and, from 1938, Balloon Command (plus a variety of other units, including certain anti-aircraft units).

At the outbreak of war Fighter Command had three operational Groups — No 11 Gp, No 12 Gp and No 13 Gp — each responsible for a specific geographic area. The catastrophe in France saw one of Dowding's greatest fears realised, he was pressured into sending more and more fighter squadrons to operate on the Continent; arguments have raged over this policy, from 'too little — too late' to 'too much'. Dowding resisted the policy as far as he could, an act which made him political enemies, but he managed to preserve what he considered to be the minimum force ready for the decisive battle over England.

The story of the 'Few' is now legend, and is outlined in the 'Campaigns' section of this book, and was the basis from which ultimate victory was assured. As the Luftwaffe turned its attention to night bombing so Fighter Command had to adapt its tactics, and introduce radar-equipped aircraft. Likewise, it had to adapt to new aspects of the daylight battle with the need to counter 'hit and run' raids.

By 1942 the squadrons of Fighter Command were generally under-employed and so turned to the offensive, flying fighter sweeps over enemy-occupied Europe. These sweeps rarely achieved their aim of drawing the Luftwaffe up to fight and so the tactic was changed to one of escort to formations of light/medium bombers — the idea being that the German forces would have to react to the bomber threat and thus expose themselves to the waiting fighters. The short range of the fighters limited the success of this tactic. With the build-up in Britain of forces for the invasion of Europe the traditional 'home defence' role of Fighter Command was considered to be at an end. On 15th November Fighter Command once more became ADGB, as an element within the Allied Expeditionary Air Force.

With Allied forces safely established on the Continent, and with a renewed threat to the home base from German lightning raids, combined with the 'mini Blitz' by flying-bombs (V-1s), the decision was taken to re-form Fighter Command. This duly took place on 15th October 1944, ADGB vanishing once more. The interception of V-1s was by no means an easy task as these weapons were faster than many of the defending fighters; nevertheless, by the end of the war, Fighter Command claimed to have destroyed over 1800 flying-bombs.

The end of the war brought a rapid run-down as the RAF tried to find a peace-time posture and force structure. By the late 1940s it was clear that the major air threat to the UK would be from the Soviet Union, although it was some years before that country acquired a credible offensive force. Subsequent decades have consisted of technological advances in both offence and defence, the introduction of effective air-to-air missiles, supersonic fighters, surface-to-air missiles, air-to-air refuelling, increasingley effective ground-based and airborne radar. Fighter Command had to maintain a high degree of flexibility in its attempts to maintain a viable air defence system.

Overall reduction in RAF strength throughout the late 1950s and into the 1960s brought a re-organisation of Command structure. On 1st May 1968 Fighter Command and Bomber Command amalgamated to form Strike Command.

MAINTENANCE COMMAND

Maintenance Command was formed on 1st April 1938 under the command of AVM J S T Bradley OBE, moving to Andover on 17th July. Its primary function was to provide supply and engineering support to the other RAF Commands, a huge and diverse area of responsibility which involved countless units performing a myriad of tasks. These 'behind the scenes' activities of the Maintenance Units and other storage and repair units played a vital role in keeping the other Commands supplied with the thousands of items essential for day to day operations. The repair and salvage units repaired hundreds of thousands of bits of equipment and returned them to service; the aircraft storage and distribution system ensured that squadrons had replacement aircraft when needed; to this end, the Command, through No 41 Gp, controlled the Ferry Pilot Pools.

The same basic range of tasks continued into the post-war period. After almost 20 years at Amport, Maintenance Command returned to Andover on 18th July 1961.

The general re-organisation of structure begun in the late 1960s continued into the following decade, one result was the disbandement of Maintenance Command on 31st August 1973, its areas of responsibility being taken over by Support Command.

BALLOON COMMAND

Balloon Command was formed on 1st November 1938 under command of AVM O T Boyd OBE MC AFC, its HQ moving to Stanmore shortly after formation. The main reason for the move was co-location with Fighter Command as for operational and 'war training' matters the reporting chain was through Fighter Command.

Balloon Command controlled all the UK and overseas balloon units.

The Balloon barrage was an important element of the overall defensive system, their major task being the defence of critical areas (from towns and cities to vital factories or ports) against low-flying aircraft. By September 1941 the Command had an authorised total of 2478 balloons of various types, a major increase on the 800 available at the ooutbreak of war. Balloon Command controlled up to five Groups, the total varying throughout the war but peaking in 1942, each covering a particular geographic area of responsibility and employing an organisation based upon 'squadrons'. It was also responsible for providing balloon squadrons for service in other theatres, and duly deployed units to France, MED/ME, India, and in support of the Allied invasion of Europe, including those on ships. The balloon itself is simply a means of supporting the steel cable, it is the latter which deters or destroys low flyers attempting to penetrate the barrage — during the first part of the flying-bomb offensive the balloon cables destroyed almost 300 of these weapons. However, the balloons proved almost as big a danger to the defending fighters and this was one of the reasons for the de-activation, in September 1944, of the balloon barrage. Balloon Command duly disbanded on 15th June 1945, a Balloon Wing taking responsibility for the few remaining tasks within Fighter Command.

RESERVE COMMAND

Formed at Hendon on 1st February 1939, moving to White Waltham in March, under the command of AM C L Courtney CB CBE DSO, Reserve Command by late September controlled three Groups (No 50, No 51 and No 54 Gp). These in turn were responsible for a wide range of flying training, primarily EFTS and AONS, as well as the Initial Training Wings.

Reserve Command disbanded on 27th May 1940. However, on 1st May 1946 the Command reformed, returning to White Waltham on 7th October. This was part of the decision to re-establish the successful pre-war concept of reserve, i.e part-time, forces — "to maintain and train adequate reserves of flying and ground personnel." The primary flying elements consisted of the squadrons of the Auxiliary Air Force , as well as the RAFVR, University Air Squadrons, and Air Training Corps.On 1st August 1950 Reserve Command was renamed Home Command.

HOME COMMAND

Home Command was formed on 1st August 1950 by renaming Reserve Command. Under the command of AM Sir Robert M Foster the new Command had responsibility for the squadrons of the R Aux AF, as well as the RAFVR, UASs, and ATC. The decision to disband the R Aux AF, effective March 1957, brought to an end the 'operational' side of the Command's responsibilities and two years later, 1st April 1959, Home Command disbanded.

FLYING TRAINING COMMAND

The rapid expansion of the training machine in the early months of World War Two brought a division in the responsibilities of Training Command, this organisation splitting to form two new Commands. Flying Training Command formed on 27th May 1940 at Shinfield Park, Reading, under the command of AVM (acting AM) L A Pattinson CB DSO MC DFC, with responsibility for all aspects of the selection and training of aircrew.

The Command controlled six Groups (Nos 21, 23, 25, 50, 51, 54), plus an interest in the training organisation in South Africa and Canada, although the administration of these overseas units came under the respective national air forces. A seventh Group, No 29 was added in July 1942.

The immense task of providing trained aircrew for the RAF, in a period of rapid expansion coupled with high loss rates, has all too often been glossed over in the histories and yet it is one of the most remarkable achievements of the war. Expansion of operational strength is not simply a matter of building more aircraft, each aircraft needs a crew, and the more crews you want

to train then the more instructors you need — and so on.

Flying Training Command did not cover the operational training aspects of aircrew training, this being the task of the OTUs and HCUs (plus various other units) incorporated within the operational Commands.

During its five years of wartime training the Command produced some 88 000 aircrew — an incredible total. The run-down of requirement commenced in late 1944 and by the end of the war the Command had already started to contract. This process continued until 1951 when the outbreak of the Korean War caused a reversal of the process. Two new Groups were formed to handle the increased training task, mainly that of refresher flying for reservists.

It was a short-lived expansion and the end of the Korean War was followed by yet another contraction of strength, albeit not so rapid as that of 1945. Further contraction and re-organisation brought the disbandment of Flying Training Command, and the re-birth of Training Command, on 1st June 1968.

TECHNICAL TRAINING COMMAND

The need to divide the responsibilities of Training Command led to the formation, on 27th May 1940, of Technical Training Command to take control of recruit, engineering and signals training. The Command formed at Wantage Hall, Reading University, under AVM (acting AM) W L Welsh CB DSO AFC. The three Groups (Nos 20, 24, 26) controlled Recruit Centres, Schools of Technical Training, various others schools and medical establishments, plus W/T stations and a few flying units. The Command gradually acquired control of ever more, and diverse, units and added another Group to its structure.

Post-war, Technical Training Command moved to Brampton, maintaining its widespread training responsibility.

Contraction and re-organisation brought a re-merger with Flying Training Command, under the title of Training Command, on 1st June 1968.

ARMY CO-OPERATION COMMAND

The increasing complexity and diversity of tactical air power led to the granting of Command status to No 22 Group which, upon the formation of Army Co-operation Command (1st December 1940), duly disbanded. Initially established at South Farnborough, the HQ moved to Bracknell, under AM Sir Arthur Barratt KCB CMG MC.

Army Co-operation Command controlled two Groups, No 70 Group being the training and development organisation with No 71 Group as the operational Group. In essence much of the work of the latter Group was also of a training nature until offensive operations re-commenced over Europe. By mid 1942 the operational side of the Command was re-organised into a Wing basis, each operational Wing being attached to an Army regional HQ. A great deal of effort was spent on developing tactics ready for the future invasion of Europe, when efficient and well organised air support would prove decisive. Whilst the never-ending stream of Army exercises seemed rather trying to the aircrew, the techniques and co-operative tactics developed during 1942 and 1943 proved to be of inestimable value.

The Command disbanded on 1st June 1943 as part of a re-organisation of tactical air power in the build up to the invasion of France.

FERRY COMMAND

The urgent need to provide aircraft for the RAF during World War Two led to extensive acquisition of American types; those capable of making the Atlantic crossing were ferried by crews of

Ferry Command took on the task of moving aircraft from America to the UK.

the civilian run ATFERO. However, the scale and complexity of the operation led to a 1941 decision to transfer the organisation to the RAF as Ferry Command. The Command formed on 20th July 1941, under ACM Sir Frederick Bowhill GBE KCB CMG DSO, and took over the task of ferrying aircraft for the RAF from the United States and for delivery flights to other Commands.

Although the Command HQ formed at Royal Bank Buildings, Montreal, Canada it soon moved to Dorval airport. Ferry Command was given three primary tasks:

1. The delivery by air of suitable types of aircraft produced in North America across the Atlantic to the UK.

2. The reception of aircraft for trans- Atlantic ferrying from the Ferry Command of the USAAC at transfer points in the eastern United States.

3. To operate as neccesary any other air routes which may develop for the delivery of aircraft from the USA.

No 44 Gp controlled a number of stations in the UK from its HQ at Gloucester, two of the most important being Kemble and Filton with their aircraft preparation units. Re-organisation of the entire RAF transport network led to the formation, on 25th March 1943, of Transport Command — Ferry Command being reduced to Group status, as No 45 Group, within the new Command.

TRANSPORT COMMAND

Re-organisation of the RAF transport network led to the formation of Transport Command on 25th March 1943 at Bush House, London, under ACM Sir Frederick Bowhill GBE KCB CMG DSO. The primary tasks were stated as, " the organisation and control of strategic air routes, for all overseas ferrying, for reinforcement moves of squadrons to and between overseas theatres, and for air movements of freight and personnel.

The new Command had cross-theatre responsibilities to control ALL major aspects of air transport, using Groups operating within other Commands. The initial establishment included No 45 Group , No 44 Group , No 216 Group and No 179 Wing. Transport Command responsibilites included all aspects of air transport, from movement of stores and equipment to supply and paratroop dropping. Although perceived by many as a non 'operational' organisation — a most unjust appraisel — the crews were present in almost every operational scenario. By mid 1944 the Command had control of five Groups (Nos 44, 45, 46, 216, 229), the latter two of which operated in the Middle East and India respectively, plus No 114 Wing operating from West Africa.

Air supply proved to be one of the most decisive factors during many of the Allied campaigns, especially in remote operational areas such as the jungles of Burma.

With the end of the war the Command faced the huge task of airlifting troops (and POWs) and equipment to their 'peace-time' stations, which in many cases was a return to the UK for demob.

The cross-Command control was abolished in March 1946 when each overseas Command was given control of its own transport elements. June 1948 brought the greatest air supply task yet seen, the requirement to keep the non-Russian sectors of Berlin supplied — the Berlin Airlift. Whilst the American contribution was by far the largest single effort, the work of the Transport Command squadrons was of enormous value, with a total lift of almost 400 000 short tons during the fifteen months of the Airlift.

A move to Upavon in April 1950 co-incided with yet another impetus in the fortunes of the Command. The post-colonial era was creating numerous problems for Britain with her world-wide commitments; inadequate level of forces meant that rapid transportation to a trouble spot was the only practicable solution. Tranpsort Command provided this vital link by providing strategic and tactical mobility.

Ten years later a specialised Group, No 38 Group, was formed within the Command to provide a tactical air transport and airborne assault capability in conjunction with the Army. Not only did this involve greater use of helicopters but it also gave Transport Command control of its own offensive support aircraft. The 1967 review of RAF organisation introduced, on 1st August, a new title for the Command — as Air Support Command.

AIR SUPPORT COMMAND

Air Support Command was formed on 1st August 1967 by renaming Transport Command, under AM Sir Thomas Prickett KCB DSO DFC.

The operational policy remained as before; however, it was a period of continuing run-down of British commitments worldwide and on 1st September 1972 the Command was reduced to Group status, as No 46 Group, and incorporated within Strike Command.

SIGNALS COMMAND

The latter war years, and into the 1950s, saw a growth in the importance of electronic aspects of the military art, especially with regard to air power. During this period such aspects had been looked after by No 90 Group; however, on 3rd November 1958, this organisation was raised to Command status, with HQ at Medmeham — as Signals Command — under AVM L Dalton-Morris CB CBE.

The responsibilites and duties of the Command were extensive and on a world-wide basis, including communications, radio, and electronic warfare. The flying units associated with Signals Command were primarily involved on calibration work, trials and development, and electronic intelligence. Signals Command disbanded on 31st December 1968 upon reduction to Group status, once more becoming No 90 Group.

STRIKE COMMAND

Formed on 30th April 1968, Strike Command was destined to absorb all the other Home-based operational Commands as RAF commitments, and strength, reduced. The initial organisation was formed by the merger of Bomber and Fighter Commands, under ACM Sir Wallace H Kyle GCB CBE DSO DFC.

A few months later, 1st January, Signals Command was absorbed followed, 28th November, by Coastal Command, all part of the continuing reduction of RAF strength. This gave

Strike Command the following Groups — No 1 (Bomber) Gp, No 11 (Fighter) Gp, No 18 (Maritime) Gp, and No 90 (Signals) Gp — and control of all UK-based offensive and defensive aircraft.

No 90 Gp transfered to Maintenance Command in 1972, but in the same year Air Support Command was disbanded, becoming No 46 Gp within Strike Command. Strike Command flying units underwent major re-equipment programmes in the 1970s and 1980s, the latter decade seeing the introduction of the Tornado S/A and AD forces and an improved variant of CAS Harriers. The ending of the Cold War and collapse of the Warsaw Pact in the early 1990s led to a major reduction in RAF strength under the so-called 'Peace Dividend'; however, an increase in out-of-area commitments, especially in support of the United Nations, meant that Strike Command units had to maintain a high degree of mobility readiness — this is likely to be the case for the forseeable future.

SUPPORT COMMAND

Support Command was formed on 31st August 1973 to take over the functions of the disbanded Maintenance Command, in addition to acquiring a number of units from the other Home-based Commands. HQ was at Andover under the command of AVM (acting AM) R Harland CB MA CEng.

With the absorbtion of Training Command on 13th June 1977 the Command was officially re-titled as RAF Support Command, although was still generally refered to simply as Support Command. This merger also saw the Command re-locate to Brampton, its current HQ. The Command has a wide range of units and tasks under its direction, ranging from the Flying Training organisations through such diverse areas as Fire and Police services. On present plans the Command is due to split into two in 1994 to form Logistics Command and Personnel & Training Command.

Transport Command Hastings provided strategic mobility.

ALLIED EXPEDITIONARY 6th JUNE 1944

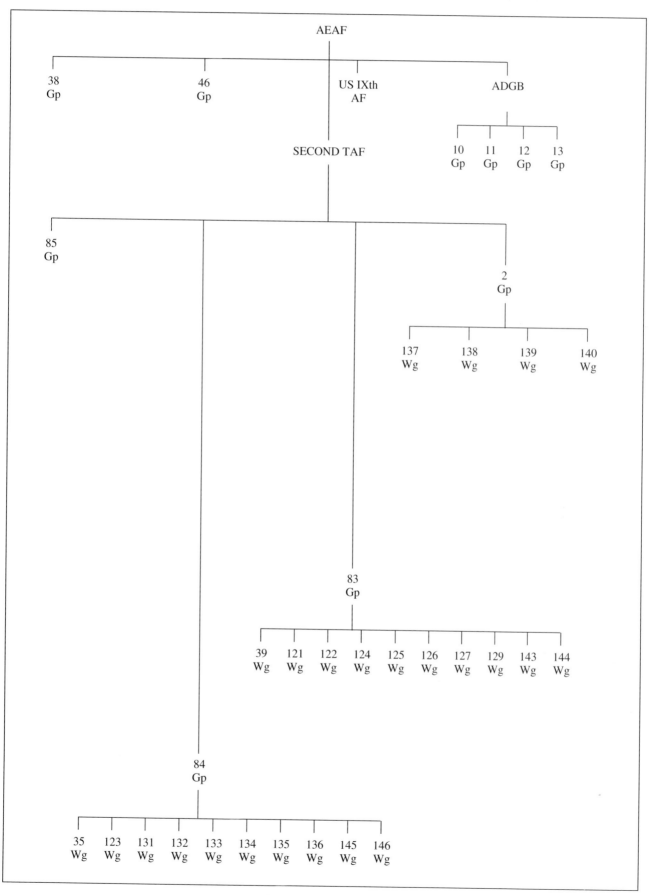

HOME COMMANDS SEPTEMBER 1939

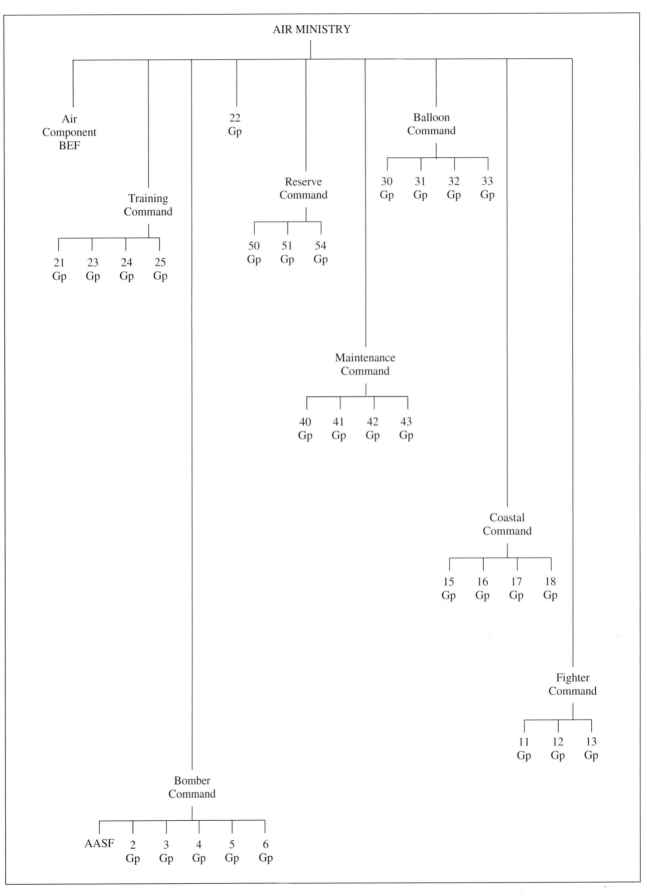

HOME COMMANDS JANUARY 1941

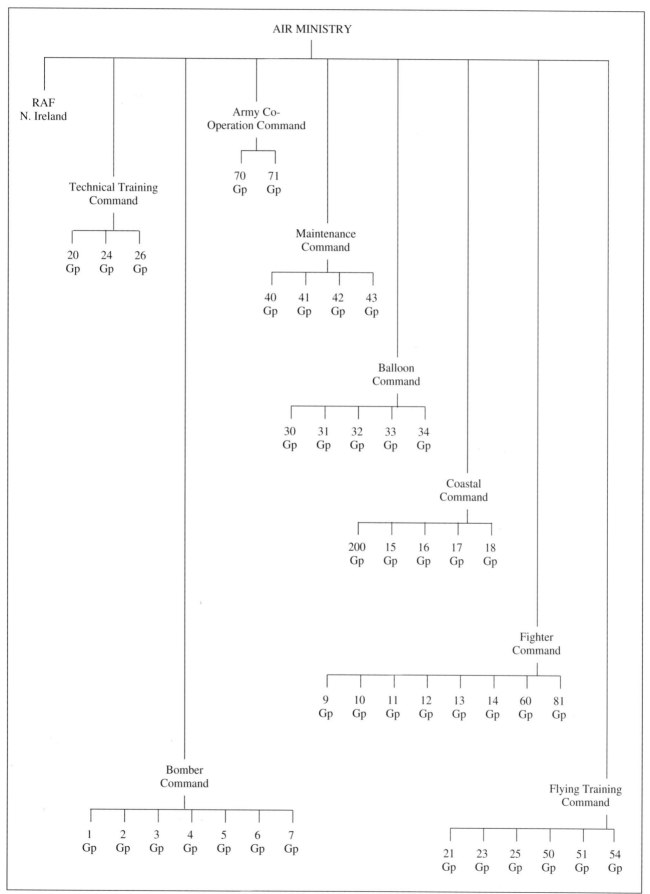

AIR MINISTRY

RAF
N. Ireland

Army Co-
Operation Command

70 Gp   71 Gp

Technical Training
Command

20 Gp   24 Gp   26 Gp

Maintenance
Command

40 Gp   41 Gp   42 Gp   43 Gp

Balloon
Command

30 Gp   31 Gp   32 Gp   33 Gp   34 Gp

Coastal
Command

200 Gp   15 Gp   16 Gp   17 Gp   18 Gp

Fighter
Command

9 Gp   10 Gp   11 Gp   12 Gp   13 Gp   14 Gp   60 Gp   81 Gp

Bomber
Command

1 Gp   2 Gp   3 Gp   4 Gp   5 Gp   6 Gp   7 Gp

Flying Training
Command

21 Gp   23 Gp   25 Gp   50 Gp   51 Gp   54 Gp

HOME COMMANDS MARCH 1943

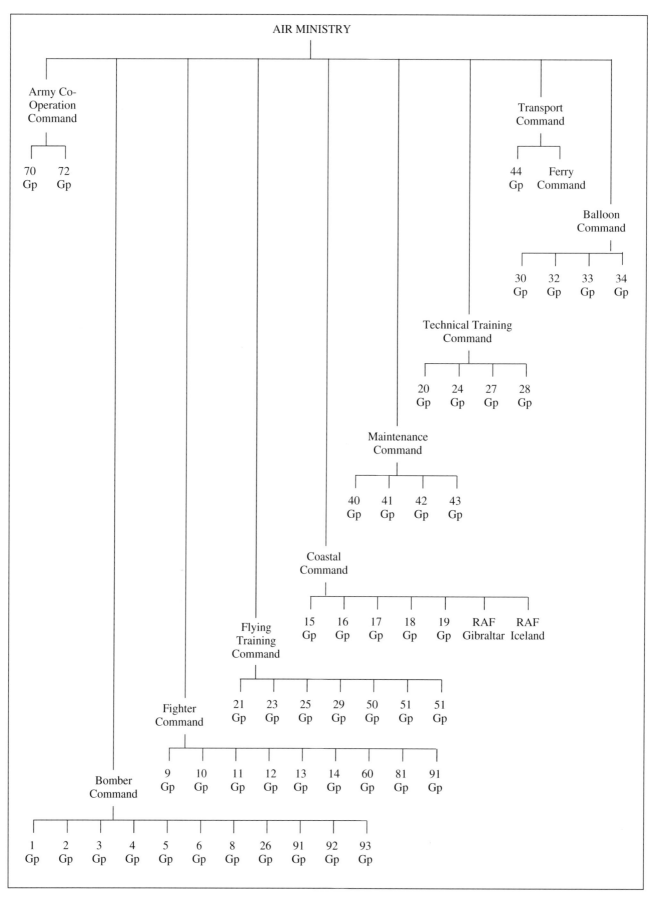

AIR MINISTRY

Army Co-Operation Command
70 Gp
72 Gp

Transport Command
44 Gp
Ferry Command

Balloon Command
30 Gp
32 Gp
33 Gp
34 Gp

Technical Training Command
20 Gp
24 Gp
27 Gp
28 Gp

Maintenance Command
40 Gp
41 Gp
42 Gp
43 Gp

Coastal Command
15 Gp
16 Gp
17 Gp
18 Gp
19 Gp
RAF Gibraltar
RAF Iceland

Flying Training Command
21 Gp
23 Gp
25 Gp
29 Gp
50 Gp
51 Gp
51 Gp

Fighter Command
9 Gp
10 Gp
11 Gp
12 Gp
13 Gp
14 Gp
60 Gp
81 Gp
91 Gp

Bomber Command
1 Gp
2 Gp
3 Gp
4 Gp
5 Gp
6 Gp
8 Gp
26 Gp
91 Gp
92 Gp
93 Gp

HOME COMMANDS JUNE 1944

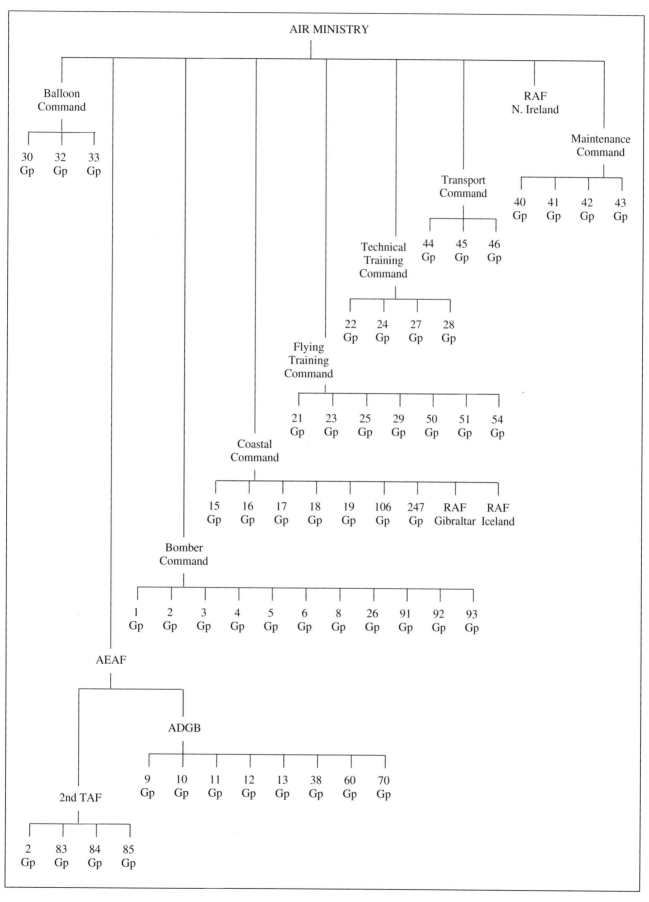

THE OVERSEAS COMMANDS

THE COMMAND STRUCTURE for RAF involvement outside of the UK is not an easy area of study as all too often the records are somewhat confused, and invariably the 'classic' chain of command does not appear to have been quite so straightforward. As was explained in the introduction to this section, the creation of the chain of command often appears somewhat arbitrary, this is particularly true of the situation overseas where certain units reported directly to London, having no regional Command structure to report through. The rapidly changing nature of the campaigns of World War Two brought many, and frequent, changes in RAF organisation, not all of which are as clear as one would like!

NORTHERN EUROPE

HQ RAF ICELAND
HQ RAF Iceland was formed March 1941, out of No 40 Wing (?). Disbanded 10th July 1945.

ALLIED EXPEDITIONARY AIR FORCE (AEAF)
Formed at Stanmore on 15th November 1943, under AM Sir Trafford Leigh-Mallory KCB DSO, the AEAF was tasked with providing air support for the invasion and consolidation of Allied forces on the European mainland. This supra-Command was formed to control all the offensive air assets allocated to the invasion plan, including ADGB, 2TAF, IXth US Air Force, including the associated Groups, plus a variety of other support units. The major RAF offensive elements were provided by ADGB and 2TAF, whose basic details, as Subordinate Commands, are covered under their respective headings. It also had temporary operational control of the heavy bomber forces — RAF Bomber Command and USSTAF (VIIIth and 15th Air Forces).

With the Allied forces established on the European mainland and advancing towards Germany the structure of tactical air power was again revised and AEAF disbanded on 15th October 1944.

2nd TACTICAL AIR FORCE
As part of the re-organisation of tactical air power 2nd TAF was formed on 1st June 1943 at Bracknell. The Command was part of Fighter Command and controlled two operational Groups (Nos 2, 83) plus No 38 Wing. On 15th November it transferred to the Allied Expeditionary Air Force as part of the build-up for the invasion of Europe. The bombers of No 2 Gp and the ground attack aircraft, primarily Spitfires and Typhoons plus the ubiquitous Auster, of No 83 Gp and, when formed, No 84 Gp, provided the on the spot fire-power that became such a decisive

feature of the Allied progress through France and into Germany following the invasion of June 1944. The squadrons undertook a wide range of tasks, building up an impressive score of enemy aircraft, tanks, vehicles and trains. The German generals were convinced that the stranglehold wielded by such tactical air power was decisive in last 12 months of the war.

With the conflict in Europe over and the RAF maintaining a presence in Germany it was decided to rename the Command; on 15th July 1945 the 2nd TAF disbanded to be replaced by British Air Forces of Occupation.

2TAF was reformed on 1st September 1951 by renaming BAFO to reflect the change in role to that of a tactical air force within the NATO alliance. The early 1950s were a time of expansion and revision of strategy, the latter reflecting the increase in nuclear capability, planning was based upon a strength of 56 squadrons by the end of 1954, although in the event the total was to fall some 20 squadrons short of this figure. New aircraft types brought a great increase in capability, the Canberra being a notable example, and allowed a partial redeployment to bases in the west of Germany. With the reforming of No 83 Gp in 1952 squadron strength stood at 25, all either light bomber of fighter/ground attack. On 22nd November 1954 the HQ moved to Monchen Gladbach.

Further expansion followed, and included the acquisition of the Sabre under the terms of the Mutual Defence Aids Programme, the peak strength of 2TAF coming in late 1955 with a total of 35 squadrons.

The previous year the HQ had moved into a new purpose-built home at Rheindahlen. However, strategic concepts continued to change and a run-down of strength began almost immediately to reflect the increased importance, and cost, of the UK-based strategic V-bombers of Bomber Command. The 'tripwire' policy of massive nuclear retaliation had arrived and so tactical air forces took a back seat; within two years 2TAF was down to 17 squadrons and both Groups had once more disbanded, airfields were handed back to the now expanding Luftwaffe.

With effect from 1st January 1959 the Command was renamed Royal Air Force Germany.

BRITISH AIR FORCES OF OCCUPATION (BAFO)
Formed 15th July 1945, under ACM Sir W Sholto Douglas KCB MC DFC, by renaming 2TAF in view of change of role to that of 'air policing' in order to "provide support of the land occupation forces, technical supervision of Luftwaffe disbandment and equipment disposal, and routine training." HQ was established at Bad Eilsen and the problems commenced almost immediately. The immediate difficulties included those of demobilisation of RAF units, as in other overseas theatres there was a general

clamour amongst the 'duration' men to get back home as soon as possible — and certainly before all the jobs were taken. There was also a need for re-organisation as American Lease-Lend aircraft were returned to the US or scrapped. By late 1945 BAFO controlled 36 operational squadrons over an area including Germany, France, Holland and Belgium, with a Command structure comprising four Groups — Nos 2, 83, 84, 85. However, within a year this structure had been drastically altered with the loss of No 83 and 84 Groups and a reduction to 15 operational squadrons. This policy continued until by late 1947 BAFO had no Groups under command and was left with a mere 10 squadrons.

The 'outbreak' of the Cold War led to a re-think of British defence posture in Europe and a decision to redeploy and strengthen BAFO. March 1948 brought the signing of the Brussels Treaty establishing the Western Union Defence Organisation, enhanced in April 1949 by the creation of NATO. In the meantime the Cold War had created its first crisis with the Soviet land blockade of Berlin. Operation PLAINFARE, the air supply of Berlin, was a major achievement, although BAFO squadrons only played a supporting role to the transport units.

The net result of the crisis was to provide impetus for expansion and re-equipment and by 1951 BAFO controlled 16 squadrons of Vampires and Meteors, with deployment of these tactical aircraft being to the east of the country — Celle, Fassberg, Gutersloh, Wahn and Wunstorf. No 85 Gp had reformed in November 1948 take operational control of BAFO units involved in the Berlin Airlift but during 1950 it disbanded once more as No 2 Gp reformed to take its place. At this time all BAFO squadrons were assigned to a NATO role under SACEUR.

The changing status of the British military in Germany from that of an occupying force to that of an ally required a change of Command title and so BAFO once more became 2TAF.

BRITISH AIR COMMAND BERLIN

Formed 17th April 1945 to control RAF elements in and around Berlin. Disbanded 28th February 1946.

RAF GERMANY

RAF Germany was formed by renaming 2TAF on 1st January 1959.

The change came at a time of diminishing resources for the Command, the low point coming in 1962 with a strength of 12 squadrons. However, the pressure for a change of NATO strategy was given impetus by continued Soviet moves in Eastern Europe and the patent limitations of the 'tripwire' mentality.

Canberras of RAFG, here B(I)8s of 59 Squadron, ranged far and wide.

The Soviet invasion of Czechoslovakia in August 1968 brought NATO, and RAFG, to a high alert state and highlighted the already known problems. It did, however, prove that RAFG needed strengthening and re-equipping. The 1970s brought a major re-equipment programme that saw the introduction of the Phantom, Harrier, Buccaneer and Lightning. The Command had to maintain a high alert and readiness posture to counter the threat of a Warsaw pact pre-emptive attack, hence fighter and bomber aircraft were kept at QRA.

At the same time NATO instigated a programme of providing hardened facilities for aircraft and personnel. All of this was in response to the growing air threat posed by the Warsaw Pact with NATO tactical air power seen as an essential element of the defence strategy. The collapse of the Warsaw Pact in the early 1990s led to a revision of defence priorities and a rapid run-down of the strength of RAFG with Tornado and Phantom units disbanding and other units returning to the UK. The reduced scale of the Command led to a reduction to Group status and the re-birth of No 2 Group (1.4.93).

MEDITERRANEAN, AFRICA AND MIDDLE EAST

MIDDLE EAST AREA

Middle East Area had control of three Groups on a regional basis — Egypt, Palestine and Iraq. Each of the Groups was small and covered the full range of RAF 'colonial' tasks, primarily reconnaissance and support of the local ground forces. However, this changed somewhat following the 1921 Cairo Conference when it was decided that the RAF should be given full control of military operations in Mesopotamia — the introduction of the so-called 'Air Control Policy'.

Expansion of the RAF organisation overseas brought two new Groups under the control of ME Area in the early 1920s, Indian Group and Mediterranean Group. Once again these Groups were quite small but the foundations of a chain of command suited for further expansion had been laid.

The command was renamed RAF Middle East in April 1922.

IRAQ COMMAND

On 1st February 1922 Iraq Group was raised to command status with HQ at Hinaidi. This was a direct result of the decision taken at the Cairo Conference to transfer operational control of Mesopotamia to the RAF. The Command had control of five squadrons — three General Purpose, one Flying Boat and one Transport — and the AOC had control of RAF, Army and Indian Army units.

The Command authority covering this area underwent a number of changes during the 1940s, mainly as a result of changing areas of responsibility and the overall strength level pertaining at any given time — if an area has few units then it may well not justify Command status. The following changes can be proved by Air Ministry directives — 1st January 1943 AHQ Iraq becomes AHQ Iraq and Persia. — 1st March 1946 AHQ Iraq and Persia becomes AHQ Iraq. — 1st May 1955 AHQ Iraq becomes AHQ Levant.

RAF MEDITERRANEAN

On 1st April 1922 Mediterranean Group was raised to command status.

By April 1932 there was only one flying squadron in theatre, plus the air element embarked on HMS Glorious.

RAF MIDDLE EAST

Formed 1st April 1922 by renaming Middle East Area. The Command had control of Egyptian Gp and Aden Flight plus, for supply and equipment purposes only, RAF Palestine and RAF Trans-Jordan.

ADEN COMMAND

During the 1920s Aden Command was under direct Air Ministry responsibility, formed February 1928 to take control of Aden area.

As with the command situation in the Iraq region, so the situation in Aden changed numerous times over the years, although this was often no more than a cosmetic change of title.

With its HQ at Steamer Point AHQ Aden was renamed HQ British Forces Aden on 14th April 1942.

During the post World War Two period the area came under HQ British Forces Aden, a reflection of the combined nature of the force structure, as an element within Middle East Command.

It was renamed HQ British Forces Arabian Peninsula (BFAP) on 6th October 1956.

BRITISH FORCES ARABIAN PENINSULA

BFAP formed on 6th October 1956 with the renaming of HQ British Forces Aden at Steamer Point, the air element becoming Air Forces Arabian Peninsula. By 1958 the AFAP main bases were Bahrain, Eastleigh (Kenya), Khormaksar, Masirah, Mauritius, Riyan, Salalah, Sharjah and Steamer Point — covering a large geographical area but with only four permanent squadrons, all of which were stationed at Khormaksar (plus a Pembroke flight at Bahrain). During the ensuing difficult years numerous changes were made to the force structure as reinforcements, usually of a temporary nature, arrived in theatre.

Another renaming took place on 1st March 1961 with BFAP becoming Middle East Command and the subordinate air element becoming Air Forces Middle East (AFME).

PALESTINE COMMAND

The Command was formed on 1st February 1922 as part of HQ RAF Middle East to control a flying section and No 2 Armoured Car Company. The primary tasks were dictated by the GOC Palestine. In November 1924 the flying section disbanded and was replaced by a flight of DH9As of No 14 Squadron. In October 1926 HQ Palestine Command moved from Bir Salem to Amman, taking over the functions of the previous HQ and absorbing the Trans-Jordan area as HQ Palestine and Trans-Jordan.

HQ RAF PALESTINE AND TRANS-JORDAN

The move of HQ Palestine Command to Amman on 1st October 1926 led to a merging of the two organisations into HQ RAF Palestine and Trans-Jordan for operational considerations, whilst general administrative matters came under the AOC Middle East; the Command remained subordinate to Middle East Command. The primary task of the new command was to be "responsible to HE the High Commissioner for such defence measures as may be neccessary for the operational control and major disposition of RAF units in Palestine and Trans-Jordan and the Trans-Jordan Frontier Force." It was a high-sounding role but at the time the sole operational unit was No 14 Squadron with its Flights at various detached locations.

The HQ moved to Jerusalem on 2nd October 1929, although it had been reduced to Group status the previous year (21st February 1928).

HQ RAF SUDAN

HQ RAF Sudan was formed 6th June 1940 but was reduced to Group status, as No 203 Gp, on 17th August.

HQ RAF EAST AFRICA

HQ RAF East Africa was formed on 25th July 1940 (some records state 19th October) by expanding the nucleus of SHQ Nairobi to control RAF and SAAF units in Kenya. It was eventually reduced to Group status as No 207 Gp.

The Command was reformed on 1st February 1961 but disbanded once more on 11th December 1964.

HQ RAF CYRENAICA

The history of this Command is somewhat confused as all of its records destroyed during the British retreat through Cyrenaica to Egypt.

Reduced to Group status, as No 204 Gp.

MALTA AIR COMMAND

Formed 18th February 1943 by renaming RAF Malta.

EASTERN AIR COMMAND

Eastern Air Command (Africa) was formed by expanding No 333 Gp to command status on 14th January 1943 to control various units in Algeria and Tunisia. This was a short-lived creation, giving way in March to North West African Coastal Air Force.

NORTH WEST AFRICAN AIR FORCE

The overall combined Command element for Allied air forces was, by early 1943, the NWAAF under Maj-Gen Spaatz. Subordinate commands comprised the NWA Strategic Air Force (NWASAF), including No 205 Gp, NWA Tactical Air Force (NWATAF), including Desert Air Force and Tactical Bombing Force (TBF), NWA PR Wing (NWAPRW), NWA Tactical Communications Command (NWATCC), and NWA Coastal Air Force (NWACAF), a combination of the old Eastern Air Command and US XII Fighter Command.

Various changes of title, some official and some not, saw the dropping of the 'West' element of the titles, plus a number of other minor changes. With the creation of MAAF towards the end of 1943 the entire structure changed again, although in most cases this was more a change of name rather than function.

BALKAN AIR FORCE (BAF)

BAF was formed at Bari 19th June 1944 out of AHQ 'G' Force, which had been formed at Bari 1st June, to "control operations in the Balkans area, primarily Yugoslavia, and associated territories such as Albania, plus the adjacent sea areas." It was also tasked to co-ordinate operations undertaken by the USAAF and Italian Air Force within this region; emphasis was placed upon the control of Special Duties work by all air forces over the Balkan region. BAF was very active, a wide range of tasks being flown by its three operational RAF Wings, which included a strong element from the SAAF.

The campaign in the Balkans and Greece was followed by a period of tension with the strident Yugoslav Communist authorities. The Command eventually disbanded on 15th July 1945.

MEDITERRANEAN ALLIED AIR FORCE

MAAF was formed on 10th December 1943 by combining the tasks of Mediterranean Air Command and North African Air Force as a combined HQ under General Ira Eaker, the RAF command element being HQ MED/ME under AM Sir John Slessor KCB DSO MC (from 1st January 1944). The AOC was responsible for direct control of all RAF formations within MAAF except for those under command of the AOC Middle East Command.

With effect from 1st February 1944 the subordinate Commands added the word 'Allied' to their title. The primary subordinate Commands thus became:

Mediterranean Allied Coastal Air Force (MACAF) — became AHQ Italy on 1st January 1945.

Mediterranean Allied Tactical Air Force (MATAF) — disbanded 6th July 1945.

MEDITERRANEAN/MIDDLE EAST COMMAND
This Command became the RAF element of the combined organisation of MAAF in January 1944.

MED/ME Command became independent at Caserta on 1st August 1945 to replace MAAF, essentially the return to single service, i.e RAF with no USAAF, organisation. October brought a move to Cairo and a defining of the area of responsibility as Central Mediterranean, North Africa, Levant, Iraq, Sudan, Aden and East Africa; this area being controlled by nine Air HQs and four Groups. However, post-war reduction in strength soon halved this total as the Command lost most of its operational tasks but acquired an important position in the air link with the Far East, providing Staging Post facilities. It was the area of transport and communications that was to prove one of the key elements for this Command, and its successors, over the ensuing three decades.

During the late 1940s further contraction took place as various AHQs were disbanded, their tasks having been completed. Both AHQ Greece and AHQ Italy went during 1947, these countries having returned to National control.

On 1st June 1949 MED/ME was renamed as Middle East Air Force, a more accurate reflection of its geographic area.

MIDDLE EAST AIR FORCE
Formed on 1st June 1949 by renaming MED/ME Command.

The next decade was to see a continued series of minor, and a few major, crises in the turbulent area of the Middle East; British forces, and the RAF in particular, were on almost permanent standby or actively engaged on operations. The primary reason for this situation was the growth of Arab Nationalism and the desire in the new world created after World War Two to 'throw off the yoke of Colonialism'. The situation in Egypt led to a revision of the Command's organisation and a move of HQ to Nicosia from Ismailia on 1st December 1954, the rear HQ moving from Abu Sueir to Ismailia and then to Episkopi, Cyprus.

The increased polarisation of Europe into two 'armed' camps, the old Western Allies against the now powerful Soviet empire, led to a new wave of mutual defence treaties, each of which brought military commitments. Under the terms of the 1955 Baghdad Pact Britain agreed to provide an air striking force, with nuclear capability, within this theatre of operations.

The same year brought a division of MEAF into a Southern Group ,covering Aden, South Arabian coast, East Africa and the Persian Gulf) and a Northern Group, covering Iraq, Jordan, Cyprus and Libya.

With the Suez crisis of 1956 MEAF provided the bases for the air tasks forces deployed from the UK, although its own squadrons were of course fully involved.

Revised concepts led to the introduction of a new unified Command structure in March 1961, with the two MEAF Groups joining separate new commands — MEAF being the RAF element of Middle East Command and NEAF that of Near East Command.

MIDDLE EAST COMMAND/MIDDLE EAST AIR FORCE
The introduction of a unified command structure on 1st March 1961 saw the old Northern Group of MEAF becoming an element of Middle East Command (Aden), with MEAF as the RAF controlling authority within MEC. The (Aden) element of the title was dropped later in the year. The final 10 years were to be difficult ones with problems throughout the area, and especially Aden. However, friendly relations were maintained with the Gulf States when MEAF closed down at Sharjah on 15th December 1971.

NEAR EAST COMMAND/NEAR EAST AIR FORCE
The introduction of a unified command structure on 1st March 1961 saw the old Southern Group of MEAF becoming an element of Near East Command (Cyprus), with NEAF as the RAF controlling authority within NEC. The (Cyprus) element of the title was dropped later in the year.

This was to a very short-lived organisation, within a year NEC had been disestablished and NEAF was left as the RAF Command structure to cover the same geographic area. The area remained active throughout the life of NEAF but continued reduction in British commitments led to disbandment on 31st March 1976.

AHQ CYPRUS
AHQ Cyprus was formed within MEAF on 9th January 1954 to control all the RAF units based on the island. As part of the general mid 1950s re-organisation responsibility was transfered to AHQ Levant when that formation moved to Cyprus on 15th January 1956.

AHQ LEVANT
This AHQ was formed on 1st May 1955 by renaming AHQ Iraq. On 15th January the HQ moved to Nicosia, Cyprus, absorbing AHQ Cyprus and assuming responsibility for Cyprus, Iraq and El Adem.

HQ DESERT AIR FORCE
As part of M(A)TAF HQ DAF was formed by renaming AHQ Western Desert. The history of this Command is covered in the relevant campaign details, the vital role it played in the prosecution of the Desert War and the development of tactical air power .

Having fought as a subordinate command through the North African and Italian campaigns, the Command eventually disbanded on 30th June 1946.

AHQ WEST AFRICA
West Africa Command formed at Freetown on 8th October 1941 Under A/C E A B Rice OBE MC. AHQ West Africa was responsible for "operational control, administration, training and efficiency of British Forces in Nigeria, Sierra Leone, Gold Coast and Gambia — with the exception of the air despatch route from Takoradi."

During 1942 various Wings were formed on a geographic basis, but most only lasted a matter of months. On 11th August 1945 the HQ moved to Accra althought the primary task now was to supervise the return to peace-time conditions and a general run-down of the RAF presence in the region. This latter was reflected in a reduction to Wing status, as No 500 Wing at Takoradi, on 1st August 1946.

AHQ EASTERN MEDITERRANEAN
Another of the short-lived subordinate Commands was AHQ E.Med, formed on 1st March 1945 to take over from No 203 Gp.

Its task was to provide operational and administrative control of fighter and GR units in Egypt and Libya, and operational training units in Egypt, Libya, Levant and Cyprus. The AHQ was disbanded on 28th February 1946 when its functions were absorbed within No 219 Gp.

HQ RAF NORTH AFRICA
This subordinate Command was formed on 30th June 1946 to take over the tasks of No 218 Gp; it was, however, very short lived, disbanding on 17th August.

AHQ AUSTRIA
Formed on 20th November 1945, AHQ Austria at Klagenfurt had control of the RAF occupation forces in that country. With effect from 15th June 1946 its functions were transfered to AHQ Italy.

AHQ ITALY
On 1st January 1945 MACAF at Caserta was renamed AHQ Italy in order to establish national, i.e RAF, control of units and to provide a more appropriate nomenclature. The Command controlled a number of subordinate Commands throughout the region but as the post-war situation stabilised, RAF strength was reduced and the AHQs began to disband. By 1st September 1947 it had been reduced to a small tactical HQ at Udine, having moved there in August 1946, providing operational control for a single Tempest Wing plus admin and technical support for various other units at Udine.

The formation disbanded on 6th October 1947.

AHQ GREECE
AHQ Greece was formed on 1st September 1944 within Force 276, a combined force organisation within MAAF, responsible for No 377 Wing and a variety of other units. The main operational task was the provision of assistance in clearing Greece of Axis forces but also countering Greek Communist (ELAS) forces in their bid to seize power during the latter months of 1944.

The formation disbanded on 11th January 1947.

AHQ GIBRALTAR
AHQ Gibraltar was formed on 1st September 1953 by renaming RAF Gibraltar. Disbanded 30th November 1966.

AF MIDDLE EAST (AFME)
As part of MEC AFME had the difficult task of looking after a turbulent area, including Aden, in the 1960s. In accordance with the planned withdrawal Aden was abandoned in October 1967, AFME becoming Air Forces Gulf as part of British Forces Gulf.

HQ RAF PERSIAN GULF/AIR FORCES GULF
As a subordinate Command within AFAP, HQ RAF Persian Gulf was formed at Bahrain on 4th July 1959.

It was renamed Air Forces Gulf on 1st September 1967 but disbanded 15th December 1971.

A major role for the units in West Africa was maritime patrol

COMMAND CHRONOLOGY — Middle East

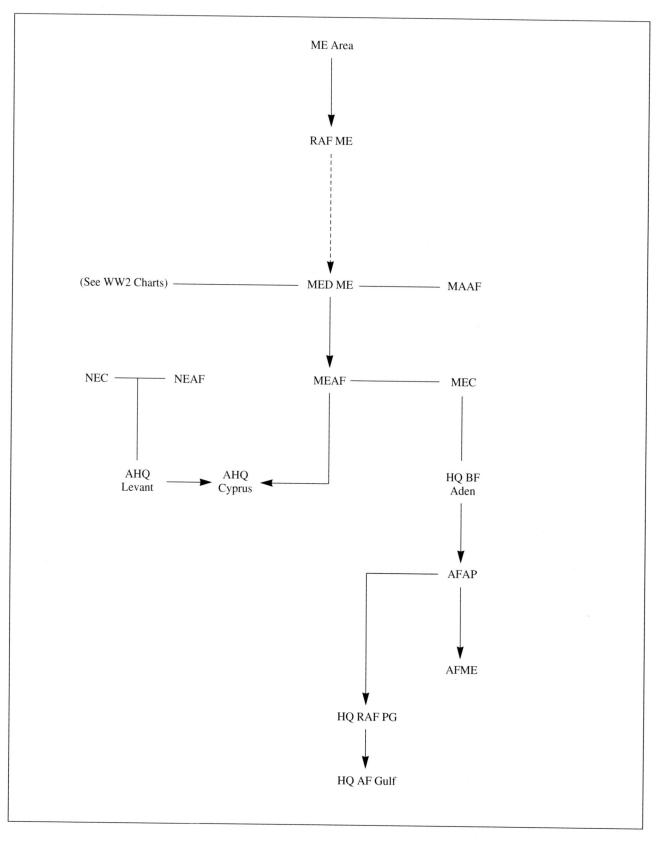

OVERSEAS COMMANDS SEPTEMBER 1939

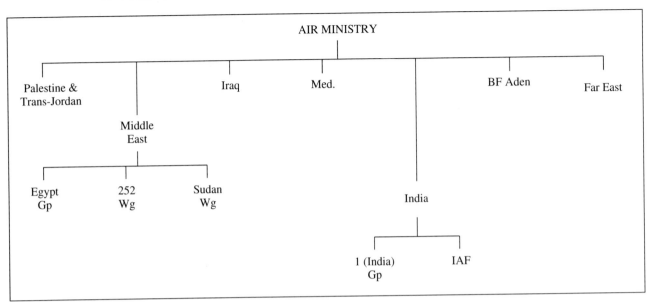

ROYAL AIR FORCE MIDDLE EAST JANUARY 1941

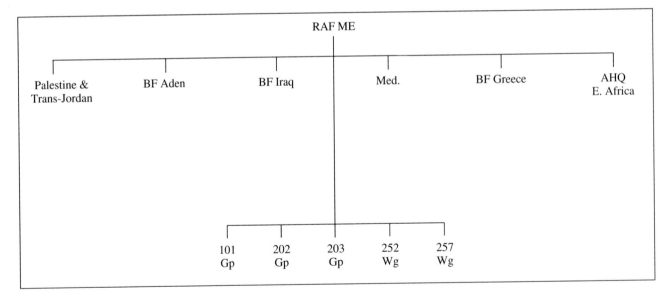

MIDDLE EAST COMMAND 11th NOVEMBER 1941

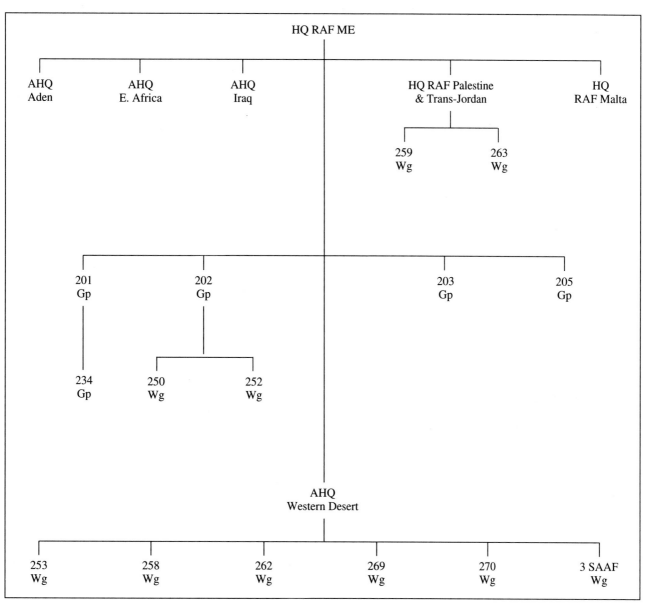

MIDDLE EAST COMMAND 27th OCTOBER 1942

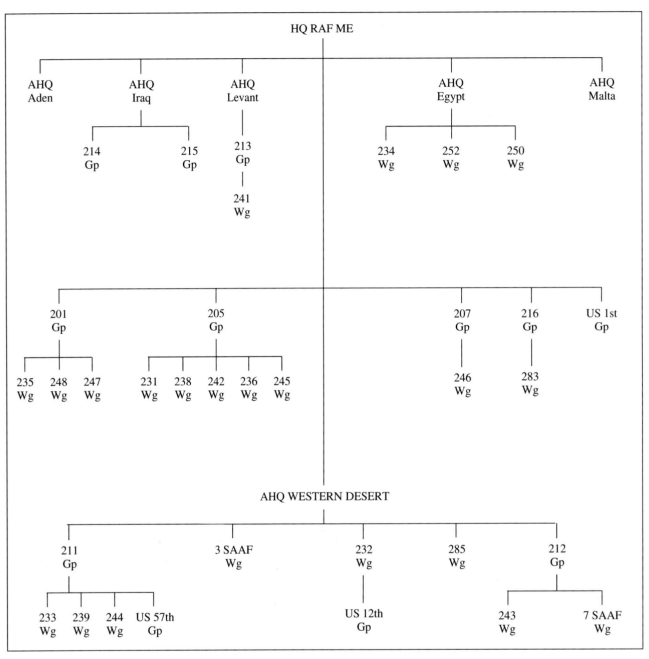

MIDDLE EAST COMMAND MARCH 1943

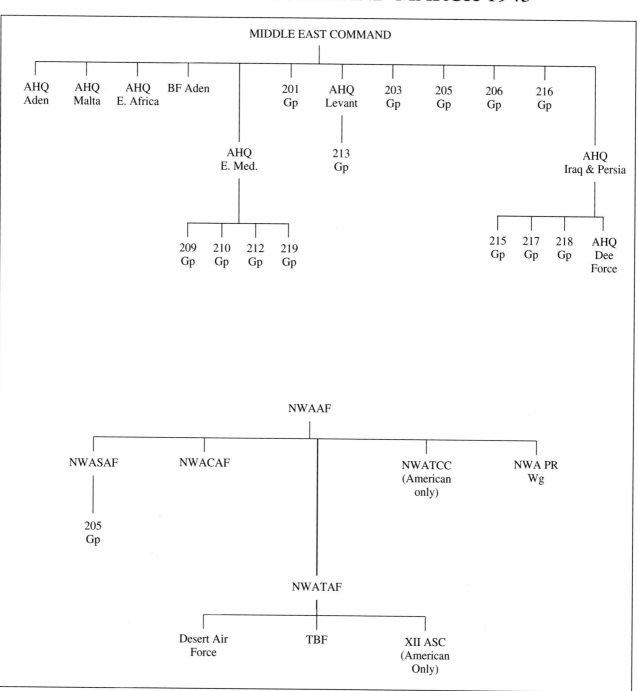

MEDITERRANEAN ALLIED AIR FORCES JUNE 1944

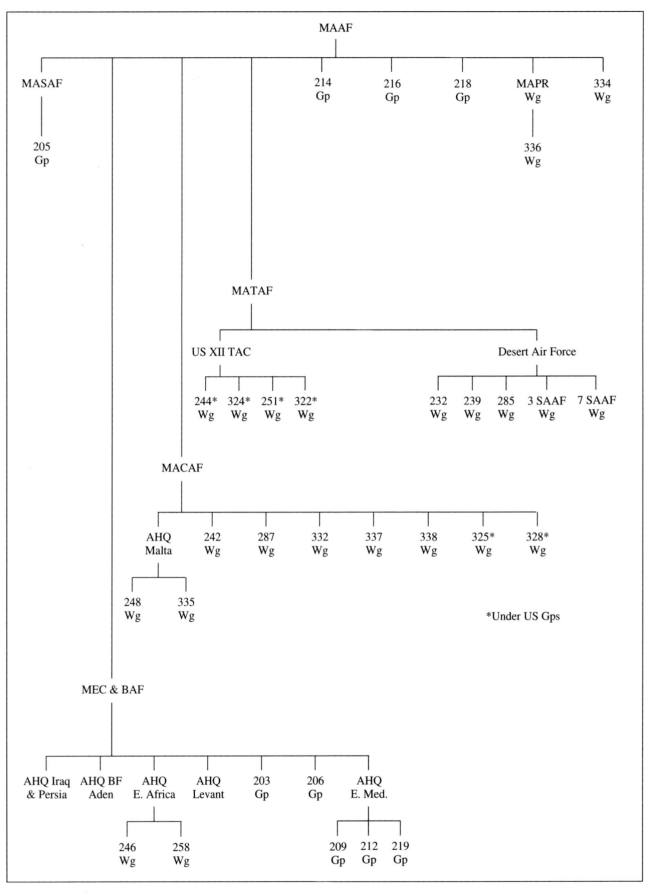

MEDITERRANEAN ALLIED AIR FORCES JANUARY 1945

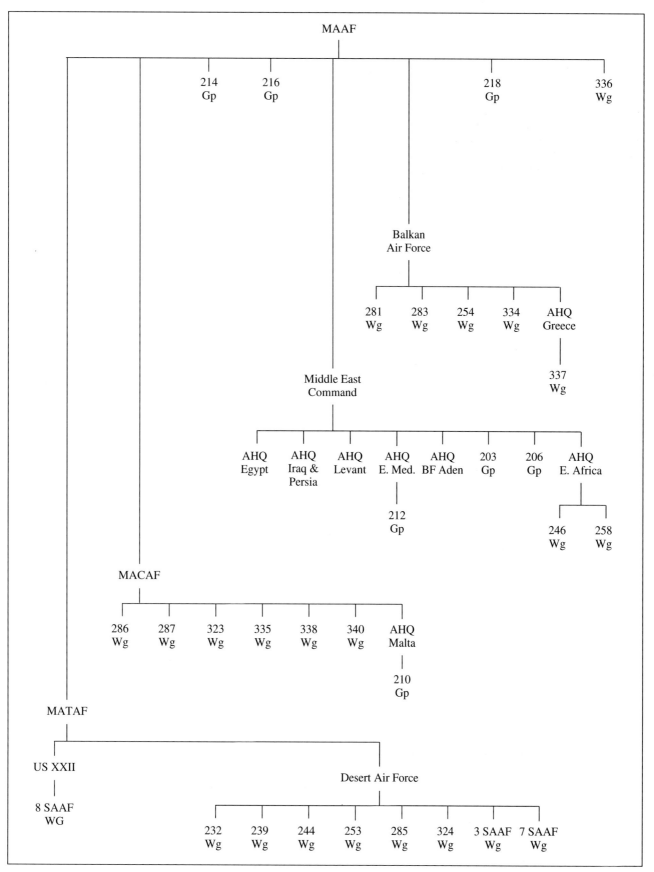

MAAF

214 Gp   216 Gp   218 Gp   336 Wg

Balkan Air Force

281 Wg   283 Wg   254 Wg   334 Wg   AHQ Greece

337 Wg

Middle East Command

AHQ Egypt   AHQ Iraq & Persia   AHQ Levant   AHQ E. Med.   AHQ BF Aden   203 Gp   206 Gp   AHQ E. Africa

212 Gp

246 Wg   258 Wg

MACAF

286 Wg   287 Wg   323 Wg   335 Wg   338 Wg   340 Wg   AHQ Malta

210 Gp

MATAF

US XXII

8 SAAF WG

Desert Air Force

232 Wg   239 Wg   244 Wg   253 Wg   285 Wg   324 Wg   3 SAAF Wg   7 SAAF Wg

THE FAR EAST

HQ RAF FAR EAST/FAR EAST COMMAND

Formed on 1st January 1930 at Seletar, HQ RAF Far East, or Far East Command,was given control of RAF operations in Singapore, Hong Kong, Malaya and Burma.

The general RAF expansion of the mid-late 1930s also affected the Far East, although with far less impetus, and a programme of airfield and landing ground construction was instigated.

On 9th January 1941 the formation was renamed AHQ Far East but continued to function in the same way. It disbanded a year later, 14th February 1942, upon the formation of ABDA.

This title of Far East Command was reborn in November 1962 with the introduction of a unified command structure, FEAF becoming the air element.

AMERICAN BRITISH DUTCH AUSTRALIAN COMMAND

A new Allied Command structure was formed under General Wavell on 14th February 1942 to cover Burma, Malaya, Dutch East Indies, Philippines and North Australia. ABDACOM consisted of five air Groups — NORGROUP (Burma), ex No 221 Gp, and WESGROUP (Singapore and parts of Sumatra), comprising No 224 and No 225 Gps, being the two main areas of RAF involvement. The overall RAF air commander was AM Sir Richard Peirse. With the fluid, and generally unfavourable, situation of 1942 the Command's units underwent numerous moves and a variety of organisational changes. By late February 1942 NORGROUP was under control of AHQ India, although it disbanded at Akyab in April, and WESGROUP had moved to Java, disbandment is usually given as 25th February.

COMMAND CHRONOLOGY — Far East

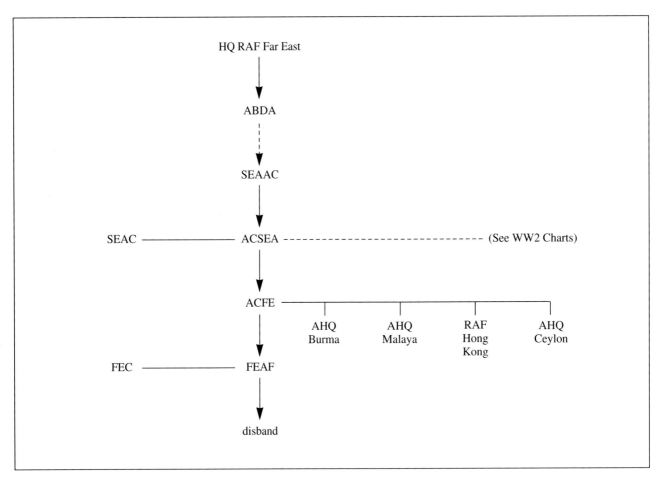

FAR EAST (ABDACOM) 14th FEBRUARY 1942

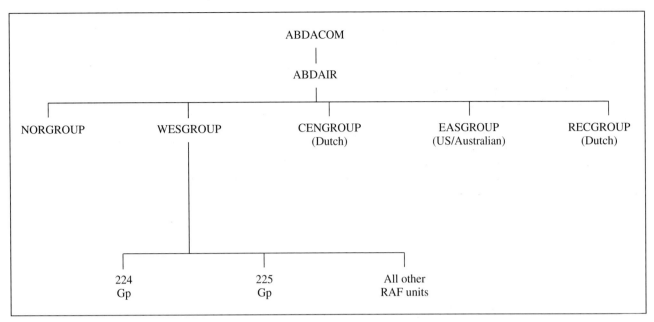

FAR EAST (ABDACOM) MARCH 1943

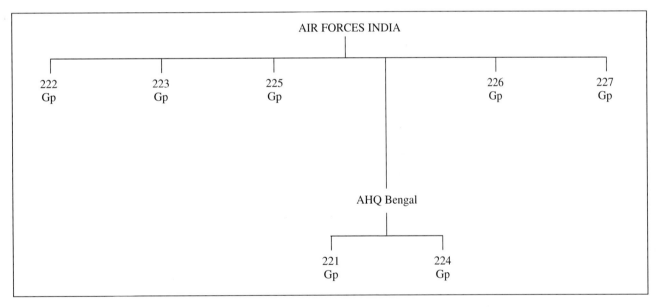

RAF India's main task in the 1930s was policing of tribal unrest, a task which suited the rugged nature of the Wapiti — 39 Squadron was based at Risalpur.

HQ RAF INDIA/AHQ INDIA

HQ New Delhi
By April 1932 all operational units under No 1 (Indian) Group, most actively engaged with anti-tribal operations in North West Frontier Province were under HQ New Dehli.

During 1947 there was a phased run-down of RAF strength in India as the Indian Air Force assumed greater responsibility; by August 1947 the RAF had two AHQs at Delhi — AHQ India and AHQ Delhi, although the former soon became a pure IAF structure.

EASTERN AIR COMMAND
This combined American/British Command formed under General Stratemeyer on 15th December 1943, absorbing AHQ Bengal, 3rd TAF, plus elements of USAAF 10th Strategic Air Force. It was later renamed Eastern Air Command (South East Asia) to avoid confusion with other Commands carrying the EAC title. By 1st June 1945 all the USAAF units had gone and so the Command disbanded, control of RAF units going to AHQ Burma.

BRITISH AIR FORCES SOUTH EAST ASIA (BAFSEA)
This HQ was formed at Delhi on 1st October 1944 for the command and control of all maintenance, supply and training support to RAF units in ACSEA, plus the control of any operational units deployed to India, but with the exception of No 222 Gp. It performed this vital behind the scenes task for the remainder of the war and into the immediate post-war period of confusion, finally disbanding on 1st April 1946 when its duties were transferred to AHQ India.

AIR COMMAND SOUTH EAST ASIA (ACSEA)
Formed 16th November 1943, as South East Asia Air Command, under ACM Sir Richard Peirse as a combined RAF/USAAF operational command covering India, Ceylon, Burma, Siam, Malaya and Sumatra. The title changed to ACSEA on 30th December 1943. An advanced HQ was formed at Kandy in April 1944 to act as a planning and liaison staff with the advanced combined HQ.

Overall strength was rapidly increased and by mid 1944 the formation had control of three subordinate Commands — EAC, 3rd TAF and BAFSEA, plus No 222 and 229 Groups. HQ moved to Kandy on 1st October 1944 and by July the following year the subordinate Commands controlled by ACSEA comprised BAFSEA and AHQ Burma, plus two additional Groups — No 222 and No 229. The area was extended during summer 1945 to include AHQ Malaya, AHQ Siam, HQ Netherlands East Indies, HQ French Indo-China, AHQ Ceylon, and HQ RAF Hong Kong. The war with Japan was over but there many unresolved problems throughout the area requiring the attention of ACSEA units. There was also the matter of demobilisation and return to the UK for the 'duration only' RAF personnel — a matter which became most contentious as the months of 'peace' went by. In December HQ ACSEA moved to Singapore.

ACSEA was re-structured to a peace-time basis, the RAF elements becoming ACFE on 30th November 1946.

AIR COMMAND SOUTH EAST ASIA 1st JULY 1944

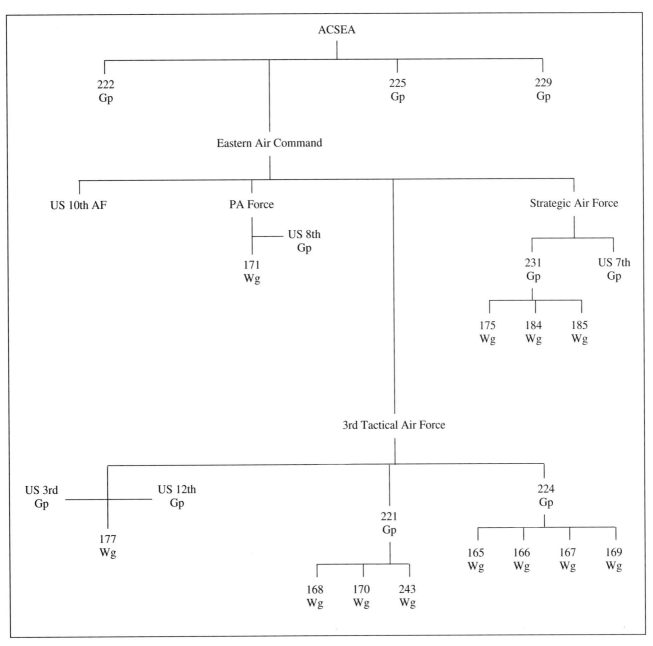

HQ RAF BURMA/AHQ BURMA/AHQ BENGAL-BURMA

HQ RAF Burma (sometimes refered to as RAF Bengal/Burma) was formed on 4th December 1944 out of 3rd Tactical Air Force under Eastern Air Command. The formation was responsible for the "functional control of all RAF units , except No 229 and No 230 Groups, east of the river Brahmaputra, plus the functional control and administrative control of of RAF units within EAC."

The command was reduced to Group status, although it is also recorded as having subordinate Command status, as AHQ Burma, on 27th February 1945 to have "functional and operational control of all RAF and Indian Air Force units, except BAFSEA, within Eastern Air Command, and RAF and Indian Air Force units in Burma". The primary task was that of air transport and the nine Dakota squadrons of No 232 Group were heavily tasked with support of 12th Army during the re-occupation campaign; there was also a heavy workload of POW repatriation and supply dropping to civilians. Another change of title, 1st August 1945,

formed HQ RAF Burma; a few weeks later this reverted to AHQ Burma, now at Rangoon, as part of ACSEA. A gradual reduction in strength led to loss of Command status, although there is some dispute as to the effective date of this; HQ moved to Mingaladon in January 1947, followed by disbandment on 31st December the same year.

HQ RAF CEYLON/AHQ CEYLON

HQ RAF Ceylon was formed 27th June 1941 at Colombo to control all RAF units in Ceylon and at bases in the Indian Ocean. In April 1942 the AOC No 222 Group became AOC Ceylon to command all RAF units on the island, although at the time this amounted to very little. The importance of Ceylon in the strategic situation of the Far East increased as other bases fell before the Japanese advance. A number of Command organisations moved to Ceylon.

AHQ Ceylon formed at Colombo on 16th October 1945 as

part of the post-war re-organisation under ACSEA.

In October 1946 the HQ moved to Katakurunda.

It moved again in November 1957 to Negombo.

AHQ MALAYA

Formed at Singapore on 1st October 1945 AHQ Malaya was part of the post-war re-organisation of ACSEA and was responsible for all RAF units in Malaya and for the provision of administrative support to HQ Netherlands East Indies and HQ Hong Kong. In February the following year its duties related to Malaya and Singapore, although in December it also acquired responsibility for air defence operations in North Borneo, Brunei and Sarawak. Having moved to Tengah in August 1946 the HQ made a further move, to Changi, in December.

AHQ Malaya was reduced to Group status, as No 224 Group, on 31st August 1957.

HQ RAF HONG KONG/AHQ HONG KONG

This HQ formed on 15th September 1945, under ACSEA, to administer all RAF units in Hong Kong and any units which operated along the China coast 'from time to time'. The formation replaced HQ Tiger Force which had formed at Hong Kong in readiness for invasion operations against Japan.

On 15th May 1946 it became AHQ Hong Kong.

AHQ SIAM

AHQ Siam formed on 1st October 1945 at Bangkok, under AHQ Burma, by the expansion and re-naming of No 909 Wing, to control all RAF units in Siam. Its primary task was the location and repatriation of Allied POWs. This task had been substantially completed by January 1946.

HQ FRENCH INDO-CHINA

Formed at Saigon on 1st October 1945, HQ French Indo-China controlled units engaged in the re-occupation of this former French territory and the supervising of its return to French control. The formation disbanded on 15th February 1946 although units for which it was responsible were operating in the area until April.

HQ NETHERLANDS EAST INDIES

As part of the ACSEA re-organisation, this Command formed at Batavia on 1st October 1945 to assist in the re-occupation of the former Dutch territories, plus the location and repatriation of POWs. The primary operational formation was No 904 (Thunderbolt) Wing. With the withdrawal of British forces from the area this formation disbanded on 30th November 1946.

AIR COMMAND FAR EAST (ACFE)

Air Command Far east was formed on 30th November 1945 out of the re-structuring of the joint ACSEA.

It had control of a number of regional-based AHQs plus other minor units under direct control. By December 1946 the structure comprised AHQs Burma, Malaya, Hong Kong and Ceylon. Continued reduction of commitments led to further re-organisation and in June 1949 ACFE was renamed FEAF.

FAR EAST AIR FORCE (FEAF)

Far East Air Force was formed on 1st June 1949 by renaming ACFE. Its major operational task during the initial period was the Malayan Emergency, this continuing until 1960. Shortly afterwards the Command was faced with the Indonesian confrontation.

1st June 1963 saw the introduction of a unified command structure for the theatre, with the formation of Far East Command, FEAF being the primary air element. The run-down of British forces in the Far East was accelerated by the Labour Government with a view to ceasing all operational commitments. Despite a number of rumours to the contrary, the run-down proceded according to the revised schedule and FEAF disbanded on 31st October 1971.

AIR COMMAND SOUTH EAST ASIA JANUARY 1945

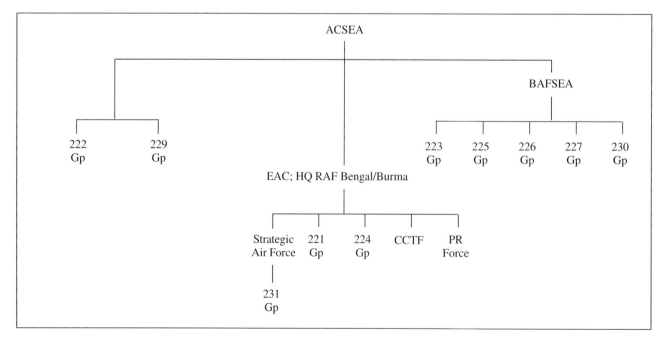

Argosy aircraft of 215 Squadron operated within FEAF.

GROUPS

The second tier of the command structure, the Group is the level at which Command instructions are turned into operational capabilities before being passed down for implementation. Throughout the history of the RAF the composition and application of the Group philosophy has changed many times — some Groups have been vast, almost like Command structures, whilst others have been quite small, little different to that of the next level down, the Wing. The original intention was to include a mini-history of each Group but space has precluded this.

Badge of No. 1 Group.

No 1 Group — TRAINING. Formed 4.18 at St James's (London). Renumbered as No 21 Group 12.4.26.

No 1 Group — BOMBER. Formed by renaming Central Area 1.5.36 at Abingdon. Disbanded 22.12.39. Reformed 22.6.40 by renaming AASF HQ at Hucknall. Current.

No 1 (Indian) Group — AC. Formed 11.28 at Peshawar. Renumbered as No 223 Group 1.5.42. Reformed at Peshawar 15.8.45. Disbanded 15.8.47.

No 2 Group — TRAINING. Formed 4.18 at Oxford. Disbanded 31.3.20 at Uxbridge.

No 2 Group — BOMBER. Formed 20.3.36 at Abingdon. Disbanded 1.5.47. Reformed in BAFO 1950. Disband 15.11.58. Reformed 1.4.93 when RAFG reduced to Gp status. Current.

No 2 (Indian) Group — Reformed 1.10.45 at Begumpet out of No 225 Gp. Reduced to Wing status 15.8.47.

No 3 Group — TRAINING. Formed 4.18 at Cambridge. Renumbered as No 23 Group 4.26.

No 3 Group — BOMBER. Formed by renaming Western Area 1.5.36 at Andover. Disbanded 1.11.67.

No 3 (Indian) Group — Formed by renumbering No 228 Group at Barrackpore 1.5.36. Reduced to Wing status 15.8.47.

No 4 Group — MARINE OPERATIONAL. Formed 1.4.18 at Felixstowe. Disbanded 24.3.19.

No 4 Group — BOMBER. Formed 1.4.37 at Mildenhall. Became TRANSPORT 7.5.45. Disbanded 2.2.48.

No 4 (Indian) Group — Formed 1.6.46 by renumbering No 227 Group at Agra, disbanded 15.7.46.

No 5 Group — OPERATIONS. Formed 1.4.18 at Dover. Disbanded 15.5.19.

No 5 Group — BOMBER. Formed 1.9.37 as an offshoot of No 4 Group at Mildenhall. Disbanded 15.12.45.

No 6 Group — OPERATIONS. Formed 4.18 at Taranto (Italy). Disbanded 20.12.18.

No 6 Group — SPECIAL RESERVE AND AAF. Formed 14.5.25. Renamed AIR DEFENCE GROUP 18.7.27. Renamed No 1 AIR DEFENCE GROUP 25.8.27. Renamed No 6 (AUXILIARY) GROUP 1.4.36. Renamed BOMBER 1.1.39 at Norwich. Became No 91 Group 11.5.42.

No 6 (RCAF) Group — Formed 25.10.42 at Allerton Park. Transferred to RCAF 17.7.45.

No 7 Group — TRAINING. Formed 4.18 at Salisbury. Disbanded 15.9.19.

No 7 Group — OPERATIONAL TRAINING. Formed 15.7.40 (effective 8.8.40) at Brampton Lodge. Became No 92 Group 11.5.42. Reformed 20.9.44 as HQ/admin for Bomber Command HCUs at Grantham. Disbanded 21.12.45.

No 8 Group — TRAINING. Formed 4.18 at Southampton. Disbanded 15.5.19.

No 8 Group — BOMBER. Formed 1.9.41 at Brampton. Disbanded 28.1.43. reformed as PFF 13.1.43 (effective 25.1.43) at Wyton. Disbanded 15.12.45.

No 9 Group — MARINE OPERATIONAL. Formed 1.4.18 at Plymouth. Disbanded 15.5.19 at Devonport.

No 9 Group — FIGHTER. Formed 9.8.40 at Barton Hall, Preston. Disbanded 18.9.44.

No 10 Group — MARINE OPERATIONAL. Formed 1.4.18 at Calshot. Disbanded 2.32.

No 10 Group — FIGHTER. Formed 15.6.40 at Rudloe Manor, Box. Disbanded 2.5.45.

No 11 Group — Formed 8.18 in Ireland. Became No 11 (Irish) Wing 5.20.

No 11 Group — FIGHTER. Formed 20.5.36 at Kenley. Disbanded 31.3.63. Reform? Current.

No 12 Group — TRAINING. Formed 4.18 at Cranwell. Disbanded 1.11.19.

No 12 Group — FIGHTER. Formed 1.4.37 at Uxbridge. Disbanded 31.3.63.

No 13 Group — TRAINING. Formed 4.18 at Birmingham. Disbanded 18.10.19 at Shotwick.

No 13 Group — FIGHTER. Formed 24.7.39 at Newcastle. Disbanded 20.5.46.

No 14 Group — MARINE OPERATIONAL. Formed 1.4.18 at Pembroke. Disbanded 19.5.19 at Haverfordwest.

No 14 Group — FIGHTER. Formed 20.1.40 from No 60 Wing at Achicourt (France). Disbanded 5.40. Reformed 1.8.40 at Drumossie Hotel, Inverness. Amalgamated with No 13 Group 15.7.43.

No 15 Group — Formed 4.18 at Mudros (Aegean). Disbanded 1.9.19.

No 15 Group — GR. Formed 15.3.39 at Lee-on-Solent. Disbanded 1.8.45.

No 16 Group — TRAINING. Formed 4.18 at York. Disbanded 18.10.19.

No 16 Group — GR. Formed 1.12.36 at Lee-on-Solent. Disbanded 8.3.46 on formation of No 16 Wing.

No 17 Group — OPERATIONAL. Formed 4.18 at Newcastle. Disbanded 18.10.19.

No 17 Group — TRAINING. Formed 1.12.36 at Lee-on-Solent. Disbanded 18.9.45.

No 18 Group — MARINE OPERATIONAL. Formed 1.4.18 at Immingham. Disbanded 18.10.19 at Harborough.

No 18 Group — GR. Formed 1.9.38 at Lee-on-Solent. Current.

No 19 Group — GR. Formed 5.2.41 at Plymouth. Disbanded 28.11.69.

No 20 Group — TRAINING. Formed 4.18 at Edinburgh. Disbanded 28.9.19.

No 20 Group — TRAINING. Formed 30.11.39 at Market Drayton. Became part of No 22 Group 1.8.43.

No 21 Group — TRAINING. Formed 4.26 from No 1 Group at West Drayton. Disbanded 2.34. Reformed 1.12.38 at Cranwell.

No 22 Group — MARINE OPERATIONAL. Formed 4.18 at Stirling. Disbanded 30.5.19.

No 22 Group — AC. Formed 12.4.26 at South Farnborough. Disbanded 1.12.40. Reformed 1.8.43 as TRAINING at Market Drayton. Disbanded 31.1.72.

No 23 Group — TRAINING. Formed 4.26 from No 3 Group at Grantham. Disbanded 1.5.68.

No 24 Group — HOME DEFENCE. Formed 7.18 at Leeds. Disbanded 13.6.19.

No 24 Group — TRAINING. Formed 10.7.36 at Halton.

No 25 Group — ARMAMENT. Formed 1.2.34 as Armament Group at Eastchurch, renamed 1.2.37. Disbanded 15.4.48. Reformed 20.3.51 as TRAINING, to control jet AFS. Disbanded 1.7.68.

No 26 Group — TRAINING. Formed 8.18 at Heliopolis (Egypt). Disbanded 12.18.

No 26 Group — SIGNALS. Formed 12.2.40 at Cranwell. Amalgamated with No 60 Group to form No 90 Group 25.4.46.

No 27 Group — Formed 8.18 at Bircham Newton as Independent Operational Air Force but never functioned as such. Disbanded 19.5.19.

No 27 Group — SIGNALS TRAINING. Formed 26.5.41 at Langley.

No 28 Group — MARINE OPERATIONAL. Formed 8.18 at Stenness. Disbanded 15.4.19.

No 28 Group — TRAINING. Formed 1.11.42 at Cirencester.

No 29 Group — Formed 27.11.18 at Edinburgh, called Fleet Group. Disbanded 4.22.

No 29 Group — TRAINING. Formed 1.7.42 at Market Drayton. Disbanded 19.7.45.

No 30 Group — OPERATIONAL. Formed 8.18 at Salonika. Became No 16 Wing 7.4.19.

No 30 Group — BALLOON BARRAGE. Formed 17.3.37. Disbanded 7.1.45.

No 31 Group — OPERATIONAL. Formed 8.18 in Mesopotamia. Disbanded 4.19.

No 31 Group — BALLOON BARRAGE. Formed 1.3.59 at HQ Balloon Command. Moved to Birmingham 1.5.39. Disbanded 13.1..41.

No 32 Group — BALLOON BARRAGE. Formed 1.3.39 in London. Disbanded 15.11.44.

No 33 Group — BALLOON BARRAGE. Formed 1.3.39(?) in London. Disbanded 4.9. 44.

No 34 Group — BALLOON BARRAGE. Formed 7.3.40 at Newcastle. Disbanded 19.7.43.

No 38 Group — AIRBORNE FORCES. Formed 11.10.43 by absorbing No 38 Wing at Netheravon. Disbanded 1.2.51. Reformed as Special Tactical Transport within Training Command. Amalgamated with No 1 Gp 18.11.83. Reformed 1.11.92. Current.

No 40 Group — MAINTENANCE. Formed 6.3.39 at Andover. Disbanded 28.7.61.

No 41 Group — MAINTENANCE. Formed 1.1.39 at Andover. Disbanded 21.7.61.

No 42 Group — MAINTENANCE. Formed 17.4.39 at Andover.

No 43 Group — MAINTENANCE. Formed 21.9.39 at Andover.

No 44 Group — FERRY SERVICE. Formed 15.8.41 at Gloucester. Disbanded 14.8.46.

No 45 Group — ATLANTIC TRANSPORT. Formed 11.4.43 by renaming Ferry Command at Dorval (Canada). Became No 45 Wing 15.2.46.

No 46 Group — TRANSPORT. Formed 17.1.44 at Harrow. Absorbed into No 47 Gp 1.5.49. Reformed 1.9.72 as TRANSPORT. Disbanded 9.11.75.

No 47 Group — TRANSPORT. Formed 1.1.45 at Hendon. Disbanded 31.3.50.

No 48 Group — TRANSPORT. Formed 1.10.45 at Milton Ernest Hall, Bedford. Disbanded 15.5.46.

No 50 Group — TRAINING. Formed 3.4.39 at London. Disbanded 31.5.47.

No 51 Group — TRAINING. Formed 11.5.39 at Hendon. 8.8.39 at Leeds. Disbanded 14.7.45.

No 54 Group — TRAINING. Formed 30.8.39 at Reading (or 12.10.39). Disbanded 17.6.46.

No 60 Group — SIGNALS. Formed 23.3.40 at Leighton Buzard. Amalgamated with No 26 Group to form No 90 Group 25.4.46.

No 61 Group — Formed 6.7.40 at Belfast. Became RAF Northern Ireland 1. 8.40. Reformed 2.5.46 as EASTERN RESERVE at Rickmansworth. Disbanded . 2.57.

No 62 Group — SOUTHERN RESERVE. Formed 2.5.46 at Exeter.

No 63 Group — WESTERN AND WELSH RESERVE. Formed 2.5.46 at Wilmslow. Disbanded 1.2.57. No 64 Group — NORTHERN RESERVE. Formed 2.5.46 at Sheffield.

No 65 Group — LONDON RESERVE. Formed 2.5.46 at London.

No 66 Group — SCOTTISH RESERVE. Formed 2.5.46 at Edinburgh.

No 67 Group — N.IRELAND RESERVE. Formed 31.3.50 at Aldergrove by renaming HQ RAF N.Ireland. Disbanded 28.2.57.

No 70 Group — AC TRAINING. Formed 1.12.40 at Farnborough. Disbanded 17.7.45.

No 71 Group — AC. Formed 1.12.40 at Hammersmith and Wentworth. Disbanded 14.8.41 at Sunningdale.

No 72 Group — AC TRAINING. Formed 16.9.42 at Farnborough. Became part of No 22 Group 1.8.43.

No 81 Group — OPERATIONAL TRAINING. Formed 16.12.40 at Sealand. Disbanded 20.4.43.

No 82 Group — FIGHTER. Formed 1.8.41 in Northern Ireland. Absorbed into RAF Northern Ireland 15.10.42.

No 83 Group — COMPOSITE. Formed 1.4.43 by renaming 'Z' Group at Redhill. Amalgamated with No 84 Group 3.46. Reformed 1952. Disbanded 16. 6.58.

No 84 Group — COMPOSITE. Formed 15.7.43 at Cowley Barracks, Oxford. Disbanded 15.12.47.

No 85 Group — BASE. Formed 17.12.43 at Uxbridge. Became No 85 Wing 1.7.46. Returned to Group status 1.12.48 for Berlin Airlift. Disbanded 15.6.50

No 87 Group — Formed 17.2.45 to assimilate RAF Units Paris. Became TRANSPORT 15.7.45. Became No 87 Wing 15.7.46.

No 88 Group — Formed 7.5.45 at Edinburgh for Operation 'Apostle' in Norway. Moved to Oslo end 5.45. Disbanded 31.12.45.

No 90 Group — SIGNALS. Formed 25.4.46 by amalgamation of No 26 and No 60 Groups at Medmenham. Reformed 1.1.69.

No 91 Group — OPERATIONAL TRAINING. Formed 11.5.42 by renaming No 6 Group at Abingdon.

No 92 Group — OPERATIONAL TRAINING. Formed 11.5.42 by renaming No 7 Group at Winslow. Disbanded 15.7.45. (also given as 27.8.46)

No 93 Group — BOMBER OPERATIONAL TRAINING. Formed 15.6.42 at Lichfield. Disbanded 14.2.45.

No 100 Group — SPECIAL DUTIES. Formed 3.12.43 at West Raynham. Disbanded 17.12.45.

No 101 Group —No data.

No 106 Group — PR. Formed 14.4.44 by renumbering No 106 Wing at Benson. Disbanded 15.8.46 on formation of Central Photographic Establishment.

No 200 Group — COASTAL. Formed 25.9.39 at Gibraltar out of GR Gp Mediterranean. Became AHQ Gibraltar 1.5.42.

No 201 Group — GR. Formed 18.9.39 on SS 'Dumana' at Alexandria out of GR Gp Middle East. Became NAVAL CO-OPERATION 7.42. Absorbed into Air Defence Eastern Mediterranean 1.2.44.

No 202 Group — OPERATIONAL. Formed 18.4.39 from HQ Egypt Group at Heliopolis. Became AHQ Egypt 12.41. Reformed 11.7.44 in Corsica. Disbanded 7.11.44.

No 203 Group — FIGHTER. Formed 17.8.40 by renaming HQ RAF Sudan at Khartoum. Reduced to number only 10.5.43. Reformed 10.5.43 at Heliopolis for operational and administrative control of various TRAINING units. Disbanded 28.2.45.

No 204 Group — OPERATIONAL. Formed 12.4.41 by renaming HQ RAF Cyrenaica at Maaten Bagush. Became AHQ Western Desert 9.10.41.

No 205 Group — HEAVY BOMBER. Formed 10.41 by renaming No 257 Wing at Shallufa (ME). 1.12.46 absorbed No 219 Group. Advanced HQ at Fayid. Disbanded 31.3.47. Reformed ...? Disbanded 15.4.56.

No 206 Group — MAINTENANCE. Formed 1.9.41 by renaming Maintenance Group which had formed 17.6.41 at HQ ME. Disbanded 28.2.46. Reformed 1.6.51 as Base Maintenance for Middle East at Abyad. Disbanded 31.8.54.

No 207 Group — GENERAL PURPOSE. Formed 12.41 by renaming AHQ East Africa at Nairobi. Became AHQ East Africa 16.11.42.

No 209 Group — FIGHTER. Formed 15.12.42 in place of No 263 Wing at Ramleh (ME). Disbanded 15.11.44.

No 210 Group — FIGHTER. Formed 3.43 at Tripoli. Disbanded 1.5.44. Reformed 6.7.44 at Algiers to control Coastal Air Force units in North Africa, Corsica and Sardinia. Disbanded 25.4.45.

No 211 Group — Formed 10.12.41 at Maaten Bagush by renaming Nucleus Group Western Desert (which had formed 5.11.41). Disbanded 3.2.42. Reformed as OFFENSIVE FIGHTER 12.3.42 at El Adem. Reduced to number only 17.9.43 and became 'Z' Sector NAAF.

No 212 Group — FIGHTER. Formed 1.12.42 at Gazala (ME). Disbanded 31.1. 46.

No 213 Group — OPERATIONAL. Formed 15.12.41 by renaming Advanced HQ Levant at Beirut. Disbanded 15.11.43.

No 214 Group — Formed 1.1.42 at Habbaniya (Iraq). Merged into No 217 Group 11.42. Reformed as MAINTENANCE 15.5.43 at Tripoli. Disbanded 31. 12.45.

No 215 Group — GR. Formed 1.5.42 at Basrah (Iraq). Disbanded 1.11.43.

No 216 Group — TRANSPORT and FERRY. Formed 9.9.42 at Heliopolis. Reduced to Care and maintenance basis 31.7.46. Disbanded 26.10.46.

No 217 Group — (PAIFORCE) Formed 18.9.42 by renaming Persian Group (formed 1.9.42) at Habbaniya (Iraq). Reduced to number only 5.43. Reformed 3.11.43 at Cairo. Disbanded 29.2.44.

No 218 Group — MAINTENANCE. Formed 1.10.42 at Habbaniya (Iraq). Reduced to number only 17.4.43. Reformed 1.1.44 by renaming NWA Air Service Command. Disbanded 30.6.46.

No 219 Group — FIGHTER. Formed 6.12.42 at Seagull Camp. Disbanded 27.7.44. Reformed 1.3.46 at Heliopolis. Amalgamated with No 205 Group 1.12.46.

No 221 Group — TACTICAL (BOMBER). Formed 21.4.41 at Rangoon. Disbanded 12.3.42 at Akyab (Burma). Reformed 12.3.42 at Calcutta. Renamed TACTICAL 1.12.42. Disbanded 30.9.45 at Rangoon.

No 222 Group — GR. Formed 1.9.41 at Colombo (Ceylon) to control all GR units in Aden, East Africa and Persian Gulf. Disbanded 15.10. 45.

No 223 Group — FIGHTER. Formed 9.8.41, also known as NORGROUP, at Singapore. Disbanded 17.12.42. Reformed as COMPOSITE 1.5.42 by renumbering No 1 (Indian) Group, to administer all units in NW India, at Peshawar. Disbanded 15.8.45.

No 224 Group — FIGHTER. Formed end.41 at Singapore. Reformed 3.2.42 at Padgate, arrived Bombay (India) 8.3.42. Renamed TACTICAL 12.42. Disbanded 30.9.45 in Malaya.

No 225 Group — FIGHTER. Formed end.41 at Singapore. Reformed as COMPOSITE 2.3.42 at Padgate and West Kirby, arrived Bombay (India) 12. 4.42 and included the old No 2 (Indian) Group. To administer all units in S.India. Renumbered No 2 (Indian) Group 1.5.46.

No 226 Group — FIGHTER. Formed 1.42 at Singapore. Last mention Sumatra 3.42. Reformed as MAINTENANCE 9.5.42 at Karachi (India). Disbanded 31. 7.46 at Palam (India).

No 227 Group — TRAINING. Formed 6.6.42 at Lahore (India). Renumbered No 4 (Indian) Group 1.5.46.

No 228 Group — Formed 27.2.45 at Calcutta to relieve AHQ Burma of some administrative responsibilities. Renumbered No 3 (Indian) Group 1.5.46.

No 229 Group — TRANSPORT. Formed 16.12.43 at Karachi and absorbed No 179 Ferry Wing. Disbanded 31.3.47.

No 230 Group — MAINTENANCE. Formed 15.12.43 at Calcutta from No 186 Wing. Absorbed into AHQ Burma 16.5.45. Reformed 1.4.52 at Seletar. Renamed AHQ Singapore 16.2.53.

No 231 Group — MEDIUM/HEAVY BOMBER. Formed 15.12.43 at Calcutta. Replaced by RAF Belvedere 30.9.45.

No 232 Group — TRANSPORT. Formed 3.45 from RAF element of Combat Cargo Task Force, at Comilla. Disbanded 15.8.46.

No 233 Group — Formed 28.3.45 at Bombay to carry out Operation 'Roger', not continued with. Disbanded 15.8.46.

No 238 Group — AIRBORNE ASSAULT. Formed 4.45 at New Delhi (India). Became No 238 Wing 11.9.45.

No 241 Group — SPECIAL OPERATIONS. Formed 1.1.42 at London for special operations in Middle East but never functioned. Disbanded 14.7.42.

No 242 Group — OPERATIONAL. Formed 24.8.42 at Algiers as Advanced Operational HQ to control two fighter wings and one bomber wing in support of First Army in North African campaign. Disbanded 14.9.44.

No 246 Group — SPECIAL OPERATIONS. Formed 3.7.43 at AM Whitehall but never functioned. Disbanded 9.8.43.

No 247 Group — COASTAL. Formed 10.43 at Azores. Disbanded 1.3.46.

No 300 Group — TRANSPORT. Formed 24.4.45 by renaming No 300 Wing in Australia. Reduced to Wing status 1.3.46.

No 333 Group — SPECIAL OPERATIONAL. Formed 8.42 at Norfolk House, London for special operations in North Africa. Some personnel sent to N.Africa 11.42 and became HQ Eastern Air Command.

No 552 Group — no data

No 561 Group — no data

NAMED GROUPS

Certain Groups were given specific name titles, these usually applied to the geographic area covered by the Group or to its specific role — e.g Adriatic Group and Rhodesian Air Training Group. Some organisations carrying the 'Group' title had no actual command function, the group refering simply to a collection of units. All of these named Groups will be covered in a future publication.

51 ROYAL AIR FORCE GROUP HEADQUARTERS
NOBIS FLAMMA ACCENDENDA

60 ROYAL AIR FORCE GROUP HEADQUARTERS
VIGILANS

61 ROYAL AIR FORCE GROUP HEADQUARTERS
BUILD IN DEPTH

63 (WESTERN & WELSH) GROUP HEADQUARTERS ROYAL AIR FORCE
VIS CELATA

64 ROYAL AIR FORCE GROUP HEADQUARTERS
PROMPTUS ET FORTIS

66 (SCOTTISH) GROUP ROYAL AIR FORCE
MAK SICCAR

67 ROYAL AIR FORCE GROUP HEADQUARTERS
PRIDE IN LOYALTY

81 ROYAL AIR FORCE GROUP HEADQUARTERS
FULMINA EX IGNE POLITIORA

83 ROYAL AIR FORCE GROUP HEADQUARTERS
A DEUX PLUS FORTS

90 ROYAL AIR FORCE GROUP HEADQUARTERS
AETHEREM VINCERE

93 ROYAL AIR FORCE GROUP HEADQUARTERS
MIHI CURA FUTURI

100 ROYAL AIR FORCE GROUP HEADQUARTERS
FIND AND DESTROY

205 GROUP HEADQUARTERS ROYAL AIR FORCE
THROUGH DARKNESS TO LIGHT

206 ROYAL AIR FORCE GROUP HEADQUARTERS
SUPPORT TO THE WINGS

GROUP HEADQUARTERS ROYAL AIR FORCE
VALOR LEALDADE E MERITO

WINGS

The third level in the command structure was that of the Wing, an organisation designed to bring together units under a single commander at a more local level, units usually having the same or complimentary functions. With flying units the system was reasonably straightforward but with ground units it was often much more complex. As with so much of RAF history this is an area that is often poorly documented and one that contains many confusions and errors. As with the Groups, only the numbered units are included here and not the named units (e.g. Akrotiri Strike Wing).

No 1 Wing — Corps formed in November 1914 to operate in France, continued in existence with formation of RAF. Disbanded 5.3.19.

No 1 Wing — GR. Formed 23.9.37 at Malta for Arzeu operation. Disbanded 23.12.37.

No 1 Wing — Formed 4.9.39 as No 1 ITW, Cambridge. Re-numbered as No 2 ITW 1.7.40 but reformed 6.41. Disbanded 29.2.44.

No 1 Wing — Balloon Barrage, formed 24.1.40 at Sutton Coldfield. Disbanded 24.6.40.

No 2 Wing — Corps formed in November 1914 to operate in France, continued in existence with formation of RAF. Disbanded 12.9.19.

No 2 Wing — Re-numbered from No 1 ITW 1.7.40 at Cambridge. Disbanded 17.5.44.

No 3 Wing — Corps formed 1.3.15 to operate in France, continued in existence with formation of RAF. Disbanded 12.18.

No 3 Wing — ITW. Formed 5.9.39 at St Leonards on Sea. Disbanded 29.2.44.

No 4 Wing — Formed 1914 as Training Wing at Netheravon. Disbanded 15.5.19.

No 4 Wing — ITW. Formed 27.9.39 at Bexhill on Sea. Disbanded 29.2.44.

No 5 Wing — Corps formed 1915 for service in Egypt. Disbanded 1.4.20.

No 5 Wing — ITW. Formed 13.11.39 at Hastings. Disbanded 23.12.43.

No 6 Wing — Formed 7.17 as Training Wing at Maidstone. Disbanded 22.11.19.

No 6 Wing — ITW. Formed 1.8.40 at Aberystwyth. Disbanded 10.5.44.

No 7 Wing — Formed 11.15 as Training Wing at Gosport. Disbanded 12.9.18.

No 7 Wing — ITW. Formed 1.10.40 at Newquay. Disbanded 10.5.44.

No 8 Wing — Formed 12.15 as Training Wing at York. Disbanded 30.6.19.

No 8 Wing — ITW. Formed 4.11.40 at Newquay. Disbanded 10.5.44.

No 9 Wing — Formed 14.5.16 as General HQ Wing for France. Disbanded 30.7.19.

No 9 Wing — Formed 20.11.40 as RECEPTION at Stratford-on-Avon, became ITW 14.6.41 at Stratford-on-Avon. Disbanded 25.5.44.

No 10 Wing — Formed 30.1.16 AC for France. Disbanded 5.3.19.

No 10 Wing — ITW. Formed 13.12.40 at Scarborough. Disbanded 23.3.44.

No 11 Wing — Formed 2.16 AC for France. Disbanded 9.9.19.

No 11 Wing — ITW. Formed 15.3.41 at Scarborough. Disbanded 11.4.44.

No 12 Wing — Formed 1.16 as Corps for France. Disbanded 20.2.19.

No 12 Wing — ITW. Formed 5.5.41 at St Andrews. Disbanded 21.4.44.

No 13 Wing — Formed 10.3.16 as AC for France. Disbanded 1.3.19.

No 13 Wing — ITW. Formed 13.6.41 at Torquay. Disbanded 1.3.44.

No 14 Wing — Formed 1.4.16 as AC for France. Disbanded 14.3.19.

No 14 Wing — ITW. Formed 23.9.41 at St Leonards-on-Sea. Disbanded 21.4.44.

No 15 Wing — Formed 22.6.16 as Corps for France. Disbanded 20.3.19.

No 15 Wing — ITW. Formed 1.11.43 at Bridlington. Disbanded 21.4.44.

No 15 Wing — FIGHTER. Formed 19.8.43 at Kingsnorth. Disbanded 12.7.44.

No 16 Wing — Formed 20.9.16 as Corps for Salonika. Disbanded 14.11.19.

No 16 Wing — ITW. Formed 1.10.43 at Whitley Bay. Disbanded 1.2.44.

No 16 Wing (RCAF) — FIGHTER-BOMBER. Formed 7.7.43 at New Romney. Disbanded 20.4.44.

No 17 Wing — Formed 1.17 as Training Wing at Beaulieu. Disbanded 14.5. 19.

No 17 Wing — ITW. Formed 23.9.41 at Scarborough. Disbanded 3.44.

No 18 Wing — Formed 25.3.16 for Home Defence, London. Disbanded 1.10.19.

No 18 Wing — ITW. Formed 16.1.43 at Bridgnorth. Disbanded 21.4.44.

No 19 Wing — Formed 10.17 as Training Wing at Jesmond. Disbanded 25.3. 19.

No 20 Wing — Formed 8.17 as Training Wing for Egypt. Disbanded 22.7.19.

No 20 Wing — ITW. Formed 31.5.43 at Bridlington. Disbanded 20.4.44.

No 20 Wing — FIGHTER. Formed 1.1.44 at Hornchurch, renamed 20 Sector HQ 12.5.44. Disbanded 12.7.44.

No 21 Wing — Formed 8.16 as Training Wing at Cirencester. Disbanded 18.2.19.

No 21 Wing — ITW. Formed 5.43 at Torquay. Disbanded 24.4.44.

No 21 Wing — BASE DEFENCE. Formed 1.1.44 at Church Fenton, renamed 21 Base Defence Sector 5.44. Disbanded 10.11.44.

No 22 Wing — Formed 14.9.16 as AC for France. Disbanded 20.5.19.

No 22 Wing (RCAF) — FIGHTER. Formed 9.1.44 at Ayr. Disbanded 12.7.44.

No 23 Wing — Formed 12.16 as Training Wing at South Carlton. Disbanded 31.5.19.

No 23 Wing — ITW (FRENCH). Formed 25.10.43 at Filey. Disbanded 1.8.46.

No 24 Wing — Formed 12.16 as Training Wing at Wyton. Disbanded 8.4.19.

No 24 Wing — BASE DEFENCE. Formed 21.2.44 at Acklington, renamed 24 Base Defence Sector 5.44. Disbanded 15.3.45.

No 25 Wing — Formed 12.16 as Training Wing at Castle Bromwich. Disbanded 8.18.

No 25 Wing — BASE DEFENCE. Formed 1.3.44 at Castle Camps, renamed 25 Base Defence Sector 5.44. Disbanded 15.3.45.

No 30 Wing — Formed 6.17 as Training Wing at Edinburgh. Disbanded 10.18.

No 30 Wing — COASTAL. Formed 25.3.41 at Iceland. Raised to Command status 2.7.41 as RAF Iceland.

No 31 Wing — Formed 20.1.17 as Corps for Mesopotamia, raised to Group status as Mesopotamian Group.

No 31 Wing — COASTAL. Formed 1.8.41 at Sydenham. Disbanded 1.12.41.

No 32 Wing — Formed 8.17 as Training Wing for Egypt. Disbanded 22.7.29.

No 32 Wing — ARMY CO-OP. Formed 19.8.41 at Edinburgh. Disbanded 1.7.43.

No 33 Wing — Formed 9.17 as Training Wing at Salisbury. Disbanded 15.5.19.

No 33 Wing — ARMY CO-OP. Formed 15.8.41 at York. Disbanded 1.7.43. Reformed as SIGNALS 7.12.44 at Malines, Belgium 7.12.44. Disbanded 20. 5.45.

No 34 Wing — Formed 10.17 as Training Wing at Stockbridge. Disbanded 9.18.

No 34 Wing — ARMY CO-OP. Formed 22.8.41 at Luton Hoo, later RECCE. Disbanded 30.9.45.

No 35 Wing — Formed 9.17 as Training Wing at Stamford. Disbanded 9.4.19.

No 35 Wing — ARMY CO-OP. Formed 15.8.41 at Reigate, later RECCE. Disbanded 21.6.46.

No 36 Wing — Formed 9.17 as Training Wing at Amesbury. Disbanded 23.6. 18.

No 36 Wing — ARMY CO-OP. Formed 15.8.41 at Welton. Disbanded 16.7.43.

No 37 Wing — Formed 3-.11.17 as Training Wing at Hooton Park. Disbanded 9.4.19.

No 37 Wing — ARMY CO-OP. Formed 8.41 at Chester but does not appear to have been activated. Disbanded 6.43.

No 38 Wing — Formed 8.17 as Training Wing for Egypt. Disbanded 15.4.19.

No 38 Wing — ARMY CO-OP. Formed 19.1.42 at Netheravon. Disbanded 11.10.43 on formation of No 38 Group.

No 39 Wing — Formed as Training Wing 10.17 at Brandon. Disbanded 4.4.19.

No 39 Wing (RCAF) — RECCE. Formed 1.8.43 at Redhill. Disbanded 7.8.45.

No 40 Wing — Formed 5.10.17 as AC for Palestine. Disbanded 1.4.20.

No 40 Wing — ITW. Formed 10.5.44 at Newquay. Disbanded 27.11.44.

No 45 Wing — Formed 15.2.46 from No 45 Gp.

No 46 Wing — HOME DEFENCE in VI Brigade 1918.

No 47 Wing — HOME DEFENCE in VI Brigade 1918.

No 48 Wing — HOME DEFENCE in VI Brigade 1918.

No 49 Wing — HOME DEFENCE in VI Brigade 1918.

No 50 Wing — HOME DEFENCE in VI Brigade 1918.

No 50 Wing — ITW. Formed 25.6.44. at Bridgnorth. Disbanded 5.46.

No 51 Wing — Formed 10.17 as Corps for France. Disbanded 30.7.19.

No 51 Wing — ARMY CO-OP. Formed 28.8.39 at Andover, became SHQ West Malling 10.6.40. Reformed 21.4.41 as MAINTENANCE at Broughton. Disbanded 21.11.42.

No 52 Wing — Formed 11.17 as Corps for India. Disbanded 1.4.20.

No 52 Wing — ARMY CO-OP. Formed 1.11.39 at Poix, France. Disbanded 14. 7.40. Reformed 21.5.41 as MAINTENANCE at Minchinhampton. Disbanded 21. 11.42.

No 53 Wing — Formed 8.2.18 for HOME DEFENCE in VI Brigade at Martlesham. Disbanded 13.6.19.

No 53 Wing — MAINTENANCE. Formed 24.3.41 at Andover. Disbanded 1.1.46.

No 54 Wing — Formed 3.18 as General HQ for France. Disbanded 5.5.19.

No 54 Wing — MAINTENANCE. Formed 25.5.42 at Andover. Disbanded 9.10.46.

No 55 Wing — Formed 8.18 in Ireland. Disbanded 25.9.19.

No 55 Wing — MAINTENANCE. Formed 1.8.42 at Derby. Disbanded 15.1.47.

No 56 Wing — Formed 11.18 as Training Wing at Chingford. Disbanded 15. 5.19.

No 56 Wing — MAINTENANCE. Formed 22.7.44 at Carlisle. Disbanded 15.10. 46.

No 57 Wing — MAINTENANCE. Formed 22.7.44 at Milton. Disbanded 15.1.47.

No 60 Wing — FIGHTER. Formed 30.8.39 at Debden. Became No 14 Group 16. 1.40. Disbanded 31.5.40.

No 61 Wing — Ex No 1 Wing RNAS, formed 1.4.18 as Operational Wing for France. Disbanded 8.18.

No 61 Wing — FIGHTER. Formed 23.9.39 at Hendon. Disbanded 31.5.40.

No 62 Wing — Formed as Marine Operational Wing for Med 4.18. Disbanded 1.10.19.

No 62 Wing — FIGHTER. Formed 13.11.39 at Hendon. Disbanded 31.5.40.

No 63 Wing — Formed as Marine Operational Wing for Med 4.18. Disbanded 21.5.19.

No 63 Wing — FIGHTER. Formed 1.40 at Hendon. Disbanded 6.40.

No 64 Wing — Ex No 4 Wing RNAS, formed 4.18 as Operational Wing at Eastchurch. Disbanded 15.9.19.

No 65 Wing — Ex No 5 Wing RNAS, formed 4.18 as Operational Wing for France. Disbanded 1.3.19.

No 66 Wing — Formed as Marine Operational Wing for Med 4.18. Disbanded 15.8.19.

No 67 Wing — Formed as Marine Operational Wing for Med 4.18. Disbanded 12.18.

No 67 Wing — FIGHTER. Formed 6.11.39 at Hendon. Disbanded 24.7.40.

No 68 Wing — Formed as Marine Operational Wing at Seaton Carew 6.18. Disbanded 1.8.19.

No 69 Wing — Formed as Training Wing for Egypt 21.7.18. Disbanded 25.7.19.

No 69 Wing — SIGNALS. Formed 15.3.45 at Everberg. Disbanded 20.10.45.

No 70 Wing — Formed as Marine Operational Wing at Felixstowe 8.18. Disbanded 1.5.19.

No 70 Wing — BOMBER. Formed 1.9.39 at Upper Heyford. Became SIGNALS 1. 7.40 at Wick. Disbanded 31.5.46.

No 70 Wing — ITW. Formed 21.4.44 at Bridlington. Disbanded 1.10.44.

No 71 Wing — Formed as Marine Operational Wing at Penzance 8.18. Disbanded 15.5.19.

No 71 Wing — BOMBER. Formed 1.9.39 at Abingdon. Disbanded 1.6.40. Reformed as SIGNALS 31.7.40 at Dyce. Disbanded 7.43.

No 72 Wing — Formed as Marine Operational Wing at Cattewater 8.18. Disbanded 1.5.19.

No 72 Wing — BOMBER. Formed 23.8.39 at Harwell. Disbanded 6.2.40. Reformed 1.7.40 as SIGNALS at Usworth. Disbanded 31.7.46.

No 73 Wing — Formed as Marine Operational Wing at Yarmouth 8.18. Disbanded 1.5.19.

No 73 Wing — SIGNALS. Formed 1.7.40 at Church Fenton. Disbanded 1.11.46.

No 74 Wing — Formed as Marine Operational Wing at Calshot 8.18. Disbanded 15.5.19.

No 74 Wing — BOMBER. Formed 2.9.39 at Benson. Disbanded 10.2.40. Reformed 1.7.40 as SIGNALS at Duxford. Disbanded 1.7.43.

No 75 Wing — Formed as Marine Operational Wing at Warsash 8.18. Disbanded 15.5.19.

No 75 Wing — BOMBER. Formed 24.8.39 at Boscombe Down. Disbanded 30.6.40. Reformed 1.7.40 as SIGNALS at Biggin Hill. Disbanded 1.11.46.

No 76 Wing — Formed as Marine Operational Wing at Felixstowe 8.18. Disbanded 11.18.

No 76 Wing — SIGNALS. Formed 10.7.40 at Filton. Disbanded 1.7.43.

No 77 Wing — Formed as Marine Operational Wing at Milford 8.18. Disbanded 11.18.

No 77 Wing — SIGNALS. Formed 17.2.41 at Liverpool. Disbanded 15.5.44.

No 78 Wing — Formed as Marine Operational Wing at Dundee 8.18. Disbanded 11.18.

No 78 Wing — SIGNALS. Formed 25.4.41 at Henbury. Disbanded 31.7.46.

No 79 Wing — Formed as Marine Operational Wing at Hornsea 8.18. Disbanded 12.18.

No 79 Wing — SIGNALS. Formed 27.9.41 at Portadown. Disbanded 7.43.

No 80 Wing — Formed as AC 6.18 for France. Disbanded 1.3.19.

No 80 Wing — SIGNALS. Formed 7.9.40 at Radlett. Disbanded 24.9.45.

No 80 Wing — ITW. Formed 21.4.44 at Bridgnorth. Disbanded 27.11.44.

No 81 Wing — Formed as AC 8.18 for France. Disbanded 1.3.19.

No 81 Wing — ITW. Formed 21.4.44 at Bridgnorth. Disbanded 6.10.44.

No 81 Wing — SIGNALS. Formed 2.6.41 at Worcester. Disbanded 30.4.46.

No 82 Wing — Formed 24.5.18 as Bombing Wing for France. Disbanded 1.3. 19.

No 82 Wing — ITW. Formed 5.44 at Bridgnorth. Disbanded 6.44.

No 83 Wing — Formed 8.18 as Bombing Wing for France. Disbanded 15.2.19.

No 84 Wing — Formed 8.18 as Training Wing for France. Disbanded 3.11.19.

No 84 Wing — SIGNALS. Formed 6.43 at Bartway. Disbanded 9.44.

No 85 Wing — Formed 1.7.46 out of No 85 Gp. Disbanded 1.12.48.

No 86 Wing — Formed 12.18 as Communications Wing at Hendon, for rapid transport connected with peace conference. Disbanded 28.10.19.

No 86 Wing — GR. Formed 5.5.39 in MV 'Dumana' (London). Became No 101 Wing 16.2.40.

No 87 Wing — TRANSPORT. Formed 15.7.46 at Paris when No 87 Group reduced to Wing status.

No 90 Wing — Formed 10.18 as AC for France. Disbanded 1.3.19.

No 90 Wing — ITW. Formed 3.5.44 at Cranage. Disbanded 28.10.44.

No 96 Wing — WIRELESS. Formed 1.10.41 at Stormont. Disbanded 10.5.44.

No 100 Wing — GR. Formed 12.5.39 in SS 'Manela' (London). Disbanded 9. 9.41.

No 101 Wing — GR. Formed 16.2.40 when No 86 Wing renumbered. Disbanded 7.41.

No 102 Wing — GR. Formed 14.4.41 in SS 'Batavier II' at

Gourock. Disbanded 31.1.42.

No 103 Wing — DISARMAMENT. Formed 12.2.45 at Bushy Park. Disbanded 30. 9.46.

No 104 Wing — PR. Formed 5.2.45 at Benson. Disbanded 1.10.45.

No 105 Wing — COMBINED OPERATIONS. Formed 28.2.43 at Ayr. Disbanded 15.8.44.

No 106 Wing — PR. Formed 3.7.43 at Benson. Disbanded 14.4.44 on creation of No 106 Gp.

No 107 Wing — TRANSPORT. Formed 16.10.44 at Hendon hall. Disbanded 1.9.45.

No 108 Wing — TRANSPORT. Formed 24.9.44 at Karachi. Disbanded 8.5.46.

No 109 Wing — TRANSPORT. Formed 10.9.44 at Bangalore. Disbanded 1.3.46.

No 110 Wing — AAC. Formed 1.3.40 at Ringway. Disbanded 5.5.41. Reformed as TRANSPORT 1.9.44 at Croydon. Disbanded 15.2.46.

No 111 Wing — TRANSPORT. Formed 4.9.44 at Northolt. Disbanded 6.4.46.

No 112 Wing — TRANSPORT. Formed 11.4.43 at Dorval. Disbanded 1.46.

No 113 Wing — TRANSPORT. Formed 11.4.43 at Dorval. Disbanded 1.46.

No 114 Wing — TRANSPORT. Formed 1.9.43 at Accra. Disbanded 1.9.45.

No 115 Wing — TRANSPORT. Formed 7.5.44 at Khartoum. Disbanded 10.4.46.

No 116 Wing — TRANSPORT. Formed 1.1.44 at Hendon Hall. Disbanded 1.1.45.

No 117 Wing — TRANSPORT. Formed 24.9.44 at New Delhi. Disbanded 1.3.46.

No 118 Wing — TRANSPORT. Formed 8.44 at Delhi. Disbanded 25.2.46.

No 121 Wing — 121 Airfield renamed Wing 23.2.43 at Middle Wallop. Became RP Typhoon 12.5.44. Disbanded 30.9.45.

No 122 Wing — 122 Airfield renamed Wing 1.4.43 at Zeals. Became FIGHTER 12.5.44. Disbanded 7.9.45.

No 123 Wing — 123 Airfield renamed Wing 1.4.43 at Stoney Cross. Became RP Typhoon 12.5.44.

No 124 Wing — 124 Airfield renamed Wing 1.4.43 at Lasham. Became RP Typhoon 12.5.44. Disbanded 30.4.46.

No 125 Wing — 125 Airfield renamed Wing 24.6.43 at Gravesend. Became FIGHTER 12.5.44. Disbanded 14.7.45.

No 126 Wing (RCAF) — 126 Airfield renamed Wing 6.7.43 at Redhill. Became FIGHTER 12.5.44. Disbanded 31.3.46.

No 127 Wing — 127 Airfield renamed Wing 11.7.43 at Kenley. Became FIGHTER 12.5.44. Disbanded 7.7.45.

No 128 Wing — 128 Airfield renamed Wing 20.7.43 at Dunsfold. Became RECONNAISSANCE 12.5.44. Disbanded 12.12.45.

No 129 Wing — 129 (RCAF) Airfield renamed Wing 4.7.43 at Gatwick. Became FB 12.5. 44. Reformed for Operation 'Apostle' (Norway) 16.5.45 at Turnhouse. Disbanded 12.12.45.

No 130 Wing — 130 Airfield renamed Wing 10.7.43 at Gravesend. Reformed 7.5.45 to take over airfields in Norway. Disbanded 15.12.45.

No 131 Wing (Polish) — 131 Airfield renamed Wing 4.10.43 at

Northolt. Became FIGHTER 12.5.44. Disbanded 25.11.46.

No 132 Wing (Norwegian) — 132 Airfield renamed Wing 1.11.43 at North Weald. Became FIGHTER 12.5.44. Transfer to Norwegian Air Force 21.11.45.

No 133 Wing (Polish) — 133 Airfield renamed Wing 1.11.43 at Heston. Became FIGHTER 12.5.44. Disbanded 7.8.45.

NO 134 Wing (Czech) — 134 Airfield renamed Wing 8.11.43 at Ibsley. Became FIGHTER 12.5.44. Disbanded 12.7.44.

No 135 Wing — 135 Airfield renamed Wing 15.11.43 at Hornchurch. Became FIGHTER 12.5.44. Disbanded

No 136 Wing — 136 Airfield renamed Wing 22.11.43 at Fairlop. Became RP Typhoon 12.5.44. Disbanded 15.9.45.

No 137 Wing — 137 Airfield renamed Wing 14.11.43 at Hartford Bridge. Became LB 12.5.44. Disbanded 30.11.45.

No 138 Wing — 138 Airfield renamed Wing 10.11.43 at Lasham. Became LB 12.5.44. Disbanded 14.4.46.

No 139 Wing — 139 Airfield renamed Wing 17.11.43 at Dunsfold. Became MB 12.5.44. Disbanded.?

No 140 Wng — 140 Airfield renamed Wing 1.12.43 at Sculthorpe. Became LB 12.5.44.

No 141 Wing — 141 Airfield renamed Wing 1.1.44 at Church Fenton. Became NF 12.5.44. Disbanded 5.11.44.

No 142 Wing — 142 Airfield renamed Wing 7.1.44 at Scorton. Became LR FIGHTER 12.5.44. Disbanded 3.8.45.

No 143 Wing (RCAF) — 143 Airfield renamed Wing 10.1.44 at Ayr. Became FB 12.5.44. Disbanded 26.8.45.

No 144 Wing (RCAF) — 144 Airfield renamed Wing 9.2.45 at Digby. Became FIGHTER 12.5.44. Disbanded 12.7.44.

No 145 Wing — 145 Airfield renamed Wing 1.2.44 at Perranporth. Became FIGHTER 12.5.44. Disbanded 15.11.45.

No 146 Wing — 146 Airfield renamed Wing 31.1.44 at Tangmere. Became FB 12.5.44. Disbanded 7.9.45.

No 147 Wing — 147 Airfield renamed Wing 16.2.44 at Acklington. Became NF 12.5.44. Disbanded 24.3.45.

No 148 Wing — 148 Airfield renamed Wing 23.2.44 at Drem. Became NF 12. 5.44. Disbanded 25.8.45.

No 149 Wing — 149 Airfield renamed Wing 1.3.44 at Castle Camps. Became LR FIGHTER 12.5.44. Disbanded 9.6.45.

No 150 Wing — 150 Airfield renamed Wing 8.3.44 at Bradwell Bay. Became FIGHTER 12.5.44. Disbanded 8.3.45.

No 151 Wing — FIGHTER. Formed 26.7.41 at Leconfield ? North Russia 30.8.41?. Disbanded. Reformed as TRANSPORT 8.4.44 at Habbaniya. Disbanded ?

No 152 Wing — GR. Formed 1.5.44 at Predannack. Disbanded 7.9.44.

No 153 Wing — GR. Formed 25.4.44 at Portreath. Disbanded 14.9.44.

No 154 Wing — GR. Formed 1.5.44 at Strubby. Disbanded 7.9.44.

No 155 Wing — GR. Formed 1.4.44 at Manston. Disbanded 11.9.44.

No 156 Wing — GR. Formed 15.4.44 at Harrowbear. Disbanded 8.8.44.

No 157 Wing — GR. Formed 14.5.44 at Hawkinge. Disbanded 25.5.45.

No 159 Wing — BALLOON. Formed 4.9.44 at Villers-le-Sec. Transfer to Fighter Command 17.6.45 for disbandment.

No 164 Wing — SIGNALS. Formed 4.5.42 at Newbold Revel (India). Disbanded 30.4.46.

No 165 Wing — TACTICAL. Formed 9.42 at Dum Dum (India). Became No 903 Wing 30.9.44.

No 166 Wing — TACTICAL. Formed 1.10.42 at Jessore (India). Became No 902 Wing 30.9.44.

No 167 Wing — TACTICAL. Formed 1.10.42 at Asansol (India). Became No 904 Wing 30.9.44.

No 168 Wing — TACTICAL. Formed 1.11.42 at Ondal (India). Became No 908 Wing 30.9.44.

No 169 Wing — TACTICAL. Formed 3.10.42 at Agertala (India). Became No 901 Wing 30.9.44.

No 170 Wing — MB. Formed 1.10.42 at Pandaveswar (India). Became No 906 Wing 30.9.44.

No 171 Wing — HB. Formed 25.11.43 at Ranchi (India), later RECCE. Disbanded 30.9.44.

No 172 Wing — COMPOSITE. Formed 18.10.42 at St Thomas Mount (India). Disbanded 1.12.44.

No 173 Wing — COMPOSITE. Formed 25.11.42 at Trichinopoly (India). Disbanded 1.3.45.

No 175 Wing — TB. Formed 1.10.42 at Cuttack (India), later BOMBER. Disbanded 30.9.45.

No 177 Wing — TRANSPORT. Formed 2.9.43 at Rawalpindi (India). Became No 900 Wing 30.9.44.

No 179 Wing — FERRY. Formed 9.10.42 at Karachi (India). Disbanded 30.11.43.

No 180 Wing — SIGNALS. Formed 9.6.43 at Calcutta (India). Disbanded 30.12.45.

No 181 Wing — SIGNALS. Formed 9.6.43 at Masinpur (India). Disbanded 10.3.46.

No 182 Wing — SIGNALS. Formed 1.8.43 at Chittagong (India). Disbanded 1.8.45.

No 183 Wing — SIGNALS. Formed 1.1.44 at Ridgeway (Ceylon). Disbanded 30.12.45.

No 184 Wing — BOMBER. Formed 23.7.43 at Salboni (India). Disbanded 20. 11.45.

No 185 Wing — FIGHTER. Formed 22.8.43 at Kalaikundah (India). Disbanded 31.10.45.

No 186 Wing — MAINTENANCE. Formed 13.1.43 at Calcutta (India). Absorbed into No 203 Group 12.43.

No 187 Wing — MAINTENANCE. Formed 28.9.43 at Peshawar (India). Disbanded 15.7.45.

No 188 Wing — MAINTENANCE. Formed 2.8.43 at Bangalore (India). Disbanded 15.7.45.

No 189 Wing — TACTICAL. Formed 5.12.43 at Palel (India). Became No 909 Wing 30.9.44.

No 190 Wing — ASSAULT. Formed 29.5.43 at Bombay (India). Disbanded 31. 1.44.

No 231 Wing — BOMBER. Formed 30.12.41 at Shallufa (ME).

No 232 Wing — BOMBER. Renumbered from No 272 Wing 10.12.41 at El Firdan (ME). Disbanded 12.12.46.

No 233 Wing — FIGHTER. Renumbered from No 273 Wing 14.12.41 at El Firdan (ME). Disbanded 25.1.44.

No 234 Wing — FIGHTER. Renumbered from No 269 Wing 24.10.41 at Sidi Heneish (ME). Disbanded 19.2.44.

No 235 Wing — GR. Formed 20.1.42 at Tobruk (ME). Disbanded 5.2.45.

No 236 Wing — BOMBER. Formed 1.2.42 at Kabrit (ME). Disbanded 20.12.46.

No 237 Wing — FIGHTER. Formed 29.5.42 at Mosul (Iraq). Disbanded 29.2. 44.

No 238 Wing — BOMBER. Formed 30.1.42 at Shallufa (ME). Disbanded 20.9. 43.

No 239 Wing — FIGHTER. Renumbered from No 262 Wing 1.4.42 at Gambut (ME). Disbanded 8.1.47.

No 240 Wing — BOMBER. Formed 28.6.42 at Helwan (Egypt). Became No 285 Wing 7.42. Reformed at Helwan 6.43. Disbanded 15.9.46.

No 241 Wing — FIGHTER. Formed 12.4.42 at Kasfareet (ME). Reduced to number only 9.43.

No 242 Wing — BOMBER. Formed 10.2.42 at Fayid (ME). Became No 332 Wing 10.43.

No 243 Wing — FIGHTER. Formed 2.4.42 at Sidi Heneish (ME). Became No 907 Wing 11.44.

No 244 Wing — FIGHTER. Formed 13.6.42 at Kasfareet (ME). Disbanded 27. 1.47.

No 245 Wing — BOMBER. Renumbered from No 249 Wing at Helwan (Egypt) 11.4.42. Disbanded 15.4.44.

No 246 Wing — FIGHTER. Formed 1.6.42 at Port Reitz (South Africa). Disbanded 10.6.45.

No 247 Wing — FIGHTER. Formed 18.4.42 at Gianaclis (ME). Disbanded 5.2.45.

No 248 Wing — GR. Formed 15.6.42 at Edku (Egypt). Later TB. Disbanded 6.10.44.

No 249 Wing — BOMBER. Formed 4.42 at Helwan (Egypt). Became No 245 Wing 23.7.42. Reformed 20.1.43 at Marble Arch (Western Desert). Disbanded 15.8.46.

No 250 Wing — SIGNALS. Formed 25.8.39 at Ismailia (Egypt). Disbanded 6.12.42.

No 251 Wing — BOMBER. Formed 19.10.39 at Helwan. Disbanded 7.3.40.

No 251 Wing — FIGHTER. Formed 22.3.44 at Naples. Disbanded 5.11.44.

No 252 Wing — FIGHTER. Formed 29.8.39 at Helwan (Egypt) ex HQ (Flying) Wing.. Disbanded 5.3.44.

No 253 Wing — BOMBER. Formed 4.8.39 at Ismailia (Egypt). Disbanded 31. 8.45.

No 254 Wing — BOMBER. Formed 2.9.39 at Khartoum. Disbanded 25.7.45.

No 256 Wing — SIGNALS. Formed 23.4.40 at Uxbridge. Disbanded 1.41.

No 257 Wing — BOMBER. Formed 20.12.40 at Shallufa. Disbanded 10.41.

No 258 Wing — FIGHTER. Formed 1.1.41 at Aboukir (Egypt). Disbanded 10. 6.45.

No 259 Wing — FIGHTER. Formed 21.7.41 at Nicosia (Cyprus). Disbanded 1.12.44.

No 260 Wing — BALLOON. Formed 15.7.41 at Cardington. Disbanded 15.1.45.

No 262 Wing — FIGHTER. Formed 11.10.41 at Sidi Heneish. Became No 239 Wing.

No 263 Wing — FIGHTER. Formed 1.11.41 in Syria. Disbanded 15.3.44.

No 264 Wing — FIGHTER. Formed 24.10.41 at Sidi Heneish. Became No 269 Wing.

No 265 Wing — BOMBER. Formed 29.11.41 at El Firdan. Became No 232 Wing.

No 269 Wing — FIGHTER. Renumbered from No 264 Wing 24.10.41? Became No 234 Wing.

No 270 Wing — TRANSPORT. Formed 11.41 at Fuka Area

(ME). Disbanded 1.42.

No 272 Wing — ? became No 232 Wing 10.12.41.

No 273 Wing — ? became No 233 Wing 14.12.41.

No 274 Wing — BALLOON. Formed 28.1.42 at Hook. Disbanded 25.5.43.

No 275 Wing — BALLOON. Formed 16.4.42 at Chessington. Disbanded 1.12.44.

No 276 Wing — SIGNALS. Formed 1.8.42 at Heliopolis. Disbanded 31.8.45.

No 281 Wing — FIGHTER. Formed 16.6.44 at Bari (Italy). Disbanded 30.9. 45.

No 282 Wing — TRANSPORT. Formed 1.2.44 at Heliopolis. Amalgamated with No 219 Group 1.6.46.

No 283 Wing — TRANSPORT. Formed 5.6.42 at Asmara.

No 284 Wing — TRANSPORT. Formed 15.8.43 at Algiers. Amalgamated with AHQ Malta 1.6.46.

No 285 Wing — RECCE. Formed from No 240 Wing at Burg-el-Arab 7.42. Disbanded 10.7.46. Reformed FIGHTER 20.1.47 at Nicosia (Cyprus).

No 286 Wing — FIGHTER. Formed 28.8.43 at La Sebala (Tunis). Disbanded 26.5.45.

No 287 Wing — FIGHTER. Formed 11.9.43 at La Sebala (Tunis) 11.9.43. Disbanded 14.7.45.

No 293 Wing — FIGHTER. Formed 1.10.42 at Allipore (India). Disbanded 30.9.44.

No 295 Wing — GR. Formed 1.3.42 at Freetown (West Africa). Disbanded 1.8.45.

No 296 Wing — SIGNALS. Formed 17.2.42 at Freetown (West Africa). Disbanded 30.4.43.

No 297 Wing — GR. Formed 7.10.42 at Freetown (West Africa). Disbanded 15.2.43.

No 298 Wing — GR. Formed 19.9.42 at Lagoa (West Africa). Disbanded 12. 6.45.

No 300 Wing — TRANSPORT. Formed 17.12.44 at Camden (Australia). Disbanded 24.4.45.

No 322 Wing — FIGHTER. Formed 7.9.42 at West Kirby. Disbanded 7.11.44.

No 323 Wing — FIGHTER. Formed 8.11.42 at Maison Blanche (North Africa). Disbanded 7.7.45.

No 324 Wing — FIGHTER. Formed 14.9.42 at Wilmslow.

No 325 Wing — GR. Formed 14.9.42 at Wilmslow. Disbanded 12.8.44.

No 326 Wing — BOMBER. Formed 5.9.42 .. disembarked Algiers 12.11.42. Disbanded 1.11.43.

No 328 Wing — GR. Formed 10.42 ... arrived Algiers 12.11.42. Disbanded 17.10.44.

No 329 Wing — SIGNALS. Formed 7.43 at Algiers. Disbanded 23.11.43.

No 330 Wing — BOMBER. Formed 5.5.43 at Fontaine Chaud (Algeria). Disbanded 26.10.44.

No 331 Wing — BOMBER. Formed 7.5.43 at West Kirby. Disbanded 18.12.43.

No 332 Wing — FIGHTER. Formed 27.10.43 at Djidjelli (North Africa). Disbanded 28.8.44.

No 334 Wing — SD. Formed 9.43 in UK. Disbanded 15.1.46.

No 335 Wing — FIGHTER. Formed 1.10.43 at Mellile (Sicily). Disbanded 15.7.45.

No 336 Wing — PR. Formed 30.10.43 at La Marsa (Tunisia). Disbanded 30. 9.45.

No 337 Wing — FIGHTER. Formed 30.11.43 at Oran (North Africa). Disbanded 15.6.46.

No 338 Wing — FIGHTER. Formed 11.11.43 at Reghaia (North Africa). Disbanded 30.9.45.

No 340 Wing — FIGHTER. Formed 6.7.44 at Bone (North Africa). Disbanded 30.9.45.

No 341 Wing — TRANSPORT. Formed 1.11.44 at West Kirby. Disbanded 15.12.45.

No 342 Wing — TRANSPORT. Formed 20.10.44 at West Kirby. Disbanded 15.12.45.

No 343 Wing — GLIDER. Formed 16.11.44 at Fateghans (India). Disbanded 31.12.45.

No 344 Wing — GLIDER. Formed 20.11.44 at Bikram (India). Disbanded 25. 10.45.

No 345 Wing — TRANSPORT. Formed 30.4.45 at Tulihal (India). Disbanded 31.1.46.

No 346 Wing — GR. Formed 8.3.45 at Akyab (Burma). Disbanded 15.12.45.

No 347 Wing — PR. Formed 24.4.45 at Calcutta (India). Disbanded 30.11. 45.

No 377 Wing — 1944.

No 500 Wing — Formed 1.8.46 from AHQ West Africa.

No 900 Wing — TRANSPORT. Renumbered from No 177 Wing 1.10.44 at Agartala (India). Disbanded 13.11.45.

No 901 Wing — TACTICAL. Renumbered from No 169 Wing 1.10.44 at Chiringa (India). Disbanded 12.45.

No 902 Wing — TACTICAL. Renumbered from No 166 Wing 1.10.44 at Chittagong (India). Disbanded 1.4.46.

No 903 Wing — TACTICAL. Renumbered from No 165 Wing 1.10.44 at Comilla (India). Disbanded 31.10.45.

No 904 Wing — TACTICAL. Renumbered from No 167 Wing 1.10.44 at Cox's Bazar (India). Disbanded 30.11.46.

No 905 Wing — TACTICAL. Formed 1.10.44 at Jaliapalong (India). Disbanded 31.10.45.

No 906 Wing — TACTICAL. Renumbered from No 170 Wing 1.10.44 at Imphal (India). Disbanded 13.11.45.

No 907 Wing — TACTICAL. Renumbered from No 243 Wing 30.11.44 at Tamu (India). Disbanded 12.45.

No 908 Wing — TACTICAL. Renumbered from No 168 Wing 1.10.44 at Kumbingian (India). Disbanded 30.9.45.

No 909 Wing — TACTICAL. Renumbered from No 189 Wing 1.10.44 at Palel (India). Disbanded 30.9.45.

No 910 Wing — TACTICAL. Formed 1.10.44 at Silcher (India). Disbanded 31.12.45.

The Airfield Construction Branch expanded rapidly during Word War Two and included a number of Airfield Construction Wings numbered in the 5000 sequence; confirmed numbers include 5351, 5352, 5353, 5354, 5355, 5356, each being attached to a Home-based Group.

ROYAL AIR FORCE SQUADRONS

SQUADRON NUMBERING

The Royal Flying Corps adopted a numbering system for its units in conjunction with the term 'Squadron', a system that continued into RAF usage. In reality this is no more than a convenient label for this organisational level, it could equally well have been called something else. RAF Squadrons have varied in size from just a few aircraft and personnel to very large and complex units with many aircraft and a wide range of support personnel; mobile squadrons in the Western Desert in 1942 were self-contained and included such elements as MT sections. If a squadron is not at full strength it may be refered to as a cadre unit, the concept being to keep the bare minimum of the unit in existence, often without aircraft, ready for expansion to full establishment. The next rung down the ladder is a reduction to a 'number only' basis whereby no equipment or personnel are kept on strength.

Squadrons may form from scratch or by creating a nucleus from an existing squadron, the commonest form of this is for the Flights of a particular squadron to be used in the formation of other units — a common practice during the rapid expansion period of 1938-40. The actual numbering process started out in a logical sequential fashion; however, incorporation of the Fleet Air Arm into the RAF brought the first major policy change, the existing FAA squadrons having '200' added to their numbers e.g No 4 Sqn FAA becoming No 204 Sqn RAF. When the maritime Flights were combined into squadrons they too received numbers in the 200 series. This policy of giving blocks of numbers became standard during the late 1930s and into World War Two. The Special Reserve squadrons were given the block 500 to 599, although only the first few numbers were taken up — the later numbers were used for new squadrons formed during World War Two. The Auxiliary squadrons had the block 600 to 616 and used all of these, the remainder of the 600 series going to new units during WW2. Expansion and the incorporation of Commonwealth and Allied units brought more block sequences (following the BCATP agreement of December 1939) — 300 to 399 going to Allied squadrons, 400 to 449 to Canadian units, 450 to 484 to Australian units, and 485 to 499 to New Zealand squadrons. The nationalities of each 'RAF' squadron are given in the listings below. It is only units so numbered that are included in this publication, although it must be appreciated that a great many other Allied and Commonwealth units played a significant part in World War Two. Many of the squadrons in the RAF sequence kept these numbers once they returned to their homelands after the war — in fact the Czech and Slovak Air Force has recently re-introduced their old RAF numbers.

With the rapid post-war run-down many squadron numbers vanished, some survived by the renumbering of other units. It has always been somewhat arbitrary as to which squadron numbers survive, although stated RAF policy has been for the preservation of the lower numbers as these, in theory, have the longest history. It is by no means always as simple as that and there is invariably a deal of 'in-fighting' with vested interest, i.e senior officers supporting 'their' old squadron, carrying much weight.

February 1949 saw the introduction of a policy to link two squadron numbers together for each unit in order to preserve squadron memory; it was a policy that met with little favour by the host squadron and the add-on was usually ignored. A total of 32 units acquired second numbers, the last one returned to single identity in October 1959. Since 1955 a similar policy was applied to training units, whereby some OCUs with an operational role acquired a shadow squadron number. This policy continues and has recently been expanded to include other non-operational training units.

A number of squadrons also received names, ranging from the regional titles adopted by Auxiliary and Reserve squadrons to special names related to sponsors or benefactors (individuals and countries). Overseas units often incorporated their home nation within their title. Other specialist titles included that of 'Eagle' given to the squadrons of American volunteers. 'Gift' squadrons were those having a "permanent association with a major donor or some other close connection", these squadrons then adopted the name of the benefactor e.g the units with 'Fellowship of the Bellows' titles. [see section on Aircraft Markings for further details.

Number	Name	Original Formation	Final Disbandment	Motto
1	—	13.5.12	Current.	'In Omnibus Princeps' First in all things.
2	—	13.5.12	Current	'Hereward' Guardian of the Army.

Crew of a 2 Squadron Hector smile for the camera.

Number	Name	Original Formation	Final Disbandment	Motto
3	—	13.5.12	Current	'Tertius primus erit' The Third shall be first.
4	—	16.9.12	Current	'In futurum videre' To see into the future.
5	—	26.7.13	Current	'Frangas non flectas' Thou mayst break but shall not bend me.
6	—	31.1.14	Current	'Oculi exercitus' The eyes of the army.
7	—	1.5.14	Current	'Per diem per noctem' By day and by night.
8	—	1.1.15	Current	'Uspiam et passim' Everywhere unbounded.
9	—	8.12.14	Current	'Per noctum volamus' Through the night we fly.
10	—	1.1.15	Current	'Rem acu tangere' To hit the mark.

Number	Name	Original Formation	Final Disbandment	Motto
11	—	14.2.15	Current	'Ociores acrierosque aquilis' Swifter and keener than eagles.
12	—	14.2.15	Current	— Leads the field.
13	—	10.1.15	Current	'Adjuvamus tuendo' We asist by watching.
14	—	3.2.15	Current	(Arabic) I spread my wings and keep my promise.
15	—	1.3.15	Current*	Aim sure.
16	—	10.2.15	Current*	'Operta aperta' Hidden things are revealed.
17	—	1.2.15	Current	'Excellere contende' Strive to excel.
18	Burma	11.5.15	Current	'Animo et fide' With courage and faith.
19	—	1.9.15	Current*	'Possunt quia posse videntur' They can because they think they can.
20	—	1.9.15	Current*	'Facta non verba' Deeds not words.
21	—	23.7.15	31.1.76	'Viribus vincimus' By strength we conquer.

Belvedere of 26 Squadron at a typical landing site in the Oman.

Number	Name	Original Formation	Final Disbandment	Motto
22	—	1.9.15	Current	'Preux et audacieux' Valiant and brave.
23	—	1.9.15	Current	'Semper aggressus' Always having attacked.

Buccaneers of 12 Squadron at Gibraltar.

Number	Name	Original Formation	Final Disbandment	Motto
24	Commonwealth	1.9.15	Current	'In omnia parati' Ready in all things.
25	—	25.9.15	Current	'Feriens tego' Striking I defend.
26	—	8.10.15	1.4.76	'N Wagter in die Lug' A guard in the sky.
27	—	5.11.15	Current	'Quam celerrime ad astra' With all speed to the stars.

Kai Tak, Hong Kong with a 28 Squadron Hunter on the ORP

Number	Name	Original Formation	Final Disbandment	Motto
28	—	7.11.15	Current	'Quicquid agas age' Whatsoever you may do,do
29	—	7.11.15	Current	'Impiger et acer' Energetic and keen.
30	—	24.3.15	Current	'Ventre a terre' All out.

The cargo bay of a 30 Squadron Beverley shows what a useful freighter this was.

Number	Name	Original Formation	Final Disbandment	Motto
31	—	11.10.15	Current	'In caelum indicum primus' First into Indian skies.
32	—	12.1.16	Current	'Adeste comites' Rally round, comrades.
33	—	12.1.16	Current	— Loyalty.

Number	Name	Original Formation	Final Disbandment	Motto
34	—	12.1.16	31.12.67	'Lupus vult, lupus volat' Wolf wishes, wolf flies.
35	Madras Presidency	1.2.16	28.2.82	'Uno animo agimus' We act with one accord.

The remote island of Gan being visited by 35 Squadron Vulcans.

Number	Name	Original Formation	Final Disbandment	Motto
36	—	1.2.16	3.11.75	'Rajawali raja langit' Eagle King of the sky.
37	—	15.4.16	5.9.67	— Wise without eyes.
38	—	1.4.16	31.3.67	'Ante lucem' Before the dawn
39	—	15.4.16	Current	'Die noctuque' By day and night

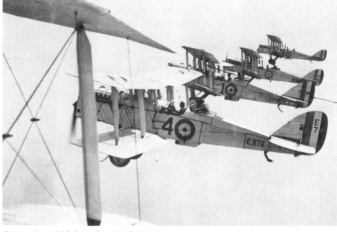

Formation of 39 Squadron D.H.9As.

Number	Name	Original Formation	Final Disbandment	Motto
40	—	26.2.16	1.2.57	'Hostem coelo expellere' To drive the enemy from the sky.
41	—	15.4.16	Current	— Seek and destroy.
42	—	26.2.16	Current*	'Fortiter in re' Bravely in action.

Number	Name	Original Formation	Final Disbandment	Motto

No. 45 Squadron pose around one of their Hornets, August 1954.

Number	Name	Original Formation	Final Disbandment	Motto
43	—	15.4.16	Current	'Gloria finis' Glory is the end.
44	Rhodesia	15.4.16	21.12.82	'Fulmina regis justa' The King's thunderbolts are righteous.
45	—	1.3.16	Current*	'Per ardue surge' Through difficulties I arise.
46	Uganda	19.4.16	31.8.75	— We rise to conquer.
47	—	1.3.16	Current	'Nili nomen roboris omen' The name of the Nile is an omen of strength.
48	—	15.4.16	7.1.76	'Forte et fidele'
49	—	15.4.16	1.5.65	'Cave canem' Beware of the dog.
50	—	15.5.16	31.3.84	— From defence to attack.
51	—	15.5.16	Current	— Swift and sure.
52	—	15.5.16	31.12.69	'Sudore quam sanguine' Through sweat other than through blood.
53	—	15.5.16	14.9.76	— United in effort.
54	—	15.5.16	Current	'Audax omnia perpeti' Boldness to endure anything.

Number	Name	Original Formation	Final Disbandment	Motto
55	—	8.6.16	Current*	'Nil nos tremefacit' Nothing shakes us.
56	Punjab	9.6.16	Current*	'Quid si coelum ruat' What if heaven falls?

An all time great, the F-4 Phantom — shown here of 56 Squadron.

Number	Name	Original Formation	Final Disbandment	Motto
57	—	8.6.16	Current*	'Corpus non animum muto' I change my body not my spirit.
58	—	8.6.16	4.6.76	'Alis nocturnis' On the wings of the night.
59	—	21.6.16	4.1.61	'Ab uno disce omnes' From one learn all.
60	—	15.5.16	Current	'Per ardua ad aethera tendo' I strive through difficulties to the sky.

Number	Name	Original Formation	Final Disbandment	Motto
61	—	25.7.17	31.3.58	'Per purum tonantes' Thundering through the clear skies.
62	—	28.7.16	30.9.64	'Inseperato' Unexpectedly
63	—	5.7.16	.9.92	'Pone nos ad hostem' Follow us to find the enemy
64	—	1.8.16	16.6.67	'Tenax propositi' Firmness of purpose.
65	East India	1.8.16	30.6.92	'Vi et armis' By force of arms.
66	—	24.6.16	20.3.69	'Cavete praemonui' Beware, I have given warning.
67	—	12.9.16	31.5.57	— No odds too great
68	—	30.1.17	20.1.59	'Vzdy pripraven' Always ready.
69	—	28.12.16	1.7.58	— With vigilance we serve.

Mobile line-hut of 69 Squadron.

Number	Name	Original Formation	Final Disbandment	Motto
70	—	22.4.16	Current	'Usquam' Anywhere.
71	Eagle	27.3.17	31.5.57	— First from the eyries
72	Basutoland	28.6.17	12.11.81	— Swift.
73	—	1.7.17	17.3.69	'Tutor et ultor' Protector and avenger.
74	Trinidad	1.7.17	Current*	— I fear no man.
75	New Zealand	1.10.16	15.10.45	'Ake ake kia kaha' For ever and ever be strong.

Number	Name	Original Formation	Final Disbandment	Motto
76	—	15.9.16	31.12.60	— Resolute.
77	—	1.10.16	10.7.63	'Ease potius quam videri' To be, rather than seem.
78	—	1.11.16	Current	'Nemo non paratus' Nobody unprepared.
79	Madras Presidency	1.8.17	Current	'Nil nobis obstare potest' Nothing can stop us.
80	—	1.8.17	28.9.60	— Strike true.

Lovely shot of 80 Squadron Gladiators at Ismailia.

Number	Name	Original Formation	Final Disbandment	Motto
81	—	7.1.17	16.1.70	'Non solum nobis' Not for us alone.
82	United Provinces	7.1.17	10.7.63	'Super omnia ubique' Over all things everywhere.
83	—	7.1.17	31.8.69	— Strike to defend.
84	—	7.1.17	Current	'Scorpiones pungunt' Scorpions sting.
85	—	1.8.17	19.12.75	'Noctu diuque venamur' We hunt by day and night.

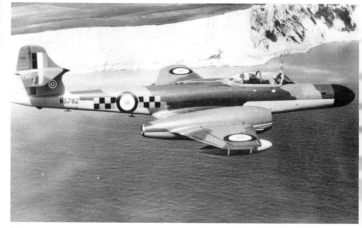

Meteor target tug of 85 Squadron.

Number	Name	Original Formation	Final Disbandment	Motto
86	—	1.9.17	25.4.46	'Ad libertates volamus' We fly to freedom.
87	United Provinces	1.9.17	3.1.61	'Maximus me metuit' The most powerful fear me.

'A' Flight of 87 Squadron Hurricanes, October 1942.

Number	Name	Original Formation	Final Disbandment	Motto
88	Hong Kong	24.7.17	17.12.62	'En garde' Be on your guard.
89	—	24.7.17	30.11.58	'Deiu auxilio telis meis' By the help of God with my own weapons.
90	—	8.10.17	1.3.65	'Celer' Swift.

Classic air-to-air shot of a 90 Squadron Valiant fuelling a Lightning.

Number	Name	Original Formation	Final Disbandment	Motto
91	Nigeria	1.9.17	31.1.47	— We seek alone.
92	East India	1.9.17	Current*	'Aut pugna aut morere' Either fight or die.
93	—	23.9.17	31.12.60	'Ad arma parati' Ready for battle.
94	—	30.7.17	30.6.63	— Avenge.
95	—	8.10.17	30.6.45	'Trans mare exivi' I went out over the sea
96	—	8.10.17	21.1.59	'Nocturni obambulamus' We prowl by night.
97	Straits Settlement	1.12.17	2.1.67	— Achieve your aim.
98	—	15.8.17	27.2.76	— Never failing.
99	Madras Presidency	15.8.17	6.1.76	'Quisque tenax' Each tenacious.
100	—	11.2.17	Current	'Sarang tebuan jangan dijolok' Never stir up a hornet's nest
101	—	12.7.17	Current	'Mens agitat molem' Mind over matter.

A rare beast — 101 Squadron Overstrand.

Number	Name	Original Formation	Final Disbandment	Motto
102	Ceylon	9.8.17	27.4.63	'Tentate et perficite' Attempt and achieve.
103	—	1.9.17	31.7.75	'Nili me tangere' Touch me not.
104	—	1.9.17	24.5.63	— Strike hard.
105	—	23.9.17	1.2.68	'Fortis in proeliis' Valiant in battles.
106	—	23.9.17	24.5.63	'Pro libertate' For freedom.
107	—	8.10.17	10.7.63	'Nous y serons' We shall be there.

Number	Name	Original Formation	Final Disbandment	Motto
108	—	11.11.17	28.3.45	'Viribus contractis' With gathering strength
109	—	1.11.17	1.2.57	'Primi hastati' The first of the legion
110	Hyderbad	1.11.17	15.2.71	'Nec timeo nec sperno' I neither fear nor despise.
111	—	1.8.17	Current	'Adstantes' Standing by.
112	—	25.7.17	1.7.57	— Swift in destruction.
113	—	1.8.17	10.7.63	'Velox et vindex' Swift to vengeance.
114	Hong Kong	22.9.17	31.10.71	— With speed I strike.
115	—	1.12.17	.10.93	— Despite the elements.
116	—	1.12.17	21.8.58	— Precision in defence.
117	—	1.1.18	17.12.45	— It shall be done.
118	—	1.1.18	31.8.62	'Occido redeoque' I kill and return.
119	—	1.1.18	25.5.45	— By night and day.
120	—	1.1.18	Current	— Endurance.
121	Eagle	1.1.18	29.9.42	— For liberty.

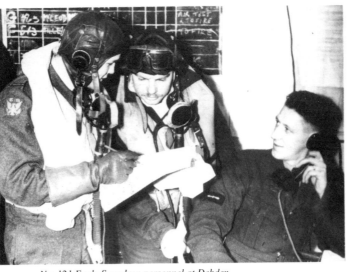

No. 121 Eagle Squadron personnel at Debden.

Number	Name	Original Formation	Final Disbandment	Motto
122	Bombay	1.1.18	1.4.46	'Victuri volamus' We fly to conquer.

Number	Name	Original Formation	Final Disbandment	Motto
123	East India	1.2.18	20.6.45	— Swift to strike.
124	Baroda	1.2.18	1.4.46	— Danger is our opportunity.
125	Newfoundland	1.2.18	10.5.57	'Nunquam domandi' Never to be tamed.
126	—	1.2.18	10.3.46	— Foremost in attack.
127	—	1.2.18	30.4.45	'Eothen' Out of the east.
128	—	1.2.18	31.3.46	'Fulminis instar' Like a thunderbolt.
129	Mysore	1.3.18	1.9.46	— I will defend the right.
130	Punjab	1.3.18	23.8.63	— Strong to serve.
131	County of Kent	15.3.18	31.12.45	'Invicta' Unconquered.
132	Bombay	1.3.18	15.4.46	'Cave leopardum' Beware the leopard.
133	Eagle	1.3.18	29.9.42	— Let us to the battle.

Blenheims of 139 Squadron in France.

Number	Name	Original Formation	Final Disbandment	Motto
134	—	1.3.18	26.6.45	'Per ardua volabimus' We shall fly through hardships.
135	—	1.4.18	10.6.45	'Pennas ubique monstramus' We show our wings everywhere.
136	—	1.4.18	8.5.46	'Nihil fortius' Nothing is stronger.
137	—	1.4.18	26.8.45	— Do right, fear naught.
138	—	30.9.18	1.4.62	— For freedom.
139	Jamaica	3.7.18	31.12.68	'Si placet necamus' We destroy at will.

141 Squadron pose with XIth Brigade trophy at Dublin, August 1919.

Number	Name	Original Formation	Final Disbandment	Motto
140	—	1.5.18 (17.9.41)	20.9.45	— Foresight.
141	—	1.1.18	31.3.64	'Caedimus noctu' We slay by night.
142	—	2.2.18	24.5.63	— Determination.
143	—	1.2.18	25.5.45	'Vincere est vivere' To conquer is to live.
144	—	20.3.18	23.8.63	— Who shall stop us.
145	—	15.5.18	15.10.57	'Diu noctuque pugnamus' We fight by day and night.
146	—	15.10.41	30.6.45	'Percutit insidians pardus' The watchful panther strikes
147	—	1.5.18 (17.10.41)	15.9.58	'Assidue portamus' We carry with regularity.
148	—	10.2.18	1.5.65	— Trusty.
149	East India	1.3.18	31.8.56	'Fortis nocte' Strong by night.
150	—	1.4.18	9.4.63	(Greek script) Always ahead.
151	—	12.6.18	.9.92	'Foy pour devoir' Fidelity unto duty.
152	Hyderabad	1.10.18	15.11.67	— Faithfull ally.
153	—	4.11.18	2.7.58	'Noctividus' Seeing by night.
154	—	7.8.18	31.3.45	'His modus ad victoriam' By this means to victory.
155	—	14.9.18	3.6.59	— Eternal vigilance.
156	—	12.10.18	25.9.45	— We light the way.
157	—	14.7.18	16.8.45	— Our cannon speak our thoughts.
158	—	4.9.18	31.12.45	— Strength in unity.
159	—	1.6.18 (2.1.42)	1.6.46	'Quo non, quando non' Whither not, when not?
160	—	1.6.18 (16.1.42)	30.9.46	'Api soya paragasamu' We seek and strike.
161	—	1.6.18 (15.2.42)	2.6.45	— Liberate
162	—	1.6.18 (4.1.42)	14.7.46	— One time, one purpose.
163	—	1.6.18 (10.7.42)	10.8.45	nil?
164	Argentine-British	6.4.42	31.8.46	'Firmes Volamos' Firmly we fly.
165	Ceylon	6.4.42	1.9.46	'Infensa virtuti invidia' Envy is the foe of honour
166	—	13.6.18	18.11.45	— Tenacity
167	Gold Coast	18.11.18	15.9.58	'Ubique sine mora' Everywhere without delay.
168	—	15.6.42	26.2.45	'Rerum cognoscere causas' To know the cause of things
169	—	15.6.42	10.8.45	— Hunt and destroy.
170	—	15.6.42	14.11.45	'Videre non videri' To see and not be seen.
171	—	15.6.42	27.7.45	'Per dolum defendimus' Confound the enemy.
172	—	4.4.42	4.6.45	'Insidiantibus insidiamur' We ambush the ambusher.
173	—	9.7.42	1.9.57	'Quocumque' Whithersoever.
174	Mauritius	3.3.42	20.4.46	— Attack.

Oops! Twin Pioneer of 152 Squadron finding yet another bad airstrip.

Number	Name	Original Formation	Final Disbandment	Motto
175	—	3.3.42	30.9.45	— Stop at nothing.
176	—	14.1.43	31.5.46	'Nocte custodimus' We keep the night watch.
177	—	11.1.43	5.7.45	'Silentur in medias res' Silently into the midst of things.
178	—	15.1.43	15.4.46	'Irae emissarii' Emissaries of wrath.
179	—	1.9.42	30.9.46	'Delentem deleo' I destroy the destroyer.
180	—	11.9.42	31.3.46	'Suaviter in modo fortiter in re' Agreeable in manner, forcible in act.
181	—	25.8.42	30.9.45	'Irruimus vastatum' We rush in and destroy.
182	—	25.8.42	30.9.45	— Fearless I direct my flight.
183	Gold Coast	1.11.42	15.11.45	— Versatility.
184	—	1.12.42	29.8.45	'Nihil impenetrabile' Nothing impentrable.
185	—	21.10.18	1.5.43	'Ara fejn hu' Look where it is.
186	—	31.12.18	17.7.45	nil?
187	—	1.4.18 (1.2.45)	2.9.57	— Versatile.
188	—	20.12.17	1.3.19	nil
189	—	20.12.17 (15.10.44)	20.11.45	nil?
190	—	24.10.17 (17.2.43)	21.1.46	'Ex tenebris' Through darkness.
191	—	6.11.17 (17.5.43)	15.6.45	'Vidi, vici' I saw, I conquered.
192	—	5.9.17 (4.1.43)	21.8.58	— Dare to discover.
193	Fellowship of the Bellows	18.12.42	31.8.45	'Aera et terram imperare' To govern the air and the earth
194	—	14.10.42	3.6.59	'Surrigere colligere' To arise and pick up.
195	—	16.11.42	14.8.45	'Velocitate fortis' Strong by speed.
196	—	7.11.42	16.3.46	'Sic fidem servamus' Thus we keep the faith

Number	Name	Original Formation	Final Disbandment	Motto
197	—	21.11.42	31.8.45	'Findimus caelum' We cleave the sky.
198	—	1.6.18 (7.12.42)	15.9.45	'Igni renatus' Born again in fire.
199	—	1.6.17 (7.11.42)	15.12.58	— Let tyrants tremble
200	—	1.7.17 (25.5.41)	15.5.45	'In loco parentis' We act as guardians.
201	—	1.4.18	Current	'Hic et ubique' Here and everywhere.
202	—	1.4.18	Current	'Semper vigilate' Be always vigilant.
203	—	1.4.18	31.12.77	'Occidens oriensque' West and east.
204	—	1.4.18	28.4.72	'Praedam man quaero' I seek my prey in the sea.
205	—	1.4.18	31.10.71	'Pertama di - Malaya' First in Malaya.
206	—	1.4.18	Current	'Nihil nos effugit' Naught escapes us.
207	—	1.4.18	30.6.84	'Semper paratus' Always prepared.
208	—	1.4.18	Current	— Vigilant
209	City of Hong Kong	1.4.18	31.12.68	— Might and main.
210	—	1.4.18	15.11.71	'Yn y nwyfre yn hedfan' Hovering in the heavens
211	—	1.4.18	15.3.46	'Toujours a propos' Always at the right moment.
212	—	20.8.18	1.7.45	'Amari ad astra' From the sea to the stars
213	—	15.1.18	31.12.69	'Irritatus lacessit crabro' The hornet attacks when roused
214	Federated Malay States	1.4.18	28.1.77	'Ulter in umbris' Avenging in the shadows
215	—	1.4.18	31.12.68	'Surgite nox adest' Arise, night is at hand.
216	—	1.4.18	Current	'CCXVI dona ferens' 216 bearing gifts.
217	—	1.4.18	13.11.59	— Woe to the unwary.
218	Gold Coast	24.4.18	23.8.63	— In time.
219	—	22.7.18	31.7.57	— From dusk till dawn

Number	Name	Original Formation	Final Disbandment	Motto
228	—	20.8.18	1.9.64	'Auxilium a caelo' Help from the sky.
229	—	20.8.18	10.1.45	— Be bold.
230	—	20.8.18	Current	'Kita chari juah' We seek far.
231	—	20.8.18	15.1.46	nil?
232	—	20.8.18	15.8.46	— Strike.
233	—	31.8.18	31.1.64	'Fortis et fidelis' Strong and faithful.
234	Madras Presidency	8.18	Current*	'Ignem mortemque despuimu' We spit fire and death.
235	—	8.18	10.7.45	'Jaculamur humi' We strike them to the ground.
236	—	8.18	25.5.45	'Speculati nuntiate' Having watched, bring word.
237	Rhodesia	8.18	1.1.46	'Primum agmen in caelo' The vanguard is in the sky.
238	—	20.8.18	4.10.48	'Ad finem' To the end.
239	—	8.18	1.7.45	'Exploramus' We seek out.
240	—	20.8.18	8.1.63	'Sjo-Vordur Lopt-Vordur' Guardian of the sea, Guardian of the sky.

Shackleton of 220 Squadron, November 1956.

Number	Name	Original Formation	Final Disbandment	Motto
220	—	1.4.18	10.7.63	(Greek script) We observe unseen.
221	—	1.4.18	25.8.45	— From sea to sea.
222	Natal	1.4.18	30.6.64	'Pembili bo'
223	—	1.4.18	23.8.63	'Alae defendunt Africam' Wings defend Africa.
224	—	1.4.18	31.10.66	'Fedele all'amico' Faithful to a friend.
225	—	1.4.18	1.11.65	— We guide the sword.
226	—	1.4.18	9.3.63	'Non sibi sed patriae' For country not for self.
227	—	1.4.18	5.9.45	nil?

223 Squadron at Foggia, October 1943, complete with Baltimore and two mascots. (Gordon Hampton).

Number	Name	Original Formation	Final Disbandment	Motto
241	—	8.18	14.8.45	— Find and forewarn.
242	Canadian	8.18	30.9.64	'Toujours pret' Always ready.
243	—	8.18	15.4.46	— Swift in pursuit
244	—	25.7.18	1.5.45	nil
245	Northern Rhodesia	8.18	18.4.63	'Fugo non fugio' I put to flight, I do not flee.
246	—	8.18	15.10.46	nil?
247	China-British	20.8.18	31.12.63	— Rise from the east,
248	—	8.18	30.9.46	'Il faut en finir' It is necessary to make an end of it.
249	Gold Coast	18.8.18	24.2.69	'Pugnis et cacibus' With fist and heels.
250	Sudan	10.5.18	30.12 46	— Close to the sun.
251	—	5.18	30.10.45	— However wind blows.
252	—	5.18	1.12.46	— With or on.
253	Hyderabad State	7.6.18	1.9.57	— Come one, come all.
254	—	5.18	23.8.63	'Fljuga vakta ok ljosta' To fly, to watch and to strike.
255	—	25.7.18	30.4.46	'Ad auroram' To the break of dawn
256	—	6.18	21.1.59	'Addimus vim viribus' Strength to strength.
257	Burma	18.8.18	31.12.63	'Thay myay gyee shin shwe hti' Death or glory
258	—	25.7.18	31.12.45	'In medias re' Into the middle of things
259	—	8.18	30.4.45	'Haya ingia napigane' Get in a fight.
260	—	8.18	19.8.45	'Celer et fortis' Swift and strong.
261	—	20.8.18	25.9.45	'Semper contendo' I strive continually.
262	—	29.9.42	15.2.45	nil?
263	—	27.9.18	30.6.63	'Ex ungue leonem' From his claws one knows the lion.
264	Madras Presidency	27.9.18	30.11.62	— We defy.
265	—	8.18	30.4.45	nil
266	Rhodesia	27.9.18	30.6.64	'Hlabezulu' The stabber of the sky.
267	—	27.9.18	30.6.70	'Sine mora' Without delay.
268	—	8.18	31.3.46	'Adjidaumo' Tail in the air.
269	—	6.10.18	24.5.63	'Omnia videmus' We see all things.
270	—	6.4.19	30.6.45	nil
271	—	27.9.18	1.12.46	— Death and life.
272	—	25.7.18	30.4.45	— On, on!
273	—	8.18	31.1.46	nil
274	—	11.18 (15.6.19)	7.9.45	'Supero' I overcome.
275	—	15.10.41	1.9.59	'Non interibunt' They shall not perish.
276	—	21.10.41	14.11.45	— Retrieve.
277	—	22.12.41	15.2.45	'Quaerendo servamus' We save by seeking.
278	—	1.10.41	14.10.45	'Ex mare ad referiendum' From out of the sea to strike again.
279	—	16.11.41	10.3.46	— To see and be seen.
280	—	10.12.41	21.6.46	— We shall be there.
281	—	29.3.42	24.10.45	'Volamus servaturi' We fly to serve.
282	—	1.1.43	19.7.45	nil
283	—	11.2.43	31.3.46	'Attende et vigila' Be alert and on guard.
284	—	7.5.43	1.8.59	— From the deep.
285	—	1.12.41	26.6.45	'Respice finem' Consider the end.

Number	Name	Original Formation	Final Disbandment	Motto
286	—	17.11.41	16.5.45	'Praesidia nostra exercemus' We exercise our defences.
287	—	19.11.41	15.6.46	'C'est en forgeant' Practice makes perfect.
288	—	18.11.41	30.9.57	— Honour through deeds
289	—	17.11.41	26.6.45	nil
290	—	1.12.43	27.10.45	nil
291	—	1.12.43	26.6.45	nil
292	—	1.2.44	14.6.45	nil
293	—	28.11.43	5.4.46	'Ex aere salus' Safety from the air.
294	—	24.9.43	8.4.46	'Vita ex undis abrepta' Life snatched from the waves.
295	—	3.8.42	31.10.48	'In caelo auxilium' Aid from the skies.
296	—	25.1.42	23.1.46	— Prepared for all things.
297	—	22.1.42	15.11.50	nil
298	—	24.8.42	21.12.46	— Silent we strike.
299	—	4.11.43	15.2.46	nil
300	Mazowiecki (Polish)	1.7.40	2.1.47	nil
301	Pomorski (Polish)	26.7.40	10.12.46	nil
302	Poznanski (Polish)	13.7.40	18.12.46	nil
303	Warsaw-Kosciusco (Polish)	22.7.40	11.12.46	nil
304	Slaski (Polish)	22.8.40	18.12.46	nil
305	Weilkopolski (Polish)	29.8.40	6.1.47	nil
306	Torunski (Polish)	28.8.40	6.1.47	nil
307	Lwowski (Polish)	5.9.40	2.1.47	nil
308	Krakowski (Polish)	5.9.40	18.12.46	nil
309	Ziemia Czerwienska (Polish)	7.10.40	6.1.47	nil
310	— (Czech)	10.7.40	15.2.46	— We fight to rebuild
311	— (Czech)	29.7.40	15.2.46	'Na mnozstui nehledte' Never regard their numbers
312	— (Czech)	29.8.40	15.2.46	'Non multi sed multa' Not many men but many deeds
313	— (Czech)	10.5.41	15.2.46	'Jeden jestrab mnoho vran rozhan' One hawk scatters many crows
315	Deblinski (Polish)	8.1.41	14.1.47	nil
316	Warszawski (Polish)	12.2.41	11.12.46	nil
317	Wilenski (Polish)	19.2.41	18.12.46	nil
318	Gdanskski (Polish)	20.3.43	12.12.46	nil
320	— (Dutch)	1.6.40	2.8.45	'Animo libere dirigimur' We are guided by the mind of liberty.
321	— (Dutch)	1.6.40	8.12.45	nil?
322	— (Dutch)	12.6.43	7.10.45	'Niet praten maar doen' Actions not words.
326	G.C2/7 Nice (French)	1.12.43	11.45	nil
327	G.C1/3 Corse (French)	1.12.43	11.45	nil
328	G.C1/7 Provence (French)	1.12.43	11.45	nil
329	G.C1/2 Cigognes (French)	3.1.44	17.11.45	nil
330	— (Norwegian)	25.4.41	21.11.45	'Trygg havet' Guarding the seas.
331	— (Norwegian)	21.7.41	21.11.45	'For Norge' For Norway
332	— (Norwegian)	16.1.42	21.11.45	'Samhold i strid' Together in battle
333	— (Norwegian)	5.5.43	21.11.45	'For Konge, Fedreland og flaggets heder' For King, country and the honour of the flag.
334	— (Norwegian)	26.5.45	21.11.45	nil
335	— (Greek)	10.10.41	31.7.45	—

Number	Name	Original Formation	Final Disbandment	Motto
336	— (Greek)	25.2.43	31.7.45	—
340	Ile-de-France (French)	7.11.41	25.11.45	—
341	G.C3/2 Alsace (French)	18.1.43	7.11.45	— Friendship
342	G.B1/20 Lorraine (French)	1.4.43	2.12.45	'Nous y sommes' Here we are.

Bostons of 342 'Lorraine' Squadron.

Number	Name	Original Formation	Final Disbandment	Motto
343	— (French)	29.11.43	27.11.45	—
344	— (French)	29.11.43	27.11.45	—
345	G.C2/2 Berry (French)	30.1.44	27.11.45	'Nil actum credo si quid supersii agendum' I think nothing done if anything remains undone.
346	G.B2/23 Guyenne (French)	16.5.44	27.11.45	—
347	G.B1/25 Tunisie (French)	20.6.44	21.11.45	—
349	— (Belgian)	9.1.43	24.10.46	— Strike hard, strike home
350	— (Belgian)	12.11.41	24.10.46	'Belgae gallorum fortissimi' The Belgae, bravest of the Gauls.
351	— (Yugoslav)	1.7.44	15.6.45	—
352	— (Yugoslav)	22.4.44	15.6.45	—
353	—	1.6.42	1.10.46	— Fear naught in unity.
354	—	10.5.43	18.1.45	nil

Number	Name	Original Formation	Final Disbandment	Motto
355	—	18.8.43	31.5.46	'Liberamus per caerula' We liberate through tropical skies.
356	—	15.1.44	15.11.45	— We bring freedom and assistance.
357	—	1.2.44	15.11.45	'Mortem hostibus' We bring death to the enemy.
358	—	8.11.44	21.11.45	'Alere flamman' To feed the flame.
360	—	1.4.66	Current	'Confundemus' We shall throw into confusion.
361	—	2.2.67	14.7.67	—
400	RCAF -	1.3.41	7.8.45	'Percussuri vigeles' On the watch to strike.
401	RCAF Ram	1.3.41	10.7.45	'Mors cellerima hostibus' Very swift death to the enemy.
402	RCAF Winnipeg Bear	1.3.41	24.7.45	— We stand on guard.
403	RCAF —	19.2.41	30.6.45	— Stalk and strike.
404	RCAF —	15.4.41	25.5.45	— Ready to fight.
405	RCAF Vancouver	23.4.41	5.9.45	'Ducimus' We lead.
406	RCAF Lynx	5.5.41	31.8.45	— We kill by night.
407	RCAF Demon	8.5.41	4.6.45	— To hold on high.
408	RCAF Goose	15.6.41	5.9.45	— For freedom.
409	RCAF —	17.6.41	1.7.45	'Media nox meridies noster' Midnight is our noon.
410	RCAF Cougar	30.6.41	9.6.45	'Noctivaga' Wandering by night.
411	RCAF —	16.6.41	21.3.46	'Inimicus inimico' Hostile to an enemy.
412	RCAF —	30.6.41	21.3.46	'Promptus ad vindtictum' Swift to avenge.
413	RCAF Tusker	1.7.41	23.2.45	'Ad vigilamus undis' We watch the waves.
414	RCAF Imperial	12.8.41	7.8.45	'Totis viribus' With all our might.
415	RCAF Swordfish	20.8.41	15.5.45	'Ad metam' To the mark.

Number	Name	Original Formation	Final Disbandment	Motto
416	RCAF -	22.11.41	19.3.46	'Ad saltum paratus' Ready for the leap.
417	RCAF City of Windsor	27.11.41	30.6.45	— Supporting liberty and justice
418	RCAF City of Edmonton	15.11.41	7.9.45	'Piyautailili' Defend even unto death.
419	RCAF Moose	15.12.41	5.9.45	'Moosa aswayita' Beware of the moose.
420	RCAF Snowy Owl	19.12.41	5.9.45	'Pugnamus finitum' We fight to the finish.
421	RCAF Red Indian	6.4.42	23.7.45	'Bellicum cecinere' They have sounded the war trumpet.
422	RCAF —	2.4.42	3.9.45	— This arm shall do it.
423	RCAF —	18.5.42	3.9.45	'Quaerimus et petimus' We search and strike.
424	RCAF Tiger	15.10.42	15.10.45	'Castigandos castigamus' We chastise those who deserve to be chastised.
425	RCAF Aloutte	25.6.42	5.9.45	'Je to plumerai' I shall pluck you.
426	RCAF Thunderbird	15.10.42	31.12.45	— On wings of fire.
427	RCAF Lion	7.11.42	31.5.46	'Ferte manus certa' Strike sure.
428	RCAF Ghost	7.11.42	5.9.45	'Usque ad finem' To the very end.
429	RCAF Bison	7.11.42	31.5.46	'Fortunae nihil' Nothing to chance.
430	RCAF City of Sunbury	1.1.43	7.8.45	'Celeriter certoque' Swiftly and surely.
431	RCAF Iroquois	11.11.42	5.9.45	'The hatiten ronteriios' Warrior of the sky.
432	RCAF Leaside	1.5.43	15.5.45	'Saeviter ad lucem' Ferociously toward the light
433	RCAF Porcupine	25.9.43	15.10.45	'Qui s'y frotte, s'y pique' Who opposes it gets hurt
434	RCAF Bluenose	13.6.43	5.9.45	'In exelsis vincimus' We conquer the heights.
435	RCAF Chinthe	1.11.44	15.3.46	'Certi provehendi' Determined on delivery.
436	RCAF Elephant	20.8.44	30.6.46	'Onus portamus' We carry the load.
437	RCAF —	1.9.44	16.6.46	'Omnia passim' Anything anywhere.
438	RCAF Wild Cat	10.11.43	26.8.45	— Going down.
439	RCAF -	31.12.43	26.8.45	— Fangs of death.
440	RCAF City of Ottawa	8.2.44	26.8.45	'Ka Ganawaitah Saguenay' He who guards the Saguenay
441	RCAF Silver Fox	8.2.44	7.8.45	— Stalk and kill
442	RCAF Caribou	8.2.44	7.8.45	'Un dieu, une reine, un coeur One God, one Queen, one heart
443	RCAF Hornet	8.2.44	15.3.46	— Our sting is death.
450	RAAF -	16.2.41	20.8.45	— Harass.
451	RAAF -	25.2.41	21.1.46	nil
452	RAAF -	8.4.41	21.6.42	nil
453	RAAF -	13.5.41	21.1.46	— Ready to strike.
454	RAAF -	23.5.41	20.8.45	nil
455	RAAF -	6.6.41	25.5.45	— Strike and strike again.
456	RAAF -	30.6.41	15.6.45	nil
457	RAAF -	16.6.41	21.6.42	nil
458	RAAF -	10.7.41	9.6.45	nil
459	RAAF -	10.2.42	10.4.45	nil
460	RAAF -	15.11.41	10.10.45	— Strike and return.
461	RAAF -	25.4.42	20.6.45	— They shall not pass unseen
462	RAAF -	7.9.42	24.9.45	nil
463	RAAF -	25.11.43	21.9.45	— Press on regardless.
464	RAAF -	15.8.42	25.9.45	'Aequo anumo' Equanimity.
466	RAAF -	15.10.42	26.10.45	nil
467	RAAF -	7.11.42	30.9.45	nil
485	RNZAF -	1.3.41	26.8.45	'Ka whawhai tonu' We will fight on.
486	RNZAF -	3.3.42	7.9.45	'Hiwa hau Maka' Beware of the wild winds
487	RNZAF -	15.8.42	19.9.45	'Ki te mutunga' Through to the end.

Number	Name	Original Formation	Final Disbandment	Motto
488	RNZAF -	1.9.41	26.4.45	'Ka ngarue ratau' We shake them.
489	RNZAF -	12.8.41	1.8.45	'Whakatanagata kia kaha' Quit ye like me, be strong
490	RNZAF -	28.3.43	30.6.45	'Taniwha kei runga' The taniwha is in the air.
500	County of Kent	16.3.31	10.3.57	'Qua fata vocent' Whither the fates may call
501	City of Bristol County of Gloucester	14.6.29	10.3.57	'Nil time' Fear nothing
502	Ulster	15.5.25	10.3.57	'Nihil timeo' I fear nothing
503	County of Lincoln	5.10.26	1.11.38	nil
504	County of Nottingham	26.3.28	10.3.57	'Vindicat in ventis' It avenges in the wind.
510	—	15.10.42	8.4.44	nil
511	—	10.10.42	6.1.76	— Surely and quickly.
512	—	18.6.43	14.3.46	'Pegasus militans' Pegasus at war.
513	—	15.9.43	21.11.43	nil
514	—	1.9.43	22.8.45	'Nil obstare potest' Nothing can withstand.
515	—	1.10.42	10.6.45	'Celeriter ferite ut hostes nacesit Strike quickly to kill the enemy.
516	—	28.4.43	2.12.44	nil
517	—	7.8.43	21.6.46	'Non nobis laboramus' We work not for ourselves.
518	—	6.7.43	1.10.46	'Thaan iuchair againn-ne' We hold the key.
519	—	7.8.43	31.5.46	— Undaunted by weather.
520	—	20.9.43	25.4.46	— Tomorrow's weather today
521	—	22.7.42	1.4.46	nil
524	—	20.10.43	25.5.45	nil
525	—	2.9.43	1.12.45	'Vinciendo vincimus' We link together to conquer.
526	—	15.6.43	1.5.45	nil
527	—	15.6.43	21.8.58	— Silently we serve.
528	—	28.6.43	1.9.44	nil
529	—	15.6.43	20.10.45	nil
530	—	8.9.42	25.1.43	nil
531	—	2.9.42	25.1.43	nil
533	—	8.9.42	25.1.43	nil
534	—	2.9.42	25.1.43	nil
535	—	2.9.42	25.1.43	nil
536	—	8.9.42	25.1.43	
537	—	2.9.42	25.1.43	nil
539	—	2.9.42	25.1.43	nil
540	—	19.10.42	31.3.56	'Sine qua non' Indispensable
541	—	19.10.42	6.9.57	— Alone above all.
542	—	19.10.42	1.10.58	— Above all.
543	—	19.10.43	24.5.74	— Valiant and vigilant.
544	—	19.10.42	13.10.45	'Quaero' I seek.
547	—	21.10.42	4.1.45	'Celer ad caedendum' Swift to strike.
548	—	15.12.43	9.10.45	nil
549	—	15.12.43	9.10.45	nil
550	—	25.11.43	31.10.45	'Per ignem vincimus' Through fire we conquer.
567	—	1.12.43	15.6.46	nil
569	—	10.1.44	1.3.44	nil
570	—	15.11.43	28.12.45	'Impetum deducimus' We launch the spearhead.
571	—	7.4.44	20.9.45	nil
575	—	1.2.44	15.8.46	— The air is our path.
576	—	25.11.43	13.9.45	'Carpe diem' Seize the opportunity.
577	—	1.12.43	15.6.46	nil
578	—	14.1.44	14.4.45	— Accuracy.
582	—	1.4.44	10.9.45	'Praecolamus designantes' We fly before marking.

Number	Name	Original Formation	Final Disbandment	Motto
586	—	10.12.43	30.12.43	nil
587	—	1.12.43	15.6.46	nil
595	—	1.12.43	11.2.46	nil
587	—	10.1.44	1.3.44	nil
597	—	10.1.44	1.3.44	nil
598	—	1.12.43	30.4.45	nil
600	City of London	14.10.25	10.3.57	'Praeter sescentos' More than six hundred.
601	County of London	14.10.25	10.3.57	nil

Superb study of 601 Squadron Avro 504; note squadron number on fuselage plus squadron badge.

Number	Name	Original Formation	Final Disbandment	Motto
602	City of Glasgow	12.9.25	10.3.57	'Cave leonem cruciatum' Beware the tormented lion
603	City of Edinburgh	14.10.25	10.3.57	'Gin ye daur' If you dare.
604	County of Middlesex	17.3.30	10.3.57	'Si vis pacem, para bellum' If you want peace, prepare for war.
605	County of Warwick	5.10.26	10.3.57	'Nunquam dormio' I never sleep.
607	County of Durham	16.3.30	10.3.57	nil
608	County of York (NR) North Riding	17.3.30	10.3.57	'Omnibus ungulis' With all talons
609	West Riding	10.2.36	10.3.57	— Tally ho!
610	County of Chester	10.2.36	10.3.57	'Alifero tollitur axe ceres' Ceres rising in a winged car.
611	West Lancashire	10.2.36	10.3.57	— Beware, beware.

Number	Name	Original Formation	Final Disbandment	Motto
612	County of Aberdeen	1.6.37	10.3.57	'Vigilando custodimus' We stand guard by vigilance
613	City of Manchester	1.3.39	10.3.57	'Semper parati' Always ready.
614	County of Glamorgan	1.6.37	10.3.57	'Codaf I geislo' I rise and search.
615	County of Surrey	1.6.37	10.3.57	'Conjunctis viribus' By our united force.
616	South Yorkshire	1.11.38	10.3.57	'Nulla rosa sine spina' No rose without a thorn.
617	—	23.3.43	Current	'Apres moi, le deluge' After me, the flood.
618	—	26.3.43	21.7.45	nil
619	—	18.4.43	18.7.45	nil
620	—	17.6.43	1.9.46	'Dona ferentes adsumus' We are bringing gifts.
621	—	12.9.43	1.9.46	— Ever ready to strike.
622	—	10.8.43	30.9.53	'Bellamus noctu' We make war by night.
623	—	10.8.43	6.12.43	nil
624	—	22.9.43	30.11.45	nil
625	—	1.10.43	7.10.45	— We avenge.
626	—	7.11.43	14.10.45	— To strive and not to yield.
627	—	12.11.43	30.9.45	— At first sight.
628	—	21.3.44	1.10.44	nil
630	—	15.11.43	18.7.45	'Nocturna mors' Death by night.
631	—	1.12.43	11.2.49	nil
635	—	20.3.44	1.9.45	'Nos ducimus ceteri secunter' We lead, others follow.
639	—	1.12.43	30.4.45	nil
640	—	7.1.44	7.5.45	nil
644	—	23.2.44	1.9.46	'Dentes draconis serimus' We sow the dragon's teeth.
650	—	1.12.43	26.6.45	nil
651	—	1.8.41	1.9.57	'Dirige' Direct.
652	—	1.5.42	1.9.47	'Sive aere sive campo' In the air and in the field.

Number	Name	Original Formation	Final Disbandment	Motto	Number	Name	Original Formation	Final Disbandment	Motto
653	—	20.6.42	15.9.45	'Ubique specula bundus' Watching everywhere.	667	—	1.12.43	20.12 45	nil
654	—	15.7.42	24.6.47	— Progressive.	668	—	16.11.44	10.11.45	nil
					669	—	16.11.44	10.11.45	nil
655	—	30.11.42	31.8.45	nil	670	—	30.12.44	1.7.46	nil
656	—	31.12.42	1.9.57	'Volans et videns' Flying and seeing.	671	—	1.1.45	25.10.45	nil
					672	—	21.1.45	1.7.46	nil
657	—	31.1.43	1.11.55	'Per terra sperque caelum' By land and sky.	673	—	27.1.45	25.10.45	nil
658	—	30.4.43	15.10.46	'Videmes delenus' We see and destroy.	679	—	1.12.43	26.6.45	nil
					680	—	1.2.43	1.9.46	nil
659	—	30.4.43	14.8.47	'Quovis per ardua' Everywhere through difficulties.	681	—	25.1.43	1.8.46	nil
660	—	31.7.43	31.5.46	nil	682	—	1.2.43	14.9.45	nil
661	—	31.8.43	10.3.57	'Designo oculis ad caedem' With my eyes I designate for slaughter.	683	—	8.2.43	30.11.53	'Nihil nos latet' Nothing remains concealed.
662	—	30.9.43	10.3.57	'Olethron omnia' Death dealing eye.	684	—	29.9.43	1.9.46	'Invisus videns' Seeing though unseen.
663	—	14.8.44	10.3.57	— We fly for the guns.	691	—	1.12.43	11.2.49	'Volamus ut serviamus' We fly to serve.
664	—	9.12.44	10.3.57	'Vae viso' I espied it, woe betide it.	692	Fellowship of the Bellows	1.1.44	20.9.45	'Polus dum sidera pascet' So long as the sky shall feed the stars.
665	—	22.1.45	10.7.45	nil	695	—	1.12.43	11.2.49	— We exercise the arms.
666	—	5.3.45	10.3.57	'Speculatus ascendimus' We ascend to observe.	1435	—	2.8.42	9.5.45	nil

Meteors of 616 Squadron on APC, Malta.

FLIGHTS

To COMPLETE THE summary of RAF organisation from Command level downwards we come to the question of Flights. This is an area of confusion and complexity, one in which many years of work await an intrepid researcher. The list presented here is very much by way of an introduction to the subject, dealing, as it does, with only the numbered specialist Flights and limiting each entry to a statement of the unit's original role and dates of existence. In the case of those Flights with more than one set of dates it is quite likely that the role changed with each new period. No mention is made of equipment as this would make the entries far too long, it being common for Flights to acquire a diverse collection of aircraft — much of it on an unoffical basis. Some, however, are far easier to consider, all the AOP units, for example, were equipped with various marks of the Auster. The policy change of March 1941 adding '1000' to all Flight numbers caused even greater confusion as it was some time before all units adopted the new style. Records of Flights are quite poor and many official sources are far from complete — leaving out quite well known Flights but then mentioning other obscure units. There are no doubt many errors in

the following list, especially with the lower numbered units. All BATFs were in the low numbers, e.g. 7 BATF at Finningley, when first formed, and later had '1500' added to their numbering. The ORBAT section provides additional detail. All RAF Groups had a communications flight and this was usually designated as, for example, No 1 Group Communications Flights — each was, therefore, a numbered Flight. Two other organisations to make extensive use of Flight numbering were the RAF Police and the Balloon units. Details of these are not included here, the Police Flights occur in the series 100 to 159, and 261-266 for VR units, and the Balloon Flights in the 50s and 101-120, both organisations often using the same number.

The final group of Flights in the low numbers were those attached to operational squadrons as conversion units, where they acquired the Squadron number e.g No 7 Conversion Flight was the Stirling element of No 7 Squadron charged with converting crews onto type. These are listed below if they eventually combined to form Conversion Units. Named Flights, such as 'Aden Flight' of the 1920s are not included.

Flt. No.	Type	Start/End Date	Remark	Flt. No.	Type	Start/End Date	Remark
7	Conversion	-.42	became 1657 CU	97	Conversion .	42-.42	became 1660 CU
9	Conversion		became 1661 CU	101	Conversion .	42-.42	became 1657 CU
10	Conversion .	42-.42	became 1658 CU	102	Conversion .	42-.42	became 1658 CU
15	Conversion .	42-.42	became 1651 CU	103	Conversion .	42-.42	became 1656 CU
26	Conversion .	41-		106	Conversion .	42-.42	became 1660 CU
28	Conversion .	41-		149	Conversion .	42-.42	became 1657 CU
35	Conversion	-.42	became 1652 CU	158	Conversion .	42-.42	became 1652 CU
44	Conversion .	42-.42	became 1661 CU	207	Conversion .	42-.42	became 1660 CU
49	Conversion .	42-.42	became 1661 CU	214	Conversion .	42-.42	became 1651 CU
50	Conversion .	42-.42	became 1654 CU	218	Conversion .	42-.42	became 1657 CU
61	Conversion .	42-.42	became 1660 CU	405	Conversion .	42-.42	became 1659 CU
76	Conversion .	42-.42	became 1658 CU	408	Conversion .	42-.42	became 1659 CU
78	Conversion .	42-.42	became 1658 CU	460	Conversion .	42-.42	became 1656 CU
83	Conversion .	42-.42	became 1654 CU				

The following series of Flight numbers were primarily those of naval units transfered to the RAF. A second element of this was the disbanding of FAA squadrons in April 1923 and the adoption of Flight numbers, these being duly transfered to the RAF on 1st April 1923. The following number sequences were used:

401-419 Fleet Fighter Flights.

420-439 Fleet Spotter Flights.

440-459 Fleet Reconnaissance Flights.

460- Fleet Torpedo Flights.

700-749 Catapult Flights.

Squadron numbers were re-introduced in April 1933, the majority of Flights taking up numbers in the 700 series, except for the Catapult Flights who maintained their identity until July 1936 at which time they adopted 700 series squadron numbers. Control of all naval aviation was returned to the Admiralty with effect from 24th May 1939.

The majority of the following were World War One naval Flights.

No	Date	Became
318	-.8.18	became No 257 Sqn
319	-.8.18	became No 257 Sqn
324	-.8.18	became No 228 Sqn
325	-.8.18	became No 228 Sqn
326	-.8.18	became No 228 Sqn
327	-.8.18	became No 230 Sqn
328	-.8.18	became No 230 Sqn
329	-.8.18	became No 231 Sqn
330	-.8.18	became No 231 Sqn
333	-.8.18	became No 232 Sqn
334	-.8.18	became No 232 Sqn
335	-.8.18	became No 232 Sqn
336	-.8.18	became No 247 Sqn
337	-.8.18	became No 247 Sqn
338	-.8.18	became No 247 Sqn
339	-.8.18	became No 261 Sqn
340	-.8.18	became No 261 Sqn
341	-.8.18	became No 261 Sqn
342	-.8.18	became No 259 Sqn
343	-.8.18	became No 259 Sqn
344	-.8.18	became No 259 Sqn
345	-.8.18	became No 240 Sqn
346	-.8.18	became No 240 Sqn
347	-.8.18	became No 238 Sqn
348	-.8.18	became No 238 Sqn
349	-.8.18	became No 238 Sqn
350	-.8.18	became No 234 Sqn
351	-.8.18	became No 234 Sqn
352	-.8.18	became No 234 Sqn
353	-.8.18	became No 234 Sqn
354	-.10.10	became No 270 Sqn
355	-.10.18	became No 270 Sqn
356	-.10.18	became No 270 Sqn
357	-.9.18	became No 271 Sqn
358	-.9.18	became No 271 Sqn
359	-.9.18	became No 263 Sqn
360	-.9.18	became No 267 Sqn
361	-.9.18	became No 267 Sqn
362	-.9.18	became No 267 Sqn
363	-.9.18	became No 267 Sqn
364	-.8.18	became No 265 Sqn
365	- 8.18	became No 265 Sqn
366	-.8.18	became No 265 Sqn
367	-.9.18	became No 271 Sqn
400	-.8.18	became No 249 Sqn
401	Met 11.40-?	
402	-.8.18	became No 249 Sqn
402	-.8.18	became No 246 Sqn
403	-.8.18	became No 246 Sqn
	11.40	became 14.03-10.41
404	-.8.18	became No 248 Sqn
405	-.8.18	became No 248 Sqn
407	-.8.18	became No 233 Sqn
410	-.8.18	became No 240 Sqn
412	-.6.18	became No 253 Sqn
413	-.6.18	became No 253 Sqn
414	-.8.18	became No 243 Sqn
415	-.8.18	became No 243 Sqn
416	-.8.18	became No 241 Sqn
	-.7.40	became No 231 Sqn
417	-.8.18	became No 241 Sqn
419	-.8.18	became No 249 Sqn
420	-.8.18	became No 237 Sqn
	-.12.40	became No 93 Sqn
421	-.8.18	became No 237 Sqn
422	-.8.18	became No 237 Sqn
	-12.40	became No 96 Sqn
423	-.8.18	became No 237 Sqn
424	-.8.18	became No 235 Sqn
425	-.8.18	became No 235 Sqn
426	-.8.18	became No 245 Sqn
427	-.8.18	became No 245 Sqn
428	-.8.18	became No 229 Sqn
429	-.8.18	became No 229 Sqn
430	AC . 40-.40 fighter element	became No 251 Sqn
431	-.10.18	became No 269 Sqn
432	-.10.18	became No 269 Sqn
433	-.8.18	became No 268 Sqn
434	-.8.18	became No 268 Sqn
435	-.9.18	became No 263 Sqn
436	-.9.18	became No 263 Sqn
437	-.9.18	became No 266 Sqn
438	-.9.18	became No 266 Sqn
439	-.8.18	became No 264 Sqn
440	-.8.18	became No 264 Sqn
441	-.9.18	became No 263 Sqn
450	-.8.18	became No 249 Sqn
451	-.8.18	became No 246 Sqn
452	-.8.18	became No 246 Sqn
453	-.8.18	became No 248 Sqn
454	-.8.18	became No 229 Sqn
455	-.8.18	became No 229 Sqn
471	-.8.18	became No 233 Sqn
472	-.4.18	became No 226 Sqn
473	-.4.18	became No 226 Sqn
474	-.4.18	became No 226 Sqn
480	.23 (ex No 230 Sqn)	
	-.1.29	became No 201 Sqn
481	-.8.18	became No 225 Sqn
	1.8.23	(ex 267 Sqn)
	-.1.29	became No 202 Sqn
482	-.8.18	became No 225 Sqn
	-.1.29	became No 203 Sqn;
	15.9.28-?	
483	-.8.18	became No 225 Sqn
485	-.8.18	became No 273 Sqn
486	-.8.18	became No 273 Sqn
487	-.8.18	became No 230 Sqn

491	-.8.18	became No 233 Sqn	527	-.6.18	became No 256 Sqn	1344	SD	(.45-?)
492	-.5.18	became No 254 Sqn	528	-.6.18	became No 256 Sqn	1353	AAC	26.6.45-15.6.46.
493	-.8.18	became No 236 Sqn	529	-.7.18	became No 258 Sqn	1357	Met	2.46-4.46
494	-.5.18	became No 250 Sqn	530	-.8.18	became No 244 Sqn	1359	VIP	1.12.45-30.6.46.
495	-.5.18	became No 252 Sqn	531	-.7.18	became No 272 Sqn	1360		6.1.58-1.2.58 became 271 Sqn
496	-.4.18	became No 224 Sqn	532	-.7.18	became No 272 Sqn			
497	-.4.18	became No 224 Sqn	533	-.7.18	became No 272 Sqn	1361	Met	16.1.46-11.2.46
498	-.4.18	became No 224 Sqn	534	-.8.18	became No 273 Sqn	1362	Met	
499	-.4.18	became No 227 Sqn	550	-.4.18	became No 227 Sqn	1363	Met	
500	-.5.18	became No 250 Sqn	551	-.4.18	became No 227 Sqn	1364	Met	
501	-.5.18	became No 250 Sqn	552	-.4.18	became No 221 Sqn	1401	Met.	40-22.7.42 became No 521 Sqn; 22.3.43- 29.6.46.
502	-.5.18	became No 260 Sqn	553	-.4.18	became No 221 Sqn			
503	-.5.18	became No 260 Sqn	554	-.4.18	became No 221 Sqn	1402	Met	.40-7.9.45; 4.12.45-1.5.46. became No 520 Sqn .9.43?
504	-.8.18	became No 251 Sqn						
505	-.8.18	became No 251 Sqn				1403	Met	.40-7.2.42;became No 520 Sqn 6.3.43-7.8.43.
506	-.8.18	became No 251 Sqn				1404	Met	.40-7.8.43.became No 517 Sqn
507	-.5.18	became No 252 Sqn				1405	Met	.40-7.2.42.became No 518 Sqn
508	-.5.18	became No 252 Sqn				1406	Met	8.41-7.8.43. became No 519 Sqn
509	-.5.18	became No 252 Sqn						
510	-.8.18	became No 251 Sqn				1407	Met	11.41-1.8.44.became 521 Sqn
511	-.6.18	became No 253 Sqn				1408	Met	11.41-.42 became No 519 Sqn
512	-.6.18	became No 253 Sqn				1409	Met	22.3.43-15.4.46.
513	-.8.18	became No 241 Sqn				1411		(.42-.43+)
515	-.8.18	became No 236 Sqn				1412		(.42-.43+)
516	-.8.18	became No 236 Sqn				1413		(.42-.43+)
517	-.5.18	became No 254 Sqn				1414		(.42-?)
518	-.5.18	became No 254 Sqn				1415		(.43-.44)
519	-.7.18	became No 255 Sqn				1416	PR	-9.41 became No 140 Sqn
520	-.7.18	became No 255 Sqn				1417		-1.43 became No172 Sqn; 11.53-11.67 became No 8 Sqn 7.77-.93
521	-.8.18	became No 244 Sqn						
522	-.8.18	became No 244 Sqn				1418	SD	
523	-.7.18	became No 258 Sqn				1419	SD	-8.41 became No 138 Sqn
524	-.7.18	became No 258 Sqn				1422		.41-3.6.44
525	-.6.18	became No 256 Sqn				1423		12.41-.43
526	-.6.18	became No 256 Sqn				1424		(1942)
			1343		(.45-?)	1425	Comms	.41-.42

The following list gives the main RAF Flight usage, given role applies to first period of existence. Some of the missing numbers in the following sequences may well have been used, but the author has not been able to find confirmation..

1300	Met	(.44-?)
1301	Met	(.44-?)
1302	Met	(.44-?)
1310	Transport	19.4.44-7.12.53; 23.7.64- 31.10.66; 8.83-1.5.86.
1311	Transport	19.4.44-21.7.44; 1.9.53- 15.2.54.
1312		8.83-Current
1315	Transport	1.1.45-1.3.46; -30.9.48.
1316	Transport	12.6.45-4.3.46.
1317	Training	13.6.45-27.6.45.
1320		8.5.44-14.6.44
1321	BDTF	1.9.44-1.11.44; 3.8.54- 15.3.56; 1.10.57-31.3.58.
1322	ADLS	9.10.44-11.12.44
1323		29.11.44-30.9.45
1340	(trials)	25.9.44-31.3.46; 31.3.53- 30.9.55.
1341	SD	(.45-?)
1342		(.45-?)
1343		(.45-?)

1426 EAC	1.12.41-17.1.45; 1.1.56-1.1.57	
1427	.41-1.4.43	
1428 Hudson	.41-6.6.42	
1429 Czech	.41-9.11.42 (to 6 OTU)	
1430		
1433	(.43-?)	
1435	(1942); 83-Current	
1437	(.43)	
1438	(.43)	
1436 Balloon	13.12.41-	
1439	1.5.57-20.11.57	
1441	.42-.4.43 became No 516 Sqn	
1442 FT	-1.8.42	
1443	(?.42-.43+)	
1444 FT	.42-3.11.42	
1445 FT	-3.11.42	
1446 FT	(1942)	
1447 Pre-OTU	19.3.42-15.12.42	
1448 Fighter	- 6.43 became No 529 Sqn	
1449 Fighter	27.3.42-17.9.44	
1451 Fighter	.7.41-9.42 became No 530 Sqn	
1452 Fighter	.8.41- 2.9.42 became No 531 Sqn	
1453 Fighter	.8.41-2.9.42 became No 532 Sqn.; 1.6.53-30.6.56; 27.7.83-30.6.85	
1454 Fighter	.8.41-2.9.42 became No 533 Sqn	
1455 Fighter	.7.41-2.9.45 became No 534 Sqn	
1456 Fighter	.8.41-2.9.42 became No 535 Sqn	
1457 Fighter	8.41-2.9.42 became No 536 Sqn	
1458 Fighter	.41-2.9.42 became No 537 Sqn	
1459 Fighter	8.41-2.9.42 became No 538 Sqn	
1460 Fighter	.8.41-2.9.42 became No 539 Sqn	

1462 (1942)		
1471 AC	.42-10.10.42	
1472	AC 15.6.42-15.11.43	
1473 SD	10.7.42-1.2.44	
1474 WI	10.7.42-4.1.43 became No 192 Sqn	
1475	2.11.42-15.5.43	
1476 AdSR	.43-1.1.44 (Advanced Ship Recce)	
1477 (Norw)	.43-5.5.43 became No 333 Sqn	
1478	15.4.43-.43 (as Signals Conv Flt)	
1479	AAC 1.5.42-1.12.43 became No 598 Sqn	
1480 AAC	.41-1.12.43 became No 290 Sqn	
1481 TTGF	?mid .42-25.11.44	
1482 BG	.42-1.4.44	
1483 BG	.42-15.2.44	
1484 BG	.42-15.2.44	
1485 BG	.42-15.2.44	
1486 FG	.41- .43	
1487 FG	.41- .43	
1488 ROTA	-15.6.43	
1488 FG	.41- .43	
1489 FG	.41- .43	
1490 FG	.41- .43; .44-?	
1491 FG	.41- .43	
1492 TT	18.10.41-	
1493 FG	.41- .43	
1494 TT	-30.6.45	
1495 TT	.42-4.11.43	
1497 TT	.43- .43	
1498 TT	.43- .43	
1499 BG	29.3.43-15.2.44	
1500 TT	4.5.43-25.1.46	
1501 BAT	-15.11.43	
1502 BAT	-6.8.43	

1503 BAT	-6.8.43	
1504 BAT	-6.8.43	
1505 BAT	-3.2.43	
1506 BAT	-6.8.43	
1507 BAT	-27.11.43	
1508 BAT	-1.4.46	
1509 BAT	-14.8.44	
1510 BAT	-1.12.46	
1511 BAT	-1.8.46	
1512 BAT	.41-1.9.44	
1513 BAT	.41-1.12.46	
1514 BAT	.41-9.1.45	
1515 BAT	.41-1.6.45	
1516 BAT	.41-11.4.46	
1517 BAT	.41-17.12.45	
1518 BAT	.41-1.9.44	
1519 BAT	.41-26.6.45	
1520 BAT	.41-3.5.45	
1521 BAT	.41-1.4.46	
1522 BAT	.41-.42	
1523 BAT	.41-17.12.45	
1524 BAT	.41-9.1.45	
1525 BAT	.41-26.6.45	
1526 BAT	.41-9.11.44	
1527 BAT	.41-28.2.46	
1528 BAT	.41-16.1.46	
1529 BAT	.41-16.1.46	
1530 BAT	.42-1.8.44	
1531 BAT	5.6.42-1.6.45	
1532 BAT	1.10.42-5.6.45	
1533 BAT	27.10.42-3.4.45	
1534 BAT	7.12.42-1.6.45	
1535 BAT	15.12.42-6.8.43	
1536 BAT	8.3.43-8.5.45	
1537 BAT	.43-4.4.47	

1538 BAT	15.4.43-18.10.44	
1539 BAT	15.4.43-1.6.45	
1540 BAT	15.4.43-17.12.45	
1541 BAT	17.5.43-11.7.45	
1542 BAT	8.6.43-1.9.44	
1544 BAT	3.11.43-1.9.44	
1545 BAT	14.2.44-17.12.45	
1546 BAT	23.5.44-9.1.45	
1547 BAT	1.6.45-1.1.47	
1551 Cal	.41-	
1552	RAT 15.9.45-26.10.46	
1553 RAT	15.9.45-1.10.46	
1554	RAT 15.9.45-1.10.45	
1555 RAT	15.9.45-9.8.47	
1556 RAT	15.9.45-1.4.46	
1559 RAT	1.10.46-9.8.47	
1560 Met	(.44-?)	
1561 Met	17.12.45-11.2.46	
1562 Met	17.12.45-11.2.46	
1563 Met	(.43-.44?); ?-Current	
1563 Helo	31.7.63(ex 103 Sqn)-17.1.72(as 84 Sqn).	
1564 Met	-15.6.46; 1.8.63-31.3.70;	
1565	(.43)	
1566 Met	(.44-?)	
1567 Met	(.44-?)	
1568 Met	(.44-?)	
1569 Met	(.44-?)	
1575	-.9.43 became No 624 Sqn	
1576	-.2.44 became No 357 Sqn	
1577	(.44-?)	
1578 Cal	(.44-?)	
1579 Cal	(.44-?)	
1580 Cal	(.44-?)	
1581 Cal	(.44-?)	
1582 Cal	(.45-?)	

1583 Cal	(.44-?)	
1586	(.44-?)	
1587 AOP	(.45-?)	
1588	9.44-?	
1589	10.44-?	
1600 AAC	13.3.39-1.12.43 became No 587 Sqn	
1601 AAC	30.6.41-1.12.43 became No 587 Sqn	
1602 AAC	15.4.39-1.12.43 became No 639 Sqn	
1603 AAC	1.5.39-1.12.43 became No 639 Sqn	
1604 AAC	.40-1.12.43 became No 639 Sqn	
1605 AAC	31.3.39-1.12.43 became No 631 Sqn	
1606 AAC	1.12.39-30.4.45	
1607 AAC	31.3.39-1.12.43 became No 595 Sqn	
1608 AAC	1.4.40-1.12.43 became No 595 Sqn	
1609 AAC	30.6.41-1.12.43 became No 595 Sqn	
1611 AAC	1.4.40-1.12.43 became No 695 Sqn	
1612 AAC	.40-1.12.43 became No 695 Sqn	
1613 AAC	-1.12.43 became No 290 Sqn	
1614 AAC	15.4.39-1.12.43 became No 650 Sqn	
1616 AAC	.39-1.12.43 became No 679 Sqn	
1617 AAC	.39-1.12.43 became No 290 Sqn	
1618 AAC	.39-1.12.43	
1620 AAC	2.5.39-1.12.43	
1621 AAC	16.5.39-1.12.43	
1622 AAC	-1.12.43	
1623 AAC	-1.12.43 became No 691 Sqn	
1624 AAC	-1.12.43 became No 567 Sqn	
1625 AAC	.43-.12.43 became No 587 Sqn	

1626 AAC	.43-1.12.43	
1627 AAC	.43-1.12.43 became No 679 Sqn	
1628 AAC	.43-1.12.43 became No 631 Sqn	
1629 AAC	.43-1.12.43 became No 291 Sqn	
1630 AAC	.43-1.12.43	
1631 AAC	.43-1.12.43 became No 667 Sqn	
1632 AAC	.43-1.12.43 became No 598 Sqn	
1634 AAC	.43-1.12.43 became No 291 Sqn	
1662	-.12.43 became No 667 Sqn	
1673	-.11.44 became No 358 Sqn	
1676	4.43-	
1677 TT	11.2.44-15.1.46	
1678 Conv.	-6.44	
1679 HC	.43-27.1.44	
1680 Comms	became No 271 Sqn 5.40? 19.5.43-18.3.46	
1681 BDT	5.6.43-21.8.44	
1682 BDT	5.6.43-21.8.44	
1683 BDT	5.6.43-21.8.44	
1684 BDT	5.6.43-21.8.44	
1685 BDT	5.6.43-21.8.44	
1686 BDT	5.6.43-21.8.44	
1687 BDT	15.2.44-31.10.46	
1688 BDT	15.2.44-30.10.46	
1689 BDT	15.2.44-7.5.45	
1689 FPT	6.3.46-9.4.53	
1690 BDT	15.2.44-12.10.45	
1691 BG	26.6.43-15.2.44	
1692 BS		
1693 AS	8.9.43-11.8.45	
1694 BDT	24.1.44-30.7.45	
1695 TT	.15.2.44-28.7.45	

1696	BDT	15.2.44-28.9.45
1697	ADLS	22.3.44-11.12.44
1698	Dev	15.4.44-15.4.44
1699	Trng	24.4.44-29.6.45

The 1900 series applied mainly to AOP/LL Auster Flights, at various times Flights were absorbed into AOP/LL squadrons, some retaining their own number during these periods, others adopting a Flight letter from their 'new' squadron, most reverted to independent status and nearly all moved over to the Army Air Corps on its formation in September 1957. Flights 1951-1970 were formed within the Auxilairy Air Force and so vanished when this organisation was disbanded in March 1957.

1900	AOP	31.12.46-1.9.57 (to AAC)
1901	AOP	31.12.46-1.9.57 (to AAC)
1902	AOP	1.1.47-1.9.57 (to AAC)
1903	AOP	1.1.47-1.9.57 (to AAC)
1904	AOP	1.1.47-1.9.57 (to AAC)
1905	AOP	1.1.47-1.9.57 (to AAC)
1906	AOP	-1.9.57 (to AAC)

1907	AOP	31.12.46-1.9.57 (to AAC)
1908	AOP	31.12.46-1.9.57 (to AAC)
1909		-1.9.57 (to AAC)
1910		31.12.46-1.9.57 (to AAC)
1911	AOP	-1.9.57 (to AAC)
1912	LL	15.8.51-
1913	AOP	12.6.51-1.9.57 (to AAC)
1914	AOP	-1.9.57 (to AAC)
1915	LL	4.4.56-1.9.57 (to AAC)
1951	AOP	1.7.49-10.3.57
1952	AOP	1.7.49-10.3.57
1953	AOP	1.7.49-10.3.57
1954	AOP	1.9.49-10.3.57
1955	AOP	1.7.49-10.3.57
1956	AOP	1.2.49-10.3.57
1957	AOP	1.5.49-10.3.57
1958	AOP	1.7.49-10.3.57
1959	AOP	1.5.49-10.3.57

1960	AOP	1.5.49-10.3.57
1961	AOP	1.5.49-10.3.57
1962	AOP	1.2.49-10.3.57
1963	AOP	1.2.49-10.3.57
1964	AOP	1.9.49-10.3.57
1965	AOP	1.9.49-10.3.57
1966	AOP	1.5.49-10.3.57
1967	AOP	1.9.49-10.3.57
1968	AOP	1.5.49-10.3.57
1969	AOP	1.9.49-10.3.57
1970	∞AOP	1.9.49-10.3.57

The higher numbers were reserved for non-flying units:

4000 - 4336 Anti-aircraft units (but included a few special flights)

4620 - 4866 Works/Airfield Construction units.

5370 - 5790 MT, Artisan, some Works.

6201 - 6208, 6211 - 6237 Bomb Disposal.

6482 - 6516 Air mobile control and reporting units (ATLWS).

UNIT BADGES

One element of the ceremonial/ heraldic attributes of RAF units is that of the unit badge, often refered to (wrongly) as the crest. The badge, once awarded, becomes a central part of the unit's identity, appearing on correspondence, aircraft or other equipment, as the major motif upon the Squadron Standard, and in a host of other uses. All RAF units, from Command size downwards, are entitled to apply for such a badge; however, they must qualify under the following provisions:

1. Have been in existence for at least 2 years — and likely to stay in existence.

2. Have a status and function which can justify the sanction of a badge.

It is obvious that both of these aspects are somewhat subjective, most minor units from World War Two had little chance of surviving the inevitable (win or lose) disbandment process — yet this did not stop them putting forward their claims. In other instances squadrons which would seem to be likely candidates appear not to have bothered. The second criterion is even more 'arbitrary', there being no detailed guidance available it was simply a question of put in the request and then wait and see.

Unit badges were only recognised as official once they had been accepted by the RAF Inspector of Badges, given sanction by the Chief of the Air Staff, and approved by the Sovereign. The initial step was to submit, via the appropriate 'chain of Command' a draft sketch of the motif and motto to the RAF Inspector of Badges, at the College of Heralds, including a statement of how the design/motto were arrived at — i.e the origin and significance. The Inspector would then make his suggestions as to amendments such that the design followed the precepts of heraldry and the motto made sense. This latter point was important as most chosen mottos were in Latin and few squadrons boasted high grade Latin scholars amongst their number. Along with the draft the unit had to send 15 guineas for the Inspector's fee!

Mottos and devices had been in use with many units, especially the flying squadrons, since the earliest days of the RAF; during the 1920s many units designed, and employed, unofficial squadron badges — in many cases these became the basis for the official badge. The example of 39 Squadron is fairly typical. During the mid 1920s the DH. 9As of 39 Squadron were frequent participants in the annual Hendon Air Pageants; just prior to the 1926 Display the Squadron Commander, Squadron Leader HV De Crespigny, devised a motif for use on the aircraft. After consultations with the other pilots it was decided to adopt a bomb, to signify the bombing role carried out by the squadron, but with the addition of wings, the initials 'RAF' and a crown (see over); to leave no doubt as to which squadron this belonged

The RAF badge showing the transition from the Tudor crown to St Edward's crown.

to, the number '39' was placed within the bomb. To complete the device a scroll was added with the inscription 'DIU NOCTUQUE' — the intended translation being 'By Day and by Night', to reflect the squadron's glorious past as a night-fighter unit and its present day role; however, it seems that the Latin was not too good and it was generally read as 'By God, By Night', not as intended but no doubt a true reflection of the 'terrors' of night operations! With the granting of an official badge in 1936 the motto was changed to 'DIE NOCTUQUE', thus ending the 'error'. To further illustrate the selection of a motif, two further examples: No 112 Squadron decided to use a black cat, the motif being chosen because of the speed of movement of this animal, and thus by implication the squadron, but also because the squadron had been based at Helwan, ancient capital of Egypt and one where the cat had been worshipped — the Egyptology was a little awry but the principle was correct. No 240 Squadron elected to use a winged Viking helmet as its recce duties took it over the northern waters once sailed by the Vikings, this concept being reinforced by an Icelandic motto — "Sjo Vordur Lopt Vordur — Guardian of the sea and air."

The general outline of the badge followed a fixed pattern of an edged circle, surmounted by a crown and with a scroll at the base. Up to 11th November 1954 it employed a Tudor crown (often refered to as a King's crown), but after that date it used St Edward's crown (the 'Queen's crown). The unit number was placed at the opposite mid points of the outer circle, the remainder of the text within the circle varying dependent upon the type of unit involved. However, in general terms the text was to include the word SQUADRON (or unit designation as appropriate) and words ROYAL AIR FORCE (or AUXILIARY AIR FORCE). Numerous changes were made to this, with, for example, the addition of squadron role (e.g Torpedo Bomber). A number of examples are included within this series of chapters.

If a unit was not eligible to apply for its own badge then it could adopt, and adapt, the badge used by its higher echelons, for example it could use the Command badge, substituting appropriate words in place of the Command title. This form was often used by Groups, the Command symbol being incorporated within the Group motif.

The whole question of unit badges became a matter for frequent discussion and the subject was a regular feature within the AMOs. Over the years, units have often made minor changes to their badges to reflect changes in title, in most cases this does not involve a change of the approved badge, i.e the original which was signed by the Sovereign, but rather just the 'in-use' badge. The commonest change was that of title with units changing role and desiring to include this change on their badge.

Origin of squadron badges — the unofficial 1926 design transformed into the 1930s official badge.

AIRCRAFT DATA

THERE ARE MANY publications which provide details of aircraft peformance, the most notable being, of course, the series of 'Jane's All the World's Aircraft'; the best single-volume published source is 'Aircraft of the Royal Air Force Since 1918' (by Owen Thetford and published by Putnam). However, in compiling the following list the author has attempted to use as much primary material as possible. This in itself presents difficulties — much of the primary material is no longer available!

A commonly-used source in most published work is the manufacturer's brochure, freely available and extolling the performance and capability of the aircraft. There are problems with this material regarding its relevance to how capable the in-service variant will be by the time the RAF has added extra bits and imposed additional limitations. The classic figures for maximum speed and 'service' ceiling published by the manufacturer would rarely be those obtainable by the average squadron aircraft. However, this does not really matter if the published figures use the same type of source as they would then provide a relative comparison if not accurate fact. Another major variation comes with the aircraft weight used when the speed/height calculations are made — is it an empty aircraft or is it loaded to an operational standard. It became evident when examining some of the primary sources, RAF trials reports for example, that some of the previously published figures are grossly in error.

As with all published material there has proved to be much variation in the numbers, ranging from a few mph to many thousands of feet. Where such variation has occured the author has tried to obtain a primary or near-primary source, and in the absence of either has elected for a concensus of opinion! With current types security classification precludes accuracy — the Tornado is often quoted as having a top speed of M2.2 but as a Tornado nav I have yet to find one capable of anything like that!

NOTES ON THE TABLES

Certain of the usual data have been intentionally omitted — height, weights, range, endurance — on the grounds that these are either of no great significance or that no single figure can prove reliable. This particularly applies to range/endurance as these figures are dependent upon operational loading, fuel weight, operating height, weather conditions etc. The Tornado Operating Data Manual, used to calculate such things, contains many pages of detailed tables — it somehow seems inappropriate to try and reduce that to a single figure!

The entries are alphabetical by aircraft name, following a numerical progression within each type. Aircraft nomenclature has been abbreviated by the removal of 'Mk' (for Mark) i.e the

Andover C.Mk.1 appears as the Andover C.1. This has been done for two reasons: firstly, simplicity; and, secondly, because in common parlance the aircraft are seldom referred to as, for example, Tornado GR.Mk.1, but rather Tornado GR.1 (or even just GR.1). This does not alter the fact that the full official designation IS Tornado GR.Mk.1, and the same for all the other RAF types.The first column states the aircraft general type using the code: Bi=Biplane, FB=Flying Boat, Gl=Glider, He=Helicopter, Mo=Monoplane. Note that the data panels do NOT include the FAA types operated by the RAF during the 1920s.

The manufacturer column gives the abbreviated name of the aircraft maker, as in the company which designed the type. It was common practise for other companies to licence-build aircraft, such a policy was vital during World War Two, with a great many companies involved in the production of components and aircraft.

A typical example of this is the Halifax production; the total of 6115 aircraft coming from five companies — HP 1539, EE 2145, London Ac Production Group 700, Rootes Securities 1070, Fairey 661.

The Spec No. (Specification Number) gives the official number under which this aircraft was provided.

Manufacturers Designation is the company coding for the type.The role states the aircraft's primary role(s).

In the case of the Gloster sequence this was simply a convenient post-war creation of a numbering sequence.

Engine details gives the abbreviated details of the power plants used.

Span and Length are the two most useful dimensions. Note that two span figures appear for swing-wing aircraft, and that the figure given for helicopters is for rotor diameter.

The armament details are amongst the hardest to confirm, partly through use of local variations but also with the introduction of multi-role aircraft capable of taking a wide range of weapons fits. The basic comment of 'various weapons' is used to cover non fixed armament if this covers a wide range of possibilities. Note also that many trainer/comms aircraft could be fitted with weapons or practice bombs if required, these circumstances are not covered at each entry.

Max speed and service ceiling are also tricky to state with any level of certainty, as discussed above.

The first flight column has two elements — prototype and production aircraft. One problem regarding first flights and prototype details is that in many instances different aircraft were used to test different aspects of a new variant — e.g Warwick BV296 was the testbed for the engines of the Mk.III whereas HF597 carried out the internal fit trials. It was not the intention to fill in both columns for every aircraft, the information is simply not available; the idea was to provide at least one entry.

IOC, Initial Operational Capability, is the type's entry to service date and unit. With operational types the unit is invariably a squadron, although in some instances the details given are for OCU-type units. An example is the Tornado GR.1 where the IOC is given as Jan 1982 for No 9 Sqn — the first squadron the receive the type — whereas the TTTE had been operating the aircraft since 1980. To the purist even the 9 Squadron date is not right as it would be some months later before the squadron could truly be considered operational.

Total build is an attempt to give details of the total to enter RAF service. The sources are not always clear as to who got what, and where this is the case it has been highlighted in the column — e.g part of the figure may be overseas or FAA use.

Last unit is an attempt to provide an 'end of active service' date for the type in regular squadron service, this does not imply a final RAF use date however as examples may well have continued in other roles for some considerable time; an example of this is the Audax with a last squadron date of February 1943 — there were still plenty still flying in the mid 1940s as 'hacks', comms and training aircraft.

US Designation gives the American equivalent designation for the aircraft, this really only applies to the American types taken up by the RAF, providing a useful cross-reference.

In the Notes various comments are made in an attempt to clarify other parts of the entry, or to explain any limitations.

There are a number of blank boxes, the result of the author being unable to find <u>acceptable</u> data for these elements.

Anson C.19 TX196 in the desert.

Type	Aircraft & Mk No.	Manufacturer	Spec. No.	Man. Design	Role	Crew	Engine	Span	Length	Armament	Max. Speed	Service Ceiling	First Flight Proto.	First Flight Prod.	IOC	Total	Last Unit	US Design	Notes
Mo	AIRACOBRA I	BELL	-	P.39	F	1	1 x Allison V-170-E4	34'	34'2"	1 x 20mm 6 x 303	358mph	35000	.39		8.41 601 Sqn	50	3.42 601 Sqn	P-400	IOC 826 Sqn FAA 3.40.
Mo	ALBACORE	FAIREY	S41/36		TB	2	1 x Bristol Taurus XII	50'	39'10"	2 x .303 2000lb bombs	110mph	15000	L7074 12.12.38		119 Sqn				
Mo	ALBEMARLE I	AW	B18/38	AW.41	B/GT	4/6	2 x Bristol Hercules XI	77'	59'11"	4/6 x .303	250mph	18000	P1360 20.3.40		10.41 161 Sqn.	600	12.44 297 Sqn		Not all RAF production Includes ST.1 and GT.1
	ALBEMARLE ST II	AW			T	4	2 x Bristol Hercules XI	77'	59'11"	2 x Vickers	265mph	18000			10.43 295 Sqn	99	12.44 297 Sqn		Similar to Mk I
	ALBEMARLE ST V	AW			T	4	2 x Bristol Hercules XI	77'	59'11"	2 x Vickers	265mph	18000			4.44 295 Sqn	49	12.44 297 Sqn		
	ALBEMARLE GT VI	AW			GT	4	2 x Bristol Hercules XI	77'	59'11"	2 x Vickers	265mph	18000			7.44 297 Sqn	117	12.44 297 Sqn		Includes ST.VI Similar to MK V; Sentes 1 e 2
Bi	ALDERSHOT III	AVRO	2/20	549	B	3	1 x RR Condor III	68'	45'	1 x Lewis 2000lb bombs	110mph	14500	J6852 early .22		8.24 99 Sqn	15	12.25 99 Sqn		
Bi	AMIENS III	DH		DH10	B	3/4	2 x Liberty 12	65'6"	39'7½"	2/4 x Lewis 900lb bombs	112½mph	16500	C8658 4.3.18		11.18 104 Sqn	220	60 Sqn 4.23		
Bi	ANDOVER	AVRO		561 563	T/AA	2	1 x RR Condor III	68'	51'3"	nil	110mph	13500	57261 .24		RAF Halton	3	.26		
Mo	ANDOVER C.1	HS		748	T	3	2 x RR Dart 201C R.Da 12	98'	77'11"	nil	302mph	23800	XS594 9.7.65		12.66 46 Sqn	31	Current		
	ANDOVER CC.2	HS		748 Srs2	VIP	3	2 x RR Dart 201C R.Da 12	98'	77'11"	nil	302mph	23800	XS789		2.69 32 Sqn	6	Current		XS790 in service with QF from 10.64.
	ANDOVER E.3/E.3A	HS			E		2 x RR Dart 201C	98'	77'11"	nil					11.76 115 Sqn	8	Current		Conversion of C.1
Mo	ANSON I	AVRO	G18/35	652A	GR/TR	3/4	2 x AS Cheetah IX	56'6"	42'3"	2 x 303 360lb bombs	188mph	19000	K4771 24.3.35	K6152 31.12.35	3.36 48 Sqn	6774	10.45 251 Sqn.		
	ANSON II	AVRO		652A	GR/TR	3/4	2 x Jacobs L6MB	56'6"	42'3"	2 x 303 360lb bombs	120mph	16200	L7069 21.8.41			1832		AT20	Canadian build
	ANSON III	AVRO		6520A			2 x Jacobs L6MB	56'6"	42'3"		190mph		N9935 .5.41						Mk I aircraft shipped to Canada without engines.
	ANSON IV	AVRO		652A			2 x Wright Whirlwind R-760-E1 or R-975-E3	56'6"	42'3"		190mph		R9816 .41			217			
	ANSON V	AVRO		652A	TR	2-6	2 x P&W Wasp Junior R-985-AN12B or AN114B	56'6"	42'3"		190mph	21450	N9943 11.42			1050			Canadian build
	ANSON VI	AVRO		652A			2 x P&W Wasp Junior R-985-AN12B/114B	56'6"	42'3"	1 x Bristol gun turret	190mph	21450	21.9.43			1			Canadian build (Anson VII, XVIII, IX not into production)
	ANSON X	AVRO		652A	T		2 x AS Cheetah IX/XIX	56'6"	42'3"	nil	175mph	19000	NK753			103	—		Conversion of Anson I. Series I and II
	ANSON 11	AVRO	OR141 OR143	652A	T/AA		2 x AS Cheetah 19	56'6"	42'3"	nil	190mph	15000	NK790	NK870 30.7.44	10.46 58 Sqn	90	7.47 58 Sqn		Conversion of Anson I
	ANSON 12	AVRO	OR141 OR143	652A	T/AA		2 x AS Cheetah 15	56'6"	42'3"	nil	190mph	15000	NL153 27.10.44		9.44 147 Sqn	246	9.57 187 Sqn		17 Conversion of Anson I includes C.12
	ANSON C.19	AVRO	OR224	652A	T		2 x AS Cheetah 15	56'6"	42'3"	nil	190mph	19000	PH806 7.47 58 Sqn.		8.52 527 Sqn	264	9.57 187 Sqn		20 Conversion of Anson 12. Includes XIX Series 1 and Series 2

Type	Aircraft & Mk No.	Manufacturer	Spec. No.	Man. Design	Role	Crew	Engine	Span	Length	Armament	Max. Speed	Service Ceiling	First Flight Proto. / Prod.	IOC	Total	Last Unit	US Design	Notes
	ANSON T.20	AVRO	T24/46	652A	TR		2 x AS Cheetah 15	57'6"	42'3"	nil	171mph	16000	VM305 5.8.47	—	59	—		
	ANSON T21	AVRO	T25/46	652A	TR		2 x AS Cheetah 15 or 17	57'6"	42'3"	nil	171mph	16000	VS562 6.2.48	—	252	—		
	ANSON T22	AVRO	T26/46	652A	TR		2 x AS Cheetah 15 or 17	57'6"	42'3"	nil	171mph	16000	VM306 21.6.48	—	34	—		
Mo	ARGOSY C.1	HS/AW		.660	T	4	4 x RR Dart 101 R.Da.8	115'	89'2"	nil	268mph	23000	G-AOZZ XN814 4.3.61	2.62 114 Sqn	56	2.75 70 Sqn		Developed from AW650 civil transport
Mo	ARGOSY E.1	HS		.660	E	4	4 x RR Dart 101 R.Da.8	115'	89'2"	nil	268mph	23000	XN814	2.68 115 Sqn	10	1.78 115 Sqn		
Mo	ARGUS I	FAIRCHILD		C-61	T	1/2	1 x Warner Super Scarab 165	36'4"	23'	nil	135mph	15700*		9.42 173 Sqn	670			User total includes ATA *or 10000ft
	ARGUS II	FAIRCHILD		UC-61A	T	1/2	1 x Warner Super Scarab 165	36'4"	23'	nil	135mph	15700						
	ARGUS III	FAIRCHILD		UC-61K	T	1/2	1 x Ranger	36'4"	23'	nil								
Bi	AW FK.8	AW			R	2	1 x Beardmore	43'4"	31'5"		95mph	13000		.19	100			
Mo	ATHENA T2	AVRO	T7/45 T14/47	.701	TR	2	1 x RR Merlin 35	40'	37'3½"	1 x .303	293mph	29700	VW890 1.8.48 / VM125 21.6.48	9.49 RAFC	15*	.56		*Or 22
Bi	ATLAS	AW	33/26		AC	2	1 x AS Jaguar IV C	39'6½"	28'6½"	1 x Vickers 1 x Lewis 4 x 112lb bombs	42½mph	16800	J8675 10.5.25 / 8.27 13 Sqn	10.27 26 Sqn	271	8.35 208 Sqn		
	ATLAS DC	AW	8/31		TR	2	1 x AS Jaguar IV C	39'6½"	28'6½"				J9435	—	175	—		
Bi	AUDAX I	HAWKER	7/31		AC	2	1 x RR Kestrel IB or X (DR)	37'3"	29'7"	1 x Vickers 1 x Lewis	170mph	21500	K1438 29.12.31 / K1995	2.32 4 Sqn	650	2.43 173 Sqn		
Mo	AUSTER I	TAYLORCRAFT		Model D	AOP	2	1 x Cirrus Minor I	35'3"	29'7"	nil			T9120 7.42	7.41 651 Sqn	100	11.43 651 Sqn		18 Taylorcraft Plus C impressed into RAF service, some mod. to C/2
	AUSTER II	TAYLORCRAFT		Model F	AOP	2	1 x Lycoming 0.290	35'3"	29'7"	nil			MZ105 30.12.42		2			Mods. to AOP.3 standard
	AUSTER III	TAYLORCRAFT		Model E	AOP	2	1 x DH Gipsy Major I	35'3"	29'7"	nil			LB319 28.9.42	?MZ100 12.42 654 Sqn	467	11.44 651 Sqn		
	AUSTER IV	TAYLORCRAFT		Model G	AOP	2	1 x Lycoming 0.290-3	36'	22'5"	nil	130mph		MT453	2.44 652 Sqn	255	3.47 654 Sqn		Includes AOP.4
	AUSTER V	TAYLORCRAFT		Model J	AOP	2	1 x Lycoming 0-290-3	36'		nil			MT356	7.44 653 Sqn	780	8.54 275 Sqn		Includes AOP.5
	AUSTER AOP 6	AUSTER		Model K	AOP	2	1 x DH Gipsy Major VII	36'	23'9"	nil	124mph	14000	TJ707 1.5.45	6.46 657 Sqn	312	3.59 209 Sqn		
	AUSTER T.7	AUSTER		Model Q	TR	2	1 x Bombardier	36'	23'9"	nil		14000	VF665 .47		77			
	AUSTER AOP 9	AUSTER		Model B5	AOP	2/3	1 x Blackburn Cirrus Bombardier 203	36'5"	23'8½"	nil	127mph	18500	WZ662 19.3.54	9.55 656 Sqn	145	9.57 656 Sqn		
Bi	AVRO 504K	AVRO		.540	TR	2	1 x Rhône or Clerget or Monosoupape	36'	29'5"	nil	95mph	16000			inc export 6350			Latter versions, still serving post-1918, of AVRO 504 Series of which 8000+ built. 504N total includes 78 conversions of 504K.
	AVRO 504N	AVRO		.582	TR	2	1 x AS Lynx IV or IV C	36'	28'6"	nil	100mph	14600	J8496	J1750	598	.33		
	AVRO 504J	AVRO			TR	2	1 x Monosoupape								1000+			

Type	Aircraft & Mk No.	Manu-facturer	Spec. No.	Man. Design	Role	Crew	Engine	Span	Length	Armament	Max. Speed	Service Ceiling	First Flight Proto.	First Flight Prod.	IOC	Total	Last Unit	US Design	Notes
Mo	BAe 125 cc.2	BAe/HS	125	125	T	2	2 x AS Viper 601-22	47'	506"	nil					4.71 32 Sqn	6			Later modified for Garrett engines
	BAe 125 cc.2	BAe/HS	125	125	T	2	2 x AS Viper 601-22	47'	506"	nil	570mph	41000			4.73 32 Sqn	2			Later modified for Garrett engines
	BAe 125 cc.3	BAe/HS	125		T	2				nil			ZD703 21.9.82		2.83 32 Sqn	6			
Mo	BAe 146 cc.1	BAe	146		T	6				nil			ZD695 20.9.82		.83 2410CU	2	–		Evaluation ac returned to BAe.
	BAe 146 cc.2	BAe	146		T	6		86'5"	85'10"	nil	400mph	30000	ZD700		4.86 QF	2	Current		
Mo	BALLIOL T.2	BP	T.7/45 T.14/47	P.108	TR	2	1 x RR Merlin 35	39'4"	35'1½"	1 x .303 4 x 60lb RP	288mph	32500	VL892 30.5.47		6.53 288 Sqn	162	–		
Mo	BALTIMORE I	MARTIN	—	.187	B	4	2 x Wright Double-Row Cyclone GR-2600-A5B	61'4"	48'5¾"	12 x 3 2000lb bombs	298mph	28000	AG685 14.6.41		1.42 223 Sqn	50	11.43 162 Sqn		
	BALTIMORE II	MARTIN	—		B	4	2 x Wright Double Row Cyclone GR-2600-A5B	61'4"	48'5¾"	12 x 3				AG735	1.42 223 Sqn	100	1.44 162 Sqn		
	BALTIMORE III	MARTIN		.187	B	4	2 x Wright Double Row Cyclone GR-2600-A5B	61'4"	48'5¾"	8-14 x .303/3 2000lb bombs	302mph	24000	AG835		3.42 223 Sqn		9.44 162 Sqn		Total RAF usage 1473
	BALTIMORE III A	MARTIN	—		B	4	2 x Wright Double Row Cyclone GR-2600-A5B	61'4"	48'5¾"				FA100		1.43 223 Sqn	281	3.44 52 Sqn		
	BALTIMORE IV	MARTIN	—		B	4	2 x Wright Double Row Cyclone GA-2600-29	61'4"	48'5¾"	7 x .5 3000lb bombs	300mph	22000	FA281	FA381	7.43 55 Sqn	294	2.45 459 Sqn		
	BALTIMORE GR V	MARTIN	—		GR/B	3-4	2 x Wright Double Row Cyclone GA-2600-29	61'4"	48'5¾"	7 x .5 3000lb bombs	300mph	22000		FW281	10.43 454 Sqn	600	7.46 680 Sqn	A-30A	
Mo	BASSET cc.1	BEAGLE		B.206	C	2	2 x RR/Continental G10-470-A	45'9"	33'9"	nil	220mph	19000	XS742 27.12.64		7.65	20	5.74 207 Sqn		
Mo	BATTLE I	FAIREY	P27/32 P23/35 P32/36 P14/36	.156	B	3	1 x RR Merlin I/II/III or IV	54'	42'1¼"	1 x .303 1 x Vickers 1000lb bombs	241mph		K4303 to 3.36	K7558 14.4.37	5.37 63 Sqn	1734	8.41 88 Sqn		Some use of Mk No. to designate Merlin variant used e.g. Battle III = Merlin III
	BATTLE TT.1	FAIREY			TT	2	1 x RR Merlin I/II/III or IV	54'	42'1¼"	nil			L5598 3.40			266			
	BATTLE T	FAIREY			TR	2	1 x RR Merlin I/II/III or IV	54'	42'1¼"	1 x .303			P2277			200			
Bi	BE 2e				R	2	1 x RAF 1a	40'9"	27'3"		82mph	11000					10.19 114 Sqn		Plus BE.12 derivatives in service post 1918
Mo	BEAUFIGHTER IF	BRISTOL	F17/39	.156	F	2	2 x Bristol Hercules III, X, XI	57'10"	41'4"	4 x 20mm 6 x .303	341mph	31200	R2052 17.7.39		8.40	(914)	7.45 577 Sqn		
	BEAUFIGHTER IC	BRISTOL	F17/39		F	2	2 x Bristol Hercules III, X, XI	57'10"	41'4"	4 x 20mm 6 x .303	330mph	30000			4.41 272 Sqn		11.43 603 Sqn		
	BEAUFIGHTER IIF	BRISTOL			F	2	2 x RR Merlin XX	57'10"	42'9"	4 x 20mm 6 x .303	337mph	32600	R2058 .740 23.3.41		4.41 600 Sqn		4.44 515 Sqn		
	BEAUFIGHTER VI C	BRISTOL			F/AS	2	2 x Bristol Hercules VI or XVI	57'10"	41'8"	4 x 20mm 7 x 303 var wpns	315mph	26000			7.42 235 Sqn	(1832)	8.44 227 Sqn		
	BEAUFIGHTER VI F	BRISTOL			F	2	2 x Bristol Hercules VI or XVI	57'10"	41'8"	4 x 20 min 7 x .303	333mph	26500	X7542		3.42 600 Sqn		8.45 176 Sqn		

Type	Aircraft & Mk No.	Manufacturer	Spec. No.	Man. Design	Role	Crew	Engine	Span	Length	Armament	Max. Speed	Service Ceiling	First Flight Proto.	Prod.	10C	Total	Last Unit	US Design	Notes
	BEAUFIGHTER X	BRISTOL			AS	2	2 x Bristol Hercules XVII or XVIII	57'10"	41'8"	4 x 20 min 1 x .303	320mph	15000	X8095		5.43 144 Sqn	2205	10.48 84 Sqn		
	BEAUFIGHTER TT.10	BRISTOL			TT	2	2 x Bristol Hercules XVII	57'10"	41'8"	nil			NT913 5.48		2.49 34 Sqn	35	9.51 20 Sqn		Conversions of Beaufighter X
	BEAUFIGHTER XI C	BRISTOL			F/AS	2	2 x Bristol Hercules XVII	57'10"	41'8"	4 x 20 min 7 x .303	320mph	21000			3.43 404 Sqn	163	8.44 227 Sqn		
Mo	BEAUFORT 1	BRISTOL	10/36; M15/35 G24/35	.152	TB	4	2 x Bristol Taurus VI	57'10"	44'2"	2-6 x .303 1500lb bombs	255mph	19000	L4441 15.10.38	L4446	11.39 22 Sqn	495	7.44 22 Sqn		
	BEAUFORT 1A	BRISTOL			TB	4	2 Bristol Taurus XI or XII	57'10"	44'2"	2-6 x .303 1500lb bombs	245mph	15000				529			
	BEAUFORT II	BRISTOL			TB	4	2 x P&W Twin Wasp R01830-S3C4-G	57'10"	44'2"	2-6 x .303 1500lb bombs	278mph	23000	N1110 9.11.40	AW244 17.8.41	10.41 217 Sqn	145	6.43 39 Sqn		
	BEAUFORT IIA	BRISTOL			TB/TR	4	2 x P&W Twin Wasp R-1830-S3C4-G	57'10"	44'2"	2-6 x .303 1500lb bombs	260mph	21000		DD945	2.42 86 Sqn	360			Last 121 built as trainers plus others converted to trainers.
Mo	BELFAST C.1	SHORTS		SC.5	T	6	4 x RR Tyne R.Ty 12 Mk 101	158'9½"	136'5"	nil	346mph	30000	XR362 5.1.64		1.66 53 Sqn	10	9.76 53 Sqn		
He	BELVEDERE HC.1	WESTLAND		.192	SH	2	2 x Napier Gazelle N.Ga 2	48'11"	89'9"	nil	138mph	10000	X9447 5.7.58		9.61 66 Sqn	26	3.69 66 Sqn		
Mo	BERMUDA	BREWSTER			TT	2/3	1 x Wright Double-Row Cyclone GR-2600	47'	39'2"	nil	284mph	23000				?750		A-34 SB2A-1	
Mo	BEVERLEY C.1	BLACKBURN	OR.161	B.101	T	4	4 x Bristol Centaurus 273	162'	99'5"	nil	238mph	16000	WZ889 17.6.53	XB259	3.56 47 Sqn	47	12.67 34 Sqn		
Mo	BISLEY	BRISTOL																	See Blenheim V
Mo	BISON I	AVRO	3/21; 33/22; 16/23	.555	R	2/3	1 x Napier Lion II	46'	36'	1 x Lewis 1 x Vickers	110mph	14000	N153 .21		.22 3 Sqn	12	.29		
Mo	BISON IA/II	AVRO		.555	R	2/3	1 x Napier Lion II	46'	36'	1 x Lewis 1 x Vickers	110mph	14200				(41)			
Mo	BLENHEIM I	BRISTOL	B28/35	.142M	B	3	2 x Bristol Mercury VIII	56'4"	39'9"	1 x Vickers 1 B rowning 1000lb bombs	285mph	32000	K7033 25.6.36	K7034	3.37 114 Sqn	30	4.42 267 Sqn		
	BLENHEIM IF	BRISTOL			F	2/3	2 x Bristol Mercury VIII	56'4"	39'9"	1 x Vickers 5 x .303			L1424		12.38 25 Sqn	23	2.42 27 Sqn		Conversions of Blenheim 1
	BLENHEIM IV	BRISTOL		.149	B	3	2 x Bristol Mercury XV or 25 or 35	56'4"	42'7"	5 x 303 1320lb bombs	295mph	31500	K7072 24.9.37	L4825	3.39 90 Sqn	3297	5.45 527 Sqn		IVL with extra fuel tanks, includes IVF.
	BLENHEIM V	BRISTOL	B6/40	.160	B	2/3	2 x Bristol Mercury 30	56'4"	44'	4 x 303 1000lb bombs	260mph	31000	AD661 ?657		10.42 139 Sqn	940	4.44 244 Sqn		Original designation. Bisley
Mo	BOMBAY I	BRISTOL	C26/31 47/36	.130A	BT	3	2 x Bristol Pegasus XXII	95'9"	69'3"	2 x Vickers 2000lb bombs	192mph	25000	K3583 23.6.35		11.39 216 Sqn	50	5.43 216 Sqn		
Mo	BOSTON I	DOUGLAS			TR	4	2 x P&W Twin Wasp T-1830-53C-G	61'4"	47'						2.41 88 Sqn	20	1.43 539 Sqn	DB-7	
	BOSTON II	DOUGLAS			NF	4	2 x Wright Double-Row Cyclone GR-2600-A5B	61'4"	47'				AH430					A-20	All converted to Havoc.
	BOSTON III	DOUGLAS			B/INT	4	2 x Wright Double-Row Cyclone GR-2600-A5B	61'4"	47'	8 x 303 2000lb bombs	304 mph	24250	W8252		7.41 88 Sqn	980	10.44 18 Sqn	A-20C	Intruder armament 4 x 20mm & 6 x .303 & 480lb bombs.
Mo	BOSTON IIIA	DOUGLAS			B	4	2 x Wright Double-Row Cyclone GR-2600-23	61'4"	48'	7 x .3 1 x .303	318mph	27000	BZ196		1.43 226 Sqn		4.45 88 Sqn		

Type	Aircraft & Mk No.	Manufacturer	Spec. No.	Man. Design	Role	Crew	Engine	Span	Length	Armament	Max. Speed	Service Ceiling	First Flight Proto.	Prod.	IOC	Total	Last Unit	US Design	Notes
	BOSTON IV	DOUGLAS			B	4	2 x Wright Double-Row Cyclone GR-2600-23	61'4"	48'4"	5 x .5 4000lb bombs	320mph	27000		BZ400	6.44 114 Sqn	(250+)	7.46 55 Sqn	A-20J	
	BOSTON V	DOUGLAS			B/INT	4	2 x Wright Double-Row Cyclone GR-2600-23 or 29	61'4"	48'	9 x .5 4000lb bombs	315mph	27000			10.44 55 Sqn		7.46 55 Sqn	A-20K	Alternative armament fit 4 x 20mm & 5 x 303 & bombs.
Mo	BOTHA I	BLACKBURN	M15/35 10/36	B.26	GR/TB	4	2 x Bristol Perseus X or XA	59'	51'1½"	3 x .303 2000lb bombs	320mph	18400	L6104 28.12.38		6.40 608 Sqn.	580			
Mo	BRIGAND B.1	BRISTOL	H7/42	164	GA	3	2 x Bristol Centaurus 57	72'4"	46'5"	4 x 20mm 2000lb bombs RPs	360mph	26000	MX988 4.12.44		2.49 84 Sqn	104			
	BRIGAND TF.1	BRISTOL			TF	3	2 x Bristol Centaurus 57	72'4"	46'5"	4 x 20mm 1 x .5 1 x torpedo	347mph	26000		TX374		13			Conversions of B.1.
	BRIGAND Met.3	BRISTOL			WR	3	2 x Bristol Centaurus 57	72'4"		nil		26000				16			
	BRIGAND T.4	BRISTOL			TR	2	2 x Bristol Centaurus 57	72'4"	46'5"	nil			RH798 .49		7.51 228 OCU	9			
	BRIGAND T.5	BRISTOL			TR		2 x Bristol Centaurus 57	72'4"	46'5"	nil						?30			Conversions of B.1.
Bi	BRISTOL FIGHTER	BRISTOL		F2A F2B	F	2	F2A - 1 x Hispano Suiza or 1 x Falcon I, F2B - 9 alternatives	39'3"	24'10" or 26'	1 x Vickers 1 x Lewis	F2A-110mph F2B-125mph	20000	A3303* 9.9.16		4.17 48 Sqn	50-F2a			Length dependent on engine type. *F2a mod. to F2b 25.10.16
	BRISTOL FIGHTER II	BRISTOL	21/21	F2B	F	2	As above or or 1 x RR Falcon III	39'3"	25'10"	1 x Vickers 1-2 x Lewis						(5125)	.31		Tropical variant.
	BRISTOL FIGHTER III	BRISTOL			F	2	1 x RR Falcon III	39'4"	25'10"	1 x Vickers 1 x Lewis 224lb bombs						(378)			
	BRISTOL FIGHTER IV	BRISTOL			F	2	21 x RR Falcon III	39'4"	25'10"	1 x Vickers 1 x Lewis + bombs									
Mo	BRISTOL M1C MONOPLANE	BRISTOL		M.1	F/R	1	1 x Le Rhône	30'9"	20'5½"	1 x Vickers	111mph	20000	1374 .16	A5138 14.7.16		125	5.17 14 Sqn*		*M1.A
Mo	BRITANNIA C.1	BRISTOL	SOP.16	253	T	5	4 x BS Proteus 255	142'3½"	124'3"	nil	360mph		XL635 29.12.58		3.59 99 Sqn	20			
	BRITANNIA C.2	BRISTOL			T	5	4 x BS Proteus 255	142'3½"	124'3"	nil						3			
Mo	BUCCANEER S.2A	HS	(NA.39)	B.103	SA	2	2 x RR RB168 Spey Mk101	44'	63'5"	16000lb bombs	690mph	40000+	XV350 11.12.69		10.69 12 Sqn	88			
Mo	BUCCANEER S.2B	HS			SA	2	2 x RR RB168 Spey Mk101.	44'	63'5"	16000lb bombs	690mph	40000+					4.94* 208 Sqn		*Planned date.
Mo	BUCKINGHAM B.1	BRISTOL	B2/41	.163	B	4	2 x Bristol Centaurus VII or XI	71'10"	46'10"	10 x .303 4000lb bombs	335mph	25000	DX249 4.2.43	KV301 12.2.44		119*			*Or 123
	BUCKINGHAM C.1	BRISTOL			T	3	2 x Bristol Centaurus VII or XI	71'10"	46'10"	nil	360mph	28000							Prob. only 3 in RAF service
Mo	BUCKMASTER T.1	BRISTOL	T13/43	.166	TR	3	2 x Bristol Centaurus VII	71'10" or (72'4")	46'5"	nil	352mph	30000	TJ714 27.10.44			110			
Mo	BUFFALO I	BREWSTER		B.339E	F	1	1 x Wright Cyclone GR-1820-G105A	35'	26'	4 x .303 or 4 x .5	294mph	30500	XF2A-2 7.39	W8131	67 3.41	170*			*Or 208
Bi	BULLDOG II/IIA	BRISTOL	F17/24 F9/26 F12/28 F11/29 F11/31	.105A	F	1	1 x Bristol Jupiter VII F or VIIF-P	33'10"	25'2"	2 x Vickers 80lb bombs	178mph	29300	J9480 21.1.28		5.29 3 Sqn	301	.37		

Type	Aircraft & Mk No.	Manufacturer	Spec. No.	Man. Design	Role	Crew	Engine	Span	Length	Armament	Max. Speed	Service Ceiling	First Flight Proto.	First Flight Prod.	IOC	Total	Last Unit	US Design	Notes
	BULLDOG TM	BRISTOL	T12/32	.124	TR	2	1 x Bristol Jupiter VI FH	34'2"	25'3"	nil	168mph	28000	K2188			69	.37		
Bi	BULLDOG T.1	SCOTTISH AVIATION			TR	2	1 Lycoming 360-A1B6	33'	23'2½"	nil	150mph	26000	XX513 30.1.73		4.73 CFS	130			
Bi	BUZZARD	MARTINSYDE	F.4		F	1	1 x Hispano-Suiza	32'9⅛"	25'5⅝"	2 x Vickers 220lb bombs	146mph	26000	Mod. F3 .18			338 *	.23		*Or 170
Bi	CAMEL	SOPWITH	F.1		F	1	1 x Clerget or Le Rhône	28'	18'9"	2 x Vickers 100lb bombs	118½mph	19000 24000	22.12.16		7.17 70 Sqn	5490			Official designation — Sopwith F.1.
Bi	CAMEL (H.D.)	SOPWITH	Type II		F	1	1 x Clerget or	28'	18'9"	2 x Lewis	117 118½mph	19000 24000							
FB	CAMPANIA	FAIREY	F.16 *		GP	2	1 x RR Eagle or Sunbeam Maori	61'7½"	43'4"	1 x Lewis + bombs	85mph	6000	N1000 16.2.17		6.18 253 Sqn	40	6.19 241 Sqn		Ex RNAS *Also F.17 & F.22
Mo	CANBERRA B.2	ENGLISH ELECTRIC	B3/45 B5/47	E.A3	B	3	2 x RR Avon 101 (RA.3)	64'	65'6"	6000lb bombs	450mph	55000	VX165 23.450	WD929 8.10.50	5.51 101 Sqn	416	7.93 360 Sqn	B-57A	Wing span with tip tanks 65'6" (all except PR.9). Includes B.2(T) and B.2(TT).
	CANBERRA PR.3	ENGLISH ELECTRIC	PR31/46	E.A2 S.D1	PR	2/3	2 x RR Avon 101 (RA.3)	64'	66'8"	nil	450mph	55000	VX181 19.3.50		12.52 540 Sqn	35	11.62 39 Sqn		
	CANBERRA T.4	ENGLISH ELECTRIC	T2/49	E.A4	TR	3	2 x RR Avon 101 (RA.3)	64'	65'6"	nil	450mph	55000	WN467 6.6.52	WE.188 31.7.52	.54 231 OCU	84	Current		Includes 16 conversions of B.2.
	CANBERRA B.6	ENGLISH ELECTRIC			B	3	2 x RR Avon 109 (RA.7)	64'	65'6"	6000lb bombs	450mph	55000	WJ754 26.1.54		6.54 111 Sqn	96	7.74 51 Sqn		Includes B.6 (Mod) and B.6(B5).
	CANBERRA B(I)6	ENGLISH ELECTRIC			B/INT	2/3	2 x RR Avon 109 (RA.7)	64'	65'6"	4 x 20mm 6000lb bombs	450mph	55000	WT307 31.3.55		7.55 213 Sqn	22	12.69 213 Sqn		
	CANBERRA PR.7	ENGLISH ELECTRIC			PR	2	2 x RR Avon 109 (RA.7)	64'	66'8"	nil	450mph	55000	WH773 28.10.53		542 Sqn 5.53	74	Current		
	CANBERRA B(I)8	ENGLISH ELECTRIC	1B.122		B/INT	2	2 x RR Avon 109 (RA.7)	64'	65'6"	4 x 20mm Various wpns.	450mph	55000	VX185 23.7.54	WT326 8.6.55	1.56 88 Sqn	80	6.72 16 Sqn		
	CANBERRA PR.9	SHORTS	SOP.5		PR	2	2 x RR Avon 206	67'10"	66'8"	nil	450mph	55000+	WH793 8.7.55	XH129 27.7.58	58 Sqn	22	Current		
	CANBERRA U/D.10	ENGLISH ELECTRIC	OR.33	S.C4	DR	1/nil	2 x RR Avon 101 (RA.3)	64'	65'6"	nil	450mph	55000	WJ624 11.6.57		6.59 LRWE	18	—		Conversions of B.2.
	CANBERRA T.11	ENGLISH ELECTRIC	SOP.17		E	2/3	2 x RR Avon 101 (RA.3)	64'	65'6"	nil	450mph	55000	WJ610 29.3.58		.59 228 OCU	8	4.69 85 Sqn		Conversions of B.2.
	CANBERRA B.15	ENGLISH ELECTRIC			B/INT	3	2 x RR Avon 109 (RA.7)	64'	65'6"	Various wpns.	450mph	55000	WH961 4.10.60		.62 73 Sqn	38	2.70 45 Sqn		Conversions of B.6.
	CANBERRA B.16	ENGLISH ELECTRIC			B/INT	3	2 x RR Avon 109 (RA.7)	64'	65'6"	Various wpns	450mph	55000	—		8.61 32 Sqn	19	3.69 ASW		Conversions of B.6(B5).
	CANBERRA T.17/T.17A	ENGLISH ELECTRIC			E	3	2 x RR Avon 101 (RA.3)	64'	65'6"	nil	450mph	55000	WJ977 9.9.65		12.66 360 Sqn	24	Current		Conversions of B.2.
	CANBERRA TT.18	ENGLISH ELECTRIC			TT	2/3	2 x RR Avon 101 (RA.3)	64'	65'6"	nil	450mph	55000	WJ632 21.3.66		5.70 7 Sqn	inc. RN 23	12.91 100 Sqn		Conversions of B.2.
	CANBERRA T.19	ENGLISH ELECTRIC			E	2/3	2 x RR Avon 101 (RA.3)	64'	65'6"	nil	450mph	55000	WH724 .65		.65 85 Sqn	8	5.18 100 Sqn		Conversions of T.11.
	CANBERRA E.15	ENGLISH ELECTRIC			E	2/3	2 x RR Avon 109	64'	65'6"	nil	450mph	55000			3.63 98 Sqn	8	12.91 100 Sqn		Conversions of B.15.
FB	CATALINA 1	CONSOLIDATED	.28		GR	8/9	2 x P&W R-1830-S13C-92 or 82	104'	65'1¼"	6 x .303 4000lb	176mph	19500	PBY proto .35	ZZ2134	3.41 240 Sqn	92	6.45 209 Sqn	PBY-5	

Type	Aircraft & Mk No.	Manufacturer	Spec. No.	Man. Design	Role	Crew	Engine	Span	Length	Armament	Max. Speed	Service Ceiling	First Flight Proto.	Prod.	IOC	Total	Last Unit	US Design	Notes
	CATALINA IB	CONSOL'D			GR	8/9	2 x P&W R-1830-S1C3-G	104'	65'1¼"	4 x .303 2000lb bombs	190mph	24000		FP100		170		PBY-5B	
	CATALINA II	CONSOL'D			GR								AM264		3.42 240 Sqn	7	6.45 209 Sqn	PBY-5	
	CATALINA IIB	CONSOL'D			GR											21		PBY-5	
	CATALINA IIIA	CONSOL'D			GR	9	2 x P&W R-1830-82	104'	65'1¼"	2 x .303 2 x .5 4000lb bombs	179mph	19500		FP525	5.42 119 Sqn	12	12.45 321 Sqn	PBY-5A	
	CATALINA IVA	CONSOL'D			GR								JB925		10.43 190 Sqn	62	12.45 321 Sqn		
	CATALINA IVB	CONSOL'D			GR								JX270			211		PBY-5	
	CATALINA VI	BOEING			GR											50		PBY-6A	
He	CHINOOK HC.1	BOEING VERTOL		CH-47	SH	4	2 x Lycoming T-SS-L-11	60'	99'	1 x GPMG	180mph	15000	YCH-47A 21.9.61	ZA670 23.3.80	8.81 18 Sqn	41	Current		ZA718 mod. to HC.2; 10C 1993.
Mo	CHIPMUNK T.10	DH	8/48	DHC-1	TR	2	1 x DH Gipsy Major 8	34'4"	25'8"	nil	138mph	16000	22.5.46	WB549	2.50 OUAS	735	Current		
Bi	CIRRUS MOTH I	DH		DH.60	TR/C	2	1 x DH Cirrus I, II or III	29'	23'5"	nil			G-EBKT 22.2.25			3			
	CIRRUS MOTH II	DH		DH.60	TR/C	2	1 x DH Cirrus I, II or III									19			
Bi	CLEVELAND	CURTISS			T	2	1 x Wright Cyclone	34'	27'6"	nil	235mph	24500	.37		24 Sqn	5		SBC4	
Bi	CLIVE II	HP	C20/27		T	2	2 x Bristol Jupiter VIIIF	75'	63'	nil	111mph	12600	J9948		HTF	2			
FB	CLOUD	SARO	15/32	A.29	TR	2	2 x A-S Serval (Double Mongoose)	64'	50'1½"	nil	118mph	14000	K2681 .31		8.33 STS	17	1.36 48 Sqn		
Mo	COMET T.2/C.2	DH	SOP.11 13/14	DH.106	T	5	4 x RR Avon 117 or 118	115'	96'	nil	480mph		27.8.53		7.56	10	5.67 216 Sqn		
	COMET R.2	DH		DH.106	E	6+	4 x RR Avon 117 or 118	115'	96'	nil					7.57 192 Sqn		1.75 51 Sqn		
	COMET C.4	DH	SOP.42	DH.106	T	5	4 x RR Avon 350	115'	118'	nil	506mph		31.10.59		2.62 216 Sqn	5	6.75 216 Sqn		
Mo	CORNELL	FAIRCHILD		PT-26FA PT-26A	TR	2	1 x Ranger	35'11½"	27'8"	nil	124mph	12500		EW341		2500			Includes Mk I & II
Mo	CORONADO GR.I	CONSOL'D			GR/T	10	4 x P&W Twin Wasp	115'	79'3"	8 x .5 12000lb bombs	200mph	20000			9.43? 231 Sqn	10	1.46 231 Sqn	PB2Y3	
Bi	CUCKOO	SOPWITH	T.1		TB	1	1 x Wolseley Viper or Sunbeam Arab	45'9"	28'6"	1 x torpedo	100mph	12000	B1496			232	4.23 210 Sqn		
Mo	DAKOTA I	DOUGLAS	C-47	C-47	T	3	2 x P&W S1C3-G	95'	64'6"	nil	230mph	23200	17.12.35 (DC-3)	FD768	11.18 185 Sqn	53	3.43 24 Sqn	C-47	NB: All Dakotas – DC-3 (+10 ex civil DC-3)
	DAKOTA II	DOUGLAS	C-53	C-53	T	3	2 x P&W R-1830-92	95'	64'6"	nil	230mph	24000				9		C-53	Includes C.2
	DAKOTA III	DOUGLAS	C-47A	C-47A	T	2/3	2 x P&W A-1830-90C	95'6"	63'9"	nil	230mph	24000		FD819		962		C-47A	Includes C.3
	DAKOTA IV/4	DOUGLAS	C-47B	C-47B	T	2/3	2 x P&W R-1830-92	95'6"	63'9"	nil	224mph	26400		KJ801		896		C-47B	Includes 21 DC-2K civil ac in temp. use & 2 C.IV/GT.IV

Argosy aircraft of 215 Squadron operated within FEAF.

2 Squadron Atlas J9956 on a message pick-up.

Avro 504N.

BAe 146 ZD696, as used by Queen's Flight for VIP transport.

Cockpit of 223 Squadron Baltimore.

Belfast.

Belvedere XG463; the type entered service in September 1966.

Blenheim I L1295 of 107 Squadron, October 1938.

Beam gun of Catalina.

Fairey Gordon, this type saw intensive use in Palestine — nine aircraft being lost.

Chinook ZD984.

Hart K2088 over the Himalayas 1932.

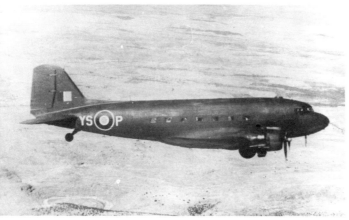

Dakota of 271 Squadron over Palestine.

FT375, Harvard trainer.

Fairey IIIF J9642 reaches 1000 hours.

Two transport workhorses — Hercules and Chinook.

Type	Aircraft & Mk No.	Manufacturer	Spec. No.	Man. Design	Role	Crew	Engine	Span	Length	Armament	Max. Speed	Service Ceiling	First Flight Proto.	First Flight Prod.	IOC	Total	Last Unit	US Design	Notes
Mo	DEFIANT I	BOULTON PAUL	F9/35 5/37	P.82	F	2	1 x RR Merlin III	39'4"	35'4"	4 x .303	303mph	30350	K8310 11.8.37		12.39 264 Sqn	713	4.45 691 Sqn		Includes NF.1A
	DEFIANT II	BOULTON PAUL			F	2	1 x RR Merlin XX	39'4"	35'4"	4 x .303	315mph	16500	N1550 20.7.40		9.41 264 Sqn	207 or 210	12.43 515 Sqn		
	DEFIANT TT.1	BOULTON PAUL			TT	1/2	1 x RR Merlin XX	39'4"	35'4"	nil			DR863 1.42			140			Based on Mk II.
	DEFIANT TT.III	BOULTON PAUL			TT	1/2	1 x RR Merlin III	39'4"	35'4"	nil			N8488		11.41	150	4.45 691 Sqn		Conversions of Mk.I.
Bi	DEMON	HAWKER	15/30 6/32 9/32		F	2	1 x RR Kestrel IIS or V (DA)	37'3"	29'7"	2 x Vickers 1 x Lewis 2 bombs	182mph	24500	J9933 3.31	K2842 10.2.33	3.31 23 Sqn	234 or 239	8.39 607 Sqn		Includes Turret Demon to Spec. 8/34 and 40/34.
Mo	DEVON C.1	DH	C13/46	DH.104	C	2	2 x DH Gipsy Queen 70	45'	37'	nil	210mph	20000	VP952		1.49 31 Sqn	40+	3.55 31 Sqn		
	DEVON C.2	DH			C	2	2 x DH Gipsy Queen 175			nil			25.9.45		2.69 207 Sqn	7	6.84 207 Sqn		Conversions of C.1.
Bi	DH.4	DH		DH.4	B	2	1 x RR Eagle VIII	42'4½"	30'8"	1 x Vickers 1-2 x Lewis 460lb bombs	136/-mph	22000 or 20000	3696 8.16		1.17 55 Sqn	1449	8.19 25 Sqn		
Bi	DH.4A	DH		DH.4A	T	2	1 x RR Eagle VI	42'4½"	30'8"	nil	121mph		F5764 .19			16*			Conversions of DH.4. *Or 7
Bi	DH.6	DH		DH.6	TR	2	1 x RAF 1a or Curtis OX-5 or Renault	35'11"	27'3½"	nil	75mph	6000	.17		9.16 76 Sqn	2282	5.19 250 Sqn		
Bi	DH.9	DH		DH.9	B	2	1 x BHP	42'4⅞"	30'6"	1 x Vickers 1-2 x Lewis 460lb bombs	111mph	17500	A7559 6.17		2.18 206 Sqn	3204 ?	9.20 55 Sqn		
Bi	DH.9A	DH		DH.9A	B	2	1 x Liberty	46'	30'	1 x Lewis 1 x Vickers 450lb bombs	114mph	16750	C6122 .17		6.18 110 Sqn	2140 ?	11.30 501 Sqn		
Bi	DH.9J	DH		DH-9J	TR	2	1 x A-S Jaguar	42'4½"	28'9"	nil	134mph		G-EBFQ			14			Used by Reserve Training Schools.
Bi	DH.86B	DH		DH.86B	TR/C	2	2 x DH Gipsy Six	64'5"	46'1"	nil	166mph	17400	14.1.34			4			
Bi	DOLPHIN	SOPWITH		5F.1	F	1	1 x Hispano-Suiza	32'6"	22'3"	2 x Vickers 1 or 2 x Lewis 100lb bombs	131½mph	21000	6.17		12.17 87 Sqn	2074	7.19 79 Sqn		
Bi	DOMINIE I	DH	18/35 29/38	.89B	TR	2-6	2 x DH Gipsy Queen	48'	34'6"	nil	157mph		K4772		3.35 24 Sqn	521 inc.			Military version of Dragon Rapide.
	DOMINIE II	DH		.89A	C	1-2				nil						FAA			
Mo	DOMINIE T.1	HS			TR	1	2 x B-S Viper 520	47'	47'5"	nil	472mph	40000	12.64		12.65 1 ANS	20	Current		
Mo	DON	DH	T6/36	DH.93	TR/C	2	1 x DH Gipsy King I	47'6"	37'4"	nil	189mph	21500	LZ387 ? 6.37			30*			*Or 50
Bi	DRAGON	SOPWITH			F	1	1 x ABC Dragonfly 1A	31'1"	21'9"	nil	150mph	25000	E7990			30			Not into sqn service.
He	DRAGONFLY HC.2	WESTLAND			AA	1	1 x Alvis Leonides 524/1 (521/1)	48'	57'6½"	nil	100mph	12400	G-AKTW 5.10.48	WF308 11.2.50	4.50 CEF	3	6.56 194 Sqn	6.51	
He	DRAGONFLY HC.4	WESTLAND			AA	1	1 x Alvis Leonides 524/1 (50)	48'	57'6½"	nil	100mph	12400		WT845		12	6.56 194 Sqn		
Bi	ELEPHANT	MARTINSYDE		G.100 G.102	GP	1	1 x Beardmore	38'	26'6"	2 x Lewis	102mph		3.18		3.18 72 Sqn				

Type	Aircraft & Mk No.	Manu-facturer	Spec. No.	Man. Design	Role	Crew	Engine	Span	Length	Armament	Max. Speed	Service Ceiling	First Flight Proto.	Prod.	10C	Total	Last Unit	US Design	Notes
Mo	ENVOY III	AIRSPEED		AS-10	T	1	2 x A-S Cheetah IX	52'4"	34'6"	nil	203mph	22000		G-AEXX	5.37 KF	3			
Mo	EXPEDITER	BEECH			T	2	2 x P&W Wasp Junior	47'8"	34'3"	nil	230mph	27000			1.45 353 Sqn	350		C-45	Beech 18
Bi	FAIREY III C	FAIREY			GP	2	1 x RR Eagle VIII	46'2"	36'	1 x Vickers 1 x Lewis bombs	110mph	15000	N2255 7.18	N9230	10.18 230 Sqn	36	3.19 230 Sqn		
Bi	FAIREY III D	FAIREY	38/22		GP	3	1 x RR Eagle VIII or Napier Lion II B or V or X A	46'1 1/4"	36'	1 x Vickers 1 x Lewis	120mph	17000	N9450 8.20		12.20 267 Sqn	207	9.30 202 Sqn		Includes Mk II.
Bi	FAIREY III F I	FAIREY	19/24		GP	3	1 x Napier Lion XI A VA or XI						N198 19.3.26		.27 45 Sqn		12.35 45 Sqn		I to III naval versions.
Bi	FAIREY III F IV C	FAIREY			GP	2	1 x Napier Lion XI A VA or XI	45'9"	36'8 5/8"	1 x Vickers 1 x Lewis 500lb bombs	120mph	20000	S1147	J9053	45 Sqn	48			Includes IV CM.
Bi	FAIREY III F IV M	FAIREY			GP	2	1 x Napier Lion XI A	45'9"	36'8 5/8"	1 x Vickers 1 x Lewis 500lb bombs	120mph	20000			207 Sqn	20			
Bi	FAIREY III F IV MA	FAIREY			GP	2	1 x Napier Lion XI A	45'9"	36'8 5/8"	1 x Vickers 1 x Lewis 500lb bombs	120mph	20000		J9637		114			All metal structure.
Bi	FAIREY III F IV B	FAIREY	3/31		GP	2	1 x Napier Lion XI A	45'9"	36'8 5/8"	1 x Vickers 1 x Lewis 500lb bombs	120mph	20000				61	2.41		
Bi	FAWN II	FAIREY	5/21 20/23		B/AC	2	1 x Napier Lion II	49'11"	32'1"	1 x Vickers 1 x Lewis 460lb bombs	114mph	13850	J6907 3.23	J7182 29.1.24	3.24 12 Sqn	48	10.29 602 Sqn		Development of Pintail amphibian.
	FAWN III	FAIREY	1/25		B/AC	2	1 x Napier Lion V	49'11"	32'1"	1 x Vickers 1 x Lewis 460lb bombs	114mph	13850	J7768		?20				Some later production called Mk IV.
FB	FELIXSTOWE F2A				GR	4	2 x RR Eagle VIII	95'7 1/2"	46'3"	2+ x Lewis 460lb bombs	95 1/2mph	9600	?8650		8.18 229 Sqn	53	267 Sqn 8.23		
FB	FELIXSTOWE F3				GR	4	2 x RR Eagle VIII	102'	49'2"		93mph	8000	N64		8.18 230 Sqn	96	9.21 230 Sqn		
FB	FELIXSTOWE F5	(various)			GR	4	2 x RR Eagle VIII	103'8"	49'3"	4 x Lewis 920lb bombs	88mph	6800	N90		11.18 231 Sqn	100	4.23 230 Sqn		
Bi	FK8	AW			R	2	1 x Beardmore	43'4"	31'5"		83.5 95mph	13000	A2683 ?	A411 .5.16	.16 35 Sqn	(488+)			
Mo	FLAMINGO	DH	20/39	.95	T	2/3	2 x Bristol Perseus XVI or XII C	70'	51'7"	nil	239mph	20900	28.12.38		12.39 24 Sqn	3	11.44 24 Sqn		
Mo	FOKKER T.8W	FOKKER	—		GR	3	2 x Wright Whirlwind	15'7"	49'10"		222mph	22300			320 Sqn	5			ex Royal Netherlands Navy.
Mo	FORTRESS I	BOEING		.299	B	6	4 x Wright Cyclone R-1820-G205A	103'9 1/2"	67'10 1/2"	7 x .3 or 1 x 303 + 6 x .5 2500lb bombs	320mph	38000		AN518	5.41	20 90 Sqn	8.42	B-17C 220 Sqn	
	FORTRESS II	BOEING			MR	8	4 x Wright Cyclone R-1820-G205A (or R-1820-97)	103'9 1/2"	11 x .5	290mph 6000 4000lb bombs	35000		FA695 9.41		7.42 220 Sqn		2.46 521 Sqn	B-17F	
	FORTRESS IIA	BOEING			MR	8	4 x Wright Cyclone R-1820-65	103'9 1/2"	73'10"	9 x .5 9 600lb bombs	295mph	32000		FK184	12.42 59 Sqn	(200)	4.43 59 Sqn	B-17E	Includes GRII

Type	Aircraft & Mk No.	Manufacturer	Spec. No.	Man. Design	Role	Crew	Engine	Span	Length	Armament	Max. Speed	Service Ceiling	First Flight Proto.	First Flight Prod.	IOC	Total	Last Unit	US Design	Notes
	FORTRESS III	BOEING			B	8–9	4 x Wright Cyclone R-1820-97	103'9"	73'	13 x .5 12 800lb bombs	280mph	31500		HB761	2.44 214 Sqn		2.46 521 Sqn	B-17G	Includes GRIII.
Bi	FOX I	FAIREY	21/25		B	2	1 x Curtiss D-12	38'	31'2"	1 x Vickers 1 x Lewis 460lb bombs	156½mph	17000	J9515 23.1.25	J7941 10.12.25	8.26 12 Sqn	28	1.31 12 Sqn		
	FOX IA	FAIREY	11/27 1/27 17/30		B	2	1 x RR Kestrel IIA	38'	31'2"	1 x Vickers 1 x Lewis 460lb bombs	160mph	17000	J9036 29.8.27		1.29 12 Sqn	7			Conversions of MkI.
Bi	FURY I	HAWKER	F20/27 13/30 13/32		F	1	1 x RR Kestrel IIs	30'	26'8"	2 x Vickers	207mph	28000	K1926	K1926 25.3.31	6.31 43 Sqn	117	1.39 43 Sqn		
	FURY II	HAWKER	114/32 6/35		F	1	1 x RR Kestrel IIs	30'	26'8"	2 x Vickers	233mph	29500	K1935	K7263 3.12.36	11.36 25 Sqn	113	1.39 41 Sqn		
Bi	GAMECOCK I	GLOSTER	37/23 18/25		F	1	1 x Bristol Jupiter VI 1 x Bristol Jupiter VII?	29'9½"	19'8"	2 x Vickers	155mph	22000	J7497 2.25	J7756	3.26 43 Sqn	91 or 90	9.31 23 Sqn		
Bi	GAUNTLET I	GLOSTER	F9/26 24/23 F20/27	SS.19B	F	1	1 x Bristol Mercury VI S2	32'9½"	26'2"	2 x Vickers	230mph	33500	J9125	K4801 17.12.34	1.35 19 Sqn	24	4.40 6 Sqn		Developed from Gloster SS.18B/SS.19B.
	GAUNTLET II	GLOSTER			F	1	1 x Bristol Mercury VI S2	32'9½"	26'5"	2 x Vickers	230mph	33500	—	K5265	5.36 56 Sqn	204	7.40 112 Sqn		
He	GAZELLE HT3	WESTLAND AEROSPATIALE	OR.33/6	SA341D	TR/C	2	1 x Turbomeca Astazou IIIA	34'5½"	39'3¾"	nil	193mph	16405	AH-1 28.4.70	XW852 .73	CFS	?220	Current		Includes 1 HCC4 VIP version.
Bi	GENET MOTH	DH		DH60	TR	2	1 x A.5 Genet	29'	23'5"	nil	90mph		22.2.25		CFS	6			
Bi	GIPSY MOTH	DH		.60M	TR/C	2	1 x DH Gipsy II or III	30'	23'11"	nil	105mph	18000	G.EBKT 22.2.25	J9922		134			
Bi	GLADIATOR I	GLOSTER	F.7/30 F14.35	SS.37	F	1	1 x Bristol Mercury IX	32'3"	27'5"	4 x .303	253mph	33000	K5200 12.9.34	K6129	2.37 1 Sqn	231	4.43 263 Sqn		
	GLADIATOR II	GLOSTER	F36/37		F	1	1 x Bristol Mercury VIIIAS	32'3"	27'5"	4 x .303	257mph	33500			3.39 94 Sqn	300	8.44 520 Sqn		Includes Sea Gladiators.
Mo	GNAT T1	FOLLAND (HS)	T.18SD	.144	TR	2	1 x B.S Orpheus 100	24'	31'9"	nil	M.97	48000	XM691 31.8.59		2.62 CFS	105			
Mo	GOOSE	GRUMMAN			C	2	2 x P&W Wasp Junior	49'	38'4"	nil	200mph	22000			1.43 24 Sqn	12	1.44 24 Sqn		
Bi	GORDON I	FAIREY	18/30		GP	2	1 x A.S Panther IIA	45'9"	36'8⅝"	1 x Vickers 1 x Lewis 500lb bombs	145mph	22000	K1697 3.3.31	K1721	4.31 40 Sqn	(246)			Total includes 68 conversions of Fairey IIIF.
	GORDON II	FAIREY	14/33		GP	2	1 x A.S Panther IIA	45'9"	36'8⅝"	1 x Vickers 1 x Lewis 500lb bombs	145mph	22000	K3577 23.5.34	K3986		24			
Bi	GREBE II	GLOSTER	2/23 37/23		F	1	1 x A.S Jaguar IV	29'4"	20'3"	2 x Vickers	152mph	23000	J6969 5.23	J7283 8.23	10.23 111 Sqn	108	7.29 25 Sqn		Plus 4 prototypes as Grebe I with as Jaguar III.
	GREBE III DC	GLOSTER			TR	2	1 x A.S Jaguar IV	29'4"	20'3"	nil	152mph	23000				21			
Gl	HADRIAN I/II	WACO		CG-4A	G	2	Nil	83'8"	48'3¾"	nil	125mph	—	.42	FR556	.43	1095			771 Mk.I; 324 Mk.II.
Mo	HALIFAX B.I	HP	P13/36 32/37	HP.57	B	7	4 x RR Merlin X	98'8"	70'1"	8–10 x .303 13000lb bombs	265mph	18000	L7244 25.10.39	L9485 11.10.40	11.40 35 Sqn	24			Includes Series I, II and III.
	HALIFAX B.II	HP		HP.59	B	6	4 x RR Merlin XX or Merlin 22	98'8"	70'1"	8 x .303 11000lb bombs	261mph	22000	V9976 25.8.41	L9609		1934			Includes Series I and IA.

Type	Aircraft & Mk No.	Manufacturer	Spec. No.	Man. Design	Role	Crew	Engine	Span	Length	Armament	Max. Speed	Service Ceiling	First Flight Proto.	Prod.	IOC	Total	Last Unit	US Design	Notes
	HALIFAX GRII	HP			GR		4 x RR Merlin XX or Merlin 22	98'8"	70'1"	7 x .303 11000 bombs	261mph	22000							
	HALIFAX B.III	HP		HP.61	B	7	4 x Bristol Hercules XVI	104'2"	71'7"	9 x .303 13000lb?	281mph	20000	R9534	HX226 7.43	10.43 466 Sqn	2238			
	HALIFAX A.III	HP			T	5	4 x Bristol Hercules XVI	104'2"	71'7"	4 x .303	289mph	20000							Includes C.III (ceiling 23,000; max speed 309mph).
	HALIFAX B.V	HP	OR.139	HP.63	B	6	4 x RR Merlin 22 or XX	98'8"	71'7"	8 x .303 11000lb bombs	261mph	22000	DG231 .42		10.42 408 Sqn	866			Includes Series I and IA.
	HALIFAX GR.V	HP			GR		4 x RR Merlin 22 or XX	98'8"	71'7"	7 x .303 11000lb bombs	261mph	22000							
	HALIFAX VI	HP	OR.166	HP.61	B	7	4 x Bristol Hercules 100	104'2"	71'7"	7–9 x .303 12000lb bombs	309mph	22000	LV838	NP715 10.10.44		557			
	HALIFAX GR.VI	HP	OR.166		GR		4 x Bristol Hercules 100	104'2"	71'7"		309mph	22000							
	HALIFAX VII	HP		HP.61	B	7	4 x Bristol Hercules XVI	104'2"	70'1½"	7–9 x .303 12000lb bombs	281mph	20000		LW196 .44		333			
	HALIFAX A.VII	HP			T	5	4 x Bristol Hercules XVI	104'2"	70'1½"	4 x .303 or 2 x .05	289mph	20000		NA311 .45	NA311 .45	(160)			Includes C.VIII – max speed 293mph. Nil armament
	HALIFAX C.VIII	HP		HP.70	T	5	4 x Bristol Hercules 100	104'2"	73'7"	nil	322mph	25000	PP217 6.45		5.46	100			
	HALIFAX A.IX	HP		HP.71	T	5	4 x Bristol Hercules XVI	104'2"	71'7"	2 x .5	289mph	2000		RT758 .45	11.45	145			
Gl	HAMILCAR I	GENERAL AIRCRAFT	X27/440	GAL.49	G	2	nil	110'	68'	nil	150mph	—	DP206 27.3.42			412			
	HAMILCAR X	GENERAL AIRCRAFT	X4/44	GAL.58	G	2	2 x Bristol Mercury 3	110'	68'	nil			LA728 2.44			20			2 prototypes + MkI conversions
Mo	HAMPDEN I	HP	B9/32 30/36	HP.52	B	4	2 x Bristol Pegasus XVIII	69'2"	53'7"	6 x .303 4000lb bombs	265mph	19000	K4240 21.6.36	L4032	2.39 44 Sqn	1453	12.43 521 Sqn		
	HAMPDEN TB.I	HP			TB	4	2 x Bristol Pegasus XVIII	69'2"	53'7"	6 x .303+ +09P	233mph	23500				144			Conversions of MkI
Bi	HP 0/400	HP			B	3–5	2 x RR Eagle VIII (some vary)	100'	62'10½"	4–5 x Lewis 2000lb bombs	975mph	8500	1455* 17.12.15		3.18 216 Sqn	554	10.21 Sqn		Includes conversions of 0/100 *0/100 prototype
Bi	HP V/1500	HP			B	5–7	4 x RR Eagle VIII	126'	64'	4–8 x Lewis 7500lb bombs	99mph	11000	B9463 5.18			20*			*Or 71
Bi	HARDY I	HAWKER	G23/33		GP	2	1 x RR Kestrel IB or X	37'3"	29'7"	1 x Vickers 1 x Lewis 224lb bombs	161mph	17000	K3013 7.3.34		4.35 30 Sqn	47	4.43 173 Sqn		
Mo	HARRIER GR.1	HAWKER (BAe)	OR356 SR.2550		GA	1	1 x B–S Pegasus 101			2 x 30mm			XV276 31.8.66	XV738 28.12.67	4.69 1 Sqn	78	12.74 3 Sqn		
	HARRIER GR.1A	HAWKER (BAe)			GA	1	1 x B–S Pegasus 103 1 x B–S Pegasus 102	25'3"	457"	5000lb bombs						40		AV-8A	Modified GR.1.
	HARRIER T.2	HAWKER (BAe)	ASR385 T.295D		TR	2	1 x B–S Pegasus 101	25'3"	55'9½"				XW174 22 or 24.4.69		233 OCU 770	-17*			*Total for T2/2A/4 (or 21).
	HARRIER T.2A	HAWKER (BAe)			TR	2	1 x B–S Pegasus 102	25'3"	55'9½"										
	HARRIER GR.3	HAWKER (BAe)			GA	1	1 x B–S Pegasus 103	25'3"	46'10"	2 x 30m 5000lb bombs	740mph	51,200			11.73	91	Current		First batch from modified GR.1/1A — 55 a/c.

Type	Aircraft & Mk No.	Manufacturer	Spec. No.	Man. Design	Role	Crew	Engine	Span	Length	Armament	Max. Speed	Service Ceiling	First Flight Proto.	First Flight Prod.	IOC	Total	Last Unit	US Design	Notes
	HARRIER T.4	HAWKER (BAe)			TR	2	1 x B–S Pegasus 103 or 104	25'3'	56'1/5'							see T.2	Current	TAV-8	
	HARRIER GR.5/5A	BAe	ASR409		GA	1	1 x RR Pegasus 105	30'4"	46'4"	2 x 25mm 9200lb bombs	720mph		ZD318 30.4.85		11.88 1 Sqn	60	Current	AV-8B	(As AV-8B first flight 5.11.81)
	HARRIER GR.7	BAe			GA	1	1 x RR Pegasus 105						29.11.89		7.90 4 Sqn	34	Current		Total is orders at late 1992; Plans to convert GR.5/5A to GR.7 standard.
	HARRIER T.10	BAe			TR	2	1 x RR Pegasus 105									14*		TAV-8B	*Planned.
Mo	HARROW I	HP	29/35		BT	5	2 x Bristol Pegasus X	88'5"	82'2"				K6933 10.10.36		1.37 214 Sqn	100	5.45 271 Sqn		
	HARROW II	HP		HP.54	BT	5	2 x Bristol Pegasus XX			4 x .303 3000lb bombs	200mph	22800		K6953*					*Or K6971
Bi	HART	HAWKER	12/26 9/29		B	2	1 x RR Kestrel IB or X (DR)	37'3"	29'4"	1 x Vickers 1 x Lewis 500lb bombs	184mph	22800	J9052 6.28	J9933	1.30 33 Sqn	415	8.43 173 Sqn		
	HART (C)	HAWKER			C	2	1 x RR Kestrel IB or X (DR)	37'3"	29'4"	nil or X (DR)				K2452	24 Sqn	(8)			
	HART (India)	HAWKER			B	2	1 x Kestrel IB or X (DR)	37'3"	29'4"				K2083 7.9.31		39 Sqn				
	HART (Special)	HAWKER	9/34			2	1 x RR Kestrel IB or X (DR)	37'3"	29'4"					K4365		(46)			
	HART (T)	HAWKER	8/32		TR	2	1 x RR Kestrel IB or X (DR)	37'3"	29'4"	nil	154mph	22800	K1996 20.4.32		6.33 *Cran	507			Includes 32 conversions.
Mo	HARVARD I	NORTH AMERICAN		NA-16	TR	2	1 x P&W Wasp R-1340-53H1	42'1/4"	28'11/8"	nil	210mph		NA-26 .37	N7000	400	500	BC-1	AT-6	
	HARVARD II	NORTH AMERICAN		NA-66	TR	2	1 x P&W 49 R-1340-47 (49)	42'1/2"	29'0"	nil	206mph			AH185					Mainly to RCAF for BCATP.
	HARVARD IIA	NORTH AMERICAN		NA-88	TR	2	1 x P&W A-1340-49	42'1/2"	29'0"	nil	206mph			EX100		945		AT-6C	
	HARVARD IIB	NORTH AMERICAN		AT-16	TR	2	1 x P&W Wasp A-1340-AN1	42'1/2"	29'0"	nil	205mph	21500		FE267		2768		AT-16	
	HARVARD III	NORTH AMERICAN			TR	2	1 x P&W R-1340-49	42'1/2"	29'0"	nil	205mph			EX847		512		AT-6D	
Mo	HASTINGS C.1	HP	C3/44	HP.67	T	5	4 x Bristol Hercules 106	113'	81'8"	nil	343mph	25000	TE580 7.5.46	TG499 25.4.47	9.48 47 Sqn	100	1.68 24 Sqn		
	HASTINGS C.2	HP		HP.67	T	5		113'	82'8"		348mph	26500		WD475	6.51 24 Sqn	43	1.68 24 Sqn		
	HASTINGS C.1A	HP			T	5				nil									Modified C.1
	HASTINGS MET.1	HP			WR	5?				nil					10.50 202 Sqn		8.64 202 Sqn		
	HASTINGS C.4	HP	C115/P	HP.94	T	5				nil				WD500 22.9.51	10.51 24 Sqn	4			
	HASTINGS T.5	HP			TR	4				nil					BCBS	8			Conversions of C.1
Mo	HAVOC I	DOUGLAS		DB-7	NF/INT	2–3	2 x P&W Twin Wasp S3C4-9	61'4"	46'11/4"	8 x .303 NF 4 x .303 INT bombs	295mph	26000	BJ464		4.41 85 Sqn	100	12.43 161 Sqn		Includes Turbinlite variant.

Type	Aircraft & Mk No.	Manu-facturer	Spec. No.	Man. Design	Role	Crew	Engine	Span	Length	Armament	Max. Speed	Service Ceiling	First Flight Proto.	Prod.	10C	Total	Last Unit	US Design	Notes
	HAVOC II	DOUGLAS		DB-7A	NF/INT	2–3	2 x Wright Double Cyclone	61'4"	46'11¼"	12 x .303 NF	300mph	30000			7.41 85 Sqn		9.42 85 Sqn		Includes Turbinlite variant.
	HAWK T.1	HSA (BAe)	ASR397	P.1182	TR	2	1 x RR/Turbomeca 151 Adour	30'9¾"	38'10½"	1 x 30mm PB	615mph	50000	XX154 21.8.74	XX156 22.4.75	11.76 4 FTS	175			
	HAWK T.1A	HSA (BAe)			TR/F	2	1 x RR/Turbomeca 151 Adour	30'9¾"	38'10½" 36'7¼"	1 x 30mm + 2 x AAM	615mph	50000				88			Conversions of T.1
Bi	HECTOR I	HAWKER	14/35		AC	2	1 x Napier Dagger III MS	36'11⅛"	29'9¾"	1 x Vickers 1 x Lewis 224lb bombs	187mph	24000	K8090 14.2.36	K3719	5.37 4 Sqn	178	8.42 296 Sqn		
Mo	HENDON II	FAIREY	B19/27 20/34		B	5	2 x RR Kestrel VI	101'9"	60'9"	3 x Lewis 1660lb bombs	155mph	21500	K1695 11.30	K5085	11.36 38 Sqn	14	1.39 38 Sqn		
Mo	HENLEY TT.III	HAWKER	P4/34		TT	2	1 x RR Merlin II or III	47'10½"	36'5"	nil	265mph	27200	K5115 10.3.37	L3243	11.38 1 AACU	200*			*Or 202
Mo	HERCULES C.1/1P	LOCKHEED		C-130K	T	5	4 x Allison T-56-A-15	132'7¼"	98'9"	nil	368mph		XV176		8.67	66	current	C-130K	Includes single W.2 of MRF.
	HERCULES C.1K	LOCKHEED			AAR	5	4 x Allison T-56-A-15	132'7¼"	98'9"	nil			XV296 8.6.82			4 or 5	current		
	HERCULES C.3	LOCKHEED			T	5	4 x Allison T-56-A-15	132'7¼"	113'9"	nil	374mph	33000	XV223 3.12.79		3.80	30	current		Conversions of C.1/1P.
Mo	HEREFORD	HP	B44/36	HP.52	B	4	2 x Napier Dagger						?L7271	L6002	8.39 185 Sqn	101	4.40 185 Sqn		
Mo	HERON C.3/C.4	DH	SOP.4	DH.114	VIP	2	4 x DH Gipsy Queen 30	71'6"	48'6"	nil	183mph		10.5.50	XH375	1.55 QF	4			The original Heron, G-AMTS, was on loan from DH.
Bi	HEYFORD I	HP	B19/27 23/32	HP.50	B	4	2 x RR Kestrel III	75'	58'	2-3 x Lewis 2660lb bombs	142mph		J9130 6.30		11.30 99 Sqn	(15)			
	HEYFORD IA	HP	B23/32		B	4	2 x RR Kestrel IIIS or IIIS-5	75'	58'	3 x Lewis 3500lb bombs	142mph	21000	K3489		8.34 10 Sqn	(23) 124*	3.39 149 Sqn		*Total Heyford.
	HEYFORD II	HP	B28/34		B	4	2 x RR Kestrel VI	75'	58'				K3492		10.35* 102 Sqn	(16)			*Or 3.35
	HEYFORD III	HP	B27/35		B	4	2 x RR Kestrel VI	75'	58'				K3503		9.35 38 Sqn	(76)	9.39 166 Sqn		
Bi	HINAIDI I	HP		HP.33	B	4	2 x Bristol Jupiter	75'	59'2"		114mph		J7745			12			
	HINAIDI II	HP	13/29	HP.36	B	4	2 x Bristol Jupiter VIII			3 x Lewis 1448lb bombs	122½mph	14500	J9478		10.29 99 Sqn	40	11.35 503 Sqn		Includes 7 conversions from . Hyderabad.
Bi	HIND I	HAWKER	G7/34 25/31 11/35		B	2	1 x RR Kestrel V	37'3"	29'7"	1 x Vickers 1 x Lewis 500lb bombs	186mph	26400	K2915 12.9.34	K4636	12.35 21 Sqn	528	4.40 613 Sqn		
	HIND T	HAWKER			TR	2	1 x RR Kestrel V (DR)	37'3"	29'7"							164			Includes 139 conversions of MkI.
Mo	HORNET F.1	DH	F12/43	DH-103	F	1	2 x RR Merlin 130/131	45'	36'8"	4 x 20mm 2000lb bombs	470mph	35000	RR915 28.7.44	PX210	4.45 64 Sqn	60	8.48 41 Sqn		*or 2.46.
	HORNET F.3	DH			F	1	2 x RR Merlin 130/131 or Merlin 133/134	45'	36'8"	4 x 20mm 2000lb bombs	438mph	35000	PX249	PX289	3.48 64 Sqn	123 133	5.55 45 Sqn		
	HORNET PR.2	DH	—	—	PR	1	2 x RR Merlin 130/131 or Merlin 133/134	45"	36'8	nil	—	—	PX216	VA962	—	5	—		Did not enter service.
Mo	HORNET FR.4	DH			FR	1	2 x RR Merlin 130/131	45'	36'8"	4 x 20mm 2000lb bombs			PX290	WF968	80 Sqn	12			

Hind K4636 light bomber.

Horsa glider taking on its load.

Lancaster RE172 served only with 37 Squadron and was SOC 3.6.47.

A selection of Javelins.

A gathering of thoroughbreds — Hunters going 'over the top'.

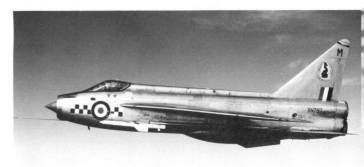

Lightning F.2 XN787.

Jaguar XZ119 of 41 Squadron.

Lerwick, a GR flying-boat produced in limited numbers.

Marauder III; the type acquired an unjustified bad reputation.

F-4 Phantom visiting Hong Kong.

Mosquito NF36 formation of 39 Squadron on the break.

Salamander J8039.

Miles Master W8825.

Latest edition to the RAF front-line inventory. E-3D sentry of 8 Squadron.

Oxfords at Finningley; the 'Oxbox' was an adaptable trainer.

Shackleton WL751 of 224 Squadron, note nose gun.

Type	Aircraft & Mk No.	Manufacturer	Spec. No.	Man. Design	Role	Crew	Engine	Span	Length	Armament	Max. Speed	Service Ceiling	First Flight Proto.	First Flight Prod.	IOC	Total	Last Unit	US Design	Notes
Gl	HORSA I/II	AIRSPEED	X26/40	AS.51 AS.58	G	2	nil	88'	67'	nil	100mph	–	DG597 12.9.41			3655			Horsa II (AS.58) with hinged nose.
Bi	HORSLEY I	HAWKER	26/23 23/25 24/25		B/TB	2	1 x RR Condor IIIA	56'6"	38'10"				J7511 .3.25		8.26 100 Sqn	(10)			
	HORSLEY II	HAWKER			B/TB	2	1 x RR Condor IIIA	56'6"	38'10"	1 x Vickers 1 x Lewis 1500lb bombs	125mph	14000		J7997	1.27 11 Sqn	–112			
	HORSLEY III	HAWKER			TB	2	1 x RR Condor IIIA Or IIIB							J8597	10.27 36 Sqn	(35)*			*or 25
Gl	HOTSPUR I	GENERAL AIRCRAFT	10/40	GAL.48	G	2	nil	61'10¼"	39'3½"	nil			BV134 ?9.40			(22)*			*or 24
	HOTSPUR II	GENERAL AIRCRAFT	X22/40		G	2	nil	45'10¼"	39'3½"	nil	130mph	–	BV199			–987			
	HOTSPUR III	GENERAL AIRCRAFT			G	2	nil	45'10¼"	39'3½"	nil					BT540	(52)			Conversions of Mk.II
He	HOVERFLY I	SIKORSKY		VS-316	C	1	1 x Warner	38'	35'5"	nil	82mph		5.45		45 HTF		10.45 529 Sqn	R-4	
	HOVERFLY II	SIKORSKY			C	1	1 x Franklin	38'	47'11"	nil	100mph	10000			4.47 657 Sqn	26	3.48 657 Sqn	R-6A	
Mo	HUDSON I	LOCKHEED		L-214	GR	5	2 x Wright Cyclone GR-1820-G012A	65'6"	44'4"	4 x .303 1400lb bombs	222mph	21000	N7205 10.12.38		5.39 224 Sqn	319 ?350	8.44 161 Sqn	A-29	Military version of Lockheed 14 Super Electra
	HUDSON II	LOCKHEED		L-414	GR	4	2 x Wright Cyclone GR-1820-G102A	65'6"	44'4"	7 x .303	223mph	21500		T9366	3.41 320 Sqn	20	8.42 206 Sqn		
	HUDSON III	LOCKHEED		L-414	GR	4	2 x Wright Cyclone GR-1820-G205A	65'6"	44'4"	7 x .303 1400lb bombs	253mph	25750		T9386	9.39 220 Sqn	428 414	1.46 520 Sqn		Includes III (LR) and III (SR).
	HUDSON IIIA	LOCKHEED		L-414	GR	4	2 x P&W Twin Wasp (Wright Cyclone R-1820-87)	65'6"	44'4"	7 x .303 1400lb bombs					6.42 200 Sqn	382	1.46 231 Sqn	A-29	Includes 2 C.III.
	HUDSON IV	LOCKHEED		L-414	GR	4	2 x P&W Twin Wasp R-1830-SC3G	65'6"	44'4"	7 x .303 1400lb bombs	252mph	25500		AE609	4.41 206 Sqn	23	9.43 117 Sqn	A-28 A-28	
	HUDSON V	LOCKHEED		L?	GR	4	2 x P&W Twin Wasp R-1830-SC34G	65'6"	44'4"	7 x .303	261mph	25500		AE639	6.41 233 Sqn	309	6.45 161 Sqn	A-28	Includes V (LR) and V (SR).
	HUDSON VI	LOCKHEED		L-414	GR	4	2 x P&W Twin Wasp S3C4-G (R-1830-67)	65'6"	44'4"	7 x .303 1000lb bombs	284mph	24500		EW873	11.41 279 Sqn	450	1.46 520 Sqn	A-28	
	HUMMINGBIRD	DH		DH.53	C	1	1 x Blackburne Tomtit	30'1"	19'8"	nil	72mph		G-LBHX 9.23			6			
Mo	HUNTER F.1	HAWKER	F3/48	P.1067	F	1	1 x RR Avon 104 (RA7/21) or 107	33'8"	45'110½"	4 x 30mm	608kts	48800	WB188 20.7.51	WT555	7.54 43 Sqn	139	11.56 43 Sqn		
	HUNTER F.2	HAWKER			F	1	1 x A–S Sapphire 101	33'8"	45'10½"	4 x 30mm	612kts	50000	WB202 14.10.53	WN888	9.54 257 Sqn	45	3.57 257 Sqn		
	HUNTER F.4	HAWKER			F	1	1 x RR Avon 113 (RA7/21) or 114	33'8"	45'10½"	4 x 30mm	608kts	48800	WT569 20.10.54	WT701	6.55 111 Sqn	363	7.58 43 Sqn		
	HUNTER F.5	HAWKER			F	1	1 x A–5 Sapphire 101	33'8"	45'10½"	4 x 30mm	612kts	50000		WN954 19.10.54	4.55 263 Sqn	105	11.58 56 Sqn		
	HUNTER F.6	HAWKER	SOP.30/32	P.1099	F		1 x RR Avon 203			4 x 30mm 2000lb bombs	621kts	50,000	XF833 22.1.54	WW592	8.56 263 Sqn	383	4.63 92 Sqn		
Mo	HUNTER T.7	HAWKER	SOP.6	P.1101	TR	2	1 x RR Avon 121	33'8"	48'10½"	1 x 30mm	608kts	48800	XJ615 8.7.55	WW563	8.58 229 OCU	51	current		Includes 6 conversions of F.4.

Type	Aircraft & Mk No.	Manufacturer	Spec. No.	Man. Design	Role	Crew	Engine	Span	Length	Armament	Max. Speed	Service Ceiling	First Flight Proto.	Prod.	IOC	Total	Last Unit	US Design	Notes
	HUNTER FGA.9	HAWKER			GA	1	1 x RR Avon 207 (RA28)	33'8"	45'10½"	4 x 30mm 2000lb bombs	621kts	50000	XE617 3.7.59		1.60 8 Sqn		7.76 45 Sqn		
	HUNTER FR.10	HAWKER			FR	1	1 x RR Avon 207 (RA28)	33'8"	46'1"	4 x 30mm	621kts	50000	XF429 7.11.58		12.60 4 Sqn	34	3.71 2 Sqn		Conversions of F.6 and FGA.9.
Mo	HURRICANE I	HAWKER	F5/34 F36/34		F	1	1 x RR Merlin II or Merlin III	40'	31'5"	8 x .303	324mph	34200	K5083 6.11.35	L1547	12.37 111 Sqn	2929			
	HURRICANE IIA	HAWKER		F	1	1	1 x RR Merlin XX or 22	40'	32'2¼"	8 x .303	340mph	41000	P3269 11.6.40		9.40 111 Sqn				Series 1 and Series 2. Series 2 and PR.I and PR.IIA.
	HURRICANE IIB	HAWKER			F	1	1 x RR Merlin XX or 22	40'	32'	12 x .303	340mph	36000				3100			Includes PR.IIB.
	HURRICANE IIC	HAWKER	OR.158		FB	1	1 x RR Merlin XX or 22	40'	32'	4 x 20mm 1000lb bombs	334mph	36000	V2461			3400			
	HURRICANE IID	HAWKER			FB	1	1 x RR Merlin XX or 22	40'	32'	2 x 40mm 2 x .303	322mph	32100	Z2326 18.9.41		184 Sqn	800			
	HURRICANE IV	HAWKER			FB	1	1 x Packard Merlin 21, 22, 24 or 27	40'	31'6"	2-4 x 40mm or 500lb bombs	330mph	32600	KX465 14.3.43		2.43 164 Sqn	524?			*280mph
	HURRICANE X	HAWKER			F	1	1 x Packard Merlin 28			12 x .303				AE958		489			Canada
	HURRICANE XI	HAWKER				1	1 x Packard Merlin 28			12 x .303 or 4 x 20mm				BW885		150			Canada (most to Russia).
	HURRICANE XII	HAWKER			F	1	1 x Packard Merlin 29			12 x .303 or 4 x 20mm				PJ660? 11.41		248			Canada (most to Russia?).
	HURRICANE XIIA	HAWKER				1	1 x Packard Merlin 29									150			Canada.
B	HYDERABAD I	HP	31/32	HP.24	B	4	2 x Napier Lion	75'	59'2"	3 x Lewis 1100lb bombs	109mph	14000	J6994 10.23	J7738	12.25 99 Sqn	38	1.34 503 Sqn		
FB	IRIS III	BLACKBURN	14/24		GR	5	3 x RR Condor IIIB	97'	67'4¼"	3 x .303 2000lb bombs	118mph	10000	N238 21.22.29		2.30 209 Sqn	8	12.32 209 Sqn		
Mo	JAGUAR GR.1/1A	SEPECAT		Type S	R/IDS	1	2 x RR/Turbomeca RT172 Adour 104	28'6"	55'1"	2 x 30mm 10500lb bombs	M1.6	45000	XXW560 29.10.69 12		3.74 54 Sqn	165	current	current	
	JAGUAR T.2	SEPECAT		Type M	TR	2	2 x RR/Turbomeca AT172 Adour 104	28'6"	55'1"				XW566			38 35	current		
Mo	JAVELIN FAW.1	GLOSTER	F5/48	GA.5	F	2	2 x A–S Sapphire Sa6	52'	56'3"	4 x 30mm	616kts	52500	WD804 26.11.51	XA544 22.7.54	2.56 46 Sqn	40	1.61 87 Sqn		
	JAVELIN FAW.2	GLOSTER			F	2	2 x A–S Sapphire Sa6	52'	56'3"	4 x 30mm	616kts	52500	XD158 31.10.55	XA768 25.4.56	8.57 46 Sqn	30	6.61 46 Sqn		
	JAVELIN T.3	GLOSTER	T.1180		TR	2	2 x A–S Sapphire Sa6	52'	59'11"	4 x 30mm	555kts	46000	WT841 26.8.56	XH390 6.1.58	.59 228 OCU	22			
	JAVELIN FAW.4	GLOSTER			F	2	2 x A–S Sapphire Sa6	52'	56'3"	4 x 30mm	610kts	50700	XA629 19.9.55		2.57 141 Sqn	50	3.62 11 Sqn		
	JAVELIN FAW.5	GLOSTER			F	2	2 x A–S Sapphire Sa6	52'	56'3"	4 x 30mm	612kts	50100	XXA641 26.7.56		5.57 151 Sqn	64	12.62 11 Sqn		
	JAVELIN FAW.6	GLOSTER			F	2	2 x A–S Sapphire Sa6	52'	56'3"	4 x 30mm	612kts	50100	XA815 14.12.56		9.57 89 Sqn	33	8.61 29 Sqn		
	JAVELIN FAW.7	GLOSTER		F	2	2	2 x B–S Sapphire Sa7 or 2 x 30mm	52'	56'3"	4 x 30mm 9.11.56 + 4 x AAM	616kts	52800	XH704 9.11.56*		7.58 33 Sqn	142	1.62		*P XA560?

Type	Aircraft & Mk No.	Manufacturer	Spec. No.	Man. Design	Role	Crew	Engine	Span	Length	Armament	Max. Speed	Service Ceiling	First Flight Proto.	First Flight Prod.	IOC	Total	Last Unit	US Design	Notes
	JAVELIN FAW.8	GLOSTER			F	2	2 x B-S Sapphire Sa7R	52'	56'3"	2 x 30mm 4 x AAM	619kts	52000	XH966 9.5.58		11.59 41 Sqn	47	12.63 41 Sqn		
	JAVELIN FAW.9/9R	GLOSTER			F	2	2 x B-S Sapphire 203 or 204	52'	56'9"	4 x 30mm 4 x AAM	610kts	52000			12.59 25 Sqn	116	4.68 60 Sqn		Conversions of FAW.7.
Mo	JET PROVOST T.1	HUNTING PERCIVAL	T16/48		TR	2	1 x A-S Viper ASV .5 (101)	35'2"	31'11"	nil	330mph		XD674 16.6.54		8.33 2 FTS	10			
	JET PROVOST T.3.T.3A	HUNTING			TR	2	1 x B-S Viper (102) ASV.8	36'11"	32'5"	nil	326mph	33000	XM346 22.6.58		6.59 2 FTS	201*			*or 201. 85 converted to T.3A.
	JET PROVOST T.4	HUNTING			TR	2	1 x B-S Viper ASV.11 (202)	36'11"	32'5"	nil	410mph	30000	15.11.60 XP547		11.61	185	7.89		
	JET PROVOST T.5/T.5/A	BAC		.145	TR	2	1 x B-S Viper 201	36'11"	37'7½"	nil	440mph	36700	XS230 28.2.67		9.69 CFS	110*			95 modified to T.5A. *or 112.
Mo	JETSTREAM T.1	SCOTTISH AVIATION	283 D&P	.201	TR	2	2 x Turbomeca Astazou XVI	52'	47'1½"	nil	285mph	26000	XX483 13.4.73		6.73 5 FTS	26			Includes Mk IIA
Bi	KANGAROO	BLACKBURN			ASW	4?	2 x RR Falcon	74'10"	44'2"		98mph	10500	B8837		8.18 246 Sqn	20			
Mo	KESTREL 1	HS			GA	1	1 x B-S Pegasus Pg.5	22'11"	42'6"	2000lb bombs	660mph		?XP831 XV276 7.3.64		10.64 Ev.Sqn	15			Evaluation Ac.
Mo	KITTYHAWK I	CURTISS			F/GA	1	1 x Allison V-1710-39	37'4"	31'9"	6 x .5 (4 x .5 1st 20)			22.5.41 AK571		12.41 450 Sqn	560		P-400	
	KITTYHAWK IA	CURTISS			GA	1	1 x Allison V-1710-39	37'4"	31'9"	6 x .5 700lb bombs	335mph				12.41 112 Sqn	1500		P-40E	
	KITTYHAWK II	CURTISS			GA	1	1 x Packard Merlin 28 (V-1650-1)			6 x .5 700lb bombs			XP-40F FL219 30.6.41		6.42 260 Sqn	?330		P-40F P-40L	
	KITTYHAWK III	CURTISS		.87A-2	GA	1	1 x Allison V-1710-73, -81, -99, or -115	37'4"	31'8'4"/ 31'2"	6 x .303 1000lb bombs	362mph	30000		FL710	9.42 450 Sqn	616	4.44 112 Sqn	P-40K P-40M P-40N	
	KITTYHAWK	CURTISS			GA	1	1 x Allison V-1710-81, or -99				360mph			FR884	10.43 450 Sqn	586	8.45 450 Sqn	P-40M	
Mo	LANCASTER I	AVRO	813/36	.683	B	7	4 x RR Merlin XX, 22, or 24	102'	69'6"	8-12 x .303 22000lb bombs	275mph	19000	BT308 9.1.41	L7527 31.10.41	12.41 44 Sqn	3689*			Includes B.1 (Special) modified for Grand Slam bombs; and B.1 (FE). *Or 3425
	LANCASTER PR.1	AVRO		.683	PR		4 x RR Merlin XX,	102'	69'6"	nil	275mph	19000			.46 541 Sqn	17+			Conversions of MkI.
	LANCASTER II	AVRO		.683	B	7	4 x Bristol Hercules VI or XVI	102'	69'6"	12 x .303 22000lb bombs	270mph	19000	DT810 26.11.44		10.42 61 Sqn	300			
	LANCASTER III	AVRO		.683	B	7	4 x Packard Merlin 28, 38, or 224	102'	69'6"	12 x .303	287mph	19000	W4114		.43	3039			
	LANCASTER GR.3/MR.3	AVRO		.683	GR/MR		4 x Packard Merlin 28, 38, or 224	102'	69'6"			19000			6.46 210 Sqn		10.56 SoMR		Conversions of ASR.3.
	LANCASTER ASR.3	AVRO		.683	ASR		4 x Packard Merlin 28, 38, or 224	102'	69'6"	2 x .303		19000	ND589		9.45 279 Sqn	130			Conversions of MkIII.
	LANCASTER VI	AVRO		.683	B/E		4 x RR Merlin 85 or 87	102'	69'6"	8 x .303		19000			.45 635 Sqn				
	LANCASTER VII	AVRO		.683	B		4 x RR Merlin 24	102'	69'6"	6 x .5 22000 lbbombs	275mph	1900	NN801			180			Includes B.VII (FE).
	LANCASTER X	AVRO		.683	B		4 x Packard Merlin 28, 38, or 224	102'	69'6"	8 x .303 14000lb bombs	287mph	19000	KB700 .43			430			Canada

Type	Aircraft & Mk No.	Manufacturer	Spec. No.	Man. Design	Role	Crew	Engine	Span	Length	Armament	Max. Speed	Service Ceiling	First Flight Proto.	First Flight Prod.	10C	Total	Last Unit	US Design	Notes
Mo	LANCASTRIAN C.2	AVRO	C16/44	.691	T/TR		4 x RR Merlin 24, 84, or 500	102'	76'10"	nil	310mph	30000	R5727	VM701	10.45 511 Sqn	33	10.49 24 Sqn		
	LANCASTRIAN C.2	AVRO		.691	T		4 x RR Merlin 24, 85, or 500	102'	76'10"	nil	315mph	25500			6.46	14			
FB	LERWICK 1	SARO	R1/36	5.36	GR	6	2 x Bristol Hercules II or IV	80'10"	63'7½"	1 x Vickers 6 x .303 2000lb bombs	213mph	25600	L7248 11.37		12.39 209 Sqn	21	422 Sqn 10.42		
Mo	LIBERATOR I	CONSOL'D	OR.186		B/GR	7	4 x P&W Twin Wasp S3C4-G	110'	63'4"	6 x .5 2 x .3 or 4 x 20mm + 5 x .303	273mph	21200	XB-24 29.12.39	AM258 17.1.41	6.41 120 Sqn	20	1.46 231 Sqn	LB-30A B-24A	
	LIBERATOR II	CONSOL'D			B/GR	8	4 x P&W Twin Wasp S3C4-G	110'	66'	11 x .303 6000lb bombs	263mph	24000	AL503		11.41 108 Sqn	139	1.46 231 Sqn	LB-30 B-24C	Includes B.IIIA.
	LIBERATOR B.III	CONSOL'D			B/GR	8	4 x P&W Twin Wasp S4C4-G	110'		9 x .303 2 x .5 5400lb bombs	275mph	33000	FK214		6.42 120 Sqn	366	6.46 159 Sqn	B-24D	
	LIBERATOR IV	CONSOL'D			B/GR										8.44 223 Sqn		6.45 223 Sqn	B-24E	
	LIBERATOR GR.V	CONSOL'D			B/GR		4 x P&W Twin Wasp R-1830-43	110'	66'	9 x .303 2 x .5 5400lb bombs	252mph	31200			4.43 59 Sqn		11.45 160 Sqn	B-24D	
	LIBERATOR B. VI/GR.VI	CONSOL'D			B/GR	8-10	4 x P&W Twin Wasp S4C4-G	110'	67'1"	9 x .5 or 6 x .5 + 4 x .303 4500lb bombs	270mph	32000			1.44 356 Sqn	1157	8.46 232 Sqn	R-24G B-24H R-24J	
	LIBERATOR C.VII	CONSOL'D			T	4	1830-43 or 65	110'	68'6"	nil	305mph	31000	EW611		7.44 511 Sqn	24	8.46 232 Sqn	C-87	
	LIBERATOR GR.VIII	CONSOL'D			GR										1.45 53 Sqn		6.47 120 Sqn		
	LIBERATOR C.IX	CONSOL'D			T	4	4 x P&W Twin Wasp GR-1830-65	110'	(66'4") 75'5"	nil						27+		RY-3 C-87C	
Mo	LIGHTNING I	LOCKHEED			F	1					357mph	40000	AE978		12-42 AAEE	3		P-38	Test aircraft only. Rejected by A&AEE (143 had been ordered).
Mo	LIGHTNING F.1/F1A	EE	F23/49	P.1B	F	1	2 x RR Avon 210	34'10"	55'3"	2 x 30mm 2 x AAM	M2.1	60000	WG760 4.8.54	XM134 29.10.59	6.60 74 Sqn	43*	9.72 5 Sqn		F.1A = AAR probe. *Or 49
	LIGHTNING F.2/2A	EE		P.25	F	1	2 x RR Avon 210	34'10"	55'3"	2 x 30mm 2 x AAM	M2.1	60000	XN723 11.7.61		12.62 19 Sqn	44	12.76 19 Sqn		
	LIGHTNING F.3	EE	SOP.33	P.26	F	1	2 x RR Avon 301	34'10"	55'3"	2 x AAM	M2.2	60000	XP693 16.6.62		4.64 74 Sqn	70 or 62	9.87 5 Sqn		
	LIGHTNING T.4	EE		P.11	TR	2	2 x RR Avon 210	34'10"	55'3"	2 x AAM	M2.1	60000	XL628 6.5.59	XM966 15.7.60	1.63 .60	20			
	LIGHTNING T.5	EE	SOP.40	P.27	TR	2	2 x RR Avon 301	34'10"	55'3"	2 x AAM	M2.3	60000+	29.3.62 XM967		4.65 OCU	22			
	LIGHTNING F.6	BAC			F	1	2 x RR Avon 301	34'10"	55'3"	2 x 30mm 2 x AAM or RP	M2.27	60000+	XP697 7.4.64	XS920	12.65 5 Sqn	62	12.87 55	5 Sqn	Includes 14 conversions of F.3. Includes F.6 (Interim).
Mo	LINCOLN 1	AVRO	B14/43	.694	B	7	4 x RR Merlin 85	120'	78'3½"	6 x .5 14000lb bombs	295mph	22000	PW925 9.6.44		8.45 57 Sqn	528			Orig. Lancaster IV.

Type	Aircraft & Mk No.	Manufacturer	Spec. No.	Man. Design	Role	Crew	Engine	Span	Length	Armament	Max. Speed	Service Ceiling	First Flight Proto.	First Flight Prod.	IOC	Total	Last Unit	US Design	Notes
	LINCOLN B.2	AVRO	.694		B		4 x RR Merlin 86	120'	78'3½"	6 x .5 14000lb bombs									Conversions of Mk.I.
	LINCOLN B.4	AVRO	.694		B		4 x RR Merlin 85	120'	78'3½"	6 x .5 14000lb bombs									(Temporary designation).
Mo	LINCOLN U.5	AVRO	.694		D	2/nil	4 x RR Merlin	120'	78'3½"	nil						2			Conversions
	LODESTAR I	LOCKHEED			T/AA	3	2 x Wright Cyclone	65'6"	49'10"	nil	272mph	26000			1.41 267 Sqn			C-56	Based on Lockheed 18.
	LODESTAR IA	LOCKHEED			T	3	2 x P&W Hornet	65'6"	49'10"	nil	230mph	18000		EW973		50	.45	C-59	
	LODESTAR II	LOCKHEED			T	3	2 x Wright Cyclone GR-1820-205A	65'6"	49'10"	nil	270mph	29000		EW983				C-60	
FB	LONDON I	SARO	R24/31	A.27	GR	6	2 x Bristol Pegasus III	80'	57'	3 x Lewis 1500lb bombs	145mph	14750	K3560 .34		10.34 209 Sqn	10	202 Sqn 4.41		
FB	LONDON II	SARO	R3/35		GR	6	2 x Bristol Pegasus X	80'	57'	3 x Lewis 2000lb bombs	155mph	19900	K3560		9.37 228 Sqn	23	6.41 202 Sqn		
Mo	LYSANDER I	WESTLAND	A39/34	P.8	AC	2	1 x Bristol Mercury XII	50'	30'6"	3 x .303 Light bombs	219mph	26000	K6127 15.6.36	L4673 25.3.38	5.38 16 Sqn	169	1.44 695 Sqn		
	LYSANDER II	WESTLAND			AC	2	1 x Bristol Pegasus XII	50'	30'6"	4 x .303 Light bombs	230mph	26000		L4739	12.38 4 Sqn	399	1.44 695 Sqn		
	LYSANDER TT.I/II	WESTLAND			TT	2	1 x Bristol Pegasus XII	50'	30'6"	nil	230mph	26000				21			Conversions.
	LYSANDER III	WESTLAND			AC	2	1 x Bristol Mercury XX or 30	50'	30'6"	4 x .303 Light bombs	212mph	21500		R8991	9.40 2 Sqn	367	6.44 277 Sqn		Includes III (SD) – 2 x .303.
	LYSANDER IIIA	WESTLAND			AC	2	1 x Bristol Mercury XX or 30	50'	30'6"	4 x .303 Light bombs				V9280	1.41 613 Sqn	347	6.45 148 Sqn		Includes IIIA (SD) – 2 x .303.
	LYSANDER TT.IIIA	WESTLAND			TT	2	1 x Bristol Mercury XX or 30	50'	30'6"	nil				V9751		100			
Mo	MAGISTER I	MILES	T40/36 37/37	M.14	TR	2	1 x DH Gipsy Major I	33'10"	24'7½"	nil	142mph	16500		L5912	9.37 CFS	1293			
Mo	MANCHESTER I/3A	AVRO	P13/36 19/37	.679	B	7	2 x RR Vulture I	90'1"	68'10"	8 x .303 10350lb bombs	294mph	19200	L7246 25.7.39	L7276	11.40 207 Sqn	199*	6.42		*Or 209
Mo	MARATHON T.11	HP		HPR.5	T	3	4 x DH Gipsy Queen 173	65'	52'3"	nil	232mph	15000	VX229 29.8.52	XA249 12.53	ANS	28			
Mo	MARAUDER I	MARTIN			B	6	2 x P&W R-2800-39	65'					11.40	FK169 8.42	14 Sqn	52	7.45 231 Sqn	B-26A	
	MARAUDER IA	MARTIN			B	5/6	2 x P&W Double Wasp R-2800-43	65'		4000lb bombs				FK362		19		B-26B	
	MARAUDER II	MARTIN			B	5	2 x P&W Double Wasp	71'	58'3"	12 x .5 4000lb bombs	305mph	32500		FB400	6.44 14 Sqn	123	8.44 14 Sqn	B-26C	
	MARAUDER III	MARTIN			B	6	2 x P&W Double Wasp	71'	56' 57'6"	8-10 x .5 4000lb bombs	305mph	28000		HD402	6.44 14 Sqn	350	9.46 39 Sqn	B-26F B-26G	
Fb	MARINER	MARTIN			GR	9	2 x Wright Double Row Cyclone	118'	78'	8 x .5 10000lb bombs	206mph 165mph	17000			10.43 524 Sqn	20+	524 Sqn 12.43	PBM.3B	
Mi	MARTINET TT.1	MILES	12/41	M.25	TT	2	1 x Bristol Mercury XX or 30	39'	30'11"	nil	232mph		LR241 24.4.42		6.43 289 Sqn	1700+	6.50 20 Sqn		
Mo	MARYLAND I	MARTIN		.167	B/R	4	2 x P&W Twin Wasp SC3-G	61'4"	46'8"	8 x .303 2000lb bombs	278mph	29000	AH205		10.40 431 GRF	155 or 145	3.43 544 Sqn		

Type	Aircraft & Mk No.	Manufacturer	Spec. No.	Man. Design	Role	Crew	Engine	Span	Length	Armament	Max. Speed	Service Ceiling	First Flight Proto.	Prod.	10C	Total	Last Unit	US Design	Notes
	MARYLAND II	MARTIN			B/R	4	2 x P&W Twin Wasp S3C4-G	61'4"	46'8"	4 x .303 / 2 x Vickers / 2000lb bombs	278mph	31000		AH280		70 or 80			Includes Mk.IA.
Mo	MASTER I	MILES	T6/36 16/38	M.9	TR	2	1 x RR Kestrel XXX	39'	30'5"	1 x Vickers	226mph	27000	N3300 .38	31.3.39 N7408	5.39	900			
	MASTER II	MILES		M.19	TR	2	1 x Bristol Mercury XX or 30	35'9"	29'6"	1 x Vickers	240mph	28000	N7422 11.39			1717	11.50		
	MASTER III	MILES		M.27	TR	2	1 x P&W Wasp Junior R-1535-584G	35'9"	30'2"	1 x Vickers	232mph	27300	N7944 .40			602			
Mo	MENTOR	MILES	24/36	M.16	TR	2	1 x DH Gipsy Six	34'9½"	26'1¼"		156mph	13800	—	L4392	10.38	45	8.44		
Mo	MESSENGER	MILES	17/43	M.38	C	1	1 x DH Gipsy Major 10	36'2"	23'9"		115mph	17000	12.9.42 44/045*		21				*RH368?
Mo	METEOR I	GLOSTER	F9/40 E28/39	G41A	F	1	2 x RR Welland I	43'	41'4"	4 x 20mm	410mph	40000	DG205 6.43	EE210	7.44 616 Sqn	20	1.45 616 Sqn		
	METEOR III	GLOSTER			F	1	2 x RR Welland or RR Derwent	43'	41'4"	4 x 20mm / 2000lb bombs	493mph	46000	EE214 9.44	EE230	1.45 616 Sqn	210	8.45 504 Sqn		
	METEOR F.3	GLOSTER			F	1		43'	41'4"	4 x 20mm / 2000lb bombs					8.45 74 Sqn		10.51		
	METEOR F.4	GLOSTER	SOP.25	G-41F	F	1	2 x RR Derwent 5	37'2"	41'	4 x 20mm / 2000lb bombs	585mph	44500	EE360 7.45	EE517	1.47 92 Sqn	545			
	METEOR T.7	GLOSTER	T1/47	G.43	TR	2	2 x RR Derwent 5 or 8	43'	43'6"	nil	590mph	45000	G-AKPK 19.3.48	VW410 26.10.48 AFS	8.49 203 AFS				
	METEOR F.8	GLOSTER	SOP.26	G.41K	F	1	2 x RR Derwent 8	43'	44'7"	4 x 20mm	598mph	45000	VT150 12.10.48	V2438	6.50 245 Sqn	1090 or 1095	3.57 616 Sqn		
	METEOR TT.8	GLOSTER			TT	1	2 x RR Derwent 8	43'	44'7"	nil					9.64 85 Sqn		8.70 85 Sqn		Conversion of F.8.
	METEOR FR.9	GLOSTER		G.41L	FR	1	2 x RR Derwent 8	43'	43'6"	4 x 20mm	595mph	44000	22.3.50 VW360		12.50 2 Sqn	126	8.59 8 Sqn		
	METEOR PR.10	GLOSTER	SOP.26	G.41M	PR	1	22 x RR Derwent 8	43'	44'3"	nil	575mph	44000	29.3.50 VS968		12.50 541 Sqn	58	7.61 81 Sqn		
	METEOR NF.11		SOP.38		NF	2	2 x RR Derwent 8	43'	48'6"	4 x 20mm	554mph	40000	WA546 31.5.50	WD585 19.10.50	7.51 29 Sqn	335	6.60 5 Sqn		
	METEOR NF.12				NF	2	2 x RR Derwent 8	43'	49'11"	4 x 20 mm	585mph	40000	WS 950 21.4.53		3.54 25 Sqn	100	6.59 72 Sqn		
	METEOR NF.13	AW			NF	2	2 x RR Derwent 8	43'	48'6"	4 x 20mm	554mph	40000	WM308 23.12.52		3.53 39 Sqn	40	9.58 39 Sqn		
	METEOR NF.14		SOP.38		NF	2	2 x RR Derwent 9	43'	51'4"	4 x 20mm	578mph	40000	WM261 23.10.53	WS722 23.12.53	3.54 25 Sqn	100	6.59 72 Sqn		
	METEOR TT.20	GLOSTER			TT	1/2		43'	48'6"	nil			WD767			19+			Conversions of NF.11
Mo	MITCHELL F I	NORTH AMERICAN		NA-62B	B	5	2 x Wright R-2600-9	67'6"	54'1"	4 x .5 / 1 x .303 / 3000lb bombs	295mph	27000	19.8.40	FK161	9.42 98 Sqn	23		B-25B	
	MITCHELL II	NORTH AMERICAN		NA-82	B	5	2 x Wright Double Row Cyclone GR-2600-A5B	67'6¼"	54'1"	6 x .5 / 6000lb bombs	292mph	23000		FL164	9.42 98 Sqn	500+	9.45 684 Sqn	B-25C / B-25D	
	MITCHELL III	NORTH AMERICAN		NA-108	B	5-6	2 x Wright Double Row Cyclone GR-2600-A5B -13 or -29	67'6¼"	53'3¾"	13 x .5 / 3200lb bombs	279mph	26000		KJ561	11.44 98 Sqn	314	12.45 342 Sqn	B-25J	

Dual control version of Sopwith Snipe.

Crew boat out to a Sunderland of 88 Squadron.

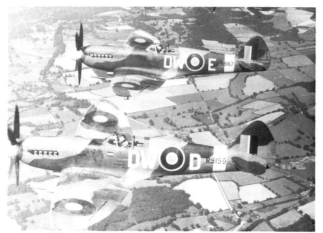

Spitfire XIVs, April 1944.

Tempest F.2 PR689 as part of 33 Squadron line-up, Gutersloh 1949.

Spitfires of 41 Squadron.

Torpedo leaves a 100 Squadron Vildebeest.

Sycamore XG502 on Internal Security operations.

The Vengeance performed well in the Far East theatre.

Vickers Vernon, the RAF's first strategic transport.

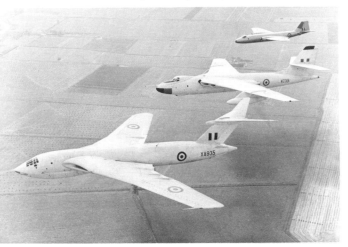

Bomber trio — Victor, Valiant, Canberra.

Virginia — the inter-war strategic bomber.

Vickers Vimy, 1921.

Walrus N9516, one of 36 aircraft used by the RAF for FSR duties.

Wapiti J9636 of 55 Squadron.

Wessex XT605 about to lift a field gun, Hong Kong.

The Whirlwind pick-up was most welcome on a dinghy drill.

Type	Aircraft & Mk No.	Manufacturer	Spec. No.	Man. Design	Role	Crew	Engine	Span	Length	Armament	Max. Speed	Service Ceiling	First Flight Proto.	First Flight Prod.	IOC	Total	Last Unit	US Design	Notes
Mo	MOHAWK III	CURTISS			F	1	1 x P&W Wasp SC3-G	37'3½"	29'	6 x .303	298mph	30400			11.41 5 Sqn				
	MOHAWK IV	CURTISS		Hawk 75A	F	1	1 x Wright Cyclone GR-1820, G-205A	37'3½"	28'7¼"	6 x .303 4000lb bombs	302mph	32700			12.41 5 Sqn		1.44 155 Sqn		
Mo	MOSQUITO B.1	DH	B11/40	DH.98	B	2	2 x RR Merlin 21	54'2"	40'9½"	nil		35000	W4050 25.11.40		1.42 69 Sqn	10	5.43 540 Sqn		
	MOSQUITO PR.1	DH			PR1	2	2 x RR Merlin 21	54'2"	40'9½"	nil	382mph	35000	W4051 10.6.41		7.41 1PRU				
	MOSQUITO F.II	DH			F	2	2 x RR Merlin 21 or 23	54'2"	41'2"	4 x 20mm 4 x .303	370mph	36000	W4052 15.5.41	W4076	1.42 157 Sqn	466	11.44 418 Sqn		Includes 4 PR conversions and (special) Intruder.
	MOSQUITO NF.II	DH	F21/40		NF	2	2 x RR Merlin 21 or 23	54'2"	42'11"	4 x 20mm 4 x .303	367mph	33500	W4052		157 Sqn	466			
	MOSQUITO T.3	DH			TR	2	2 x RR Merlin 21, 23, or 25	54'2"	40'9½"	nil	384mph	37500	1.42 W4053		9.42 MTU	358			
	MOSQUITO B.IV	DH			B	2	2 x RR Merlin 21 or 23	54'2"	40'9½"	no guns 2000lb bombs (1 x 4000lb bomb)	380mph	28800	W4072 *	3.42	11.41 105 Sqn	273	9.45 627 Sqn		*or W4057 Includes 9 Series I
	MOSQUITO PR.IV	DH			PR	2	2 x RR Merlin 21 or 23	54'2"	40'9½"	nil	381mph	35000		DZ422	12.42 PRU	32			Conversions of B.IV.
	MOSQUITO FB.VI/6	DH			FB	2	2 x RR Merlin 21, 23, or 25	54'2"	41'2"	4 x 20mm 4 x .303	380mph	36000	HJ662* 1.6.42	2.43	5.43 233 Sqn	2718	8.50 11 Sqn		*or DZ434
	MOSQUITO B/PR.VII	DH			PR	2		54'2"	42'11"				KB300 24.9.42			5?			Canada
	MOSQUITO PR.VIII	DH			PR	2	2 x RR Merlin 61	54'2"	42'11"	nil	436mph	38000	DK324 20.10.42		11.42 540 Sqn	5			
	MOSQUITO B.IX	DH	3/47		B	2	2 x RR Merlin 72		44'6"	5000lb bombs	408mph	37000	D2540 24.3.43		4.43 109 Sqn	50	9.45 109 Sqn		Based on PR.IX.
	MOSQUITO PR.IX	DH			PR	2	2 x RR Merlin 72		41'6"	nil	408mph	38000	4.43	LR405	5.43 540 Sqn	90			
	MOSQUITO NF.XII	DH			NF	2	2 x RR Merlin 21 or 23	54'2"	40'6"	4 x 20mm	370mph	36000	8.42 DD715		2.43 85 Sqn	97	9.45 256 Sqn		Conversion of NF.II.
	MOSQUITO NF.XIII	DH			NF	2	2 x RR Merlin 21	54'2"	40'6"	4 x 20mm	370mph	34500	8.43		5.43 256 Sqn	270	9.45 256 Sqn		
	MOSQUITO NF.XV	DH			NF	2	2 x RR Merlin 73 or 77	59'	44'6"	4 x .303	412mph	43000	MP469		3.43 85 Sqn	5	8.43 85 Sqn		
	MOSQUITO B.XVI	DH			B	2	2 x RR Merlin 72, 73, 76 or 77	54'2"	44'6"	4000lb bombs	415mph	40000	MP469 14.9.42	ML926	12.43 109 Sqn	1200			
	MOSQUITO PR.XVI	DH			PR	2	2 x RR Merlin 72, 73, 76 or 77	54'2"	44'6"	nil	408mph	38000	7.43 DZ540		12.43 140 Sqn	432			
	MOSQUITO NF.XVII	DH			NF	2	2 x RR Merlin 21 or 23	54'2"	40'6"	4 x 20mm	370mph	36000	3.43		11.43 85 Sqn	99	3.45 125 Sqn		Conversion of NF.II
	MOSQUITO FB.XVIII	DH			FB	2	2 x RR Merlin 25		40'9½"	1 x 6 pdr	368mph	37000	HJ732 8.6.43		10.43 248 Sqn	27	5.45 254 Sqn		
	MOSQUITO NF.XIX	DH			NF	2	2 x RR Merlin 25	54'2"	40'6"	4 x 20mm	372mph	34500	5.44 DZ659		2.47 500 Sqn	220			Includes PR.19.
	MOSQUITO B.XX	DH			B	2	2 x Packard Merlin 31 or 33	54'2"	40'6"	5000lb bombs	380mph	34000	KB100	KB161	12.43 139 Sqn	145	7.46 162 Sqn	F-8	Canada

Type	Aircraft & Mk No.	Manufacturer	Man. Design	Spec. No.	Role	Crew	Engine	Span	Length	Armament	Max. Speed	Service Ceiling	First Flight Proto. / Prod.	IOC	Total	Last Unit	US Design	Notes
	MOSQUITO B.XXV	DH			B	2	2 x Packard Merlin 225			4000lb bombs	380mph	32000	KA930	10.44 139 Sqn		1.48 502 Sqn		Canada.
	MOSQUITO FB.26	DH			FB	2	2 x Packard Merlin 225	54'2"		4 x 20mm 4 x .303			KA103 10.44	222.46 39 Sqn	338	11.46 55 Sqn		Canada
	MOSQUITO T.XXVII	DH			T	2	2 x Packard Merlin 225						KA877					
	MOSQUITO T.29	DH								nil				2.46 85 Sqn	8	4.47 65 Sqn		Canada
	MOSQUITO XXX	DH												6.44 219 Sqn		11.46 307 Sqn		
	MOSQUITO NF.30	DH			NF	2	2 x RR Merlin 72 or 76	54'2"	41'9" 44'6"	4 x 20mm	407mph	39000	3.44 MM686	11.45* 264 Sqn	380	5.49 616 Sqn		*or 6.44 219 Sqn.
	MOSQUITO PR.32	DH			PR	2	2 x RR Merlin 113	54'2"	40'6"	nil	430mph	42000	.44 MM328	10.44 544 Sqn	5	10.45 544 Sqn		Conversion of PR.XVI.
	MOSQUITO XXXIV	DH												4.45 544 Sqn		10.46 540 Sqn		Canada.
	MOSQUITO PR.34	DH			PR	2	2 x RR Merlin 76 or 113	54'2"	41'6"	nil	425mph	43000	4.12.44	9.46* 13 Sqn	50			*or 4.45 544 Sqn.
	MOSQUITO PR.34A	DH			PR	2	2 x RR Merlin 114A	54'2"	41'6"	nil	425mph	43000		4.49 58 Sqn		9.53 540 Sqn		Conversion of PR.34.
	MOSQUITO B.35	DH			B	2	2 x RR Merlin 113/114	94'	40'6"	5000lb bombs	422mph	42000	AS699* VR793 12.3.45 ?	12.47 14 Sqn	276	1.54 527 Sqn		Includes TT.35. *or RV364.
	MOSQUITO PR.35	DH			PR	2	2 x RR Merlin 113/114	94'	40'6"	nil				11.51 58 Sqn		3.54 58 Sqn		Conversion of B.35.
	MOSQUITO NF.36	DH			NF	2	2 x RR Merlin 113/114 113A/114A	94'	40'6"	4 x 20mm 1000lb bombs	415mph	43000	RK955 5.45	1.46 85 Sqn	266 163	10.53 199 Sqn		
	MOSQUITO NF.38	DH			NF	2			411'5"½	4 x 20mm	404mph	36000	18.11.47 RL.248		101			Not into RAF Service. (60 to Yugoslavia).
Mo	MUSTANG I	NORTH AMERICAN	NA-73 NA-83		F/R	1	1 x Allison V-1710-39 (F3R)	37'¼"	32'2½"	4 x .5 4 x .3	390mph	32000	NX19998 AG345 26.10.40 1.5.41	26 Sqn 1.42	600*		P-51	Plus 5 mod with Merlin 65. (*or 620) as Mustang X.
	MUSTANG IA	NORTH AMERICAN	NA-91		F/R	1	1 x Allison V-1710-39 (F3R)	37'¼"	32'2½"	4 x 20mm	390mph	32000	FD418		93*		P-51	*or 97
	MUSTANG II	NORTH AMERICAN			F/R	1	1 x Allison V-1710-81	37'¼"	32'2½"	4 x .5 1000lb bombs	402mph	34000	FR890		50		P-51A	
	MUSTANG III	NORTH AMERICAN	NA-102		FB	1	1 x Packard Merlin V-1650-7	37'¼"	32'3"	4 x .5 1000lb bombs	442mph	42500	AL975 FB100	12.43 65 Sqn	900+		P-51B P-51C	
	MUSTANG IV	NORTH AMERICAN	NA-109		FB	1	1 x Packard Merlin V-1650-7	37'¼"	32'3"	6 x .5 1000lb bombs	437mph	41500	KH641	9.44	280	1.47 213 Sqn	P-51D/H	
	MUSTANG IVA	NORTH AMERICAN	NA-111		FB	1	1 x Packard Merlin V-1650-7	37'¼"	323'3"	6 x .5 1000lb bombs	430nog	40000			594	1.47 213 Sqn	O-51K -NT	
Mo	NEPTUNE MR.1	LOCKHEED	.26		MR	7	2 x Wright Turbo-Cyclone R-3350-30W	104'	78'3"	4 x .5 2 x 20mm 8000lb bombs	353mph	26000	XP2V-1 WX493 17.5.45	1.52 217 Sqn	52		P2V-5	
Bi	NIEUPORT				F	1	1 x Le Rhône	26'11½"	18'10"	1 x Lewis 1 x Vickers	110mph	17400						
Bi	NIGHTHAWK	MILES			TR	2	1 x DH Gipsy Six	35'	25'		180mph			7.37 24 Sqn		9.38 24 Sqn		

Type	Aircraft & Mk No.	Manufacturer	Spec. No.	Man. Design	Role	Crew	Engine	Span	Length	Armament	Max. Speed	Service Ceiling	First Flight Proto.	Prod.	IOC	Total	Last Unit	US Design	Notes
Bi	NIGHTHAWK	NIEUPORT	35/22	Mars VI	F	1	1 x A-S Jaguar II or Bristol Jupiter III	28'	18'	2 x Vickers	150mph	27000	F2909 4.19		4.23 1 Sqn	70	9.23 1 Sqn		ABC Dragonfly 1 of 320hp.
Bi	NIGHT JAR	NIEUPORT		Mars X	F	1	1 x Bentley BR.2	28'	18'4"	2 x Vickers	120mph	19000	HB535 .21		8.22 203 Sqn	18	4.23 203 Sqn		Main service with FAA. Conversion of surplus Nighthawks by GAC.
Mo	NIMROD MR.1	HSA		HS.801	MR	10/12	4 x RR RB168 Spey	114'10"	129'1"	Torpedo, DC,			XV148 23.5.67	28.6.68	10.70 201 Sqn	46	6.84 42 Sqn		Some converted to AEW.3, then project cancelled.
	NIMROD MR.2/2P	HSA			MR	12	4 x RR RB 168-20 Spey 250	114'10"	129'1"	9 x torpedo AAM	575mph	42000	?	13.2.79	2.80 206 Sqn	35	current		Conversion of MR.1.
	NIMROD R.1	HSA			E	10+	4 x RR RB168 Spey	114'10"					XW664		7.71 51 Sqn	3	current		Conversion of MR.1 Includes R.1P.
Mo	NOMAD	NORTHROP			B	2	1 x P&W Twin Wasp Twin				225mph	20700				60		A-17A	Handed to SAAF.
Mo	N2P-B	NORTHROP			GR	2/3	1 x Wright Cyclone	47'9"	38'	2-4 x .5 2 x .3	228mph	24000	J9186 .33		6.41 320 Sqn	18	6.43 330 Sqn		
Bi	OVERSTRAND I	BOULTON PAUL	29/33 23/34	P.75	B	5	2 x Bristol Pegasus IIM 3	72'	46'	3 x Lewis 1600lb bombs	153mph	22500	K4546		1.35 101 Sqn	24	8.38 101 Sqn		
Mo	OXFORD I	AIRSPEED	T23/26	AS.10	TR	3	2 x A-S Cheetah IX or X	53'4"	34'6"	A-W Turret	182mph	19200	L4534 19.6.37		11.37 CFS	8570	10 AFTS .54		
	OXFORD II	AIRSPEED		AS.10	TR	3	2 x A-S Cheetah X	53'4"	34'6"	nil	188mph	19500	N91						
	OXFORD V	AIRSPEED		AS-46	TR	3	2 x P&W Wasp Junior R-985-AN6	53'4"	34'6"	nil	202mph		AS592						
Bi	PANTHER	PARNALL			FR	2	1 x Bentley BR.2			1 x Lewis	108mph	14500			4.20 205 Sqn	150	4.23 205 Sqn		
Mo	PEMBROKE C.1	HUNTING PERCIVAL		P.66	C	2	2 x Alvis Leonides 127	64'6"	46'	nil	224mph	22000	WV698 21.11.52		9.54 267 Sqn	45	1.76 21 Sqn		
	PEMBROKE C(PR)1				PR	3	2 x Alvis Leonides 127	64'6"	46'	nil	224mph	23000			1.56 81 Sqn	6	8.60 81 Sqn		
FB	PERTH	BLACKBURN	20/32		GR	5	3 x RR Buzzard II MS	97'	70'	3 x .303 1 3 37mm 2000lb bombs	132mph	11500	K3580 .33		1.34 209 Sqn	4	12.34 209 Sqn		
Mo	PETREL	PERCIVAL	25/38	P.16E	C	2	2 x D4 Gipsy Six II	46'8"	32'3"	nil	195mph	21000	—		6.39 24 Sqn	8			
Mo	PHANTOM FG.1	McD		F-4K	F	2	2 x RR RB168-25R Spey 202	38'4¼"	58'3"	8 x AAM 1 x 20mm	M2.1	58050	XT852 17.2.67		9.69 43 Sqn	23		F-4K	Ex-Royal Navy
	PHANTOM FGR.2	McD		F-4M	GA/R	2	2 x RR RB169-25R	38'4¼"	57'7"	11000lb bombs 4 x AAM	M2.1	58050			.5.69 6 Sqn	118	10.92 74 Sqn	F-4M	
	PHANTOM F.3	McD		F-4J	F	2	2 x GE 579-GE-10	38'4¼"	57'7"	8 x AAM 1 x 20mm	1430mph	58750	27.5.66	?ZE350 *	.83 74 Sqn	15	1.91 74 Sqn	F-4J	*or XE512.
Mo	PIONEER CC.1	SCOTTISH AVIATION	A4/45	Pioneer II	C/AA	1-2	1 x Alvis Leonides 502/4	49'9"	34'4"	nil	145mph	16000	VL515		2.54 267 Sqn	40	12.69 20 Sqn		
Mo	PREFECT	AVRO	32/34	.626	TR	2	1 x A-S Lynx IV C	34'	26'4½" or 26'6"	nil	130mph	14000			1.357 ANS				
Mo	PRENTICE T.1	PERCIVAL	T23/43 20/46 21/46	P.40	TR	2	1 x DH Gipsy Queen 32	46'	31'3"	nil	143mph	18000	TV163 31.3.46			370			

Type	Aircraft & Mk No.	Manufacturer	Spec. No.	Man. Design	Role	Crew	Engine	Span	Length	Armament	Max. Speed	Service Ceiling	First Flight Proto.	First Flight Prod.	IOC	Total	Last Unit	US Design	Notes
Mo	PROCTOR I	PERCIVAL	20/38	P.28	TR/C	3–4				nil			P5998 8.10.39			245			Includes IA
	PROCTOR II	PERCIVAL		P30	TR	3				nil				2719					Includes IIA
	PROCTOR III	PERCIVAL		P.34	TR	2–3				nil				R7530					
	PROCTOR IV	PERCIVAL	T9/41	P.31	TR/C	3–4	1 x DH Gipsy Queen II	39'6"	28'2"	nil	160mph	14000	LA586	NP156		256			Original designation – Preceptor
Mo	PROVOST T.1	HUNTING PERCIVAL	T16/48	P.56	TR	2	1 x Alvis Leonides 126	35'2"	28'8"	nil	200mph	25000	WE522 24.2.50	WH418	CFS .51	397*			*or 461
He	PUMA HC.1	WESTLAND/AEROSPATIALE		SA.330	SH	2–3	2 x Turbomeca Turmo III C4	51'2½"	48'5"	2 x GPMG	174mph	15090	WX198 25.11.70		6.71 33 Sqn	48	current		
Bi	QUEEN BEE	DH		DH.82B	D	nil	1 x DD Gipsy Major	29'3"	23'9"	nil	109mph		K3584 5.1.35	L5888		320			Radio-controlled target.
Mo	QUEEN MARTINET	MILES	Q10/43		D	nil	1 x Bristol Mercury XX or XXX	39'	30'11"	nil			PW99			65			Radio-controlled target.
FB	RANGOON	SHORT	R18/29	8.8/8	GR	5	3 x Bristol Jupiter XI F	93'	66'9½"	3 x Lewis 1000lb bombs	115mph	12000	51433 24.9.30		4.31 203 Sqn	6	9.36 210 Sqn		
Bi	RE.8				R	2	1 x Raf 4A	42'7"	27'10"		102mph	13000			1.17 34 Sqn	200	11.20 208 Sqn		
He	ROTA I	AVRO	16/35	.671	AC	1	1 x Genet Major	37'	19'8½"	nil	100mph	8000	K4230		6.43 529 Sqn	12	10.45 529 Sqn		Cierva C-30A Autogyro.
Mo	SABRE F.4	NORTH AMERICAN		C1-13	F	1	1 x General Electric J-47 GE-13	37'1"	37'6"	6 x .5	670mph	53000	XP-86 1.10.47	X530	5.53 3 Sqn	430	6.56 3 Sqn	F-86	
Bi	SALAMANDER	SOPWITH		TF.2	GA	1	1 x Bentley BR2	31'2⅝"	19'6"	2 x Vickers	125mph	13000	E5429 27.4.18		11.18 96 Sqn	210	2.19 157 Sqn		
FB	SCAPA 1	S'MARINE	R20/31 19/33	.221	GR	5	2 x RR Kestrel III MS	75'	53'	3 x Lewis 1000lb bombs	142mph	15500	S1648 8.7.32		5.35 202 Sqn	12	1.39 240 Sqn		Original designation – Southampton V.
Bi	SE.5A	RAF (various)			F	1	1 x Hispano-Suiza or Wolseley Viper	26'7½"	20'11"	1 x Vickers 1 x Lewis 100lb bombs	132mph	20000	A4563 .17		6.17 56 Sqn	5180	1.20 81 Sqn		
FB	SEAFORD	SHORT	R8/42	S.45	GR	6+	4 x Bristol Hercules 100				242mph	13000	MZ269 30.8.44		3.46 201 Sqn	8	4.46 201 Sqn		Original designation – Sunderland IV. Trials only.
He	SEA KING HAR.3	WESTLAND			SAR	4	2 x RR Gnome H.1400-1	62'	72'8"	nil	131mph	14000	XZ585 6.9.77		.79 202 Sqn	19	current	S-61	
FB	SEA OTTER	S'MARINE	5/35, 52/38 514/39, 512/40	.309	ASR	3–4	1 x Bristol Mercury XXX	46'	39'10/4"	1000lb bombs	163mph		K8854 23.9.38		11.43 277 Sqn	290	10.45 281 Sqn		
Bi	SEA TUTOR	AVRO	26/32	.646	TR	2	1 x A-S Lynx IV C			nil			K2893		STS	14			
Mo	SENTINEL	VULTEE-STINSON			AA	1	1 x Lycoming			nil			.41		1.45 117 Sqn	100	1.46 27 Sqn	L-5	
Mo	SENTRY	BOEING			AEW	17	4 x GE/SNECMA CFM-56 2A3	145'9"	152'11"	nil	530mph	40000		2H101	3.91 8 Sqn	7			
Mo	SHACKLETON MR.1	AVRO	R5/46 42/46	.696	MR	10	4 x RR Griffin 57A	120'	77'6"	2 x 20mm 12000lb bombs			VW126 9.3.49	VP254 28.3.50	4.51 120 Sqn	77	9.62 206 Sqn		Includes MR.1A.
	SHACKLETON MR.2	AVRO			MR	10	4 x RR Griffin 57A	120'	87'3"	4 x 20mm 20000lb bombs 300mph	272mph	25700	WB833 17.6.52		1.53 42 Sqn	70	4.72 204 Sqn		Includes MR.2C.
Mo	SHACKLETON T.2	AVRO			TR		4 x RR Griffin 57A	120'	87'3"	nil					.68	10			Conversion of MR.2.

Type	Aircraft & Mk No.	Manufacturer	Spec. No.	Man. Design	Role	Crew	Engine	Span	Length	Armament	Max. Speed	Service Ceiling	First Flight Proto.	First Flight Prod.	IOC	Total	Last Unit	US Design	Notes
	SHACKLETON AEW.2	AVRO			AEW		4 x RR Griffon 57A	120'	87'3"				WL745		1.72	12	6.91 8 Sqn		Conversion of MR.2.
	SHACKLETON MR.3	AVRO			MR	10	4 x RR Griffon 57A	119'10"	92'6"	2 x 20mm 2000lb bombs	302mph	19200	WR970 2.9.55		8.57 220 Sqn	34	12.71 203 Sqn		
	SHACKLETON T.4	AVRO			TR		4 x RR Griffon 57A	120'	77'6"	nil						17			Conversion of MR.1A.
	SHORT 184	SHORT		.184	GR	2	1 x Sunbeam	63'6"	40'7½"	520lb bombs	88mph	3706			6.18 253 Sqn	300	5.21 202 Sqn		
	SHORT 320	SHORT			GR	2	1 x Sunbeam Cossack?	74'6"	45'9"		80mph	5500	8317		8.18 229 Sqn	50	10.19 268 Sqn		
Bi	SIDESTRAND II	BOULTON PAUL	9/24		B	3–4	2 x Bristol Jupiter VIII						J7938 .26	J9176	3.29 101 Sqn	⌉ –18	—		P was mod. Mk II.
	SIDESTRAND III	BP		P.29	B	3/4	2 x Bristol Jupiter VIII F	71'11"	46'	3 x Lewis	140mph	24000	J9176		101 Sqn	⌋	7.36		
FB	SINGAPORE III	SHORT	R3/33	S.5 S.19	GR	6	2 x RR Kestrel IV (RR)	90'	64'2"	3 x Lewis 2000lb bombs	132mph	15500	K3592 15.6.34		1.35 210 Sqn	37	10.41 205 Sqn		Singapore II – 209 Sqn 8.32–11.32 for evaluation.
He	SIOUX AH.1	BELL			T/TR	2	1 x Lycoming TVO-435-A1A	37'1½"	31'7"	nil	105mph	16100	9.3.65 *			79?		TH-13T	*Model 47, 8.12.45
He	SIOUX HT.2	BELL	T							nil					CFS ⌋15				
Bi	SISKIN III	A–W	14/22	SR.2	F	1	1 x A–S Jaguar III	33'1"	23'	2 x Vickers 80lb bombs	134mph	20500	J6583 5.5.23		8.24 41 Sqn	102	3.27 41 Sqn		Developed from Siddley SR.2 includes IIDC.
	SISKIN III A	A–W	25/25		F	1	1 x A–S Jaguar IV	33'2"	25'4"	2 x Vickers 80lb bombs	156mph	27000	J8428 21.10.25		9.26 111 Sqn	353	10.32 56 Sqn		
	SISKIN III DC	A–W	32/23 1/28		TR	2	1 x A–S Jaguar IV	33'1"	23'	nil	140mph	21000							Includes 32 conversions.
He	SKEETER	SARO			TR	2	1 x DH Gipsy Major	32'	28'5"	nil	101mph				CFS	3			
Mo	SKYMASTER	DOUGLAS			T	3/4	4 x P&W R–2000	117'6"	93'11"	nil	265mph	26600	EW999		6.44 Northolt	23	4.46 232 Sqn	DC-4 C-54	
Bi	SNIPE	SOPWITH	A.1A/1917 7F.1		F	1	1 x Bentley BR2	30'1"	19'9"	2 x Vickers 100lb bombs	121mph	20000	B9962 11.17		8.18 43 Sqn	1100	11.26 1 Sqn		
Bi	SOPWITH 1½ STRUTTER	SOPWITH			F	1	1 x Clerget	33'6"	25'3"	1 x Vickers 1 x Lewis	100mph	15000	.3686 12.15		4.16 70 Sqn	1315	7.18 78 Sqn		Called Sopwith Two-Seater by RFC.
FB	SOUTHAMPTON I	S'MARINE	R18/24	.189	GR	5	2 x Napier Lion V	75'	51'1½"	3 x Lewis 1100lb bombs			N9896 10.3.25		8.25 480 Flt	18			All completed to MkII.
FB	SOUTHAMPTON II	S'MARINE		.190	GR	5	2 x Napier Lion Va	75'	51'1½"	3 x Lewis 1100lb bombs	95mph	5950			1.29 201 Sqn	48	12.36 201 Sqn		
Bi	SPAD SCOUT VII				F	1	1 x Hispano–Suiza	25'8"	20'3½"	1 x Vickers	119mph	18000							
Mo	SPITEFUL F.14	S'MARINE	F1/43	.382	FB	1	1 x RR Griffon 65	35'6"	32'4"	4 x 20mm 2000lb bombs	483mph	42000	6.44 NN660 ?NN664 30.6.44			⌉ –17			
	SPITEFUL XV	S'MARINE				1	1 x RR Griffon 85	35'6"	32'4"										
	SPITEFUL XVI	S'MARINE		.371		1	1 x RR Griffon 101	35'6"	32'4"				RB516			⌋			
Mo	SPITFIRE I	S'MARINE	F7/30 F5/34 F37/34	.300	F	1	1 x RR Merlin II or III	36'10"	29'11"	4 x .303 (nil on PR)	364mph	31500	K5054 5.3.36	K9787	8.38 19 Sqn	⌉ –1567			General for Spitfire – wide variety of engine marks and armament fits. Includes PR.1 variants (PR.1A–PR.1C).
	SPITFIRE IA	S'MARINE		.300	F	1	1 x RR Merlin II or III	36'10"	29'11"	8 x .303	367mph	31500				⌋			

Type	Aircraft & Mk No.	Manufacturer	Spec. No.	Man. Design	Role	Crew	Engine	Span	Length	Armament	Max. Speed	Service Ceiling	First Flight Proto.	First Flight Prod.	IOC	Total	Last Unit	US Design	Notes
	SPITFIRE IB	S'MARINE	.300		F	1	1 x RR Merlin, II, III	36'10"	29'11"	4 x .303 2 x 20mm	328mph	31500	L1007		.38 19 Sqn				
	SPITFIRE IIA	S'MARINE	.329		F	1	1 x Merlin XII	36'10"	29'11"	8 x .303	370mph	31500	K9788	P7280	8.39 612 Sqn	750			
	SPITFIRE IIB	S'MARINE	.329		F	1	1 x RR Merlin XII	36'10"	29'11"	4 x .303 2 x 20mm	370mph	31500				170			
	SPITFIRE IIC	S'MARINE	.375		F/ASR	1	1 x RR Merlin XX	36'10"	29'11"	?4 x .303	365mph	31500			.43	50			Conversions of MK II.
	SPITFIRE PR.IV	S'MARINE	.353		PR	1	1 x RR Merlin 46, 50, 50A, 55, or 56	36'10"	29'11"	nil	372mph	38000	BP888		9.41 140 Sqn	229	11.44 681 Sqn		PR version of MkV. Often called PR.10.
	SPITFIRE V.A	S'MARINE	.332		F	1	1 x RR Merlin 45, 46, 50, or 50A	36'10"	29'11"	8 x .303	369mph	36500	X4922 20.2.41		92.5qn 2.41	6487			The MkV was also seen in a number of other versions, e.g. PA.V D converted in ME.
	SPITFIRE V.B	S'MARINE	.331		F	1	1 x RR Merlin 45, 46,	36'10"	29'11"	4 x .303 2 x 20mm	372mph	38000	W3134			(3923)			32'7" span = clipped wing.
	SPITFIRE V.C	S'MARINE	.349		F	1	1 x RR Merlin 45, 46, 50, or 50A	36'10"	29'11"	4 x .303 2 x 20mm	357mph	36500	W3217*		10.41	(2482) or (2447)			*or W3237
	SPITFIRE LF V.B	S'MARINE			F	1	1 x RR Merlin 45, 46 or 50	32'2"	29'11"	4 x .303 2 x 20mm	357mph	35500							
	SPITFIRE F.VB TROP.	S'MARINE	.352		F	1	1 x RR Merlin 45 or 46		29'11"	4 x .303	346mph	35000	X4922*						*or AB320
	SPITFIRE VI	S'MARINE	.350		F	1	1 x RR Merlin 47 or 49	40'2"	29'11"	4 x .303 2 x 20mm	364mph	39000	X4942 4.7.41	AB176	4.42 616 Sqn	100			
Mo	SPITFIRE VII	S'MARINE	.351		F	1	1 x RR Merlin 61, 64, or 71	40'2"	31'	4 x .303	408mph	43000	AB450*		9.42 HAF	140			*X4786
	SPITFIRE HF.VII	S'MARINE	.360		F	1	1 x RR Merlin 71	40'2"	31'	4 x .303 2 x 20mm	416mph	44000			9.42 HAF				
	SPITFIRE PR.VII	S'MARINE	.353		PR	1	1 x RR Merlin 45, 46			8 x .303 or nil	349mph	44000					25		
	SPITFIRE VIII	S'MARINE	.359 .360		FB	1	1 x RR Merlin 61, 63 or 63A	36'10"	30'4½"	4 x .303 2-4 x 20mm 1000lb bombs	410mph	43000	X4942* 4.7.41	JF299 4.42	6.43 145 Sqn		5.47 253 Sqn		*or JF299
	SPITFIRE HF.VIII	S'MARINE	.359		FB	1	1 x RR Merlin 70	36'10"	30'4½"	4 x .303 2-4 x 20mm	408mph	43000				(1658)			
	SPITFIRE LF.VIII	S'MARINE	.359		FB	1	1 x RR Merlin 66	36'10"	30'4½"	4 x .303 2-4 x 20mm	404mph	41500							
	SPITFIRE HF.VIII	S'MARINE	.359		FB	1	1 x RR Merlin 70	35'6"	30'4½"	4 x .303 2-4 x 20mm	416mph	44000							
	SPITFIRE IX	S'MARINE	.361		F	1	1 x RR Merlin 61, 63 or 63A	36'10"	30'6"	4 x .303 2 x 20mm	416mph	44000	MH874		7.42 64 Sqn				Includes IX.B and FR.IX.
	SPITFIRE IX.E	S'MARINE			F	1	1 x RR Merlin 61, 63 or 63A	36'10"	31'½"	2 x .5 2 x 20mm	416mph	44000				(5665)*			Includes 280 conversions of Mk.V. *or 5710
	SPITFIRE HF.IX	S'MARINE	.361		F	1	1 x RR Merlin 70	36'10"	30'	2 x .5 2 x 20mm	416mph	45000	AB505						
	SPITFIRE LF.IX	S'MARINE	.361		F	1	1 x RR Merlin 66	36'10"	30'	4 x .303 2 x 20mm	404mph	42500	MJ823						
	SPITFIRE PR.IX	S'MARINE			PR	1													

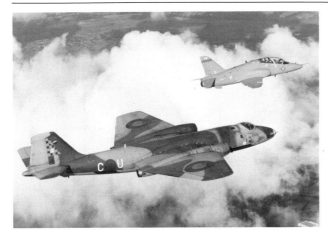

Canberra of 100 Squadron with target tow plus Hawk.

Dramatic shot of GR.5 leaving a forest road.

Jetstream XX496 of METS in standard Support Command training scheme.

Classic Hunter lines.

Dominie XS709 as above.

Spitfire.

Jaguars of 6 Squadron. Note squadron markings on intake and fin aerial.

Puma in Gulf ARTF.

Mosquito RR299.

No mistaking the SAR Wessex of 22 Squadron.

Lightning of 56 Squadron on guard at Akrotiri, Cyprus.

Maritime finish on a Catalina.

43 Squadron Phantom on APC, Cyprus.

Silver dope suits this Hawker Hind.

Rare shot of 80 Squadron Hornets, 1954.

Meteor T7, with 39 Squadron markings, leads NF13 of the same squadron.

Type	Aircraft & Mk No.	Manu-facturer	Spec. No.	Man. Design	Role	Crew	Engine	Span	Length	Armament	Max. Speed	Service Ceiling	First Flight Proto.	First Flight Prod.	IOC	Total	Last Unit	US Design	Notes
	SPITFIRE PR.X	S'MARINE		.362 .387	PR	1	1 x RR Merlin 64, 71 or 77	36'10"		nil	417mph	42000	MD191		5.44 541 Sqn	16	8.45 542 Sqn		Conversions of VII.
	SPITFIRE PR.XI	S'MARINE		.365	PR	1	1 x RR Merlin 61, 63, 63A, or 70	36'10"	31'4½"	nil	422mph	44000			12.42 541 Sqn	471	12.47 13 Sqn		
	SPITFIRE XII	S'MARINE		.366	FB	1	1 x RR Griffon III or IV	32'7"	31'10"	4 x .303 2 x 20mm	393mph	40000	DP845 27.11.41	EN221	2.43 41 Sqn	100	7.45 595 Sqn		Orig. designation Mk.IV.
	SPITFIRE PR.XII	S'MARINE			PR	1	1 x RR Griffon III or IV												
	SPITFIRE XIII	S'MARINE			FB	1	1 x RR Merlin 32	36'10"		4 x .303			L1004			18			
	SPITFIRE PR.XIII	S'MARINE		.367 .353	PR	1	1 x RR Merlin 32	36'10"	30'	4 x .303	348mph	38000	L1004			26			
	SPITFIRE XIV	S'MARINE		.369 .379	FB	1	1 x RR Griffon 65, 67, 85, 87	36'10"	32'8"	4 x .303 2 x 20mm 1000lb bombs	448mph	43500	JF316		1.44 610 Sqn		10.49 612 Sqn		
	SPITFIRE XIV E	S'MARINE		.379	FB	1	1 x R. Griffon 65, 67,	36'10"	32'8"	2 x .5 2 x 20mm 1000lb bombs	439mph	43550				(957)			
	SPITFIRE FR.XIV E	S'MARINE			FR	1	1 x RR Griffon 88	32'8"	32'8"	2 x .5 2 x 20mm 1000lb bombs	439mph	43500			1.44 2 Sqn				
	SPITFIRE XVI	S'MARINE		.380	FB	1	1 x Packard Merlin 266	32'8"	31'4"	4 x .303 2 x 20mm 1000lb bombs						1054			
	SPITFIRE XVI E	S'MARINE			Fb	1	1 x Packard Merlin 266			2 x .5 2 x 20mm									
	SPITFIRE LF.XVI	S'MARINE			FB	1	1 x Packard Merlin 266			*2 x 20mm 4 x .303	406mph	41500				(100)			*or 2 x .5 500lb bombs.
	SPITFIRE XVIII	S'MARINE		.394	FB	1	1 x 44 Griffon 65 or 67	36'10"	33'3¾"	2 x .5 2 x 20mm 1000lb bombs	437mph	43000	NH872 6.45		8.46 208 Sqn		4.51 208 Sqn		
	SPITFIRE FR.XVIII	S'MARINE		.394	FR	1	1 x RR Griffon 65 or 67	36'10"	33'3¾"	2 x .5 2 x 20mm 1000lb bombs	437mph	43000				(200)			
	SPITFIRE PR.XVIII	S'MARINE		.394	PR	1	1 x RR Griffon 65 or 67	36'10"	33'3¾"	2 x .5 2 x 20mm 1000lb bombs	437mph	43000			7.47 607 Sqn				
	SPITFIRE PR.XIX	S'MARINE		.389 .390	PR	1	1 x RR Griffon 65 or 66	36'10"	32'8"	nil	457mph	44500	SW777 *		3.45 16 Sqn	225	6.54 81 Sqn		*542 Sqn or 5.44.
	SPITFIRE F.21	S'MARINE		.356	FB	1	1 x RR Griffon 61, 64, or 85	36'11"	32'8"	4 x 20mm 1000lb bombs	454mph	44000	DP851 4.10.42	LA187 15.3.44	1.45 91 Sqn	122	1.51 602 Sqn		DP851 first flew as Mk.XX 8.8.42.
	SPITFIRE F.22	S'MARINE		.356	FB	1	1 x RR Griffon 61, 64 or 85	36'11"	32'11"	4 x 20mm 1000lb bombs	454mph	45500		PK312	7.47 607 Sqn	278	8.51 610 Sqn		
	SPITFIRE F.24	S'MARINE		.356	Fb	1	1 x RR Griffon 61, 64, or 85	36'11"	32'11"		454mph	43000	VN302		1.48 80 Sqn	81	12.51 80 Sqn		Includes 27 conversions of F.22.
Mo	STIRLING I	SHORT	B12/36	S.29	B	7	4 x Bristol Hercules XI	99'1"	87'3"	8–10 x .303 14000lb bombs	260mph	20500 16500	L7600	N3635 14.5.39	8.40 7 Sqn	722 or 712	2.44 214 Sqn		
	STIRLING III	SHORT			B	7–8	4 x Bristol Hercules VI or XVI	99'1"	87'3"	8–10 x .303 14000lb bombs	270mph	18000	R9309 6.42		12.42 15 Sqn	1047	3.45 199 Sqn		

Type	Aircraft & Mk No.	Manufacturer	Spec. No.	Man. Design	Role	Crew	Engine	Span	Length	Armament	Max. Speed	Service Ceiling	First Flight Proto.	First Flight Prod.	IOC	Total	Last Unit	US Design	Notes
	STIRLING IV	SHORT			B/T	6	4 x Bristol Hercules VI or XVVI	99'1"	87'3"	4 x .303	269mph	18000	LJ512 8.43		1.44 190 Sqn	594	3.46 196 Sqn		
	STIRLING V	SHORT			T	5	4 x Bristol Hercules VI or XVI	99'1"	90'6¼"	nil	280mph	18700	LJ530 8.44		1.45 46 Sqn	160	5.46 46 Sqn		
FB	STRANRAER II	S'MARINE	P24/31 17/35	.237 437	GR	6	2 x Bristol Pegasus X	85'	54'10"	3 x Lewis 1000lb bombs	165mph	18500	K3973 27.7.34		4.37* 228 Sqn	17	4.41 240 Sqn		Original designation – Southampton V. *or 210 Sqn 10.35.
FB	SUNDERLAND I	SHORT	A2/33 22/36	S-25	GR	6-7 -11	4 x Bristol Pegasus 22	112'8"	85'3"	7-8 x .303 2000lb bombs	206mph	11400/14800	K4774 16.10.37		6.38 230 Sqn	90	4.41 240 Sqn		
	SUNDERLAND II	SHORT			GR	11	4 x Bristol Pegasus XVIII	112'8"	85'3"	7 x .303 2000lb bombs	211mph	12600/16100	8.41	S1160		43			
	SUNDERLAND III	SHORT			GR	11	4 x Bristol Pegasus XVIII	112'8"	85'3"	10 x .303 2 x .5 2000lb bombs	210mph	11700/15600/16000	T9042	W3999		461			Includes IIIA.
	SUNDERLAND IV	SHORT			GR	10	4 x Bristol Hercules XIX	112'8"	88'6"	8 x .5 4 x .303	247mph	10500/15000	MZ269 30.8.44			8			Became S.45 Seaford.
	SUNDERLAND V	SHORT			GR	10-13	4 x P&W Twin Wasp R-1830-90B	112'9½"	85'4"	7 x .303 4000lb bombs	234mph	19700/22600	ML765 3.44		2.45 228 Sqn	155 or 150			
Mo	SWIFT F.1	S'MARINE	F.105	.541	F	1	1 x RR Avon RA.7	32'4"	41'5½"	2 x 30mm	660mph	45500	WJ960 1.8.51	WK196 3.53	2.54 56 Sqn	18 or 20	3.55 56 Sqn		
	SWIFT F.2	S'MARINE			F	1		32'4"	41'5½"	4 x 30mm			WK214		56 Sqn	16	8.54 56 Sqn	17	355
	SWIFT F.3	S'MARINE			F	1		32'4"	41'5½"				WK247			25			
	SWIFT F.4	S'MARINE		.546	F	1	1 x RR Avon RA.7R	32'4"	41'5½"		709mph	39000	WK198 2. 27.5.53			6 or 8			
	SWIFT FR.5	S'MARINE		.549	FR	1	1 x RR Avon RA.7R/114	32'4"	42'3"	nil	712mph	45800	XD903 27.5.55		2.56 2 Sqn	94	3.61 4 Sqn		Includes 35 conversion of F.4?
	SWIFT F.7	S'MARINE			F	1	1 x RR Avon RA.7/116	35'	43'	AAM	700mph	41600	XF774 4.56		4.57 1GWDS	12			
He	SYCAMORE HC.11				C+	2				nil					9.51 657 Sqn		9.57 651 Sqn		
	SYCAMORE HA.12	BRISTOL	E20/45	.171	ASW/SAR	2				nil			VL958 24.7.47		2.52 St Mawgan				
	SYCAMORE HR.13	BRISTOL		SAR	SAR	2				nil									
	SYCAMORE HR.14	BRISTOL			SAR	2	1 x Alvis Leonides 73	48'7"	46'2"	nil					4.53 275 Sqn	2	11.55 275 Sqn		
	SYCAMORE HC.14					2									4.54 194 Sqn / 1.60 225 Sqn	90	10.64 110 Sqn / 8.72 32 Sqn		
Mo	TEMPEST II	HAWKER			FB	1	1 x Bristol Centaurus V or VI	41'	34'5"	4 x 20mm 2000lb bombs	442mph	37500	LA602 28.6.43		10.45 183 Sqn	452	4.49 26 Sqn		Includes F.2 designation. Some conversions to TT.II.
	TEMPEST V	HAWKER	F10/41		FFB	1	1 x Napier Sabre IIA or IIB	41'	33'8"	4 x 20mm	426mph	36500	HM595 2.9.42		1.44 486 Sqn	800	4.48 3 Sqn		Original designation – Typhoon II series 1 and 2. Includes F.5 designation.
	TEMPEST TT.5	HAWKER			TT	1	1 x Napier Sabre IIA or IIB	41'	33'8"	nil	nil		.45	SN329					Conversion of MkV.
	TEMPEST VI	HAWKER			FB	1	1 x Napier Sabre V	41'	33'10½"	4 x 20mm	438mph	38000	HM595		12.46	142	3.50		Includes F.6 designation.

Type	Aircraft & Mk No.	Manufacturer	Spec. No.	Man. Design	Role	Crew	Engine	Span	Length	Armament	Max. Speed	Service Ceiling	First Flight Proto.	Prod.	IOC	Total	Last Unit	US Design	Notes
	TEMPEST TT.6	HAWKER			TT	1	1 x Napier Sabre V			nil									Conversion of Mk.VI.
Mo	THUNDERBOLT I	REPUBLIC			FB	1	1 x Wright R-2800-21	40'9"	34'10"	6-8 x .5 2000lb bombs	420mph	35000/36000	XP-47B FL731 6.5.41		5.44 133 Sqn	240	2.46 5 Sqn	P-47D P-47B	
	THUNDERBOLT II	REPUBLIC			FB	1	1 x P&W Double Wasp R-2800-59	40'9/4"	36'1/4"	8 x .5 2000lb bombs	427mph	36500	MD182		6.44 79 Sqn	590	11.46 60 Sqn	P-47D	
Bi	TIGER MOTH I	DH	T15/31 T23/31	.82	TR	2	1 x DH Gipsy III	29'4"	23'11"	nil	105mph	15800	G-ABRC K2567 26.10.31		11.31 3FTS				
	TIGER MOTH II	DH	26/33	.82A	TR	2	1 x DH Gipsy Major I	29'4"	23'11"	nil	104mph	13600	G-ACDA K4242 .34		FTS	4668			
Mo	TOMAHAWK I	CURTISS		.81A-1	F/GA	1	1 x Allison V-1710-33	37'4½"	31'8½"	2 x .5 (4 x .303)	338mph	30500	XP-40 AH741 14.10.38		2.41 26 Sqn	140		P-40	
	TOMAHAWK IA	CURTISS			F/GA	1	1 x Allison V-1710-33	37'4½"	31'81½"	2 x .5 (4 x .303)									
	TOMAHAWK IB	CURTISS			F/GAS	1	1 x Allison V-1710-33	37'4½"	31'8½"	2 x .5 (4 x .303)									
	TOMAHAWK IIA	CURTISS		81A-2	F/GA	1	1 x Allison V-17110-23	37'4½"	31'8½"	2 x .5 4 x .303	345mph	29500	AH881			110		P-40C	
	TOMAHAWK IIB	CURTISS			F/GA	1	1 x Allison V-17110-33	37'4½"	31'8½"	6 x .303 (4 x .3)	345mph	29500	AH991			635			
	TOMTIT	HAWKER			TR	2	1 x A-S Mongoose IIIC	28'6'8"	23'8"	nil	124mph	19500	J9772		7.30 24 Sqn	25			
Mo	TORNADO GR.1	PANAVIA		IDS	IDS	2	2 x Turbo Union RB-199-34R Mk101/103	45'7½"	54'10"	2 x 27mm 18000lb bombs	M2.2	50000	P.01 14.8.74	ZA319 10.7.79	1.82 9 Sqn		current		45'7'/2" = wings forward at 25° sweep.
	TORNADO GR.1B	PANAVIA			S/AS	2	2 x Turbo-Union RB 199-34R	45'7½"	54'10"	2 x 27mm 18000lb bombs Sea Eagle	M2.2	50000		ZA407		24*			*GR.1 conversion planned total.
	TORNADO GR.1A	PANAVIA			IDS/R	2	2 x Turbo Union RB-199-34R Mk101/103	45'7½"	54'10"	18000lb bombs 1 x 27mm	M2.2	50000			2 Sqn 1.89		current		Total GR prod. 199.
	TORNADO GR.1(T)	PANAVIA			IDS/TR	2	2 x Turbo Union RB-19-34R Mk101/103			2 x 27mm 18000lb bombs	M2.2	50000			7.80		current		
	TORNADO F.2	PANAVIA		ADV	F	2	2 x Turbo Union RB-199-34R Mk104/105	45'7½"	54'10"	1 x 27mm	M2+	50000	ZA254		11.84	18	in store		Includes F.2(T).
	TORNADO F.3	PANAVIA	ASR.395		F	2			61'1"	1 x 27mm 8 x AAM	M2.27	70000	ZA267		11.87 29 Sqn	147	current		
Mo	TRISTAR K.1	LOCKHEED	L-1011 -500		T/AAR	3+	3 x RR RB211-254 B4	164'6"	164'2½"	nil	545mph	43500	20948 9.7.85		.83 216 Sqn	9	current		
	TRISTAR KC.1	LOCKHEED			T/AAR	3+	3 x RR RB-211-254 B4	164'6"	164'2½"	nil						6	current		Conversions of K.1 (ex-British Airways)
	TRISTAR KC.2	LOCKHEED			T/AAR	3+	3 x RR RB211-254 B4	164'6"	164'2½"	nil			ZE706		3.93 216 Sqn	3	current		Conversions of K.1 (ex Pan-American)
Mo	TUCANO T.1	SHORT	AST 412	S-312 EMB .312G	TR	2	1 x Garrett TPE-331-12B	36'6½"	34'4"	nil	310mph	25000	G-14-007 11.4.86	ZF135 30.12.86 CFS	9.88 CFS	130	current		
Bi	TUTOR I	AVRO	3/30, 25/32.621 18/31, 24/34		TR	2	1 x A-S Lynx IV.C	34'	26'6"	nil	122mph	16000 97mph	K1797			380			
Mo	TWIN PIONEER CC.1	SCOTTISH AVIATION	SOP.20		C/AA	2-3	2 x Alvis Leonides 514 or 531	76'6"	45'3"	2 x Browning 2000lb bombs	165mph	20000	XL966 10.58 *29.8.57			32	11.67		*Proto. ANTP 25.6.55.

Type	Aircraft & Mk No.	Manufacturer	Spec. No.	Man. Design	Role	Crew	Engine	Span	Length	Armament	Max. Speed	Service Ceiling	First Flight Proto.	First Flight Prod.	IOC	Total	Last Unit	US Design	Notes
	TWIN PIONEER CC.2	SCOTTISH AVIATION			C/AA	2–3	2 x Alvis Leonides 514	76'6"	45'3"	2 x Browning 2000lb bombs	165mph	20000	XN320 14.7.59		10.60 209 Sqn	7	12.68 209 Sqn		
Mo	TYPHOON 1A	HAWKER	F18/32		FB	1	1 x Napier Sabre IIA, IIB, or IIC	41'7"	31'11"	12 x .303 2000lb bombs	412mph	35200	P5212 24.2.40	R7576	9.41 56 Sqn	3300 *	5.43 257 Sqn		*Or total 3317.
	TYPHOON FR.1A	HAWKER			FR	1	1 x Napier Sabre IIA, IIB, or IIC	41'6"	31'11"	3 x 20mm	405mph	33000/34000							Only 2 x 20mm with camera fit.
	TYPHOON 1B	HAWKER			FB	1	1 x Napier Sabre IIA, IIB, or IIC	41'6"	31'11"	4 x 20mm 2000lb bombs	375mph	32500/33500	P5216 3.5.41		3.42 56 Sqn		9.45 175 Sqn		
	TYPHOON FR.1B	HAWKER			FR	1	1 x Napier Sabre IIA, IIB, or IIC	41'6"	31'11"	2000lb bombs					7.44 268 Sqn		1.45 4 Sqn		
Bi	HP V/1500	HP			B	5–7	4 x RR Eagle VIII	126'	64'	4–8 Lewis 7500lb bombs	99mph	11000	5.18 F8285		10.18 166 Sqn	20	1.20 274 Sqn		
Bi	VALENTIA	VICKERS		.264	T	2	2 x Bristol Pegasus IIL3 or IIM3	87'4"	59'6"	2200lb bombs	120mph	16250	K2340	K3599	2.35 216 Sqn	82	9.41 216 Sqn		Includes 54 conversions of Victoria. P was Victoria Mk VI mod.
Mo	VALETTA C.1	VICKERS	C9/46	.637 .651	T	4	2 x Bristol Hercules 230	89'3"	62'11"	nil	258mph	22200	VL249 30.6.47		5.49	199			
	VALETTA C.2	VICKERS		.659	T/VIP	3/4	2 x Bristol Hercules 230	89'3"	62'11"	nil	258mph	22200	VL262	VX571		40			
	VALETTA T.3	VICKERS	T1/49	.664	TR	3+	2 x Bristol Hercules 230	89'3"	62'11"	nil	258mph	22200	VX564 31.8.50			39			
	VALETTA T.4	VICKERS			TR	3+	2 x Bristol Hercules 230	89'3"	62'11"	nil	258mph	22200	WJ465 15.3.56		228 OCU	16*			*Or 18, most conversions of T.3.
Mo	VALIANT B.1	VICKERS	B9/48	.706	B	5	4 x RR Avon 204	114'4"	108'3"	21000lb bombs	414mph	54000	WB210 18.5.51		1.55 138 Sqn	29	12.64 148 Sqn		
	VALIANT B(PR).1	VICKERS		.710	SR	5	4 x RR Avon 204	114'4"	108'3"	21000lb bombs	414mph	54000			7.55 543 Sqn	11	12.64 543 Sqn		
	VALIANT B (K).1	VICKERS		758	AAR+	5	4 x RR Avon 204	114'4"	108'3"	nil	414mph	54000			6.56 138 Sqn	45	12.64 90 Sqn		
	VALIANT B.PR (K).1	VICKERS		733	AAR+	5	4 x RR Avon 204	114'4"	108'3"	nil	414mph	54000			3.56 138 Sqn	14	12.64 214 Sqn		
Mo	VAMPIRE F.1	DH	E6/41	.100	F	1	1 x DH Goblin D Gn 2	40'	30'9"	4 x 20mm	540mph	50000	LZ548 9.43		4.46 247 Sqn	170			
	VAMPIRE F.3	DH	3/47		F	1	1 x DH Goblin D Gn 2	40'	30'9"	4 x 20mm		54000	TG275 4.11.46		4.48 54 Sqn	117			
	VAMPIRE FB.5	DH			Fb	1	1 x DH Goblin D Gn 2	38'	30'9"	4 x 20mm 2000lb bombs	535mph	40000		W213 23.6.48	.48	473			
	VAMPIRE FB.9	DH			Fb	1	1 x DH Goblin D Gn 3	38'	30'9"	4 x 20mm 2000lb bombs			G-5-2 28.8.49		1.52 (FEAF)	297 or 300+			Tropical version of FB.5
	VAMPIRE NF.10	DH		.113	NF	2	1 x DH Goblin 3	38'	34'7"	4 x 20mm	538mph				7.51 25 Sqn	78			
	VAMPIRE T.11	DH	T.111	.115	TR	2	1 x DH Goblin 35	38'	34'6"	2 x 20mm 1000lb bombs	538mph	40000	WW456 WW458 15.11.50 1.12.51		AFS	530	11.67 Leeming		
Mo	VARSITY T.1	VICKERS	T13/48	.668	TR	3+	2 x Bristol Hercules 264	95'8"	67'6"	nil	288mph	28700	VX838 17.7.49		10.51 201 AFS	160			
Mo	VC10 C.1	BAC	C.239		T	4	4 x RR Conway 301	146'2"	158'8"	nil	550mph		XR806 26.11.65		7.66 10 Sqn	14	current		Includes C-1K to ASR.416 1st a/c XV101 11.6.92.

Type	Aircraft & Mk No.	Manu-facturer	Spec. No.	Man. Design	Role	Crew	Engine	Armament	Span	Length	Max. Speed	Service Ceiling	First Flight Proto.	First Flight Prod.	IOC	Total	Last Unit	US Design	Notes
	VC 10 K.2/K.3	BAC	K294DP	.1112 .1164	AAR	4	4 x RR Conway 550B	nil	146'2"	158'8" 171'8" K.3	550mph		ZA141 22.6.82		5.84 101 Sqn	5 K.2 4 K.3	current		Conversion of ex civil aircraft. IOC 2.85 for K.3 101 Sqn; first flight ZA148 3.7.84.
	VC 10 K.4	BAC			AAR	4	4 x RR Conway 550B	nil	146'2"	178'8"	550mph		20242 30.7.93		11.93 101 Sqn	5	current		(ex Super VC-10).
Mo	VEGA GULL III	PERCIVAL	26/38		C	1	1 x DH Gipsy Six II	nil	39'6"	25'4"					11.38 24 Sqn	12	4.44 510 Sqn		
Mo	VENGEANCE I	VULTEE		V.72	DB	2	1 x Wright Double Row Cyclone GR–2600–ASB–5	6 x .303 2000lb bombs	48'	40'	279mph	24300		AF745 *7.41		400			*or AN838
	VENGEANCE II	VULTEE			DB	2										300			
	VENGEANCE III	VULTEE			DB	2							FB918		3.44 82 Sqn	100?	1.45 110 Sqn	A–31	
	VENGEANCE IV	VULTEE			DB	2							FD118		6.44 110 Sqn	562?	5.47 695 Sqn	A–35	Includes conversion to TT.IV.
Mo	VENOM FB.1	DH		.112	FB	1	1 x DH Ghost 103	4 x 20mm 2000lb bombs	41'9"	33'	640mph 597mph	48000	VV612 2.9.49		8.52 11 Sqn	370	11.59 28 Sqn		
	VENOM NF2/2A	DH			NF	2	1 x DH Ghost 103	4 x 20mm	42'11"	33'1"	630mph		WP227 22.8.50		11.53 23 Sqn	90	8.57 253 Sqn		
	VENOM NF3	DH		.112	NF	2	1 x DH Ghost 104	4 x 20mm	42'10"	36'8"	630 595mph	45000	WV928 22.2.53		6.55 141 Sqn	129	11.57 89 Sqn		
	VENOM FB.4	DH			FB	1	1 x DH Ghost 104	4 x 20mm 2000lb	41'9"	31'10"	640mph		WE381 29.12.53		7.55 5 Sqn	150	7.62 28 Sqn		
Mo	VENTURA I	LOCKHEED		V–146	B	5	2 x P&W Double Wasp S1A4G	6–8 x .303	65'6"	51'5"	312mph	25000	AE658 31.7.41		5.42 21 Sqn	394	10.44 251 Sqn		Including modifications to GR.I.
	VENTURA II/IIA	LOCKHEED		PV–1	B	5	2 x P&W Double Wasp GR–2800–31	2 x .5 6 x .303 2500lb bombs	65'6"	51'2½"	300mph	25000	AE846		5.42 21 Sqn		1.44 299 Sqn	B–34	
	VENTURA GR.V	LOCKHEED		237– 27– 01						65'6"	51'9"	322mph	26300			9.43 519 Sqn	387	12.44 521 Sqn		Not all production taken up. Includes CV.
Bi	VERNON I	VICKERS	6/20		T	2/3	2 x RR Eagle VIII	nil	68'1"	43'8"			J6855	J6864	3.22 45 Sqn	20			
	VERNON II	VICKERS	43/22		T	2/3	2 x Napier Lion II	nil	68'1"	43'8"	118mph	11000	J7133			25			
	VERNON III	VICKERS			T	2/3	2 x Napier Lion III	nil	68'1"	43'8"			J7539			12	1.27 45 Sqn		Includes 2 conversions of Mk II.
Mo	VICTOR B.1	HP		HP.80	B	5	4 x AS 202 or 207	35000lb bombs	110'	114'11"	M.9	55000	WB771 24.12.52	(XA917) 1.2.56	11.57 232 OCU	25	6.66 57 Sqn		Includes B(PR)1.
	VICTOR B.1A	HP			B	5	4 x AS Sapphire 202 or 207	35000lb bombs	110'	114'11"						24			
	VICTOR B(K) 1A	HP			AAR	4/5	4 x AS Sapphire 202 or 207	nil	110'	114'11"	630mph	50000			5.65 55 Sqn	6	4.67 55 Sqn		
	VICTOR K.1	HP			AAR	4/5	4 x AS Sapphire 202 or 207	nil	110'	114'11"					2.66 57 Sqn	10	5.77 57 Sqn		
	VICTOR K.1A	HP			AAR	4/5		nil	110'	114'11"					2.67 55 Sqn	14	8.76 55 Sqn		
	VICTOR B.2	HP			B	5	4 x RR Conway A–Co 17 Mk 201	35000lb bombs	120'	114'11"	M.92	60000	XM668 20.2.59		2.62 139 Sqn	34	12.68 139 Sqn		Includes B.2R.

Type	Aircraft & Mk No.	Manufacturer	Spec. No.	Man. Design	Role	Crew	Engine	Span	Length	Armament	Max. Speed	Service Ceiling	First Flight Proto.	First Flight Prod.	10C	Total	Last Unit	US Design	Notes
	VICTOR B/SR.2	HP			B/SR		4 x RR Conway A-Co 17 Mk201	120'	114'11"						5.65 543 Sqn	8	5.74 543 Sqn		
	VICTOR K.2	HP			AAR	4	4 x RR Conway A-Co 17 Mk201	113'		nil			1.3.72		7.75 55 Sqn	24	10.93 55 Sqn		Conversion of B.2 and B.2R.
Bi	VICTORIA III	VICKERS	5/20 13/25	.117	T	2	2 x Napier Lion V or II			nil	100mph		J6860 22.8.22	J7921 1.26	2.26 70 Sqn	(46)	4.35 216 Sqn		
	VICTORIA IV	VICKERS		.145	T	2	2 x Napier Lion IIB			nil	110mph		J9250		70 Sqn	14			Conversions of MK III.
	VICTORIA V	VICKERS	7/29	.169 .241	T	2	2 x Napier Lion XIB	87'4"	59'6"	nil	110mph	16200		J9760	2.29 216 Sqn	96	8.35 70 Sqn		
	VICTORIA VI	VICKERS	25/33	.262	T	2	2 x Bristol Pegasus JM3	87'4"	59'6"	nil	130mph	18300		K3159	7.31 70 Sqn		11.35 70 Sqn		Some redesignated Valentia I.
Mo	VIGILANT	VULTEE-STINSON			AOP	1	1 x Lycoming	51'	34'	nil	123mph	20000			651 Sqn	100	.41	0.49	
Mo	VIKING C.II	VICKERS	OR.198	.498	T/VIP	3	2 x Bristol Hercules 634	89'3"	65'2"	nil	210mph		VL226		.46 KF	4*			*or 12.
Bi	VILDEBEEST I	VICKERS	22/31	.244	TB	2	1 x Bristol Pegasus IM3	49'	368"	1 x Vickers 1 x Lewis 1100lb bombs	140mph	19000	N230 4.28		11.32 100 Sqn	22	11.39 22 Sqn		
	VILDEBEEST II	VICKERS		.258	TB	2	1 x Bristol Pegasus II M3	49'	368"						8.33 100 Sqn	30	1.41 100 Sqn		
	VILDEBEEST III	VICKERS	15/34	.267	TB	3	1 x Bristol Pegasus II M3	49'	36'8"	1 x Vickers 1 x Lewis 1000lb bombs	143mph	17000			5.34 36 Sqn	83	3.42 36 Sqn		
	VILDEBEEST IV	VICKERS		.286		2	1 x Bristol Perseus VIII	49'	37'8"	1 x Vickers 1 x Lewis 1000lb bombs	156mph	17000	K4164		3.37 22 Sqn	17	4.40 42 Sqn		
Bi	VIMY IV	VICKERS		FB.27	B	3	2 x RR Eagle VIII	68'1"	43'6½"	4 x Lewis 2476lb bombs	103mph	7000	B9952 30.11.17		7.19 58 Sqn	22	7.28 502 Sqn		Redesignated Vimy II in 1923
Bi	VINCENT	VICKERS		.266	GP	3	1 x Bristol Pegasus II M3	49'	36'8"	1 x Vickers 1 x Lewis 1000lb bombs	142mph	17000	K2945		1.35 84 Sqn	197	1.43 244 Sqn		
Bi	VIRGINIA III	VICKERS	1/21	.79	B	4	2 x Napier Lion II	86'6"	50'7"	2-3 x Lewis 1900lb bombs	102mph	9450		J6992	5.24 7 Sqn	6	3.27 9 Sqn		
	VIRGINIA IV	VICKERS	28/23	.99	B	4	2 x Napier Lion II	86'6"	50'7"	2-3 x Lewis 1900lb bombs	102mph	9450		J7274		3			
	VIRGINIA V	VICKERS	19/24	.100	B	4	2 x Napier Lion II	86'6"	50'7"	? 1900lb bombs	98.5mph	6200		J7418	1.25 7 Sqn	32*	11.26 58 Sqn		*or 22.
	VIRGINIA VI	VICKERS		.108	B	4	2 x Napier Lion II	86'6"	50'7"		98.5mph	6200		J7558	6.25 7 Sqn	31	5.27 58 Sqn		
	VIRGINIA VII	VICKERS		.112	B	4	2 x Napier Lion V	86'6"	50'7"		102.5mph	7420	J6993 28.8.25		7.26 9 Sqn	50	1.33 7 Sqn		Includes 38 conversions.
	VIRGINIA IX	VICKERS		.139	B	4				102.5mph	7420		J7131		4.27 58 Sqn	35	4.34 58 Sqn		Includes 27 conversions.
	VIRGINIA X	VICKERS	5/31	.139	B	4	2 x Napier Lion V B or XI	87'8"	62'2¼"	3 x Lewis 3208lb bombs 108	102.5mph	7420 15530	J7439 .5.27		1.28 58 Sqn	103	2.38 51 Sqn		Includes 53 conversions.
Mo	VULCAN B.1/1A	AVRO	B35/46	.698	B	5	4 x Bristol Olympus 101 or 102 or 104	99'	97'1"	21000lb bombs 625mph	55000		VX770 30.8.52		7.57 83 Sqn	45	12.67 101 Sqn		

Type	Aircraft & Mk No.	Manufacturer	Spec. No.	Man. Design	Role	Crew	Engine	Span	Length	Armament	Max. Speed	Service Ceiling	First Flight Proto. / Prod.	IOC	Total	Last Unit	US Design	Notes
	VULCAN B.2/2A	AVRO	SOP.21		B	5	4 x Bristol Olympus 201 or 301	111'	99'11"	21000lb bombs	645mph	60000	XH533 19.8.58	10.90 83 Sqn	89	3.84 50 Sqn		
	VULCAN B.2 (MRR)	AVRO			MR		4 x Bristol Olympus 201 or 301	111'	99'11"					11.73 27 Sqn	9	3.82 27 Sqn		Conversion of B.2
	VULCAN K.2	AVRO					4 x Bristol Olympus 201 or 301	111'	99'11"	nil				6.82 50 Sqn	6	3.84 50 Sqn		Conversion of B.2
Bi	WALLACE I	WESTLAND	19/32 7/33 9/33	PV.6	GP	2	1 x Bristol Pegasus II M3	46'5"	34'2"	1 x Vickers 1 x Lewis 580lb bombs	158mph	24100	G-AANA K3562 31.10.31	1.33 501 Sqn	67			Includes 58 conversions of Wapiti
	WALLACE II	WESTLAND	G31/35		GP	2	1 x Bristol Pegasus IV	46'5"	34'2"				K3488 K3436		107			
	WALLACE TT				TT	1				nil								
Bi	WALRUS I	S'MARINE	2/35 32/36	.236	ASR	4	1 x Bristol Pegasus VI	45'10"	37'7"	2 x Vickers K	135mph	18500	K4797 21.6.33 K5772 18.3.36	10.41 275 Sqn	746			Original designation Seagull V
	WALRUS II	S'MARINE			TR/ASR4		1 x Bristol Pegasus VI	45'10"	37'7"	3 x Vickers K 760lb bombs	135mph	18500	X1045 2.5.40			4.46 293 Sqn		
Bi	WALRUS	WESTLAND			GR	3	1 x Napier Lion II	46'2"	29'9" 30'	1 x Vickers 1 x Lewis	124mph	19000	N9500 .2.21	1.22 3 Sqn	36	4.23 3 Sqn		
Bi	WAPITI I	WESTLAND	26/27 1/29 13/30	.460	GP	2	1 x Bristol Jupiter VI	46'5"	31'8"	1 x Vickers 1 x Lewis 580lb bombs	110mph	20600	J8495 7.3.27 J9078	8 Sqn	25			
	WAPITI II	WESTLAND	16/32		GP	2	1 x Bristol Jupiter VIII	46'5"	31'8"	1 x Vickers 1 x Lewis 580lb bombs			J9327	84 Sqn	10			
	WAPITI IIA	WESTLAND	12/30		GP	2	1 x Bristol Jupiter VIII or VIII F or X Fa	46'5" 46'5"	31'8" 31'8"	1 x Vickers 1 x Lewis 580lb bombs			J9247	3.30 60 Sqn	430			
	WAPITI V	WESTLAND			AC	2	1 x Bristol Jupiter VIII Fa	46'5"	34'2"	1 x Vickers 1 x Lewis 580lb bombs			J9728		35			
Mo	WAPITI VI	WESTLAND	17/31		TR	2	1 x Bristol Jupiter IX F	46'5"	31'8"	nil			K2236		16			
Mo	WARWICK ASR.I	VICKERS	B1/35	.462 .456	ASR	6	2 x P&W Double Wasp R-2800-SIALG or -25BG	96'8½'	72'3"	8 x .303	224mph	21500	BV214 1.5.42	10.43 280 Sqn	275	6.46 280 Sqn		Includes B.I and C.I Type 284 P K8178
	WARWICK GR.II	VICKERS	OR.178	.413 .611	GR	6	2 x Bristol Centaurus VII or VI	96'8½'	72'3"	8 x .303 8000lb bombs	262mph	19000	BV216		133			Includes GR.II Met (not into service)
	WARWICK C.III	VICKERS	OR.138	.460	T	4	2 x P&W Double Wasp R-2800-51A4-G	96'8½'	72'3"	nil	260mph	15000	BV296 HG215	6.44 525 Sqn	100	5.46 304 Sqn		
	WARWICK GR.V	VICKERS	OR.130	.475 .474	GR	6	2 x Bristol Centaurus VII or VIII	96'8½'	70'6"	7 x .5 2000lb bombs	290mph	19000	PN697 4.44	11.44 179 Sqn	211	8.46 621 Sqn		
	WARWICK ASR.VI	VICKERS		.485			2 x P&W Double Wasp R-2800-25BG						HF983	4.45 281 Sqn	95			Often referred to as ASR.1
Mo	WASHINGTON B.1	BOEING		.345	B	10	4 x Wright Cyclone R-3350	141'3"	99'	8 x .5 17500lb bombs	350mph	35000	21.9.42 WF434	8.50 115 Sqn	88*	2.58 192 Sqn	B-29 B-29A	*or 88
Mo	WELKIN	WESTLAND	F4/46 F7/41	P.14	F	1	2 x RR Merlin 72, 73, 76 or 77	70'4"	41'7"	4 x 20mm	387mph	44000	DG558 1.11.42	—	67	—		Stored at No.5 MU; did not enter service
Mo	WELLESLEY I	VICKERS	G4/31 22/35	.287	B	2	1 x Bristol Pegasus XX	74'7"	39'3"	2 x Vickers 2000lb bombs	228mph	33000	K7556 19.6.35	4.37 7 Sqn	176	3.43 47 Sqn		
Mo	WELLINGTON I	VICKERS	B9/32 29/36	.285 .290	B	5	2 x Bristol Pegasus XVIII	85'10"	60'6"	6 x .303 4500lb bombs	265mph	26300	K4049 15.6.36 L4212 23.12.37 99 Sqn	10.38 99 Sqn	183			

Serial No.	Aircraft & Mk No.	Manufacturer	Spec. No.	Man. Design	Role	Crew	Engine	Span	Length	Armament	Max. Speec	Service Ceiling	First Flight Proto.	Prod.	IOC	Total	Last Unit	US Design	Notes
	WELLINGTON IA	VICKERS		.408 .409	B		2 x Bristol Pegasus X			6 x .303 4500lb bombs	265mph	26300			10.39 37 Sqn	187			Includes IB Includes 4 DW.I
	WELLINGTON IC	VICKERS		.450 .415	B	5/6	2 x Bristol Pegasus XVIII	86'2"	64'7"	6 x .303 4500lb bombs	235mph	18000	23.12.37		2.40 9 Sqn	2685			
	WELLINGTON II	VICKERS		.298 .406	B	5	2 x RR Merlin X	86'2"	60'10"	6-8 x .303 4500lb bombs	270mph	23500	L4250 3.3.39		11.40 12 Sqn	400	8.43 104 Sqn		
	WELLINGTON III	VICKERS		.440 .417	B		2 x Bristol Hercules III	86'2"	60'10"	8 x .303 4500lb bombs	255mph	19000	L4251 16.5.39		7.41 9 Sqn	1519	1.45 192 Sqn		
	WELLINGTON IV	VICKERS		.410 .424	B		2 x P&W Twin Wasp R-1830-S3C4G	86'2"		6 x .303 4500lb bombs	229mph	20000	R1220 12.40		8.41 300 Sqn	220	5.43 305 Sqn		
	WELLINGTON V	VICKERS	B23/39 17/40	.407 .421	B		2 x Bristol Hercules VIII	86'2"					R3298 8.40			3			
	WELLINGTON VI	VICKERS		.431 .442 .449	B	4	2 x RR Merlin 60 or 62	86'2"	61'9"	4 x .303 4500lb bombs	300mph	38500	W5795 .41		3.42 109 Sqn	63			
	WELLINGTON GR.VIII	VICKERS		.429	GR	6/7	2 x Bristol Pegasus XVIII	86'2"	64'7"	4 x .303 DC/torp	235mph	19000	W5674		1.42 221 Sqn	394	9.43 36 Sqn		Includes TOR VIII and TT.VII
	WELLINGTON X	VICKERS		.440	B	5/6	2 x Bristol Hercules VI or XVI	86'2"	64'7"	6-8 x .303 4000lb bombs	255mph	22000	X3374* DF609		11.42 466 Sqn	3084	4.46 527 Sqn		*Or X3595
	WELLINGTON T.10	VICKERS			T	4+	2 x Bristol Hercules VI or XVI	86'2"	64'7"	nil							ANS		Conversions
	WELLINGTON XI	VICKERS		.454 .458	GR	6/7	2 x Bristol Hercules VI or XVI	86'2"	64'7"	4500lb bombs	255 mph	22000		HF720	1.43 407 Sqn	180			
Mo	WELLINGTON XII	VICKERS		.455	B/GR	6/7	2 x Bristol Hercules VI or XVI	86'2"	64'7"	5 1000lb bombs 6 .303	251 mph	13400			12.42 172 Sqn	58	2.44 407 Sqn		
	WELLINGTON XIII	VICKERS		.466	GR	6/7	2 x Bristol Hercules XVII	86'2"	64'7"	6 x .303 Torp	250mph	16000		HZ551	3.43 612 Sqn	843	4.46 294 Sqn		
	WELLINGTON XIV	VICKERS		.467	GR	6/7	2 x Bristol Hercules XVII	86'2"	64'7"	6 x .303 4000lb bombs	250mph	16500			6.43 612 SQN	841	12.46 38 SQN		
	WELLINGTON XV	VICKERS			T		2 x Bristol Pegasus XVII	86'2"	64'7"	nil	235mph								
	WELLINGTON XVI	VICKERS			T			86'2"	64'7"	nil	235mph								
	WELLINGTON T.XVII	VICKERS			TR	3+	2 x Bristol Hercules VI	86'2"	64'7"	nil									Conversions of Mk.XI
	WELLINGTON T.XVIII	VICKERS			TR	3+	2 x Bristol Hercules XVII	86'2"	64'7"	nil						80			Conversions of Mk.XIII
	WELLINGTON T.19				TR	3+	2 x Bristol Hercules VI or XVI	86'2"	64'7"	nil									Conversions of Mk.X
He	WESSEX HC 2	WESTLAND			SH	2-3	2 x B-5 Gnome H.1200 Mk 110/111	56'	65'10"	GPMG ATM	132mph	12000	XR588	XR497	1.64 18 sqn	68	Current	S-58	Includes conversions to HCSC for SAR
	WESSEX HAR.2	WESTLAND			SAR	2-3	2 x B-5 Gnome H.1200 Mk 110/111	56'	65'10"	nil				X5674	6.55 22 Sqn	6	Current		
	WESSEX HCC.4	WESTLAND			VIP	2-3	2 x B-5 Gnome H.1200 Mk 110/111	56'	65'10"	nil			XV732 17.3.69		6.69 QF	2	Current		
	WHIRLWIND I	WESTLAND	F9/35 F10/35 F37/35	P.9	FB	1	2 x RR Peregrine I	45'	32'9"	4 x 20mm 1000lb bombs	355mph	30300	L6844 11.10.38		.40 263 Sqn	114	12.43 263 Sqn		
He	WHIRLWIND HAR.2	WESTLAND			SAR	3	1 x P&W R-1340-40	53'	62'1½"	nil	99mph	8600	G-AMHK 6.6.51		22 Sqn	2.55	33 22 Sqn	8.62	

Type	Aircraft & Mk No.	Manufacturer	Spec. No.	Man. Design	Role	Crew	Engine	Span	Length	Armament	Max. Speed	Service Ceiling	First Flight Proto.	Prod.	10C	Total	Last Unit	US Design	Notes
	WHIRLWIND HAR.4	WESTLAND			SAR	3	1 x P&W R-1340-57	53'	62'1½"	nil	99mph	8000	XD1063		9.54 155 Sqn	24	12.62 228 Sqn		
	WHIRLWIND HCC.8	WESTLAND	SOP.28		VIP	2	1 x Alvis Leonides Major 160	53'	62'1½"	nil	109mm	1300	XN126		11.59 QF	2			
	WHIRLWIND HAR.10	WESTLAND	SOP.35		SH/SAR	3	1 x B-5 Gnome H.1000	53'	62'4"	4 x ATM	109mph	16600	XJ398 28.2.59	XP299 28.3.61	6.59 110 Sqn	70+	3.82 84 Sqn		Conversions of HR2 and HR4
	WHIRLWIND HC.10	WESTLAND			C	3	1 x B-5 Gnome H.1000	53'		nil	110mph	16600			11.61 225 Sqn		12.72 103 Sqn		
	WHIRLWIND HCC.12	WESTLAND	SOP.55		VIP	2	1 x B-5 Gnome	53'		nil	110mph	16600	XR486		64 QF	2			
Mo	WHITLEY I	AW	B31/34	.188 .38	B	5	2 x A-5 Tiger IX	84'	69'3"	2 x .303	183mph	19200	K4586 17.3.36	K7183 .37	3.37 10 Sqn	34	4.40 166 Sqn		
	WHITLEY II	AW		.197	B	5	2 x A-S Tiger VIII	84'	69'3"	2 x .303	209mph	23000	K7209 *		2.38 51 Sqn	46	4.40 97 Sqn		*Or K7217
	WHITLEY III	AW	20/36	.205	B	5	2 x A-S Tiger VIII	84'	69'3"	4 x .303	209mph	23000	K7211		8.38 51 Sqn	80	4.40 58 Sqn		
	WHITLEY IV/IVA	AW		.209 .210	B	5	2 x RR Merlin IV or X	84'	69'3"	5 x .303	244mph	18000	K7209	5.4.39	5.39 10 Sqn	40	6.40 78 Sqn		First ac with 4-gun turret
	WHITLEY V	AW		.207	B	5	2 x RR Merlin X	84'	72'6"	5 x .303 7000lb bombs	230mph	26000	N1345		9.39 77 Sqn	1466	2.44 297 Sqn		
	WHITLEY GR VII	AW		.217	GR	6	2 x RR Merlin X	84'	72'6"	5 x .303 2000lb+ bombs	215mph	20000	P4949		9.41 612 Sqn		6.43 612 Sqn		Includes conversions of Vs
Bi	WOODCOCK	HAWKER	25/22 3/24		F	1	1 x Bristol Jupiter IV	32'6"	26'2"	2 x Vickers	138mph	20000	J6987 7.23		5.25 3 Sqn	63	8.28 3 Sqn		
Mo	YORK C.1	AVRO	C1/42	.685	T	5	4 x RR Merlin T24	102'	78'6"	nil	298mph	26000	LV626 5.7.42	MW100 11.43	511 Sqn	208	12.51 24 Sqn		

Colourful schemes appeared in the 1920s — Gauntlet of 17 Squadron.

AIRCRAFT MARKINGS

NOTE: This chapter draws together a wealth of material on what is a very wide topic where standardisation was often attempted but seldom achieved. Throughout the period since 1918, and particularly during World War Two, there was enormous local variation on the general principles outlined here. It would require a consideration of each aircraft type within each theatre to arrive at a complete reference and even then there would be numerous instances of 'one-offs' which did not fit the general pattern; nevertheless, an overview of this subject is essential in a reference work such as this.

The basic aircraft as delivered by the manufacturer is a fairly boring artifact, ignoring the 'classic' lines of certain aircraft which make them aesthetic in their own right. There are numerous concepts behind the various schemes of 'decorating' aircraft. The major elements to be covered here are:

1. Camouflage.
2. National markings.
3. Serial numbers.
4. Squadron codes and markings.
5. Personal codes.
6. Named aircraft.
7. Nose art.

This is not an exhaustive list but, as will be seen, it covers the major elements applicable to the RAF. It would be impossible within the scope of this book to provide a complete analysis of all these aspects. However, the general principles within each category will be covered, followed by list of appropriate data.

1. CAMOUFLAGE

One of the oldest of military desires was that of being able to hide from the enemy — and then pounce when the time was right. This was only true up to a point, a point at which the desire not to be found gave way to that of brashness and show — and the need for identification through the use of colour and style of uniforms and standards. For the British Army the latter began to give way to the former during the disasters of the Boer Wars of the late 19th Century. With the arrival of the aeroplane the military art had a new branch, one that would need to consider the same range of options as its associates, including those of identification and concealment.

Throughout World War One the impetus for camouflage and markings changed a number of times, although the RFC tended to maintain its basic concept of giving its aircraft drab schemes to provide a measure of concealment when viewed from above. There were also special schemes devised for such as night fighters and maritime patrol aircraft. The gaudy 'here I am come and get me' schemes favoured by certain German aircraft did not find favour with the RFC, much to the chagrin of some if its pilots. By the latter months of the war most operational aircraft were finished in khaki-green, khaki or brown dopes.

A distinct change was brought about in 1919 with a move to the use of clear varnish or aluminium dope for home based aircraft and a continuation of khaki/brown dopes for use overseas. However, the latter was soon dropped in favour of aluminium dope — although in a wide range of shades that made it look as if many different schemes were in use. In 1926 a number of more colourful schemes appeared, especially the adoption by Home-based units, led by the fighter squadrons, of bright fuselage and upper wing markings. The standard airframe remained dope.

The increase in tension in the mid 1930s, with the likliehood of a European war, led to yet another re-think on camouflage and a move back towards tone-down schemes. A standard trainer scheme was authorised in 1936 of all-over yellow, except for engine cowlings which were burnished metal.

By 1937 the standard finish applied by manufacturers to operational aircraft was specified as brown/green disruptive pattern. The following year this was extended to all front-line aircraft, and later the same year to all aircraft at operational stations. Two disruptive patterns were specified, Scheme A and Scheme B, the former being applied to aircraft whose serials ended in a even number, whilst, logically, the latter was applied to those with odd numbered serials. Remember, however, that this applied to aircraft as finished by the manufacturer and that in-service repaints would not always follow this plan. The standard scheme for the underside of the aircraft was silver for fighter and army co-operation aircraft, this being changed to sky-grey in 1938 and shortly afterwards to all black for bombers and a split scheme of black (port) and sky-blue (starboard) for fighters; again, a number of variation were in use. The fighter split scheme was short-lived, giving way in June 1940 to a light blue finish and a few months later to a duck-egg blue finish (sometimes called duck-egg green). Most aircraft were also given a diamond-shaped patch of gas detector paint, usually yellow, although this concept was discontinued after mid 1940.

WORLD WAR TWO

With the outbreak of World War Two the number of camouflage schemes proliferated and in many instances it is difficult to even talk of a 'standard' scheme — despite the fact that such standard schemes were promulgated in quite unequivocal terms in Air Ministry Orders. The problem came with local variation, often brought about by such simple problems as availability of materials, although there were also instances of direct disobedience of official instructions. By 1941 there were five main camouflage schemes in use, associated with six patterns dictated by the type of aircraft to which the scheme was applied.

SCHEME:
1. Temperate Land — Dark Green/Dark Earth.
2. Temperate Sea — Dark Slate Grey/Extra Dark Sea Grey.
3. Middle East — Dark Earth/Middle Stone.
4. Command — variation as required.
5. PRU — Overall blue.

PATTERNS:
1. Single-engined monoplanes.
2. Twin-engined monoplanes of less than 70 ft span.
3. Twin-engined monoplanes of greater than 70 ft span.
4. Four-engined aircraft.
5. Single-engined bi-planes.
6. Twin-engined bi-planes.

The system gradually evolved into one whereby camouflage schemes were dictated by aircraft role/type, although this quite logical process did not always apply to overseas Commands and there was still a plethora of local variations. AMO A.664 of July 1942 provided a revised list of camouflage schemes, national markings and miscellaneous markings:

Indent marking	Type of aircraft	Width of flash, in inches	Outside diameter of each colour band, in inches, or width of each colour band, in inches				Height, in inches
			Red	White	Blue	Yellow	
Roundel ...	Small ...	—	6	8	16	18	—
,,	Medium ...	—	12	16	32	36	—
,,	Large ...	—	18	24	48	54	—
Flash ...	Small ...	18	8	2	8	—	24
,,	Medium ...	24	11	2	11	—	24
,,	Large ...	36	17	2	17	—	24

(A.M.Os. A.513/41 and A.687/41 cancelled.)

FIGHTER. The standard fighter scheme was for a Temperate Land pattern with a 50% white/black underside. In June the underside scheme was changed to shades of Duck Egg Blue (or almost green) although some aircraft kept the old scheme and some appear to have been given a silver finish. However, the black underside returned, temporarily, in December. By mid 1941 the general finish was Dark Green/Ocean Grey with a Medium Sea Green underside. December 1940 brought in an ident band for day fighters, this being an 18 inch band in Sky Type S around the fuselage forward of the tailplane and spinner, this latter item having been black in the previous scheme. A different ident band was applied from July 1942 with fighters being given a narrow yellow strip on the leading edges of the wings. As usual there were a great many variations on the basic concept and specialist aircraft had their own series of schemes; for example, high altitude aircraft were given a Medium Sea Green upper and PR Blue under finish. During the last few months of the war some fighter types appeared in a polished natural metal finish.

Hurricane of 87 Squadron, June 1942, with a somewhat coarse 'paint job'.

Two varieties of Spitfire finish — FR.XIVs in tone-down and PR.XIXs in high-speed finish.

NIGHT FIGHTER. A special night-fighter paint was introduced in 1940 with a 'velvety non-reflective surface' (officially RDM2), a stealth feature to help the aircraft vanish at night even when illuminated by searchlights. In general terms this lasted until October 1942 when the scheme was changed to Dark Green/Medium Sea Grey upper surfaces with a sea grey underside.

INTRUDER. These aircraft carried the night fighter scheme until late 1942 when a change to the standard day fighter scheme was introduced, although with black underside. The medium bombers of No 2 Gp adopted a Temperate Sea or Dark Sea Grey colour instead of the Dark Earth; the Mosquito intruders had as many different schemes as their were squadrons! Many of the American types delivered from 1943 onwards retained their Olive Drab/Neutral Grey finish. 1943 also brought a more general introduction of the now standard Dark Green/ Medium Sea Grey upper surfaces, but still keeping the black underside.

BOMBER. Bomber aircraft carried a wide variation of scheme depending upon the specific role, and many of course were multi-role; from December 1939 the day bombers were given sky blue undersides whilst the 'night' bombers had their black undersides extended up the side of the fuselage, by late 1940 this encompassed some 75% of the fuselage and included the fins and rudders. The four-engined bombers tended to use the Temperate land scheme or Special Night adaptations. Not all units followed the Bomber Command standard, the B-17s of No 90 Squadron were given an azure blue underside — their concept of operations being ultra high level bombing. The bomber aircraft of Tiger Force were given a white upper and fuselage finish with matt black undersides.

MARITIME. The greatest variation of all came with the maritime types, partly because this covered such a wide range of roles. The commonest scheme in use was the Temperate Land one which was applied to most land-based GR aircraft (with a light grey underside) and strike aircraft, although the latter changed to a Temperate Sea scheme in 1942. Many of the specialist units, such as the PRU, devised and used their own schemes. The Flying Boats are even harder to specify, using a variety of Battleship Grey and Sea Green schemes, although by 1941 most had adopted a Temperate Sea variation with Sky, Sky Grey or Silver undersides.

ARMY CO-OPERATION AND AOP. The ubiquitous Lysanders carried the Dark Green/Dark Earth scheme with silver under the wings, although this latter had changed to Sky by late 1940. The AOP Austers carried the Temperate Land scheme. The more offensive orientated aircraft, such as the Mustangs, tended to adopt the Fighter Command schemes, with the inclusion of a yellow wing band from 1942.

TRANSPORTS. Communications aircraft in general carried a silver dope on fabric-covered aircraft or a clear varnish on metal aircraft. However, examples can be found of comms aircraft in almost every scheme ever devised, plus numerous 'one-offs', especially where the comms aircraft was also the squadron 'hack' — the commonest scheme, however, was Dark Green/Drak Earth with yellow under. . In 1943 it was ordered that all transport aircraft outside of the UK should be Temperate Sea with Azure Blue underside, although this was by no means universally adopted. Transport aircraft such as the Dakota often carried Olive Drab or Khaki finish, with neutral grey underside.

Although the finish is tatty, this 84 Squadron Dakota was all-over Drab.

GLIDERS AND TUGS. Undersides of gliders carried broad yellow and black stripes. Most tugs were in standard bomber camouflage. All target tow aircraft carried black/yellow 'don't shoot me' stripes although the extent and pattern of these varied greatly throughout the war as did the extent of any standard camouflage scheme carried.

TRAINERS. Another area with a range of variation; however, the basic official policy was for camouflaged upper surfaces, the scheme extending half way down the fuselage (later, down the whole fuselage side) , with the rest of the aircraft painted yellow. In general terms the scheme adopted tended to be dictated by the Command and/or role, OTUs, for example, moving towards standard operational schemes. One of the primary aims with trainer schemes was that of ease of ident to reduce the risk of mid-air collision, hence the large percentage of surface area finished in yellow.

MISCELLANEOUS. Air Ambulances carried the Temperate Land Scheme with white underside, and the addition of a red cross within a white circle.

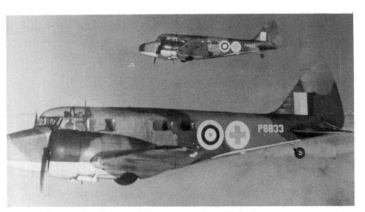

Special Red Cross markings on ambulance Oxfords.

MIDDLE EAST. There was great variation in the Middle East theatre although the standard ME camouflage scheme was the Tropical Land one of Dark Earth/Middle Stone with Azure undersides. Aircraft also carried standard 'role' colours e.g night bombers having black undersides. Reinforcement aircraft from the UK appeared in their original UK scheme and many never received an in-theatre repaint. Likewise, American types arrived in their standard finishes. By the time of the campaigns in Italy most fighters had adopted an Ocean Grey/Dark Green/Medium Sea Grey scheme whilst GR aircraft appeared in Extra Dark Sea Grey/White.

FAR EAST. The standard UK schemes predominated in the early years, as was also true of reinforcement aircraft from UK — however, some aircraft from the Middle East carried ME schemes. From 1944 to the end of the war fighters and ground attack aircraft in the Far East theatre carried a Grey/Green scheme. American aircraft, such as the P-47, arrived in Olive Drab/Neutral Grey. In the latter months of the war some aircraft appeared in natural metal finish.

OTHER MARKINGS

Throughout the war various other identification markings were added to RAF aircraft, some of these have been covered above, one of the most significant was the 'invasion stripes' given to aircraft of the AEAF in June 1944 for the D-Day operations. These consisted of alternate black and white stripes on wings (usually adjacent to the fuselage) and rear fuselage. Similar markings, although black and yellow were painted on RAF aircraft during the Suez conflict.

Others included a 6 inch yellow wing leading edge strip given to day fighters in late 1941 and a one foot yellow band around the wings of Army Co-operation Mustangs. Training aircraft and other of such ilk, BATF units for example, carried a variety of ident markings. Many other identification markings have been used, often theatre-based (black bands on NWFP aircraft 1930s) at various times.

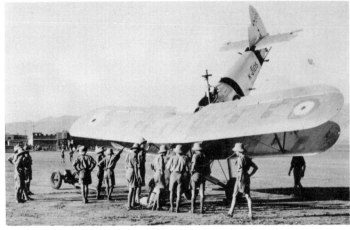

Identity markings took many forms. This sad Hart carried black identity bands of No. 2 (India) Wing.

POST WAR

FIGHTER. Fighter units were amongst the first to get rid of the 'drab' wartime camouflage in favour of somewhat brighter finishes — the favourite being silver/polished metal. It was a short-lived change as camouflage schemes were soon re-introduced, the commonest being Dark Green/Dark Sea Grey and Light Slate Grey/Medium Sea Grey, both having Light Blue undersides. The night fighter force adopted the first of these two schemes but combined it with Medium Sea Grey underside.

However, a standard scheme for UK-based fighters was introduced in 1953 (AMO 228/53) with Dark Green/Dark Sea Grey with silver underside for day fighters and Dark Green/Dark Sea Grey with Dark Sea Grey underside for night fighters. The schemes changed rapidly and there was much local variation. The late 1970s brought a new wave of schemes such as the 'countershading' with its attempt to break up the harsh angular shadows of the aircraft, all of these adopted shades of so-called Air Defence Grey to give a neutral appearance.

Meteors of 141 Squadron with standard camouflage.

Meteor camouflage trials — NF.11s trying to hide.

BOMBER. It was mid 1947 before Bomber Command adopted a new standard scheme of Medium Sea Grey. Other types, such as the B-29 Washington which appeared in a silver finish, adopted other schemes. The introduction of the V-bombers brought a move to a new all-white anti-flash scheme devised to suit the nuclear role of these bombers. The switch to low level tactics in 1964, a result of improved missile defence capability, brought a return to more 'traditional' schemes of Dark Green/Medium Sea Grey with white undersides. Different types adopted different schemes to suit their operational environment, the Canberras, for examples having frequent changes of scheme in the early 1950s.

MARITIME. By 1947 most Coastal Command aircraft were being given a Medium Sea Grey upper surface with matt White fuselage and gloss White underside. In the early 1950s certain types, e.g Shackletons were seen with an overall Medium Sea Grey finish.

TRANSPORT. There was a general move to an aluminium finish, often with White upper surfaces.

PHOTO RECCE. In the immediate post-war period Cerulean Blue was the favoured overall scheme, although this changed to 'high-speed' silver in 1947. Within a few years this gave way to a Medium Sea Grey upper and Azure Blue underside scheme. However, silver became the primary option again from 1952 onwards.

TRAINING. Training aircraft followed the general move towards an all silver finish, whilst keeping yellow bands around the fuselage and wings, the size of the bands being dictated by overall aircraft size.

FAR EAST. Camouflage schemes were maintained on aircraft in this theatre although by the late 1940s certain types had begun to adopt other schemes — Dakotas appeared in silver as did some Austers (but soon returned to Dark Green/Dark Earth), whilst most trainers sported an overall Yellow scheme.

MIDDLE EAST. The silver finish appeared on aircraft from 1947 onwards and in this theatre then followed the UK schemes and patterns until a more general return to role and theatre specific camouflage in the late 1950s.

Camouflage patterns are all very well but the markings show up really well. Hunters of 2 Squadron.

1980s

FIGHTER. The latter years of the Lightning saw a Medium Sea Green upper and Barley Grey underside adopted. However, in general terms fighter aircraft moved to an overall low visibility grey scheme, usually simply called 'Camouflage Grey', sometimes making use of toning to provide an element of shading.

BOMBER. The majority of bomber types appeared in Dark Green/Dark Sea Grey finish. However, theatre schemes have been seen (e.g. use of 'snow' camouflage for Norway). Some types now appearing in Camouflage Grey.

Special finishes are often applied in a temporary paint — such is the case with the Harrier winter camouflage.

MARITIME. No 18 Gp adopted a low visibility hemp or eggshell finish, in matt, semi-matt or satin. Some types, e.g. Buccaneer, also seen in Camouflage Grey.

TRANSPORT

A wide variety of schemes dependant upon the aircraft and role, the tactical types tending to appear in grey/green and the strategic and comms aircraft in white/cream or, in more recent times, grey schemes.

TRAINING

The standard training scheme retained the overiding principle of visibility and so used various degrees of red banding on wings and fuselage. Weapons Training Units and OCUs adopted operational schemes.

GULF WAR

With the Iraqi invasion of Kuwait in August 1990 and the decision to deploy RAF aircraft to the area, it was decided to apply new camouflage schemes to the participating aircraft. A variable shade of pink, often called 'desert pink' but officially designated as ARTF (Alkali Removable Temporary Finish), was applied to all those types likely to operate at low level, particularly the Tornado GR.1 and GR.1A, Jaguar and Buccaneer, Puma. Other specials schemes appeared, such as the disrupted pattern adopted by the Chinook support helicopters.

2. NATIONAL MARKINGS

There were various changes brought in during the 1930s, the most significant being the reversal of colours on the rudder to avoid confusion with French aircraft, from October 1930 all British aircraft were to adopt the Red nearest to the rudder post. 1935 brought a standardisation in wing roundel size and an instruction that roundels were not to overlap any control surfaces.

WORLD WAR TWO

As part of the tone-down of aircraft the roundel colours on operational aircraft were given a matt finish, although the white reamined bright, this was followed by the addition of a yellow

outer ring to the roundel — the matt roundels blending too well with the camouflage! Greater variation soon began to creep in, both in general terms regarding aircraft role, with a dull red/blue roundel for night operations, and on a more local basis. It was the same story with the fin marking, although by late 1940 this had been given some degree of standardisation. Various official pronouncements were made concerning the size and positioning of roundels to suit particular aircraft and roles in an attempt to get something distinctive and yet not too conspicuous.

In 1942 aircraft in the Far East adopted a new roundel and fin scheme removing the red to avoid confusion with Japanese markings, the new colours being Dark Blue and Azure.

SUMMARY OF ROUNDELS:

1914-42	Red/White/Blue	— bright.
1937-42	Red/White/Blue	— matt.
1937-42	Red/White/Blue/Yellow	— matt.
1915-37	Red/White/Blue/White	— bright.
1923-81	Red/Blue	— matt.
1939	Red/Blue/Yellow	— matt.
	Dark Blue/Azure	
1942-47	Red/White/Blue	— dull.
1942-47	Red/White/Blue/Yellow	— dull.
1947-	Red/White/Blue	— bright.

Style, size and colour of roundels have undergone many changes over the past 40 years, usually dictated by the requirements of tone-down, the national markings almost vanishing at times. The latest concepts are for small, pale insignia (pale pink and blue being favourite).

Standard roundel on 83 Squadron aircraft, March 1942 — RAF roundels pre tone-down provided excellent aiming marks for enemy fighters. (Note flak damage — this aircraft was nicknamed 'pepperpot').

3. SERIAL NUMBERS

By April 1918 the system for the allocation of serial numbers to identify individual aircraft was well established, since 1916 this had comprised a single letter followed by up to four numbers. The system had reached E1600 and so it could be argued that E1601, an Avro 504, was the first RAF aeroplane! With the start of the 'K' series of aircraft serials, mid 1929, a new policy was adopted of having a five digit group, the first aircraft being 1000 e.g K1000 (this particular one being an Armstrong Whitworth Atlas I).The colour used for these serial numbers varied greatly, usually in conjunction with changes in the aircraft's overall scheme — black, white, medium grey, red, yellow all being used; some units even adopted different colours for different Flights. By 1938 most had adopted grey, from 1941 dull red was used by aircraft involved with night operations.

Amongst the local variations was that employed by the aircraft depots in the Middle East between 1923 and 1936 whereby an 'R', for rebuild, was added to the serial after the initial letter.

Another major change came in the 'L' series with the introduction of blocks of serial numbers, allocated in batches of 10 to 50 numbers, with missing sequences, refered to as 'blackout blocks', between them. This system commenced following L7272 (a Vega Gull), the first 'missing' aircraft being L7273-L7275. The letter 'M' was not used as a prefix as it was already in use as a suffix on airframes being used for ground instructional purposes. 'N', on the other hand, was used by both the RNAS and RAF, hence N1000 could be either an RAF Beaufort I or an RNAS Fairey Campania. For obvious reasons of confusion the letters 'O' and 'Q' were not used. 'S' had already been used as a follow-on from 'N' for naval type aircraft, the 'S' being taken to represent sea, and so it was not taken up again in logical sequence once R9988, the last of the 'R' series, was reached. Amongst the last letters of the alphabet 'U' and 'Y' were not used.

Z9978, allocated to a Blenheim IV but cancelled, was the last of the single letter four number combinations; the last actual aircraft was Blenheim IV Z9836. The solution adopted in 1940 was to use a two letter three number sequence, starting with AA100 (a Blenheim IV), with each block running from 100 to 999. The concept of Blackout blocks was continued as was the omission of certain combinations that might prove confusing; thus in the 'A-' series 'AC', 'AQ', 'AU' and 'AY' were left out, as were combinations involving 'I' or 'O' as these could be confused with numbers. The same omissions applied to the 'B-' series. There was no 'C-' series and 'DA' to 'DD' and 'DH' were not used, in addition to the usual set of omissions. Serials ET100 to HD776 were allocated to American aircraft provided under Lend-Lease, the first example being ET100 an ex-USAAF Curtiss Kittyhawk; a second batch of Lease-Lend serials ran from JS100 to KV300 and included orders placed in Canada. For the rest of the alphabet the following combinations were not used:

E- : EA, EC, EI, EO, EQ, EU, EY.

F- : FC, FI, FO, FQ, FU, FY.

G- : only GA was used and then for captured aircraft.

H- : HA, HC, HI, HO, HQ, HS, HU, HY.

I- : not used. J- : JC, JE, JH, JI, JJ, JO, JQ, JU, JY.

K- : KC, KI, KO, KQ-KU, KY.

L- : LC, LI, LO, LQ, LU, LY.

M- : MC, MI, MO, MQ, MR, MU, MY.

N- : NI, NO, NQ, NU, NY.

O- : not used.

P- : PC, PI, PO, PQ, PU, PY.

Q- : not used.

R- : RC, RI, RO, RQ, RU, RY.

S- : SA-SK, SO, SQ, SU, SY.

T- : TC, TI, TO, TQ, TU, TY.

U- : not used.

V- : VC, VI, VO, VQ, VU, VY.

W- : WC, WI, WO, WQ, WU, WY.

X- : XC, XI, XO, XQ, XU, XY.

Y- : not used.

Z- : ZC (current sequence is up to ZH).

The position, size and colouring of the aircraft serial went through a number of changes and, like almost all other aspects of aircraft marking, was subject to widespread local variation.

During 1918 an underwing serial was added to Avro 504 trainers, the standard being black lettering 4 in wide (i.e each 'stroke') and 30 in high. This scheme was extended to all RAF aircraft in March 1927 with the proviso that serials were to be at least one foot clear of roundels and in opposite directions on each

wing. This system remained in place until the outbreak of war, although colouring changed with the re-introduction of general camouflage schemes in 1937. However, the outbreak of war brought a decision to remove the underwing serials from all operational types and in most cases to tone down and/or reduce the size of other serials around the aircraft.

The style of presentation also had many variations: for example, India Command between 1934 and 1939 used the style J-.... for the fin serial whereas most other Commands put the letter above the number.

A return to peace brought a return to larger and more distinctive serials, including re-introduction of the underwing serial. By April 1946 a standard had been promulgated for underwing serials:

> Single-engined aircraft — 24 in x 15 in x 3 in.
> Twin-engined aircraft — 36 in x 22 in x 4 in.
> Multi-engined aircraft — 48 in x 30 in x 6 in.

Despite the attempts at standardisation there remained a large number of variations, different types and different roles presenting cases for their own patterns. The Canberra force is a classic example of how many alternatives were in general use; this was often simply a result of changing fashions in camouflage.

By the late 1960s NATO was very much into a camouflage/tone down scenario and this was reflected in the application of serial letters, both in size, colour and position. One part of this process was the removal of the underwing serial, firstly by only putting it under one wing and then by leaving it off completely. The ultimate stage of this has been reached in the Tornado whereby the aircraft carries a small serial in black on each side of the rear fuselage (on GR.1/1A); the new camouflage scheme used during the Gulf War saw these serials painted in white.

Peaceful days, squadron numbers carried on aircraft — Tutors of 616 Squadron and Hind of 90 Squadron.

4. SQUADRON CODES AND MARKINGS

The use of markings to denote a particular squadron started during World War One as an identification system to prevent the aircraft being shot-down by its own side, in which task it was no means always a success. Since 1918 the use of squadron markings has come and gone many times, often at the whim of the Air Ministry, despite the desire of most squadrons to paint their aircraft and so advertise their identity. The few squadrons lucky enough to survive the headlong disbandment of 1918/19 had weightier matters to contend with but with the gradual expansion in the early 1920s an interest in squadron markings was re-born and various unofficial schemes appeared, the fighter squadrons taking the lead in this venture. An Air Ministry review of 1924 failed to come up with a firm policy and it was left to AOCs to approve, or not, the ideas put forward by the squadrons — although a standard policy on Flight colours was introduced with Red for 'A Flight', Yellow for 'B Flight' and Green for 'C Flight', these colours to be painted on wheel discs and other areas as required.

Many squadrons adopted their old wartime markings, albeit usually in brighter colours, and there was an increase in the number of unofficial squadron badges or numbers appearing on various parts of the airframe; a typical example of this was the badge designed by No 39 Sqn and painted on the nose of the unit's DH.9As for the Hendon Pageants of the mid 1920s (for further details on badges see the relevant section).

Squadron motifs were placed inside 'role'-specific devices on the fin — here a six-pointed star for the AC role.

Aircraft sported many other markings, especially with modern types — this Buccaneer shows a few related to the escape system. Similar devices/notices are stencilled over many areas.

A further attempt at standardisation came in 1936 with the first official squadron badges receiving Royal approval, these to become the basis for all use by squadrons of such devices. During 1936 a role-related outline was decreed for squadron motifs, the motif to be enclosed within a spearhead for fighter aircraft, a grenade for bomber and torpedo-bomber aircraft, and a six-pointed star for general reconnaissance and army co-operation aircraft. This, however, was a short-lived policy and within 2-3 years had vanished.

The return to a more overt military stance in the late 1940s was reflected not only in a return to camouflage schemes but also the adoption, with a few exceptions, of new methods of displaying squadron identity.

According to CD0302(3) of 1946 the object of using squadron code letters was to "provide a means of air/air or ground/air visual identification of squadrons and other formations and of individual aircraft." The use of such letter and number codes had been introduced in 1938 as a result of increased military tension during the Munich Crisis, up to that point aircraft had simply carried the squadron number of the side of the fuselage. The adoption of the new system was well established by spring 1939 with units being given a two letter identifier and then adding an individual letter for each aircraft. The standard style of presentation was to be the two letter code on one side of the fuselage roundel and the individual aircraft letter on the other, it was, however, left to AOCs to decide "whether the code marking or the single letter is to be forward of the national marking".

With the outbreak of war all the codes were changed for security reasons.

By 1941 the possible combinations were running out and so the decision was taken to adopt number/letter combinations and to use 'C' and 'I' which had previously been omitted to prevent confusion.

An additional letter 'G', for 'Guard', appeared at the end of the code in the latter years of the war to denote an aircraft requiring higher security protection, a good example being the Meteor IIIs delivered to No 616 Squadron at Farnborough — such as EE213/G. A number of other special markings appeared from time to time, such as 'SNAKE' on aircraft bound for India during the critical period of 1943 — the basic meaning being don't take this aircraft as it is needed elsewhere; the Middle East squadrons having a justified reputation for poaching aircraft bound for the Far East.

A 1946 policy amendment introduced the use of three letter codes. Some units were given a single letter code.

The use of squadron codes was on the way out by 1949 although some squadrons retained them for much longer. In more recent years it has been the fashion with some squadrons to re-adopt wartime codes, for example, the Tornado GR.1s of No 617 Squadron all carry the ex-Lancaster 'AJ' code.

5. PERSONAL CODES

A special variant of such codes was that of personal codes whereby an individual identified himself and his aircraft by using an obvious combination of letters — usually the initials of his name. Amongst the most famous was that of 'DB' carried by Douglas Bader on his Spitfires; the list of such codes is now quite long, thanks to research carried out by Air Britain; however, space precludes inclusion of the full list.

During the 1950s there was a trend towards use of station and Wing motifs, often with the device being colour coded to denote a particular squadron. A good example of this is the Canberra bomber wing at Binbrook in the early 1950s, the station/wing symbol was a lightning flash on the nose of the aircraft, this being

Mosquito VI, mount of Station Commander Lubeck.

Spitfire F.XIV, mount of Wg. Cdr. Flying, Lubeck 1947.

blue for No 9 Squadron, gold for No 12 Squadron, orange for No 50 Squadron and white (later white and black) for No 101 Squadron. At times this was taken to extremes and all squadron identity vanished, such was the case with the Akrotiri Strike Wing in the late 1960s where all aircraft simply had the wing symbol and were used as a pool by the four squadrons — although the groundcrew were quick to re-paint squadron markings whenever opportunity presented itself. Certain Commands, notably Transport, Signals, Middle East, Near East, Far East, took the opportunity of painting the Command title on the aircraft, usually on the upper fuselage or nose.

At various times all such markings and motifs changed from bright colours to dull colours, and back again, with the changing fashion of conspicuity.

Motifs and flashes have appeared on almost all parts of aircraft,although the trend in the 1950s was towards fin decoration, including use of a flash to denote the squadron commander's aircraft, but also making use of tip tanks when these were fitted. However, the fuselage remained the major area of decoration with flashes appearing around the roundel.

Fighter squadrons have generallly managed to retain their squadron markings even at times when other units have been ordered to remove such devices, but overall there is a definite arbitrary feel to the way such decisions are made. It is also a subject creating much heated debate as to what manner of markings a particular unit should be allowed. When 39 Squadron became a PR unit it attempted to retain the old Meteor black/yellow dogtooth device — much to the chagrin of certain fighter units who decreed that such motifs were only for fighter squadrons!In spite of the general NATO tone-down of the 1980s,

the Tornado force has managed to maintain a tradition of exhibiting squadron flashes and other such markings, most following the colour-coded arrowhead pattern around the forward fuselage roundel. Amongst the variations appearing in recent years has been the 'conspicuity tail', various fast-jets being given brightly coloured fins as an aid to low level visibility — most were on a trial basis and little has come of the policy.

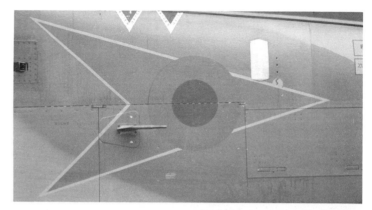

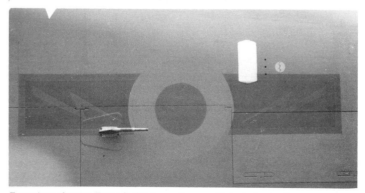

Four views showing Tornado GR.1 squadron markings on forward fuselage. a – 9 Squadron. b — 17 Squadron. C — 45 Squadron/TWCU. d — 617 Squadron.

Anniversary schemes take many forms — Tornado of 9 Squadron and Hawk of 234 Squadron.

SPECIAL COLOUR SCHEMES

This is perhaps the biggest single subject within the heading of aircraft colour schemes and markings and so we will only touch upon it briefly and include only those schemes which were designed for special events. There are two broad categories for this — display aircraft and anniversary schemes.

The most famous of the former category must be the Red Arrows with their all-red Gnats and Hawks but they are, of course, only one of a long line of such distinctively painted display aircraft; other classics have included the Hunters of the Black Arrows and the yellow Gnats of the Yellowjacks. Solo display aircraft are rarely painted in the same way but rather adopt an individual scheme, often changed from one season to the next, and usually only painted on two aircraft (as primary and secondary).

Commemmorative schemes have been in use for some time, for example the 'Alcock and Brown' Phantom, but received a major impetus as squadrons reached their 75 anniversaries. The last five years has seen an amazing array of colour scemes, ranging from entire aircraft re-paints, such as the all-black Tornado GR.1 of No 16 Squadron, to quite simple devices including the wording '75th anniversary'. When a squadron desires to paint any such scheme it must present a case, and a design, to higher authority for approval; it is often a major battle to make any progress and much depends upon the attitude of individual AOCs.

There have been a number of other special schemes, some official and some not quite so official, to mark aircraft anniversaries or the end of a particular 'era' of type or role.

Special schemes adorn display aircraft — here Jet Provosts of 1 FTS 1992 solo aerobatic display. Two aircraft are usually painted up, one to act as a spare.

NAMED AIRCRAFT AND GIFT SQUADRONS

It is quite common when looking at photographs of World War Two aircraft to notice a name inscribed on the nose of the aircraft e.g 'Manchester Civil Defender', a Spitfire used by No 616 Sqn. This policy of Named Aircraft was instituted to provide visible 'credit' to the donors of aircraft, or rather the money to provide aircraft. The donor's name was inscribed on the front of the aircraft, sometimes along with a crest or other motif of the donor organisation. This policy was most widespread with single-seat fighters and during the war thousands of such aircraft entered service. It was stated that such named aircraft should not be sent to 'Gift' squadrons, the latter being units with a permanent association with a major donor or some other close connection. In this case all aircraft on the squadron were to carry the appropriate name, e.g No 92 (East India) Squadron, and all replacement aircraft were to be marked on arrival — likewise, all aircraft leaving the squadron were to have the name removed. Such links often brought other rewards, No 139 (Jamaica) Squadron received an annual 'issue' of rum from Jamaica, an arrangement that continued until the squadron disbanded in December 1959 (the author has no eevidence that the arrangement was re-started when the squadron reformed with Victors).

Named aircraft — donor squadron, 'Nigeria' carried on all Spitfires of 91 Squadron.

7. NOSE ART AND MISSION SYMBOLS

The temptation to draw symbols and motifs on military aircraft has proved irresistable since the genesis of military aviation. The official attitude to decorating aircraft has never been easy to fathom, different organisations and different commanders taking very different stances.

Throughout World War Two aircraft of Bomber Command 'sprouted' nose art — both the standard use of symbols to denote missions completed (usually bombs in the case of bombers), and an aircraft name/symbol at the whim of the crew. There were, of course, other motif types such as the national designations favoured by certain of the Allied, especially Polish, squadrons. There were also special devices such as that on the Stirling 'McRoberts Reply'. The majority of nose art was, however, of the decorative sort devised by the crew and painted on the aircraft by the nearest thing to an artist that the crew could lay hands on — and some of the artwork was of a very high standard. There was no hard and fast rule to the creation of designs ... . "decided to name and paint artwork, needed official permission but this was informal and caused no delay. ... to be of feminine sex, and therefore pilot's name and aircraft letter (C), therefore had to be 'Charlies's Aunt'. Chose a Varga pin-up from Esquire magazine — curvaceous redhead in a seductive green dress."

The range of nose art was very impressive and much of it followed the same basic precepts as those applied to 'Charlie's Aunt' with the female form being a favoured design. Two other widely used types were the 'political' statement — Hitler or other characters being kicked or bombed — and make-believe crests comprising symbols representing each member of the crew. Although other types adopted nose art it was very much Bomber Command that 'led' the field; the fighter squadrons tended to be much more circumspect (for once) although certain units in the Desert Air Force sprouted sharks-mouth designs around the forward fuselage.

Where the bombers carried mission symbols the fighters tended to display kill markings, the range of depictions being quite extensive but usually based upon a miniature flag representing the aircraft shot down — hence a swastika for a German aircraft.

The next major outburst of nose art came with the Gulf War when squadrons went back to the World War Two concepts for both motifs and mission symbols. Once again the female form predominated, although political statements, Saddam being booted, cartoon characters, such as Snoopy and Dennis the Menace, were also used. Other types included an aircraft-eating shark and sharks mouth. Even the TIALD pods were given their own painted characters, a tradition retained, although with different characters, on the pods in use on Op JURAL — although nose art has not returned.

Mission symbols varied widely from base to base and type to type and almost every aircraft was decorated in one way or another.

Of the same ilk are the messages scrawled on bombs, a popular pastime during WW2 and one that has been seen during many other operational sceanarios, including the Gulf War. These messages tend to be either a rude comment adressed to the recipient or some formula including the name of the 'sender'.

Lancaster of 619 Squadron with typical female adornment.

Wellington 'The Sundowner'.

Wellington 'Ritchies Wonder' of 69 Squadron.

Kill markings on Hurricane of R.P. Beamont.

Halifax 'Intuition', including Hitler cartoon and mission symbols.

Artist at work on Canberra PR.3 of 69 Squadron.

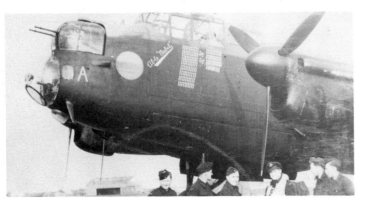

Lancaster 'Able Mabel' with 121 mission symbols.

Buccaneer 'Miss Jolly Roger'.

SQUADRON CODES

A final few words on the problems involved with squadron codes ...codes were not always applied to the squadron 'hack', and most wartime squadrons seemed to acquire a variety of additional one-offs; the converse is that codes appear on aircraft never officially on charge to a particular unit, leading to the comment that 'x' squadron did not have this type and so the code must be wrong. The final area of confusion comes with the habit of decorating visiting or temporary aircraft, in the former case this usually involves the ground crew adding the requisite host squadron details whilst the visitors are not looking, the latter case is far more widespread and variable and often results in aircraft appearing with one squadrons codes and another's markings. Thus it is obvious that a photograph claiming to represent a particular unit cannot always be seen as proof that the depicted code is correct! In the absence of 100% accurate official records, however, these confusions will no doubt remain. In the following list single letter/number codes are not included and there is no reference to the wartime codes, using this system, adopted by the USAAF. Other unusual combinations, where, for example, a diverse unit had a 2-letter code but then gave a third letter to denote aircraft type and a fourth letter or number to define the particular aircraft, are also excluded.

AA — ATA TU.	Anson
AA — 10 AOS.	Anson
AA — 75 Sqn.	Wellington, Stirling, Lancaster, Lincoln, Anson.
AB — 423 Sqn RCAF.	Sunderland.
AB — 1557 RATF.	Oxford.
AC — 138 Sqn.	Lancaster.
AD — 113 Sqn.	Blenheim, Hurricane, Thunderbolt.
AD — 251 Sqn.	Hudson, Fortress, Halifax, Anson.
AD — 60 Sqn.	Hart.
AE — 402 Sqn RCAF.	Hurricane, Spitfire.
AE — 1409 Flt.	Mosquito, Liberator.
AE — 59 Sqn.	Liberator
AF — 611 Sqn.	Spitfire
AF — 607 Sqn.	Spitfire.
AF — AFDU.	Spitfire, Hurricane, + various.
AG — ?.	Stirling, Lysander, Dakota.
AG — CFE.	Anson
AH — 332 Sqn.	Spitfire.
AJ — 1653 CU?	Oxford.
AJ — 617 Sqn.	Lancaster, Mosquito.
AJ — SF N.Luffenham.	
AK — 213 Sqn.	Hurricane, Spitfire, Mustang, Tempest, Harvard.
AK — 1657 CU.	Lancaster, Stirling.
AL — 79 Sqn.	Hurricane.
AL — 429 Sqn.	Wellington, Halifax, Lancaster.
AM — 14 OTU.	Wellington, Anson, Hurricane, Martinet.
AM — 131 OTU	Catalina
AN — 417 Sqn RCAF.	Spitfire.
AN — SF Gt Dunmow.	Oxford.
AN — 13 Sqn.	Lysander.
AO — 223 Sqn.	Wellesley.
AP — 186 Sqn.	Hurricane, Spitfire, Typhoon.
AP — 130 Sqn.	Spitfire, Vampire.

AP — 80 Sqn?	Hurricane.
AQ — 276 Sqn.	Lysander, Walrus, Spitfire, Tiger Moth, Magister, Master, Defiant, Anson.
AR — 460 Sqn.	Lancaster.
AR — 309 Sqn.	Lysander
AR — 331 Sqn.	Spitfire.
AS — 166 Sqn.	Whitley, Wellington, Lancaster.
AS — 100 Sqn.	Lincoln.
AT — 60 OTU.	Blenheim, Mosquito, Oxford.
AU — 421 Sqn.	Spitfire.
AU — 148 Sqn.	Lancaster, Lincoln.
AV — 121 Sqn.	Hurricane, Spitfire.
AW — 42 Sqn.	Beaufort, Vildebeest, Hurricane, Thunderbolt.
AW — 504 Sqn.	Blenheim.
AW — 664 Sqn.	
AX — 202 Sqn.	Sunderland, Catalina.
AX — 77 OTU?	Wellington.
AY — 17 OTU.	Anson, Lysander, Hurricane, Martinet, Spitfire, Wellington.
AY — 110 Sqn.	Blenheim.
AZ — 234 Sqn.	Spitfire, Mustang.
AZ — 627 Sqn.	Mosquito.
A1 — 11 AGS.	Anson
A2 — 514 Sqn.	Lancaster.
A3 — 1653 CU.	Lancaster.
A3 — 230 OCU.	Lincoln, Mosquito, Lancaster.
A4 — 115 Sqn.	Lancaster.
A4 — 195 Sqn.	Lancaster.
A4 — 12 AGS.	Anson.
A5 — 3 LFS.	Lancaster.
A6 — 257 Sqn.	Meteor.
A9 — SF Woodbridge	Oxford.

2A — SF St Eval.	Oxford, Martinet, Dominie.
4A — 2 Gp CF.	
5A — 329 Sqn.	Spitfire, Vampire.
7A — 614 Sqn.	Spitfire, Meteor.
8A — 298 Sqn.	Halifax.
BA — 277 Sqn.	Lysander, Defiant, Walrus, Spitfire.
BB — 27 OTU.	Wellington.
BB — 226 OCU.	Vampire.
BC — 511 Sqn?	
BD — 43 OTU.	Auster.
BD — 227 OCU.	Oxford, Tiger Moth, Chipmunk.
BD — 51 OTU.	Blenheim.
BE — 8 OTU?	Spitfire.
BF — 54 OTU.	Blenheim, Beaufighter.
BF — 14 Sqn.	Wellington.
BF — 28 Sqn.	Lysander, Hurricane, Spitfire.
BF — ?	Spitfire, Typhoon.
BG — 660 Sqn.	Auster.
BH — 300 Sqn.	Wellington, Lancaster.
BH — 215 Sqn.	Harrow, Wellington, Anson.
BI — SF Holme.	
BJ — 271 Sqn.	Bombay, Albatross, Harrow.
BJ — ?	Lancaster.
BK — ?	Hurricane.
BK — 115 Sqn.	Harrow, Wellington.
BK — SFS CF.	Oxford, Prentice, Vampire.
BL — 609 Sqn.	Hind, Spitfire.
BL — 1656 CU.	Halifax, Manchester, Lancaster, Hurricane, Spitfire.
BL — 40 Sqn.	Lancaster
BM — 433 Sqn	Halifax, Lancaster.
BN — 240 Sqn.	London, Stranraer, Catalina.
BN — 170 Sqn.	Mustang.
BN — 1401 Met Flt.	Spitfire.
BP — 457 Sqn.	Spitfire.
BP — 458 Sqn.	Hind, Ventura, Baltimore.
BQ — 600 Sqn.	Blenheim, Beaufighter.
BQ — 550 Sqn.	Lancaster.
BQ — 451 Sqn.	Hurricane, Spitfire.
BR — 184 Sqn.	Hurricane, Typhoon.
BR — 550 Sqn.	Lancaster
BS — 1651 CU.	Lancaster, Stirling.
BS — 148 Sqn.	Wellington, Anson.
BS — 120 Sqn.	Liberator, Lancaster.
BS — 160 Sqn.	Liberator.
BT — 30 OTU.	Wellington, Hurricane, Tomahawk.
BT — 252 Sqn.	Beaufighter.
BT — 113 Sqn.	Blenheim.
BU — 214 Sqn.	Wellington, Stirling, Fortress.
BW — 58 Sqn.	Whitley.
BX — 86 Sqn.	Beaufort, Blenheim.
BX — ?	Halifax.
BX — 666 Sqn.	
BY — 58 Sqn.	Halifax.
BY — 59 Sqn.	Liberator, York.
BY — 23 OTU?	Wellington.
BZ — 107 Sqn.	Blenheim.
BZ — 127 Sqn?	
BZ — 82 OTU.	Wellington.
B3 — SF Wyton.	Oxford.
B4 — 282 Sqn.	Anson, Walrus, Warwick.

B6 — SF Spilsby.	
B7 — SF Waddington.	
B8 — SF Woodhall Spa.	
B9 — 1562 Met Flt.	Spitfire.
1B — 43 Gp CF.	Anson.
2B — 272 MU.	
3B — 23 MU.	
4B — 5 Gp CF.	Anson Oxford.
6B- SF Tempsford.	
7B — 5 Sqn.	Spitfire, Harvard, Oxford.
7B — 595 Sqn.	Martinet, Spitfire, Beaufighter, + various.
8B — Acclimisation Flt.	
CA — 131 OTU	Sunderland.
CA — 189 Sqn.	Lancaster.
CA — 2TAF CF.	Anson.
CB — MCS.	Dominie, Anson, Devon, Chipmunk.
CB — 31 Sqn.	Anson, Devon.
CC — SF Holmsley South.	
CE — 5 LFS.	Lancaster.
CF — 625 Sqn.	Lancaster.
CG — SF Binbrook.	
CH — SF Swinderby.	
CJ — 203 Sqn.	Liberator, Lancaster.
CL — SF Little Rissington.	
CM — 107 OTU.	Wellington.
CM — 42 Gp CF.	
CO — ?	Mosquito.
CP — SF Topcliffe.	
CR — 162 Sqn.	Mosquito, Oxford.
CS — 513 Sqn?	Stirling.
CS — SF Upwood.	Oxford.
CT — 52 OTU.	
CV — SF Tuddenham.	
CW — 214 Sqn.	Lincoln.
CX — 14 Sqn.	Wellington, Mosquito, Vampire.
CY — SF Ludford Magna.	
CZ — 84 OTU.	Martinet.
C1 — 6 OTU.	Anson.
C2 — BCIS.	Oxford.
C2 — ?	Hastings.
C3 — ?	Meteor.
C5 — SF Tibenham.	Proctor.
C6 — 51 Sqn.	Halifax.
C7 — 1 Ferry Pool	Anson, Oxford.
C8 — 640 Sqn.	Halifax.
1C — SF Scampton.	Anson, Oxford.
3C — 1 LFS.	Lancaster.
6C — PRDU.	Mosquito, Spitfire, Hornet.
7C — 296 Sqn.	Halifax, Albemarle.
8C — 12 MU.	
DA — 210 Sqn.	Sunderland, Catalina.
DA — 237 MU.	Stirling?
DB — 411 Sqn.	Spitfire.
DC — 131 OTU	Sunderland
DC — SF Oakington.	
DD — 22 OTU.	Wellington.

DD — 45 Sqn.	Wellington.
DE — 61 OTU.	Spitfire.
DF — 221 Sqn.	Wellington.
DF — CBE.	Lancaster, Lincoln, Mosquito.
DG — 150 Sqn.	Battle.
DG — 155 Sqn.	Mohawk, Spitfire.
DG — 422 Sqn.	Sunderland.
DH — 540 Sqn.	Mosquito.
DH — 1664 HCU.	Halifax, Lancaster.
DI — SF Kemble.	
DJ — 15 Sqn.	Stirling.
DJ — 612 Sqn.	Hector, Anson.
DJ — 57 Sqn.	Lancaster.
DJ — ?	Kittyhawk.
DK — 158 Sqn.	Stirling.
DL — 92 Sqn.	Meteor.
DL — 54 Sqn.	Spitfire.
DL — 91 Sqn.	Spitfire, Meteor.
DM — 248 Sqn.	Mosquito.
DN — 416 Sqn.	Spitfire.
DN — 512 Sqn?	Dakota.
DP — 30 Sqn.	Blenheim.
DP — 193 Sqn.	Typhoon.
DQ — 228 Sqn.	Sunderland.
DQ — 1402 Met Flt.	Hurricane, Master.
DR — 1697 ADLF/S.	Hurricane.
DR — 1555 RATF.	Oxford.
DS — SF LLanbedr.	
DT — 192 Sqn.	Wellington, Halifax, Mosquito, Anson.
DT — 257 Sqn.	Hurricane.
DU — 70 Sqn.	Valentia.
DU — 312 Sqn.	Hurricane, Spitfire.
DV — 129 Sqn.	Spitfire, Mustang.
DV — 237 Sqn?	
DV — ?	Mustang.
DV — 77 Sqn?	Dakota.
DW — 610 Sqn.	Spitfire, Meteor.
DX — 57 Sqn.	Blenheim, Wellington, Lancaster, Lincoln.
DX — 245 Sqn.	Baltimore, Hurricane.
DX — 230 Sqn.	Sunderland.
DY — 102 Sqn.	Whitley, Halifax.
DZ — 151 Sqn.	Hurricane, Defiant, Mosquito.
DZ — SF Broadwell.	
D2 — 1606 Flt.	Martinet.
D4 — 620 Sqn.	Stirling, Halifax.
D6 — SF Hethel.	
D8 — 22 MU.	
2D — 24 Sqn.	
3D — 48 MU.	Proctor, Oxford, Anson.
3D — 4 FP.	Anson.
4D — 74 Sqn.	Spitfire, Meteor, Oxford.
5D — SF Gibraltar.	
5D — 31 Sqn?	Dakota.
6D — 631 Sqn.	Spitfire, Hurricane, Martinet, Vengeance, Oxford.
6D — 20 Sqn.	
7D — 57 MU.	
8D — 220 Sqn.	Liberator.

EA — 49 Sqn.	Hampden, Manchester, Lancaster, Lincoln.
EB — 41 Sqn.	Spitfire, Hornet.
EC — SF Odiham.	Proctor.
EC — PRDU	Meteor.
ED — 78 Sqn.	Whitley.
ED — 21 OTU.	Wellington.
EE — SF Elvington.	
EE — 404 Sqn.	Blenheim, Beaufighter.
EE — 295 Sqn.	Halifax.
EE — 16 Sqn.	Lysander
EE — 31 Sqn.	Valentia
EF — 15 Sqn.	Battle.
EF — 232 Sqn.	Hurricane, Spitfire.
EF — 102 Sqn.	Liberator.
EG — 34 Sqn.	Thunderbolt, Blenheim.
EG — 16 Sqn.	Spitfire, Tempest, Vampire.
EG — 27 Sqn?	Blenheim.
EG — 355 Sqn.	Liberator
EG — 487 Sqn.	Ventura, Mosquito.
EH — 55 OTU.	Hurricane, Typhoon.
EH — 3 TEU.	Hurricane.
EJ — CCFIS.	Beaufighter, Wellington, Mosquito, Sunderland, Catalina, Liberator.
EK — 1656 HCU.	Halifax, Lancaster.
EK — 168 Sqn.	Tomahawk.
EL — 181 Sqn.	Hurricane, Typhoon.
EL — 10 OTU?	
EM — 17 APC?	Martinet.
EM — 207 Sqn.	Battle, Manchester, Hampden, Lancaster, Lincoln, Anson.
EN — 18 OTU	
EN — 27 OTU.	Wellington.
EO — 15 OTU.	Wellington.
EO — 404 Sqn.	Mosquito.
EP — 104 Sqn.	Blenheim, Wellington, Liberator, Lancaster, Anson.
EP — 84 Gp CF.	Messenger, Anson, Proctor, Auster.
EQ — ?	Liberator
EQ — 408 Sqn.	Hampden, Halifax, Lancaster.
EQ — 57 Sqn.	Battle, Blenheim.
ER — 1552 RATF.	Oxford.
ES — 82 Sqn.	Spitfire.
ES — 541 Sqn.	Spitfire.
ES — 229 OCU.	Vampire, Meteor, Hunter.
ET — 662 Sqn.	Auster.
EU — 26 OTU.	Wellington, Martinet.
EV — 180 Sqn.	Mitchell, Mosquito.
EW — 47 Sqn.	Vincent, Gordon, Wellington.
EW — 307 Sqn.	Defiant, Beaufighter, Mosquito, Oxford.
EX — 11 Sqn.	Vampire.
EX — 199 Sqn.	Wellington, Halifax, Stirling.
EX — 171 Sqn?	
EY — 80 Sqn.	Hurricane, Spitfire.
EY — 233 Sqn.	Anson.
EY — 78 Sqn.	Whitley, Halifax, Dakota.
EZ — 81 OTU.	Whitley, Wellington, Dakota, Anson, Spitfire, Hurricane, Oxford, Proctor.
EZ — 1380 TSCU.	
E2 — SF Warboys.	
E4 — SF Wickenby.	

E7 — 570 Sqn.   Albemarle, Stirling.
E9 — SF Westcott.

3E — 100 Gp CF.
4E — 1687 BD Flt.   Spitfire,Martinet, Hurricane.
7E — 327 Sqn.   Spitfire.
8E — 295 Sqn.   Whitley, Halifax, Stirling,
                                Albemarle.
9E — BAFO CW.

FA — 236 Sqn.   Whitley, Wellington.
FA — 281 Sqn.   Anson, Warwick.
FB — WCU.   Washington.
FB — 24 OTU.   Whitley.
FC — SF Northolt   Hurricane.
FC — SF Kenley.
FD — 114 Sqn.   Blenheim.
FD — 1659 HCU.   Halifax, Lancaster, Oxford.
FE — 56 OTU.   Typhoon.
FF — 132 Sqn.   Spitfire.
FG — 72 Sqn.
FG — 335 Sqn.   Hurricane.
FG — ?   Walrus.
FG — 282 Sqn.   Anson.
FH — 46 Sqn.   Beaufighter.
FH — 53 Sqn.   Liberator.
FH — 15 OTU.   Wellington, Martinet, Defiant.
FI — 83 OTU?   Hurricane.
FI — Warwick TU.   Warwick.
FJ — 261 Sqn.   Hurricane, Thunderbolt.
FJ — 37 Sqn.   Harrow, Wellington.
FJ — 164 Sqn.   Spitfire, Hurricane, Typhoon,
                                Auster.
FK — 209 Sqn.   Stranraer.
FK — 219 Sqn.   Blenheim, Beaufighter, Mosquito.
FL — 81 Sqn.   Spitfire, Thunderbolt.
FM — 238 Sqn.   Dakota.
FM — 257 Sqn.   Hurricane, Typhoon.
FN — 331 Sqn.   Hurricane, Spitfire.
FN — 453 Sqn?
FO — 75 Sqn.   Harrow. Anson.
FO — SF Wick.
FO — 1665 CU.   Stirling.
FP — 1683 BDTF.   Tomahawk.
FP — 35 Sqn?
FQ — 12 OTU.   Battle, Anson, Wellington.
FR — SF Manston.
FS — 35 Sqn.
FS — 148 Sqn.   Halifax, Liberator, Lysander.
FT — 43 Sqn.   Hurricane, Spitfire.
FT — SF Mildenhall.
FU — 458 Sqn.   Wellington.
FU — 453 Sqn.   Spitfire.
FV — 1659 HCU.   Halifax.
FV — 81 Sqn.   Hurricane.
FV — 205 Sqn.   Singapore, Catalina.
FV — 230 Sqn.   Sunderland.
FV — 13 OTU.   Blenheim, Mitchell, Mosquito,
                                Tempest.
FW — SF Rivenhall.
FX — 62 Sqn.   Blenheim.
FX — 234 Sqn.   Spitfire, Meteor.
FX — 266 Sqn.   Spitfire, Meteor.

FY — 611 Sqn.   Spitfire, Mustang, Meteor.
FY — 4 Sqn.   Lysander.
FZ — 65 Sqn.   Spitfire.
FZ — 23 OTU.   Wellington, Oxford.
FZ — 100 Sqn.   Lancaster.

F2 — 635 Sqn.   Lancaster.
F3 — 438 Sqn.   Hurricane, Typhoon.

3F — BAFO CW.
5F — 147 Sqn.   Halifax.
6F — 1669 HCU.   Halifax, Lancaster.
8F — 105 OTU.   Wellington, Dakota.
9F — SF Stradishall.

3-letter 'F' codes given to Flying Training Command units in 1946: Most of these units operated such types as Anson and Oxford or Harvard, plus a range of other comms and training types.

FAA-FAG.   19 SFTS/FTS.
FAI-FAM.   20 SFTS/2 FTS.
FAN-FAQ.   21 SFTS.
FAS-FAY.   16 PFTS.
FBA-FBE.   7 SFTS/FTS.
FBG-FBN.   6 SFTS/FTS.
FBP-FBY.   3 SFTS/FTS.
FCA-FCG.   17 SFTS/FTS/ 1 FTS.
FCI-FCM.   22 SFTS/FTS.
FCN-FCR.   5 PAFU.
FCT-FCX.   ECFS/EFS/RAFFC.
FDA-FDG.   21 PAFU/ 21 PRFS/ 1 PRFU.
FDI-FDO.   CFS.
FDQ-FDT.   10 FIS/ 8 EFTS.
FDU-FDW.   BAS.
FDW? CFS
FDX. BAS.

FDY.   SoFC/ SoATC
FEA-FEE.   1 GTS.
FEG-FEN.   3 GTS.
FEP-FET.   2 HGCU.
FFA-FFD.   10 AGS.
FFE-FFG.   11 AGS.
FFI-FFK.   5 ANS/ 1 ANS.
FFM-FFP.   7 ANS/2ANS
FFR-FFU.   10 ANS.
FGA-FGC.   EAAS/ RAFFC.
FGE-FGG.   EANS/ CNS/CNCS
FGI-FGN.   A&AEE.
FGP-FGR.   ETPS.
FGT-FGX.   AFEE.
FHA-FHC.   1 EFTS.
FHE-FHG.   2 EFTS.
FHI-FHK.   3 EFTS.
FHM-FHO.   4 EFTS.
FHQ-FHT.   6 EFTS.
FHV-FHY.   7 EFTS.
FIA-FID.   11 EFTS.
FIJ-FIL.   15 EFTS.
FIN-FIP.   16 EFTS.
FIR-FIT.   18 EFTS.
FIV-FIY.   21 EFTS.
FJA-FJD.   22 EFTS.

FJF-FJH.	24 EFTS. ?	
FJJ-FJL.	28 EFTS.	
FJN-FJQ.	29 EFTS.	
FJS-FJX.	CGS.	
FKA	1511 BATF.	
FKD.	1537 BATF.	
FKF.	1547 BATF.	
FKN.	FTC CF.	
FKO.	21 Gp CF.	
FKP.	23 Gp CF.	
FKQ.	25 Gp CF.	
FKR.	54 Gp CF.	
FKS.	SF Cranwell.	
FLA.	Cambridge UAS.	
FLB.	Aberdeen UAS.	
FLC.	Edinburgh UAS.	
FLD.	Glasgow UAS.	
FLE.	Queens UAS.	
FLF.	St Andrews UAS.	
FLG.	L UAS.	
FLH.	Manchester UAS.	
FLI.	Leeds UAS.	
FLJ.	Durham UAS.	
FLK.	Birmingham UAS.	
FLL.	Nottingham UAS.	
FLM.	Bristol UAS.	
FLN.	Swansea UAS.	
FLO.	London UAS.	
FLP.	Southampton UAS.	
FLQ.	Oxford UAS.	
FLR.	Perth UAS.	
FLS.	Wolverhampton UAS.	
FLT.	Derby UAS.	
FLU.	Yatesbury UAS.	
FLV.	Cambridge UAS.	
FMA-FMC.	201 AFS.	
FME-FMG.	202 AFS.	
FMI-FMK.	203 AFS.	
FMO.	204 AFS.	
GA — 16 OTU.	Anson, Lysander, Oxford, Master, Mosquito, Buckmaster.	
GA — 21 Sqn.		
GA — 112 SQN.	Tomahawk, Kittyhawk, Mustang.	
GA — 208 Sqn.	Lysander.	
GB — 105 Sqn.	Battle, Blenheim, Mosquito.	
GB — 166 Sqn.	Heyford, Whitley.	
GC — SF Pershore.		
GD — SF Horsham St Faith	Oxford, Prostor, Mustang.	
GE — 58 Sqn.	Whitley.	
GE — 349 Sqn.	Tomahawk, Spitfire, Tempest.	
GF — 56 OTU/1 TEU.	Hurricane, Typhoon, Tempest.	
GG — 1667 HCU.	Halifax, Lancaster.	
GG — 151 Sqn.	Hurricane.	
GI — 622 Sqn.	Stirling, Lancaster.	
GJ — SF Duxford.		
GK — 162 Sqn.		
GK — 52 OTU.	Spitfire.	
GK — 80 Sqn.	Gladiator.	
GK — 459 Sqn.	Hudson.	
GL — 185 Sqn.	Hampden, Kittyhawk, Anson.	
GL — 14 OTU.	Hereford, Wellington.	
GL — 1529 RATF.	Master, Oxford.	

GM — 42 OTU?	Blenheim, Mosquito.	
GM — 55 Sqn.	Blenheim.	
GN — CBE.	Lancaster, Mosquito.	
GN — 249 Sqn.	Hurricane, Spitfire, Mustang, Mosquito, Tempest.	
GO — 94 Sqn.	Gladiator, Hurricane, Kittyhawk, Spitfire.	
GO — 42 OTU.	Whitley.	
GO — CFE.	Spitfire, Vampire, Tempest.	
GP — 1661 HCU.	Halifax, Lancaster, Stirling, Manchaster.	
GQ — 134 Sqn.	Spitfire, Hurricane, Thunderbolt.	
GQ — SF N.Killingholme.		
GR — 301 Sqn.	Baltimore, Wellington, Warwick, Halifax.	
GR — 64 Sqn.	Blenheim.	
GR — 92 Sqn.	Blenheim, Spitfire.	
GR — 1586 Flt.	Halifax, Liberator.	
GS — 83 OTU.	Wellington, Martinet, Anson.	
GS — 330 Sqn.	Catalina.	
GS — ?	Halifax.	
GT — 156 Sqn.	Wellington, Lancaster.	
GU — 18 Sqn.	Blenheim.	
GV — 134 Sqn.	Hurricane, Spitfire.	
GV — 103 Sqn.	Battle.	
GV — 1652 HCU.	Halifax.	
GW — 340 Sqn.	Spitfire.	
GX — 415 Sqn.	Beaufort, Blenheim, Hampden.	
GX — SF Broadwell.		
GY — 1383 TSCU.	Halifax, Wellington, Dakota.	
GZ — 12 Sqn.	Lancaster.	
GZ — 32 Sqn.	Hurricane, Spitfire.	
G2 — 19 Gp CF.	Anson, Proctor.	
G4 — SF Skellingthorpe.		
G5 — 190 Sqn.	Stirling, Halifax.	
G6 — MCCS	Anson.	
G7 — BCFU.	Lancaster.	
G8 — SF Wing.		
G9 — 430 Sqn.	Spitfire.	
3G — 111 OTU.	Halifax, Mitchell, Liberator.	
5G — 299 Sqn.	Stirling, Ventura.	
6G — 223 Sqn.	Liberator, Fortress.	
7G — SF Northolt.		
HA — 218 Sqn.	Battle, Blenheim, Wellington, Stirling, Lancaster.	
HA — 261 Sqn.	Hurricane.	
HB — 229 Sqn.	Hurricane, Spitfire.	
HB — 239 Sqn.	Lysander, Tomahawk, Hurricane, Mustang, Mosquito, Beaufighter, Oxford, Gladiator.	
HC — 241 Sqn.	Dakota.	
HC — ?	Proctor.	
HC — 512 Sqn.	Dakota, Anson.	
HD — 466 Sqn.	Wellington, Halifax.	
HD — 38 Sqn.	Wellington.	
HE — 605 Sqn.	Gladiator.	
HE — 263 Sqn.	Hurricane, Whirlwind, Typhoon, Meteor.	
HF — 183 Sqn.	Hurricane, Typhoon, Tempest.	
HF — 54 Sqn.	Tempest, Vampire.	
HG — 322 Sqn.	Spitfire.	
HH — 321 Sqn.	Catalina.	
HH — 273 Sqn.	Vildebeest.	

HH — 175 Sqn.   Hurricane, Typhoon.
HI — 66 Sqn.   Meteor.
HI — 63 OTU.
HJ — 100 Sqn?   Vildebeest.
HK — 269 Sqn.   Warwick.
HK — FLS.   Spitfire, Hurricane.
HL — SF Gransden Lodge.
HL — 26 Sqn.   Lysander.
HM — 216 Sqn.   Dakota.
HM — 136 Sqn.   Hurricane.
HM — 1677 TTF.   Martinet.
HN — 20 Sqn.   Audax, Lysander, Hurricane,
                             Spitfire.
HN — 93 Sqn.   Havoc, Spitfire.
HO — 143 Sqn.   Beaufighter, Blenheim.
HO — ?   Hurricane.
HP — 247 Sqn.   Gladiator, Hurricane.
HP — GRU.   Hurricane, Henley, Spitfire,
                             Defiant, Wallace, Battle,
                             Wellington.
HP — SF Full Sutton.
HQ — 56 OTU.   Typhoon, Tempest, Hurricane.
HR — 304 Sqn?   Wellington.
HR — NEFS Flt.
HS — 260 Sqn.   Hurricane, Kittyhawk, Tomahawk,
                             Mustang.
HS — 109 Sqn.   Anson, Wellington, Mosquito,
                             Lancaster.
HS — 192 Sqn.   Whitley.
HT — 154 Sqn.   Spitfire.
HT — 601 Sqn.   Spitfire.
HU — 220 Sqn.   Anson.
HU — 406 Sqn.   Blenheim, Beaufighter, Mosquito.
HV — 73 Sqn.   Hurricane.
HV — 8 Sqn.   Vincent, Blenheim.
HV — SF East Kirkby.
HW — 100 Sqn.   Lancaster, Lincoln.
HX — 41 OTU.
HX — 61 OTU.   Spitfire, Master, Havoc, Mustang.
HX — 203 AFS   Spitfire, Meteor.
HX — 226 OCU.   Meteor, Vampire.
HY — 88 Sqn.   Battle.
HY — 342 Sqn?
HZ — 44 Gp CF.   Hurricane.

H3 — 111 OTU.   Halifax, Liberator.
H4 — 1653 HCU.   Lancaster, Stirling.
H7 — 346 Sqn.   Halifax.
H9 — SF Shepherds Grove. Oxford.

2H — SF Brawdy.
3H — 80 OTU.   Spitfire.
4H — 142 Sqn.   Mosquito.
5H — SF Chivenor.   Beaufighter.
6H — 96 Sqn.   Halifax.
6H — 1688 BDTF.   Hurricane, Spitfire, Oxford, Tiger
                          Moth.
7H — 84 Gp CF.   Proctor.
8H — 8 Gp CF.

IA — SF Syerston.   Wellington.
IB — Glider pick-up Flt   Dakota.
IB — 43 Gp CF.   Anson.

IC — 623 Sqn.   Stirling.
IC — SF Scampton.   Anson, Oxford.
IF — 84 OTU.   Wellington, Anson.
IG — 1668 HCU.   Halifax.
II — 59 OTU.   Hurricane, Typhoon.
II — 116 Sqn.   Lysander, Anson, Hurricane,
                           Oxford.
IJ — ?   Blenheim.
IK — BCIS.   Lancaster, Halifax.
IL — 115 Sqn.   Lancaster.
IL — 195 Sqn?   Lancaster.
IM — 90 Sqn.
IN — SF Valley.   Wellington.
IO — 41 OTU.   Tomahawk, Mustang, Master,
                           Spitfire.
IP — BCIS.   Spitfire.
IP — 434 Sqn.   Halifax.
IQ — 150 Sqn.   Lancaster.
IT — ?   Mosquito.
IV — SF Upper Heyford.   Anson.
IW — SF Chilbolton.
IY — SF Dunsfold.

I2 — 48 Sqn.   Dakota.
I4 — 567 Sqn.   Vengeance, Martinet, Oxford,
                           Hurricane, Defiant, Spitfire,
                           Wellington, Tiger Moth.
15 — 105 OTU
I5 — 1381 TSCU.   Wellington, Dakota.
I6 — 32 MU CF.
I8 — 440 Sqn.   Typhoon, Hurricane.
I9 — 575 Sqn.   Dakota, Anson.

2I — 443 Sqn.   Spitfire.
5I — SF Benson.   Anson, Proctor.
7I — SF Acklington.
8I — APS Spilsby.   Mosquito, Master, Martinet,
                           Spitfire, Mustang.
9I — 326 Sqn.   Spitfire.

JA — 1652 HCU.   Halifax.
JB — 81 OTU.   Spitfire, Whitley, Anson.
JB — 1380 TSCU.   Anson.
JC — 11 Gp CF.   Oxford.
JD — SF Grimsetter.
JE — 195 Sqn.   Typhoon, Lancaster.
JE — 610 Sqn.   Hind.
JF — 3 Sqn.   Tempest.
JF — 1654 HCU.   Lancaster, Stirling.
JG — 17 OTU.   Wellington, Spitfire, Blenheim,
                           Anson.
JH — 203 AFS.   Spitfire.
JH — 317 Sqn.   Hurricane, Spitfire.
JH — 74 Sqn.   Spitfire.
JI — 514 Sqn.   Lancaster.
JJ — 274 Sqn.   Spitfire, Tempest.
JL — 10 OTU.   Whitley.
JM — 20 OTU.   Wellington.
JN — 75 Sqn.   Stirling, Lancaster.
JN — 30 Sqn.   Dakota, Valetta.
JN — 90 Sqn.   Lancaster.
JN — 150 Sqn.   Wellington, Battle.
JO — 463 Sqn.   Lancaster.
JO — ?   Spitfire.

JP — 21 Sqn.	Blenheim.	
JP — 12 OTU.		
JP — 60 OTU/132 OTU.	Defiant, Blenheim.	
JQ — 2 AACU.	Battle, Hector, Roc.	
JQ — SF Breighton.		
JR — 161 Sqn.	Lysander.	
JR — 1654 HCU.	Halifax.	
JS — 16 OTU.	Wellington, Hampden, Mosquito.	
JT — 256 Sqn.	Defiant, Beaufighter, Mosquito.	
JO — 62 Sqn.	Blenheim.	
JU — 111 Sqn.	Hurricane, Spitfire.	
JU — 202 Sqn.	London.	
JV — 6 Sqn.	Hurricane, Spitfire, Tempest.	
JV — SF Finningley.	Oxford.	
JW — CFE.	Spitfire.	
JW — 44 Sqn.	Blenheim, Hampden, Anson.	
JX — 1 Sqn.	Hurricane, Typhoon, Spitfire, Meteor, Oxford.	
JY — 10 OTU.		
JZ — 57 OTU.	Spitfire.	
J5 — 3 Sqn.	Tempest, Vampire.	
J6 — 1521 RATF.	Oxford.	
J7 — 8 MU.		
J8 — 24 MU.		
J9 — 1668 HCU.	Lancaster.	
3J — 13 MU.	Oxford, Tiger Moth, Halifax, Dakota.	
4J — 5 MU.		
5J — 126 Sqn.	Spitfire, Mustang.	
6J — 34 Sqn.	Spitfire, Mustang.	
8J — 435 Sqn.		
9J — 227 Sqn.	Lancaster.	
JAM — 511 Sqn?	Hastings.	
KA — 1661 HCU.	Mosquito.	
KA — 2 Sqn.	Lysander.	
KA — 9 Sqn.	Wellington.	
KA — 82 OTU.	Wellington, Hurricane, Martinet.	
KB — 142 Sqn.	Battle.	
KB — 1661 HCU.	Halifax, Lancaster.	
KC — 238 Sqn.	Hurricane, Spitfire.	
KC — 617 Sqn.	Lancaster, Lincoln.	
KD — 30 OTU.	Wellington, Moth Minor.	
KD — 226 OCU.	Meteor.	
KE — MSFU.	Hurricane.	
KE — BLEU.	Dominie, Proctor.	
KF — 1661 HCU.	Halifax, Lancaster.	
KG — 204 Sqn.	Sunderland.	
KG — 3 OTU.	Whitley, Anson, Blenheim, Beaufort.	
KG — 81 OTU.	Whitley.	
KG — 1380 TSCU.	Wellington.	
KH — 11 OTU?	Hurricane.	
KH — 403 Sqn.	Tomahawk, Spitfire.	
KI — SF Coningsby.	Oxford.	
KJ — 11 OTU.	Wellington, Master, Martinet, Anson.	
KJ — 16 Sqn.	Lysander.	
KK — 15 OTU.	Wellington, Anson.	
KK — 1477 Flt.	Catalina, Mosquito.	

KK — 333 Sqn.	Catalina, Mosquito.	
KL — 54 Sqn.	Spitfire.	
KL — 269 Sqn.	Anson.	
KM — 44 Sqn.	Hampden, Lancaster, Lincoln, Washington.	
KM — 205 Sqn.	Singapore.	
KN — 77 Sqn.	Whitley, Halifax, Dakota.	
KO — 2 Sqn.	Lysander, Tomahawk.	
KO — 115 Sqn.	Wellington, Lancaster, Lincoln.	
KP — 226 Sqn.	Battle.	
KP — 409 Sqn RCAF.	Defiant, Beaufighter, Mosquito.	
KQ — 13 OTU.	Blenheim, Boston, Mosquito, Mitchell.	
KQ — 502 Sqn.	Hind, Anson.	
KR — 61 OTU.	Spitfire, Mustang, Harvard, Master.	
KR — 1667 HCU.	Lancaster.	
KR — 226 OCU.	Vampire, Meteor.	
KS — SF Tarrant Rushton.		
KT — 32 Sqn?	Hurricane.	
KU — 47 Sqn.	Wellington, Beaufort, Mosquito.	
KW — 425 Sqn RCAF.	Wellington, Halifax, Lancaster.	
KW — 615 Sqn.	Gladiator, Hurricane, Spitfire, Thunderbolt.	
KW — 267 Sqn.	Anson, Lysander, Hudson, Lodestar.	
KX — 311 Sqn.	Wellington.	
KX — 529 Sqn.	C30a, Hoverfly, Hornet Moth.	
KY — 242 Sqn.		
KZ — 287 Sqn.	Lysander, Hurricane, Tempest, Oxford, Defiant, Beaufighter, Spitfire, Martinet.	
K2 — 2 Gp CF.	Anson.	
K5 — SF Pocklington.		
K7 — 6 OTU.	Warwick, Mosquito, Lancaster, Hurricane, Beaufighter.	
K7 — 236 OCU.	Lancaster.	
K8 — SF Wymeswold.		
K9 — SF Tain.		
1K — BCIS.	Halifax, Lancaster.	
2K — 1 BDTU	Spitfire, Beaufighter.	
2K — 1668 HCU.	Lancaster, Halifax.	
3K — 1695 BDTF?	Hurricane, Spitfire.	
4K — SF West Malling.	Oxford, Meteor, Mosquito.	
5K — 39 MU.	Anson, Tiger Moth.	
7K — (A)SR TU	Sea Otter, Walrus, Catalina.	
8K — 571 Sqn.	Mosquito.	
9K — 1 TTU.	Beaufighter, Oxford.	
LA — 235 Sqn.	Blenheim, Beaufighter, Mosquito.	
LA — 607 Sqn.	Spitfire, Harvard, Vampire.	
LB — 34 Sqn.	Blenheim.	
LB — 20 OTU.	Wellington.	
LC — SF Feltwell.		
LD — 108 Sqn.	Blenheim, Anson.	
LD — 117 Sqn.	Hudson.	
LD — 216 Sqn.		
LD — 250 Sqn.	Tomahawk, Hurricane, Kittyhawk, Mustang.	
LE — 242 Sqn.	Hurricane, Spitfire.	
LE — 630 Sqn.	Lancaster.	
LE — 40 Sqn.	York.	

LF — 37 Sqn.	Wellington, Liberator.	
LF — SF Predannack.		
LG — 215 Sqn.	Wellington, Anson.	
LG — 13 Gp CF.		
LJ — 211 Sqn.	Hind, Blenheim.	
LJ — 614 Sqn.	Audax, Hind, Lysander.	
LJ — 600 Sqn.	Meteor.	
LK — 87 Sqn.	Hurricane, Spitfire.	
LK — 578 Sqn.	Halifax, Mosquito.	
LL — 1513 RATF.	Oxford, Anson.	
LM — SF Elsham Wolds.		
LN — 99 Sqn.	Wellington.	
LN — ?	Spitfire.	
LN — 83 Gp CF.		
LN — ?	Blenheim.	
LO — 602 Sqn.	Spitfire, Harvard, Vampire, Meteor.	
LP — 8 OTU.	Spitfire, Mosquito, Maryland.	
LP — 237 OCU.	Oxford, Spitfire, Mosquito, Meteor.	
LP — 283 Sqn .	Warwick.	
LQ — 117 Sqn.	Hudson.	
LQ — 405 Sqn.	Halifax, Lancaster, Wellington.	
LR — 56 Sqn.	Hurricane.	
LR — 146 Sqn.	Hurricane.	
LR — 1667 HCU.	Lancaster, Halifax.	
LS — 15 Sqn.	Battle, Blenheim, Wellington, Stirling, Lancaster, Lincoln, Washington.	
LS — 61 Sqn.	Blenheim, Hampden.	
LT — 7 Sqn.	Whitley, Anson.	
LT — 22 OTU.	Wellington, Martinet.	
LU — MSFU.	Hurricane.	
LU — 101 Sqn.	Blenheim.	
LV — 57 OTU.	Spitfire, Master.	
LW — 607 Sqn.	Gauntlet, Gladiator.	
LW — Signals Wing.	Blenheim, Hornet Moth.	
LW — 318 Sqn.	Spitfire.	
LX — 225 Sqn.	Lysander.	
LX — 54 OTU.	Beaufighter, Mosquito.	
LY — 14 Sqn.	Blenheim.	
LY — 149 Sqn.	Wellington.	
LY — PDU/ 1 PRU.	Spitfire, Mosquito, Wellington, Hudson, Anson, Blenheim.	
LZ — 421 Flt/ 66 Sqn.	Spitfire, Hurricane.	
L4 — 27 MU.		
L5 — 297 Sqn.	Tiger Moth, Whitley, Halifax.	
L6 — 1669 HCU.	Halifax, Lancaster.	
L7 — 271 Sqn.	Dakota.	
L8 — 347 Sqn.	Halifax.	
L9 — 190 Sqn.	Stirling, Halifax.	
2L — 9 MU.		
3L — 584 TU?		
4L — SF Melton Mowbray.		
5L — 187 Sqn.	Dakota.	
8L — 92 Sqn.	Meteor.	
MA — 161 Sqn.	Lysander, Albemarle, Havoc, Hudson, Halifax.	
MB — 52 Sqn.	Battle, Anson.	
MB — 51 Sqn.	Whitley.	
MB — 236 Sqn.	Beaufighter.	

MB — 220 Sqn.	Fortress.
MC — SF Fiskerton.	
MD — 526 Sqn.	Blenheim, Oxford, Dominie.
MD — 133 Sqn.	Spitfire.
MD — 458 Sqn.	Wellington.
ME — 280 Sqn.	Warwick.
ME — 488 Sqn.	Beaufighter, Mosquito.
MF — FLS/CFE.	Typhoon, Tempest.
MF — 108 Sqn.	Blenheim, Anson.
MF — 260 Sqn.	Hurricane.
MF — 280 Sqn.	Anson.
MG — 7 Sqn.	Stirling, Lancaster, Anson.
MH — 51 Sqn.	Whitley, Halifax, York.
MJ — 1680 Flt.	Anson, Dominie, Dakota.
MK — 500 Sqn.	Anson, Blenheim, Hudson.
MK — 20 OTU.	Anson.
MK — 126 Sqn.	Spitfire.
ML — 132 OTU.	
MN — 350 Sqn.	Spitfire.
MN — 1665 HCU.	Stirling.
MP — 76 Sqn.	Halifax, Dakota, Anson.
MQ — 226 Sqn.	Battle, Blenheim, Boston, Mitchell.
MR — 5 Sqn.	Audax.
MR — 97 Sqn.	Heyford, Whitley, Anson.
MR — 245 Sqn.	Hurricane, Typhoon.
MS — 23 Sqn.	Hart, Demon, Blenheim.
MS — 273 Sqn.	Hurricane, Spitfire.
MS — SF Linton on Ouse.	Hornet, Mosquito.
MT — 122 Sqn.	Spitfire, Mustang.
MT — 105 Sqn.	Battle.
MT — 126 Sqn.	Spitfire.
MU — 60 Sqn.	Blenheim, Hurricane, Thunderbolt.
MV — 600 Sqn.	Blenheim.
MV — 278 Sqn.	Sea Otter.
MV — 53 OTU.	
MW — 217 Sqn.	Anson, Beaufort.
MW — 101 Sqn.	Halifax.
MW — 1641 Flt.	
MX — 1653 CU.	Liberator.
MX — SF Glatton.	
MY — 278 Sqn.	Anson, Lysander, Walrus, Defiant, Sea Otter, Spitfire.
MZ — 83 OTU.	Wellington.
MZ — 299 Sqn.	
M2 — 33 MU.	
M4 — 587 Sqn.	Spitfire, Oxford, Harvard, Hurricane, Martinet, Vengeance.
M5 — 128 Sqn.	Mosquito.
M6 — 83 Gp CF.	Anson.
M7 — 41 Gp CF.	Tutor.
M8 — 4 Gp CF.	
M9 — 1653 HCU.	Lancaster.
2M — 520 Sqn.	Halifax, Martinet.
3M — 679 Sqn.	Martinet, Hurricane.
3M — 48 Gp CF.	
4M — 695 Sqn.	Hurricane, Henley, Oxford, Martinet, Spitfire, Beaufighter, Harvard, Vengeance.
7M — 1 PTS.	
8M — 266 Sqn.	
9M — 1690 BDTF.	Hurricane, Martinet.

MOHA — 297 Sqn.	Halifax.	
MOHC — 113 Sqn.	Halifax.	
MOHC — 620 Sqn.	Halifax.	
MOHD — 47 Sqn.	Halifax.	
MOHD — 644 Sqn.	Halifax.	
NA — 1 Sqn.	Hurricane.	
NA — 146 Sqn.	Hurricane, Thunderbolt.	
NA — 408 Sqn.	Lancaster?	
NA — 428 Sqn.	Wellington, Halifax, Lancaster.	
NB — FCCS.		
NC — 4 Sqn.	Mosquito.	
ND — 236 Sqn.	Blenheim, Beaufighter.	
ND — 1666 HCU.	Halifax, Lancaster.	
NE — 143 Sqn.	Beaufighter, Mosquito.	
NE — 63 Sqn.	Battle, Anson.	
NF — 138 Sqn.	Whitley, Halifax, Lancaster, Oxford, Lincoln.	
NF — 488 Sqn.	Buffalo.	
NG — 604 Sqn.	Blenheim, Beaufighter, Mosquito, Spitfire, Vampire.	
NG — 2 BANS.	Anson.	
NH — 274 Sqn.		
NH — 38 Sqn.	Wellington.	
NH — 119 Sqn.	Albacore.	
NH — 530 Sqn.	Boston, Havoc.	
NI — 451 Sqn.	Spitfire.	
NI — 6 Sqn.	Anson.	
NJ — MSFU.	Hurricane.	
NJ — 207 Sqn.	Battle, Anson.	
NK — 100 Sqn.	Beaufort, Vildebeest.	
NK — 118 Sqn.	Spitfire, Mustang.	
NL — 341 Sqn.	Spitfire.	
NM — 76 Sqn.	Wellington, Anson.	
NM — 230 Sqn.	Sunderland.	
NM — 268 Sqn.	Lysander, Tomahawk, Mustang.	
NN — 310 Sqn.	Hurricane, Spitfire.	
NO — 320 Sqn.	Hudson, Mitchell, Anson.	
NO — 85 Sqn.	Hurricane.	
NP — 158 Sqn.	Wellington, Halifax.	
NQ — 43 Sqn.	Hurricane.	
NQ — 24 Sqn.	Wellington, Dakota.	
NR — 220 Sqn.	Hudson, Fortress, Anson.	
NR — 605 Sqn.	Vampire.	
NS — 201 Sqn.	Sunderland.	
NS — 52 OTU.	Spitfire, Martinet.	
NT — 203 Sqn.	Singapore.	
NT — 29 OTU.	Wellington, Anson.	
NU — 1382 TCU.	Dakota.	
NU — 240 OCU.	Dakota, Devon, Valetta, Anson.	
NU — 242 OCU	Valetta.	
NV — BLEU.		
NV — 79 Sqn.	Hurricane, Thunderbolt.	
NV — 144 Sqn.	Hampden.	
NW — 33 Sqn.	Gladiator, Hurricane.	
NW — 286 Sqn.	Defiant, Oxford, Hurricane, Master.	
NX — 131 Sqn.	Spitfire, Thunderbolt.	
NX — CFE.	Master, Martinet.	
NY — 1665 HCU.	Stirling.	
NZ — 304 Sqn.	Wellington.	
N7 — SF Lyneham.		
N8 — SF Waterbeach.		

N9 — SF Blackbushe.		
2N — SF Foulsham.	Spitfire.	
5N — 38 Gp CF.		
7N — SFU.	Anson, Wellington, Beaufighter.	
9N — 127 Sqn.	Spitfire.	
OA — 22 Sqn.	Beaufort, Vildebeest.	
OA — 342 Sqn.	Boston, Mitchell.	
OB — 45 Sqn.	Blenheim, Vengeance, Buckingham, Brigand, Hornet.	
OB — 53 OTU.	Spitfire.	
OC — SF Sandtoft.		
OD — 80 Sqn.		
OD — 6 OTU.	Hudson.	
OD — 56 OTU.	Typhoon, Tempest.	
OE — 36 Sqn.	Vildebeest.	
OE — 168 Sqn.	Tomahawk, Mustang.	
OE — 661 Sqn.	Auster.	
OE — 98 Sqn.	Battle.	
OF — 97 Sqn.	Whitley, Manchester, Lancaster, Lincoln, Anson.	
OG — 1665 HCU.	Halifax, Stirling.	
OG — 172 Sqn.	Wellintgon.	
OG — 1332 HTCU.	Halifax.	
OG — 1651 HCU	Stirling.	
OH — 120 Sqn.	Liberator.	
OI — 2 Sqn.	Spitfire.	
OJ — 149 Sqn.	Wellington, Stirling, Lancaster, Lincoln, Washington.	
OK — 450 Sqn.	Hurricane, Kittyhawk.	
OK — 1674 HCU.	Halifax, Anson.	
OK — 3 GRS.		
OL — 83 Sqn.	Hampden, Manchester, Lancaster, Lincoln.	
OM — 11 Sqn.	Mosquito.	
OM — 107 Sqn.	Blenheim, Boston, Mosquito.	
ON — 56 Sqn.	Meteor.	
ON — 63 Sqn.	Battle, Anson.	
ON — 124 Sqn.	Spitfire, Meteor, Tiger Moth.	
OO — 13 Sqn.	Blenheim, Lysander.	
OO — 1663 HCU.	Halifax.	
OP — 3 Sqn.	Gladiator, Hurricane.	
OP — 11 OTU.	Wellington.	
OP — 32 OTU.		
OQ — 5 Sqn.	Hart, Tempest, Thunderbolt.	
OQ — 52 OTU/FLS.	Spitfire.	
OR — BBDU.	Halifax, Lancaster.	
OS — 279 Sqn.	Hudson.	
OS — 528 Sqn.	Blenheim.	
OS — SF Sturgate.		
OT — 58 Sqn.	Anson, Mosquito.	
OT — 1 BDU.	Halifax.	
OT — 540 Sqn.		
OU — 485 Sqn RNZAF.	Spitfire, Typhoon, Tempest.	
OV — 197 Sqn.	Typhoon.	
OW — 426 Sqn RCAF.	Wellington, Lancaster, Halifax, Liberator.	
OX — 40 Sqn.	Battle.	
OX — 22 OTU.	Wellington.	
OX — ORTU.	Halifax.	
OY — 48 Sqn.	Beaufort, Anson, Hudson.	

OY — 13 OTU.	Mosquito.	
OY — 11 Sqn.	Hart, Blenheim.	
OZ — 82 Sqn.	Blenheim.	
OZ — 179 Sqn	Warwick, Lancaster.	
OZ — 219 Sqn.	Lancaster.	
O3 — BCDU.		
O5 — BSDU.	Mosquito.	
O6 — 298 Sqn.	Halifax.	
O8 — SF Merryfield.	Anson.	
O9 — S & FCS.		
2O — 84 Gp CS.		
3O — SF Wratting Common.		
5O — 521 Sqn.	Hurricane, Halifax, Fortress.	
6O — 582 Sqn.	Lancaster.	
8O — BAFO Comms Wg.		
9O — 44 MU.		
OAA — 437 Sqn.	Anson.	
OAA — 24 Sqn.	Anson.	
OAF — 147 Sqn.	Anson.	
PA — 55 OTU/3 TEU.	Hurricane, Typhoon.	
PB — 26 OTU.	Wellington.	
PB — ?	Auster.	
PB — 10 Sqn.	Whitley.	
PD — 87 Sqn.	Hurricane.	
PD — 450 Sqn.	Hurricane.	
PD — 303 Sqn.	Mustang.	
PE — 1662 HCU.	Halifax, Lancaster.	
PF — 51 OTU.	Blenheim.	
PF — 42 OTU/227 OCU.	Auster.	
PG — 608 Sqn.	Anson.	
PG — 619 Sqn.	Lancaster.	
PI — SF Silverstone.		
PH — 12 Sqn.	Battle, Wellington, Lancaster, Lincoln.	
PJ — 59 Sqn.	Hector, Blenheim.	
PJ — 130 Sqn.	Spitfire.	
PK — 220 Sqn.	Anson.	
PK — 315 Sqn.	Spitfire, Mustang.	
PL — 144 Sqn.	Hampden, Beaufighter.	
PM — 20 Sqn.	Lysander.	
PM — 103 Sqn.	Wellington, Halifax, Lancaster.	
PN — 41 Sqn.	Spitfire.	
PN — 252 Sqn.	Blenheim, Beaufighter.	
PN — 1552 RATF.	Oxford.	
PO — 46 Sqn.	Hurricane.	
PO — 467 Sqn.	Lancaster.	
PO — 104 Sqn.	Blenheim, Anson.	
PP — 25 OTU.	Hampden, Wellington.	
PP — 203 Sqn.	Singapore.	
PP — 311 Sqn.	Liberator.	
PQ — 58 OTU.	Spitfire.	
PQ — 206 Sqn.	Liberator.	
PQ — 2 TEU.	Spitfire.	
PR — 609 Sqn.	Spitfire, Typhoon, Harvard.	
PS — 264 Sqn.	Defiant, Mosquito, Oxford.	
PT — 15 FTS	Hart.	
PT — 27 Sqn.	Blenheim.	
PT — 62 Sqn.	Blenheim.	
PT — 420 Sqn.	Hampden, Wellington, Halifax, Lancaster.	
PU — 53 Sqn.	Dakota.	

PU — 187 Sqn.	Dakota, Halifax.	
PV — 275 Sqn.	Walrus, Lysander, Defiant, Anson, Spitfire.	
PW — 224 Sqn.	Anson, Hudson.	
PW — 57 OTU.	Spitfire.	
PX — 295 Sqn.	Whitley.	
PY — 84 Sqn.	Mosquito.	
PY — 1527 RATF.	Oxford.	
PZ — 456 Sqn.	Defiant.	
P2 — SF Marston Moor.	Oxford.	
P3 — 692 Sqn.	Mosquito.	
P4 — 153 Sqn.	Lancaster.	
P5 — 296 Sqn.	Albemarle, Halifax.	
P6 — 489 Sqn.	Beaufighter, Mosquito.	
P6 — SF Banff.		
P7 — 87 Gp CF.	Oxford.	
P8 — 87 Gp CF.	Anson.	
P9 — ASWDU.	Halifax, Wellington, Hoverfly, Anson, Lancaster, Brigand, Tiger Moth, Lincoln, Beaufighter, Proctor, Sea Otter, Mosquito, Sunderland, Warwick,	
P9 — 58 OTU.	Spitfire.	
1P — BCIS.	Halifax.	
2P — 644 Sqn.	Halifax.	
3P — 516 Sqn.	Mosquito.	
8P — 525 Sqn.		
9P — 85 OTU.	Wellington.	
QA — 224 Sqn.	Hudson, Liberator.	
QB — 424 Sqn.	Wellington, Halifax, Lancaster.	
QC — 168 Sqn.	Typhoon.	
QD — 304 Sqn.	Wellington, Warwick, Halifax.	
QD — 654 Sqn.	Auster.	
QE — 12 Sqn.	Battle.	
QE — CFE.	Mustang, Mosquito.	
QF — 97 Sqn.	Battle.	
QF — 1323 AGLT Flt.	Lancaster.	
QF — PFF NTU.	Mosquito, Oxford.	
QG — 53 OTU.	Spitfire.	
QH — ?	Spitfire.	
QI — SF Swanton Morley.		
QJ — 616 Sqn.	Gauntlet, Battle, Spitfire.	
QJ — 92 Sqn.	Spitfire.	
QJ — 613 Sqn.	Spitfire, Vampire.	
QJ — BAFO Comms Wg.		
QK — PTPS.	Spitfire, Dominie.	
QK — 12 APC.	Master, Martinet.	
QL — 413 Sqn.	Catalina.	
QL — 76 Wg?	Blenheim.	
QM — 254 Sqn.	Beaufighter, Mosquito.	
QM — 42 Sqn.	Beaufighter.	
QN — 214 Sqn.	Lancaster, Lincoln.	
QN — 28 OTU.	Wellington, Spitfire.	
QN — 5 Sqn.	Wapiti.	
QO — 432 Sqn.	Wellington, Lancaster, Halifax.	
QO — 3 Sqn.	Hurricane, Typhoon, Tempest.	
QO — 167 Sqn.	Harvard, Anson, Meteor, Valetta.	
QO — 52 Sqn.	Valetta.	
QO — 42 Sqn.	Vildebeest.	
QP — SF Kirmington.		

QQ — 83 Sqn.	Hampden.	
QQ — 321 Sqn.	Catalina.	
QQ — 1651 HCU.	Lancaster, Stirling.	
QR — 15 Sqn.	Lancaster.	
QR — 61 Sqn.	Hampden, Manchester, Lancaster, Lincoln.	
QR — 223 Sqn.	Wellington.	
QS — 620 Sqn.	Stirling, Halifax.	
QT — 142 Sqn.	Battle, Wellington.	
QT — 57 Sqn.	Lancaster, Lincoln, Oxford.	
QU — RAF NI CF.	Hurricane, Anson, Proctor, Oxford.	
QU — 432 Sqn.	Halifax.	
QU — 67 Gp CF.	Anson.	
QV — 19 Sqn.	Spitfire, Mustang, Hornet.	
QW — 1516 RATF.	Oxford.	
QX — 224 Sqn.	Hudson, Liberator.	
QX — 50 Sqn.	Hampden.	
QX — CC CF.		
QY — 254 Sqn.*	Blenheim. (*poss. 235 Sqn.)	
QY — 1666 HCU.	Halifax, Lancaster.	
QY — 452 Sqn.	Spitfire.	
QZ — 4 OTU.		
Q3 — 613 Sqn.	Spitfire, Vampire, Harvard, Meteor.	
Q6 — 1384 TCU.	Oxford.	
Q7 — 29 MU.		
Q8 — BAFO Comms Wg.		
2Q — 88 Gp CF.	Anson.	
4Q — 59 OTU.	Typhoon.	
4Q — CC FATU.	Vengeance, Martinet.	
6Q — SF Pembroke Dock.		
8Q — 34 Sqn.	Beaufighter, Spitfire, Harvard, Vengeance, Oxford, Tiger Moth, Martinet, Hurricane.	
RA — 410 Sqn.	Defiant, Mosquito.	
RA — 100 Sqn.	Vildebeest.	
RB — 66 Sqn.	Spitfire.	
RC — 5 LFS.	Lancaster.	
RD — 67 Sqn.	Buffalo, Spitfire.	
RD — 32 OTU.		
RE — 229 Sqn.	Blenheim, Hurricane.	
RE — CFE.	Tempest.	
RF — 303 Sqn.	Mustang, Hurricane, Spitfire.	
RF — 204 Sqn.	London, Sunderland.	
RF — 1510 ABST Flt.	Anson, Oxford.	
RG — 208 Sqn.	Lysander, Hurricane, Spitfire.	
RG — 1472 DB Flt.	Battle, Tomahawk.	
RG — TC Met Flt.	Spitfire.	
RH — 88 Sqn.	Battle, Blenheim, Boston.	
RJ — SF Thornaby.		
RJ — 46 Sqn.	Gladiator, Hurricane.	
RK — 10 OTU.	Whitley, Wellington, Anson.	
RL — SLAIS	Hurricane, Typhoon.	
RL — 38 Sqn.	Warwick, Lancaster.	
RL — 279 Sqn.	Warwick, Lancaster.	
RL — 603 Sqn.	Gladiator.	
RM — 26 Sqn.	Lysander, Tomahawk, Mustang.	
RN — 72 Sqn.	Spitfire.	
RN — 1674 HCU.	Fortress.	
RO — 29 Sqn.	Blenheim, Beaufighter, Mosquito.	
RP — 288 Sqn.	Hurricane, Spitfire, Oxford, Mosquito.	

RQ — SF Colerne.		
RR — 407 Sqn.	Blenheim, Hudson.	
RR — ?	Warwick.	
RR — 615 Sqn.	Gauntlet, Gladiator.	
RR — SF Filton.		
RS — 157 Sqn.	Mosquito.	
RS — 33 Sqn.	Hurricane, Spitfire.	
RS — 30 Sqn.	Hurricane, Thunderbolt.	
RS — 229 OCU.	Beaufighter, Oxford, Tempest, Vampire, Hunter.	
RT — 8 Sqn.	Mosquito, Tempest.	
RT — 114 Sqn.	Blenheim, Mosquito, Boston.	
RT — 112 Sqn.	Gladiator.	
RU — 414 Sqn RCAF.	Lysander, Tomahawk, Mustang.	
RU — SF Hendon.		
RV — 1659 HCU.	Halifax, Lancaster.	
RW — 36 Sqn.	Wellington.	
RX — 407 Sqn.	Lancaster.	
RX — 456 Sqn.	Beaufighter, Mosquito.	
RX — 25 Sqn.	Blenheim.	
RY — 314 Sqn.	Spitfire.	
RY — 313 Sqn.	Beaufighter, Mosquito.	
RZ — 241 Sqn.	Lysander, Tomahawk, Mustang, Spitfire.	
R2 — PAU.	Queen Bee, Proctor.	
R4 — 18 APC.	Master, Martinet.	
R7 — AEU.		
R8 — 274 MU.		
5R — 33 Sqn.	Spitfire, Typhoon, Tempest, Hornet.	
6R — 41 OTU.		
7R — 524 Sqn.	Wellington.	
9R — 229 Sqn.	Spitfire.	

Most of the following units also operated comms/'hacks' such as Harvards.

RAA — 500 Sqn.	Mosquito, Meteor, Spitfire.	
RAB — 501 Sqn.	Spitfire, Vampire.	
RAC — 502 Sqn.	Spitfire.	
RAD — 504 Sqn.		
RAG — 600 Sqn.		
RAH — 601 Sqn.		
RAI — 602 Sqn.		
RAJ — 603 Sqn.		
RAK — 604 Sqn.		
RAL — 605 Sqn.		
RAN — 607 Sqn.		
RAO — 608 Sqn.		
RAP — 609 Sqn.		
RAQ — 610 Sqn.		
RAR — 611 Sqn.		
RAS — 612 Sqn.		
RAT — 613 Sqn.	Spitfire.	
RAU — 614 Sqn.		
RAV — 615 Sqn.		
RAW — 616 Sqn.	Mosquito, Oxford, Meteor.	

RCA — Reserve Command CF.
RCB/RCC/RCD — 12 RFS.
RCE — 61 Gp CF.
RCF — 62 Gp CF.

RCG — 63 Gp CF.
RCH — 64 Gp CF.
RCI — 66 Gp CF.
RCJ — 17 RFS.
RCK — 3 RFS.
RCL — 14 RFS.
RCM — 1 RFS.
RCN — 4 RFS.
RCO — 6 RFS.
RCP — 7 RFS.
RCQ — 8 RFS.
RCR — 11 RFS.
RCS — 16 RFS.
RCT — 18 RFS.
RCU — 22 RFS.
RCV — 24 RFS.
RCW — 25 RFS.
RCX — 2 RFS.
RCY — 5 RFS.
RCZ — 9 RFS.

ROA — 661 Sqn.	Auster.
ROB — 662 Sqn.	Auster.
ROC — 663 Sqn.	Auster.
ROD — 664 Sqn.	Auster.
ROG — 666 Sqn.	Auster.

RSA — 23 RFS.
RSB — 10 RFS.

RUA — Aberdeen UAS.
RUB — Birmingham UAS.
RUC — Cambridge UAS.
RUD — Durham UAS.
RUE — Edinburgh UAS.
RUG — Glasgow UAS.
RUL — London UAS.
RUM — Manchester UAS.
RUN — Nottingham UAS.
RUO — Oxford UAS.
RUQ — Queens UAS.
RUS — St Andrews UAS.
RUY — Leeds UAS.
RUZ — Southampton UAS.

SA — 486 Sqn.	Hurricane, Typhoon, Tempest.
SA — ?	Whitley.
SB — 464 Sqn.	Ventura, Mosquito.
SC — SF Prestwick.	
SD — 501 Sqn.	Hurricane, Spitfire, Tempest, Harvard, Meteor, Vampire.
SD — 72 Sqn.	Gladiator, Spitfire.
SE — 95 Sqn.	Sunderland.
SE — 431 Sqn.	Wellington, Halifax, Lancaster.
SF — 39 Sqn.	Hart.
SF — 137 Sqn.	Hurricane, Typhoon, Whirlwind.
SG — ?	Whitley.
SG — SF Lincolnshire Fighter Sector.	
SH — 64 Sqn.	Blenheim, Spitfire, Mustang, Hornet.
SH — 216 Sqn.	Valentia, Bombay.
SH — 240 Sqn.	Singapore, London.
SJ — 21 OTU.	Wellington.
SJ — 70 Sqn.	Valentia.

SJ — 244 Sqn.	Valentia.
SK — 165 Sqn.	Spitfire, Mustang.
SL — 13 OTU.	Anson, Havoc, Tempest, Mosquito.
SM — 305 Sqn.	Battle, Wellington, Mitchell, Mosquito.
SN — 243 Sqn.	Spitfire.
SN — 230 OCU.	Lincoln, Oxford.
SO — SF South-east fighter sector.	Oxford.
SP — 400 Sqn.	Lysander, Tomahawk, Mustang.
SP — SF Doncaster.	
SQ — 500 Sqn.	Anson.
SR — 33 Sqn.	Spitfire.
SR — 101 Sqn.	Wellington, Lancaster, Lincoln, Oxford.
SS — 1552 RATF.	Oxford.
ST — 228 OCU	Martinet, Wellington, Blenheim.
ST — 54 OTU.	Beaufort, Beaufighter, Spitfire, Wellington, Hurricane, Anson, Martinet.
SU — SF Turnhouse.	
SV — 1663 HCU.	Halifax.
SV — 218 Sqn.	Battle.
SW — 253 Sqn.	Hurricane, Spitfire.
SW — 43 Sqn.	Meteor.
SW — 1678 HCU.	Lancaster.
SX — 1 CACU	Spitfire.
SX — SF Methwold.	
SY — 467 Sqn.	
SY — 139 Sqn.	Blenheim.
SY — 613 Sqn.	Mustang, Mosquito.
SZ — 316 Sqn.	Hurricane, Spitfire, Mustang.
S6 — MC CS.	Anson.
S7 — 500 Sqn.	Meteor, Harvard.
S8 — 328 Sqn.	Spitfire.
S9 — 16 Gp CF.	Proctor, Dominie, Oxford.
3S — 3 Gp CF.	Proctor, Anson.
4S — CSE/RWE.	Mosquito, Lancaster, Oxford.
5S — 691 Sqn.	Spitfire, Oxford.
6S — 190 Sqn.	Halifax.
7S — 83 GSU	Spitfire, Tempest.
9S — MAEE.	
TA — 4 OTU.	
TA — 358 Sqn.	Wellington, Liberator.
TB — 77 Sqn.	Halifax.
TB — 153 Sqn.	Beaufighter.
TB — 51 Sqn.	Stirling, York.
TC — 170 Sqn.	Lancaster.
TD — 126 Sqn.	Spitfire.
TD — 453 Sqn.	Buffalo.
TD — 82 OTU.	Wellington.
TD — 320 Sqn.	T-8W, Anson?
TE — 53 Sqn.	Blenheim.
TE — 521 Sqn.	Spitfire.
TE — 1401 Flt.	Hurricane.
TE — SF Desborough.	
TF — 29 OTU.	Wellington.
TG — 502 Sqn.	Whitley.
TH — 418 Sqn.	Boston, Mosquito.
TH — 20 Sqn.	Spitfire, Harvard, Tiger Moth, Beaufighter.

TJ — 52 OTU.	Spitfire.	
TJ — 202 Sqn.	Catalina.	
TJ — 272 Sqn.	Beaufighter.	
TK — 149 Sqn.	Lancaster, Stirling.	
TL — 170 Sqn.	Lancaster.	
TL — 35 Sqn.	Halifax, Anson, Lancaster, Lincoln.	
TM — 111 Sqn.	Hurricane.	
TM — 504 Sqn.	Hurricane, Spitfire, Meteor, Harvard.	
TN — 30 OTU.	Wellington.	
TN — 33 Sqn.	Gladiator.	
TO — 61 OTU/228 OCU.	Master, Harvard, Martinet, Tiger Moth.	
TO — 203 AFS.	?	
TO — 228 Sqn.	Stranraer.	
TP — 73 Sqn.	Hurricane, Spitfire.	
TP — 198 Sqn.	Typhoon.	
TQ — 102 Sqn.	Whitley.	
TQ — 202 Sqn.	London, Swordfish, Sunderland.	
TQ — 276 Sqn.	Spitfire.	
TQ — SF Bramcote.		
TR — 59 Sqn.	Blenheim, Hudson, Liberator.	
TR — 265 Sqn.	Catalina.	
TS — 548 Sqn.	Spitfire.	
TS — 657 Sqn.	Auster, Hoverfly, Proctor.	
TT — 1658 HCU.	Halifax, Oxford.	
TU — 1 TTU.	Beaufort.	
TU — SF Dyce.		
TV — 4 Sqn.	Lysander, Mustang.	
TV — 1660 HCU.	Halifax, Lancaster, Manchester, Stirling, Spitfire.	
TW — 90 Sqn.	Blenheim.	
TW — 141 Sqn.	Defiant, Beaufighter, Mosquito.	
TX — 11 OTU.	Anson, Wellington.	
TY — 24 OTU.	Whitley, Wellington, Anson.	
TZ — 310 Sqn.		
T2 — 46 MU.		
T5 — SF Abingdon.		
T6 — SF Melbourn.		
T7 — 650 Sqn.	Martinet.	
T7 — 1614 Flt.	?	
3T SF Acaster Malbis.		
4T — SF Portreath.		
5T — 233 Sqn.	Anson, Dakota.	
6T — 608 Sqn.	Mosquito, Harvard, Spitfire, Mosquito, Oxford.	
7T — 196 Sqn.	Stirling.	
8T — 298 Sqn.	Halifax.	
9T — SFU.	Anson, Hudson.	
TAL — Aldermaston CF.		
TBR — Staff College, Andover.		
TCA — 1 Radio School.	Halifax.	
TCE — SF Carew Cheriton.		
TCN — SF Cranwell.		
TCO — SF Cosford.		
TCR — 1 Radio School.	Anson, Halifax.	
TCW — SF Carew Cheriton.		
TDE — EARS, Debden.	Anson.	
TFA/TWM — 1 SofP.		
TGX — 27 Gp CF.	Anson.	

THA — SF Halton.		
THE — Parachute test Flt, Henlow.		
THI — A&AEE.		
THL — 24 Gp CF.	Anson.	
THO — SF Hornchurch.		
TIH — FPU.		
TLO — SF Locking.		
TML/TMA/TMD/TME — 4 Radio School. Anson.		
TOC — 2 ITS.		
TSA — SF St Athan.		
TSI/TSN — RAF Training (Belgian) School.		
TSM — 4 Radio School.	Anson.	
TSO — 27 Gp CF.	Anson.	
TTE — 22 Gp CF.	Anson.	
TWY — TTC CF.	Anson.	
UA — 269 Sqn.	Anson, Hudson.	
UB — 164/63 Sqn.	Spitfire, Meteor.	
UB — 455 Sqn.	Hampden, Beaufighter.	
UC — 3 ANS.	Anson.	
UD — 452 Sqn.	Spitfire.	
UE — 228 Sqn.	Sunderland.	
UF — 601 Sqn.	Blenheim, Spitfire, Hurricane, Airacobra, Martinet, Oxford.	
UF — 24 OTU.	Wellington, Hurricane.	
UG — 16 Sqn.	Lysander, Mustang, Gladiator.	
UG — 1654 HCU.	Halifax, Manchester, Stirling, Lancaster.	
UH — 21 OTU/202 CTU.	Anson, Wellington, Oxford, Martinet.	
UH — 1654 HCU	Lancaster.	
UH — 1682 Flt.	Spitfire, Hurricane.	
UJ — 27 OTU.	Wellington.	
UK — CFE.	Proctor.	
UL — 576 Sqn.	Lancaster.	
UL — 608 Sqn.	Anson, Botha, Blenheim, Hudson.	
UM — 626 Sqn.	Lancaster.	
UM — 152 Sqn.	Gladiator, Spitfire.	
UM — 21 OTU.	Anson.	
UN — SF Faldingworth.		
UO — 19 OTU.	Whitley, Wellington.	
UO — 266 Sqn.	Spitfire, Typhoon.	
UP — 605 Sqn.	Boston?	
UP — 21 Sqn.	Blenheim.	
UP — 4 Sqn.	Mosquito, Vampire.	
UQ — 211 Sqn.	Blenheim.	
UQ — 1508 Flt.		
UR — 84 Sqn.	Blenheim.	
UR — 13 OTU	Mitchell.	
US — 56 Sqn.	Hurricane, Typhoon, Tempest, Spitfire, Meteor.	
US — 27 Sqn.	Hart, Blenheim.	
US — 28 Sqn.	Audax.	
UT — 17 Sqn.	Spitfire, Beaufighter, Oxford, Harvard.	
UT — 461 Sqn.	Sunderland.	
UT — 51 Sqn.	Whitley.	
UU — 321 Sqn.	Catalina.	
UU — 61 OTU/226 OCU.	Spitire, Mustang, Meteor, Vampire.	
UV — 17 Sqn.	Gauntlet, Hurricane.	
UV — 460 Sqn.	Wellington, Halifax, Lancaster.	
UW — 3 TEU.	Typhoon.	
UW — 55 OTU.	Hurricane.	

UX — 82 Sqn.	Blenheim, Mosquito.
UX — 214 Sqn.	Wellington.
UX — CFE.	Spitfire, Meteor.
UX — 1476 Flt?	Anson.
UY — 10 OTU.	Whitley, Lysander, Master, Martinet, Anson, Spitfire, Wellington.
UZ — 306 Sqn.	Hurricane, Spitfire, Mustang.
U2 — SF Talbenny	
U3 — RWE.	Halifax, Fortress.
U4 — 667 Sqn.	Defiant, Vengeance, Spitfire.
U5 — 51 MU.	
U5 — 3 FP.	Anson.
U6 — 436 Sqn.	Dakota.
U7 — 1697 ADLS Flt.	Anson, Hurricane.
4U — 30 MU.	
6U — 415 Sqn CAF.	Halifax.
7U — SF Bardney.	
8U — SF Ballykelly.	
9U — 644 Sqn.	Halifax.
VA — 84 Sqn.	
VA — 113 Sqn.	Blenheim.
VA — 125 Sqn.	Defiant, Beaufighter, Mosquito.
VA — 264 Sqn.	Mosquito.
VB — 14 OTU.	Wellington, Anson.
VB — 334 Sqn.	Mosquito.
VE — 110 Sqn.	Blenheim, Mosquito.
VE — SF Kirton-in-Lindsey.	
VF — SF Lindholme.	Oxford.
VF — 99 Sqn.	Wellington.
VG — 285 Sqn.	Oxford, Defiant, Martinet, Anson.
VG — 286 Sqn.	Oxford.
VG — 210 Sqn.	Sunderland.
VH — ?	Hudson.
VI — 169 Sqn.	Mosquito.
VJ — ?	Wellington.
VK — 85 Gp CF.	Anson.
VK — 238 Sqn.	Hurricane.
VL — 167 Sqn.	Spitfire.
VL — 322 Sqn.	Spitfire.
VM — 231 Sqn.	Lysander.
VM — 243 Sqn.	Dakota.
VM — 1561 Flt.	
VN — 50 Sqn.	Hampden, Manchester, Lancaster, Lincoln.
VO — 98 Sqn.	Mitchell, Mosquito.
VP — SF Exeter.	Dominie.
VP — ?	Dakota.
VQ — 201 Sqn.	London.
VQ — 28 OTU?*	Wellington, Martinet, Lysander (*poss. 18 OTU).
VR — 22 Sqn.	Vildebeest.
VR — 419 Sqn.	Wellington, Halifax, Lancaster.
VS — MCS/31 Sqn.	Anson, Proctor.
VT — 30 Sqn?	Blenheim.
VT — 1556 RATF.	
VT — 216 Sqn.	Valentia.
VU — 246 Sqn.	York.
VU — 36 Sqn.	Vildebeest.
VV — SF Sumburgh.	Mosquito.
VV — 235 Sqn.	Mosquito.

VW — ?	Anson.
VW — SF Chedburgh.	
VX — 206 Sqn.	Anson, Hudson, Fortress.
VY — 85 Sqn.	Hurricane, Havoc, Mosquito.
VZ — 42 Sqn.	Spitfire.
V2 — ? 18 Gp CF	Anson.
V4 — 6 MU.	Dominie.
V6 — 615 Sqn.	Spitfire, Harvard, Meteor.
V7 — RWE.	Halifax, Anson, Lancaster.
V7 — CSE.	Anson.
V8 — 570 Sqn.	Albemarle, Stirling.
V9 — 502 Sqn.	
V9 — ?	Martinet.
2V — 547 Sqn.	
2V — 18 Gp CF.	Anson.
3V — 1 Gp CF.	Anson, Proctor.
4V — 302 FTU.	
5V — 439 Sqn RCAF.	Hurricane, Typhoon.
6V — SF Cottesmore.	
8V — 60 OTU.	
WA — ?	Whitley.
WA — SF Manorbier.	
WB — BCIS.	Lancaster, Lincoln.
WB — CSE.	Lancaster.
WC — 309 Sqn.	Hurricane, Mustang.
WD — 206 Sqn.	Anson.
WD — SF Leeming.	
WE — 18 OTU?	
WE — 23 OTU.	Wellington.
WE — 59 Sqn.	Liberator.
WF — 525 Sqn.	Dakota.
WF — 238 Sqn.	Dakota.
WG — 26 OTU.	Wellington, Hurricane.
WH — 330 Sqn.	Sunderland.
WH — APS Acklington.	
WI — 69 Sqn.	Mosquito.
WJ — 17 OTU.	Blenheim, Anson, Wellington.
WK — 81 Sqn.	Tiger Moth.
WK — 1316 Flt.	
WK — 135 Sqn.	Thunderbolt.
WL — 612 Sqn.	Anson, Whitley, Wellington.
WL — 434 Sqn.	Halifax, Lancaster.
WL — SF Celle.	Vampire.
WM — 68 Sqn.	Beaufighter, Mosquito.
WN — 172 Sqn.	Wellington.
WN — 527 Sqn.	Blenheim, Hurricane, Spitfire, Oxford, Wellington.
WO — 90 Sqn.	Fortress.
WP — 90 Sqn.	Fortress, Stirling, Lancaster, Lincoln, Washington.
WP — 89 Sqn.	Beaufighter.
WP — 243 Sqn.	Buffalo.
WQ — 209 Sqn.	Stranraer, Lerwick, Catalina.
WQ — 12 Gp CF.	Anson, Oxford, Proctor, Spitfire.
WQ — 604 Sqn.	Blenheim.
WR — 248 Sqn.	Blenheim, Mosquito.
WR — SF Moreton-in-the-Marsh.	
WS — 9 Sqn.	Wellington, Lancaster.
WT — 35 Sqn.	Battle, Anson.
WT — SF Stornoway.	
WU — 225 Sqn.	Spitfire.

WV — 18 Sqn.	Blenheim, Mosquito.	
WW — 1382 TSCU.		
WX — 302 Sqn.	Spitfire.	
WY — 541 Sqn.	Spitfire, Meteor, Harvard.	
WY — 28 OTU.	Master, Wellington.	
WZ — SF Graveley.		
WZ — 19 Sqn.	Spitfire.	
W2 — 80 Sqn.	Spitfire, Tempest, Hornet.	
W3 — 322 Sqn.	Spitfire. (or 3W?)	
W3 — SF Coningsby.	Oxford.	
W3 — SF Hemswell.		
W4 — Glider pick-up flight.		
W5 — SF Castle Camps.		
W6 — 18 MU.		
W9 — 24 MU.		
2W — 3 GRS.	Anson.	
3W — 322 Sqn?		
3W — ?	Spitfire.	
5W — SF Snaith.		
8W — 612 Sqn.	Wellington, Spitfire, Vampire, Meteor.	
9W — 296 Sqn.	Halifax, Albemarle.	
XA — SF Essex sector.		
XA — 489 Sqn.	Hampden, Blenheim.	
XB — 58 OTU.	Spitfire.	
XB — 224 Sqn.	Liberator, Lancaster, Halifax.	
XB — 2 TEU.	Spitfire.	
XB — 457 Sqn.	Spitfire.	
XC — 26 Sqn.	Mustang, Spitfire, Tempest, Vampire.	
XD — 139 Sqn.	Blenheim, Mosquito.	
XD — 13 OTU.	Boston.	
XE — 6 Sqn.	Hardy.	
XE — 123 Sqn.	Spitfire, Thunderbolt.	
XE — CBE.		
XF — 19 OTU.	Whitley, Anson, Lysander, Martinet, Defiant, Hurricane, Wellington.	
XG — 16 OTU.	Wellington.	
XH — 218 Sqn.	Lancaster.	
XH — 295 Sqn.	Whitley.	
XJ — 13 OTU.		
XJ — 261 Sqn.	Hurricane.	
XK — 46 Sqn.	Stirling, Dakota.	
XK — 272 Sqn.	Blenheim.	
XL — 20 OTU.	Wellington.	
XL — 1335 CU/226 OCU.		
XM — 182 Sqn.	Hurricane, Typhoon.	
XM — 652 Sqn.		
XN — 22 OTU.	Anson, Wellington.	
XO — 112 Sqn.	Gladiator.	
XP — 174 Sqn.	Hurricane, Typhoon.	
XQ — 64 Sqn.	Blenheim.	
XQ — 86 Sqn.	Liberator.	
XR — 71 Sqn.	Hurricane, Spitfire.	
XR — 2 Gp CF.		
XS — 106 Sqn.	Anson, Hampden.	
XT — 603 Sqn.	Spitfire.	
XT — 1657 HCU.	Stirling.	
XU — 49 Sqn.	Hampden.	
XU — 7 Sqn.	Stirling.	

XV — 2 Sqn.	Mustang.	
XW — 18 OTU.	Anson, Defiant, Wellington, Martinet..	
XY — 90/186 Sqn.	Lancaster.	
XZ — 39 Sqn.	Blenheim.	
X2 — SF Stoney Cross.		
X3 — 111 OTU.	Halifax, Liberator, Wellington.	
X6 — 290 Sqn.	Spitfire, Martinet.	
X8 — 6 Gp CF.	Anson, Oxford.	
X9 — 517 Sqn.	Halifax.	
X9 — 299 Sqn.	Halifax, Stirling.	
2X — 85 OTU.	Master, Martinet.	
3X — 38 MU.		
4X — 230 Sqn.	Sunderland, Sea Otter.	
4X — 1692 Flt.	Mosquito.	
7X — SF Aldergrove.		
9X — 1689 Flt.		
9X — 20 MU.		
YA — SF Netheravon.		
YB — 29 Sqn.	Blenheim.	
YB — 17 Sqn.	Hurricane, Spitfire.	
YB — SF Bentwaters.		
YC — 18 OTU.		
YD — 255 Sqn.	Defiant, Beaufighter, Mosquito.	
YE — 289 Sqn.	Hurricane, Oxford, Martinet, Vengeance, Spitfire.	
YE — 1353 TCU.		
YF — SF Scampton.		
YF — 280 Sqn.	Anson.	
YG — 502 Sqn.	Anson, Whitley, Halifax.	
YG — 156 Sqn.		
YH — 11 Sqn.	Blenheim.	
YH — 21 Sqn.	Blenheim, Ventura, Mosquito.	
YI — 423 Sqn.	Sunderland.	
YK — 80 Sqn.	Hurricane.	
YJ — SF Metheringham.		
YL — 27 OTU?		
YM — 1528 RATF.		
YN — 601 Sqn.	Gauntlet, Blenheim.	
YN — 20 OTU?		
YO — 401 Sqn.	Hurricane, Spitfire.	
YO — SF Down Ampney.		
YO — 8 Sqn.	Vincent.	
YP — 23 Sqn.	Blenheim, Havoc, Mosquito.	
YQ — 616 Sqn.	Spitfire, Meteor.	
YQ — 217 Sqn.	Anson.	
YR — ?	Hurricane.	
YR — 20 OTU.	Wellington.	
YS — 271 Sqn.	Dominie, Dakota.	
YS — 77 Sqn.	Dakota.	
YT — 65 Sqn.	Spitfire, Mustang, Hornet.	
YU — SF Lossiemouth.		
YV — 48 Gp CF.		
YW — 1660 HCU.	Halifax, Lancaster.	
YX — 54 OTU.		
YY — 78 Sqn.	Whitley.	
YY — 1332 HTCU.	Halifax.	
YY — 1381 HTCU.	York.	
YX — 614 Sqn.	Lysander, Hector.	
YZ — 617 Sqn.	Lancaster.	
YZ — 1651 HCU.	Stirling.	

Y2 — 442 Sqn.	Spitfire, Mustang.	
Y3 — 202 Sqn.	Halifax, Hastings.	
Y3 — 518 Sqn.	Halifax, Anson.	
Y5 — SF Dallachy.		
2Y — 345 Sqn.		
3Y — 577 Sqn.	Oxford, Beaufighter, Spitfire, Anson.	
6Y — 171 Sqn.	Stirling, Halifax.	
8Y — 15 MU.		
9Y — 20 MU.		
9Y — 132 OTU.		
ZA — 10 SQN.	Whitley, Halifax, Dakota.	
ZA — 15 Sqn.	Anson.	
ZA — 31 Sqn/MCS.	Valentia.	
ZA — 3 ANS.	Anson.	
ZC — 284 Sqn.	Walrus.	
ZB — 1658 HCU.	Halifax.	
ZD — 6 Sqn.	Hardy.	
ZD — 222 Sqn.	Blenheim, Spitfire, Tempest, Meteor.	
ZE — 293 Sqn.	Walrus, Warwick.	
ZE — CFE/NFLS.		
ZF — 549 Sqn.	Spitfire.	
ZF — 308 Sqn.	Spitfire.	
ZG — 10 OTU.	Whitley.	
ZG — 94 Sqn.	Gladiator.	
ZH — 266 Sqn.	Typhoon.	
ZH — 501 Sqn.	Hurricane.	
ZH — ?	Dakota, Proctor.	
ZJ — 96 Sqn.	Defiant, Beaufighter, Mosquito.	
ZK — 25 Sqn.	Blenheim, Beaufighter, Mosquito.	
ZK — 24 Sqn.	Dakota.	
ZL — 427 Sqn.	Halifax, Lancaster.	
ZL — 77 Sqn.	Wellington.	
ZM — 106 Sqn.	Lancaster.	
ZM — 201 Sqn.	Sunderland.	
ZM — 185 Sqn.	Hampden.	
ZN — 106 Sqn.	Hampden, Manchester, Lancaster.	

ZO — 195 Sqn.	
ZP — 74 Sqn.	Spitfire.
ZP — 1473 Flt.	
ZQ — FIU.	
ZQ — BCIS.	
ZR — 613 Sqn.	Hind, Hector.
ZR — 309 Sqn?	Lysander.
ZR — ?	Blenheim.
ZR — 1333 TSCU.	Dakota.
ZS — 1336 TSCU.	Dakota.
ZS — 233 Sqn.	Hudson.
ZT — 258 Sqn.	Thunderbolt.
ZT — 602 Sqn.	Gauntlet, Spitfire.
ZT — 97 Sqn.	Lancaster.
ZT — 20 OTU.	Wellington.
ZU — 1664 HCU.	Lancaster.
ZV — 19 OTU.	Whitley.
ZV — 18 Gp CF.	Anson.
ZW — ?	Halifax.
ZW — 140 Sqn.	Blenheim.
ZW — 1359 Flt.	
ZW — 1416 Flt.	Spitfire.
ZW — 48 Sqn.	Anson.
ZX — 145 Sqn.	Spitfire.
ZX — 3 TEU.	
ZY — 247 Sqn.	Hurricane, Typhoon, Tempest, Vampire.
ZZ — 220 Sqn.	Liberator.
Z2 — 437 Sqn.	Dakota, Anson.
Z4 — 10 MU.	Anson.
Z5 — 462 Sqn.	Halifax.
Z8 — 45 MU.	
Z9 — 519 Sqn.	Hampden, Spitfire, Hudson, Ventura, Fortress, Halifax.
4Z — 1699 Flt.	Fortress.
4Z — BCCS.	Anson.
6Z — 19 MU.	
7Z — 1391 TCU.	
8Z — 295 Sqn..	Hurricane, Typhoon.

SQUADRON CODES — BY AIRCRAFT TYPE

AIRACOBRA.
UF - 601 Sqn.

ALBACORE.
NH - 119 Sqn.
NH - 415 Sqn.

ALBATROSS.
BJ - 271 Sqn.

ALBEMARLE.
7C - 296 Sqn.
PE7 - 570 Sqn.
8E - 295 Sqn.
MA - 161 Sqn.
V8 - 570 Sqn.
9W - 296 Sqn.

ANSON.
AA - 10 AOS.
AA - ATA TU.
AA - 75 Sqn.
AD - 251 Sqn.
AM - 14 OTU.
AQ - 276 Sqn.
AY - 17 OTU.
A1 - 3 AGS.
A4 - 12 AGS.
BM - 215 Sqn.
BH - 215 Sqn.
BS - 148 Sqn.
4B - 5 Gp CF.
B4 - 282 Sqn.
CA - 2TAF CF.
CB - MCS/31 Sqn.
C1 - 6 OTU.
C7 - 1 FP.
1C - SF Scampton.
DA - ?.
DJ - 612 Sqn.
DT - 192 Sqn.
3D - 4 FP.
EM - 207 Sqn.
EP - 84 Gp CF.
EP - 104 Sqn.
EY - 233 Sqn.
EZ - 81 OTU.
FA - 281 Sqn.

FDO - CFS.
FDY - SoATC.
FFI/FFJ - 5 ANS.
FFM - 2 ANS.
FG - 282 Sqn.
FGF - CNCS.
FGF - RAF FC.
FGG - EANS.
FKP - 23 Gp CF.
FKQ - 25 Gp CF.
FKN - FTC CF.
FKO - 21 Gp CF.
FO - 75 Sqn.
FQ - 12 OTU.
FCV - EFS.
GA - 16 OTU.
GL - 185 Sqn.
GS - 83 OTU.
G2 - 19 Gp CF.
G6 - ?.
HC - 512 Sqn.
HS - 109 Sqn.
HU - 220 Sqn.
I3 - 43 Gp CF.
IF - 84 OTU.
IV - SF Upper Heyford.
II - 116 Sqn.
5I - SF Benson.
I9 - 575 Sqn.
JB - 81 OTU.
JB - 1380 TSCU.
JG - 17 OTU.
JW - 44 Sqn.
KG - 3 OTU.
KJ - 11 OTU.
KK - 15 OTU.
KL - 269 Sqn.
KQ - 502 Sqn.
KW - 267 Sqn.
5K - 39 MU.
K2 - 2 Gp CF.
LD - 108 Sqn.
LG - 215 Sqn.
LL - 1513 RATF.
LT - 7 Sqn.
LY - PDU/1 PRU.
MB - 52 Sqn.
MF - 108 Sqn.

MF - 280 Sqn?.
MG - 7 Sqn.
MJ - 1680 Flt.
MK - 500 Sqn.
MK - 20 OTU.
MP - 76 Sqn.
MR - 97 Sqn.
MW - 217 Sqn.
MY - 278 Sqn.
M6 - 83 Gp CF.
NE - 63 Sqn. NG - 2
   BANS.
NI - 6 Sqn.
NJ - 207 Sqn.
NM - 76 Sqn.
NO - 320 Sqn.
NR - 220 Sqn.
NT - 29 OTU.
NU - 240 OCU.
7N - 5 FU.
7O - ?.
O8 - SF Merryfield.
OF - 97 Sqn.
OK - 3GRS.
ON - 63 Sqn.
OT - 58 Sqn.
OY - 48 Sqn.
OAA - 24 Sqn.
OAA - 437 Sqn.
OAF - 147 Sqn.
PG - 608 Sqn.
PK - 220 Sqn.
PO - 104 Sqn.
PV - 275 Sqn.
PW - 224 Sqn.
P8 - 87 Gp CS.
P9 - ASWDU.
QO - 167 Sqn.
QU - 67 Gp CF.
QU - RAF NI CF.
2Q - 88 Gp CF.
RCE - 61 Gp CF.
RCF - 62 Gp CF.
RCG - 63 Gp CF.
RCH - 64 Gp CF.
RCI - 66 Gp CF.
RF - 1510 ABST Flt.
RK - 10 OTU.

SL - 13 OTU.
SQ - 500 Sqn.
ST - 54 OTU.
3S - 3 Gp CF.
TCR - 1 RS.
TD - 320 Sqn?.
TDE - ERS.
TGX - 27 Gp CF.
THL - 24 Gp CF.
TMA - 4 RS.
TSM - 1 ASS.
TSO - 27 Gp CF.
TTE - 22 Gp CF.
TWY - TTC CF.
TL - 35 Sqn.
TY - 24 OTU.
TX - 11 OTU.
5T - 233 Sqn.
9T - SFU.
UA - 269 Sqn.
UC - 3ANS.
UH - 21 OTU.
UL - 608 Sqn.
UM - 21 OTU.
UX - 1470 Flt?.
UY - 10 OTU.
U5 - 3 FP.
U7 - 1697 ADLS Flt.
VB - 14 OTU.
VG - 285 Sqn.
VK - 85 Gp CF.
VS - MCS/31 Sqn.
VW - ?.
VX - 206 Sqn.
V2 - ?.
V7 - CSE.
V7 - RWE.
2V - 18 Gp CF.
3V - 1 Gp CF.
WD - 206 Sqn.
WJ - 17 OTU.
WL - 612 Sqn.
WT - 35 Sqn.
WQ - 12 Gp CF.
W7 - 35 Sqn.
WD - 206 Sqn.
2 W - 3 GRS.
XN - 22 OTU.

XF - 19 OTU.
XS - 106 Sqn.
XW - 18 OTU.
X8 - 6 Gp CF.
9X - 2 FP.
YF - 280 Sqn.
YG - 502 Sqn.
YQ - 217 Sqn.
3Y - 577 Sqn.
ZA - 3 ANS.
ZA - 5 FTS.
ZA - 15 Sqn.
ZK - 24 Sqn.
ZS - 233 Sqn.
ZW - 48 Sqn.
Z2 - 437 Sqn. 4Z - BC CF,

AUDAX.
HN - 20 Sqn.
LJ - 614 Sqn.
MR - 5 Sqn.
U5 - 28 Sqn.

AUSTER.
BD - 43 OTU/227 OCU.
BG - 660 Sqn.
ET - 662 Sqn.
EP - 84 GP CF.
FJ - 164 Sqn.
OE - 661 Sqn.
PF - 42 OTU/227 OTU.
QD - 654 Sqn.
TS - 657 Sqn.
ROA - 661 Sqn.
ROB - 662 Sqn.
ROC - 663 Sqn.
ROD - 664 Sqn.
ROG - 666 Sqn.

BALTIMORE.
BP - 458 Sqn.
DX - 245 Sqn.
GN - 249 Sqn.
GR - 301 Sqn.

BATTLE.
DG - 150 Sqn.
EF - 15 Sqn.

EM - 207 Sqn.
EQ - 57 Sqn.
FQ - 12 OTU.
GB - 105 Sqn.
GV - 103 Sqn.
HA - 218 Sqn.
HP - GRU.
HY - 88 Sqn.
JN - 150 Sqn.
JQ - 2 AACU.
KB - 152 Sqn.
KP - 226 Sqn.
LS - 15 Sqn.
MB - 52 Sqn.
MQ - 226 Sqn.
MT - 105 Sqn.
NE - 63 Sqn.
NJ - 207 Sqn.
OE - 98 Sqn.
ON - 63 Sqn.
OX - 40 Sqn.
PH - 12 Sqn.
QE - 12 Sqn.
QF - 97 Sqn.
QJ - 616 Sqn.
QT - 142 Sqn.
RH - 88 Sqn.
RG - 1472 Flt.
SM - 305 Sqn.
SV - 218 Sqn.
WT - 35 Sqn.

LA - 235 Sqn.
LX - 54 OTU.
MB - 236 Sqn.
ME - 488 Sqn.
4M - 695 Sqn.
ND - 236 Sqn.
NE - 143 Sqn.
NG - 604 Sqn.
7N - SFW.
PL - 144 Sqn.
PN - 252 Sqn.
P6 - 489 Sqn.
P9 - ASWDU.
QM - 254/42 Sqn.
8Q - 34 Sqn.
RO - 29 Sqn.
RS - 229 OCU.
RX - 456 Sqn.
RY - 313 Sqn.
ST - 54 OTU.
TB - 153 Sqn.
TH - 20 Sqn.
TJ - ?.
TW - 141 Sqn.
UB - 455 Sqn.
UT - 17 Sqn.
VA - 125 Sqn.
WM - 68 Sqn.
WP - 89 Sqn?.
YD - 255 Sqn.
3Y - 577 Sqn.

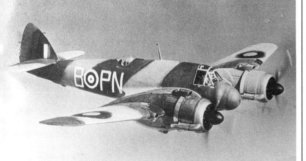

107 Squadron Blenheim 'OM-J'.

Beaufighter 'PN-B' of 252 Squadron.

BEAUFIGHTER.
BF - 54 OTU.
BQ - 600 Sqn.
BT - 252 Sqn.
7B - 595 Sqn.
EE - 404 Sqn.
EW - 307 Sqn.
FK - 219 Sqn.
FH - 46 Sqn.
HB - 239 Sqn.
HO - 143 Sqn.
HU - 406 Sqn.
5H - SF Chivenor.
JT - 256 Sqn.
KP - 409 Sqn.
KZ - 287 Sqn.
K7 - 6 OTU.
2K - 1 BDTU.
9K - 1 TTU.

ZJ - 96 Sqn.
ZK - 25 Sqn,

BEAUFORT
AW - 42 Sqn.
BX - 86 Sqn.
EJ - CCFIS.
GX - 415 Sqn.
KG - 3 OTU.
KU - 47 Sqn.
MW - 217 Sqn.
NK - 100 Sqn.
OA - 22 Sqn.
OY - 48 Sqn.
ST - 54 OTU.
TU - 1 TTU,

BLENHEIM.
AD - 113 Sqn.

AT - 60 OTU.
AY - 110 Sqn.
AW - 504 Sqn.
BD - 51 OTU.
BF - 54 OTU.
BL - 40 Sqn.
BQ - 600 Sqn.
BT - 113 Sqn.
BZ - 107 Sqn.
BX - 86 Sqn.
DP - 30 Sqn.
DX - 57 Sqn.
EE - 404 Sqn.
EP - 104 Sqn.
EQ - 57 Sqn.
EG - 27 Sqn?.
EG - 34 Sqn.
FD - 114 Sqn.
FK - 219 Sqn.
FV - 13 OTU.
FX - 62 Sqn.
GB - 105 Sqn.
GM - 42 OTU?.
GM - 55 Sqn.
GR - 64 Sqn.
GR - 92 Sqn.
GU - 18 Sqn.
GX - 415 Sqn.
HA - 218 Sqn.
HO - 143 Sqn.
HU - 406 Sqn.
IJ - ?.
JG - 17 OTU.
JO - 62 Sqn.
JP - 21 Sqn.
JP - 60 OTU/132 OTU.
JW - 44 Sqn.
KG - 3 OTU.
KQ - 13 OTU.
LA - 235 Sqn.
LB - 34 Sqn.
LD - 108 Sqn.
LJ - 211 Sqn.
LN - ?.
LS - 15 Sqn.
LS - 61 Sqn.
LU - 101 Sqn.
LW - Signals Wg.
LY - PDU/1 PRU.
MF - 108 Sqn.
MK - 500 Sqn.

MQ - 226 Sqn.
MS - 23 Sqn.
MU - 60 Sqn.
MV - 600 Sqn.
ND - 236 Sqn.
NG - 604 Sqn.
OB - 45 Sqn.
OM - 107 Sqn.
OS - 528 Sqn.
OU - 13 Sqn.
OY - 11 Sqn.
OZ - 82 Sqn.
PF - 51 OTU.
PJ - 59 Sqn.
PN - 252 Sqn.
PT - 27 Sqn.
PT - 62 Sqn.
PU - 104 Sqn.
PZ - 53 Sqn.
QL - 76 Sqn?.
QY - 254 Sqn.
RE - 229 Sqn.
RH - 88 Sqn.
RO - 29 Sqn.
RR - 407 Sqn.
RT - 114 Sqn.
RX - 25 Sqn.
SH - 64 Sqn.
SO - 145 Sqn.
ST - 228 OCU.
SY - 139 Sqn.
TE - 53 Sqn.
TR - 59 Sqn.
TW - 90 Sqn.
UF - 601 Sqn.
UL - 608 Sqn.
UP - 21 Sqn.
UQ - 211 Sqn.
UR - 84 Sqn.
US - 27 Sqn.
UX - 82 Sqn.
VA - 113 Sqn.
VE - 110 Sqn.
VT - 30 Sqn?.
WJ - 17 OTU.
WN - 527 Sqn.
WQ - 604 Sqn.
WR - 248 Sqn.
WV - 18 Sqn.
XA - 489 Sqn.
XD - 139 Sqn.

XK - 272 Sqn.
XQ - 64 Sqn.
XZ - 39 Sqn.
YB - 29 Sqn.
YH - 11 Sqn.
YH - 21 Sqn.
YN - 601 Sqn.
YP - 23 Sqn.
ZD - 222 Sqn.
ZK - 25 Sqn.
ZR - ?.
ZW - 140 Sqn,

BOMBAY.
BJ - 271 Sqn.
SH - 216 Sqn.

BOSTON.
KQ - 13 OTU.
MQ - 226 Sqn.
NH - 530 Sqn.
OA - 342 Sqn.
OM - 107 Sqn.
RH - 88 Sqn.
RT - 114 Sqn.
TH - 418 Sqn.
UP - 605 Sqn.
XD - 13 OTU.

BOTHA.
UL - 608 Sqn.

BRIGAND.
OB - 45 Sqn.

BUCKINGHAM.
OB - 45 Sqn.

BUCKMASTER.
GA - 16 OTU.

BUFFALO.
NF - 488 Sqn.
RD - 67 Sqn.
TD - 453 Sqn.
WP - 243 Sqn.

CATALINA.
AM - 131 OTU.

AX - 202 Sqn.
BN - 240 Sqn.
DA - 210 Sqn.
EJ - CCFIS.
FV - 205 Sqn.
GS - 330 Sqn.
HH - 321 Sqn.
7K - SRTU.
KK - 333 Sqn.
KK - 1477 Flt.
QL - 413 Sqn.
QQ - 321 Sqn.
TJ - 202 Sqn.
TR - 265 Sqn.
UU - 321 Sqn.
WQ - 209 Sqn,

CHIPMUNK
BD - 43 OTU/227 OCU.
CB - 31 Sqn/MCS

DAKOTA.
AG - ?.
CM - 1333 TCU.
DN - 512 Sqn?.
DV - 77 Sqn.
5D - 31 Sqn?.
EY - 78 Sqn.
EZ - 81 OTU/138 OTSCU.
FM - 238 Sqn.
GY - 1383 TSCU.
HC - 241 Sqn.
HC - 512 Sqn.
HM - 136 Sqn.
IB - Glider pick-up Flt.
I2 - 48 Sqn.
I5 - 1381 TSCU.
I9 - 575 Sqn.
JN - 30 Sqn.
3J - 13 MU.
KN - 77 Sqn.
L7 - 271 Sqn.
5L - 187 Sqn.
MP - 76 Sqn.
MJ - 1680 Flt.
NQ - 24 Sqn.
NU - 1382 TCU.
NU - 240 OCU.
PU - 53/187 Sqn.
5T - 233 Sqn.
U6 - 436 Sqn.
VM - 243 Sqn.
VP - ?.
WF - 238 Sqn.
WF - 525 Sqn.
XK - 46 Sqn.
YS - 271 Sqn.
YS - 77 Sqn.
ZA - 10 Sqn.
ZH - ?.
ZK - 24 Sqn.
ZR - 1333 TSCU.
ZS - 1336 TSCU.
Z2 - 437 Sqn.

DEFIANT.
BA - 277 Sqn.
DZ - 151 Sqn.
EW - 307 Sqn.
FH - 15 OTU.
HP - GRU.
I4 - 567 Sqn.
JP - 60 OTU/132 OTU.
JT - 256 Sqn.
KP - 409 Sqn.
KZ - 287 Sqn.
MY - 287 Sqn.
NW - 286 Sqn.
PS - 264 Sqn.
PV - 275 Sqn.
PZ - 456 Sqn.
RA - 410 Sqn.
TW - 141 Sqn.
U4 - 667 Sqn.
VA - 125 Sqn.
VG - 285 Sqn.
XF - 19 OTU.
XW - 18 OTU.
YD - 255 Sqn.
ZJ - 96 Sqn.

DEMON.
MS - 23 SQN.

DEVON.
CB - 31 Sqn/MCS.
NU - 240 OCU

DOMINIE.
ZA - SF St Eval.
CB - MCS/31 Sqn.
KE - BLEU.
MD - 526 Sqn.
MJ - 1680 Flt.
QK - PTPS.
VP - SF Exeter.
S9 - 16Gp CF.
V4 - 6MU.
YS - 271 Sqn,

FORTRESS.
AD - 251 Sqn.
BU - 214 Sqn.
6G - 223 Sqn.
MB - 220 Sqn.
NR - 220 Sqn.
RN - 1674 HCU.
U3 - RWE.
VX - 206 Sqn.
WO? - 90 Sqn.
WP - 90 Sqn.
Z9 - 519 Sqn.
4Z - 1699 Flt..
50 - 521 Sqn.

GAUNTLET.
LW - 607 Sqn.
QJ - 616 Sqn.
RR - 615 Sqn.

UV - 17 Sqn.
YN - 601 Sqn.
ZT - 602 Sqn.

GLADIATOR.
GK - 80 Sqn.
GO - 94 Sqn.
HB - 239 Sqn.
HE - 605 Sqn.
HP - 247 Sqn.
KW - 615 Sqn.
LW - 607 Sqn.
NW - 33 Sqn.
OP - 3 Sqn.
RJ - 46 Sqn.
RL - 603 Sqn.
RR - 615 Sqn.
RT - 112 Sqn.
SD - 72 Sqn.
SO - 33 Sqn.
TN - 33 Sqn.
UG - 16 Sqn.
UM - 152 Sqn.
XO - 112 Sqn.
ZG - 94 Sqn.

GORDON.
EW - 47 Sqn.

Halifax 'H7-N' of 346 Squadron.

HALIFAX.
AD - 251 Sqn.
AL - 429 Sqn.
8A - 298 Sqn.
BL - 1656 HCU.
BM - 433 Sqn.
BX - ?.
BY - 58 Sqn.
7C - 296 Sqn.
C8 - 640 Sqn.
C6 - 51 Sqn.
DH - 1664 HCU.
DT - 192 Sqn.
DY - 102 Sqn.
D4 - 620 Sqn.
EE - 295 Sqn.
EK - 1656 HCU.
EY - 78 Sqn.
EQ - 408 Sqn.
EX - 199 Sqn.
8E - 295 Sqn.
FD - 1659 HCU.
FS - 148 Sqn.

FEP/FEQ/FER/FES/FET -
   21 HGCU.
FGE - EANS.
FGF - ERS.
5F - 147 Sqn.
6F - 1669 HCU.
GG - 1667 HCU.
GP - 1661 HCU.
GR - 1586 Flt.
GR - 302 Sqn.
GS - ?.
GV - 1652 HCU.
GY - 1383 TSCU.
3G - 111 OTU.
G5 - 190 Sqn.
HD - 466 Sqn.
6H - 96 Sqn.
H3 - 111 OTU.
H7 - 346 Sqn.
8H - 8GP CF.
IG - 1668 HCU.
IP - 434 Sqn.
JA - 1652 HCU.
JR - 1654 HCU.
3J - 13 MU.
KN - 77 Sqn.
KB - 1661 HCU.
KW - 425 Sqn.

IK - BCIS.
2K - 1668 HCU.
LK - 578 Sqn.
LQ - 405 Sqn.
LR - 1667 HCU.
L5 - 297 Sqn.
L6 - 1669 HCU.
L8 - 347 Sqn.
L9 - 190 Sqn.
MA - 161 Sqn.
MH - 51 Sqn.
MP - 76 Sqn.
MW - 101 Sqn.
2M - 520 Sqn.
NA - 428 Sqn.
ND - 1666 HCU.
NF - 138 Sqn.
NH - 415 Sqn.
NP - 158 Sqn.
OF - 97 Sqn.
OG - 1665 HCU.
OG - 1332 HTCU.
OK - 1674 HCU.

OO - 1663 HCU.
OT - 1 BDU.
OR - BBDU.
OX - ORTU.
ODY - 1333 TSTU.
5O - 521 Sqn.
O6 - 298 Sqn.
OW - 426 Sqn.
PD - 450 Sqn.
PE - 1662 HCU.
PM - 103 Sqn.
PT - 420 Sqn.
PU - 187 Sqn.
1P - BCIS.
2P - 644 Sqn.
P5 - 297 Sqn.
P9 - ASWDU.
QB - 424 Sqn.
QD - 304 Sqn.
QO - 432 Sqn.
QS - 620 Sqn.
QU - 432 Sqn.
QY - 1666 HCU.
RV - 1659 HCU.
SE - 431 Sqn.
SV - 1663 HCU.
TB - 77 Sqn.
TL - 35 Sqn.

TT - 1658 HCU.
TV - 1660 HCU.
8T - 298 Sqn.
TCA/TCR - 1 Radio
   School.
UG - 1654 HCU.
UV - 460 Sqn.
U3 - RWE.
6U - 415 Sqn.
9U - 644 Sqn.
VR - 419 Sqn.
VU - 246 Sqn.
V7 - RWE.
WL - 434 Sqn.
9W - 296 Sqn.
XB - 224 Sqn.
X3 - 111 OTU.
X9 - 517 Sqn.
X9 - 299 Sqn.
YG - 502 Sqn.
YW - 1660 HCU.
YY - 1332 HTCU.
Y3 - 202 Sqn.

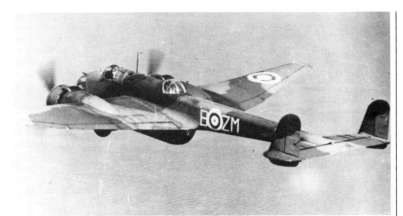

Hampden 'ZM-B' of 185 Squadron.

Y3 - 518 Sqn.
6Y - 171 Sqn.
ZA - 10 Sqn.
ZB - 1658 HCU.
ZL - 427 Sqn.
ZW - ?.
Z5 - 462 Sqn.
Z9 - 519 Sqn. MOHA - 297 Sqn.
MOHC - 113 Sqn.
MOHC - 620 Sqn.
MOHD - 47 Sqn.
MOHD - 644 Sqn.

HAMPDEN.
EA - 49 Sqn.
EM - 207 Sqn.
EQ - 408 Sqn.
GL - 185 Sqn.
GX - 415 Sqn.
JS - 16 OTU.
JW - 44 Sqn.
KM - 44 Sqn.
LS - 61 Sqn.
NV - 144 Sqn.
OL - 83 Sqn.
PL - 144 Sqn.
PP - 25 OTU.
PT - 420 Sqn.
QQ - 83 Sqn.
QR - 61 Sqn.
QX - 50 Sqn.
UB - 455 Sqn.
VN - 50 Sqn.
XA - 489 Sqn.
XS - 106 Sqn.
XU - 49 Sqn.
ZM - 185 Sqn.
ZN - 106 Sqn.
Z9 - 519 Sqn.

HARDY.
XE - 6 Sqn.
ZD - 6 Sqn.

HART.
AD - 60 Sqn.
MS - 23 Sqn.

OY - 11 Sqn.
PT - 1 SFTS.
SF - 39 Sqn.
OQ - 5 Sqn.
US - 27 Sqn.

HARROW.
BH - 215 Sqn.
BJ - 271 Sqn.
BK - 115 Sqn.
FJ - 37 Sqn.
FO - 75 Sqn.

HARVARD.
AK - 213 Sqn.
7B - 5 Sqn.
FCA - 1 FTS.
FBP - 3 FTS.
FBG - 6 SFTS.
FCD - 1 FTS.
FCT - EFS.
FDA - 1 RFU.
FKO - 21 Gp CF.
HX - 61 OTU.
JX - 1 Sqn.
KR - 61 OTU.
LA - 607 Sqn.
LO - 602 Sqn.
LP - 237 OCU.
4M - 695 Sqn.
M4 - 587 Sqn.
PR - 609 Sqn.
QO - 167 Sqn.
Q3 - 613 Sqn.
8Q - 34 Sqn.
RAA - 500 Sqn.
RAB - 501 Sqn.
RAC - 502 Sqn.
RAD - 504 Sqn.
RAG - 600 Sqn.
RAH - 601 Sqn.
RAK - 604 Sqn.
RAL - 605 Sqn.
RAN - 607 Sqn.
RAO - 608 Sqn.
RAQ - 610 Sqn.
RAS - 612 Sqn.
RAT - 613 Sqn.

RAU - 614 Sqn.
RCA - RC CS.
SD - 501 Sqn.
S7 - 500 Sqn.
TH - 20 Sqn.
TM - 504 Sqn.
TO - 61 OTU/228 OCU.
6T - 608 Sqn.
UT - 17 Sqn.
V6 - 615 Sqn.
WY - 541 Sqn.
9X - 1689 Flt.
YT - 65 Sqn,

HASTINGS.
C2 - ?.
Y3 - 202 Sqn.
JAM - 511 Sqn?

HAVOC.
HN - 93 Sqn.
MA - 161 Sqn.
NH - 530 Sqn.
SL - 13 OTU.
VY - 85 Sqn.
YP - 23 Sqn.

HECTOR.
DJ - 612 Sqn.
JQ - 2 AACU.
PJ - 59 Sqn.
YX - 614 Sqn.
ZR - 613 Sqn

HENLEY.
6D - 20/631 Sqn.
HP - GRU.
4M - 695 Sqn.

HEREFORD.
GL - 14 OTU.

HEYFORD.
GB - 166 Sqn.
MR - 97 Sqn.

HIND.
BL - 609 Sqn.

JE - 610 Sqn.
KQ - 502 Sqn.
LJ - 614 Sqn.
LJ - 211 Sqn.
ZR - 613 Sqn.

HORNET.
6C - PRDU.
EB - 41 Sqn.
MS - SF Linton-on-Ouse.
OB - 45 Sqn.
QV - 19 Sqn.
SH - 64 Sqn.
SR - 33 Sqn.
W2 - 80 Sqn.
YT - 65 Sqn.

HORNET MOTH.
KX - 529 Sqn.
LW - Signals Wing.

HOVERFLY.
KX - 529 Sqn.
P9 - ASWDU.
TS - 657 Sqn.

In its pen at Digby. 'DZ' coded Hurricane of 151 Squadron.

HUDSON.
AD - 251 Sqn.
BP - 458 Sqn.
GK - 459 Sqn.
HZ - ?.
KW - 267 Sqn.
LD - 117 Sqn.
LQ - 117 Sqn.
LY - PDU/1 PRU.
MA - 161 Sqn.
MK - 500 Sqn.
ND - 320 Sqn.
NR - 220 Sqn.
OD - 6 OTU.
OS - 279 Sqn.
OY - 48 Sqn.
PW - 224 Sqn.
PZ - 53 Sqn.
QA - 224 Sqn.
QX - 224 Sqn.
RR - 407 Sqn.
TR - 59 Sqn.
9T - Signals FU.
UA - 269 Sqn.

UL - 608 Sqn.
VH - ?.
VX - 206 Sqn.
ZS - 233 Sqn.
Z9 - 519 Sqn,

HUNTER.
ES - 229 OCU.
RS - 229 OCU.

HURRICANE.
AD - 113 Sqn.
AE - 402 Sqn.
AF - AFDU.
AK - 213 Sqn.
AL - 79 Sqn.
AM - 14 OTU.
AP - 186 Sqn.
AP - 80 Sqn?.
AV - 121 Sqn.
AW - 42 Sqn.
AY - 17 OTU.
BF - 1656 HCU.
BR - 184 Sqn.
BT - 30 OTU.

BQ - 451 Sqn.
DQ - 1402 Met Flt.
DR - 1697 ADLF/S.
DT - 257 Sqn.
DU - 312 Sqn.
DX - 245 Sqn.
DZ - 151 Sqn.
6D - 20/631 Sqn.
EF - 232 Sqn.
EH - 55 OTU.
EH - 3 TEU.
EL - 181 Sqn.
EY - 80 Sqn.
EZ - 81 OTU/138 OTSCU.
4E - 1687 BDF.
FC - SF Northolt.
FG - 335 Sqn.
FI - 83 OTU?.
FJ - 261 Sqn.
FJ - 164 Sqn.
FM - 257 Sqn.
FN - 331 Sqn.
FT - 43 Sqn.
FV - 81 Sqn.

F3 - 438 Sqn.
GF - 56 OTU/1 TEU.
GG - 151 Sqn.
GN - 249 Sqn.
GO - 94 Sqn.
GQ - 134 Sqn.
GV - 134 Sqn.
GZ - 32 Sqn.
HA - 261 Sqn.
HB - 229 Sqn.
HB - 239 Sqn.
HE - 263 Sqn.
HF - 183 Sqn.
HH - 260 Sqn.
HQ - 56 OTU.
HV - 73 Sqn.
HO - ?.
6H - 1688 BDTF.
II - 59 OTU.
II - 116 Sqn.
I4 - 567 Sqn.
I8 - 440 Sqn.
JH - 317 Sqn.
JT - 256 Sqn.
JU - 111 Sqn.
JV - 6 Sqn.
JX - 1 Sqn.
KA - 82 OTU.
KC - 238 Sqn.
KH - 11 OTU.
KT - 32 Sqn.
KW - 615 Sqn.
KZ - 287 Sqn.
KE - MSFU.
3K - 1695 BDTF?.
K7 - 6 OTU.
LD - 250 Sqn.
LE - 242 Sqn.
LK - 87 Sqn.
LR - 56 Sqn.
LR - 146 Sqn.
LU - MSFU.
LZ - 421 Flt/66 Sqn.
MF - 59 OTU.
MF - 260 Sqn.
MR - 245 Sqn.
MS - 273 Sqn.
MU - 60 Sqn.
ML - 605 Sqn?.
M4 - 587 Sqn.
3M - 679 Sqn.
4M - 695 Sqn.
9M - 1690 BDTF.
NA - 1 Sqn.
NA - 146 Sqn?.
NJ - MSFU.
NN - 310 Sqn.
NO - 85 Sqn.
NQ - 43 Sqn.
NV - 79 Sqn.
NW - 33 Sqn.
NW - 286 Sqn.
OK - 450 Sqn?.
OP - 3 Sqn.

2O - 84 Gp CF.
5O - 521 Sqn.
PA - 55 OTU/3 TEU.
PD - 87 Sqn.
PD - 450 Sqn.
PO - 46 Sqn.
QO - 3 Sqn.
QU - RAF NI CF.
8Q - 34 Sqn.
RE - 229 Sqn.
RF - 303 Sqn.
RG - 208 Sqn.
RJ - 46 Sqn.
RL - 1 SLAIS.
RP - 288 Sqn.
RS - 33 Sqn.
RS - 30 Sqn.
SA - 486 Sqn.
SD - 501 Sqn.
SF - 137 Sqn.
SO - 145 Sqn.
ST - 54 OTU.
SW - 253 Sqn.
SZ - 316 Sqn.
TE - 1401 Flt.
TM - 111 Sqn.
TM - 504 Sqn.
TP - 73 Sqn.
UF - 601 Sqn.
UF - 24 OTU.
UH - 1682 Flt.
US - 56 Sqn.
UV - 17 Sqn.
UW - 55 OTU.
UZ - 306 Sqn.
U7 - 1697 ADLS.
VK - 238 Sqn.
VY - 85 Sqn.
SV - 439 Sqn.
WC - 309 Sqn.
WG - 128 Sqn.
WN - 527 Sqn.
XE - 123 Sqn.
XF - 19 OTU.
XM - 182 Sqn.
XP - 174 Sqn.
XR - 71 Sqn.
YB - 17 Sqn.
YE - 239 Sqn.
YK - 80 Sqn.
YO - 401 Sqn.
ZY - 247 Sqn.
ZH - 401 Sqn.

KITTYHAWK.
GA - 112 Sqn.
GL - 185 Sqn.
GO - 94 Sqn.
HS - 260 Sqn.
LD - 250 Sqn.
OK - 450 Sqn.

LANCASTER.
AA - 75 Sqn.

At Pomigliano November 1945 for repatriation of POWs, a variety of Lancasters including 12 Squadron ('PH'), 100 Squadron ('HW') and 106 Squadron ('ZN').

AC - 138 Sqn.
AJ - 617 Sqn.
AK - 1657 HCU.
AL - 429 Sqn.
AP - 186 Sqn.
AP - 460 Sqn.
AR - 460 Sqn.
AS - 166 Sqn.
AU - 148 Sqn.
A2 - 514 Sqn.
A3 - 230 Sqn.
A3 - 1653 HCU.
A4 - 195 Sqn.
A5 - 3 LFS.
BA - 550 Sqn.
BH - 300 Sqn.
BJ - ?.
BL - 40 Sqn.
BL - 1656 HCU.
BM - 433 Sqn.
BQ - 550 Sqn.
BS - 120 Sqn.
BS - 1651 HCU.
CA - 189 Sqn.
CE - 5 LFS.
CF - 625 Sqn.
CJ - 203 Sqn.
3C - 1 LFS.
DF - CBE.
DH - 1664 HCU.
DJ - 57 Sqn.
DX - 57 Sqn.
EA - 49 Sqn.
EK - 1656 HCU.
EM - 207 Sqn.
EP - 104 Sqn.
EQ - 408 Sqn.
FD - 1659 HCU.
FDI - CFS.
FDI to FDO - CFS.
F2 - 635 Sqn.
6F - 1669 HCU.
GG - 1667 HCU.
GI - 622 Sqn.
GP - 1661 HCU.
GT - 156 Sqn.
GZ - 12 Sqn.

G7 - BCFU.
HA - 218 Sqn.
HW - 100 Sqn.
HV - SF East Kirkby.
HH - 1653 HCU.
IK - BCIS.
IL - 115 Sqn.
IL - 195 Sqn.
IQ - 150 Sqn.
JE - 195 Sqn.
JF - 1654 HCU.
JI - 514 Sqn.
JN - 75 Sqn.
JN - 90 Sqn.
JO - 463 Sqn.
J9 - 1668 HCU.
9J - 227 Sqn.
2K - 1668 HCU.
KB - 1661 HCU.
KC - 617 Sqn.
KF - 1662 HCU.
KM - 44 Sqn.
KO - 115 Sqn.
KR - 1667 HCU.
KW - 425 Sqn.
K7 - 6 OTU.
K7 - 236 OCU.
LE - 630 Sqn.
LQ - 405 Sqn.
LR - 1667 HCU.
LS - 15 Sqn.
1L - 115 Sqn.
L6 - 1669 HCU.
MG - 7 Sqn.
M9 - 1653 HCU.
NA - 428 Sqn.
ND - 1666 HCU.
NF - 138 Sqn.
6O - 582 Sqn.
OF - 97 Sqn.
OJ - 149 Sqn.
OL - 83 Sqn.
OR - BBDU.
OW - 426 Sqn.
OZ - 179 Sqn.
OZ - 210 Sqn.
6O - 582 Sqn.

PE - 1662 HCU.
PG - 619 Sqn.
PH - 12 Sqn.
PM - 103 Sqn.
PO - 467 Sqn.
PT - 420 Sqn.
P4 - 153 Sqn.
P9 - ASWDU.
QB - 424 Sqn.
QF - 1323 AGLTF.
QN - 214 Sqn.
QO - 432 Sqn.
QQ - 1651 HCU.
QR - 15 Sqn.
QR - 61 Sqn.
QT - 57 Sqn.
QY - 1666 HCU.
RC - 5 LFS.
RL - 38 Sqn.
RV - 1659 HCU.
RX - 407 Sqn.
RX - 470 Sqn.
SE - 431 Sqn.
SR - 101 Sqn.
SW - 1678 HCU.
4S - CSE.
TC - 170 Sqn.
TK - 149 Sqn.
TL - 170 Sqn.
TL - 35 Sqn.
TV - 1660 HCU.
UG - 1654 HCU.
UH - 1654 HCU.
UL - 576 Sqn.
UM - 626 Sqn.
UV - 460 Sqn.
VN - 50 Sqn.
VR - 419 Sqn.
V7 - RWE.
WB - CSE.
WB - BCIS.
WL - 434 Sqn.
WP - 90 Sqn.
WS - 9 Sqn.
XB - 224 Sqn.
XH - 218 Sqn.
XY - 90 Sqn.

XY - 186 Sqn.
YW - 1660 HCU.
YZ - 617 Sqn.
ZL - 427 Sqn.
ZM - 106 Sqn.
ZN - 106 Sqn.
ZT - 97 Sqn.
ZU - 1664 HCU.

LERWICK.
WQ - 209 Sqn.

LIBERATOR.
AE - 59 Sqn.
AE - 1409 Flt.
BL - 40 Sqn.
BS - 120 Sqn.
BS - 160 Sqn.
BY - 59 Sqn.
CJ - 203 Sqn.

Liberators of 220 Squadron carry their 'ZZ' code.

8D - 220 Sqn.
EJ - CCFIS.
EP - 104 Sqn.
EF - 102 Sqn.
EG - 355 Sqn.
FH - 53 Sqn.
FS - 148 Sqn.
GR - 1586 Flt.
3G - 111 OTU.
6G - 223 Sqn.
LF - 37 Sqn.
MX - 1653 CU.
OH - 120 Sqn.
H3 - 111 OTU.
OW - 426 Sqn.
PP - 311 Sqn.
PQ - 206 Sqn.
QA - 224 Sqn.
QX - 224 Sqn.
TA - 358 Sqn.
TR - 59 Sqn.
WE - 59 Sqn.
XB - 224 Sqn.
XQ - 86 Sqn.
X3 - 111 OTU.
ZZ - 220 Sqn.

LINCOLN.
AA - 75 Sqn.

AU - 148 Sqn.
A3 - 1653 CU/230 OCU.
CW - 214 Sqn.
DF - CBE.
DX - 57 Sqn.
EA - 49 Sqn.
EM - 207 Sqn.
HW - 100 Sqn.
KC - 617 Sqn.
KM - 44 Sqn.
KO - 115 Sqn.
LS - 15 Sqn.
NF - 138 Sqn.
OF - 97 Sqn.
OJ - 149 Sqn.
OL - 83 Sqn.
PH - 12 Sqn.
QN - 214 Sqn.
QR - 61 Sqn.
QT - 57 Sqn.

SR - 101 Sqn.
SN - 230 OCU.
TL - 35 Sqn.
VN - 50 Sqn.
WB - BCIS.
WP - 90 Sqn.

LODESTAR.
KW - 267 Sqn.

LONDON.
BN - 240 Sqn.
JU - 202 Sqn.
RF - 204 Sqn.
SH - 240 Sqn.
TQ - 202 Sqn.
VQ - 201 Sqn.

LYSANDER.
AG - ?.
AN - 13 Sqn.
AR - 309 Sqn.
AQ - 276 Sqn.
AY - 17 OTU.
BA - 277 Sqn.
BF - 28 Sqn.
EE - 16 Sqn.
FS - 148 Sqn.
FY - 4 Sqn.

GA - 16 OTU.
GA - 208 Sqn.
HB - 239 Sqn.
HN - 20 Sqn.
HL - 26 Sqn.
II - 116 Sqn.
JR - 161 Sqn.
KA - 2 Sqn.
KJ - 16 Sqn.
KO - 2 Sqn.
KW - 267 Sqn.
KZ - 287 Sqn.
LJ - 614 Sqn.
LX - 225 Sqn.
MA - 161 Sqn.
MY - 278 Sqn.
NM - 268 Sqn.
OO - 13 Sqn.
PM - 20 Sqn.
PV - 275 Sqn.
RG - 208 Sqn.
RM - 26 Sqn.
RU - 414 Sqn.
RZ - 241 Sqn.
Sp - 400 Sqn.
TV - 4 Sqn.
UG - 16 Sqn.
UY - 10 OTU.
VM - 231 Sqn.
VQ - 18/28 OTU.
XF - 19 OTU.
YX - 614 Sqn.
ZR - 309 Sqn.

MAGISTER.
AQ - 276 Sqn.

MARTINET.
AM - 14 OTU.
AY - 17 OTU.
2A - SF St Eval.
7B - 595 Sqn.
C2 - 84 OTU.
D2 - 1606 Flt.
6D - 20/631 Sqn.
EM - 17 APC?.
EU - 26 OTU.
4E - 1687 BD Flt.
FH - 15 OTU.
GS - 83 OTU.
HM - 1677 TTF.
8I - APS Spilsby.
I4 - 567 Sqn.
KA - 82 OTU.
KZ - 287 Sqn.
KJ - 11 OTU.
LT - 22 OTU.
ML - 12 OTU.
M4 - 587 Sqn.
2M - 520 Sqn.
3M - 679 Sqn.
4M - 695 Sqn.
9M - 1690 BDTF.
NS - 52 OTU.

NX - CFE.
4Q - CC FATU.
QK - 12 APC?.
8Q - 34 Sqn.
R4 - 18 APC.
ST - 54 OTU.
ST - 228 OCU.
TO - 61 OTU/228 OCU.
T7 - 650 Sqn.
UH - 21 OTU/202 CTU.
UF - 24 OTU.
UY - 10 OTU.
VG - 286 Sqn.
VQ - 18/28 OTU.
V9 - ?.
XF - 19 OTU.
XW - 18 OTU.
X3 - 111 OTU.
X6 - 290 Sqn.
2X - 85 OTU.
YE - 289 Sqn,

MANCHESTER.
BL - 1656 HCU.
EA - 49 Sqn.
EM - 207 Sqn.
GP - 1661 HCU.
OF - 97 Sqn.
OL - 83 Sqn.
QR - 61 Sqn.
TV - 1660 HCU.
UG - 1654 HCU.
VN - 50 Sqn.
ZN - 106 Sqn.

MARYLAND.
LP - 8 OTU.

MASTER.
AQ - 276 Sqn.
DQ - 1407 Flt.
GA - 16 OTU.
GL - 1529 RATF.
HX - 61 OTU.
IO - 41 OTU.
8I - APS Spilsby.
KR - 61 OTU.
KJ - 11 OTU.
LV - 57 OTU.
MF - 59 OTU.
NW - 286 Sqn.
NX - CFE.
QK - 12 APC.
R4 - 18 APC.
TO - 61 OTU/228 OCU.
UY - 10 OTU.
ZX - 85 OTU.

MESSENGER.
EP - 84 GP CF.

METEOR
A6 - 257 Sqn.
7A - 614 Sqn.

C3 - ?.
DL - 92 Sqn.
DL - 91 Sqn,DW - 610 Sqn.
4D - 74 Sqn.
EC - PRDU.
ES - 229 OCU.
FX - 234 Sqn.
FX - 266 Sqn.
FY - 611 Sqn?.
HE - 263 Sqn.
HI - 66 Sqn.
HX - 203 AFS.
HX - 226 OCU.
JX - 1 Sqn.
KR - 226 OCU.
KD - 226 OCU.
4K - SF West Malling.
LJ - 600 Sqn.
LO - 602 Sqn.
LP - 237 OCU.
8L - 92 Sqn.
ON - 56 Sqn.
ON - 124 Sqn.
QO - 167 Sqn.
Q3 - 613 Sqn.
RAA - 500 Sqn.
RAW - 616 Sqn.
SD - 501 Sqn.
SW - 43 Sqn.
S7 - 500 Sqn.
TM - 504 Sqn.
UB - 164/63 Sqn.
US - 56 Sqn.
UU - 61 OTU/226 OCU.
UX - CFE.
V6 - 615 Sqn.
WY - 541 Sqn.
8W - 612 Sqn.
YQ - 616 Sqn.
ZD - 222 Sqn.

MITCHELL.
EV - 180 Sqn.
FV - 13 OTU.
3G - 111 OTU.
KQ - 13 OTU.
MQ - 226 Sqn.
NO - 320 Sqn.
OA - 342 Sqn.
SM - 305 Sqn.
UR - 13 OTU.
VO - 98 Sqn.

MOHAWK.
DG - 155 Sqn.

MOSQUITO.
AE - 1409 Flt.
AJ - 617 Sqn.
AT - 60 OTU.
AZ - 627 Sqn.
A3 - 1653 CU/230 OCU.
CO - ?.

CR - 162 Sqn.
CX - 14 Sqn.
6C - PRDU.
DH - 540 Sqn.
DM - 248 Sqn.
DF - CBE.
DT - 192 Sqn.
DZ - 151 Sqn.
EG - 487 Sqn.
EJ - CCFIS.
EO - 404 Sqn.
EW - 307 Sqn.
EV - 180 Sqn.
FK - 219 Sqn.
FV - 13 OTU.
GA - 16 OTU.
GB - 105 Sqn.
GM - 42 OTU?.
GN - CBE.
GN - 249 Sqn.
G7 - BCFU.
HB - 239 Sqn.
HS - 109 Sqn.
HU - 406 Sqn.
4H - 142 Sqn.
IT - ?.
8I - APS Spilsby.
JT - 256 Sqn.
JS - 16 OTU.
KA - 1661m
KK - 333 Sqn.
KK - 1477 Flt.
KP - 409 Sqn.
KQ - 13 OTU.
KU - 47 Sqn.
4K - SF West Malling.
8K - 571 Sqn.
K7 - 6 OTU.
LA - 235 Sqn.
LK - 578 Sqn.
LP - 8 OTU.
LX - 54 OTU.
LP - 237 OCU.
ME - 488 Sqn.
MS - SF Linton-on-Ouse.
M5 - 128 Sqn.
NC - 4 Sqn.
NE - 143 Sqn.
NG - 604 Sqn.
O5 - BSDU.
OM - 107 Sqn.
OM - 11 Sqn.
OT - 58 Sqn.
OY - 13 OTU.
PS - 264 Sqn.
PY - 84 Sqn.
3P - 516 sqn.
P3 - 692 Sqn.
P6 - 489 Sqn.
P9 - ASWDU.
QE - CFE.
QF - PFF NTU.
QM - 254/42 Sqn.
RA - 410 Sqn.

RO - 29 Sqn.
RS - 157 Sqn.
RT - 8 Sqn.
RT - 114 Sqn.
RX - 456 Sqn.
RY - 313 Sqn.
SB - 464 Sqn.
SL - 13 OTU.
SM - 305 Sqn.
SY - 613 Sqn.
4S - CSE.
TH - 418 Sqn.
TW - 141 Sqn.
6T - 608 Sqn.
UP - 4 Sqn.
UX - 82 Sqn.
VA - 125 Sqn.
VA - 264 Sqn.
VB - 334 Sqn.
VE - 110 Sqn.
VI - 169 Sqn.
VO - 98 Sqn.
VV - SF Sumburgh.
VV - 235 Sqn.
VY - 85 Sqn.
WI - 69 Sqn.
WM - 68 Sqn.
WV - 18 Sqn.
XD - 139 Sqn.
4X - 1692 Flt.
YD - 255 Sqn.
YH - 21 Sqn.
YP - 23 Sqn.
2J - 96 Sqn.
ZK - 25 Sqn. RAA - 500
   Sqn.
RAL - 605 Sqn.
RAP - 609 Sqn.
RAW - 616 Sqn.

MOTH MINOR.
KD - 30 OTU.

MUSTANG.
AK - 213 Sqn.
AZ - 234 Sqn.
BN - 170 Sqn.
DV - 3 Sqn.
DV - 129 Sqn.
FY - 611 Sqn.
GA - 112 Sqn.
9G - 441 Sqn.
GD - SF Horsham St Faith.
GN - 249 Sqn.
HB - 239 Sqn.
HS - 260 Sqn.
HX - 61 OTU.
IO - 41 OTU.
8I - APS Spilsby.
5J - 126 Sqn.
6J - 34 Sqn.
KR - 61 OTU.
LD - 250 Sqn.
LY - PDU/1 PRU.

ML - 605 Sqn?.
MT - 122 Sqn.
NK - 118 Sqn.
NM - 268 Sqn.
OE - 168 Sqn.
PD - 303 Sqn.
PK - 315 Sqn.
QE - CFE.
QV - 19 Sqn.
RF - 303 Sqn.
RM - 26 Sqn.
RU - 414 Sqn.
RZ - 241 Sqn.
SH - 64 Sqn.
SK - 165 Sqn.
SP - 400 Sqn.
SY - 613 Sqn.
SZ - 316 Sqn.
TV - 4 Sqn.
UG - 16 Sqn.
UZ - 306 Sqn.
UU - 61 OTU/226 OCU.
WC - 309 Sqn.
XC - 26 Sqn.
XV - 2 Sqn.
YT - 65 Sqn.
Y2 - 442 Sqn.

OXFORD.
AB - 1557 RATF.
AJ - 1653 CU.
AT - 60 OTU.
AN - SF Great Dunmow.
A9 - SF Woodbridge.
2A - SF St Eval.
BD - 43 OTU/227 OTU.
BK - SFSCF.
B3 - SF Wyton.
4B - 5 Gp CF.
7B - 5 Sqn.
CR - 162 Sqn.
C5 - SF Upwood.
C2 - BCIS.
C7 - Ferry Pool?.
1C - SF Scampton.
DR - 1555 RATF.
D2 - 151 Sqn.
3D - 48 MU.
4D - 74 Sqn.
6D - 631 Sqn.
ER - 1552 RATF.
EW - 307 Sqn.
E2 - 81 OTU/138 OTSCU.
F2 - 23 OTU.
FD - 1659 HCU.
9F - SF Stradishall.
GA - 16 OTU.
GD - SF Horsham St Faith.
GL - 1529 RATF.
HB - 239 Sqn.
6H - 1688 BDTF.
7H - 84 Gp CF.
H9 - Shepherds Grove SF.
II - 116 Sqn.

V - SF Upper Heyford.
I4 - 567 Sqn.
JC - 11 Gp CF.
JV - SF Finningley.
JX - 1 Sqn.
J6 - 1521 RATF.
3J - 13 MU.
KI - SF Coningsby.
K2 - 287 Sqn.
4K - SF West Malling.
9K - 1 TTU.
LL - 1513 RATF.
LP - 237 OCU.
MD - 526 Sqn.
M4 - 587 Sqn.
4M - 695 Sqn.
NF - 138 Sqn.
NW - 286 Sqn.
PN - 1552 RATF.
PY - 1527 RATF.
P2 - SF Marston Moor.
P7 - 87 Gp CF.
QF - PFF NTU.
QT - 57 Sqn.
QU - RAF NI CF.
QW - 1516 RATF.
Q6 - 1384 TCU.
8Q - 34 Sqn.
RP - 288 Sqn.
RF - 1510 ABST Flt.
RS - 229 OCU.
R2 - PAU.
SR - 101 Sqn.
SS - 1552 RATF.
SN - 230 OCU.
SO - SF SEFS.
SS - 691 Sqn.
4S - CSE.
S9 - 16Gp CF.
TT - 1658 HCU.
6T - 608 Sqn.
UF - 24 OTU.
UH - 21 OTU/202 CTU.
UT - 17 Sqn.
VF - SF Lindholme.
VG - 285 Sqn.
VG - 286 Sqn.
WN - 527 Sqn.
WQ - 12 Gp CF.
W3 - SF Coningsby.
YE - 289 Sqn.
3Y - 577 Sqn.
ZH - ?

PROCTOR.
BK - SFSCF.
C5 - SF Tibbenham.
3D - 48 MU.
EC - SF Odiham.
EP - 84 Gp CF.
EZ - 81 OTU/138 OTSCU.
GD - SF Horsham St Faith.
GZ - 19 Gp CF.
HC - ?.

7H - 84 Gp CF.
5I - SF Benson.
KE - BLEU.
3M - 48 Gp CF.
5N - 38 Gp CF.
P9 - ASWDU.
QU - RAF NI CF.
R2 - PAU.
S9 - 16 GP CF.
3S - 3 GP CF.
TS - 657 Sqn.
UK - CFE?.
VS - 31 Sqn/MCS.
3V - 1 GP CF.
WQ - 12 GP CF,

SEA OTTER.
MV - 278 Sqn.
7K - SRTU
P9 - ASWDU.
4X - 230 Sqn.

SPITFIRE.
AE - 402 Sqn.
AF - 607 Sqn.
AF - AFDU.
AH - 332 Sqn.
AK - 213 Sqn.
AN - 417 Sqn.
AP - 130 Sqn.
AP - 186 Sqn.
AQ - 276 Sqn.
AU - 421 Sqn.
AV - 121 Sqn.
AZ - 234 Sqn.
AY - 17 OTU.
7A - 614 Sqn.
5A - 329 Sqn.
BA - 277 Sqn.
BL - 1656 HCU.
BP - 457 Sqn.
BL - 609 Sqn.
BN - 1401 Flt.
BQ - 451 Sqn.
7B - 5 Sqn.
7B - 595 Sqn.
B9 - 1562 Flt.
6C - PRDU.
DB - 411 Sqn.
DG - 155 Sqn.
DL - 91 Sqn.
DL - 54 Sqn.
DN - 416 Sqn.
DU - 312 Sqn.
DV - 129 Sqn.
DW - 610 Sqn.
DE - 61 OTU.
4D - 74 Sqn.
6D - 20/631 Sqn.
EB - 41 Sqn.
EF - 232 Sqn.
EG - 16 Sqn.
ES - 82 Sqn.
ES - 541 Sqn.

June 1944 with Spitfires of 56 Squadron ('US'), 332 Squadron ('AH') and 411 Squadron ('DB').

EY - 80 Sqn.
EZ - 81 OTU/138 OTSCU.
4E - 1687 BDF.
7E - 327 Sqn.
FF - 132 Sqn.
FJ - 164 Sqn.
FL - 81 Sqn.
FN - 331 Sqn.
FT - 43 Sqn.
FU - 453 Sqn.
FX - 234 Sqn.
FZ - 65 Sqn.
FX - 266 Sqn.
FY - 611 Sqn.
GE - 349 Sqn.
GK - 52 OTU.
GN - 249 Sqn.
GO - CFE.
GO - 94 Sqn.
GQ - 134 Sqn.
GR - 92 Sqn.
GV - 134 Sqn.
GW - 340 Sqn.
GZ - 611 Sqn.
GZ - 32 Sqn.
9G - 441 Sqn.
G9 - 430 Sqn.
HB - 229 Sqn.
HK - FLS.
HN - 20 Sqn.
HN - 93 Sqn.
HP - GRU.
HT - 154 Sqn.
HT - 601 Sqn.
HX - 61 OTU.
HG - 332 Sqn.
HX - 203 AFS.
3H - 80 OTU.
6H - 1688 BDTF.
IO - 41 OTU.
IP - BCIS.
2I - 443 Sqn.
8I - APS Spilsby.
9I - 326 Sqn.

I4 - 567 Sqn.
JB - 81 OTU.
JG - 17 OTU.
JH - 203 AFS.
JH - 317 Sqn.
JJ - 274 Sqn.
JO - ?.
JU - 111 Sqn.
JV - 6 Sqn.
JX - 1 Sqn.
JZ - 57 OTU.
JW - CFE.
5J - 126 Sqn.
6J - 34 Sqn.
KC - 238 Sqn.
KH - 403 Sqn.
KL - 54 Sqn.
KR - 61 OTU.
KW - 615 Sqn.
KZ - 287 Sqn.
2K - 1 BTU.
3K - 1695 BDTF.
LA - 607 Sqn.
LE - 242 Sqn.
LK - 87 Sqn.
LO - 602 Sqn.
LP - 8 OTU.
LV - 57 OTU.
LW - 318 Sqn.
LY - PDU/1 PRU.
LZ - 421 Flt/66 Sqn.
LN - ?.
LP - 237 OCU.
MD - 133 Sqn.
MK - 126 Sqn.
MN - 350 Sqn.
MT - 122 Sqn.
MJ - ?.
ML - 605 Sqn?.
MO - ?.
MS - 273 Sqn.
MT - 126 Sqn.
MV - 53 OTU.
MY - 278 Sqn.

M4 - 587 Sqn.
4M - 695 Sqn.
NG - 604 Sqn.
NK - 118 Sqn.
NL - 341 Sqn.
NN - 310 Sqn.
NS - 52 OTU.
NX - 131 Sqn.
ND -?.
NI - 451 Sqn.
9N - 127 Sqn.
2N - SF Foulsham?.
OB - 53 OTU.
OI - 2 Sqn.
ON - 124 Sqn.
OU - 485 Sqn.
OQ - 52 OTU/FLS.
PJ - 130 Sqn.
PQ - 2 TEU.
PQ - 58 OTU.
PR - 609 Sqn.
PV - 275 Sqn.
PK - 315 Sqn.
PN - 41 Sqn.
PW - 57 OTU.
P9 - 58 OTU.
QG - 53 OTU.
QH - ?.
QJ - 616 Sqn.
QJ - 92 Sqn.
QJ - 613 Sqn.
QK - PTPS.
QN - 28 OTU.
QV - 19 Sqn.
QY - 452 Sqn.
Q3 - 613 Sqn.
8Q - 34 Sqn.
RAA - 500 Sqn.
RB - 66 Sqn.
RAB - 501 Sqn.
RAC - 502 Sqn.
RD - 67 Sqn.
RF - 303 Sqn.
RG - 208 Sqn.

RG - TC Met Flt.
RN - 72 Sqn.
RP - 288 Sqn.
RS - 33 Sqn.
RY - 314 Sqn.
RZ - 241 Sqn.
5R - 33 Sqn.
9R - 229 Sqn.
SD - 501 Sqn.
SD - 72 Sqn.
SH - 64 Sqn.
SK - 165 Sqn.
SN - 243 Sqn.
SO - 145 Sqn.
ST - 54 OTU.
SW - 253 Sqn.
SX - 1 CACU.
SZ - 316 Sqn.
5S - 691 Sqn.
S8 - 328 Sqn.
7S - ?.
TE - 521 Sqn.
TH - 20 Sqn.
TJ - 52 OTU.
TM - 504 Sqn.
TQ - 276 Sqn.
TS - 548 Sqn.
TV - 1660 HCU.
6T - 608 Sqn.
UB - 164/63 Sqn.
UD - 452 Sqn.
UF - 601 Sqn.
UH - 1682 Flt.
UM - 152 Sqn.
UO - 26 Sqn.
US - 56 Sqn.
UT - 17 Sqn.
UZ - 306 Sqn.
UU - 61 OTU/226 OCU.
UX - CFE.
UY - 10 OTU.
U4 - 667 Sqn.
VL - 167 Sqn.
VL - 322 Sqn.
VZ - 412 Sqn.
V6 - 615 Sqn.
WN - 527 Sqn.
WQ - 12 Gp CF.
WU - 225 Sqn.
WX - 302 Sqn.
WY - 541 Sqn.
WZ - 19 Sqn.
WZ - 80 Sqn.
3W - 322 Sqn.
8W - 612 Sqn.
XB - 58 OTU.
XB - 457 Sqn.
XC - 26 Sqn.
XE - 123 Sqn.
XR - 71 Sqn.
XT - 603 Sqn.
X6 - 290 Sqn.
YB - 17 Sqn.
YE - 289 Sqn.

YO - 401 Sqn.
YQ - 616 Sqn.
YT - 65 Sqn.
2Y - 345 Sqn.
3Y - 57 Sqn.
Y2 - 442 Sqn.
ZF - 549 Sqn.
ZF - 308 Sqn.
ZP - 74 Sqn.
ZT - 602 Sqn.
ZW - 1416 Flt.
ZX - 145 Sqn.
Z9 - 519 Sqn.
RAG - 600 Sqn.
RAH - 601 Sqn.
RAI - 602 Sqn.
RAJ - 603 Sqn.
RAK - 604 Sqn.
RAN - 607 Sqn.
RAO - 608 Sqn.
RAQ - 610 Sqn.
RAR - 611 Sqn.
RAS - 612 Sqn.
RAU - 614 Sqn.
RAV - 615 Sqn.

SINGAPORE.
FV - 205 Sqn.
KM - 205 Sqn.
NT - 203 Sqn.
PP - 203 Sqn.
SH - 240 Sqn.

STIRLING.
AA - 75 Sqn.
AK - 1657 CU.
BS - 1651 HCU.
BU - 214 Sqn.
CS - 513 Sqn.
DA - 237 MU.
DJ - 15 Sqn.
DK - 158 Sqn.
D4 - 620 Sqn.
EX - 199 Sqn.
E7 - 570 Sqn.
8E - 295 Sqn.
FD - 1665 HCU.
FO - 1665 HCU.
GI - 622 Sqn.
GP - 1661 HCU.
G5 - 190 Sqn.
5G - 299 Sqn.
HA - 218 Sqn.
H4 - 1653 HCU.
IC - 623 Sqn.
JN - 75 Sqn.
KT - ?.
KY - 242 Sqn.
LS - 15 Sqn.
L9 - 190 Sqn.
MG - 7 Sqn.
MN - 1665 HCU.
OG - 1651 HCU.
OJ - 149 Sqn.

QQ - 1651 HCU.
QS - 620 Sqn.
TB - 51 Sqn.
TK - 149 Sqn.
TV - 1660 HCU.
7T - 196 Sqn.
V8 - 570 Sqn.
WP - 90 Sqn.
XK - 46 Sqn.
XU - 7 Sqn.
YZ - 1651 HCU.
6Y - 171 Sqn.

STRANRAER.
BN - 240 Sqn.
KK - 209 Sqn.
TO - 228 Sqn.
WQ - 209 Sqn.

SUNDERLAND.
AB - 423 Sqn.
AX - 202 Sqn.
CA - 131 OTU.
DA - 210 Sqn.
DC - 131 OTU.
DG - 422 Sqn.
DQ - 228 Sqn.
DX - 230 Sqn.
EJ - CCFIS.
FV - 230 Sqn.
KG - 204 Sqn.
NM - 230 Sqn.
NS - 201 Sqn.
P9 - ASWDU.
RB - 10 RAAF Sqn.
RF - 204 Sqn.
SE - 95 Sqn.
TQ - 202 Sqn.
UE - 228 Sqn.
UT - 461 Sqn.
VG - 210 Sqn.
WH - 330 Sqn.
4X - 230 Sqn.
YI - 423 Sqn.
ZM - 201 Sqn.

TEMPEST.
AK - 213 Sqn.
EG - 16 Sqn.
FV - 13 OTU.
GE - 349 Sqn.
GF - 56 OTU/1 TEU.
GN - 249 Sqn.
GO - CFE.
HF - 183 Sqn.
HF - 54 Sqn.
HQ - 56 OTU.
JF - 3 Sqn.
JJ - 274 Sqn.
JV - 6 Sqn.
J5 - 3 Sqn.
KZ - 287 Sqn.
MF - FLS/CFE.
OD - 56 OTU.

OQ - 5 Sqn.
OU - 485 Sqn.
QO - 3 Sqn.
RE - CFE.
RS - 229 OCU.
RT - 8 Sqn.
SR - 33 Sqn.
SA - 486 Sqn.
SD - 501 Sqn.
SL - 13 OTU.
7S - ?.
US - 56 Sqn.
W2 - 80 Sqn.
XC - 26 Sqn.
ZD - 222 Sqn.
ZY - 247 Sqn.

TIGER MOTH.
AQ - 276 Sqn.
BD - 43 OTU/227 OCU.
6H - 1688 BDTF.
I4 - 567 Sqn.
3J - 13 MU.
5K - 39 MU.
L5 - 297 Sqn.
ON - 124 Sqn.
8Q - 34 Sqn.
TH - 20 Sqn.
TO - 61 OTU/228 OCU.
WK - 81 Sqn,

THUNDERBOLT.
AD - 113 Sqn.
AW - 42 Sqn.
EG - 34 Sqn.
FJ - 261 Sqn.
FL - 81 Sqn.
GQ - 134 Sqn.
KW - 615 Sqn.
MU - 60 Sqn.
NA - 146 Sqn.
NV - 79 Sqn.
NX - 131 Sqn.
ON - 124 Sqn.
OQ - 5 Sqn.
RS - 30 Sqn.
WK - 135 Sqn.
XE - 123 Sqn.
ZT - 258 Sqn.

TOMAHAWK.
BT - 30 OTU.
EK - 168 Sqn.
FP - 1683 BDTF.
GA - 112 Sqn.
GE - 349 Sqn.
HB - 239 Sqn.
HS - 260 Sqn.
IO - 41 OTU.
KH - 403 Sqn.
KO - 2 Sqn.
LD - 250 Sqn.
NM - 268 Sqn.
RG - 1472 Flt.

RM - 26 Sqn.
RU - 414 Sqn.
RZ - 241 Sqn.
SP - 400 Sqn.

TUTOR.
M7 - 41 Gp CF.

Typhoon 'MR-?' of 245 Squadron.

TYPHOON.
AP - 186 Sqn.
BR - 184 Sqn.
DP - 193 Sqn.
EH - 55 OTU.
EL - 181 Sqn.
FE - 56 OTU.
FJ - 164 Sqn.
FM - 257 Sqn.
FM - 245 Sqn.
F3 - 438 Sqn.
GF - 56 OTU/1 TEU.
HE - 263 Sqn.
HF - 183 Sqn.
HH - 175 Sqn.
HQ - 56 OTU.
II - 59 OTU.
I8 - 440 Sqn.
JE - 195 Sqn.
JX - 1 Sqn.
MF - FLS/CFE.
MR - 245 Sqn.
OU - 485 Sqn.
OV - 197 Sqn.
OD - 56 OTU.
PA - 55 OTU/3 TEU.
PR - 69 Sqn.
QC - 168 Sqn.
QO - 3 Sqn.
4Q - 59 OTU.
RL - 1 SLAIS.
5R - 33 SQN.
SA - 486 SQN.
SF - 137 SQN.
TP - 198 SQN.
UO - 266 SQN.
US - 56 SQN.
UW - 3 TEU.
5V - 439 Sqn.
XM - 182 Sqn.
XP - 174 Sqn.
ZH - 266 Sqn.
ZY - 247 Sqn.

VALENTIA.
DU - 70 Sqn.
EE - 31 Sqn?.
SH - 216 Sqn.
SJ - 70 Sqn.
VT - 216 Sqn.
ZA - 31 Sqn.

VALETTA.
JN - 30 Sqn.
NU - 240 OCU.
NU - 242 OCU.
QO - 52 Sqn.
QO - 167 Sqn.
SJ - 204 Sqn?

VAMPIRE.
AP - 130 Sqn.
BB - 226 OCU.
BK - SFS CF.
CX - 14 Sqn.
EG - 16 Sqn.
ES - 229 OCU.
EX - 11 Sqn.
GO - CFE.
HF - 54 Sqn.
HX - 226 OCU.
J5 - 3 Sqn.
KR - 226 OCU.
LA - 607 Sqn.
LO - 602 Sqn.
NG - 604 Sqn.
NR - 605 Sqn.
QJ - 613 Sqn.
Q3 - 613 Sqn.
RS - 229 OCU.
SA - 329 Sqn?.
SD - 501 Sqn.
TH - 20 Sqn.
UP - 4 Sqn.
UU - 61 OTU/226 OCU.
WL - SF Celle.
8W - 612 Sqn.
XC - 26 Sqn.
ZY - 247 Sqn. RAB - 501
   Sqn.
RAL - 605 Sqn.

VENGEANCE.
6D - 20/631 Sqn.
I4 - 567 Sqn.

M4 - 587 Sqn.
4M - 695 Sqn.
OB - 45 Sqn.
4Q - CC FATU.
8Q - 34 Sqn.
RP - 288 Sqn.
U4 - 667 Sqn.

YE - 289 Sqn.

VENTURA.
BP - 458 Sqn.
EG - 487 Sqn.
SB - 464 Sqn.
SG - 299 Sqn.
YH - 21 Sqn.
Z9 - 519 Sqn.

VILDEBEEST.
AW - 42 Sqn.
HH - 273 Sqn.
HJ - 100 Sqn?.
NK - 100 Sqn.
OA - 22 Sqn.
QD - 42 Sqn.
OE - 36 Sqn.
RA - 100 Sqn.
VR - 22 Sqn.
VU - 36 Sqn,

VINCENT.
EW - 47 Sqn.
YO - 8 Sqn.

WALLACE.
HP - GRU.

WALRUS.
AQ - 276 Sqn.
BA - 277 Sqn.
B4 - 282 Sqn.
FG -?.
7K - SRTU.
MY - 278 Sqn.
PV - 275 Sqn.
ZC - 284 Sqn.
ZE - 293 Sqn.

WAPITI.
MY - 27 Sqn.
QN - 5 Sqn.

WARWICK.
B4 - 282 Sqn.
FA - 281 Sqn.
FI - WTU.
GR - 301 Sqn.
HK - 269 Sqn.
K7 - 6 OTU.
LP - 283 Sqn.
ME - 280 Sqn.
MF - 280 Sqn.
OZ - 179 Sqn.
P9 - ASWDU.
QD - 304 Sqn.
RL - 38/279 Sqn.
RR - ?.
ZE - 293 Sqn,

WASHINGTON.
FB - WCU.
KM - 44 Sqn.
LS - 15 Sqn.
OJ - 149 Sqn.
WP - 90 Sqn.

WELLESLEY.
AO - 223 Sqn.

BY - 23 OTU?.
CM - 107 OTU.
CM - 1333 TCU.
CX - 14 Sqn.
DD - 22 OTU.
DD - 45 Sqn.
DF - 221 Sqn.
DT - 192 Sqn.
DX - 57 Sqn.
ED - 21 OTU.
EJ - CCFIS.
EN - 27 OTU.
EP - 104 Sqn.
EU - 15 OTU.
EU - 26 OTU.
EW - 47 Sqn.
EX - 199 Sqn.
EZ - 81 OTU.
FA - 236 Sqn.
FH - 15 OTU.
FJ - 37 Sqn.
FQ - 12 OTU.
FU - 458 Sqn.
FW - 458 Sqn.
FZ - 23 OTU.
8F - 105 OTU.

JN - 150 Sqn.
JS - 16 OTU.
KA - 9 Sqn.
KA - 82 OTU.
KD - 30 OTU.
KG - 1380 TSCU.
KJ - 11 OTU.
KK - 15 OTU.
KO - 115 Sqn.
KW - 425 Sqn.
KU - 47 Sqn.
KW - 425 Sqn.
KX - 311 Sqn.
KY - 242 Sqn.
LB - 20 OTU.
LF - 37 Sqn.
LG - 215 Sqn.
LN - 99 Sqn.
LQ - 405 Sqn.
LS - 15 Sqn.
LT - 22 OTU.
LY - PDU/1 PRU.
LY - 149 Sqn.
MD - 458 Sqn.
ML - 12 OTU.
MZ - 83 OTU.

PM - 103 Sqn.
PP - 25 OTU.
PT - 420 Sqn.
P9 - ASWDU.
9P - 85 OTU.
QB - 424 Sqn.
QD - 304 Sqn.
QO - 432 Sqn.
QT - 142 Sqn.
QN - 28 OTU.
QR - 223 Sqn.
RW - 36 Sqn.
RK - 10 OTU.
7R - 524 Sqn.
SE - 431 Sqn.
SM - 305 Sqn.
SR - 101 Sqn.
SJ - 21 OTU.
ST - 54 OTU.
ST - 228 OCU.
TA - 358 Sqn.
TD - 82 OTU.
TF - 29 OTU.
TN - 30 OTU.
TX - 11 OTU.
TY - 24 OTU.
UF - 24 OTU.
UH - 21 OTU.
UJ - 27 OTU.
UO - 19 OTU.
UV - 460 Sqn.
UX - 214 Sqn.
UY - 10 OTU.
VB - 14 OTU.
VF - 99 Sqn.
VJ - ? VQ - 28 OTU?.
VR - 419 Sqn.
WE - 23 OTU.
WG - 26 OTU.
WJ - 17 OTU.
WL - 612 Sqn.
WN - 172 Sqn.
WN - 527 Sqn.
WS - 9 Sqn.
8W - 612 Sqn.
XF - 19 OTU.
XG - 16 OTU.
XL - 20 OTU.
XN - 22 OTU.
XW - 18 OTU.
X3 - 111 OTU.
YR - 20 OTU.
ZT - 20 OTU.
ZL - 77 Sqn.

WHIRLWIND.
HE - 263 Sqn.
SF - 137 Sqn.

WHITLEY.
BW - 58 Sqn.
DY - 102 Sqn.
EY - 78 Sqn.
EZ - 81 OTU/138 OTSCU.

8E - 295 Sqn.
FA - 236 Sqn.
GB - 166 Sqn.
GE - 58 Sqn.
GO - 42 OTU.
HS - 192 Sqn.
JB - 81 OTU.
JL - 10 OTU.
KG - 30 OTU.
KG - 81 OTU?.
KN - 77 Sqn.
LT - 7 Sqn.
LS - 297 Sqn.
MB - 51 Sqn.
MH - 51 Sqn.
MR - 97 Sqn.
NF - 138 Sqn.
OF - 97 Sqn.
PB - 10 Sqn.
RK - 10 OTU.
SA - ?.
SG - ?.
TG - 502 Sqn.
TQ - 102 Sqn.
TY - 24 OTU.
UO - 19 OTU.
UT - 51 Sqn.
UY - 10 OTU.
WA - ?.
WL - 612 Sqn.
XF - 19 OTU.
XH - 295 Sqn.
YG - 502 Sqn.
YY - 78 Sqn.
ZA - 10 Sqn.
ZV - 19 OTU.

YORK.
BY - 59 Sqn.
KY - 242 Sqn.
LE - 40 Sqn.
MH - 51 Sqn.
TB - 51 Sqn.
VU - 246 Sqn.119 Sqn.
NH - 415 Sqn.
YY - 1381 HTCU.

'KX' coded Wellingtons of 311 Squadron.

WELLINGTON.
AA - 75 Sqn.
AL - 429 Sqn.
AS - 166 Sqn.
AM - 14 OTU.
AX - 77 OTU?.
AY - 17 OTU.
BB - 27 OTU.
BH - 215 Sqn.
BK - 115 Sqn.
BS - 148 Sqn.
BT - 30 OTU.
BU - 214 Sqn.
BZ - 82 OTU.
BF - 14 Sqn.
BH - 300 Sqn.

GR - 301 Sqn.
GT - 156 Sqn.
GS - 83 OTU.
GY - 1383 TSCU.
HD - 38 Sqn.
HD - 466 Sqn.
HH - 218 Sqn.
HR - 304 Sqn?.
HS - 109 Sqn.
IA - SF Syerston.
IF - 84 OTU.
IN - SF Valley.
I4 - 567 Sqn.
I5 - 1381 TSCU.
JG - 17 OTU.
JM - 20 OTU.

NA - 428 Sqn.
NH - 38 Sqn.
NH - 415 Sqn.
NM - 76 Sqn.
NP - 158 Sqn.
NQ - 24 Sqn.
NT - 29 Sqn.
NZ - 304 Sqn.
7N - SFU.
OG - 172 Sqn.
OJ - 149 Sqn.
OP - 11 OTU.
OW - 426 Sqn.
OX - 22 OTU.
PB - 26 OTU.
PH - 12 Sqn.

Honours and Awards to the RAF Since 1918

(with Peter Jacobs)

Since the formation of the RAF many Orders, Decorations and Medals have been awarded to members of the Service. The list is long and the variations in why they were awarded are complex. The majority, the Campaign awards, were awarded to personnel present in a theatre of operations during a period of conflict or war. This chapter covers all the British awards which a serving member of the RAF might have obtained, both during wartime and so-called 'peacetime.' All the basic data relating to each award is covered — type, description, number awarded (although this can vary according to the source) and, in the case of the gallantry awards and Orders, includes 'illustrative examples.' The awards covered are in order of precedence.

For gallantry awards, there are immediate and non-immediate awards. An immediate award being for an act of gallantry worthy of instant recognition whereas a non-immediate award would be for a period of gallantry or devotion to duty. How awards are recommended, particularly in the case of gallantry awards, is interesting. In some cases it is all too easy to think that an award has simply been 'given' away but every award must be taken on its own individual merit. Yet why, for example, were some decorated with the supreme award of a Victoria Cross while others received a Distinguished Flying Cross or, in many cases, nothing? Quite often an individual had not performed quite to the level required for a particular award, or it may have been considered that one area of operations should not be more favoured than another.

In the case of Orders bestowed upon members of the RAF (or WRAF), an individual's long and distinguished career is rewarded by the State. There are many variations depending on the rank and services of the individual. For campaign medals, rank and service career make no difference. The same medal is awarded to an 'other rank' as to a commander in a theatre of conflict or war.

THE VICTORIA CROSS

The Victoria Cross is the most coveted decoration and takes precedence of all other Orders, decorations and medals. It was instituted in January 1856 and is awarded for very exceptional gallantry to officers and men alike. The award is open to women although no award has ever been made.

The VC consists of a bronze cross patte 1.5 inches wide. On the obverse is a lion standing upon the Royal Crown below which is 'FOR VALOUR' on a semi-circular scroll. The reverse has the date of the act engraved in a circle in the centre. The cross is suspended from a 'V' which is part of the clasp ornamented with laurel leaves. On the reverse of the clasp is the recipient's name, rank and unit. The ribbon is crimson. All awards are verified in the London Gazette.

A total of just 51 awards have been made to airmen of which 19 were for the First World War and 32 for the Second World War. The first recipient of an air VC was 2nd Lieutenant William Rhodes Moorhouse, 2 Squadron RFC, for gallantry whilst bombing Courtrai rail junction in FE2b 687 on 22 April 1915 during the First Battle of Ypres.

Captain A. Ball VC DSO MC — 56 Squadron

Probably the most famous of the RFC's air aces was Albert Ball. by the time he was posted to 56 Squadron on 25 February 1917, he had already been awarded the Military Cross and the Distinguished Service Order and two bars. The Squadron was newly formed and equipped with the new SE5. Ball scored the Squadron's first victory, on 23 April, and during the next two weeks he scored 14 victories.

Flying SE5 A4850, on 7 May 1917, Ball was engaged in a series of combats between Cambrai and Douai. He was last seen chasing an enemy aircraft into cloud. German eyewitnesses state that his aircraft emerged from cloud emitting black smoke and plunged into the ground. The Germans buried him with full military honours at Annoeulin Cemetery. Soon after it was announced that Albert Ball was awarded the VC. The citation for his VC stated that Ball had scored 44 combat victories, but was later confirmed to be 47. Albert Ball was just 20 years old.

All but four of the First World War air VCs were awarded for action before the formation of the RAF (including two to the RNAS and one to the AFC). The first award after this date was to Captain 'Freddie' West, 8 Squadron, for gallantry during a reconnaissance sortie in FK8 C8594 near Roye on 10 August 1918.

The first awards of the Second World War, and the only occasion when two members of the same crew received a VC, went to Flying Officer Donald Garland, pilot, and Sergeant Thomas Gray, observer, 12 Squadron, who were both posthumously awarded the VC following their attack in Battle P2204 on a bridge at Veldwezelt on 5 May 1940.

Flight Lieutenant E. J. Nicolson VC — 249 Squadron

Despite the heroics of 'The Few' during the Battle of Britain, Fighter Command's sole VC was awarded not to an 'ace', but to a man experiencing combat for the very first time.

249 Squadron had moved south to Boscombe Down on 14 August 1940. Just two days later, in Hurricane P3576, James Nicholson was leading a section on patrol over the Southampton area at 18,000 feet when they were jumped by BF109s. Nicholson's aircraft was hit in the fuel tank and on fire. Wounded above the eye and in the foot, he prepared to bale out but then saw a BF110 ahead and, getting back into his seat, he carried out an attack. By now his cockpit had become a furnace, badly burning his face and hands. Realising that he did not have much

Sqn Ldr J. B. Nicolson with VC ribbon. Note this also includes a miniature cross.

time, he carried out one final attack before abandoning his aircraft. The sortie had lasted just 47 minutes. Nicholson eventually recovered from his injuries, but sadly lost his life in the Far East on 2 May 1945.

The youngest recipient of a VC for aerial operations was Sergeant John Hannah, 83 Squadron, a wireless operator who was just 18 years old when he was awarded the VC following a raid in Hampden P1355 against the port of Antwerp on the night of 15/16 September 1940. The oldest recipient of an air VC was 34 year old Flight Lieutenant David Hornell, a pilot of 162 Squadron, who was posthumously awarded the VC following an attack in Canso 9754 against a U-boat on 24 June 1944. Hornell was one of just four VCs to be awarded to Coastal Command.

Although generally regarded as a British award, half of the Second World War air VCs went to airmen born outside Britain from Australia, New Zealand, Canada, Eire and South Africa. Of the British recipients, six were born in Scotland.

Flight Lieutenant W. Reid VC — 61 Squadron

Born in Scotland, Bill Reid was just 21 when he was awarded the VC following a raid against Dusseldorf, in Lancaster LM360, on the night of 3/4 November 1943.

Outbound, his aircraft was attacked by a BF110 resulting in several instruments, including the compass, being made useless also the port elevator had been hit and the hydraulics damaged. Reid was wounded in the head and shoulder but decided to continue. Soon after, a FW190 attacked killing the navigator and fatally wounding the wireless operator. The mid-upper turret was hit and the oxygen system put out of action. Reid was wounded again but, determined only to reach the target, continued, using the Pole Star and ground features to navigate. Holding the aircraft steady, he flew directly over the target and released his bombs. With only a short supply of emergency oxygen, short of fuel and with ruptured hydraulics, he held the aircraft steady until coasting in back home. Unsure of exactly where he was and growing weaker through the loss of blood, Reid landed at the first airfield. The undercarriage collapsed before the aircraft finally came to rest. He had landed at Shipdham and was taken to hospital where he recovered from his injuries. Soon after came the announcement that Bill Reid was awarded the VC.

Bill Reid was one of ten VCs won by Lancaster airmen and one of 19 VCs to Bomber Command. The only transport pilot to receive the VC was Flight Lieutenant David Lord, flying Dakota

KG374 of 271 Squadron, who was posthumously awarded the VC during the Allied airborne invasion of Arnhem, on 19 September 1944.

Just five air VCs were awarded for action outside the European theatre. The only air VC won in North Africa was to Wing Commander Hugh Malcolm, 18 Squadron, who was posthumously awarded the VC after leading a daylight attack near Chougui in Blenheim BA875 on 4 December 1942. Flying Officer Lloyd Trigg, 200 Squadron, was posthumously awarded the VC following an attack on a U-boat, in Liberator BZ832, 240 miles to the west of Dakar, on the west coast of Africa, on 11 August 1943.

Three other air VCs out of the European theatre were awarded to heroes of the 'forgotten war' in the Far East.

Flying Officer A. S. K. Scarf VC — 62 Squadron

On 9 December 1941, Flying Officer 'John' Scarf took off from Butterworth in Blenheim L1134 detailed to attack a Japanese airfield at Singora in Siam. Immediately after he got airborne, Butterworth was attacked by Japanese bombers preventing any further aircraft from getting airborne. At that point, Scarf would have been fully justified in abandoning his mission but, against all the odds, decided to press on to his target. Overhead Singora he was attacked by 12 Japanese fighters. With great determination he carried out his attack despite being hit several times. Grievously wounded, Scarf evaded the enemy fighters and nursed the Blenheim back to safety before making an emergency landing at Alor Star. Soon after arriving at hospital, Scarf died of his terrible injuries. Following the chaos in the Far East at that time, it was not until after the war that the full story was told and in June 1946 it was announced that 'John' Scarf was posthumously awarded the VC.

The second Far East air VC was won by Flight Lieutenant Bill Newton, 22 (RAAF) Squadron, flying Boston A28-15 against a Japanese base at Salamaua, New Guinea, on 16 March 1943. He survived the ordeal only to be shot down two days later and captured by the Japanese. Following intensive interrogation, Newton was callously beheaded by the Japanese on the 29 March. The third, and also the last action of the war for which an air VC was won, was awarded to Lieutenant Robert Gray, 1841 Squadron. He was posthumously awarded the VC following an attack in Corsair KD658 against two Japanese destroyers on 9 August 1945.

THE GEORGE CROSS

The George Cross was instituted in September 1940. It is awarded only for 'acts of the greatest heroism or of the most conspicuous courage in circumstances of extreme danger'. It is intended primarily for civilians, men and women, but has been awarded to members of the Services for cases where military awards are not applicable. There was also a provision for living recipients of the Empire Gallantry Medal to exchange their original award for the GC.

The GC consists of a plain silver cross with a circular medallion in the centre bearing St. George and the dragon, surrounded by 'FOR GALLANTRY'. In the angle of each limb of the cross is the Royal cypher 'CVI'. The reverse is plain and contains the name of the recipient and the date of the award. The GC hangs from a dark blue ribbon by a silver bar adorned with laurel leaves. When awarded to women, the GC is worn on the left shoulder from a ribbon tied in a bow. Bars may be awarded for further acts of heroism. All awards are notified in the London Gazette, although the award has been very sparingly given. Excluding exchange awards, only some 150 awards of the GC have been made.

THE MOST HONOURABLE ORDER OF THE BATH

The Order of the Bath was originally founded in 1399. Since the formation of the RAF the Order has been awarded for senior officers for services in wartime and peacetime. Today, all officers are eligible for appointment to the Military Division but the Order is generally only awarded to the most senior officers for peacetime services. Admission to the Order is still granted sparingly. There are three classes:-

1. Knight Grand Cross — GCB
2. Grand Commander — KCB
3. Companion — CB

KCB — neck badge and breast star.

The Military Badge is a gold Maltese cross of eight points, enamelled white, each point tipped with a gold ball. Between the arms of the cross is a gold lion. In the centre is a rose, thistle and shamrock and three Imperial Crowns, surrounded by a red enamel circle on which is the motto 'TRIA JUNCTA IN UNO' in gold. This circle is surrounded by two branches of laurel, enemelled green, below which is a blue enamel scroll with 'ICH DIEN' in gold.

A Knight Grand Cross wears the Military Badge around the neck from a gold Collar. Also he wears a star on the left breast consisting of a gold Maltese cross of the same pattern as the badge, mounted on a flaming star. A Knight Commander wears a smaller badge around the neck from a crimson ribbon and also a star on the left breast. The star of the KCB has no Maltese cross and is in the shape of a cross Pattee. The Companion wears just a smaller sized badge around the neck from a crimson ribbon.

Marshal of the RAF Sir Michael Beetham GCB CBE DFC AFC

Born in 1923, Michael Beetham joined the RAF in 1941. As a Lancaster pilot, he flew a tour of operators with 50 Squadron during which he was awarded the DFC. Beetham's career in the RAF was undoubtedly as distinguished as one will ever read about. He achieved every rank possible and commanded at the highest levels. As a Wing Commander he was awarded the AFC in 1960. As a Group Captain he commanded Khormaksar, Aden, between 1964-66 for which he was made a Commander of the British Empire in 1967. Many senior appointments followed before he was appointed Chief of the Air Staff in 1977 and made a Knights Grand Cross of the Order of the Bath in 1978 in recognition of his outstanding career. Sir Michael served as CAS for five years and was in-post during the Falklands Conflict of 1982.

Air Chief Marshal Sir Charles Medhurst KCB OBE MC

Born in 1896, Charles Medhurst was commissioned into the Royal Inniskillin Fusiliers in 1915. Soon after, he transferred as a pilot into the RFC. He was awarded the Military Cross early in 1918 and was amongst the very first recipients of the new Military Division of the Order of the British Empire when he was awarded the OBE on 1 January 1919. Medhurst served with the RAF between the wars reaching the rank of Group Captain by 1939. Several senior Air Ministry appointments followed, and he quickly became an Air Vice-Marshal. In 1941, he was appointed Vice Chief of the Air Staff to Sir Charles Portal and was made a Companion of the Order of the Bath in 1942, and became a member of the Air Council in 1943. In 1946 he was made a Knight Commander of the Order of the Bath. Sir Charles' next appointment was Commander-in-Chief RAF Mediterranean and Middle East, a position he held until the end of 1948. As Air Chief Marshal, he retired from the RAF in 1950.

Air Vice-Marshal Leslie Cannon CB CBE

Born in 1904, Leslie Cannon joined the RAF as an apprentice in 1920. Commissioned as a pilot in 1925, he served with the RAF during the inter-war years. During the Second World War, he was promoted to Group Captain and commanded RAF Watton. Cannon continued to fly on operations throughout 1943, not only with the RAF, but also with the United States 8th Air Force as Air Officer Administration No. 2 Group, and this led to him being awarded the United States Silver Star. After the war, he was appointed Air Officer Commanding 85 Group and made a Commander of the British Empire in June 1946. As an Air Vice-Marshal, he became Commander-in-Chief of the Royal Pakistan Air Force in 1951. Cannon was made a Companion of the Order of the Bath in January 1952, before retiring from the RAF in 1958.

OBE group to Wg Cdr Gordon Hampton — OBE, DFC, 1939-45 Star, Africa Star plus clasp, Italy Star, Defence Medal, War Medal 1939-45. Note incorrect mounting of DFC ribbon.

THE ORDER OF THE BRITISH EMPIRE

Founded in 1917, the Order of the British Empire was introduced owing to the large demand for honours and awards created by the First World War. The Order is conferred upon officers for services of a non-combatant character and all commissioned officers and warrant officers of the RAF or WRAF are eligible for the Military Division of the award. The five classes are as follows:-

1. Knights (or Dames) Grand Cross — GBE
2. Knights (or Dames) Commanders — KBE or DBE
3. Commanders — CBE
4. Officers — OBE
5. Members — MBE.

For members of the first three classes, the cross patonce is of silver gilt with the arms enamelled pearl grey. In the centre, within a circle enamelled crimson, was originally a representation of Britannia but from 1937 the busts of King George V and Queen Mary. The circle contains the motto 'FOR GOD AND THE EMPIRE'. The badge of the fourth class is similar, but is smaller and in silver gilt and not enamelled. That of the fifth class is silver. In addition, members of the first two classes wear a star with the central device the same as that for the badge. The ribbon was originally purple with a narrow scarlet stripe down the centre but in 1936 was changed to rose pink, edged with pearl grey, and a central stripe in pearl grey.

There are several variations on how the Order is worn. Simply, the first class is worn with the badge mounted on a ribbon worn over the shoulder, and the star worn on the left side. For men, the second class is worn with the badge worn around the neck, suspended from a ribbon, with the star worn on the left side. Women wear a bow of ribbon, with the badge attached, on the left side with the star being fixed just below the badge. For the third class, men wear the badge suspended around the neck from the ribbon and the women wear a bow of ribbon, with the badge attached, on the left side. For the fourth and fifth classes, the badge is worn from the ribbon as with other medals and decorations.

Group Captain C. Spink CBE

Cliff Spink joined the RAF in 1963. Following pilot training, he flew lightnings with 111 and 56 Squadrons in the UK and Cyprus. He later flew Phantoms, as a Flight Commander with 111 Squadron and then as Officer Commanding 74 Squadron. In 1989, Cliff Spink was appointed as an Officer of the Order of the British Empire for his services to the RAF. He later commanded RAF Mount Pleasant in the Falkland Islands before taking command of RAF Coningsby in December 1990. Within days, he was sent to the Gulf as overall Detachment Commander of the RAF forces at Dhahran, and remained there until the end of the Gulf War before returning to Coningsby to resume his command in March 1991. For his distinguished career, and in particular his fine leadership in command at Dhahran during the Gulf War, Cliff Spink was made a Commander of the Order of the British Empire in January 1992.

Wing Commander G. Hampton OBE DFC

Born in 1919, Gordon Hampton joined the RAF as a pilot in 1941. Whilst serving with 223 Squadron during the Sicily campaign, he was awarded the DFC in march 1944. After the war, he continued a career in the RAF. Among his many appointments was a tour as Officer Commanding 50 Squadron and an exchange tour with the USAAF Strategic Air Command flying B-52s. In 1959, he was made an Officer of the Order of the British Empire in recognition of his distinguished career in the RAF.

Flying Officer D. Dines MBE — 276 Squadron

In August 1943, Dines was observer of an Anson which, owing to engine failure, came down in the sea. The pilot sustained injuries to his head and Dines took command of the crew. As a result of his untiring efforts the dinghy was recovered from the wreckage. Then, in order to save an airman who was a non-swimmer. Dines swam over to a petrol tank which had broken loose and succeeded in getting the airman onto it. He eventually inflated the dinghy and assisted all the crew into it safely. All were rescued several hours later. The lives of Dines' comrades were undoubtedly saved by his courage and coolness in extremely difficult circumstances.

THE BRITISH EMPIRE MEDAL

A silver medal of the Order of the British Empire was instituted in 1917. It had a purple ribbon with a central red stripe. In 1922 the award of the medal was discontinued and two other medals were issued in its place:-

1. The medal of the Order of the British Empire for gallantry — EGM (Empire Gallantry Medal).

2. The medal of the Order of the British Empire for meritorious service.

The Empire Medal for gallantry was abolished on the institution of the George Cross in September 1940. At the same time, the rule for the award of the BEM was laid down that it was to be awarded only to persons who rendered meritorious service who were not already members of any of the five classes of the Order of the British Empire, and were not eligible for appointment thereto.

The medal is silver. The obverse has a representation of Britannia with the motto of the Order, and at the base 'FOR MERITORIOUS SERVICE'. The reverse has the Royal and Imperial cypher and 'INSTITUTED BY KING GEORGE'. It is suspended from a clasp ornamented with oak leaves, the ribbon being the same as that for the Order. Bars may be awarded for further acts of meritorious service. All BEMs are issued named and all awards are notified in the London Gazette, although few have citations.

Total numbers of awards show that some 2,000 of the original medal were awarded between 1917-22. Only 130 EGMs and approximately 850 Medals for Meritorious Service were awarded between 1922-40. Since 1941 numerous awards have been made.

Corporal W. Lush BEM — RAF Regiment

In October 1943 an aircraft, which had sustained damage during an attack on Hanover, crashed near an airfield. The aircraft disintegrated on impact and immediately burst into flames. The rear gunner was injured and trapped in his turret. A high explosive bomb was in the blazing wreckage just ten yards away from the gunner. Lush hastened to the scene of the accident. Although fully aware that the heat might cause the bomb to detonate, he spent over half an hour trying to relieve the gunner's pain and free him. A crane was brought to the scene and the wreckage lifted. Displaying complete disregard for his own safety he crawled under the wreckage and released the trapped gunner. Corporal William Lush was awarded the BEM for 'fine courage and determination in circumstances of great danger.'

THE DISTINGUISHED SERVICE ORDER

The DSO was established in 1886 to reward individual instances of meritorious or distinguished service in war. It is only awarded to commissioned officers whose services have been marked by the special mention in despatches for 'distinguished services under fire, or under conditions equivalent to service in actual combat with the enemy.' Any recipient of the Order who subsequently performs a further approved act of gallantry is awarded a bar and for every additional such act, a further bar.

The badge consists of a gold cross, enamelled white, and edged gold. On the obverse is the Imperial Crown in gold within a wreath of laurel enamelled green. On the reverse is the Royal cypher in gold within a similar wreath. It hangs from the ribbon by a gold clasp ornamented with laurel, while another similar clasp is worn at the top of the ribbon. The ribbon is red with narrow blue borders.

The number of members of the Order is unlimited, although awards to the RAF are scarce. All awards are verified in the London Gazette, the first Air Ministry awards being gazetted on 3 June 1918. The number of awards to the RAF for the First World War is 52 with seven first bars and one second bar.

Captain J. Gilmour DSO MC — 65 Squadron

On 1 July 1918, a patrol of 65 Squadron Sopwith Camels was attacked by a large formation of 40 enemy aircraft over Morlancourt. During the following action, Captain Gilmour destroyed five enemy machines, an act which brought him an immediate award of the DSO on 16 July. By the end of the war, Gilmour had shot down 44 enemy aircraft and in addition to the DSO he had been awarded two bars to his Military Cross.

Between 1920-39, a total of 163 DSOs were awarded for operations worldwide. During the Second World War 870 DSOs were awarded to the RAF with 62 first bars, eight second bars and two third bars. the two recipients of third bars were Air Vice-Marshal Sir Basil Embry and Wing Commander J. B. 'Willie' Tait.

Squadron Leader A. Spooner DSO DFC — 53 Squadron

A veteran of Malta, for which he was awarded the DFC, Tony Spooner became one of Coastal Command's great U-boat hunters. He and the crew of his Liberator became highly decorated — two DFCs, four DFMs and Spooner's DSO in 1944. His citation reads —

'This officer has participated in a large number of sorties and has invariably displayed a high degree of skill and courage. One night recently he piloted an aircraft which attacked two U-boats. The vessels were surfaced and in close proximity, and Spooner released several depth charges over both of them in the same attacking run. Some nights later Spooner attacked two more U-boats. In all his encounters with the enemy, this officer has displayed great determination and has pressed home his attacks in the face of enemy opposition. He has set a very fine example to all.'

Since 1945 about 170 DSOs have been awarded for operations worldwide although it is unclear how many awards have been made to the RAF. Most of these awards were made during 1949-58 for Malaya and 1951-54 for Korea.

DSO group to Sqn Ldr Tony Spooner — DSO, DFC, 1939 Star, Atlantic Star plus clasp, Africa Star, Defence Medal, War Medal 1939-45, Air Efficiency Award.

THE DISTINGUISHED FLYING CROSS

The DFC was established on 3 June 1918 for award to officers and warrant officers for an act or acts of valour, courage or devotion to duty performed whilst flying in active operations against the enemy.

The cross is silver and consists of a cross flory surmounted by another cross of aeroplane propellers, with a roundel within a wreath of laurels 'RAF'. On the reverse is the Royal cypher above the date 1918. Suspension is by a straight silver bar,

ornamented with sprigs of laurel. The ribbon was originally violet and white alternate stripes. From July 1919, the stripes were changed to run at an angle of 45 degrees from left to right. Awards made during and after the Second World War have the year of the award engraved on the reverse lower limb. Bars may be awarded for further acts of bravery, and awards made during and after the Second World War have the year of the award engraved on the reverse of the bar. All awards appear in the London Gazette. Citations appear for a number of awards, although the majority during the Second World War do not have citations.

Between 1918 and 1939, a total of 1,215 crosses were awarded with 88 first bars and 7 second bars. During the Second World War, over 20,000 DFCs were awarded with 1,550 first bars and 42 second bars thus making it the most frequent award of the war.

Pilot Officer A. S. Ramsay DFC — 105 Squadron

On 4 July 1941, 15 Blenheims were tasked with a daring daylight raid, at low level, against the industrial complex at Bremen. Chosen to lead the raid was Wing Commander Hughie Edwards, and for this special raid he picked Alastair Ramsay as his navigator.

In Blenheim V6028, they proceeded to the target at a height of about 50 feet mostly under conditions of poor visibility. The area was heavily defended against air attack on account of its great industrial importance. Flying at chimney-height, in between barrage balloon cables, they pressed home a most determined attack. Direct hits were scored on factories, timber yards and derricks. A barrage of flak opened up and four aircraft were immediately destroyed. Ramsay's aircraft was under constant attack for some 10 minutes and repeatedly hit. Every Blenheim suffered flak damage as they withdrew at rooftop height. After a reconnaissance of the target they turned for home. They were the last to return.

Edwards was awarded the VC and Ramsay the DFC. Ramsay's citation includes — 'There is no doubt that Ramsay's skill in navigation and cool determination contributed very materially towards the success of a most hazardous operation.' Sadly Alastair Ramsay was killed just three weeks later during an operation in Malta.

Squadron Leader H. T. Gilbert DFC — 65 Squadron

At the age of just 22 years old Humphrey Gilbert was tragically killed in a flying accident on 2 May 1942. At the time he was OC 65 Squadron, a fighter ace and a 'veteran' of the Battle of Britain — one of 'The Few'. Later that month came the announcement of a posthumous award of the DFC to Gilbert. His citation reads —

'This officer has been engaged on operational flying since August 1940 and fought through the Battle of Britain. He has completed numerous operational sorties over enemy occupied territory and although he has been shot down and wounded, he has always displayed great keenness to engage the enemy. Since February 1942 Gilbert has participated in a number of operational sorties, including an attack on German battleships. In this operation he destroyed one enemy aircraft and damaged another. He has led his squadron, and occasionally the Wing, with considerable success and his fine leadership and determination have been an inspiration to his pilots.'

Since 1946, approximately 280 DFCs have been awarded with 26 first bars and 3 second bars, the majority of which were for operations in Malaya (118 awarded between 1949-60) and Korea (89 awarded between 1951-54). Nine awards were made following the Falklands Conflict of 1982 and 12 awards following the Gulf War of 1991.

Wing Commander P. T. Squire DFC AFC — 1 Squadron

Peter Squires of OC 1 Squadron, with Harrier GR3s, embarked on HMS *Hermes* during the Falklands Conflict of 1982. His citation reads — 'Wing Commander Squire led his Squadron with great courage from the front, flying 24 attack sorties. He flew many daring missions including an attack at low level with rockets at Port Stanley airfield in the face of heavy anti-aircraft fire when both he and his wingman returned damaged. Also a bombing attack on an HQ position when a bullet passed through his cockpit which temporarily distracted him, but he quickly found an alternative target and bombed that instead.

THE AIR FORCE CROSS

The AFC was established on 3 June 1918 for award to officers and warrant officers for an act or acts of valour, courage or devotion to duty performed whilst flying, though not in active service against the enemy.

The cross is silver and consists of a thunderbolt in the form a cross, the arms conjoined by the wings, surmounted by another cross of aeroplane propellers, the four ends enscribed with the Royal cypher. In the centre is Hermes mounted on a hawk bestowing a wreath. On the reverse is the Royal cypher above the date 1918. The cross is suspended by a straight silver bar, ornamented with sprigs of laurel. The ribbon was originally crimson and white alternate horizontal stripes. From July 1919, the stripes were changed to run at an angle of 45 degrees from left to right. Awards made during and after the Second World War have the year of the award engraved on the reverse lower limb. Bars may be awarded for further acts of courage, and awards made during and after the Second World War have the date of the award engraved on the reverse of the bar. All awards are found in the London Gazette, although very few have citations.

Between 1918 and 1939, a total of 837 awards were made with 12 first bars and 3 second bars. During the Second World War, only 2000 AFCs were awarded with 26 first bars and just one second bar — awarded to Wing Commander H. J. Wilson AFC in 1944. Since 1945, approximately 2000 awards have been made with about 150 first bars and 20 second bars.

Squadron Leader P. Day AFC — 229 Operational Conversion Unit

In a remarkable flying career with the RAF, Paul Day has flown fighters since 1963, having achieved 2000 hours flying the Hawker Hunter and 3000 hours on the F4 Phantom. His tours of operations included the Middle and Far East, Germany and the USA. Since 1980, he has flown with the Battle of Britain Memorial Flight based at RAF Coningsby and is currently Fighter Leader with nearly 1000 hours flying time on the Spitfire and Hurricane. In 1987 Paul Day was awarded the AFC for 'Services to RAF air combat training in the F4 and services to the Battle of Britain Memorial Flight.' He is currently flying as an instructor on the Tornado F3 at RAF Coningsby.

THE CONSPICUOUS GALLANTRY MEDAL

Until 1942, the only medal available to 'other ranks' of the RAF as a reward for gallantry during flying duties in action was the Distinguished Flying Medal. To make good this deficiency, in November 1943, the Conspicuous Gallantry Medal (previously a Royal Navy award only) was extended to RAF and Army personnel for gallantry 'whilst flying in active operations against the enemy.' The award is superior to the DFM.

The medal is silver and has on the obverse the effigy of the Sovereign and on the reverse 'FOR CONSPICUOUS GALLANTRY' with a crown above, all surrounded by laurel branches. The ribbon is of light blue with dark blue edges. Bars may be awarded for further actions of gallantry, although none have yet been awarded. The medal is issued named and all awards are verified in the London Gazette. Since its institution, only 110 CGMs (flying) have been awarded.

Flight Sergeant L. B. Wallace CGM — 83 Squadron

Leslie Wallace was the wireless operator of a Lancaster detailed to attack Munich in December 1942. Outbound his aircraft was attacked by an enemy fighter, wounding Wallace in the leg. Some flares inside the aircraft were set alight causing a severe fire in the fuselage. Despite his injury, and with complete disregard for his own safety, he immediately attempted to quell the flames. The heat and stifling fumes compelled him to desist several times, but undaunted he jettisoned all moveable burning material through the rear turret and finally subdued the fire. For his bravery, Leslie Wallace was awarded the CGM — the first time a CGM as awarded for gallantry whilst flying.

Warrant Officer M. G. Clynes CGM — 431 Squadron

Michael Clynes was an air gunner with 431 Squadron RCAF and had completed 47 'ops' when he was recommended for a CGM in June 1943. All but two of his 'ops' were flown with 104 Squadron in the Middle East. He was credited with having shot down and destroyed two enemy aircraft. His CGM was approved and gazetted in August 1943. Soon after, he took off in a Halifax detailed to attack Frankfurt on the night of 25/26 November but failed to return.

Sergeant D. J. Allen CGM — 367 Squadron

Derrick Allen was the mid-upper gunner of a Lancaster detailed to attack Dusseldorf in November 1944. His aircraft was attacked by a fighter, Allen opened fire but the bomber was struck causing much damage. A second attack followed and the bomber was again hit, resulting in the port outer engine catching fire. All efforts to extinguish the fire were unavailing, the aircraft lost height and began to lose control, and so the captain ordered the crew to bale out. The rear gunner was unable to open the turret doors and was trapped. With complete disregard for his own safety, Allen promptly went to assist his comrade. The aircraft was now on fire and falling rapidly. Nevertheless, he hacked away at the turret doors with an axe and finally succeeded in freeing his comrade. Just as Allen was about to jump the aircraft broke in two. However, he fell clear and pulled his ripcord and descended safely. For this brave action, Derrick Allen was awarded the CGM and his citation concludes — 'In the face of extreme danger, this airman displayed conduct in keeping with the best traditions of the Royal Air Force.'

THE GEORGE MEDAL

The George Medal was instituted in September 1940 to reward men and women for 'great bravery', where the services are not so outstanding as to merit the award of the George Cross. It is primarily a civilian award although awards have been made to members of the Armed Services when a military award is not applicable.

The medal is silver with on the obverse the Sovereign's effigy and on the reverse St. George slaying the dragon on the coast of England, surrounded by 'THE GEORGE MEDAL.' The ribbon is red with five equidistant narrow vertical blues strips. Bars are awarded for subsequent acts and all awards are verified in the London Gazette, some of which have citations. Since it's institution in 1940, a total of approximately 1900 GMs and 25 first bars have been awarded, of which 200 (no bars) have been awarded to members of the RAF.

THE DISTINGUISHED FLYING MEDAL

The DFM was instituted on 3 June 1918 and is awarded to non-commissioned officers and other ranks for 'a act or acts of valour, courage, or devotion to duty performed whilst flying in active operations against the enemy.'

It is oval shaped and in silver. On the obverse is the Sovereign's effigy and on the reverse is Athena Nike seated on an aeroplane with a hawk rising from her right hand above the words 'FOR COURAGE'. The medal is surmounted by a bomb attached to the clasp and ribbon by two wings. The ribbon was originally thin violet and white alternate horizontal stripes. From July 1919, the stripes were similar but running at an angle of 45 degrees from left to right. Bars are awarded for subsequent acts and since 1939 the year of award engraved on the reverse. All awards are verified in the London Gazette, some of which have citations. There were 104 DFMs with two first bars awarded for the First World War. The bars were awarded to —

Sergeant Observer A. Newland DFM — 3 December 1918

Sergeant Mechanic J. Chapman DFM — 3 June 1919

DFM group showing obverse and reverse.

Private A. E. Humphrey DFM

'When escorting an important reconnaissance, his machine was attacked by eight enemy aeroplanes. After firing several rounds his gun jammed, when he immediately picked up his spare gun and, firing from his shoulder, brought down one of the enemy machines and continued firing on the others until he was severely wounded. Aerial gunner Humphreys has been 23 times engaged over enemy territory, and has proved himself gallant and resourceful on all occasions.'

Air Mechanic 1st Class C. H. Palmer DFM

'This airman displays conspicuous gallantry and devotion to duty. On six occasions he has been shelled whilst on observation duty in a balloon, but he has invariably completed his task. In one attack, his balloon was punctured in nine places.'

Between the wars just 79 DFMs with two first bars were awarded of which the majority were awarded for gallantry on the North West Frontier. The bars were awarded to —

Corporal R. W. Ellis DFM — 8 September 1933, For operations in the Chitral Reliefs

Sergeant J. Coggins DFM — 14 April 1939, For operations in Palestine

During the Second World War 6638 DFMs were awarded with 58 first bars and just one second bar. The unique recipient of the DFM and two bars was a Spitfire pilot, Flight Sergeant Donald Kingaby of 92 Squadron.

Flight Sergeant D. E. Kingaby DFM — 92 Squadron

DFM (6 December 1940) — 'This airman has displayed great courage and tenacity in his attacks against the enemy. He has destroyed at least nine hostile aircraft, four of which he shot down in one day.'

Bar to DFM (29 July 1941) — 'This airman pilot has continued to prove himself a very able section leader who fights with coolness and courage. He has now destroyed at least 14 enemy aircraft and damaged others.'

2nd Bar to DFM (11 November 1941) — 'This airman leads his section, and occasionally the flight, with great skill and courage. He has participated in 38 operational sorties during which he has destroyed 17, probably destroyed six, and damaged a further seven enemy aircraft. Flight Sergeant Kingaby has at all times displayed the greatest determination and sound judgement, combined with a high standard of operational efficiency.'

Flight Sergeant A. L. Bartlett DFM — 50 Squadron

Les Bartlett served with 50 Squadron during the Berlin Offensive of the winter of 1943/44. On the night of 28/29 January 1944, he was bomb aimer of a Lancaster detailed to attack Berlin. Whilst over the target his aircraft was attacked by an enemy fighter. On hearing the gunner's warning, Bartlett promptly manned the front turret. His shots were seen to strike the enemy aircraft and it was subsequently claimed as damaged. For this and his previous successful 18 'ops', Les Bartlett was awarded the DFM.

Flight Sergeant K. E. Ladds DFM — 58 Squadron

Kenneth Ladds was mid-upper gunner of a Halifax engaged on an anti-submarine patrol in September 1943. A surfaced U-boat was sighted and his aircraft immediately attacked. During the approach, Ladds used his guns to good effect, pouring a hail of bullets into the U-boat's gun positions. The aircraft sustained severe damage during the action and, a little later, the captain had to bring the aircraft down into the sea. The crew boarded the dinghy in which they subsequently drifted for 11 days before being rescued. Despite being short of food and water, Ladds displayed great heart and fortitude, setting an example which proved an inspiration to his comrades. For this action, Ladds was awarded the DFM.

Sergeant W. J. McKerracher DFM — 113 Squadron

An Australian, Walter McKerracher was a Blenheim wireless operator serving with 113 Squadron in the Far East where the Squadron was involved in attacking Japanese positions. During one raid, McKerracher was in the leading aircraft detailed to attack shipping at Akyab. Whilst over the target area, his aircraft was repeatedly attacked by enemy fighters but, in spite of this, they made a most determined attack at low level. During this action, McKerracher was wounded but he used his gun most effectively. For this action and the rest of his tour of operations,

Walter McKerracher was awarded the DFM.

Since the Second World War 88 DFMs have been awarded of which 42 were for operations in Malaya, 28 for Korea and ten awarded to Australians for operations in Vietnam. Less than half of the awards since 1945 have been to members of the RAF. Other than Australians, 17 awards have been made to members of various Army units, one award to the Royal Navy and one award to the Royal Marines during the Falklands Conflict of 1982.

THE AIR FORCE MEDAL

The AFM was instituted on 3 June 1918 for award to non-commissioned officers and other ranks for 'an act or acts of valour, courage or devotion to duty whilst flying, though not in active operations against the enemy.'

It is silver and oval shaped. On the obverse is the Sovereign's effigy, and on the reverse is Hermes mounted on a hawk bestowing a wreath. The ribbon was originally thin red and white alternate stripes but since July 1919 the stripes run at an angle of 45 degrees from left to right. Bars are awarded for subsequent acts and, since 1939, the year of the second award is engraved on the reverse of the bar. All awards are issued named and can be verified in the London Gazette although they are generally found without citations.

The number of awards have been relatively few since its institution, with probably only some 850 AFMs in total and maybe 10 first bars awarded. Approximately just over 100, with two first bars, were awarded for the period of the First World War. A further 100 awards with three first bars were awarded between the wars. The four members of the RAF awarded first bars during the period 1918-39 were:-

Sergeant J. M. Bennett AFM — 26 December 1919
Sergeant W. H. Shiers AFM — 26 December 1919
Flight Sergeant S. J. Heath AFM — 4 June 1921
Flight Sergeant G. W. Hunt AFM — 19 May 1925

During the Second World War 259 AFMs were awarded, but no bars. Since 1946, approximately 400 AFMs have been awarded with only a handful of bars. The largest number of awards for any one event was in 1948 when ten AFMs were awarded for the Berlin Airlift.

Sergeant H. H. Parker AFM — 51 Squadron

Herbert Parker was bomb aimer of a Halifax returning from an operational sortie in 1943. The aircraft developed a fault in one engine and was unable to gain height. On heading out to sea, the aircraft was engaged by heavy flak and the petrol tanks and second engine set on fire. While the aircraft was descending towards the water, and already burning fiercely, another hit was sustained severely wounding Sergeant Parker, who had throughout rendered great assistance. The captain succeeded in bringing the aircraft down on the water and Parker then assisted the rest of the crew in boarding the dinghy. Both Herbert Parker and the captain Flight Sergeant John Collins, were awarded the AFM.

FIRST WORLD WAR CAMPAIGN MEDALS

Due to the formation of the RAF late in the First World War, the only two campaign medals issued named to members of the RAF are the British War Medal and the Victory Medal. Other earlier Campaign Stars ware found with groups to the RAF but will be named to other Units. Generally, both medals were issued together although there are a few occasions when just the BWM as issued. The VM was never issued on its own.

British War Medal 1914-20

This medal is made in silver. On the obverse is the head of King George V and on the reverse is the figure of St. George on horseback. The horse is trampling on a shield, representing the Central Powers, and on a skull and crossbones, symbolic of death. Above the horse's head is the sun, symbolic of victory. Around the edges are the dates '1914 and '1918'. The ribbon is a broad orange watered band down the centre, bordered with white, black and blue stripes. All medals were issued named.

The medal was issued to all members of the RAF serving in a theatre of war. It was also awarded to all members of the RAF who were actively engaged in the air against the enemy whilst borne on the strength of an operational unit based in Great Britain, or were employed in flying new aircraft to France, or formed part of the complement of an aircraft-carrying ship. The qualification period was later extended to cover service in Russia during 1919-20. A total of 6.5 million silver BWMs were issued.

Victory Medal 1914-19

This medal is made of bronze. On the obverse is the winged, full-length figure of Victory, with her arm extended and holding a palm in her right hand. The ribbon is watered and (from the centre outwards) the colours of red, yellow, green, blue and violet are merged into a rainbow pattern.

The medal was issued to commemorate the Allied victory over the Central Powers. The medal was issued to all members of the RAF who served in a unit in a theatre of war within specified dates. It was also issued to those who served with an operational unit in the British Isles or overseas and who were actively engaged in the air against the enemy. Those who flew new planes from Britain to France and those who formed part of the complement of an aircraft-carrying ship were also eligible. The medal was issued named, and those awarded a Mention in Despatches during the First World War were entitled to wear an oakleaf on the ribbon. Approximately 5,735,000 British VMs were issued.

AFRICA GENERAL SERVICE MEDAL 1902-56

This medal is silver and never issued without a bar. Only the George V or Elizabeth II obverse issues are eligible for members of the RAF. On the reverse is the standing figure of Britannia and in the exergue 'AFRICA'. The ribbon is yellow edged with black and with two green stripes towards the centre. All medals were issued named. A total of 45 bars were issued with this medal but only two of which were awarded to members of the RAF.

Somaliland 1920 — Awarded for the final expedition against the 'Mad Mullah' between 21 January and 12 February 1920.

Kenya — Awarded for 91 days or more service against the Mau Mau within designated operational areas. Known units — 30, 152 and 208 Squadrons and the WRAF.

INDIA GENERAL SERVICE MEDAL 1908-35

This medal is in silver and never issued without a bar. On the obverse is the crowned bust of King George V and on the reverse is the fort of Jamrud with mountain in the background, below which is 'INDIA'. The ribbon is green with a central dark blue band. All medals were issued named. After 11 August 1920, those awarded a Mention in Despatches were entitled to wear a bronze oakleaf on the ribbon. a total of 12 bars were issued, nine of which are known to members of the RAF.

Afghanistan NWF 1919 — This was the first time that the RAF took part in operations in the India campaigns and was awarded for service in the Third Afghan War between 6 May and 8 August 1919. 850 bars were issued to the RAF. Known units — 20, 31, 48 and 114 Squadrons.

Mahsud 1919-20 — Awarded to those who served west of, and including, Jandola or under the GOC Waziristan Force north of Jandola, between 18 December 1919 and 8 April 1920. 175 bars were issued to the RAF, nearly always found on medals with the bar 'Wariristan 1919-21'.

Waziristan 1919-20 — For operations against the Tochi and Wana Wazirs and Mahsuds between 6 May 1919 and January 1921. 600 bars were issued to the RAF. Known units — 5, 20, 27, 28, 31, 60, 97 and 99 Squadrons.

Waziristan 1921-24 — Awarded to those who served in North and South Waziristan (and other surrounding areas) between 21 December 1921 and 31 March 1924. 600 bars were issued to the RAF. Known units — 5, 27, 28, 31 and 60 Squadrons.

Waziristan 1925 — For operations against the Waziris between 9 March and 1 May 1925. Those who had already qualified for the bar 'Waziristan 1921-24' and who took part in these operations were given the option of receive one bar OR the other. This bar was only awarded to the RAF with a maximum of 263 issued. Known units — 5, 27 and 60 Squadrons.

North West Frontier 1930-31 — For services in Kohat, Waziristan and the Peshawar District between 23 April and 30 September 1930, and also for services in a designated area on the North West Frontier between 1 October 1930 and 22 March 1931. 1,350 bars were issued to the RAF. Known units — 5, 11, 20, 27, 28, 39 and 60 Squadrons.

Burma — Awarded to those who were despatched from India and served in Burma between 22 December 1930 and 25 March 1932. Only 14 bars were awarded to the RAF. Known units — 36 and 205 Squadrons.

Mohmad 1933 — For operations against the Upper Mohmands between 28 July and 3 October 1933. Only 180 bars were awarded to the RAF and the only known unit was 230 Squadron.

North West Frontier 1935 — For operations on the North West Frontier between 12 January and 3 November 1935. Only bars to 20 Squadron are known for the RAF.

INDIA GENERAL SERVICE MEDAL 1936-39

This medal is silver and never issued without a bar. On the obverse is the head of King George VI and on the reverse is a tiger standing astride mountains, above which is 'INDIA'. The ribbon has a grey sandy-coloured central band flanked by red and green stripes. Those awarded a Mention in Despatches were entitled to wear a bronze oakleaf on the ribbon. All medals are issued named. Just two bars were issued, both of which were available to members of the RAF.

North West Frontier 1936-37 — For operations on the North West Frontier between 24 November 1936 and 16 December 1937. Known units — 5, 11, 20, 27, 28, 31, 39, 60 and 70 Squadrons.

GENERAL SERVICE MEDAL 1916-62

This medal is awarded for services other than for India or Africa. It is silver and never issued without a bar. On the obverse is the head of the Sovereign and on the reverse is the standing figure of Victory who is placing a wreath on the emblems of the Army and the RAF (the Navy had its own GSM). The ribbon is purple with a green stripe down the centre. From 11 August 1920, those awarded a Mention in Despatches were entitled to wear a bronze oakleaf on the ribbon. All medals are issued named. A total of 16 bars were issued, all of which were available to members of the RAF. The qualifying criteria is most often expressed as a start/stop date for a given geographic area(s), usually with a requirement of some 30 days within this area. However, variations are quite common and include the proviso that the qualifying period is not valid if an individual has been awarded a BEM or higher award on termination of ????. Therefore service is due to injury or death. For aircrew the qualification was invariably at least one operational sortie.

S. Persia — For services at or near Bushire between 12

November 1918 and 22 June 1919, or at or near Bandar Abbas between 12 November 1918 and 3 June 1919. The only unit known to qualify for this bar is 30 Squadron.

Kurdistan — For operations in Kurdistan between 23 May and 6 December 1919 and for operations against the Kurdish Sheik Mahmoud between 19 March and 18 June 1923. Known units — 6, 30 and 63 Squadrons.

Iraq — For services at Ramadi and in Iraq between 10 December 1919 and 17 November 1920. Known units — 6, 30, 55, 63 and 84 Squadrons.

N. W. Persia — Awarded to members of the North Persia Force between 10 August and 31 December 1920. Known units — 6, 30 and 63 Squadrons.

Southern Desert: Iraq — For operations against the Akhwan in the Southern Desert between 8 January and 3 June 1928. This bar was mainly awarded to the RAF only. Known units — 30, 55, 70 and 84 Squadrons.

Northern Kurdistan — For operations in Northern Kurdistan between 15 March and 21 June 1932. This bar is mainly awarded to the RAF only, and only a maximum of some 350 could have been issued. Known units — 30, 55 and 70 Squadrons.

Palestine — For service in Palestine between 19 April 1936 and 3 September 1939. Known units — 6, 14, 33, 80, 208, 211 and 216 Squadrons.

S.E. Asia 1945-46 — Awarded to personnel involved in South East Asia after the Japanese surrender on 15 August 1945. Qualifications for the RAF are to have flown one operational sortie, or a sortie in removing prisoners of war and internees. Non-aircrew personnel who served in specified areas between 3 September 1945 and 30 November 1946 qualified. At least 22 squadrons are known to have served.

Bomb and Mine Clearance 1945-49 and 1945-56 — The qualification for either of these bars was 6 months active engagement in the clearance of bombs and mines in the UK and Northern Ireland between 9 May 1945 and 31 December 1949. In May 1956, the period was extended for service in the Mediterranean. Any member of the RAF employed in this work would have qualified for either of these bars.

Palestine 1945-48 — For service in Palestine between 27 September 1945 and 30 June 1948. At least 18 squadrons are known to have served plus numerous ground and support units.

Cyprus — For service in Cyprus between 1 April 1955 and 18 April 1959. Qualification was by four months service with a unit in Cyprus, with the addition of aircrew from 37 to 38 Squadrons based at Malta who flew ten or more sorties over Cyprus waters.

Malaya — For operations against communist insurgents in Malaya between 16 June 1948 and 31 July 1960. Qualification was one or more days service with a unit in Malaya or Singapore. Service with detached squadrons based elsewhere, but involved in operations, qualified.

Near East — Awarded for Operation Musketeer, the seizure of the Suez Canal in the Port Said area, between 31 October and 22 December 1956. This involved some 300 aircraft from 34 RAF squadrons involved in the support of the operation. Qualification was by one day's service ashore in Egypt or off the Egyptian coast, or participation in one or more operational sorties from Cyprus over the area of operations.

Arabian Peninsular — Awarded to those who had served one month in the Aden Coony or Protectorate and the Sultanates of Muscat and Oman, or any of the adjacent Gulf States, between 1 January 1957 and 30 June 1960.

Brunei — Awarded for one or more day's service in Brunei and/or North Borneo and Sarawak between 8-23 December 1962. RAF recipients of this bar are unlikely.

Kuwait — For operations in Kuwait and Northern Gulf in the period 8 March to 30 September, 1991.

N. Iraq and S. Turkey — In recognition of service on Op Haven 6 April to 17 July 1991; for 30 days service or three operational air sorties.

SECOND WORLD WAR CAMPAIGN STARS & MEDALS

A total of eight campaign stars were awarded for services during the Second World War. They were all of similar design and made of a copper zinc alloy in the form of a six-pointed star. In the centre of the star is the Royal and Imperial cypher, surmounted by a crown. The cypher is surrounded by a circlet bearing the name of the particular star.

No one person could receive more than five campaign stars. In cases when a recipient qualified for two or three stars, and only one star of which could be issued, a bar was issued to represent the second star. No one individual was awarded more than one bar or emblem to any one campaign star. A total of nine bars were issued. All campaign stars were issued unnamed.

1939-45 Star

This star was awarded for service between 3 September 1939 and 2 September 1945. The ribbon is (from left to right) equal bands of dark blue, red and light blue, representing the colours of the Navy, Army and the RAF. Qualification for the RAF was for carrying out operations against the enemy provided that two months service had been completed in an operational unit. Non-aircrew personnel had to complete six months service in an area of an operational command. Operational service curtailed by death, disability or wound qualified for the award irrespective of the length of service. Also, a recipient of an honour, decoration, Mention in Despatches or King's Commendation qualified for the award irrespective of the length of service. Service in areas where personnel were evacuated, such as Dunkirk, were also eligible. Members of the crews of fighter aircraft who took part in the Battle of Britain, between 10 July and 31 October 1940, were awarded the bar 'Battle of Britain' affixed to the ribbon of the star.

1939-45 Star with Battle of Britain clasp.

The Atlantic Star

This star was awarded to commemorate the Battle of the Atlantic between 3 September 1939 and 8 May 1945. The ribbon is the watered type of (from left to right) dark blue, white and sea-green symbolic of the Atlantic. Qualification for the RAF was for aircrew who had taken part in active operations within the specified area, providing they had completed two months service in an operational unit after qualifying for the 1939-45 Star. Two bars were issued — 'Air Crew Europe' and 'France and Germany'.

The Air Crew Europe Star

This star was awarded for operational flying from UK bases over Europe between 3 September 1939 and 5 June 1944. The ribbon is light blue with black edges and two yellow stripes, representing continuous service by day and by night. The time qualification was two months as aircrew and the recipient must have previously qualified for the 1939-45 Star. Two bars were issued — 'Atlantic' and 'France and Germany'.

The Africa Star

This star was awarded for one or more days service in North Africa between 10 June 1940 and 12 May 1943. The ribbon is pale buff with a central red stripe and two narrow stripes, one of dark blue and the other of light blue, representing the desert, the Navy, Army and RAF. Qualification was to have landed in, or flown over, any of the areas which qualified for the award, or territory occupied by the enemy. Areas which qualified for the award were — North Africa, Abyssinia, The Somalilands, Eritrea, Sudan and Malta. Three bars were issued with the Africa Star, one of which was to the 1st Army and another to the 8th Army. A third bar, however, was available to members of the RAF. The bar 'North Africa 1942-43' was awarded to those who served under the command of AOC Western Desert, AOC NW African Forces, AOC Malta, or any others who operated against the Germans or Italians between 23 October 1942 and 12 May 1943.

The Pacific Star

This star was awarded for service in the Pacific theatre of operations between 8 December 1941 and 2 September 1945. The ribbon is dark green with red edges with a central yellow stripe, also a thin one of dark blue and another light blue. The green and yellow symbolise the forests and beaches, with the Navy, Army and the RAF all represented. Qualification was for RAF crews to have completed at least one operational sortie over the appropriate land or sea. These areas were generally the Pacific Ocean, South China Sea and the Indian Ocean east of a line running south from Singapore. The overland areas included territories which had been subjected to enemy or allied invasions, and Malaya. A bar, 'Burma', was issued with this star.

The Burma Star

This star was awarded for service in the Burma Campaign between 11 December 1941 and 2 September 1945. The ribbon is dark blue with a wide red stripe down the centre. The blue edges each have a central orange stripe. The red symbolises the British Commonwealth Forces and the orange the sun. Qualification was one operational sortie. Non-aircrew qualified for service in any part of Burma between the required dates. Service in Bengal, Assam, China and Malaya between certain dates also qualified for the award. A bar, 'Pacific', was issued with this star.

The Italy Star

This star was awarded for operational service in Sicily or Italy between 11 June 1943 and 8 May 1945. The ribbon represents the Italian colours and is of equal stripes of red, white, green, white red. Qualification consisted of participation in aircrew service within the Mediterranean theatre, including sorties from the

Mediterranean islands and Yugoslavia. There were no bars issued with this star.

The France and Germany Star

This star was awarded for either service in France, Belgium, Holland or Germany, or any operations flown over Europe (except those which qualified for the Italy Star) between 6 June 1944 and 8 May 1945. The ribbon is of equal stripes of blue, white, red, white and blue, representing the Union flag and those of France and the Netherlands. A bar, 'Atlantic', was issued with this star.

The Defence Medal

This medal is made of cupro-nickel. On the obverse is the uncrowned head of King George VI and on the reverse the Royal Crown resting on a stump of an oak tree, flanked by two lions. The years '1939' and '1945' are at the top left and top right respectively. At the base is 'THE DEFENCE MEDAL'. The ribbon is flame coloured with green edges, symbolic of the enemy attacks on our green land. The black-out is commemorated by two thin black stripes down the centre of the green ones. The medal was generally awarded for service in non-operational areas subject to air attack, or closely threatened, provided such service lasted for three or more years. It was also awarded for service overseas, provided that service lasted for one year, except in territories threatened by the enemy or bomb attacks, in which case it was six months. Service curtailed by death or wound due to enemy action was considered eligible. Also, those who received a personal award conferred by the King were eligible, irrespective of their length of service, providing they were serving in a category that qualified for the medal. The medal was issued unnamed.

The War Medal

This medal is made of cupro-nickel. On the obverse is the crowned head of King George VI and on the reverse is a lion standing on a dragon with two heads, above which are the years '1939' and '1945'. The ribbon is symbolic of the colours of the Union Flag and has a narrow stripe down the centre with a narrow white stripe either side of it. The rest of the ribbon is equally divided into blue and red stripes, with the blue ones next to the white. The medal was awarded to all personnel wherever they served during the war. Operational and non-operational service counted provided that it was of 28 days or more duration. Operational service curtailed by death or wounds also qualified for the medal even if service did not total 28 days. For anyone who was awarded a Mention in Despatches during the war, an oakleaf was worn on the ribbon. The medal was issued unnamed.

CAMPAIGN MEDALS TO THE RAF — POST WWII
Korea Medal

This medal was awarded for service in the operations in Korea between 2 July 1950 and 27 July 1953. The medal was made of cupro-nickel and on the obverse was the bust of Queen Elizabeth II facing right. On the reverse is Hercules, armed with a dagger, his left arm out holding the Hydra. The word 'KOREA' is in the exergue. The medal was issued named with the ribbon of yellow with two blue stripes. Qualification for the RAF was for one operational sortie over Korea or Korean waters, or service of one or more days on land or service of 28 days afloat in the operational areas of the Yellow Sea and Sea of Japan. Known RAF recipients were fighter pilots who flew with the USAAF, photographic interpreters and members of the Far East Flying Boat Wing based at Seletar. No bars were issued but those Mentioned in Despatches wore a bronze oakleaf on the ribbon.

British War Medal with Mention-in-Despatches oak leaf.

Campaign Service Medal 1962-

This campaign medal superceded the General Service Medal 1918-62. It is made of cupro-nickel with the crowned bust of Queen Elizabeth II on the obverse and a wreath of oak surrounded by 'FOR CAMPAIGN SERVICE', with a crown above, on the reverse. The medal is issued named and never awarded without a bar. The ribbon is purple with green edges and recipients who have received a Mention in Despatches wear a bronze oakleaf on the ribbon. The medal is still on issue to the RAF and, so far, nine bars have been awarded, seven of which are known to have been awarded to members of the RAF.

Borneo

This bar was awarded for services against the rebels of what was known previously as North Borneo (now Sabah, Sarawak or Brunei) between 24 December 1962 and 11 August 1966. Qualification for the RAF was 30 days, not necessarily continuous, ashore in specified areas or one sortie in direct support of operations. Approximately 11,000 bars were awarded to the RAF.

Radfan

Awarded for service of 14 continuous days or more in the mountainous area of the Radfan, north of Aden, including those who took part in a supporting role in Aden itself, between 25 April and 31 July 1964. Approximately 5,000 bars were awarded to the RAF.

South Arabia

This bar was awarded for 30 continuous days in the Federation of South Arabia between 1 August 1964 and 30 November 1967. Some 15,000 bars were awarded to the RAF.

Malay Peninsular

Awarded for operations against Indonesian infiltrators between 17 August 1964 and 11 August 1966. Qualification for the RAF was for service of 30 days, not necessarily continuous, on land in the Malay Peninsular/Singapore or completion of 30 sorties on operational patrols over the waters surrounding the Malay Peninsular/Singapore between 13 June 1965 and 11 August 1966. Approximately 6,500 bars were awarded to the RAF.

Northern Ireland
This bar, still being awarded, is for recognition of service in Northern Ireland since 14 August 1969. Qualification is 30 days, not necessarily continuous, on the posted or attached strength of any RAF unit in the area.

Dhofar
Awarded in recognition of service in the Dhofar Province of Oman between 1 October 1969 and 30 September 1976. Qualification is by 30 days service, not necessarily continuous, in the Province of Oman or 30 Flights into Salahah airfield in support of operations.

Lebanon
A rare bar as only a total of 700 were awarded to HM Forces, although awards to the RAF are known. It was awarded for 30 days service either within the territory of Lebanon and its territorial waters in support of the Multi-national force between 7 February 1983 and 9 March 1984. In addition, aircrew who carried out three operational sorties landing in, or overflying, Lebanese territory qualified.

South Atlantic Medal
This medal was awarded for service during the Anglo-Argentine war of 1982. It is made of cupro-nickel and has the crowned head of Queen Elizabeth II facing right on the obverse and the Falkland Islands coat-of-arms encompassed by 'SOUTH ATLANTIC MEDAL' and sprigs of laurel on the reverse. The medal was issued named and the ribbon is watered bands of blue, white, green, white, blue. The operational area for which the medal was awarded is one of the largest for which any campaign medal has been awarded, covering the vast area from just below the equator to the Antarctic Circle. Personnel who served ashore or afloat below 35 degrees South, or who flew operationally below Ascension Island, were entitled to wear a small white metal rosette sewn to the ribbon.

Gulf Medal
Awarded for service during the Gulf War, the defining dates being 2 August 1990 to 7 March 1991. It is generally similar to the South Atlantic Medal on the obverse but on the reverse carries the Combined Services badge and the words 'THE GULF MEDAL 1990-91'. All medals issued named.

Other Medals
In addition to the campaign medals already listed, many other medals can be found to members of the RAF, brief details are listed below:

Meritorious Service Medal — Issued between 1919 and 1924 (then replaced by the British Empire Medal) and again since 1977 for non-commissioned officers and other ranks for outstanding meritorious service. It is nowadays a very rare medal and qualification is by 27 years service of a very high standard. Recipients must now be of the rank of Sergeant or above and only 70 awards are made each year. All medals are named and the ribbon is currently dark blue and maroon with white edges and a central white stripe.

Long Service and Good Conduct Medal — Awarded since 1919 to NCOs and men for, originally, 18 years, and more lately 15 years, service of exemplary conduct. Officers who have completed 12 years in the ranks can also receive the medal. A bar is awarded for a further 18/15 years service. All medals are named and the ribbon is dark blue and maroon with white edges.

Air Efficiency Award — Awarded since 1942 for 10 years service in the Auxiliary and Volunteer Air Forces. Conduct had to be good and officers and men were eligible. All awards are named and the ribbon is green with two pale blue stripes in the centre.

Coronation & Jubilee Medals — Various have been awarded throughout the history of the RAF including the Jubilee Medals of 1935 and 1977 and the Coronation Medals of 1937 and 1953. All medals were issued unnamed.

United Nations Medals — Various including the UN Medal for service in Korea 1950-53 and Cyprus 1964-65.

Foreign Orders, Decorations and Medals — A number of awards have been made to members of the RAF since 1918 particularly during time of war or tension. These awards are issued unnamed and the more distinctive are generally confirmed in the London Gazette.

Sqn Ldr Tony Spooner, note method of wearing ribbons on battledress.

SEQUENCE IN WHICH RIBBONS OF ORDERS, DECORATIONS AND MEDALS ARE TO BE WORN.
The list quoted below is taken from AMOs of various dates.

VICTORIA CROSS

GEORGE CROSS

Most Noble Order of the Garter
Most Ancient and Most Noble Order of the Thistle
Most Illustrious Order of St Patrick
Knights Grand Cross, Most Honourable Order of the Bath (GCB)

Order of Merit
Baronet's Badge
Knight Grand Commander, Most Exalted Order of the Star of
    India (GCSI)
Knights Grand Cross, Most Distinguished Order of St Michael
    and St George (GCMG)
Knight Grand Commander, Most Eminent Order of the Indian
    Empire (GCIE)
Order of the Crown of India
Knights Grand Cross, Royal Victorian Order (GCVO)
Knights Grand Cross, Most Excellent Order of the British Empire
    (GBE)
Order of the Companions of Honour (CH)
Knight Commander, Most Honourable Order of the Bath (KCB)
Knight Commander, Most Exalted Order of the Star of India
    (KCSI)
Knight Commander, Most Distinguished Order of St Michael and
    St George (KCMG)
Knight Commander, Most Eminent Order of the Indian Empire
    (KCIE)
Knight Commander, Royal Victorian Order (KCVO)
Knight Commander, Most Excellent Order of the Bath (KBE)
Knight Bachelor's Badge
Companion, Most Honourable Order of the Bath (CB)
Companion, Most Exalted Order of the Star of India (CSI)
Companion, Most Distinguished Order of St Michael and St
    George (CMG)
Companion, Most Eminent Order of the Indian Empire (CIE)
Commander, Royal Victorian Order (CVO)
Commander, Most Excellent Order of the British Empire (CBE)

(BRITISH ORDER):
Distinguished Service Order
Lieutenant, Royal Victorian Order (Class IV) (LVO)
Officer, Order of the British Empire (Class IV) (OBE)
Imperial Service Order (ISO)
Member, Royal Victorian Order (Class V) (MVO)
Member, Order of the British Empire (Class V) (MBE)
Indian Order of Merit — Military

DECORATIONS
Royal Red Cross, Class I
Distinguished Service Cross
Military Cross
Distinguished Flying Cross
Air Force Cross
Royal Red Cross, Class II
Albert Medal
Order of British India
Kaiser-I-Hind Medal
Order of St John

MEDALS FOR GALLANTRY AND DISTINGUISHED
    CONDUCT
Distinguished Conduct Medal
Conspicuous Gallantry Medal
George Medal
Queen's Police Medal for Gallantry
Queen's Fire Service Medal for Gallantry
Edward Medal
Royal West African Frontier Force Distinguished Conduct Medal
King's African Rifles Distinguished Conduct Medal
Indian Distinguished Conduct Medal
Union of South Africa King's Medal for Bravery, in silver

Distinguished Service Medal
Military Medal
Distinguished Flying Medal
Air Force Medal
Constabulary Medal (Ulster)
Medal for Saving Life at Sea
Indian Order of Merit (Civil)
Indian Police Medal for Gallantry
Colonial Police Medal for Gallantry
British Empire Medal (previously Medal of the Order of the
    British Empire for Meritorious Service)
Canada Medal
Queen's Police Medal for Distinguished Service
Queen's Fire Service Medal for Distinguished Service
Queen's Medal for Chiefs

War Medals 1914-19
    1914 Star
    1914-15 Star
    British War Medal
    Mercantile Marine War Medal
    Victory Medal
    Territorial Force War Medal
    India General Service Medal (1908)

1939-45
    1939-45 Star
    Atlantic Star
    Air Crew Europe Star
    Africa Star
    Pacific Star
    Burma Star
    Italy Star
    France and Germany Star
    Defence Medal
    Volunteer Service Medal of Canada
    War Medal 1939-45
    Africa Service Medal of Union of South Africa
    India Service Medal
    New Zealand War Service Medal
    Southern Rhodesia Service Medal
    Australia Service Medal (1939-45)

    General Service Medal
    India GSM (1902)
    India GSM (1908)
    Naval GSM (1915)
    GSM (Army and RAF) (1918)
    India GSM (1936)
    Pakistan GSM
(the order of wearing of GSMs will vary dependent upon the
    dates of participation in the relevant campaigns).
Polar Medals (in date order)
Royal Victorian Medal (Gold, Silver and Bronze)
Imperial Service Medal

POLICE MEDALS FOR VALUABLE SERVICES

JUBILEE AND CORONATION MEDALS
King George V's Silver Jubilee Medal 1935
King George VI's Coronation Medal 1937
King George V's Long and Faithful Service Medal
King George VI's Long and Faithful Service Medal
Queen Elizabeth II's Long and Faithful Service Medal

Queen Elizabeth II's Coronation Medal
Queen Elizabeth II's Silver Jubilee Medal

EFFICIENCY AND LONG SERVICE DECORATIONS AND
MEDALS
(Numerous awards)

FOREIGN ORDERS (in date order)

FOREIGN DECORATIONS (in date order) — need Sovereign's
permission.

FOREIGN MEDALS (in date order) — need Sovereign's
permission.

RAF No. 1 Dress

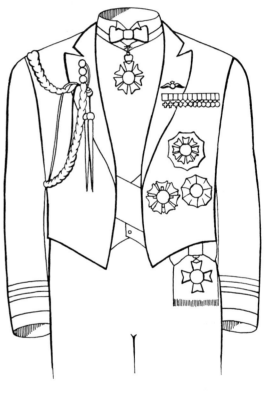

RAF Mess Dress

BATTLE HONOURS

NOTE: The primary source for information regarding this subject is AP 3327, ' Colours and Standards in the Royal Air Force.' Individual squadron details, i.e the Battle Honours to which a unit can lay claim, and those it actually chooses to display upon its Standard, come from squadron records. Entitlement to, and presentation of, squadron standards is usually covered by an AMO.

Whilst individuals, and in the unique case of Malta, islands (!), could receive various gallantry and campaign awards, RAF squadrons were entitled to place appropriate 'Battle Honours' upon their Standards. Before we look at these in detail it is necessary to say a few words about the Standards themselves. The system was instituted on 1st April 1943 by King George VI to mark the 25th anniversary of the Royal Air Force. The basic requirement for a squadron to receive a Standard is completion of 25 years service; however, a Standard might also be granted to a squadron which "earned the Sovereign's appreciation for especially outstanding operations."

The Standard itself is a 4 ft by 2 ft 8 in rectangle of RAF light-blue silk, fringed and tasselled in gold and blue. It has a border of roses, thistles, shamrocks and leeks — devices of the countries which comprise the United Kingdom — and a central motif of the approved squadron badge. The only other motifs on the Standard are the Battle Honours to which the squadron is entitled, these being depicted in scrolls. The Standard is mounted on an 8 ft 1 in staff, surmounted by a gold eagle with outstretched (elevated) wings.

Once the squadron has satisfied the qualifying requirements it receives a list, from the Air Ministry/MoD, of the Battle Honours to which it is entitled, with a note of those that may be placed upon the Standard. The squadron then selects the honours it wishes to display, to a maximum of eight, and this, along with the formal request for a Standard is forwarded to the Sovereign for approval. A typical example is that of No 39 Squadron .. S/L Coghill as CO in 1954 when the first Standard was due to the squadron had to choose from the following list of Battle Honours to which the squadron was entitled: Home Defence 1916-18, North-West Frontier 1930-31, Mohmand 1933, North-West Frontier 1935-39, East Africa 1940, Egypt and Libya 1940-43, Greece 1941, Mediterranean 1941-43, Malta 1942, North Africa 1942-43 and South-east Europe 1944-45. However, with the policy decision that the operations on the North-West Frontier of India could not be displayed upon the Standard he was left with no choice and all the other Honours were duly represented.

The limit of eight Honours appears to have been dictated by purely aesthetic considerations of space and balance on the Standard. As many squadrons had qualified for the limit of eight by their involvement in the two World Wars it meant that any subsequent award would have to be at the expense of an Honour already displayed. However, it appears to have been policy that the conflicts of the so-called post-colonial period should not be recognised in this way and so the problem did not arise. The two major conflicts of the past 10 years — the Falklands and the Gulf — appear likely to be in a different category, being somewhat more politically 'acceptable'. There was much debate following the Falklands War as to the granting of a Battle Honour, in the end an award was made and certain units given entitlement to add to their list of Battle Honours. So far, the Gulf War has not been so recognised.

The presentation of the Standard follows a set formal pattern, including dedication ceremony; the same applies to the presentation of any replacement Standard. In essence the Standard is the ceremonial flag of the squadron and is only paraded on special occasions — formal parades, Freedom Parades, Dining-in nights, for example.

OFFICIAL BATTLE HONOURS

The following list gives ALL those Battle Honours which may be used on squadron standards, including the limiting dates (i.e the period within which the squadron must have been employed in the appropriate campaign/theatre) and brief details of the operations. It is important to note that the dates are limiting dates and that the dates applied by the squadron are those which the squadron actually spent involved in the particular operation (but NOT outside of the limiting dates).

BATTLE HONOUR CONDITIONS

Home Waters 1914-1918	Operations over home waters, whether by land-based or carrier-borne aircraft.
Home Defence 1916-1918	Interception operations against enemy aircraft and Zeppelins raiding Great Britain.
Western Front 1914-1918	Operations in support of Allied armies in Belgium and France.
Independent Force and Germany 1914-1918	Squadrons based in France as part of the Independent Force; and for operations over Germany, whether by squadrons based in France (as part of the Independent Force or not) or by carrier-borne aircraft.

Standards of the Bruggen Wing on display in the Officers Mess, mid 1960s.

Italian Front and Adriatic 1917-1918	Operations over the Trentino and neighbouring areas, in support of the Allied armies on theItalian front; and for operations over the Adriatic and attacks on targets on the Dalmatian coast.
Aegean 1915-1918	Operations in the Aegean area against the German/Turkish land, sea and air forces, including the attempt to force the Dardenelles, the Gallipoli campaign, and the various operations over the Aegean Sea and against Turkish coastal targets.
Macedonia 1916-1918	Operations in support of the Allied Forces at Salonika and in their eventual advance and defeat of the Bulgarian armies in Macedonia and adjoining territories.
Mesopotamia 1915-1918	Operations over Mesopotamia and Persia in the liberation of Mesopotamia from the Turks.
Palestine 1916-1918	Operations over Palestine, Transjordan and Syria, in the liberation of those territories from the Turks.

Arabia 1916-1917	Operations over Arabia, in support of the Arab Revolt against the Turks.
Egypt 1914-1917	Operations by squadrons based in Egypt during the Turkish advance on the Suez Canal across Sinai; and for operations in the Western Desert against the Senussi.

Not to be placed on the Standard:

East Africa 1915-1917	Operations over German East Africa during its conquest from the enemy, whether by aircraft based in the country or operating from exterior seaplane bases.
South-West Africa 1915	Operations by South African Personnel during the conquest of German South-West Africa.

The numerous inter-war campaigns, especially in India, entitled squadrons to Battle Honours but these could NOT be placed on the Squadron Standard. The eligibility was also not so clear cut and was determined by an Air Council committee which examined squadron records then announced its decision. For details of the campaigns listed below see the relevant chapter.

South Persia 1918-1919

Iraq 1919-1920

Kurdistan 1919

Kurdistan 1922-1924

North-West Persia 1920

Afghanistan 1919-1920
Mahsud 1919-1920

Waziristan 1919-1920

North-West Frontier 1930-1931

Burma 1930-1932

Northern Kurdistan 1932

Mohmand 1933

North-West Frontier 1935-1939

Palestine 1936-1939

North Russia 1918-1919

South Russia 1919-1920

Somaliland 1920

Sudan 1920

Iraq 1923-1925

Iraq 1928-1029

Transjordan 1924

Mohmand 1927

Aden 1928

Aden 1929

Kurdistan 1930-1931

Aden 1934

East

RAF squadrons were also entitled to lay claim to Army Battle Honours, the Air Ministry would approve such claims if the squadron could prove its 'intimate participation in the land battle'.

WORLD WAR TWO:

Battle of Britain	Interception operations by fighter squadrons 1940 in the Battle of Britain (August to October 1940).
Home Defence 1940-1945	Interception operations after the Battle of Britain, in defence of Great Britain and Northern Ireland against enemy aircraft and flying bombs.
Invasion Ports 1940	Bombing operations against German-occupied Channel ports, to dislocate enemy preparations for the invasion of England.
France and Low Countries	Operations in France and the Low Countries between the outbreak of war 1939-1940 and the Fall of France (3rd September 1939 to 25th June 1940). Applicable both to squadrons based in France (the Air Component and the Advanced Air Striking Force) and to squadrons operating from home bases.
Dunkirk	Operations covering the evacuation of the British Expeditionary Force and the French from Dunkirk 26th May to 4th June 1940.
Meuse Bridges	Squadrons which participated in bombing against the crossings of the Meuse during the German breakthrough between Sedan and Dinant (12th to 14th May 1940.)
Atlantic 1939-1945	Operations by aircraft of Coastal Command and others employed in the coastal role over the Atlantic Ocean from the outbreak of war to VE Day.

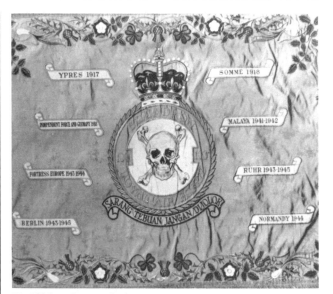

No. 100 Squadron standard.

Bismarck	Operations by aircraft of Coastal Command associated with the action against the *Bismarck* (24th to 29th May 1941).
Channel and North Sea 1939-1945	Ship attack, anti-submarine, and mining operations over the English Channel and North Sea from the outbreak of war to VE Day.
Tirpitz	Operations resulting in the sinking of the Tirpitz.
Norway 1940	Operations over Norway during the German invasion (9th April to 9th June 1940): applicable both to squadrons based in Norway and to those operating from home bases.
Baltic 1939-1945	Operations over the Baltic and its approach by squadrons of Bomber and Coastal Commands from the outbreak of war to VE Day.
Fortress Europe 1940-44	Operations by aircraft based in the British Isles against targets in Germany, Italy and enemy-occupied Europe, from the Fall of France to the invasion of Normandy.
The Dams	Squadrons participating in the operations for breaching the Moehne, Eider, Sorpe and Kembs Dams(May 1943 to October 1944).
Dieppe	Squadrons which participated in the combined operations against Dieppe on 19th August 1942.
France and Germany 1944-45	Operations over France, Belgium, Holland and Germany during the liberation of North-West Europe and the advance into the enemy's homeland, from the initiation

of air action preparatory to the invasion of France to VE Day (April 1944 to 8th May 1945).

Biscay Ports 1940-45
Operations over the Bay of Biscay ports from the Fall of France to VE Day.

Ruhr 1940-1945
Bombardment of the Ruhr by aircraft of Bomber Command.

Berlin 1940-45
Bombardment of Berlin by aircraft of Bomber Command.

German Ports 1940-1945
Bombardment of the German ports by aircraft of Bomber and Coastal Commands.

Normandy 1944
Operations supporting the Allied landings in Normandy the establishment of the lodgement area, and the subsequent break-through (June to August 1944).

Arnhem
Squadrons participating in the operations of the Allied Airborne Army (17th to 26th September 1944).

Walcheren
Operations in support of the capture of the Island of Walcheren (3rd October to 9th November 1944).

Rhine
Operations in support of the battle for the Rhine crossing (8th February to 24th March 1945)

Biscay 1940-1945
Operations over the Bay of Biscay by aircraft of Coastal Command and Fighter Command, and Bomber Command aircraft loaned to Coastal Command, between the fall of France and VE Day (25th June 1940 to 8th May 1945).

East Africa 1940-1941
Operations over Kenya, the Sudan, Abyssinia, Italian Somaliland, British Somailand, Eritrea, and the Red Sea, during the campaign which resulted in the conquest of Italian East Africa (10th June 1940 to 27th November 1941).

Greece 1940-1941
Operations over Albania and Greece during the Italian and German invasion, whether carried out by squadrons based in Greece or operating from external bases (28th October 1940 to 30th April 1941).

South-East Europe 1942-1945
Operations over Yugoslavia, Hungary, Romania, Bulgaria and Greece.

Egypt and Libya 1940-1943
Operations in the defence of Egypt and the conquest of Libya, from the outbreak of war against Italy to the retreat of the Axis forces into Tunisia (10th June 1940 to 6th February 1943).

El Alamein
Operations during the retreat to El Alamein and subsequent actions (June to November 1942).

El Hamma
Operations at El Hamma in support of the Battle of the Mareth Line by squadrons operationally controlled by Air Headquarters Western Desert (including No 205 Group squadrons engaged in tactical bombing), during the period 20/21st March to 28th March 1943.)

Malta 1940-1942
Squadrons participating in defensive, offensive, and reconnaissance operations from Malta during the period of enemy action against the island (10th June 1940 to 31st December 1942).

North Africa 1942-1943
Operations in connection with the campaign in French North Africa, from the intitial landings in Algeria to the expulsion of the Axis Powers from Tunisia (8th November 1942 to 13th may 1943).

Mediterranean 1940-43
Operations over Italy, Sicily and the Mediterranean and Aegean Seas by aircraft based in the Mediterranean area (including reconnaissance, convoy protection, mining, and attacks on enemy ports and shipping) between the entry of Italy into the war and the initiation of air action preparatory to the Sicilian campaign (10th June 1940 to 30th June 1943).

Sicily 1943
Operations in furtherance of the conquest of Sicily (1st July to 17th August 1943) by aircraft based in Africa, Malta and Sicily.

Italy 1943-1945
Operations over Italy.

Salerno
Operations in support of the Allied landings in Italy (9th to 16th September 1943).

Anzio and Nettuno
Operations in support of the Allied landings at Anzio and Nettuno (January 1944).

Gustav Line
Squadrons participating in the operations against the Gustav Line (May 1944).

Gothic Line
Air Operations in support of the breaching of the Gothic Line (August to September 1944).

Pacific 1941-1945
Operations against the Japanese in the Pacific theatre, throughout the war with Japan (8th December 1941 to 15th August 1945).

No. 58 Squadron standard.

Malaya 1941-1942	Operations against the Japanese in Malaya, Sumatra and Java, from 8th December 1941, until the final capitulation in Java on 12th March 1942.
Ceylon April 1942	Operations against Japanese aircraft and naval units by squadrons based in Ceylon during the Japanese attacks of April 1942.
Eastern Waters 1941-1945	Operations over waters east of the Mediterranean and Red Sea, including the Indian Ocean, the Bay of Bengal the Java Sea, and the South China Sea, throughout the war with Japan.
Burma 1941-1942	Operations in defence of Rangoon and in support of British Forces during the Japanese invasion of Burma (December 1941 to May 1942).
Arakan 1942-1944	Operations by fighter, bomber and transport squadrons in support of the first and second Arakan campaigns (November 1942 to February 1943, and November 1943 to March 1944).
North Burma 1943-1944	The supply by air of General Wingate's first long-range penetration into North Burma (February to June 1943) and for the air supply and support of his second expedition (5th March to 26th June 1944).
Manipur 1944	Operations in support of the besieged forces at Imphal (March to July 1944).

Burma 1944-1945	Operations during the 14th Army's advance from Imphal to Rangoon, the coastal amphibious assaults, and the Battle of Pegu Yomas (August 1944 to August 1945).
Special Operations	Operations by squadrons regularly assigned to special duties, i.e the succour of resistance movements in enemy-occupied countries by dropping supplies and by introducing and evacuating personnel by air, from the formation of the first special duty flight (20th August 1940) after the Fall of France to VE and VJ Days.
Arctic 1940-1945	Operations over the Arctic by squadrons of Coastal Command based in Iceland, Russia and the Shetlands.
Russia 1941-1945	Operations from Russian bases.
Iraq 1941	Operations in the defeat of Rashid Ali's rebellion (2nd to 31st May 1941).
Habbaniya	Units engaged in the defence of Habbaniya (30th April to 6th May 1941).
Syria 1941	Operations over Syria during the campaign against the Vichy French (8th June to 12th July 1941).
Madagascar 1942	Operations by squadrons of SAAF during and after the landings in Madagascar.

POST WORLD WAR TWO:

It is a sad fact of 20th Century politics that the RAF has rarely been 'at peace' for more than a few years at a stretch since 1945 (see the campaigns chapter). However, the granting of Battle Honours played no part in any of these 'post-colonial' conflicts. As has been explained above, this is in large part due to the politics of any given situation; Suez should, by all normal military standards, have earned a Battle Honour for the participating squadrons.

South Atlantic 1982	The standard of No 1 Squadron carries this battle honour below the squadron badge; the scroll having been modified to make it fit. Although a number of RAF units, including RAF Regiment units, have been awarded the battle honour, only two flying squadrons — No 1 and No 18 Squadrons — can display it upon their standards.
Gulf	A battle honour for the Gulf War has now been agreed. One problem will be to decide which squadrons qualify — the Gulf conflict used composite squadrons; some 20 flying units are at present scheduled to be granted authority to display the honour upon their standards.

(Note: RAF Regiment squadrons also qualify for Standards of this type along with the appropriate Battle Honours.)

OTHER STANDARDS

The Royal Air Force Ensign flies on every RAF unit worldwide; however, it is not a ceremonial flag and so cannot be paraded. It was instituted on 24th March 1921 and consists of a rectangle of blue silk with a small Union flag in the canton (corner) and with a red/white/blue roundel at the fly (i.e the side away from the pole). The regulations regarding the flying of the Ensign are too complex to be covered here (details can be found in Queen's Regulations and Air Council Instructions).

Before leaving the subject of ceremonial flags, it is essential to mention the Queen's Colours which have been presented to the Royal Air Force. Colours are awarded by the Sovereign in recognition of achievement, no qualifying period is required, and the RAF, to date, has six 'active' Colours and three 'redundant' Colours.

1. Colour of the RAF College, Cranwell — presented 6th July 1949.
2. Colour of the RAF in the United Kingdom — Presented 26th May 1951.
3. Colour of No 1 SoTT, RAF Halton — presented 25th July 1952.
4. Colour of the RAF Regiment — presented 17th March 1953.
5. Colour of the Auxiliary Air Force.
6. Colour of the Central Flying School.

The three 'redundant', i.e. laid up, Colours are:
1. Colour of the Far East Air Service.
2. Colour of the Middle/Near East Air Force.
3. Colour of Royal Air Force, Germany.

Standard presentation to 18 and 101 Squadron, Finningley 1962.

ROYAL AIR FORCE FLYING BREVETS

INTRODUCTION:

To distinguish aircrew from other members of the RAF a system of brevets was devised; as each new aircrew trade was created, so a new brevet was introduced. The details given here are for the main brevets worn by RAF aircrew trades, certain other 'flying badges' have existed but are not of direct relevance here (e.g. the ATA badge), as well as special badges worn by aircrew achieving a particular qualification (such as the 'Pathfinder' crews of Bomber Command).

PILOT:

The double wing with the central laurel wreath containing the letters 'RFC' (for Royal Flying Corps) and surmounted by a Royal crown, was inaugurated in 1913 to be the symbol worn by qualified pilots. It has changed very little since that date, except that the original wing shape, based on that of a swift, was changed in 1918 to that of an eagle (a more aggressive and majestic bird); at the same time, with the formation of the RAF, the central lettering was changed to 'RAF'. During 1919 a rule was introduced whereby airship pilots were not entitled to wear a pilot brevet unless they had completed a specific airship course. With the coronation of Queen Elizabeth II, the crown was changed from a King's crown to a Queen's crown. The RAF wings have been used as the pattern for pilot wings by a great many other air forces, in the case of Commonwealth air forces the central letters usually incorporated national identity.

The original RAF brevet was given Royal approval by King George V in February 1913 (as Army Order 40/13).

OBSERVER:

There has been dispute for many years as to the origin of the Observers badge, some writers claiming that this was the first flying badge to be inaugurated, its origins going back to the late 19th Century and the era of the Royal Engineer balloon companies. However, the more commonly accepted version gives an introduction of September 1915 (as Army Order 327), the brevet being awarded to qualified officers who performed the duties of second aircrew member — for navigation (although the pilot was to remain the primary navigator until the introduction of a specialist), bombing, and a host of other tasks. This second seat was often occupied by a qualified pilot, who thus was, in theory, entitled to both brevets! By November 1915 wearing of the brevet had been extended to suitably qualified Warrant Officers and NCOs. The first of the 'half-wing' style of brevets, it is also unique in that it has no laurel wreath surround to its lettering; instead, the 'O' is an integral part of the wing. The post-war reduction in RAF strength, along with a number of other considerations, led to a return to the pre-1915 situation whereby

Lancaster crew of 44 Squadron — note brevets, especially Observer 2nd from left.

the only fully-trained crew member was the pilot, all others being 'part-timers' who received a minimum of on-squadron training. New aircraft introduced in the late 1930s, and a change of philosophy, led to a re-appraisal of aircrew training; one outcome was the re-introduction, in October 1937 (AMO 347) of the 'O' brevet. Qualification for the brevet involved:

1. Passing an Observers course.
2. Service on a squadron for 6 months.
3. Flying 50 hours an an Observer.
4. Recommendation by the Squadron Commander.

This answered the situation for a short while, but continued developments in aircraft and tactics meant that the old Observer concept was ill-suited to all but a few aircraft — it would, for example, have been fine in a Beaufighter or Mosquito but of no use in a Lancaster or Dakota. Observers were (are!) fiercely proud of their qualification, and their brevets, a fact that led to a certain amount of ire when the brevet was replaced by the Navigator brevet in 1942; many insisted on wearing their old brevets — a distinguishing feature.

Before leaving the subject of the Observer there are two special groups to mention — the Observer (Radio) and the Meteorological Observer. The former specialisation was introduced to cover the second crew-man in the night-fighters, his primary task being that of radar operator to work the AI set. A specialist training course was introduced and succesful completion brought award of the the 'RO' brevet. The final Second World War brevet to be introduced was that for the Meteorological Observer — a standard half-wing containing the letter 'M'.

Crew at 1657 HCU model brevets — pilot, AG, N, E, B. Note shoulder flashes of 'Canada' and 'Netherlands'. (Peter Rowlands).

AIR GUNNER:

Throughout the RAF's history there appears to have been a reluctance on the part of the 'hierarchy' to change established patterns of behaviour; a classic example of this has been the attitude towards recognition of additional aircrew trades. By the latter years of World War One air power had developed into many different roles, including the advent of the long-range strategic bomber with its multi-man crew. One of the new breed of (unrecognised) aircrew was the air gunner, usually volunteer armament tradesmen. In the post-war RAF inventory strategic bombers were seen as an essential element, designs such as the HP V/1500 carried four gunner positions. Various discussions took place in the early 1920s, culminating in AMO 204/23 establishing the trade of air gunner and authorising the wearing of a trade badge, to comprise a winged bullet, in brass, to be worn on the right sleeve.

As with the Observers brevet, this badge became an item of contention when a new brevet was introduced in 1939; the 'old hands' prefered to keep the existing bullet. The new design for a half-wing brevet along the lines of that worn by Observers was submitted for consideration in 1938; having had one of its thirteen feathers removed (superstition?) it was approved and inaugurated under AMO 547/39, dated 21st December 1939. A significant change over that of the Observers brevet was the inclusion of a laurel wreath surround for the 'AG' lettering. This was to become the standard pattern for all subsequent brevets — a half-wing of twelve feathers and lettering with a laurel wreath surround.

A rare variety of AG brevet was that worn by some WOP/AGs, the standard half-wing containing the initials 'WAG'. This is the hardest of all brevets to track down in the records, although it is attested as having been worn (examples are still extant). Increasing specialisation of aircraft to roles led to further changes in the nomenclature of aircrew trades. A training conference held in Ottowa in early 1942 recognised eleven primary aircrew trades, three of which fell under the Air Gunner bracket:

1. Wireless Operator/Air Gunner.
2. Wireless Operator/Air Gunner (ASV) — specific to GR aircraft.

Both of the above were universally refered to as 'WOP/AGs'.

3. Air Gunner.

Post World War Two the era of the Air Gunner was short-lived in the RAF, the last operational type to be equipped with gun 'turrets' being the Shackleton.

FLIGHT ENGINEER:

Technology has always served to make aircraft more complex and in due course the large aircraft — bombers, transports, and maritime types — acquired more engines, with associated dials, controls and fuel, plus items such as retractable undercarriages and associated hydraulic systems. The net result was a requirement for another specialist, although official acceptance of this was somewhat slow in coming. Bomber Command held a conference in January 1940 to address the question of a crew member in the heavy bombers to be responsible for fuel and engine monitoring, and to act as an extra air gunner. It was thought, however, that "any intelligent flight mechanic" could do the job after a short engineering and gunnery course. In the meantime, squadrons continued the ad hoc arrangements already in operation, such as selecting 'likely' candidates and putting them through a training course on the squadron. The first officially trained personnel reached Bomber Command squadrons in April 1941, the trade having been established by AMO on 20th March. Two months later it was agreed that these crew members should wear the 'AG' brevet; many within the Commands soon 'amended' these brevets to read 'FE', thus reflecting what they saw as the true nature of the job! The increasing number of heavy aircraft entering RAF service, especially with Bomber Command, during 1942 led to a re-appraisel of the situation. A more rigorous, and appropriate, training course was instituted at St Athan and the Flight Engineer 'came of age' — with due recognition coming in September 1942 and the introduction of the specialist 'E' brevet (although many of the modified 'FE' brevets remained firmly in place on tunics for some time).

90 Squadron crews at briefing, note the sleeve brevets.

NAVIGATOR:

From the earliest days of aviation the pilot was responsible for navigation and the introduction of a second crew member did nothing to change this situation. This continued to be the case into the early years of World War Two, the pilot of a Bomber Command Wellington was still responsible for the navigation. However, it was soon realised that for the long-range operational aircraft a specialist was required.

The Ottowa conference produced a list of five tradesmen entitled to wear the new Navigator brevet:

1. Observer.
2. Observer (W/T).
3. Navigator.
4. Navigator (W/T).
5. Navigator (Radio).

The above list makes obvious the wide range of duties expected of the Navigator, often entailing far more than the simple abbreviations would suggest. A good example of this is the Nav of a Beaufighter on 39 Squadron in the period 1943-44, a time when the squadron was engaged on anti-shipping duties in the Mediterranean, as well as RP strikes against land targets in Yugoslavia. In the Beaufighter the Nav not only had the task of getting the aircraft to and from the target (with no nav aids to speak of and fairly poor met forecasts), but also of managing the radio and handling the rear cockpit guns.

The 'N' brevet, which followed the now standard design, was authorised by AMO 746/42. (or AMO 1019) Once again, there was opposition from the 'old hands' who were most reluctant to give up their hard-won Observer brevets. An official dispensation was granted to those who had been awarded their brevets before the outbreak of war, hence the Observer brevet was to be seen on RAF uniforms for many more years — although no new ones were granted. The Navigator brevet has remained the same since its introduction, and amongst its recipients has acquired the same status — to the extent that when a recent suggestion was made that the brevet should be given a double wing, in the fashion of pilot wings, the navigator 'union' firmly voted to keep the established pattern.

A proud moment — the award of a brevet; presentation at 6FTS.

AIR BOMBER

The situation whereby the pilot, or in some cases Observer/Navigator, was also responsible for bomb aiming was quite suitable in the era before the appearance of more advanced medium and heavy bombers. However, these new aircraft, with their greater number and variety of weapons, plus the introduction of more complex bombsights, required a re-appraisel of the existing arrangement. To this was added the analysis of the Bomber Command raids of 1939 and 1940, evidence which showed the need for two specialists in the crew — the Navigator to get the bomber to the target area and an Air Bomber to take-over and make the final run-in to hit the actual target.

SIGNALLER

Introduced on 2nd December 1943, the Signaller brevet was awarded to specifically qualified wireless operators — i.e those who spent most of their time at the radio station within the aircraft, this particularly applied to Coastal Command flying boats.

AIR ELECTRONICS OPERATOR

Introduced in 1956, the AE brevet was recognition of the growing part played by electronic warfare in air combat.

AIR QUARTERMASTER/AIR LOADMASTER

This particular trade was in existence for many years before it was recognised by the provision of a specialist brevet, a standard half-wing bearing the initials 'AQ'. In due course it was superceded by the Air Loadmaster brevet, a standard half-wing with the initials 'LM'. The Quartermaster, 'QM', brevet was introduced on 16th May 1962 as, "the qualities required of an air quartermaster and the responsibility attaching to their duties are such as to merit aircraw status." It followed the standard half-wing pattern.

FIGHTER CONTROLLER (AIRBORNE)

One of the newest categories, designed for the airborne fighter controllers aboard the AWACs (E-3 Sentry). A standard half-wing with the initials 'FC'.

AIR TECHNICIAN

As with the FC category, this is a new 'aircrew' branch introduced with the AWACs. A standard half-wing with the initials 'AT'.

THE '1947' EXPERIMENT

AMO 498/47 introduced a complete new series of non-commissioned aircrew ranks, each with a variety of categories and accompanied by a new set of distinguishing badges. There were five ranks in Category A, each applicable to the aircrew trades of Pilot, Navigator, Signaller, Engineer, Gunner:

1. MASTER. (as in Master Pilot, Master Navigator etc) — the distinguishing badge was an eagle within a laurel wreath, surmounted by the Royal Arms — all elements being produced in light blue silk.
2. AIRCREW I. (as in PI, NI etc) — the distinguishing badge being three six-pointed stars within a laurel wreath, surmounted by an eagle and crown — all elements being in light blue silk.
3. AIRCREW II. (as in PII, NII etc) — the distinguishing badge being as for the Aircrew I but without the crown.
4. AIRCREW III. (as in PIII, NIII etc) — the distinguishing badge being as for Aircrew II but with only two stars.
5. AIRCREW IV. (as in PIV, NIV etc) — the distinguishing badge being a for Aircrew II but with only one star.

As part of the system a Cadet element was included — Cadet Pilot etc, the distinguishing badge being a laurel wreath surmounted by an eagle.

The final part of the system applied only to Signallers, Engineers, and Gunners; this provided for AIRCREW I to IV ranks but in Category B and C — the distinguishing badges were as for the Category A ranks except that the stars were of white silk not light blue silk. All except the Master's badge were worn on the upper arm, the Master badge being worn on the lower sleeve. It was a short-lived structure, only the Master Aircrew element survived beyond 1950. A re-assessment came into effect on 31st August 1950 whereby Aircrew 1 was regraded as Flight Sergeant and Aircrew 2-4 as Sergeant. The Master element from then on included the word 'air' in the full title — hence Master Air Loadmaster (MALM), Master Air Electronics Operator (MAEOp) etc. The badge for these categories was later modified to include a brass eagle.

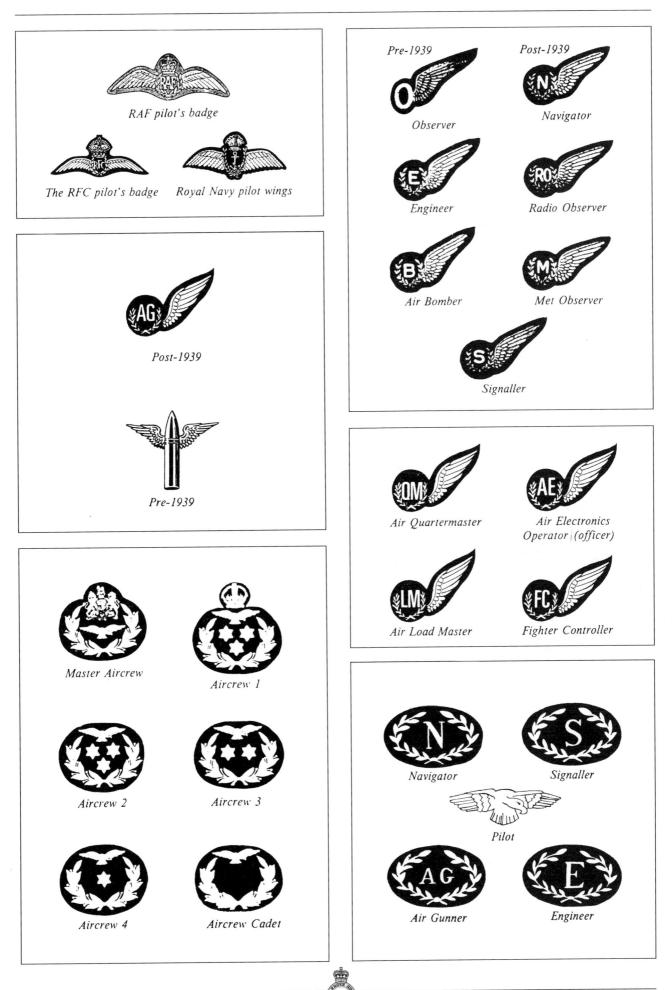

RAF pilot's badge

The RFC pilot's badge

Royal Navy pilot wings

Post-1939

Pre-1939

Pre-1939

Observer

Post-1939

Navigator

Engineer

Radio Observer

Air Bomber

Met Observer

Signaller

Master Aircrew

Aircrew 1

Aircrew 2

Aircrew 3

Aircrew 4

Aircrew Cadet

Air Quartermaster

Air Electronics Operator (officer)

Air Load Master

Fighter Controller

Navigator

Signaller

Pilot

Air Gunner

Engineer

The following seven sections cover a number of elements that would not otherwise feature in such a reference work; they are selected from many hundreds of similar 'data files' that provide basic information. The selection was based upon historical importance (e.g. Chief of Air Staff list and Expansion Plan details) and a number of other factors, such as that of illustrating wartime use of codenames (e.g. minelaying).

1. RAF Equipment Types — 1st March 1922

AMWO 73/22 defined the types of 'air equipment' available to the RAF, these being the descriptions to be used in all official documentation.

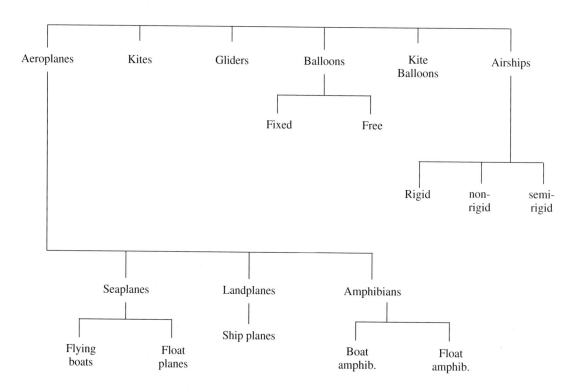

2. Codes for Minelaying Areas (1940-45)

In the interests of security almost every operational aspect of World War Two, or any other operational period, was covered by the use of code-words. One operation that made great use of this technique was the sowing of mines in enemy-held waters. Aircraft undertaking mine-laying sorties were said to be 'gardening', during which they planted 'vegetables' of various descriptions, e.g 'melons', in specific areas, e.g 'Forget-me-Nots'. To read an account of such an operation (see below) makes almost no sense without some basic understanding of what any of it means! The two elements which need decoding are the weapons and the target locations; the following list covers the former aspect. As will become readily apparent, the code-words follow the general horticultural association implied by gardening and vegetables; although a small group of targets use marine animal names.

Anemones — Le Havre
Artichokes — Lorient
Asparagus — Great Belt
Barnacle — Zeebrugge
Beech — St Nazaire
Bottle — Haugesund
Broccoli — Great Belt
Carrots — Little Belt
Cinnamon — La Rochelle
Cypress — Dunkirk
Daffodil — The Sound
Deodar — Bordeaux
Dewberry — Boulogne
Eglantine — Heligoland approaches
Elderberry — Bayonne
Endives — Little Belt
Flounder — Maas and Scheldt
Forget-me-Nots — Kiel Canal
Furze — St Jean De Luz
Hawthorne — Esbjerg approaches
Hollyhock — Travemunde
Hyacinth — St Malo
Geranium — Swinemunde
Gorse — Quiberon
Greengage — Cherbourg
Jasmine — Trevemunde
Jellyfish — Brest
Juniper — Antwerp
Krauts — Lim Fjord
Lettuces — Kiel Canal
Limpets — Den Helder
Melon — Kiel Canal

Mullet — Spezia
Mussels — Terschilling Gat
Nasturtiums — The Sound
Nectarines — Friesian Islands
Newt — Maas and Scheldt
Onions — Oslo
Oysters — Rotterdam
Prawns — Calais
Privet — Danzig
Pumpkins — Great Belt
Quinces — Great Belt
Quinces — Kiel Bay
Radishes — Kiel Bay
Rosemary — Heligoland
Scallops — Rouen
Silverthorne — Kattegat areas
Sweet Peas — Rostock and Arcone Light
Tangerine — Pillau
Tomato — Oslo fjord approaches
Trefoils — Texal (South)
Turbot — Ostend
Undergrowth — Kattegat
Verbena — Copenhagen approaches
Vine Leaves — Dieppe
Wallflowers — Kiel Bay
Whelks — Zuider Zee
Willow — Arcona to R.Dievenow
Xeranthemums — R.Jade
Yams — Heligoland approaches
Yewtree — Kattegat
Zinneas — R.Jade

3. PHONETIC ALPHABET

IT HAS ALREADY BEEN shown in the section on abbreviations that RAF history is full of 'shorthand', both in text and speech. The abbreviations section covers the major element of this but one important aspect is that of letters used with reference to such things as aircraft identity. The most obvious use here is for the letter given to each individual aircraft e.g a Lancaster in 1944 coded 'PM-M' would be announced as 'M for Mike' (in full, although rarely applied it would be 'Peter Mike-Mike'). A Tornado in 1992 coded 'JM' would be announced as 'Juliet Mike'. The use of this phonetic alphabet extends into other areas, most commonly being used for the aircraft radio call-sign — an item which has taken a variety of forms over the years. Formations tend to be refered to by a formation name e,g 'DESPOT' (thus not making use of the phonetic system), with individual aircraft being given a formation number or letter. However, single aircraft, and in certain circumstances formations, take a call-sign comprising a number of phonetic letters (the commonest form in use now being the trigraph — i.e 3 three letters); thus, 'FYR 42' would be announced as ' Foxtrot Yankee Romeo four two'. The phonetic alphabet used by civilian agencies was at variance with that of the RAF until 1956 when the two came into line.

Phonetic Alphabet used by RAF:

1924-42	1942-1943	1943-56	1956-
A — Ac	Apple	Able-Afirm	Alfa
B — Beer	Beer	Baker	Bravo
C — Charlie	Charlie	Charlie	Charlie
D — Don	Dog	Dog	Delta
E — Edward	Edward	Easy	Echo
F — Freddie	Freddy	Fox	Foxtrot
G — George	George	George	Golf
H — Harry	Harry	How	Hotel
I — Ink	In	Item/Interrogatory	India
J — Johnnie	Jug/Johnny	Jig/Johnny	Juliett
K — King	King	King	Kilo
L — London	Love	Love	Lima
M — Monkey	Mother	Mike	Mike
N — Nuts	Nuts	Nab/Negat	November
O — Orange	Orange	Oboe	Oscar
P — Pip	Peter	Peter/Prep	Papa
Q — Queen	Queen	Queen	Quebec
R — Robert	Roger/Robert	Roger	Romeo
S — Sugar	Suga	Sugar	Sierra
T — Toc	Tommy	Tare	Tango
U — Uncle	Uncle	Uncle	Uniform
V — Vic	Vic	Victor	Victor
W — William	William	William	Whiskey
X — X-ray	X-ray	X-ray	X-ray
Y — Yorker	Yoke/Yorker	Yoke	Yankee
Z — Zebra	Zebra	Zebra	Zulu of 'shorthand'

Hawks of the Red Arrows.

4. ROYAL AIR FORCE DISPLAY TEAMS

AEROBATIC AND FORMATION displays have been part of the RAF 'heritage' since the earliest days, often on an informal basis but also with official sanction. The latter grouping covers all the acknowledged formation teams whose task it has been to display to the public the expertise of the RAF, both as a show of ability and also as an aid to recruiting. During the 1920s this concept was mainly seen at the annual Hendon Pageants when squadron formations teams would astound the air-minded public with feats of close formation manoeuvring. In general terms a squadron was chosen for a particular year and then expected to devise and rehearse a suitable routine. The shows would also include solo routines, either by a member of the formation team or by another display machine. However, our interest here is only with the named formation teams. World War Two brought an end to all such public shows, but the post-war period saw a great upsurge in public displays held at RAF stations in the form of an annual Battle of Britain 'At Home' Day. These would feature a wide range of air and ground displays; with the resident squadrons providing a range of solo and formation displays and visiting aircraft adding extra interest. The 1950s saw the development of 'official' formation teams who toured the shows. The following list gives the major teams since 1956:

NAME	AC TYPE	No of ac	DATES	UNIT
Black Arrows	Hunter F.4	4/5	1956	111 Sqn
Black Arrows	Hunter F.6	7/9	1957	111 Sqn
Black Arrows	Hunter F.6	9/16	1958-60	111 Sqn
Black Knights	Hunter F.4	4	1956	54 Sqn
Blades	Jet Provost T.5	4	1970-73	CAW
Blue Chips	Chipmunk T.10	2	1960s-74	
Blue Diamonds	Hunter F.6	16	1961-2	92 Sqn
Bulldogs	Bulldog T.1	2		3 FTS
Firebirds	Lightning F.1	9	1963-65	56 Sqn
Fighting Cocks	Hunter F.4	4	1950s	43 Sqn
Gazelles	Gazelle HT.3	4	1970s	CFS
Gemini Pair	Provost T.4/T.5	2	1970-73	Leeming
Gin/Linton Gin	Jet Provost T.4		1968-70	CAW
Green Marrows	Canberra T.4/B.2	4	1989	231 OCU
Lincolnshire Poachers	Jet Provost		1969?	
Linton Blacks	Vampire T.11	4	1960	1 FTS
Macaws	Jet Provost T.4		1968-72	CAW
Meteorites	Meteor T.7	3	1952	CFS
Poachers	Jet Provost T.4/T.5	4	1963-76	Cranwell
Red Arrows	Gnat T.1	7	1965	CFS
Red Arrows	Gnat T.1	9	1966-1980	CFS
Red Arrows	Hawk T.1	9	1980-	CFS
Red Pelicans	Jet Provost T.4	4/6	1962-70	CFS
Red Pelicans	Jet Provost T.5	4/6	1970-73	CFS
Redskins	Jet Provost	2	1959	CFS
Skylarks	Chipmunk T.10	4	1968-70	CFS
Swords	Jet Provost T.5	4	1974	3 FTS
Tigers	Lightning F.1		1961-62	74 Sqn
Tigers	Phantom F-4J	4	1991-92	74 Sqn
Tomahawks	Sioux HT.3	3	1967-69	CFS(H)
Vintage Pair	Meteor T.7	1	1972-81/1986-88	CFS
	Vampire T.11	1		
Vipers	Jet Provost T.4	4	1968-69	2 FTS
Yellowjacks	Gnat T.1	4	1964	

5. STRENGTH TABLE

For certain years accurate statistics are not available. Wherever possible the best source has been used and cross checked. At the time of publication, the figures for 1992 had not been released.

Date	Personnel		Aircraft		Remarks
1918	Officer:	28846	Op:	3300	
	Airmen:	211410	Other:	19347	
	Total:	240256	Total:	22647	
1923	Officer:	3155	Op: (36 Sqns)		
	Airmen:	27033	Other:		
	Total:	30188	Total:		
1928	Officer:	3350	Op: (67 Sqns)		
	Airmen:	27564	Other:		
	Total:	30914	Total:		
1933	Officer:	3188	Op:		
	Airmen:	27812	Other:		
	Total:	31000	Total:		personnel total +1335 Aux AF
1938	Officer:	6218	Op:	1982	
	Airmen:	67049	Other:		
	Total:	73267	Total:		
1942	Officer:	65151	Op:	4287	
	Airmen:	1006982	Other:		
	Total:	1072133	Total:		
1945	Officer:	109256	Op:	8752	
	Airmen:	1006267	Other:	18691	96% 'Duration only'
	Total:	1115523	Total:	27443	(Airmen)
1948	Officer:	21395	Op:	1124	
	Airmen:		Other:	2635	
	Total:		Total:	3759	
1952	Officer:	26773	Op:	1717	8200 Airmen
	Airmen:	245899	Other:	4353	National Service
	Total:	272672	Total:	6070	
1958	Officer:	24279	Op:	1249	
	Airmen:	160579	Other:	2009	
	Total:	184858	Total:	3258	

Date	Personnel		Aircraft		Remarks
1963	Officer:	21553	Op:	920	
	Airmen:	123036	Other:	1343	
	Total:	144589	Total:	2263	
1968	Officer:	21242	Op:	780	
	Airmen:	100173	Other:	1122	
	Total:	121415	Total:	1902	
1973	Officer:		Op:	662	
	Airmen:		Other:	969	
	Total:	105900	Total:	1631	
1978	Officer:	14682	Op:	620	
	Airmen:	69489	Other:	804	
	Total:	84171	Total:	1424	
1983	Officer:	14900	Op:	577	
	Airmen:	74800	Other:	894	
	Total:	89700	Total:	1471	
1988	Officer:	15400	Op:	606	
	Airmen:	77900	Other:	853	
	Total:	93300	Total:	1459	
1992	Officer:		Op:		
	Airmen:		Other:		
	Total:		Total:		

Variations in statistics. The aircraft strength would, one would think, be a matter of fact and so easy to determine.This, unfortunately, is not the case! The author has uncovered a wide range of statistical variations, a few of which are reproduced below. A typical example is that for 1950 ... a statement in Parliament, recorded in Hansard, gives details of aircraft strength for the years 1950 to 1967; for 1950 it states a strength of 4510 aircraft. An RAF statistical document gives a figure of 4594 for the same year, broken down into 1338 operational, 404 communications, 332 miscellaneous, 2248 training, 272 in store. A second RAF source of 'aircraft held on charge' gives a total of 9941! This latter document gives the following figures for 1945 to 1976:

1945 — 61584
1946 — 38730
1947 — 20430
1948 — 14504
1949 — 11417
1950 — 9941
1951 — 8990
1952 — 9681
1953 — 10100

1954 — 9146
1955 — 8690
1956 — 8397
1957 — 7554
1958 — 6174
1959 — 5194
1960 — 4178
1961 — 3770
1962 — 3374
1963 — 3175
1964 — 3122
1965 — 3073
1966 — 2967
1967 — 2823
1973 — 2030
1968 — 2526
1974 — 2019
1969 — 2359
1975 — 1914
1970 — 2296
1976 — 1841
1971 — 2192
1972 — 2152

6. CHIEF OF THE AIR STAFF

THE MOST SENIOR officer within the RAF structure is CAS, the following list of occupants of this post gives their rank upon entering the post — many were promoted in post.

Maj-Gen Sir Hugh Trenchard KCB DSO	3.1.18 —
Maj-Gen Sir Frederick Sykes CMG	14.4.18 —
Maj-Gen Sir Hugh Trenchard KCB DSO	11.1.19 —
ACM Sir John Salmond KCB CMG CVO DSO	1.1.30 —
ACM Sir Geoffrey Salmond KCB KCMG DSO	1.4.33 —
ACM Sir Edward Ellington KCB CMG CBE	22.5.33 —
ACM Sir Cyril Newall KCB CMG CBE AM	1.9.37 —
MRAF Sir Charles Portal KCB DSO MC	25.10.40 —
MRAF Sir Arthur Tedder GCB	1.1.46 —
ACM Sir John Slessor GCB DSO MC ADC	1.1.50 —
ACM Sir William Dickson GCB DSO MC ADC	1.1.53
ACM Sir Dermot Boyle KCVO KBE CB AFC	1.1.56 —
ACM Sir Thomas Pike KCB CBE DFC	1.1.60 —
ACM Sir Charles Elworthy GCB CBE DSO MVO DFC AFC MA	1.9.63 —
ACM Sir John Grandy GCB KBE DSO	1.4.67 —
ACM Sir Denis Spotswood GCB CBE DSO DFC ADC	1.4.71 —
ACM Sir Andrew Humphrey GCB OBE DFC AFC ADC	1.4.74 —
ACM Sir Michael Beetham KCB CBE DFC AFC	10.8.77 —
ACM Sir Keith Williamson GCB AFC DFC	15.10.82
ACM Sir David Craig GCB OBE	15.10.85
ACM Sir Peter Harding GCB ADC FRAeS	14.11.88
ACM Sir Michael Graydon GCB CBE ADC	6.11.92

7. THE EXPANSION SCHEMES 1934-1938

ALTHOUGH A VARIETY of expansion plans had been put forward during the latter 1920s there was no political motivation to provide the requisite funding and so the RAF continued to languish, short of equipment and with with little prospect of improvement. The rising European political crises of the early 1930s, in conjunction with an improving home economy, led to yet another batch of expansion proposals, each new scheme being motivated by developments in Germany and the perceived threat from the German Air Force. A study of these proposals is essential to an understanding of the position in which the RAF found itself in the late 1930s; each scheme addressed a number of questions such as total number of squadrons, squadron strength (i.e aircraft establishment) and role, and the proportion of war reserve to be provided. The latter aspect is a key element often ignored in RAF histories where consideration is only given to available aircraft 'in the shop window', but without an efficient and well-stocked reserve organisation failure in the Battle of Britain would have been guaranteed; in the event, the supply of Spitfires and Hurricanes never dried up and the major crisis became one of pilots not aircraft.

The data below provides the basic numbers game for each of the major expansion schemes — note the effective dates (i.e date at which the scheme was to be complete) and the authorisation date when it was approved by the Cabinet.

SCHEME A — Effective date 31.3.39, approved 18.7.34. To provide a maximum front-line strength this scheme proposed a major reduction in war reserve.

Home based squadrons —	84 with 960 aircraft.	
(F) Fighter 28 + 5 aux		12 ac per sqn
(LB) Light Bomber 25 + 8 aux		12 ac
(MB) Medium Bomber 8		12 ac
(HB) Heavy Bomber 8		10 ac
(TB) Torp. Bomber 2		12 ac
(GP) General Purpose 4		12 ac
(FB) Flying Boat 4		4 ac
(AC) Army Co-op 5		12 ac
Overseas squadrons —	27 with 292 aircraft	

SCHEME C — Effective date 31.3.37, approved 21.5.35. To achieve parity with the German Air Force; this scheme was a direct outcome of the Berlin visit of 26.3.35 and talks with Hitler.

Home based squadrons —	123 with 1512 aircraft.	
F 35 + 5aux		12 ac per sqn
(LB 30 + 11 aux		12 ac

MB 18		12 ac
HB 20		12 ac
TB 2		12 ac
GP 7		18ac
FB 6		6 ac
AC 5		18 ac
Overseas squadrons —	27 with 292 aircraft	

SCHEME F — Effective date 31.3.39, approved 25.2.36. An overall increase in aircraft strength and the first increase in overseas establishment. This scheme also made provision for war reserves of 150% of front-line strength.

Home based squadrons —	124 with 1736 aircraft.	
F 30 + 5 aux		14 ac per sqn
MB 29		18 ac
MB 19 + 11 aux		12 ac
HB 20		12 ac
TB 2		16 ac
GR 7		18 ac
FB 6		6 ac
AC 11 + 4		12 ac
Overseas squadrons —	37 with 468 aircraft.	

SCHEME H — Effective date 31.3.39, approved 14.1.37. An increase in the fighter element to meet the probable scale of an attack and to produce a strike force not inferior to that of Germany. This was seen as an interim scheme and included a reduction in war reserve in order to increase front-line numbers.

Home based squadrons —	145 with 2422 aircraft.	
F 34 + 9 aux		14 ac per sqn
M/HB 8		14ac
MB 47 + 17		21 ac
HB 20		14 ac
TB 2		21 ac
GR 7		21 ac
FB 6		6 ac
AC 11 + 4		12 ac
Other* 10		21 ac

(* the role of these units was not specified).
Overseas squadrons — 27 with 348 aircraft.

SCHEME J — Effective date summer.41, approved 22.12.37. To achieve offensive parity with German Air Force rather than simple numbers, a major effect of this was the decision to concentrate on HB production. Major increase, almost double, in overseas strength.

Home based squadrons —   154 with 2331 aircraft.

        F 38 + 9 aux................ 14 ac per sqn
        MB 26 + 7....................... 21 ac
        HB 64............................ 14 ac
        GR 9............................. 21 ac
        FB 6............................. 6 ac
        AC 11 + 4....................... 12 ac
        TD* 4............................ 14 ac

(* Trade Defence squadrons, to be based in UK or overseas.)

Overseas squadrons —   45 with 644 aircraft.

SCHEME K — Effective date 31.3.41, approved 14.3.38. A more realistic scheme than that proposed by Scheme J, including further cuts in war reserve to most types — except fighter.

Home based squadrons —   145 with 2305 aircraft.

        F 38 + 9 aux............... 14 ac per sqn
        MB 16............................ 24 ac
        MB 3............................. 16 ac
        HB 58............................ 16 ac
        GR 9............................. 21 ac
        FB 6............................. 6 ac
        AC 11 + 4....................... 12 ac

Overseas squadrons —   39 with 490 aircraft.

SCHEME L — Effective date 31.3.40, approved 27.4.38. An increase in the percentage of fighters at the expense of heavy bombers but also a much more realistic programme in that it allowed for a move towards a war economy by diverting effort from domestic production to military provision.

Home based squadrons —   141 with 2373 aircraft.

        F 38 + 9 aux............... 16 ac per sqn
        MB 23............................ 24 ac
        MB 3............................. 16 ac
        HB 47............................ 16 ac
        GR 9............................. 21 ac
        GR 4............................. 14 ac
        FB 6............................. 6 ac
        AC 11 + 4....................... 12 ac

Overseas squadrons —   39 with 490 aircraft.

SCHEME M — Effective date 31.3.42, approved 7.11.38. Impetus to greater effort following Munich Crisis of September. Larger fighter force, to be based around the newest types (Whirlwind, Typhoon, Tornado) and massive HB strike force.

Home based squadrons —   163 with 2549 aircraft.

        F 50 + 14 aux.............. 16 ac per sqn
        HB 85............................ 16 ac
        TB/GR 2.......................... 21 ac
        GR 7............................. 21 ac
        GR 4............................. 14 ac
        GR/FB 6.......................... 6 ac
        AC 9 + 2........................ 12 ac

Overseas squadrons —   49 with 636 aircraft.

ROYAL AIR FORCE CAMPAIGN HISTORIES

SINCE ITS FORMATION in April 1918, the Royal Air Force has been involved in two World Wars, a number of United Nations actions, and a host of minor, mainly 'Colonial' conflicts. There has rarely been a single year since 1918 that the RAF has not been involved in 'operations' of one type or another. The scale of this historical involvement demands many tomes to do it full justice; here, however, we must content ourselves with outlines of each campaign and, in particular, the RAF involvement. Rather less detail has been provided for the campaigns of World War Two for the reason that these, in the most part, have been well covered in print. There are many 'one line' operational events which have also been left out, a typical example being the deployment of a Hunter detachment to Gibraltar following the May 1967 imposition by Spain of a prohibited Air Zone effecting approaches to the Gibraltar; also the many relief operations undertaken by the RAF, almost an annual event for the Hercules squadrons in recent years, have been omitted. As our story is not taken up until April 1918 it is pertinant to say a few words about the period leading up to this date.

GENESIS OF AIR POWER

The desire to employ the 'third dimension' for military purposes was not new to the 20th Century; as early as the 5th Century BC the Chinese had employed kites to place observers aloft, although the writers tell us little of the military value of these kites. Napoleon was the first great military mind to consider the full application of air power, with a concept for a combined arms invasion of England, where a balloon force would land picked troops behind the coastal defences whilst naval landings were taking place. It was, of course, with balloons that the first practical application of air power was forthcoming. A man could be placed in a balloon above the battlefield and so be able to observe the movements of friend and foe, relaying this intelligence to the General and so having a significant impact on the outcome of the battle. By the late 19th Century most European nations used military balloons for just such a purpose, the first significant conflict in which they were employed being the Franco-Prussian war of 1870.

The British Army was slow to take up the idea but the Royal Engineers did employ observation balloons during the Boer War. Most military authorities were agreed as to the value of this work but also realised the limitations imposed by lack of mobility and poor communications (air to ground). It would require a breakthough in technology to overcome these difficulties; it would also require a suitable impetus and this was lacking amongst the traditionalists who still saw light cavalry as the intelligence-gathering arm of the military. This dogma was to keep Britain behind in the development of air power, despite the

presence, in the lower officer ranks, of some free-thinkers who recognised the critical part that this element would play in any future major conflict. The appearance of practical heavier-than-air machines during the first decade of the 20th Century meant that air power had truly arrived — although some still failed to realize the significance of this development. Probably the first serious shock to the British establishment came in 1909 when Bleriot made his flight from France to England; still it did not seem too critical as these early flimsy machines could carry no useful military payload.

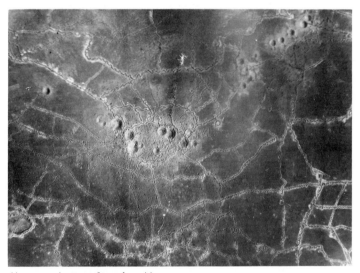
Air reconnaissance of trench positions.

BE2c — multi-role aircraft of the RFC.

A series of Army manoeuvres did, however, convince the Army command that the presence of observation aircraft could play a useful role in the conduct of a campaign or battle, albeit as an adjunct to the existing land-based reconnaissance. Other European nations were much more enlightened in respect of the employment of air power, the Italians had already foreseen the potential of the aircraft as an offensive weapon and were soon using it as such in their colonial conflicts.

It was not until 1911 that the first British military air formation came into being with the creation of the Air Battalion of the Royal Engineers, comprising No 1 (Airship) Company and No 2 (Aeroplane) Company. The same year a crucial report was made by the Haldane Committee, one of whose recommendations was the formation of a British Aeronautical Service. This Royal Flying Corps was formed in 1912 and comprised a Military Wing, a Naval Wing (soon to become the Royal Naval Air Service), and a Central Flying School. The latter opened at Upavon in June 1912 to train pilots to man the planned seven squadrons. However, it was a slow start and by August 1914 it was still very much a paper force with only the nucleus of the squadrons in existence — a report drawn up in 1913 showed that of the RFC's notional 120 machines only 46 were 'ready to fly', with the rest under repair or damaged. Likewise, the equipment itself was by no means startling, with the majority of machines being BE2s or Maurice Farmans. In June 1914 virtually the entire strength of the RFC gathered at Netheravon for summer camp (No 2, 3, 4, 5 and 6 Squadrons). The primary role of all the squadrons was that of reconnaissance.

Two months later the world was at war. The RNAS (this designation being approved in June 1914) squadrons were designated for Home Defence as this area of responsibility had been given to the Admiralty, although RNAS units were soon stationed on the other side of the Channel. In August four RFC squadrons were sent to Amiens, France in support of the British Expeditionary Force (BEF). The first operational sortie was flown on 19th August and the airborne eyes of the land commander soon became crucial amidst the confusion of the mobile warfare of these early months. Before long, rival recce aircraft met over the Front Lines and combat was joined — to protect ones own aircraft and to prevent the enemy gaining intelligence. Aircraft armament was developed and so was born the fighter. At the end of 1914 artillery spotting (fall-of-shot and corrections) became a major task for the still limited number of aircraft in France. 1915 was a year of developments and expansion and by September the RFC strength stood at twelve squadrons, with a notional 161 aircraft. New roles were developed and weapons and tactics devised to fit the changing requirments. In May, Lt Rhodes-Moorhouse, of No 2 Squadron, became the first airman to be awarded the Victoria Cross — following his lone attack on the important marshalling yards at Courtrai. In the summer of 1915 the first true fighters appeared and the German 'Fokker Scourge' began to take its toll of the slow and virtually unarmed RFC aircraft.

1916 brought a doubling of RFC strength to 27 squadrons and over 400 aircraft, plus the introduction of newer more capable types which in large part redressed the balance of the previous year and enabled the RFC to renew the fight. It was short-lived, however, as the German advantage was soon re-established. The operational use of aircraft was not confined to the Western Front; RFC machines saw service in almost all theatres of the war — from Africa to the Balkans, although never on the scale of the air battles over the Western Front.

By 1916 the Home Defence of Britain had proved impotent in the face of German airship raids and there was great public outcry that something should be done. Responsibility was transferred from the Admiralty to the RFC and the latter set about establishing a more co-ordinated defence shceme of aeroplanes, guns and searchlights. In September William Leefe Robinson, of No 39 Squadron, brought down an airship over London — much to the delight of the thousands of witnesses — and for this achievement he was awarded the Victoria Cross. Within weeks No 39 Squadron had claimed three more of the previously immune giants and, for a while, this strategic bombing threat receded. Unfortunately the defences did not develop as rapidly as its opponents and the start of the raids by long range heavy bombers brought renewed terror to English cities. This led to such a public outcry that an inquiry, headed by General Jan Smuts, was initiated and which, through a variety of debates and changes, in due course recommended the creation of an independent air force. Thus was drafted the Air Force (Constitution) Act which was given Royal Assent on 29th November 1917, leading to the creation of the Royal Air Force on 1st April 1918.

WESTERN FRONT
APRIL — NOVEMBER 1918

After the stagnation of their early Spring offensive towards Amiens, the Germans launched the Battle of the Lys on 9th April to push the British forces back at Hazebrouck. The attack was proving effective in certain areas and RAF squadrons were heavily involved with ground support work, there being no shortage of worthwhile targets. The air over the Front was also the scene of heavy fighting and on one day, 12th April, the RAF claimed 49 enemy aircraft and six balloons shot down, no less than six aircraft falling to the guns of Captain Woollett of No 43 Squadron. Ten days later the famous Baron von Richthofen was killed. This campaign and associated fighting on the French sector, where the squadrons of IXth Brigade were lending a hand, continued into July with air power proving decisive. The German offensive petered out, the troops were exhausted but had almost achieved a breakthrough. However, it was now the turn of the Allied armies to launch themselves forwards — it was to prove too much for the now shattered German forces. The Battle of Amiens commenced on 8th August and was to be the start point of the final victorious push. All four RAF Brigades — I, III, V and IX — were involved on a wide range of tasks, although certain squadrons now began to acquire specialist duties, No 43 Squadron, for example, using its Camels as a night fighter force to counter the nightly raids by German heavy bombers, whilst No 84 Squadron specialised in anti-balloon work and No 6 Squadron went in for co-operation with cavalry forces.

Almost all of the so-called 'gentlemens' war had now vanished from the air campaign; No 80 Wing mounted a major attack on German airfields which proved to be highly effective and at very little cost. As the Allied force continued to advance, winning the Second Battle of the Somme (21st August to 3rd September), RAF aircraft wrought havoc amongst the retreating German columns, such ground attack missions playing a great part in the rapid advance. French and Belgian troops who found themselves short of supplies were grateful for the RAF air-dropped rations, including the all-important beer supply! A typical day of activity was 30th October with the RAF flying 45 recce sorties, 59 combat patrols, 18 artillery counter-battery operations, dropping 23.5 tons of bombs by day and 13 tons by night, and claiming the destruction of 68 enemy aircraft and one balloon.

By November the Allies were paused for the final push from the Sambre to Valenciennes; this offensive by 4th, 3rd and 1st

Armies met with immediate success and on 11th of the month Mons was captured.

INDEPENDENT FORCE

Reinforcements arrived throughout the summer, many of these going to build up the Independent Force for its strategic campaign against Germany. The intention was for long-range bombers to strike at the industries and transportation system of Germany itself, thus bringing the war to an end. A variety of units was incorporated within this new force, although most consisted of standard day bombers such as the DH9 with its limited range and bomb load. The larger bomber aircraft essential to the success of this policy were only just becoming available in the latter months of the war.

An Air Council summary of late November stated that, " in recent months the work of the Independent Air Force has had moral and material effects which have contributed powerfully to the disintegration of the enemy's capacity for resistance."

BELGIAN COAST

Despite the renumbering of the Naval Wings and their incorporation into the RAF the basic tasks remained the same, the primary one being support of naval operations to shut down German use of the naval base at Bruges. During the actual assault aircraft operating from Dover and Dunkirk were engaged attacking coastal batteries and dropping flares to help in the positioning of block ships. With the latter in place a regular task was that of bombing the area to prevent the enemy making repairs.

During the summer the main workload comprised attacks on communications targets as preparation for the Allied offensive. These attacks took on an intensive nature and aircraft ranged far and wide destroying key rail and road targets as well as taking every opportunity of strafing and bombing road and rail traffic. With the opening of the offensive in early September most squadrons were attached to support the Belgian army as it moved forward to liberate its homeland. As the German retreat gathered momentum the columns were harrassed by Allied aircraft, great destruction and confusion was created and total collapse was only prevented by a period of bad weather.

HOME DEFENCE AND MARITIME OPERATIONS

After the defeat of the Zeppelin menace in late 1916, the German strategic bombing effort had relied on their long-range bombers. These continued to pose a threat into 1918 until suitable home defence fighters were made available.

The German U-boat menace required a substantial British counter-effort, including the use of aircraft, airships and balloons operating in conjunction with surface forces. One expert opinion stated that a force of 1185 aeroplanes and seaplanes would be required for this task in 1918, the actual strength being no more than 314 as the year opened. Hours of anti-submarine patrol were rewarded with only a few sightings and even fewer attacks, the first definite sinking being that of UC49 on 31st May. However, another important task for the patrol aircraft was the surveying of minefields to check the position of cleared channels. Seaplanes often operated from lighters towed into position by destroyers of the Harwich Force, although aircraft also used the carrier HMS *Furious*, additionally some cruisers carried Sopwith Camels. These latter elements were usually employed on offensive sweeps including attacks on land targets such as Zeppelin bases and seaplane stations.

MIDDLE EAST

The most significant of the Middle East campaigns was that of General Allenby with his thrust into Palestine designed to eliminate the Turkish presence. An important aspect of this was the air offensive, albeit with limited resources of SE5A and DH9, against garrisons. The main offensive was launched on 19th September and during the Battle of Nablus aircraft bombed and strafed the retreating Turkish columns causing great confusion and destruction. As the retreat passed through Wadi el Far'a the seven British squadrons flew constant patrols over the columns, as one group of aircraft ran out of bombs so the next group arrived to take their place. By 25th September Amman had been captured and the other Turkish Army, 4th Army, isolated and subjected to air attack. Damascus fell on the 30th as Allenby's forces swept onwards. The Turks signed an Armistice on 31st October.

ARMISTICE

The 'Great War' ended in November 1918 but Europe was still not at peace.

CAMPAIGN 1918-1939
RUSSIA 1918-20

THE BOLSHEVIK REVOLUTION in Russia rapidly led to that country seeking peace with Germany, thereby freeing German forces to move to the Western Front. This was a major blow to the Allied forces, and was made even more disheartening by the prospect of Russo-German co-operation. Thus, any possibility of restoring Russia to the Allied side to keep her in the war was greeted with enthusiasm. The presence of anti-Bolshevik 'white' Russian forces provided just such an opening and so became a focus of Allied, particularly British and Japanese, involvement.

Northern Russia.

In August 1918 British forces, accompanied by an assortment of aircraft, occupied the northern port of Archangel. An offensive was launched towards Obozerskaya with the aircraft providing close support to the advancing infantry.

By the middle of December the RAF had operational units stationed at Archangel and Murmansk; however, the following month most British forces were withdrawn from Russia.

Although World War One was now over there was still a strong feeling in the capitals of western Europe that the Bolsheviks should be overthrown, especially as the 'Whites' appeared to be achieving major successes! A 'Relief Force' was sent to north Russia in mid 1919 to resume operations where the previous expedition had left off. Within a matter of weeks two squadrons of 'volunteers' (there being no shortage of RAF personnel who were finding peace-time conditions not to their liking) had been established at Bereznik. The squadrons were numbered '2' and '3', with a mix of Snipes, DH9s and DH9As. Operations commenced in July with ground support sorties on the Dvina and Vaga Fronts. Although there was no air opposition, the Bolsheviks having almost no air assets, the strafing and bombing missions were hazardous in the face of intense ground fire. It was, however, a losing battle and the following month all air units were withdrawn to Archangel and evacuated.

Southern Russia.

With the Armistice in November 1918 British forces were in occupation of parts of the Caucasus previously held by German and Turkish forces. The decision to support the 'Whites' in the Russian Civil War led to their attachment to the army of General Deniken, the most successful of the royalist generals. The major operational unit was No 221 Sqn which left for Russia aboard HMS *Riveria* and HMS *Empress* in December 1918, arriving at Batum on 5th January. Over the next few weeks the unit operated from a number of bases — Baku, Petrovsk Kaskar, Chechen, Lagan — in support of ground forces in the Astrakhan area. Reinforcements arrived in March when the Short 184s of No 266 Sqn commenced operations from Petrovsk Port and Chechen.

A 'training and advisory' mission arrived at Taganrog in April to teach the Russians how to operate the RE8s donated by the British Government. Meanwhile No 47 Sqn added its weight to the RAF effort with its DH9s moving to Novorossik in April, although by June the HQ unit was at Ekaterinodar. Over the next few months this squadron was heavily involved with support missions in a number of areas, detached flights flying from Gniloaksaiskaya, Velikoknya-jaskaya, Zimovniki, Kotelnikovo and Beketovka. The squadron also operated an assortment of aircraft types including DH9s, DH9As and Camels; they also scored one of the few victories, shooting down a Nieuport Scout.

October was the high-water mark of the White forces, Deniken having won a series of victories which were promptly squandered through internal bickering and lack of strategic appreciation. It was a most frustrating time for the British 'advisers', especially as it led to the inevitable withdrawals. All three RAF squadrons disbanded, No 47 Sqn being the last to go, in October, although the elements of the latter were redesignated as 'A' Squadron and continued to operate alongside the Russian forces which had received the ex RAF equipment. The last operational sortie was flown on 29th March 1920. The same month saw the final withdrawal of the training mission.

BRITISH SOMALILAND 1919-21

British Somaliland had been a source of military difficulty for the British ever since its acquisition as a Protectorate in 1898. It was a large country with inhospitable climate and terrain, the type of conditions which the Victorian soldier of the British Empire had been battling for years in an attempt to keep the native tribes at peace. The tribal rebellion in this area was under the leadership of the 'Mad Mullah' (Mohammed bin Abdullah Hassan) and had grown to such an extent that a major land expedition was planned in an effort to restore stability. In the event, however, the British Empire was otherwise occupied between 1914 and 1918 and the Mullah was left to increase his power and authority.

A Colonial Office appraisel in early 1919 came up with two options; give up the area, or, mount a major expedition, although the latter according to the War Office, would be expensive and would tie up three divisions for at least a year. At a time when there were other pressing colonial problems this was simply not viable. More in hope than expectation, the Colonial Office approached the RAF for ideas. This was a time when the RAF, under the leadership of Trenchard, was looking for a role to justify its peace-time existence (under pressure from both Army and Navy). The idea it came up with was for the RAF to mount an expedition in conjunction with existing local forces — a much cheaper option. It was also a gamble, although anti-tribal operations by small numbers of aircraft had proved practicable in similar situations.

The idea was given the go-ahead and a special unit, 'Z Force', was formed under the command of Gp Capt R Gordon; by October 1919 the advance party was in Egypt, arriving at Berbera, British Somaliland, the following month. The initial task was to select suitable landing grounds, arrange for support facilities and liaise with the local land force commanders. The main party arrived at Berbera on 30th December and within two weeks the ten DH9s were ready for action, including two having been fitted-out as air ambulances. The operational flight deployed

to Eil dur Elan in late January and commenced bombing missions against rebel forts. In the ensuing days the DH9s flew bombing, recce, strafing and supply missions both as independent actions and in direct support of the Somaliland Field Force. To keep pace with the ground operations a number of landing grounds were brought into use, some being little more than semi-cleared patches of scrub. The use of aircraft to harrass the rebel forces proved to be a total success, the Mullah was given no chance to mount an offensive and every time his forces assembled they were attacked from the air. In the face of this he fled fled across the border into Abyssinian Somaliland.

The RAF units were back at Berbera by 18th February, the campaign having been concluded in record time and with very few casualties — although the air ambulances had more than proved their worth in the ferrying of wounded. The Colonial Office expressed their delight at the outcome — and low financial cost — and the RAF had the first solid evidence to support its case for air policing of colonial disturbances.

CHANAK CRISIS 1922-23

The collapse of the old empires with the end of World War One brought many problems in south-east Europe and Arabia; in particular amongst the old territories of the Ottoman Empire. One facet of this was to be the re-birth of Turkish nationalism under Mustapha Kemal Bey (better known as Kemal Ataturk), a charasmatic leader who stirred up the various warlike tribes to 'restore lost Turkish authority and pride'. During an offensive against Greek forces, as part of his offensive on Constantinople, his army entered the Allied-controlled neutral area around Gallipoli. The British Prime Minister, Lloyd George, was determined to preserve the sanctity of the neutral area and ordered mobilisation of reinforcements. The Allied zone was jointly controlled by the British, French and Italians.

A number of RAF squadrons were mobilised and sent to the area. The Fairey IIIDs and Nieuport Nightjars of No 203 Sqn left Southampton aboard the carrier HMS *Argus* on 18th September 1922, landing at Kilia some weeks later, having picked up more Fairey IIIDs at Malta.

By October the Constantinople Wing, under the command of Group Captain R M Fellowes, consisted of seven squadrons (No 4 Sqn — F2B, No 25 Sqn — Snipe, No 56 Sqn — Snipe, No 203 Sqn — Nightjar, No 207 Sqn — DH9A, No 208 Sqn — F2B, No 267 Sqn — Fairey IIID) and an aircraft park at San Stefano. During the build-up period the Turks agreed to an armistice, this being signed at Mudaria on 11th October, but the Allied leadership required positive proof that the conditions were being obeyed before they would agree to a withdrawal of forces. Thus, the squadrons maintained their operational stance and continued to fly reconnaissance missions.

The winter of 1922/23 was severe and heavy rains caused serious flooding on the Allied airfields, whilst many aircraft were damaged by frost. The deployment schedule of the squadrons was as follows:

No 4 Sqn — Aboard HMS Argus and HMS *Ark Royal* 26th September arrived Kilya Bay 11th October, moved to Kilid el Bahr 11th December, depart for UK 5th September 1923.

No 25 Sqn — Departed UK 28th September, arrived San Stefano 11th October, departed for UK 22nd September 1923. No 56 Sqn — Based at Aboukir, detachment to San Stefano, depart August 1923 (the squadron having disbanded and reformed in the UK in the meantime).

No 203 Sqn — Aboard HMS Argus 18th September 1922, arrived Kilya Bay 27th September, left again on HMS *Argus* 19th December.

No 207 Sqn — Departed UK on 29th September and arrived San Stefano 11th October, departed for UK 22nd September 1923.

No 208 Sqn — Departed UK on 28th September for San Stefano, departed 26th September 1923 for Egypt.

No 267 Sqn — Departed Malta on HMS *Argus* for Kilya Bay. The squadron disbanded on 1st August but the operational detachment was redesignated as No 481 Flight.

The formal peace treaty was signed at Lausanne on 23rd August 1923.

MESOPOTAMIA 1919-1939

The post-war carve-up of the Ottoman Empire gave Britain control of various parts of the Middle East — all of which were potentially volatile, especially as their native leaders had not been consulted as to the new situation. The Turks had faced revolts in many of the Arab provinces; the British now faced the same problems. One of the most vociferous anti-British leaders was Sheik Mahmud, with his dream of an independent Kurdistan. This particular revolt had been simmering for some time but broke into full-scale rebellion in May 1919.

The Bristol Fighters and RE.8s of No 6 Sqn arrived in Basrah in June 1919 to join the varied types which had been operating in Mesopotamia as detached flights of No 30 Sqn since 1915, although by 1919 the main base was Baghdad West.

Although Sheik Mahmud's rebellion was easily contained, and the Sheik himself imprisoned, the general tribal disturbances increased until by July 1920 most areas of Mesopotamia were affected. The aircraft and crews were kept very busy supporting the many isolated garrisons which were easy targets for the rebel tribesmen. Operating from a number of landing grounds, often in harsh conditions, the basic remit for the crews was to attack any tribal gathering within the proscribed areas. There was too much work for too few aircraft and so the decision was taken to double the RAF presence. No 84 Sqn reformed with DH9As at Baghdad West on 13th August 1920, with the DH9As of No 55 Sqn arriving at the same base on 23rd September.

D.H.9As of 47 Squadron over Mesopotamia.

All four units were heavily engaged throughout the remainder of 1920, flying over 4000 operational hours and dropping almost 100 tons of bombs, as well as expending large quantities of ammunition.

February 1921 brought further reinforcement with the arrival of No 8 Sqn, also equipped with the ubiquitous and hard-wearing DH9A. Although the year was generally fairly quiet there were a number of operational periods; including action against Turkish incursions — the Turks were, like the native tribes, not happy with the post-war arrangements!

1921 was a significant year for a different reason. During March the Cairo Conference was summoned to try and seek a solution to the various tribal problems. One of the major considerations was the need to police these areas as 'economically as possible' — both in terms of money and manpower. Once more the RAF put forward a proposal to use air control as the prime policing method. This was duly accepted and an RAF supremo was put in charge of the military operations in Mesopotamia.

RAF armoured car.

Sulaimaniyah after a bombing raid.

The choice of General Officer Commanding, an RAF 'supremo' with control of air and land forces, was AVM Sir John Salmond; he duly took post in October 1922 and was allocated a force of eight flying squadrons plus assorted support units. The existing five squadrons were joined by No 1 Sqn (Snipe), No 45 Sqn (Vernon) and No 70 Sqn (Vernon); the major significance being that the latter two brought an air transport/supply, and following modification, bombing, capability. Main bases were established at Hinaidi, Mosul, Baghdad West and Shaibah.

The latter months of 1922 and into early 1923 brought a renewed, and more serious, series of Turkish-inspired revolts, with Sheik Mahmud and his Kurds being particularly active. A number of air-supported ground columns moved into the area and by late April Turkish forces had retired over the border, the revolt being terminated by the capture of Sulaimania on 17th May. An attempted revolt in southern Iraq was nipped in the bud by the Vernon 'bombers' of No 45 Squadron. However, Sheik Mahmud was destined not to remain peaceful for long and operations began again in late summer the same year, the scale increased following the declaration of 'jihad' in May 1924. Squadrons redeployed to Kingerban and Kirkuk to support the ground forces in yet another advance on Sulaimania, which at one point was subjected to a 48-hour bombardment. The town was re-occupied in July bringing an effective end to the campaign. September brought renewed Turkish involvement with an attack on the Mosul area, this, however, was broken up by a determined series of attacks by the Bristol Fighters of No 6 Squadron.

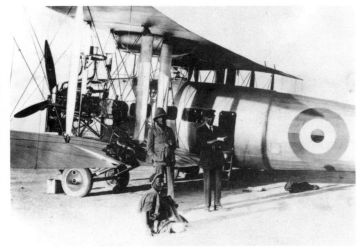

Mesopotamia brought rapid development of air transport.

With the arrival of spring 1925 Mahmud decided to try his luck again but with no more success than on previous occasions, any concentration of tribesmen was soon under air attack and so the Sheik retired across the border into Persia. It was only a short retirement. A raid of September 1925 was followed in spring 1926 by another widespread rebellion which required intensive air operations against rebel villages. After this latest series of setbacks the Sheik agreed a truce to run from 1927 to 1930. This did not mean peace in Mesopotamia as Sheik Ahmad of Barzan chose 1927 to cause trouble, although this was soon crushed.

The British were still learning the lesson that inter-tribal conflict , and thus dislike of central authority, was a natural state of affairs in Mesopotamia and that to prevent such happenings would mean almost continual operations. The situation was exasperated by external influences promoting tribal unrest; in the southern part of Iraq this was often prompted by Ibn Saud from the Nejd (later Saudi Arabia) who had pretensions of extending his authority to the north. In January 1928 four squadrons and the Armoured Car Wing gathered at Ur Junction to form 'Akforce' to combat one such inter-tribal disturbance that looked like getting out of hand. Operating from a number of advanced bases, aircraft dropped warning notices on the tribes and as these produced no result active operations commenced on 27th January. The area of ops was gradually extended into Kuwait as 'Akforce' increased in size to combat an estimated 50,000 rebel tribesmen. After months of intensive operations, over 7000 hours being flown, the rebels were persuaded to desist and 'Akforce' disbanded on 3rd June.

His three year truce up, Sheik Mahmud took to the field again in September 1930, to be met by the Iraqi Army supported by the RAF. For three months the conflict dragged on with bombing of rebel forces preventing them making any secure gains but being

unable to prevent a growing wave of support for Mahmud. The scale of RAF involvement was increased both to harass the existing rebels and dissuade any other villages from joining the fray. This had the desired effect and Mahmud rapidly lost support until by April it was obvious that his revolt could not suceed; he sought terms and duly surrendered on 13th May, rapidly followed by other tribal leaders.

It was then Sheik Ahmad of Barzan's turn to cause trouble and this he duly did in March 1932. The Iraqi Army moved against the rebels but required intensive RAF support in order to achieve success; during these operations a tannoy system was fitted to at least one Victoria to broadcast warnings of air action. The bombing of villages and attacks on even small groups of tribesmen brought results and at the end of May the Sheik fled to Turkey.

In September 1932 Iraq became an independent nation and from that point on the RAF provided assistance as an ally, operating from its new main base at Dhibban (later Habbaniya), Shaibah and Basrah.

PALESTINE 1918-1948

Palestine, as a mandated territory, was another part of the old Ottoman Empire to come under British control — it was to be a troublesome area up to the final withdrawal in 1948. Operations in the area continued after the war, mainly due to what many have seen as British betrayal of Arab aspirations. RAF aircraft and armoured cars supported local troops in quelling unrest although these were usually small-scale operations. Much of the trouble was of a standard tribal nature with a tribal leader raiding a road or town for profit, others were more serious. In August 1924 aircraft attacked a large group of Wahabis pushing towards Amman; in the face of this intense air attack the Arab force dispersed.

Similar operations continued to the early 1930s with combined air-land operations taking place each year. However, the nature of the disturbances changed in the 1930s with an increase in Arab-Jewish tension, a political aspect creating a national, eventually supra-national, conflict rather than simple tribal unrest. RAF strength gradually increased to cope with the additional tasks and in the period 1936 to 1938 the squadrons were heavily involved with recce, air cordon/blocking missions, and attacks on Arab gatherings. The policy of hitting any trouble early and hard paid off in that by 1939 the scale of operations had reduced, with an Arab (and Jewish) move towards terrorist style activities rather than overt action. This provided short-term relief, especially with the Jewish agreement to back the Allies in the war against Germany; however, it was merely a postponement of the troubles and with the end of World War Two they returned with a renewed vigour.

ADEN 1917-1939

RAF and FAA detachments had been active in Aden since 1917 in support of allied tribal leaders but it was not until 1927 that a permanent squadron was provided. In February of that year No 8 Squadron moved its DH.9As to Khormaksar. At the end of the year tribesmen from Yemen spilled over the border raiding villages; the RAF responded with air attacks that continued, on and off, until the middle of 1928 with attacks around Taiz, Kataba, Mafalis, Yerim and Dhala Fort. Over 1200 operational hours were flown as the pattern of these operations followed that already seen in Mesopotamia. Demonstration Flights over prospective trouble spots were a regular feature and no doubt prevented many disturbances. The most serious outbreak in 1929 was by the Suhebi and air ops were mounted from 30th January to 5th March, bombing villages and crops.

So it continued into the mid 1930s when an upsurge in regional tension, the result of Italian aggression in Abyssinia, led to an increase in British military strength, including the arrival of three more squadrons in 1935. It was not only Aden that received reinforcements, additional squadrons moved to Palestine, Egypt and the Sudan to counter any threat to British possesssions in this part of Africa. Most of the units became involved in anti-tribal ops in the areas to which they were attached, which must have come as quite a shock to the tribesmen.

It was a short-lived reinforcement and all these units had left again by early 1937.

Anti-tribal operations continued up to the outbreak of World War Two.

CHINA 1927

In June 1925 the population of Shanghai took to the streets with cries of "Kill the English", it was the culmination of years of discontent against the level of Western influence in China. Central authority deteriorated in the early 1920s with the rise of powerful local warlords and the outbreak of civil war as Nationalist forces under Chiang Kai-Shek endeavoured to seize power from the weak government. In 1926 the British became involved when gunboats were sent up the Yangtse to rescue five merchant officers. The following January the British forces around Shanghai were reinforced by a 12 000-strong Division which set up defensive positions around the International Settlement; meanwhile naval forces were increased to 21 warships plus the carrier *Hermes*. A number of FAA Flights (404, 406, 422, 441, 443) had departed the UK in February and were deployed to various parts of the operational theatre.

No 2 Squadron received orders to send a detachment of Bristol Fighters from Manston to China, the squadron duly arriving at Shanghai on 30th May 1927 after a long, arduous journey by troopship. Operating from the race-course the squadron flew recce sorties around the local area and undertook co-operation exercises with army units. When Bristol Fighter J7652 force-landed at Kiangwan the local commander refused to let an RAF party recover the wings; the British responded with a threat to attack the railway line and a number of Bristols were armed ready for action. The matter was duly resolved and a few weeks later, 30th August, the squadron commenced its departure from Shanghai. However, its place was taken by six Fairey IIIDs of No 441 (FR) Flight. The FAA Flights departed the area in early May 1928.

INDIA 1918-39

As with Mesopotamia, India, and in particular the North West Frontier Province (NWFP), was to involve the RAF in active operations almost every year between 1918 and 1939, albeit most of the actions were small-scale anti-tribal affairs. It was an area in which many future RAF leaders, including Arthur Harris, gained experience, and it also saw the development of air power theory in such critical areas as combined operations.

Since the earliest days of British rule in India the tribesmen of the North West Frontier had proved troublesome having no respect for central authority, banditry and rebellion being almost a way of life. Air power arrived to assist the land forces in 1915 with the BE2c of No 31 Squadron at Nowsherra. Expansion of the RFC in India was slow, one of the problems being the need to chose and prepare landing grounds. However, by April 1918 air power had proved itself to be an essential element of British control of the rebellious tribal areas and the two squadrons, No 31 and No 114, were well established.

The scale of involvement varied from the support of local forces to suppress riots, such as those in Amritsar in mid 1919, to a major role in more serious conflicts, such as the Third Afghan War.

Afhganistan was a routine trouble spot threatening peace on the frontier; a standard ploy of the rulers being to incite trouble with the British in India in order to avoid internal problems. Such was the case with the Third Afghan War of May to August 1919. The army columns which advanced into Afghanistan were supported by aircraft which undertook recce, ground strafing and bombing tasks, the latter having a major impact on the Afghan forces. Meanwhile, the only 'strategic' bomber in the area, a borrowed HP V/1500 (J1936) attacked Kabul on 24th May, the aircraft dropped a mix of 112 lb and 20 lb bombs and managed to score a few hits on the palace — enough to convince the Amir of the power of the British! An armistice followed a few days later although a formal peace treaty was not signed until 8th August. It had been an amazing victory for strategic bombing — even though J1936 was then grounded having been defeated by termites.

Over the next twelve months further squadrons arrived in India, and some were renumbered, so that by the end of 1920 there were six operational squadrons.

It was also a period of almost continual operations, as soon as one tribal disturbance was quelled another broke out, it certainly kept the squadrons very busy. In the period up to 1922 the main trouble spots were Waziristan and Mahsud, although the Afghans continued to make border raids from time to time. Sir John Salmond, as AOC India, highlighted the vital role of the RAF in India but also pointed out the poor state of equipment and facilities; he also emphasised the need for the RAF to be independent from the Army and to have its own budget. This was to become a regular complaint and would lead to acrimony between the two Services and, eventually, a major Inquiry in 1931.

Waziristan remained the major operational area into 1924 even though much of the frontier district was peaceful. The decision was taken to mount a major operation against the rebel heartland in southern Waziristan, a campaign that came to be known as 'Pink's War' after its commander, Wg Cdr R Pink. Operations commenced on 9th March with No 27 and No 60 Squadrons operating from Miranshah and No 5 Squadron and a detachment of No 20 Squadron operating from Tank. Bombing ops continued into early April, with No 31 Squadron undertaking night ops, until the rebel leaders agreed to talk with the Political Officers. Over a period of 54 days the squadrons had flown over 2700 hours — for the loss of only one aircraft. No ground forces had been involved.

NWFP, home to many remote landing grounds — here at Gilgit.

Returning from a raid 1930 — Wapitis over Kohat Pass.

The ensuing three years were amongst the most peaceful ever experienced in the frontier region and it gave the RAF a chance to improve its organisation and facilities, and undertake a training programme.

By the outbreak of the next major crisis, in 1928, the RAF in India was still awaiting re-equipment with new types, the Bristol Fighters and DH.9As having to soldier on in the hostile Indian environment. It was not until early the following year with the arrival of two new units, No 11 and No 39 Squadrons, that the first 'new' type arrived — the Westland Wapiti, a rugged aircraft that proved ideal for frontier ops. The major activity in 1928 was the evacuation of the British Legation at Kabul when internal conflict erupted in Afghanistan. On 18th December a DH.9A was flown to Kabul to make arrangements for the air evacuation of British and allied personnel; the first such evacuation flights taking place on 23rd of the month using a landing ground at Sherpur. The evacuation continued until 25th February with a wide range of types, including Victoria, Hinaidi, Wapiti and DH.9a, being involved. It was a major achievement with 586 people and over 24 000 lbs of freight being taken back to India.

Other than minor disturbances caused by supporters of Gandhi's civil disobedience policy the remainder of 1929 was quiet; it was to an extent the lull before the storm as 1930 brought intensive operations in the Mohmand areas. Major ops commenced in May with squadrons carrying out demonstration flights and recce sorties, the first bombing sorties taking place on the 10th. The standard policy of dropping warning notices about 48 hours in advance of the actual bombing served to keep tribal casualties low whilst impressing the tribesmen with the power of the government. However, unrest continued to spread and before long the squadrons were operating in Mohmand, Utman Khel, Tirah and Waziristan with raids being up to Group strength of four squadrons. To give some idea of the scale of involvement .. up to mid August No 39 Squadron alone flew almost 1100 operational hours, dropped 107 tons of bombs plus 28512 BIBs (Baby Incendiary Bombs) and fired thousands of rounds of .303 ammunition. As with most of these tribal 'conflicts' it simply petered out as the tribesmen decided to call it a day — and wait for another chance to cause trouble.

1931 was a significant year in that it saw the oft heralded Frontier Defence Inquiry take place. The RAF and Army presented cases as to the best way, in terms of effect and money, of controlling the frontier; each cited examples of previous operations, often arriving at different conclusions from the same data. The RAF also stressed the success of the air control policy in Mesopotamia. The outcome was very much a compromise as the RAF gained a greater degree of independence, although few of the extra resources requested.

One of the routine operations was the biennial relief of the garrison at Chitral, an event that involved a large body of troops moving through a hostile terrain of narrow defiles under almost constant enemy fire — sniping at such columns being considered a 'good day out' by the hill tribes. Aircraft performed a wide range of tasks in support of the column, warning of ambushes and providing close support when requested. Tribal disturbances continued throughout the 1930s with operations against the 'Red Shirts' in Mardan, Swabi and Nowsherra (1932), the Tochi and Mohmand areas (1933), major raids into Mohmand in 1935 — a year that also saw the airfield at Quetta devastated by an earthquake. A jihad, or holy war, was proclaimed in 1936 by the Fakir of Ipi, the start of a widespread, but usually small scale, revolt that lasted on and off until 1939. A ground force moved into the Fakirs stronghold of the Khaisora valley in November 1936, with two squadrons in direct support and others, including Valentia, 'bombers' providing additional firepower. These operations peaked in April the following year but continued until June when the Fakir was forced to move to the Mahsud area. Squadrons were given a general clearance to bomb any village thought to be sheltering the Fakir, this policy kept the rebel leader on the move and prevented him gaining any secure base as he moved through Waziristan and Maddha Khel. The situation quietened down at the end of 1937 but burst to life again the following spring and continued until the outbreak of World War Two, at which point the Indian Air Force took over responsibility for frontier operations.

ALGERIA 1937

In September 1937 the Singapore flying boats of No 209 and No 210 Squadrons arrived at the French base of Arzeu, Algeria to undertake 'anti-piracy patrols' in the Mediterranean. This operational deployment was a result of Italian aspirations in the area and Fascist support of the right-wing elements in the Spanish Civil War. The main task of the flying boats was to conduct anti-submarine patrols, it being suspected that Italian submarines posed a threat to British and French shipping in the Mediterranean. The detachment left Pembroke Dock in mid September with 210 Squadron going direct to Arzeu and 209 Squadron going to Kalafrana, Malta — and then at the end of the month moving to Arzeu. Both units returned to the UK in December, the detachment having flown 414 operational hours with no sightings of hostile submarines.

210 Squadron at Arzeu, 1937.

WORLD WAR TWO
FRANCE 1939-40

FOLLOWING THE MUNICH CRISIS of September 1938 when war was only narrowly averted, the British and French authorities made ever greater efforts to co-ordinate defensive plans. It was obvious that France would become an early target for the German army, although many planners were of the opinion that Britain would be first on the enemy agenda. Bomber Command's strategic plan for attacks on German industry required it to base its shorter range bombers, such as the Battles of No. 1 Group, on the continent: the presence of a British land force in France would also call for an RAF contribution to provide ground support and fighter cover. All that remained was for these plans to be put into effect.

During the early months of the war the Advanced Air Striking Force (AASF) and Air Component (of the British Expeditionary Force) squadrons were confined to reconnaissance sorties along the border; the vulnerability of the Battles being shown on more than one instance — on 30th September four out of five aircraft had been shot down by enemy fighters near Saarbrucken. It was a similar story for the rest of the RAF units in France, numerous sorties but very few combats; however, the Hurricanes did prove able to look after themselves on the occasions that that they clashed with the Luftwaffe. There was the added problem of Belgian and Dutch neutrality — aircraft were not allowed to overfly these territories and if forced down were likely to be interned.

With the German western offensive launched on 10th May the pace of operations soared, and soon revealed inadequacies in numbers, equipment and tactics.

RAF squadrons deployed to France. 114 Squadron on the move 1940.

The heroic, yet tragic, role played by the Battles of the AASF has seldom been matched in the annals of warfare. These obsolete aircraft were thrown into a lost battle in an attempt to stem the rapid advance being made by German ground forces. On most such missions they received no air cover and so were easy prey for the ever-present Luftwaffe fighters; many of those who survived these attacks fell to the highly efficient German flak defences. The Battles attacked road convoys and important bridges and despite achieving some success the cost was always too high. Within weeks the force had been decimated and had to be withdrawn. It was a similar story with the Blenheims of No. 2 Group operating from Britain, similar types of target and some horrendous loss rates.

The Hurricanes did their best to provide air cover to British ground forces but they were always too few. It was now that one of the crisis points occurred — should more fighters, including Spitfires, be sent to France, would they make the difference or, as Dowding argued, would this policy simply erode Britain's own defences. In the event a compromise was made — but it still cost Fighter Command the better part of 1,000 aircraft by the end of the British involvement.

The German army continued to advance and soon the majority of British forces were holed up at Dunkirk awaiting evacuation to England. In the mind of the British soldier the RAF played no part in the Dunkirk story, all they ever saw were German aircraft. This is a great untruth as the RAF put much effort into providing offensive sorties against the German land forces and provided extensive fighter cover around the beach area. The losses of British and French troops would have been far greater, and perhaps the whole evacuation a disaster, but for the air effort expended.

The Dunkirk evacuation was not the end of this first involvement in France as other forces had retreated further west, although these too withdrew to England in early June.

NORWAY 1940

Amongst the many plans beloved by Churchill was one which entailed Allied control of Norway, partly to control, indeed terminate, the iron ore supply to and from Sweden, via Norwegian ports, to Germany, and also as a route to assist the Finns in the struggle against Russia. Certain strategic planners were also of the view that the Germans desired to control this region in order to protect the iron ore shipments and also to provide another vase for attacks against Britain — it is a matter of some debate as to who had the idea first! In the event, however, the Germans moved first, taking over Denmark and then, on 8th April, invading Norway.

The initial British counter-reaction consisted of sorties mounted to locate, track and attack German shipping in the seas around Norway. This air effort brought little result, although the mine-laying ops were somewhat more successful. As the Luftwaffe established itself on Norwegian airfields, such as Stavangar, these became the targets for frequent bombing missions. Meanwhile, a British force landed at Nansos on 14th April as part of a plan to seize the Trondheim area and so cut Norway in half, the Allies controlling the northern half. Other landings took place at Narvik and Aandalsnes. The primary air element of this move consisted of the Gladiators of No. 263 Squadron which deployed from HMS *Glorious* to operate off a frozen 'strip' at Lake Lesjakog from 23rd April. Within 48 hours ten of the aircraft had been destroyed by German air attacks; on 25th only five of the original eighteen aircraft were able to move to Setnesmoen prior to evacuation of the air and ground crews. During the few days in which the Gladiators had been operational they had coped well with the bad weather conditions and made some, albeit small, impact on the Luftwaffe.

A few weeks later, 22nd May, a reformed 263 Squadron flew its Gladiators off HMS *Furious* to Bardufoss in north Norway. On 26th May the Hurricanes of No. 46 Squadron arrived at Skaanland. Both units then operated in support of ground troops in the Narvik region, this town being captured on 27th May. However, it was a short-lived deployment as evacuation of British forces commenced on 2nd June. The surviving aircraft were flown onto HMS *Glorious* — no mean feat for the Hurricanes — but in one of the sad twists of fate this vessel was sunk by German warships. Lack of adequate air cover during the British operations in Norway was one of the main reasons for failure.

The RAF continued to mount anti-shipping, mining, bombing and special support operations over Scandinavia.

THE BATTLE OF BRITAIN

IN A FAMOUS speech the Prime Minister, Winston Churchill, said, "the Battle of France is over. I expect the Battle of Britain is about to begin". British forces had been forced out of France and

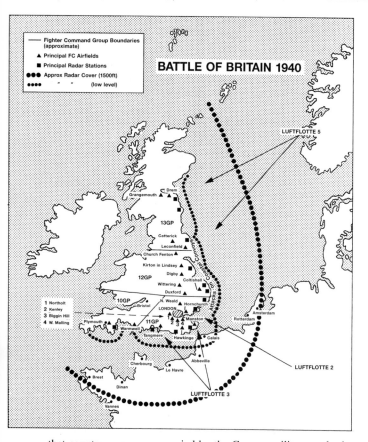

The two main fighter types of the Battle of Britain — Spitfire 1 (616 Squadron) and Hurricane (73 Squadron).

that country was now occupied by the German military, only the Channel stood between the German Army and the conquest of England. Firstly, however, the Luftwaffe had to achieve a measure of air superiority. The Battle of Britain was truly a turning point in World War Two.

In essence the Battle can be split into a number of reasonably distinct phases:

Phase I — early July to 12th August, attacks on coastal shipping and installations (the 'Kanalkampf') plus limited attacks on radar installations and airfields.

Phase II — 13th August to 6th September, attacks on airfields and associated installations.

Phase III — 7th September to late September, switch to London.

Phase IV — Late September onwards, daylight fighter sweeps and fighter-bomber raids, increased weight of night bombing.

On 16th July Hitler issued Directive No 16 for the invasion of England, Operation Sealion, with the proviso that before invasion could take place, "the British Air Force must be eliminated to such an extent that it will be incapable of putting up any sustained opposition to the invading troops."

The dates used for the Battle are the RAF's declared period of 10th July to 31st October 1940 although it is true to say that the lone recce aircraft and convoy raiders were around before that start date and that operations continued well after the end date. Later in the day the main action began to develop with a sweep by Me109s, followed sometime later by a bomber attack on a convoy near Dover.

Damage to the convoy was negligible and in this, the first 'dogfight' involving over 100 aircraft, the RAF came out best.

Convoy attacks along this pattern continued to the end of July with mixed fortunes, although in general terms it was proving far harder than many of the Luftwaffe planners had expected. Daily combats were taking their toll of both sides but the score sheet favoured the RAF.

Hitler was not convinced that the campaign was proceeding as it should and so on 1st August issued his Directive No17 for the Luftwaffe "to overpower the English Air Force with all the forces at its command, in the shortest possible time", and with the proviso that all preparation for the invasion was to be complete by 15th September. This was translated into a strategy for *Adlerangriff* (Eagle Attack), a progressive campaign to destroy the RAF in the air and on the ground with the opening date, *Adler Tag* (Eagle Day) to be decided upon when plans were complete and the weather forecast suitable.

Whilst this planning process was underway the conflict over the Channel convoys continued. On 7th August convoy CW9, the first westbound convoy for some time, left Southend bound for Portsmouth; with the dawning of 8th August the Germans had clearly decided to wipe out this convoy and the scene was set for the heaviest air battles to date. The Hurricanes of 145 Squadron were in the same area and were able to position themselves to dive out of the sun and hit the Stukas at their most vulnerable as they began their dives. In a rapid and confusing conflict the Hurricanes claimed no less than 21 enemy aircraft (EA) shot down (the actual figure for Ju87s lost was nearer to 8).

12th August dawned fine and bright, the Battle had still not touched the peaceful English countryside and to most it was still a remote event .. all that was about to change. The Luftwaffe was now ready for Phase One of its plan and had targetted a number of radar stations and airfields for destruction on this opening day. The radar sites had been identified as key elements in the Fighter Command organisation; attacks were made on the radar stations at Pevensey, Rye, Dunkirk and Dover.

However, the overall damage proved to be not as bad as, certainly, the attackers thought and the three stations were soon operational with emergency power supplies. Meanwhile a force of Ju88s was attacking Ventnor with similar accuracy but greater effect and this station was to be off the air for 11 days. The Luftwaffe desire to destroy the radar stations was a sensible one but the inability to knock down the towers themselves or to create damage of such magnitude that the radar station was written off totally led to rapid disillusionment amongst the Luftwaffe planners, and attacks on radar stations became few and far between.

The same day brought the first wave of attacks against airfields in Southern England ... Lympne, Hawkinge and Manston. Lympne was hit twice during the day so that by the end of the second raid there was hardly a clear space left on which to land, the airfield being pockmarked with craters. Hawkinge was hit around 5pm as the Ju88s destroyed two hangars, workshops and other buildings as well as leaving the airfield surfaces badly damaged, although a number of aircraft did manage to find a long enough clear stretch on which to land.

This pattern of airfield attacks was to continue until the end of the first week of September.

In the latter part of August the attacks concentrated on what the Luftwaffe thought were a number of key airfields and, in recognition of the losses being suffered by the bombers increased the level of fighter support. It now became even harder to break through the swarms of Me109s and the attempted tactic of Spitfires against the escort whilst the Hurricanes dealt with the bombers was hardly ever possible. What was more likely was that one section of a squadron would be tasked with holding off the escorts whilst the rest tried to get at the bombers! Significantly, from the last week of the month to the end of this phase of the Battle German and British losses ran at about the same levels. During this period to 6th September RAF fighter losses (Spitfire/Hurricane) were 295, plus a further 18 lost in accidents and a further 171 badly damaged. Production during the same period gave 269 aircraft and so there was a substantial drain on reserves.

Hugh Dowding, head of Fighter Command and architect of its victory.

On the night of 24/25th August London was bombed by mistake (at the time it was a prohibited target) and Churchill demanded a return bombing of Berlin. So, the following night a force of Bomber Command Wellingtons and Hampdens attacked industrial targets around Berlin. Although damage was light the effect on Berliners, the Nazis and Hitler was enormous. The Battle of Britain was about to enter a new phase.

The huge raid of 400 bombers, escorted by 600 figters, was picked up as it formed over France and set course for England. It soon became obvious that the target was no longer the airfields and that this air armada was aimed at London. Once more it was a day of mixed fortunes, the Luftwaffe lost 41 aircraft and the RAF 28 but the bombers devastated the East End and 450 people were killed. Although London and other cities had been bombed before it had been on a small scale, usually at night, but from now on London was to undergo trial by fire by day and, increasingly, by night as well.

After a week of large raids followed by days when almost nothing happened the Battle was set to reach its climax. The Luftwaffe planners, under pressure from Goering and Hitler to achieve a breakthrough, had decided upon one massive blow to try and destroy the last remnants (as their statistics had it) of Fighter Command and clear the way for the invasion. In actual fact Fighter Command was in good shape after the quiet week and squadrons were at their most effective for some time. As the raid built up the controllers scrambled more and more fighters until the RAF had its strongest ever numbers airborne; also, with no problem of having to work out the target squadrons could be positioned to achieve the most ideal intercepts. As soon as the waves of German aircraft crossed the coast they were met in force by the Hurricanes and Spitfires and formations dispersed. A second, even bigger, raid later in the day was met in the same way and broken up without achieving its primary target — although on both raids a certain amount of damage was done to the suberbs of London. It had been a great shock to many of the German aircrew who had been operating over Britain for some time, where had all these British fighters come from? At the end of the day German losses were estimated at 183 aircraft against 40 RAF losses (the actual figure being 60 and 26). It had been a vital day and probably deserves its recognition as Battle of Britain Day — not so much for what happened just on that day but as a marker of the change of fortunes, from that point on it was most unlikely that the Battle would be lost or that Britain would be invaded.

Two days later ..... "The enemy air force is by no means defeated. On the contrary, it shows increasing activity. The Fuhrer therefore decides to postpone 'Sea Lion' indefinitely".

The last of the mass daylight raids came on the 30th September and was promptly seen off by the resurgent Fighter Command. From then until the 'official' end of the Battle in October the main attacks were pinpoint raids, often by lone aircraft, and 'nuisance' raids by Me109s acting as fighter-bombers. These could still, however, be large scale in that as many as 1000 such sorties appeared in a single day. By their very nature such raids were hard to counter and Fighter Command had to resort to the undesirable practice of keeping standing patrols airborne. In effect the Battle simply petered out and the end date is somewhat arbitrary as it was well into 1941 before daylight attacks on Britain ceased.

Many different explanations have been put forward as to why the invincible Luftwaffe lost the Battle, or in other terms why the RAF won the Battle. Was it Hitler's fault for decreeing a switch of target priority to London? Was Dowding the architect of victory with his determination not to see Fighter Command bled to death in France? Did the Spitfire turn the tables by being better than everything else (in fact Hurricanes shot down the most enemy aircraft and it was a Hurricane squadron which was the top scorer)? And so the list could be continued ... as with so much of history the true answer is no doubt a combination of all of them, plus a bit of luck. Whatever the truth of the matter the bottom line was that a few hundred pilots and aircraft helped prevent the invasion of Britain and the probable loss of the War.

Truly, as Churchill said, "Never in the field of human conflict was so much owed by so many to so few."

STRATEGIC BOMBING OFFENSIVE

BOMBER COMMAND was involved in active operations from day one of the war with Wellingtons and Blenheims tasked against enemy naval installations and shipping. At the outbreak of war the Command tried to implement its pre-war plans — the so-called 'Western Air' (WA) Plans.

However, there was a reluctance to commit their strategic force (in concept if not capability) to combined tactical operations, although No 1 Group, ten Battle squadrons, was detached to France as part of the Advanced Air Striking Force in September 1939. Even so, the intention was simply to put the bombers within range of targets inside Germany.

There were two main problems facing those in Bomber Command who favoured a strategic bombing offensive: firstly, a lack of the right aircraft in type or quantity to pursue such a strategy; and, moreover, a reluctance in certain quarters to start a 'total war' against an enemy that appeared to have great potential to hit back hard! Thus, in the early months of the war, and excepting the force comitted to France, the main aspects of the Command's operations were:

★ Leaflet dropping over Germany at night, primarily by the Whitleys of No 4 Group.
★ Daylight attacks on German shipping, primarily by the Wellingtons of No 3 Group.

However, losses amongst the Wellingtons were high, as high as 50% in some instances — a totally unsupportable loss rate. The losses amongst the Whitleys were far lower, a statistic used by some to prove that the only prospects for the future lay with night bombing. Whilst Bomber Command never abandoned daylight operations, it is true that from this point on the emphasis, especially with the strategic campaign, moved towards night operations.

The first significant 'change' in the air bombing policy came with a Directive issued to Portal on 13th April 1940; in the event of general air action being called for Bomber Command was to implement the basic provisions of plan WA8 (the night attack on Germany) — attacks on various industrial installations and ports. To carry out this plan the C-in-C was to use Nos 3 and 4 Groups, plus that part of No 5 Group not engaged on mining tasks. If the situation so permitted he could also call upon the squadrons of the AASF. However, if the Germans had invaded the Low Countries then the entire plan changed, the emphasis being "to attack vital objectives in Germany, starting in the Ruhr, to cause the maximum dislocation to lines of communication of the German advance through the Low Countries."

On 15th May, Churchill authorised bombing east of the Rhine, up to this point crews had been risking the journey to Germany just to drop propaganda leaflets. With the attack the same night by 99 bombers on oil and rail targets in the Ruhr the strategic bombing offensive, which was to reach its crescendo in late 1944/early 1945, was underway.

With the German assault on the West the Battles of the AASF were thrown into the fray in an effort to stem the flood of German armour and troops; un-cordinated, and often un-escorted, attacks were made against such targets as the bridges over the Meuse. Losses were high and yet time after time the gallant crews returned to try and destroy their targets. It was hopeless, and despite some successes, a one-sided battle.

As operations moved into France the depleted squadrons were withdrawn to Britain to rest and reform. It was the end of an episode for Bomber Command.

The Blenheim squadrons of No 2 Group had been as heavily involved and after a series of gallant attacks, often with heavy losses for little result, it was obvious that the situation could not continue. An urgent Directive was sent to Air Marshal Barratt, AOC-in-C BAFF, on 30th May ... "it is imperative that some reduction in their effort should be made in order that the force be maintained at its present operational strength and efficiency."

Although the Blenheims would continue to support the land operations it would be on a reduced scale. Barratt had the not enviable task of explaining this to the French High Command, at the same time having to pass on the news that the RAF's heavy bombers were switching away from direct support — but with the guarantee that if a 'critical situation' developed the full weight of Bomber Command would be immediately available. The Air Staff had decided that , "in the absence of moonlight, experience proves that the heavy bombers cannot operate with sufficient accuracy against road objectives and defiles in the forward area to make an effective contribution to the land situation by this means." They decided, therefore, to concentrate on industrial targets in Germany, "to cause the continuous interruption and dislocation of industry, particularly where the German aircraft industry is concentrated."

It is interesting to see that oil had vanished from the target systems under consideration and that the German aircraft industry had replaced it. Over the next 4 years this variance in priority, amongst many others, was to re-appear time after time, much to the frustration of those who sought a clear single strategic aim.

The loss of France and the now direct threat to the British Isles led to much re-thinking of policy, evinced by the stream of directives which reached Bomber Command — varying priorities and target areas almost weekly.

As the military situation continued to deteriorate invasion looked imminent. Bomber Command had been attacking enemy shipping in the occupied ports of Europe for some time but a review of bombing policy in early July led to a new Directive on 4th July. This called for an increased effort against enemy ports and shipping — from the Capital Ships, such as the Scharnhorst at Kiel and Bismark at Hamburg, to barges and merchant shipping in the occupied ports. The mining effort, which had been one squadron of Hampdens, was to be trebled, with the Hampdens now to concentrate on Kiel Canal, Kiel Bay and the Belts.

In April 1940 Hampdens began laying mines ('planting vegetables') off the Danish coast. During the first full year of these ops (1941) 1250 sorties were flown and 1055 mines laid. When Harris took over in 1942 he agreed with the Admiralty for his Command to lay 1000 mines a month, covering the Baltic to the Spanish frontier. Just under 10,000 mines were laid that year, sorties which represented almost 15% of Bomber Command's total effort.

With rising losses and no (apparent) major success, the work of Bomber Command came under continual scrutiny. Surely, these squadrons could be better utilized elsewhere, what about the all-important U-boat war, a few more bombers in the Middle

Wellingtons bore the brunt of the early bombing ops (this is a 1944 shot showing leaflet preparation).

5 Group state boards for ops against Genoa 22/23 October 1942.

Blenheims of 2 Group made a significant contribution to the anti-shipping war.

Lancasters of 50 Squadron.

Invasion barges, here at Antwerp, became a major target.

Halifax of 35 Squadron en route to attack warships at Brest.

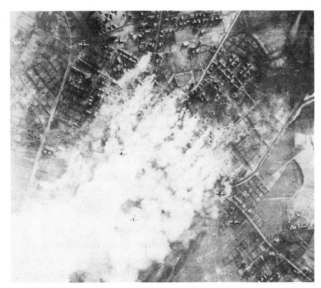

Crescendo of air power. Bomber Command lays waste German industry in 1944/45.

east might prevent the loss of Egypt — and so on. Bomber Command operations remained varied but generally small scale, despite gradual improvement in equipment with the introduction of the first four-engined heavy bombers, Stirling (first op February 1941) and Halifax (first op March 1941), and the promising, but ill-fated, twin-engined Manchester (first op February 1941). The planners still favoured small pinpoint targets at night despite the lack of accurate navigation and bombing aids; the exponents of the Command claimed an average error of just 1000 yards but an enquiry , based on air photography taken on and after the raids, suggested that only one in three of the bombers dropped within 5 miles of the target, and for Ruhr targets this dropped to one in ten.

1942 was to be the turning point. After fairly frequent changes of Commander, in February 1942 Bomber Command acquired at its head the man who was to inspire and lead it for the rest of the war — Air Marshal Arthur T Harris. Harris was convinced of the value, and necessity, of the Offensive and he gave a valuable boost to the morale of the Command at a time when its fortunes were at a low ebb. With the change of command came a new Air Ministry directif, dated 14th February 1942, 'to focus attacks on the morale of the enemy civilian population and, in particular, of the industrial workers.'

One of Harris's first aims was to convince the doubters that the Offensive was essential to the success of the war effort; to do this he planned a 1000-bomber raid as a demonstration of the full power of a co-ordinated bombing plan. The target was the city of Cologne and the date the night of 30/31 May 1942. By scraping together every possible aircraft, including crews still in training, a force of 1046 bombers was sent against the target. Fortunately for Harris and Bomber Command the raid was a major success.

Bomber Command was given a higher priority for aircraft and, more importantly, scientific development of navigation aids and radar — vital for the accurate delivery of bombs to their targets. Developments came thick and fast: firstly, 'Gee' then later the same year the much better 'Oboe' system. Finally, in early 1943, came the introduction of the superlative H2S radar.

Unfortunately, with improvements for the attackers came improvements in the defences, and the German night-fighters continued to take a heavy toll of bombers. To try and redress the balance the bombers flew in compact streams to swamp small areas of the defences, diversionary raids were mounted, deception plans instigated; and other countermeasures, such as dropping 'window' to confuse enemy radar screens, were used. Yet another of the 1942 advances was the adoption of 'Pathfinder' aircraft and target marking, again with the aim of improving bombing accuracy.

There was much heated debate over the question of forming a specialist unit. All were agreed on the need for 'expert crews' to mark, in some way, a target for the main force of bombers to attack; the variance came with how this should be implemented.

Last, but not least, for 1942 was the introduction of the four-engined Avro Lancaster, destined to become the most significant of all Allied bombers of the war. By Spring 1943 Bomber Command had been largely re-equipped with Lancasters and modified Halifaxes. Furthermore, the Command had been given a new Directive arising out of the Chiefs of Staff Conference at Casablanca in January 1943:

"Your primary object will be the progressive destruction and dislocation of the German military, industrial and economic system, and the undermining of the morale of the German people to a point where their capacity for armed resistance is fatally weakened."

This directive was a clear call to the advocates of strategic bombing to prove their case; in March 1943 Bomber Command launched a sustained attack on Germany. The first part was the 'Battle of the Ruhr', from March to July, aimed at destroying the vital war industries of the Ruhr; this caused extensive damage but on a short-term basis as the Germans effected rapid repairs.

Harris saw the Essen raid of 5/6 March 1943 as a turning point. Led by an Oboe-equipped PFF force, 442 bombers attacked the industrial city of Essen and this elusive target received heavy damage for the loss of only 14 aircraft — "years of endeavour, of experiment, and of training in new methods have at last provided the weapons and the force capable of destroying the heart of the enemy's armament industry."

Next it was the turn of Hamburg and in late July/early August this city received four very heavy and accurate attacks, causing Goebbels to comment on the resulting damage as a "catastrophe, the extent of which simply staggers the imagination." The third part of this offensive was the 'Battle of Berlin' from November to March 1944.

By the close of 1943 Bomber Command was at last able to show the destructive power of large numbers of heavy aircraft. Nevertheless, continued improvements in defences took a heavy toll and in May 1943 at the Washington Conference a policy was declared proposing the destruction of the Luftwaffe and the German aircraft industry. The twin prongs of this offensive were to be the daylight raids by American bomber units and the night raids by Bomber Command. At last realisation had dawned that air superiority was a basic pre-requisite for succesful bombing operations.

At the beginning of 1944 the Command had 1600 front-line aircraft, virtually all 'heavies', but in the Spring of that year the major effort was diverted from the Strategic Offensive over Germany to the softening up of German defences and disruption of lines of communications as part of the build-up to D-Day and the Allied invasion. Furthermore, the heavy bombers were being called upon to attack the V-bomb sites and factories as a counter to what was being called the Second Blitz. There was much high-level arguement and disagreement over the employment of the strategic bombers, various experts came up with 'master plans' which would end the war — 'the Oil Plan, 'the Transportation Plan' and so on. Harris argued that any diversion from his overall Offensive was counter-productive and that his bombers should be left alone to bring Germany to its knees rather than be given a multitude of other tasks. It was a cogent arguement and a firm Principle of War regarding selection of an Aim and sticking to it. From May to September 1944, 85% of Bomber Command effort had been diverted to OVERLORD and post-invasion support targets.

By the time the Command returned to the Offensive in the Autumn of 1944 the tide had definitely turned. Although Germany contrived to produce aircraft at a great rate, a masterpiece of industrial improvisation, the support arms could not cope, fuel was in dire shortage due to the destruction of oil plants. It is worth noting here that the German economy did not go onto a full war footing until 1943, hence the apparent ease with which production was maintained or even increased — the spare capacity was there. It was against oil production and transport targets that the renewed Offensive was aimed, causing widespread destruction and fatally disrupting the German war economy. A veritable Armageddon of destruction rained from the skies over Germany in early 1945 as city after city was devastated.

Many critics have said that the Strategic Bombing Offensive contributed little to final victory, others have commented on the 'moral' implications of such a style of warfare. In practical terms the Offensive tied down vast amounts of men and material, particularly aircraft, in the defence of the German homeland and occupied territories that otherwise could have been used in an offensive nature thus making the Allied advance even harder. Also, there can be little doubt that the disruption of communications within Germany and between the fighting fronts was of vital importance in destroying the cohesion of German forces. Add to this the widespread destruction of the means of production of war materials and the picture is complete — that Bomber Command and the American strategic bombing units played a SIGNIFICANT part in bringing the was to a close. The 'moral' argument is of a different nature, the War became 'Total War', a matter of survival, and as such the fine lines of 'morality' became blurred.

The cost had been very high. Bomber Command casualties were 57,000 killed, the Americans 65,000 killed — a staggering total. It must also be remembered that Bomber Command strength included large numbers of Commonwealth and Allied aircrew, particularly Canadian (the 14 squadrons of No 6 Group), Australian, Polish, French and many others. The part played by Bomber Command is often distilled in a single phrase — "made a decisive contribution to victory" — but behind this lies a wealth of history.

MIDDLE EAST AND MEDITERRANEAN

IN THE VAST area covered by the 'Middle East' theatre — stretching from the western Mediterranean to the centre of Africa, air power played a crucial role in almost every campaign.

Campaigns within the Middle East/Mediterrean theatre went well for the British whilst they were engaged against the Italians, although these forces were invariably larger and better equipped; however, the arrival of combat experienced German forces in 1941 was a turning point which almost brought disaster. A point that must be made is the degree of contribution made by the South African Air Force (SAAF) in most of the following campaigns, in the later stages of the war in the Middle East and into Italy numerous SAAF squadrons operated within the Allied air forces, often as integral parts of RAF Wings (or vice versa); the fact that these accounts give them scant mention is no reflection on the value of their contribution but rather a matter of space in an account dealing with the RAF.

The following divisions are somewhat articial in that certain campaigns were inextricably linked — the Greek campaign and the initial Western Desert offensive, the Malta campaign (and associated anti-shipping activity) and the ability of Rommel to operate in the Desert. The divisions used are simply for convenience of reference.

EAST AFRICA 1940

With the Italian entry into the war in June 1940 the previously quiet east African states were under immediate threat from superior Italian forces. The outnumbered British forces were forced to withdraw from British Somalia as the Italians advanced

Gladiators and Blenheims fought the desert war against Italy.

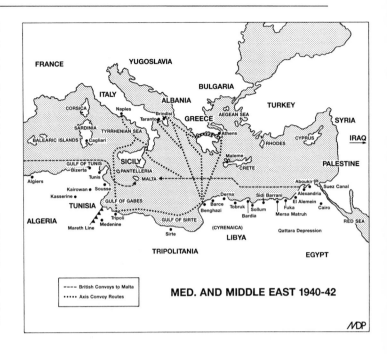
MED. AND MIDDLE EAST 1940-42

---- British Convoys to Malta
••••• Axis Convoy Routes

in August and captured Berbera. However, it was only a temporary move whilst the British were re-organised and reinforced. The RAF presence was very small, although Wellesleys did undertake a number of bombing missions. The major effort was applied by the squadrons based at Sheikh Othman, Aden and this became a critical factor in denying the Italian forces access to other British states in the area and in keeping control of the all-important Red Sea communications route. The Aden base had received new squadrons in June with the arival of the Blenheim equipped units, No 11 and No 39 Squadrons, of No 2 (Indian) Wing. These aircraft were heavily involved with recce of ports and airfields as well as bombing missions on a wide range of Italian targets in Abyssinia and Somaliland, the airfield at Diredawa being a particular favourite. Losses mounted in the face of opposition from CR.42 fighters but overall the squadrons gave a good account of themselves by keeping up the pressure on the Italians.

The build-up of forces in Sudan and Kenya was prompted by Churchill's insistence that the lost territory be regained as soon as possible. After a swift campaign the area was regained, along with Abyssinia — Addis Ababa being captured on 6th April 1941.

WESTERN DESERT 1940-42

The Western Desert campaign, and the creation of the Desert Air Force, saw air-land operations brought to a peak of efficiency and provided many lessons for the later operations in northern Europe by the tactical air forces. Operations against the Italians commenced on 11th June with bombing sorties against targets in Cyrenaica, Blenheims with a Gladiator escort attacking by day and Bombays by night. The Italians launched an offensive which by 10th September took them into Egypt. The understrength British ground and air forces managed to weaken the attack and it petered out — at which point, December 9th, a counter-attack was put in which achieved immediate success, driving the Italians back as far as Agheila before it in turn ran out of steam. During this offensive the squadrons of No 202 Group provided essential air support. By 30th January Derna was captured and whilst the ground forces took a short halt to re-supply and re-organise, the air elements kept up the pressure on the Italians. The offensive restarted on 3rd February and four days later Tobruk fell.

The major reason for the termination of the offensive was a political decision by Churchill to send forces to Greece, and the only forces available were those busily driving back the Italians. This has remained one of the great debatable points of World War Two.

Whilst the British reinforcements did little to effect the military outcome of the conflict in Greece the weakening of the forces in the Western Desert certainly had an impact. By late February RAF recce aircraft had picked up clear evidence of large-scale German reinforcement, the opportunity to clear Cyrenaica had been lost. On 31st March Rommel launched his attack, the advance was rapid and ably supported by the Luftwaffe. As the British fell back the RAF attempted to stem the advance by attacking supply lines and providing CAS for beleagured ground units. German troops swept past Tobruk encircling its garrison, and two RAF squadrons, as they raced on towards the Egyptian frontier. As this corresponded with the virtual end of the involvement in Greece it did at least enable a re-organisation to take place in the Egyptian main base areas. This latter was aided by a sudden surge in new equipment, released by the stabilsing of the situation in Western Europe but also by British realisation that they could not afford for Egypt to be lost. During this low point for British forces two other problems arose — a revolt in Iraq and the need to take control of Syria. The German-inspired revolt in Iraq was led by Rashid Ali and opened on 3rd April 1941. By the end of the month his forces were besieging the airfield at Habbaniya, home of No 4 FTS. This became a spirited little action during which the training aircraft — Audax, Oxford, Gladiator — of the FTS were modified for offensive action and in which capacity they flew over 1400 sorties! The revolt was over by 31st May as British forces regained control of the rebel areas. Vichy French control of Lebanon/Syria provided problems with supply of British areas and also provided a potential line of attack for German forces. The decision was taken to seize these areas and an offensive was launched on 8th June, the ground forces being supported by 4 1/2 squadrons, these being primarily engaged on a counter-air campaign to negate the French air presence as well as providing ground support on the few occasions that the situation so demanded. A cease-fire was declared on 12th July.

4 FTS at Habbaniya had its own mini war against Iraqi rebels.

Meanwhile, the front-line in Egypt had stabilised, largely because the German offensive had out-run its logistic support. As both sides prepared for the next round it was a question of who would be first onto the attack. A British attack of mid May stalled as soon as it began, as did an attempt to relieve Tobruk; however, the CRUSADER offensive was launched in November and the newly constituted Desert Air Force soon gained a measure of air

superiority. Ground support techniques were developed and proved effective, Hurribombers being responsible for the destruction of large amounts of enemy equipment. The air phase had commenced in mid October with anti-shipping and anti-air sorties aimed at achieving a dominant situation in these aspects before the ground attack opened. Whilst the tactical aircraft moved forward with the ground troops the strategic bombers attacked more distant targets, especially those connected with supply. By mid December the advance had reached a point 1000 miles from Cairo. This offensive, like so many in the vast Western Desert theatre, was defeated by lack of supplies and support facilities, German forces were able to disengage from their pursuers and establish a defensive line.

Once again the race was on to see who would be ready first for the next move. Rommel, ever ready to take a gamble, struck first even though he had received little in the way of reinforcement. By the early summer Tobruk had fallen and he was back in Egypt, where the Allied defense line at El Alamein managed to halt the offensive. But for the work of the Desert Air Force squadrons the retreat would quite likely have become a disastrous rout.

Rommel was brought to a halt at a pre-planned defence line, but it is equally true to say that lack of supplies was a major factor in the termination of his offensive. A great deal of the credit for this must go to the anti-shipping squadrons operating from Malta and the Western Desert. These aircraft, especially Beauforts, Blenheims and Wellingtons, hunted down Axis shipping throughout the Mediterranean, paying particular attention to the routes from Italy and Greece across to North Africa.

It was this element that now played the dominant role in ensuring success for the Allied forces. Whilst the Afrika Korps was starved of supplies the British forces were receiving a veritable plethora of men and equipment, the new British commander, Bernard Montgomery, insisting on overwhelming superiority before he would take the offensive. The Battle of El Alamein was launched on 19th October with massive air support provided by the Desert Air Force. Air superiority was immediate and after that the squadrons ranged over the battlefield causing chaos and widespread destruction. After an initial defenive battle, and attempted counter-offensive, the German line collapsed and the retreat began — during which German columns were under almost constant air attack. Tobruk was relieved on 13th November. A second major blow fell with the invasion of Tunisia/Algeria (Operation TORCH), Allied forces making an amphibious assault aimed at knocking out the Vichy French territories and then hitting the Germans from west as well as east.

The German High Command decided to try and hold Tunisia and sent large bumbers of reinforcements, although these had some initial impact it was wasted effort. In April the German air corridor became the scene of what can only be described as a massacre as lumbering German transport aircraft, with little or no escort, were shot to pieces by Allied fighters. German forces in Tunisia surrendered on 12th May 1943, North Africa had been liberated.

GREECE 1941

On 28th October 1941 Italian forces invaded Greece from Albania. In response to Greek requests British air and land forces were despatched from Egypt. The diversion of resources to Greece at a time when the British forces in the Western Desert were in a position to oust the Italians from Africa has been seen as a turning point in the fortunes of the Desert war — and has caused much detailed and often bitter argument. However, many

German scholars have seen Hitler's insistence on sending troops to the Balkan/Greek theatre as a significant factor in the failure of the invasion of Russia. The initial RAF effort comprised three squadrons of Blenheims plus the Gladiators of No 80 Squadron, all were soon engaged on successful operations against the Italians as the latter found their 'simple' conquest turning into defeat. Additional squadrons arrived in January and the situation appeared quite promising. However, Hitler decided to take a hand and ordered German forces to assist his Italian ally. The German offensive opened on 6th April, driving the Allies away from the Metaxa Line and into headlong retreat. Most of the Blenheims were destroyed on the ground by Luftwaffe attacks, against which the few RAF fighters could make no impact. In a daring and risky evacuation a large proportion of the British (and New Zealand) troops were evacuated to Crete, part of this work being undertaken by Sunderland which would appear at remote bays to lift key personnel to safety.

Beauforts on anti-shipping ops from the Western Desert and Malta wrecked Axis supply routes.

Marylands provided vital reconnaissance during the desert campaigns and the disaster in Greece/Crete.

Unfortunately Crete was not to be a safe haven. In the absence of adequate reinforcement, and a critical lack of air resources, the defence of Crete became impossible. The island fell to a spirited airborne assault by German paratroops — but it was the last such operation these forces made, the cream of this elite body was decimated.

MALTA 1940-43

As part of the general Italian assault on British bases, Malta received its first air attack on 11th June 1941. This was the start of a two-month air assault designed to destroy the air and naval installations on the island and break the morale of the population. The sole air defence consisted of three airworthy Sea Gladiators — *Faith*, *Hope* and *Charity* — and these put up a determined defence against the Italian air armadas. A few Hurricanes arrived at the end of June, joined by another batch in August flown off HMS *Argus*. This hand-to-mouth reinforcement was to remain a feature of the air battle for Malta. Whilst the fighters were essential to the defence of the island, Malta's great strategic value lay in its ability to strike back, especially against the N.African supply routes.

A new offensive was launched against Malta at the end of 1940 as the Luftwaffe joined in the battle in a determined effort to destroy the island's defences. Intensive attacks on the airfields caused enormous difficulties for the defenders and most of the strike aircraft departed for the relative safety of Egypt. It was now that the nature lent a hand in that Malta, being little more than a solid but easily workable rock was turned into a veritable fortress. The airfields were strengthened and new aircraft pens

constructed, as much as possible of the support elements went underground and so by dint of hard work and adaptability the island remained operational. The first Spitfire reinforcements arrived in March, followed by a second batch off the USS *Wasp* on 20th April. Although the problems remained immense, not least in the matter of supplies, the defenders were able to maintain their resistance. The withdrawal of German air strength in May (for the invasion of Russia) provided Malta with an essential recovery period. More Spitfires arrived and the offensive aircraft returned to resume their attacks on Axis shipping and bases in Sicily. The part played by the anti-shipping units cannot be too highly stressed, it was a decisive factor in the defeat of the Afrika Korps, as Rommel, starved of supplies as tanker after tanker was sunk, could not support a mobile campaign. During one ten-month period a single squadron claimed over 100 000 tons of Axis shipping!

By the time that the Luftwaffe returned a few months later the defences had grown too strong, although the attacks brought a new round of hardship to the people of Malta. The island went through a number of other crisis periods but none as great as those of the first Luftwaffe offensive when defeat seemed inevitable. As the defences managed once again to gain a measure of control then Malta assumed an even greater offensive role, providing an ideal base to support the landings of Operation TORCH.

ITALY AND BALKANS 1943-45

With the whole of North Africa in Allied hands the commanders now looked to the invasion of Italy as the next step in their offensive. During the summer of 1943 the joint RAF/American elements of Mediterranean Allied Air Forces were re-organised and strengthened, commencing anti-air operations in June for the invasion of Sicily. One element of this was to be the capture of the defended islands of Lampedusa and Pantelleria; both were subjected to heavy air attack, which proved so successful that the garrison commanders surrendered as soon as Allied ground forces landed. Malta now provided a key base for the attacks on Sicily, Sardinia and southern Italy; whilst the bombers attacked a wide range of targets, the fighter squadrons roamed the skies searching for the somewhat elusive enemy, and the anti-shipping squadrons sank anything that moved.

The assault force hit the beaches of Sicily on 10th July, under the cover of a huge air umbrella which prevented not only enemy offensive air operations but also enemy reconnaissance. Amongst the airborne forces employed was 1st Airborne, their target being the Ponte Grande bridge at Syracuse. This operation did not go well, 50% of the gliders ended up in the sea. As bridgeheads were

ITALY AND BALKANS 1943-45

Map legend:
- Approx Position of German Defence Line
- Amphibious Assault
- Front Line (with dates)
- Main Rail Lines

The German defence established on the Gustav Line was proving hard to overcome, the area around Monte Cassino being seen as a key position by the Allied planners. It was decided to apply massive bombing against the area around the Monastery in an effort to blast the German defenders out of their positions and enable the advance to be resumed.

In the end it was an assault by Polish troops which led to the capture of Monte Cassino in mid May, allowing 5th Army to push forward.

The overall offensive had not, however, been stalled for all these months. A daring plan was put into action in an effort to cut off the German defenders, the landings at Anzio (22nd January) were aimed slicing through the weak rear echelons and isolating the strong forces further south. Without air support the landings would have failed. The German reaction was swift and powerful but it ran into Allied tactical air power employed on an almost undreamt-of scale.

Strategic aircraft caused equal havoc to the supply lines as Op STRANGLE gained an increasing hold of the German supply network. An element of this latter campaign was the mining of the Danube, one of the great communications routes of Europe. Late Spring saw a decrease in the air strength available to the RAF as squadrons were returned to the UK to be incorporated within the air forces being built-up for the invasion of France. Nevertheless, combined land and air pressure at last broke the Gustav Line in May 1944, the retreating German forces providing a wealth of targets for the tactical aircraft. On 4th June Allied forces entered Rome.

With typical German inventiveness a new defence line was established, the Gothic Line, this becoming the scene of the summer campaign. The ground forces could make little headway in the Appennine mountains and although the air forces continued to create supply problems for the defenders they could make little direct impact on the overall situation. In the meantime, a new air campaign opened in conjunction with Op DRAGOON, the landing in southern France. Pre-invasion bombing softened up the area before the first troops went ashore on 15th August. The same month saw the Allied air forces involved in one of the most heart-breaking 'campaigns' of the war. Partisans in the ghetto of Warsaw, Poland rose against the German garrison in the expectation that the the Red Army would soon be in the city. Bomber aircraft from bases in the UK and Italy flew supply missions to Warsaw in an effort to provide the partisans with weapons and medical supplies. Losses were very heavy and it was obvious that the sorties could not continue. The expected Russian assistance did not materialise and the uprising was put down with great ferocity.

In Italy the arrival of one of the worst winters of recent years provided many problems for the Allied air forces, not least being the poor condition of many of the airfields. Much of the air effort was concentrated against the remaining supply lines to weaken the enemy before the Spring offensive was launched. This duly opened on 9th April, preceded by an air bombardment and supported by wave after wave of CAS aircraft. The ground forces made good progress and it is likely that the final German defences would have collapsed had a cease-fire not been called in early May.

BALKANS

Yugoslavia was a country in which partisan forces had always been strong, resisting the German presence with numerous acts of sabotage and exerting control over the more remote areas of their country. Air supply was instituted as soon as contact was made with the various groups, Special Duties operations being a regular

established so temporary landing strips were constructed to enable the tactical aircraft to provide even more intensive cover; the work of the RAF servicing commandos in re-arming and re-fuelling aircraft IN the front line is deserving of great praise. After the initial shock the Axis air arm joined the fray day and night but before long the Allied squadrons had gained air superiority, a factor that was to remain constant in all the subsequent campaigns in Italy. The advance through Sicily continued, aircraft providing support every time the Germans endeavoured to hold a defensive line. A great deal of attention was paid to closing the Straits of Messina to prevent reinforcements arriving and, as the retreat continued, enemy forces escaping. Sicily was subdued by 15th August but despite intense air bombardment of the Straits a substantial portion of the German garrison escaped.

Strategic and tactical air forces had been conducting an offensive against lines of communication in south Italy and this campaign was now intensified, as Operation STRANGLE it was later to become the key element in Allied air strategy in Italy. The first ground troops landed in Italy on 3rd September, only a few days before the Italian capitulation. This latter event had little immediate impact as it was half expected by the German commanders, who moved swiftly to occupy all the key areas held by their recent 'ally'. Other amphibious assaults took place, all with massive air support, the landing at Salerno requiring close support to suppress shore batteries and then to counter a determined German thrust. With waves of Allied aircraft dominating the area the German forces could only deploy at night, any movement by day was sure to be pounced upon by RAF and American fighter-bombers. The standard policy of contructing landing grounds in the area of the main thrusts once more paid dividends and Spitfires and Kittyhawks were soon operating from a series of rough strips. The capture, and repair, of major airfields, such as the clutch of airfields around Foggia, enabled the strategic aircraft to move from their bases in North Africa.

feature in this area. Tactical aircraft carried out attacks on a wide range of targets, often in support of partisan operations. However, one of the favoured target groups was that of communications and the road and rail systems of Yugoslavia, and Albania, were regular hunting grounds for Beaufighters.

This theatre of ops had grown in importance as the advance up Italy continued, enabling squadrons to operate from bases on the east coast of Italy across the Adriatic against Albania and Yugoslavia. As German fortunes worsened so the partisan forces in Yugoslavia applied ever increasing pressure in an effort to liberate their country. Tactical air power was used to add to this pressure and to support partisan operations whilst air supply, especially by Dakota, provided essential supplies and even flew out wounded partisans. The BAF, which included substantial elements from the SAAF and the Italian Air Force, kept up the pressure and by March 1945 aircraft were operating from bases in Yugoslavia in support of the Yugoslav 4th Army. The campaign ended on 4th April when this partisan force linked up with elements of British 8th Army advancing from Italy.

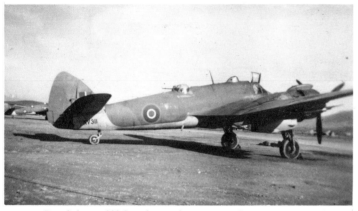

Beaufighters of 39 Squadron took part in anti-Communist ops in Athens, December 1944.

GREEK ISLANDS AND GREECE

During the second half of 1943 the main aim of the air forces operating in the eastern Med had been the harrassing of the German garrisons on Crete and the Greek islands, as well as attacks on the Greek mainland. Cyprus provided an important base for these operations but it could only support a limited number of squadrons, most of the strategic units still having to operate from Egypt. The Aegean area was one in which the Luftwaffe was still quite active and losses amongst the RAF squadrons remained high, although the anti-shipping squadrons continued to dominate the coastal waters. It was this latter factor that enabled the Allied forces to ignore the German garrisons on the various islands, they were to all intents wasted resources unable to move from their locations. The same was not true of the German forces on mainland Greece, they were expected to provide stiff opposition to the landings planned for Autumn 1944. However, it became apparent from air reconnaissance that most movement in Greece was of convoys and trains making their way to the north of the country, escaping before the Russian advance in eastern Europe could cut off the land corridor to Germany.

Allied troops landed at Araxos in September and tactical aircraft occupied the abandoned airfields — from where they harrassed the retreating German columns, a favoured tactic being to drop bridges at either end of a column and then deal with the trapped remnants. With the situation under control operations were mounted to re-take certain of the main islands. However, Greece was not to be liberated without a final struggle between various internal factions. Communist unrest erupted in Athens in

December as ELAS forces attempted to seize power. The RAF was called in to help the recognised government and detachments operated from various airfields around the city. Beaufighters flew close support missions against single buildings in Athens, the RPs having a deadly effect. At one point the Communist forces captured AHQ Greece but in the face of overwhelming odds their struggle was doomed to failure. A cease-fire was declared on 15th January, bringing to an end RAF offensive ops in Greece.

BATTLE OF ATLANTIC 1939-1945

ON MORE THAN one occasion Churchill stated that victory in the Battle of the Atlantic was the single most important factor in the conduct of the war and that all available resources must be expended to ensure this victory. The Germans employed three main offensive weapons against the shipping lifelines — surface raiders, U-boats, and long-range aircraft.

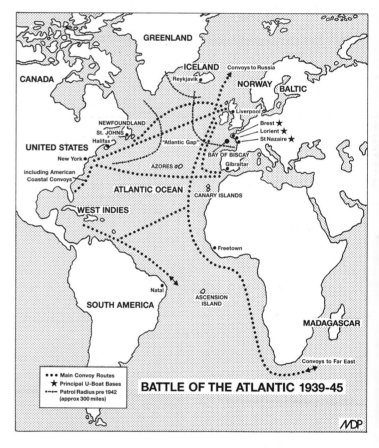

The first sinking took place on the first day of the war and by the end of September 41 ships had been lost to U-boats and surface raiders. However, the German U-boat service was still fairly weak and most damage was caused by the surface raiders, the German battlecruisers became a priority target for the Admiralty. It was not until late 1940 that the losses of merchant shipping began to assume alarming proportions, in October some 350,000 tons of shipping was sunk. At the outbreak of the war Coastal Command strength comprised a number of flying boat and Anson squadrons and these aircraft took on the mantle of trying to protect shipping around the UK and, as far as was possible, out into the Atlantic. These very limited air resources were soon supplemented by detachments from Bomber Command.

The introduction in early 1941 of new tactics, especially the 'Wolf Packs', brought a new dimension to the threat and there

The anti-submarine war was critical in the Battle of the Atlantic.

Ansons were the major Coastal Command element at the outbreak of war

was a distinct possibility that Britain would lose control of the vital sea supply lanes. Although the convoy system had reduced the loss rate for a while it was now an invitation for the Wolf Packs to gather on such lucrative targets, guided by a shadowing U-boat or by one of the long-range Kondor aircraft. The major problem for the naval commanders was lack of air cover both for reconnaissance and for offensive action — if the shadower could be destroyed or at least driven away then the convoy had a chance of escaping into the vastness of the Atlantic. Longer-range aircraft such as the Catalina were introduced but they were always in short supply and still suffered operational limitations; the entry to service in Spring 1941 of the Liberator was a major step forward. Nevertheless, there was still a gap in the central Atlantic outside of land-based air cover. One attempted solution, in the absence of escort carriers, was placing a 'one-shot' protective fighter on a number of ships (the so-called CAM — Catapult Armed Merchantmen — ships), the idea being that the Hurricane would be launched to shoot down the Kondor and then ditch alongside its ship for the pilot to be picked up. Coastal Command aircraft were also involved with air combat against He.111s, Ju.88s and the Kondors. Another vital role for the patrol aircraft was that of Search and Rescue and the escorting of damaged ships. Sunderlands made a number of dramatic rescues, landing near survivors from a ship and taking them on board.

By 1942 increased numbers of U-boats began to make the lack of air cover even more damaging. The total losses in 1942

amounted to 1664 ships, an incredible 7,790,000 tons (and thousands of lives) — more than the total of new-build shipping entering service. This was largely due to the wolf-packs concentrating on the Greenland Gap where no air cover was able to reach the convoys.

One of the topics discussed at the Casablanca Conference of January 1943 was the critical situation in the Atlantic. Churchill insisted that greater effort was to be expended on solving the problem and that Coastal and Bomber Commands MUST co-operate more readily; up to this point Bomber Command insisted that the best way of attacking the U-boat force was to destroy the building yards. However, the Command did expend a great deal of effort attacking the U-boat bases in France, although these were so well constructed that conventional bombing was of little value. The real battle was won by Coastal Command aircraft on its endless convoy patrols, hours of searching rewarded by a few sightings and even fewer attacks — but enough by mid 1943 to have an impact on the campaign. In mid 1943 the U-boats were withdrawn from the North Atlantic as losses were too high whilst sinkings were insignificant. However, one of the areas in which the air campaign was even more succesfull was in attacking U-boats as they transited the Bay of Biscay to and from their bases. This became a vicious campaign as German air strength was increased to counter the patrols, which in turn led to an increase in air combats and participation by Fighter Command.

59 Squadron Liberator on patrol.

Between June and August 1943 only 58 ships were lost to German submarines, whilst the latter suffered 79 losses, including 58 to aircraft. Air cover was further improved in August with operations from bases on the Azores, thus decreasing the 'gap'. The Allies had certainly gained the upper hand in technology with improved ASV to detect U-boats, the Leigh-Light to enable night attacks to be made, and improved weapons. In the face of increased air capability many submarine commanders chose to stay on the surface and fight it out with the attacking aircraft, U-boats began to sprout ever-increasing defensive armament and aircraft losses rose, although Coastal Command crews continued to press home their attacks. By early summer 1943 the U-boats had been ordered out of the North Atlantic and into 'safer' waters; they returned for a brief spell in September-October but achieved little for a high loss rate — 20 were sunk in October.

The technology war swung back and forth as each side introduced new equipment or counter-measures. However, the balance remained with the aircraft and by Spring 1944 the U-boat campaign in the Atlantic was virtually terminated. Coastal Command had a stranglehold on the German submarine service, U-boats were attacked wherever they tried to operate. Even the advent of such devices as the Schnorkel, which enabled submarines to remain submerged, could not redress the balance;

not enough new submarines were being completed (thanks in large measure to Bomber Command attacks on Germany) and losses of experienced crews had been so heavy that it was hard for the new boats to find suitable manpower. With the invasion of France, most U-boats were ordered to move to bases in Denmark and Norway. It was a futile manoeuvre and U-boat losses in the coastal waters of those countries rose to alarming proportions.

Air supply was much used during the advance towards Germany.

EUROPE 1941-1945

AFTER THE COLLAPSE of France and the frantic defence of Britain, the RAF was left as the only Allied force capable of striking back at enemy-occupied Europe and at Germany itself. Until 1944 the main element of this offensive rested with Bomber Command (see above for the Strategic Bombing Offensive), although other RAF elements, notably Coastal Command, were involved with operations on the fringes of Europe. The Fighter Command contribution was limited by aircraft performance, the single-engined fighters being unable to reach far into Europe. Nevertheless, and within months of the end of the Battle of Britain, Fighter Command commenced operations over N. Europe in an attempt to bring the Luftwaffe to battle. These operations met with mixed success, the Germans often refusing to respond, and loss rates were roughly equal on both sides. The longer range types, such as the Mosquito and Beaufighter, proved adept at intruder missions, attacking a wide range of targets.

The first major tactical air effort in this theatre came with the Dieppe Raid of August 1942, an operation which has been the subject of much debate; losses amongst the Canadian troops were high — was the knowledge and experience gained worth the cost? The RAF supported each stage of the operation, providing air cover and support.

Total air superiority allowed aircraft such as this Typhoon to dominate the land battle.

The proposed 1942 invasion went into North Africa and that for 1943 was postponed, despite protests from Stalin, as the Allied force in the UK expanded and trained, and with an ever-increasing number of American air and ground units coming into play. Whilst the pressure was maintained on the German-held territories a great deal of attention was also paid to training and the development of tactics and procedures for the close co-ordination of air and ground forces. With the invasion set for early summer 1944, the pressure on German forces was increased throughout northern Europe but particularly around Normandy and the Pas de Calais. Allied aircraft swept the skies clear of German aircraft and attacked almost anything that moved by road, rail or river. It was a taste of things to come when air supremacy was to dominate the European battlefield.

The D-Day landings of 6th June 1944 went in under the largest air umbrella ever seen, aircraft performing a huge variety of tasks — including such unusual tasks as pretending to be an invasion fleet by dropping radar-deceiving metal strips ('window'). At any point that the landings were held up, the fighter-bomber types, such as the rocket-firing Typhoon, would appear to blast a way through. The German commanders found it impossible to move units in daylight so total was the Allied domination of the air over the battlefield. Tactical air power worked hand-in-hand with the advancing troops, fighters adding the weights of their cannon and machine-guns to the land battle in the absence of much 'trade' in the air war. The Luftwaffe did appear from time to time and achieved a few notable successes but it was a virtual one-sided conflict and Luftwaffe losses were high. It was not only the fighter types which had a role to play, the transport squadrons were involved at every stage of the battle, performing a heroic role in the ill-fated airborne operations around Arnhem.

Brief appearance on the continent of Allied jet aircraft towards the end of the war — a white Meteor or 616 Squadron.

The German employment of V-weapons led to the 'second Blitz' of London and created a threat to the advancing ground forces. Strategic bombers and tactical aircraft were given the task of destroying the launch sites and other installations; whilst over southern England fighters, including the RAF's first operational jet aircraft (Meteor) hunted down the flying-bombs.

And so the Allied advance continued through France, Belgium and Holland and on into Germany; a mix of tactical and strategic power providing the basis for success, albeit with the ground forces facing stout resistance from the German Army and having to fight every inch of the way. The central role of air power was proven during the German counter-offensive through the Ardennes, a master-stroke aided by a period of bad weather which hampered Allied air operations. One of the major reasons for its eventual failure was an improvement in the weather and the return of tactical air to the battlefield. In the face of such overwhelming Allied air superiority it is amazing that the German land forces were able to put up the degree of resistance that they did. However, the ultimate Allied victory was by now a foregone conclusion and many German commanders were in favour of seeking surrender terms. The insistence upon unconditional surrender can certainly be said to have lengthened the war. During the closing months Germany was assaulted from east and west, air elements being to the fore in all the battles as the Luftwaffe had to all intents and purposes ceased to exist.

FAR EAST - MALAYA AND BURMA

FAR EAST 1941-1945

THE CAMPAIGNS IN the Far East have often been called the 'Forgotten War' and there is much truth in this statement, it was an area remote from the life-and-death struggle in Europe and so in many minds took a back seat. However, it was yet another area in which air power was to prove a decisive factor in eventual victory.

The Japanese entry into the war brought a new set of problems for the British commanders — a complete new theatre of operations to consider with yet more demands on the already stretched resources. It was a theatre which had been starved of resources in the face of so many crises elsewhere, although the land forces were reasonably strong they too were ill-equipped. However, the worst element by far was that of air power, although some reinforcements had been sent these had all too often been 'borrowed' on their way through the Middle East.

With Pearl Harbor and the American fleet neutralised the way was clear for a Japanese invasion of the Far East.

Japanese forces landed at Khota Bharu on the east coast of Malaya as part of a strategy to capture key airfields in their thrust towards the British naval base at Singapore. The expansion programme underway for the RAF included the construction of airfields and landing grounds; unfortunately, there was little in the way of modern aircraft for these new sites (total strength in Malaya was 158 aircraft). As the Japanese invasion fleet approached it was spotted by air recce and a naval force was sent to intercept. An almost total lack of air cover led to the loss of

HMS *Repulse* and HMS *Prince of Wales* under a determined Japanese air assault. Some reinforcements arrived in Singapore, as batch of Hurricanes proving particularly useful in countering Japanese bombing raids, although the balance shifted once more with the arrival of Zero escort fighters. The antiquated Vildebeest torpedo bombers were destroyed in valiant attempts to strike at Japanese shipping.

By late January inferior Japanese forces, but with adequate air support, had pushed the Allied army back into Singapore. The final assault began on 8th January 1942 and within a week Singapore had fallen: although what remained of the air assets had already moved to Sumatra. Singapore was the second major British base to be taken, Hong Kong having been captured on 25th December. Sumatra and then Java fell and RAF units, having tried to counter overwhelming Japanese strength, retreated to Burma. Air attacks on Burma had been underway since December, Rangoon having been bombed on 23rd. The major RAF effort, what was left of it, was tasked with supporting the defence line on the river Salween plus the defence of Rangoon. Blenheims and Hurricanes attacked Japanese airfields, with some success but also mounting losses; whilst Buffalos and Hurricanes provided air defence for the British forces. Under increasing air attack and with the inexorable Japanese advance, Rangoon was evacuated on 7th March. During the retreat RAF units provided whatever air support they could, often operating from rough strips hacked out of the jungle. The major elements of 'Burwing' concentrated at Magwe and Akyab, where they were caught by Japanese raids and virtually wiped out — this, "taught us the first lesson on the Burma campaign, namely that air supremacy is a requisite for victory on land." By mid April the survivors were back at bases in India but still operating over the Burma front. The Dakotas of No 31 Sqn undertook numerous supply missions as well as air evacuation, a hint of the vital importance that such operations were to play in the Burma campaigns.

Whilst the front line was being stabilised on the frontier of India, attention was being paid to another area where the Japanese threatened to wreak havoc. With their domination of the open sea it seemed likely that a seaborne attack would be launched at India. Ceylon was in a position to prevent this — but only if air and naval forces could be built up to a satisfactory level. Both these elements were addressed and by the time of the first enemy air attacks (5th April) the defences of the isalnd were strong enough to prevent any major damage to base facilities.

The remainder of 1942 was a period of relative quiet as the Japanese consolidated their hold on Burma and pushed the last remnants of British forces back into Burma. The first air raids on Calcutta took place in December, the arrival of a number of night-fighter Beaufighters put a stop to these night raids. The RAF organisation was reformed and strenghtened, realisation at last of the dire state of affairs in this theatre, as the commanders planned for a counter-offensive to re-take Burma in 1943. The first part of this plan was to be the capture of airfields on Akyab island; this First Arakan campaign was launched on 9th December, the attack started well but soon stalled — largely due to an inadequate level of air support. The Blenheims and Hurricanes had fought well, at one stage the four fighter squadrons had been flying over 150 missions a day. It had, however, provided valuable lessons for the future. The same offensive was also the start of the 'Chindit' raids, these penetration raids became a regular element of future campaigns but were only successful when provided with adequate air supply and support.

The build-up of forces continued and by mid 1943 there were 53 Allied squadrons available, the majority being RAF. Not only were more aircraft available but they were also better types — Hurricane, Beaufighter and Vengeance, soon to be joined by Spitfires. One of the most impressive aspects of this build-up was the provision of facilities — over 300,000 tons of concrete was used in the contruction of all-weather airfields, plus the construction of many other fair-weather strips. The new air forces were given five main tasks — CAS of Allied troops, air supply, interdiction of enemy supply routes, troop transport and aeromedical, and the air defence of India.

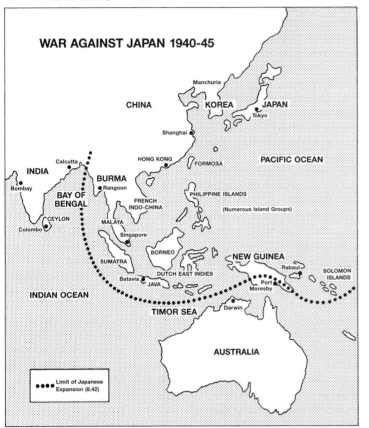

The combined Allied air forces began a programme of attacks on Japanese airfields in an effort to achieve air superiority. By early 1944 this had been successful and the ground forces were able to operate under the air umbrella. The second Battle of Arakan was launched on 4th February 1944 but floundered almost immediately as the Japanese executed a brilliant counter move. However, rather than retreat the Allied forces adopted a new tactic of establishing a defensive stronghold and relying on air power to both provide fire support and supplies. The system worked well and the Japanese manoeuvre was defeated leaving them no option but retreat, although the battles around Imphal had been tense, the final deciding factor being overwhelming Allied air power. During the three-month seige of Imphal the defenders had received over 8000 supply sorties bringing in 850,000 gallons of petrol, 1300 tons of grain, 400 tons of sugar, plus a wide range of other food and logistical supplies — as well as 12,000 bags of mail and 43 million cigarettes!

In March a strong 'Chindit' force was moved by glider to 'Broadway', deep behind enemy lines. An airstrip was constructed and by 13th March over 9000 troops had been flown in. Air support/supply remained essential to the success of this venture, RAF liaison officers accompanied Chindit expeditions to provide expert advice.

By July 1944 British troops had reached the Chindwin river although the overall timetable of re-conquest had been delayed by the Japanese counter-attacks. During the summer the Allied

commanders laid plans for the final moves in Burma, to be combined with an offensive by Chinese forces. The offensive re-opened in Autumn with 15th Corps moving against Akyab, another attempt to seize vital air bases. They found the Japanese forces already retreating and so by early January this vital area was in Allied hands. From that point on the offensive rarely faltered, leap-frogging through Burma seizing air bases and driving the Japanese back towards Rangoon. The RAF was ever in the forefront of the attack, hitting enemy installations and troop concentrations and destroying lines of communication. On 20th March 1945 Mandalay was recaptured; six weeks later (1st May) air and sea landings were made around Rangoon, the city being entered on the following day. The remainder of May and most of June was taken up with clearing out the rest of Burma and consolidating the position ready for the offensive into Malaya and back to Singapore. These latter plans were cancelled when the Japanese surrendered on 2nd September.

CAMPAIGNS 1945-1970

PALESTINE 1945-1948

The 'conflict-in-waiting' that was Palestine flared again as the chaos caused by World War Two subsided. All the old resentments came to the surface once more but there was also a new factor — the moral pressure that Jewish activists were able to apply to world opinion over the question of Jewish immigration to Palestine — the need for a Jewish homeland for the survivors of the Holocaust. Terrorist attacks had re-commenced in 1944 with extremist Jewish organisations such as Irgun and the 'Stern Gang' attacking government and police buildings; although it must be emphasised that at this time the extremists were very much a minority amongst the Jewish community. It was, however, enough to persuade leaders such as Churchill to support a pro-Arab stance, especially in view of the perceived importance of Palestine as a secure base in the post-war period.

The moderate Jews expected the British to negotiate; however, it became clear that the British Foreign Office had no real intention of giving ground and was determined to limit Jewish immigration. The revolt which opened in October 1945 brought the British into direct confrontation with their recent allies and led to an unhappy compromise.

Operational RAF strength in Palestine stood at six squadrons, half of them being offensive support types, plus six RAF Regiment squadrons. However, this was increased from mid January by detachments plus aircraft operating from other areas; the major task being Operation SUNBURN, the search for ships running to Palestine with illegal immigrants. This task involved RAF aircraft flying long patrols over the Med and then directing RN ships to intercept and turn back any suspect vessels.

The well-trained, and British equipped, Jewish forces attacked a wide range of targets and in February 1946 managed to destroy a number of aircraft at Qastina, Peta Tiqva and Lydda. The situation rapidly deteriorated with off-duty soldiers being murdered, which in turn led to an hardening of the British attitude. A round up of Jewish leaders was followed by the bombing of the GHQ at King David Hotel, with the loss of 91 lives. During the internal security operations the Austers played an important role in both the recce and light liaison roles whilst the Spitfires hovered around the area to provide air support as required.

The main stumbling blocks remained those of immigration quotas and the establishment of a self-governing Jewish 'state'. The London Conference of September 1946 to February 1947 went over all the old arguments and came up with no new solutions. In exasperation Britain took the problem to the United Nations; during the subsequent UN Special Commission visit the extremists increased their attacks — as proof of Jewish feeling and power — which caused the British to impose martial law in some areas. As part of a clearing the decks for action policy, a major airlift of service dependents took place in February. The final UN solution was in favour of partition, an idea which appealed to the Jews but caused consternation in the entire Arab world. Britain refused to oversee the transition and determined to leave when the mandate ran out on 15th May 1948. It was not be that simple, the Arab-Jewish conflict erupted on 30th November 1947, the day after the UN General Assembly approved the partition plan. Over the next few months the British forces tried to extricate themselves from between the two factions without showing favour — and without casualties. The Spitfires of No 32 Sqn and No 208 Sqn continued to fly operational sorties escorting road convoys and providing fighter cover of key areas, whilst Nos 37 and 38 Sqns maintained their maritime patrols. The aircraft were called into action from time to time to prevent ground troops being hampered in their moves back to the final enclave areas around Ramat David and Haifa. Egyptian aircraft attacked the airfield at Ramat David on 22nd May, the second and third waves losing five of their number. The attacks were almost certainly a mistake as the Arab forces had no desire to prevent the British leaving.

The last British troops left Haifa on 30th June, glad to see the back of Palestine.

SUDAN 1946

A Sudan Defence Squadron was established to provide air support for local ground forces, the task being undertaken by No 39 Squadron's Mosquito aircraft until the 'wooden wonder' proved itself unsuited to the climate. Returning in June 1948 with Tempests, the squadron was soon involved in anti-bandit operations against Shifta terrorists in Eritrea. The primary task was that of recce to provide information for the ground force, although some offensive sorties were flown. Similar policing actions were required at various times during the late 1940s and early 1950s.

BERLIN AIRLIFT 1948

The first post-war crisis in Europe was not long in coming. Berlin had been divided into sectors by the victorious occupying powers and immediately became a source of tension between the Western Allies and the Soviet Union. In the face of growing Soviet intransigence over the use of road and rail links into Berlin, in March 1948 the Allies cancelled all movements except those by food trains. This left only the three air corridors into the city and so air power was called upon to sustain the military and civilian population of this major city — a mammoth task and one without precedent. The city would need 4500 tons of supplies a day. On 28th June the USAF commenced air transport operations into Berlin — the Berlin Airlift was in business. Although the American contribution was by far the largest, the RAF was soon involved and a Transport Wing was established at Wunstorf to control the Dakota and York transports which provided the major RAF element. Other forces in BAFO were put on alert as a precaution against Soviet interference with the airlift. In the early part of the operation Sunderlands had flown into Lake Havel so urgent was the need for air transport. By August the RAF was averaging 1340 lift tons a day.

On 15th October the Combined Airlift Task Force had been established to control all Allied contributions; No 85 Gp was reformed to ease the RAF administrative workload in BAFO.

Although the blockade was lifted on 12th May 1949, supply missions were continued into September to build up stocks of food and other supplies. The RAF had moved 17% of the total lift, a very significant contribution.

KENYA — MAU MAU 1952-1956

Another of the so-called 'post-Colonial' struggles, the Mau-Mau uprising in Kenya was one of the most vicious of small-wars. It was fortunate that the British were able to use the experience gained in Malaya to contain and then defeat the terrorists. The large and powerful Kikuyu tribe had long resented the British presence in Kenya and during the 1930s the Kikuyu Association, under Jomo Kenyatta, had been pushing for land reforms. In 1946 there was renewed activity, including the growth of the extremist Mau Mau secret society with its rituals and reform through violence policy. Over the next few years there were attempts at achieving political settlements but without result; meanwhile the Mau Mau were extending the series of regional cells throughout Kenya, with the Aberdare forests as a safe base.

Lincoln detachments participated in Kenyan Mau Mau ops.

The Eastleigh Comms Flight aircraft flew leaflet-dropping sorties over Kikuyu heartlands trying to persuade the tribesmen to support the government. To add a little muscle to this proposal, demonstration flights were made by Tempests of No 6 Sqn, a detachment of which had been at Eastleigh since March 1947, and Lancasters of No 82 Sqn.

Continued unrest led to the Mau Mau being declared an illegal body in August 1950, a move which did nothing to ease tension but did lead to an increase in attacks on European farms. By Spring 1952 arson and murder had become commonplace leading in October to the declaration of a State of Emergency. Reinforcements were flown in by Hastings to support the King's African Rifles. Terrorist ringleaders were arrested and an anti-terrorist campaign instituted. The initial moves against the forest gangs in Aberdare met with little success and an increase in the overall level of terrorist activity brought additional reinforcements. The air element at this time was quite limited, comprising a few Harvards equipped to drop light bombs (No 1340 Flt had formed at Eastleigh in March 1953) and a variety of types operated by the Kenya Police Reserve (mainly ex RAF pilots). It soon became obvious that a heavier air offensive would be needed and so detachments of Lincolns from Bomber Command were planned, initial trials with just two aircraft proving the value of this option. The air strength built up to include six Lincolns, two Meteor PR.10s, of No 13 Sqn, and a variety of support aircraft including a Sycamore for CASEVAC and Auster and Pembroke detachments testing out the use of tannoys to broadcast messages to the terrorists ('Skyshout').

1954 was a busy year for the security forces in an effort to persuade the Mau Mau leadership to negotiate a settlement, the RAF flew over 5000 operational sorties in support of the ground forces. The overall result was disappointing and little progress was made. General Sir George Erskine therefore planned a series of major offensives for 1955, the first being launched in January against the Aberdare region — with air support of the advancing ground forces in addition to area denial bombing. This operation petered out in February but was followed in April by a push into the area around Mount Kenya and then, in July, into the southern Aberdares. This series of assaults broke up the forest gangs and kept them on the move, the number of defections increased and the terrorists rapidly lost popular support. The mopping-up ops continued to the latter part of 1956 but withdrawal of British forces had already commenced in August.

PERSIAN CRISIS 1951

The nationalisation of the Anglo-Iranian Oil Company in June 1951 brought an immediate British response with the deployment of Transport Command aircraft to Fayid ready to airlift troops in and civilians out. Air support was to be provided by the Venoms of No 6 and No 249 Squadrons, having moved to Shaibah, and the Brigands of No 8 Squadron. The crisis failed to develop and no airlift was required, the air units returning to their home bases.

EGYPT 1947-1956

During 1947 British forces in Egypt moved into the re-vamped base areas in the Suez Canal Zone as part of the planned abandonement, under Egyptian pressure, of the main bases in Egypt. Fayid, Deversoir, Shallufa and Kabrit became home to a strong force of aircraft — the transport wing at Kabrit, for example, having no less than five, albeit low strength, Dakota squadrons. By Spring 1948 the move was virtually complete. The Israeli offensive into Egypt in January 1949 was monitored by RAF aircraft, but on 4th January four Spitfires of No 208 Squadron were shot down, three by Israeli fighters, a Tempest of No 213 Squadron being lost later the same day. This was a severe shock to the RAF and was largely blamed on poor Rules of Engagement which put unarmed British aircraft in vulnerable positions.

British policy still saw the area as a vital one both in respect of the Suez Canal itself and for the general strategic position. However, the prospect of conflict between Egypt and the new state of Israel, which would inevitably involve the Suez Canal area, caused a re-think on the basing policy and an attempt to reduce the drastic overcrowding whilst maintaining a strong presence.

SUEZ 1956

From the middle of 1951, nationalist fervour had been on the increase in Egypt, leading to a campaign of terror and no co-operation designed to put pressure on Britain to withdraw from her bases in Egypt. In 1952 Neguib and Nasser came to power following the Colonels Revolt, the restlessness grew as Britain suggested a phased withdrawal and guarantees of intervention rights should the Suez Canal be threatened. When Nasser seized absolute control in April 1954 he was determined to oust the British as soon as possible. The Anglo-Egyptian Agreement of October 1954 led to the gradual withdrawal of British forces in line with this proposal, the last troops leaving in June 1956. Despite the withdrawal, however, a virulent campaign of anti-British propaganda continued. Nasser increased his drive for Egyptian control of Egypt and its resources, and in a fiery and dramatic speech on 26th July 1956 announced that the Suez Canal had been nationalised and that Egyptian forces were taking control "as he spoke".

Outside intervention seemed to be almost inevitable following this "slap in the face by a Hitlerite bandit", as Nasser's action was described in Parliament in a phrase soon taken up by the media. As the most directly affected countries, both France and Britain sought a diplomatic solution, whilst at the same time examining military options. During September and October joint Anglo-French military planning took place and, eventually, Operation MUSKETEER emerged. Despite frequent changes and arguments, the air plan was formulated with three specific phases:

1. Neutralisation of the Egyptian Air Force.

2. A psychological warfare programme for a continual air offensive to disrupt Egyptian economy, morale and armed forces.

3. Domination of the Canal Zone and its occupation by land, sea and air forces as might be necessary.

The primary task of the Air Task Force, under Air Marshal Barnett, was the neutralisation phase. Egypt had received substantial amounts of modern weapons from Czechoslovakia, including MiG-15 fighters and Il-28 bombers and it was considered essential that a British bombing force destroy these assets at the earliest opportunity. Bombing was ti be selective, to avoid civilian casualties or excessive material damage, and so Phase 2, the aero-psychological element, was virtually abandoned. The bomber element of the Air Task Force was to consist of Bomber Command Canberras and Valiants, and plans were laid to deploy squadrons to the operational area, using airfields on Cyprus and Malta. Nicosia was earmarked as the major airfield for the operation and the build-up of squadrons commenced; it was obvious from the early stages of planning that additional airfield space would be needed — so the longer range Valiants and Canberra B.6s of Bomber Command deployed to airfields in Malta (Luqa and Hal Far). The new airfield at Akrotiri was made the home for the Tangmere Hunter wing as well as the PR Canberras of No 13 and No 58 Squadrons. Although Tymbou airfield was re-surfaced it was given over to the French for use as a transport base.

On 20th October a Canberra PR.7 flew the first recce sortie over Egypt, ten days later the Egyptians refused a final Anglo-French ultimatum. The following night the Canberras and Valiants went into action against Almaza, Kabrit, Abu Sueir, Inchas and Cairo West, although most aircraft were recalled because of confusion over clearance to bomb certain of the targets. During 1st November the ground attack aircraft attacked a wide range of targets, concentrating on the Egyptian Air Force and scoring numerous hits on parked aircraft. It took only one more day for the planners to consider that the EAF was no longer a viable threat and to switch air attacks to other military targets such as barracks, troop concentrations and communications. By 5th November the effort had switched to preparing the way for the planned sea and air landings, the latter taking place at Gamil airfield where a successful drop was made by Hunter-escorted Hastings and Valletas — whilst Venoms swept ahead to suppress any ground targets. It was a similar story the next day with the naval landings around Port Said, although this also involved one of the first helicopter air assault operations.

American-led political pressure had, however, reached such a level as to force a cease-fire, effective at 1700 GMT on the 6th. The military operations had gone reasonably well, allied losses had been very light and there was no doubt that the rest of the Canal Zone could have been taken. Anglo-French forces remained in place until the arrival of a United Nations force on 13th, after which time the run-down of strength was as rapid as the build-up had been.

There has been much debate as to the effectiveness of the RAF effort, especially the medium level bombing by the Canberras and Valiants; it is true to say that the majority of Egyptian aircraft were destroyed by the GA aircraft and that the level of damage inflicted by the other bombers was less than expected. However, it must be born in mind that the medium bombers were using out-dated equipment and techniques, having to rely on the Second World War concept of a marker force; furthermore, this type of operation was subject to severe political constraint to avoid 'co-latteral' damage.

JORDAN 1948-1958

The 1948 Arab attacks on the new state of Israel involved all of its neighbours, Israeli aircraft attacked Amman in June, damaging two Ansons in a hangar. Jordanian resentment of the British presence grew and restrictions were placed on servicemen to prevent resentment turning to violence. Reinforcements were flown in to protect the airbases and other facilities. In 1951 Hussein took control of Iraq after the assasination of King Abdullah.

The RAF's presence in Jordan, with major bases at Amman and Mafraq, was considered a vital element of the MEAF strategic position in the 1950s, Jordan being considered a stable and relaible ally. However, as part of a general swell of Arab nationalism in the mid 1950s there were demonstrations in Amman in early 1955. British reinforcements were flown into Cyprus where air and land forces were placed on high alert to move into Jordan. Some reinforcements were moved into the country and plans were laid for an air evacuation. The sacking of General Glub, the British head of the Arab Legion, increased the already high level of tension. Although the situation remained tense the British forces had to released from readiness in January 1956. Within a year the Anglo-Jordan treaty was terminated (March 1957) and British forces withdrawn from the country, Mafraq being handed over in May. It was a reasonably amicable arrangement and good relations were maintained with King Hussein.

The latter 1950s was a period of increased inter-Arab tension with new power groupings being formed; an alliance between Egypt and Syria being countered by an Iraq-Jordan link, the latter with British support. During 1958 rioting broke out in Lebanon, the pro-Western government being supported by Britain and America. A revolution in Iraq ended the Arab Federation, Hussein was concerned over the possible spread of the unrest and urged Britain to send aircraft to Mafraq; on 17th July transport aircraft moved 16th Para Brigade to Amman, air support being provided by the Hunters of No 208 Squadron. The major problem for the RAF was that of obtaining diplomatic clearance for routes to and from the area, with many instances of aircraft having to fly long and circuitous routes having been refused an overflight of various countries. There was now a very real risk of a coup attempt in Jordan and so British forces in Jordan and Cyprus were put on high alert. However, a political solution was found — Hussein requested the withdrawal of British forces to placate his anti-British opponents, all done under the auspicies of a United Nations plan for peace in the region. The airlift took place at the end of October and the RAF was once more out of Jordan.

CYPRUS (EOKA) 1946-1960

The first series of EOKA terrorist bombs went off on 1st April, 1946 opening a campaign that was to last until 1960. This outburst of terrorist activity had been anticipated and measures were introduced to try and curb the flow of supplies and arms. The existing air patrols around the island were increased, additional sorties being flonn by the Anson Flight from Nicosia

and by Malta-based Shackletons. Aircraft had also been flying IS patrols for some time and these were also increased. With the arrival in October of Sir John Harding, the new Governor, a tougher policy was adopted, including 'cordon and search' operations in areas suspected on being EOKA hide-outs. The newly arrived Sycamores were to play a vital role in this type of operation and the EOKA leader, Colonel Grivas, was to have numerous lucky escapes after security forces literaly descended upon his hiding place.

Following the banishing in March 1956 of Archbishop Makarios there was a general increase in violence, including the murder of British personnel. In an error of judgement the Turkish element of the Police force was increased and used on IS operations in Greek villages thus sparking off even greater violence.

Over the next two years the situation improved, firstly through the availability of extra troops released from the Suez War and, secondly, from the increased use of aircraft in a wide range of support roles. It was the light aircraft — Austers, Pioneers, Chipmunks, and Sycamore helicopters — which proved so invaluable, carrying out recce, liaison, comms, supply, CASEVAC, and even psyops missions. Nevertheless, and despite numerous successes in destroying EOKA groups, the problem refused to go away. This, and a Turkish threat of intervention to protect its ethnic brethren, provided impetus for a new round of talks — the Lancaster House Conference of February 1959. An agreement was signed and implemented for an immediate end to hostilities. Cyprus became a Republic on 21st September 1960 although Britain retained control of two Sovereign Base Areas.

1974 — The Turkish invasion of July 1974 had no direct impact on British forces in the island but did provoke an evacuation of all personnel from outlying areas into the SBAs, followed by an airlift out of Cyprus of over 10 000 dependents and non-essential personnel. A second airlift took place in August following the break down of peace talks. The RAF bases were put on alert it was made known to the Turks that overflights of British bases would be viewed with extreme disfavour. With the establishment of a divided Cyprus the British bases returned to normality; although a final airlift, of Turkish Cypriot refugees to Turkey, took place in January the following year.

OMAN AREA 1952-1965

The desert wastelands around the shores of the Arabian Gulf have been the scene of much dispute (an on-going problem) with many different claims being made to a number of areas within the region. The heart of the problem lay in the unsatisfactory way in which 'borders' wer drawn up and the nomadic life of the tribesmen which refused to recognise such borders; however, until the major exploration of oil resources this did not cause too great a problem.

In August 1952 a Saudi Arabian force occupied the villages around the Buraimi oasis in Oman, a move countered by the Trucal Oman Levies (TOL) supported by Vampires of No 6 Squadron and leaflet dropping by Valettas. Whilst negotiations continued the RAF reinforced the TOL with an armoured car company and continued to fly recce sorties in the area, co-operating with ground forces in intercepting any movement towards the Oasis. A variety of aircraft were involved with these missions, including for a time Shackletons deployed from Malta and PR Lancasters of No 683 Squadron. The RAF's major problem was the unsuitability of the runway at Sharjah, the main base, for the operation of jet aircraft. The situation dragged on through 1954 but worsened with the arrival of Saudi reinforcements, leading to a decision by the government forces to

Tactical transport was key factor on ops in Aden and Oman; a wide range of types took part — including the Argosy.

settle the matter through military action. The TOL moved forward, air support Lincolns, Valettas, Pembrokes, Ansons and Venoms being placed on readiness. In the event the Saudi force capitulated and the only air action was taken by the transport aircraft which landed at Buraimi to collect POWs and wounded.

The Saudis continued to promote discontent amongst tribal leaders within Muscat and Oman, culminating in a revolt by Imam Ghalib in central Oman — an inhospitable area centred upon Nizawa. The latter place was duly taken by the Sultan's forces, supported by RAF aircraft. Aircraft also patrolled the border area to prevent infiltration by the so-called Omani Liberation Army. The unsettled period continued into 1957 when, in June, rebel forces occupied a number of fortified towers in Jebel Kavr. On 22nd July Shackletons dropped warning notices on six towers, two days later Venoms commenced to RP each one in turn. As ground forces moved into the area a 'shoot-on-sight' policy was instituted allowing aircraft to attack any suitable targets. A number of rebels moved into the remote Jebel Akhdar region where they were promptly attacked by Shackletons of No 37 Squadron dropping 1000lb bombs. Such harrassing raids and propaganda drops, plus 'skyshout', continued through 1958 it being considered too difficult to assault the area. However, a new tactic was employed in early 1959 with assault parties led by Special Air Service teams — supported by Shackletons and Venoms, as well as Pembrokes and Beverleys for a host of communications and supply duties.

OMAN 1974

A detachment of four Wessex of No 72 Sqn operated in Dhofar during mid 1974 in support of Omani ground forces. The aircraft were flown to Masirah by Belfast and then deployed to Salalah as a Main Operating Base, being in place by early April. Over the eight months of the detachment the unit flew 1487 hours, moved 2750 tons of freight and 15 000 passengers. The major tasks involved supply, artillery positioning, aeromed, troop deployment, and airborne FAC (for SOAF Strikemasters).

KUWAIT 1961

In the early 1960s Iraq was going through a traumatic political period, one manifestation of this was an Iraqi claim, on 25th June 1961, to the territory of Kuwait. In early July Iraqi troops moved up to the border. Kuwait was an established British ally and a plea for help was made on 30th June — it was decided to move the Hunters of No 8 Sqn and No 208 Sqn to Bahrain. This was simply the first element in what was planned to be a major air and ground reinforcement, the Hunters being joined in due course by Canberras (at Sharjah) from Germany, whilst additional Canberras held readiness in Cyprus. The airlift of ground forces

was made difficult by the political stance of various countries in the region, overflight agreements proving somewhat tricky. Nevertheless, the Britannias, Beverleys and Hastings of Transport Command managed to move the troops and equipment into place such that a reasonable force was established by the end of the first week of July. It proved sufficient and the Iraqi threat lessened although the internal situation in that country remained fluid. The run-down of British forces was equally rapid and the offensive support aircraft had gone by the end of July.

ADEN 1959-1967

Aden was to prove a source of continual trouble for the British forces until an abandonment, with no regrets, of this inhospitable location in November 1967.

The intervention by Egyptian troops in the political upheaval in Yemen brought another disturbing influence into the region. In December 1963 the High Commissioner was attacked, leading to the declaration of a State of Emergency, whilst the National Liberation Front (NLF) promoted rebellion in the Radfan area — with Egyptian support and encouragement. Hunters, Shackletons and Belvederes were involved in operations in the affected area, the helicopters proving valuable during Operation NUTCRACKER (January 1964) with positioning 105mm guns on remote hilltops.

Yemeni aircraft attacked the village of Beihan on 13th March 1963, the local ruler demanded retalliation and so Hunters attacked the fort at Harib.

The Radfan troubles continued and ground forces had to be moved in to control the area, a task requiring a wide range of air support by Hunters, Shacks, Belvederes and Twin Pioneers (as well as Army Air Corps aircraft); on more than one occasion a ground party would be trapped by rebels — the appearance of ultra low-flying Hunters in a CAS role providing a rapid solution. Without this fire and movement support the task would have been impossible. This particular series of campaigns came to a conclusion in June 1964 when the tribesmen made the mistake of trying to fight a static conventional battle at Djebel Huriyah, allowing the government forces to employ superior firepower. Offensive operations had virtually ceased by October although the 'official' end was declared in March the following year.

Britain announced its intention of giving up the Aden base by the late 1960s but the internal unrest continued to grow under the control of FLOSY (Front for the Liberation of South Yemen) and its external supporters. The Radfan remained a centre of trouble although there was also an increase in unrest in the urban area of Aden itself. During 1965 the 'hearts and minds' campaign within the Radfan was having an impact. However, extremist factions grew more powerful during 1966 and offensive action increased, often trying to keep two of the opposing rebel factions apart. By early 1967 the internal security situation had been handed to British control, local police forces being unable or unwilling to provide security. The decision was taken in May to evacuate British dependants; at the same time there was an upsurge in anti-British feeling and sections of the Police and Army began to support the rebels. In June 1967 a revolt amongst the security forces, during which one helicopter was shot down, required British reinforcements to be airlifted to Aden. It was very much an expedient designed to allow British forces to disengage and then hold the Khormaksar area until the final evacuation could be effected. The last troops left on 29th November.

RHODESIA 1965-1979

On 11th November 1965 the government of Rhodesia declared independence from Britain in reponse to white minority perceptions that any deal agreed by Britain would favour the black population. This Unilateral Declaration of Independence was greeted with dismay but the Labour Government was reluctant to take action. An air and sea blockade was imposed as part of a series of economic sanctions, a primary aim being to deny oil imports to Rhodesia. Shackletons were involved in flying maritime patrols and co-operating with the Royal Navy. It was no more than a token effort as Rhodesia received a steady flow of supplies from South Africa. At the same time Zambia, ex Northern Rhodesia, was concerned over Rhodesian pressure and requested military assistance. The scale of this was limited to deployment of Javelin fighters, and an RAF Regiment contingent, but no ground forces.

Fifteen years later, November 1979, the Lancaster House Agreement was signed for the transfer of power to the black majority, the process to be supervised by a Commonwealth Monitoring Force. The RAF provided Hercules and Puma support for this tricky mission, most returning to their home bases the following February.

THE FAR EAST
NETHERLANDS EAST INDIES 1945-1946

The ending of the war with Japan did not signal the end of all hostilities in the area; many of the pre-war Colonial powers wished now to re-establish their control of various territories. However, in the NEI certain groups, armed and trained by the Japanese, had no desire to see the return of Dutch authority. An Allied Task Force was assembled to recover the area, especially Batavia and Sumatra, and to expedite the release of Allied POWs believed to be held on these islands. No 904 (Thunderbolt) Wing moved to Kemajoran, this airfield becoming the main base for the entire air striking force — which at one stage reached over 100 aircraft (reinforcements being Spitfires, Mosquitos, Dakotas, Beaufighters, Liberators and Catalinas.) The initial deployment to Sumatra was of Spitfires to Medan.

The first major operation took place against the town of Soerabaya in November with air support for 5th Division's ground assault. Dakotas provided air supply for this and for an encircled Gurkha detachment at Magelang. Ground forces moving towards the POW camps were also attacked by rebels and so air strikes were called in to keep the offensive moving. The worst incident was 23rd November when the 22 crew and passengers on a force-landed Dakota of No 31 Squadron were murdered by rebels. By late December the urban areas were reasonably quiet but rural areas still harboured rebel groups and all road movements had to be air escorted.

The new year opened with a period of bad weather restricting air operations but by March the situation was once again quite active, although negotiations were making some progress. On the air side the major problem was the rapid deterioration of the Mosquitos due to extreme humidity — they were quite simply falling apart. An air evacuation of POWs was agreed and the first such flight took place on 20th May. From that date onwards there was a gradual hand-over of control from British forces to Dutch forces and by late November the RAF had left the NEI.

FRENCH INDO-CHINA 1945-1946

On 8th September 1945 an advanced party landed at Tan Son Nhut airfield, Saigon as part of the Allied force taking control of the country from the Japanese. Allied forces were instructed to hand control back to the French as soon as the situation was stable. In the meantime Spitfires of No 273 Squadron and Mosquitos of No 684 Squadron flew routine patrols of the area around Saigon. French forces arrived in October and conflict broke out with the anti-French Viet Minh. Although the RAF started to withdraw on handing over to the French, Spitfires did fly support missions for the French garrison at Banme Thuet when this was attacked by Viet Minh forces. Nevertheless, the withdrawal went ahead as planned and by April 1946 the last significant RAF contribution was over.

'AMETHYST' INCIDENT

When HMS *Amethyst* was attacked by Chinese artillery on 20th April 1949 as it sailed up the Yangtze river, there began a 3-month 'siege' of the trapped vessel. Amongst the British relief units were Sunderlands of No 88 Squadron, which flew missions to land alongside the ship.

KOREAN WAR 1950-

American and Soviet forces occupied South and North Korea respectively at the end of World War Two and despite UN efforts to bring about re-unification of the country it remained divided, and fortified, at the 38th parallel. The southern part of the country became the Republic of Korea as American forces withdrew. However, on 25th June 1950 the North Koreans invaded intent on seizing control of the entire country. The offensive was rapid as South Korean forces collapsed. The aggression was condemned in the UN and American forces were deployed to shore up the defenders whilst a UN force was assembled. Britain joined the task force on 28th June and Hong Kong became a major supply point and staging post. RAF participation in the conflict was never large, Spitfires defended Hong Kong and Sunderlands of the Far East Flying Boat Wing joined in the blockade of North Korean ports as well as providing mine surveillance and weather recce.

The formation in July 1951 of the 1st Commonwealth Division included air support from two Auster units (1903 and 1913 Flights), both units saw extensive operational employment, flying almost 3000 sorties. A number of RAF 'experts' were attached to the American 5th Tactical Air Force and others flew Meteors with No 77 Squadron RAAF.

MALAYAN EMERGENCY 1948-1960

During the Second World War the British had armed the anti-Japanese communist guerillas in Malaya; after the war these same guerillas used their power, and the presence of one million Chinese in Malaya, to try and seize power. As the situation deteriorated a State of Emergency was declared on 16th June 1948; reinforcements were flown in to assist in the restoration of law and order.

100 Squadron Lincoln on detachment to Malaya 1950.

The Malayan Communist Party (later MRLA -Malayan Races Liberation Army) comprised some 2500 terrorists in 1948, their strongholds being the rubber plantations where a majority of the workers were Chinese who provided support, such as food supplies. The initiative in the early years lay with the guerillas, their numbers increased to around 8000 and they held a firm grip on many of the rural districts, although failing to acquire a firm base in the towns and cities. The British Director of Operations, Lt Gen Sir Harold Briggs, devised a two-fold plan — to cut the terrorists off from their sources of supply (and recruits) and then to seek and destroy the forest bands themselves. This plan was to remain the essence of the British campaign throughout the Emergency and as resources became available to make it viable so it began to take effect. Initial air resources were inadequate for the proposed type of operation and facilities in Malaya were few and afar between, an important task during the first two years of the Emergency was the provision of new airfields and landing strips.

Neither side made much impact in the early months of the conflict although by mid 1950 the Communist organisation was well established and efficient, averaging 500 incidents a month, despite a high casualty rate. The government response was to accelerate the move of villagers to new secure sites and to concentrate on the control of key areas. The air element of the original Task Force at Kuala Lumpur comprised three Spitfires

Air strike on a patch of Malayan jungle 1949.

Brigands of 45 Squadron, 1950.

from No 60 Squadron, the first air strike being mounted against a CT base in Perak. This offensive element was gradually increased with the arrival of more Spitfires, Beaufighters, Tempests and even Sunderlands. A major increase in strike capability came with the first medium bomber detachment from Bomber Command; under Operation MUSGRAVE eight Lincolns of No 57 Squadron deployed to Tengah in March 1950. This was the start of a routine of Bomber Command squadron rotation, first by Lincoln and then Canberra (as Operation MILEAGE) aircraft, which lasted throughout most of the Emergency. June 1950 also brought Australian involvement with the arrival of Lincolns from No 1 Squadron RAAF. It was a similar story with the transport force, the need to increase the range of types and so enhance overall capability. The primary aims of the transport force were to aid the mobility and flexibilty of ground forces, sustain operations in areas of deep jungle for prolonged periods, and provide communications for command and control elements. Dakotas and Valettas provided the bulk of the medium range transport, operating from January 1951 as the Far East Transport Wing, for movement of supplies within the theatre but also for air-dropping to jungle outposts and patrols. During the five weeks of Operation HAYSTACK in mid 1948 the Dakotas of No 110 Squadron operating from Taiping dropped 220 containers of supplies; in the first two months of 1949 the total supply drop was 156,000 lb, these figures were small in comparison to the effort expended at later stages of the conflict (eg Operation VALIANT November 1953 with 728, 647 lb of supplies). The other side of the transport force was that provided by the light aircraft, primarily Austers. These aircraft performed a wide range of roles and as their numbers increased in the early years of the Emergency so they came to play an increasing part in the overall success. Of similar importance, but often ignored, were the photo recce aircraft employed on 'Firedog' missions, No 81 Squadron operating throughout the period of the conflict, flying thousands of sorties to provide valuable intelligence for air and ground operations. During the conflict the Squadron was equipped with Spitfire and Mosquito aircraft, acquiring Meteors and Pembrokes in 1953 and 1956 respectively. The Auster units also carried our visual and photo recce. The only PR reinforcement was towards the later years with the presence of Canberra detachments on Operation PLANTERS PUNCH, the first such being No 542 Squadron in May 1955.

These control policies were having an effect by late 1951 and the CTs withdrew to their jungle bases to try and recover; however, the security forces were not prepared to sit and wait and began a series of successful jungle operations in which air power proved significant.

Overall air offensive strength was affected during the early 1950s by a series of re-equipment programmes which introduced a new range of aircraft types to the conflict, the most important being the Hornet and Vampire. One air element which developed during this period was the helicopter, the success of the Dragonfly equipped Far East CASEVAC flight led to its expansion to squadron status as No 194 Squadron, February 1953. This unit, along with Whirlwinds of 848 NAS, provided a new type of air mobility for ground forces, as well as performing a range of other tasks. The helicopter Wing was strengthened by the arrival of No 155 Squadron in October 1954 and despite a number of serviceability problems proved its worth in the difficult jungle terrain moving supplies and troops to remote areas and carrying out numerous CASEVACs.

By 1955 the rate of terrorist incidents had dropped to around 65 a month and the CT leaders were prepared to negotiate a settlement, although this broke down without any progress having been made. The programme of airfield development in Malaya had by now provided eleven airfields suitable for medium transports plus an extensive network of grass strips and helicopter landing sites. This was to prove decisive in the control of jungle areas as security force bases could be supplied and reinforced by air.

The mid 1950s were also the peak of air offensive strength, the Bomber Command detachments now being flown by Canberras, and with techniques established and effective. Two main types of offensive action were taken, direct bombing of CT camps — often applied to sites beyond the reach of a ground force, and selective bombing to push a terrorist group towards an ambush zone. A variety of techniques were applied to assist the attackers in finding their targets in the dense jungle, one of the most successfull was the Auster Mark, whereby an Auster would use smoke to mark the target area. A 'typical' maximum effort attack might consist of an initial wave of Lincolns dropping 1000 lb bombs, followed by bomb/RP attacks from Vampires and Hornets, plus possible strafing of the area. A subsequent series of attacks over the next 48 hours would involve dropping anti-personnel bombs in order to, "harrass the survivors and create the greatest feeling of anxiety and uncertainty." This latter element was all part of the pysops element of the conflict, an element that included the use of propaganda leaflets and broadcasts ('skyshout'). The air transport force remained a key element and was enhanced by the arrival of Pioneers and Pembrokes, aircraft capable of using the remote strips, relieving the Austers of some of this work and increasing payload capability.

The continued failure of the CT to achieve any lasting success and the general percepetion that the government was winning the campaign led to a further decline in terrorist strength as surrenders increased and the civilian population withdrew their support. 1956 onwards saw a gradual reduction in air strength, partly as a result of other commitments but also as targets became fewer and less profitable.

Malaya became independent on 31st August 1957 but the conflict continued until the last of the guerilla groups fled into Thailand; the Malayan Emergency was declared to be at an end on 31st July 1960.

BORNEO-INDONESIA CONFRONTATION 1962-1966
During 1961 an agreement was reached for a federation of Malaya, Singapore and the territories of north Borneo to be established by mid 1962. However, President Sukarno of Indonesia also had plans for a 'Greater Indonesia' which included various claims in Borneo; a third factor was an independence movement in Borneo (the TNKU, North Borneo National Army). The revolt opened in Borneo on 8th December 1962 and to quell the disturbances a detachment of the Gurkha Rifles was airlifted to Brunei and Labuan.

Other areas of the country were also effected and so Twin Pioneers were used to deploy troops to trouble spots; meanwhile, Hunters provided air support and harrassed rebel areas. By 14th December the revolt in Brunei was over but the border regions of Sarawak and Sabah were still tense as Indonesian support for the rebels became more obvious. Despite continued, but generally small-scale, disturbances moves towards federation continued, the London Agreement of July 1963 providing the basis for the new Federation of Malaya to come into effect on 16th September. Infiltration across the border from Indonesia increased, as did the number of deep penetration raids many of which now included Indonesian regular troops. The main counter to these raids was provided by jungle patrols and the use of ambush set-ups, troops having been flown into position by helicopter.

A four-month cease-fire in early 1964 was followed by signs of a major build-up of Indonesian forces, which was countered by a reinforcement of both air and ground forces. As the infiltrations continued to grow in number and size the use of air mobility of troops and weapons became vital to the British policy of containment; the initiative in such hostile territory always lay with the attacker and so rapid reaction by the defender was essential. Fire-bases were established in the jungle and numerous helicopter and light aircraft operating strips were built.

After a further round of failed talks in Japan (Tokyo Summit June 1964) Indonesian forces landed on the mainland of Malaya to try and exploit divisions within the Federation. In August Indonesian troops landed in Johore and there was an airborne landing at Labis — both were rapidly defeated. Further similar operations over the following months were equally unsuccesful. During the same period large numbers of Indonesian troops made attacks on the fire-bases, more British reinforcements were sent to the area and an air and naval task force was assembled. British forces were now given authority to penetrate up to 11 miles inside Indonesia on hot pursuit operations.

In August 1965 Singapore left the Federation but this had no impact on the conduct of operations. The end of the conflict came when growing political discontent in Indonesia created a climate whereby negotiations could proceed.

The period of Confrontation was declared to be at an end on 4th August 1966.

Air power had played a vital role — e.g average troop lift of 19,000 a month, 2 million lbs of supplies air landed and a further 2 million air dropped.

THAILAND 1962
As part of the SEATO defence involvement against a possible invasion of Thailand by Pathet Lao guerillas, the RAF sent six Hunters and one Canberra to Thailand in support of a small ground force. In the event no action was needed and these forces soon withdrew.

INDIA 1962
The Chinese invasion of northern India in October 1962 brought a call from the Indian government for assistance. British response to this request included twelve Javelins deployed, along with American forces, on an air defence 'exercise' of key Indian cities.

COD WARS
During the various fishing limits disputes with Iceland, often called the 'Cod Wars', Nimrod MPA flew numerous patrols.

CAMPAIGNS 1971-1992
FALKLANDS CONFLICT 1982
When Vulcan XM607 dropped its load of 1000lb bombs on Port Stanley airfield in the early hours (0745 GMT) of 1st May 1982 it must have, at last, been obvious to the Argentinian Government that Britain was prepared to fight to regain the islands. Although the Falklands War could very much be considered a naval operation, including the major air effort being provided by RN Sea Harriers and helicopters, the RAF did play a major role in certain aspects of the campaign.

The Argentinian invasion of 2nd April had taken the military planners by surprise but the reaction was rapid as contingency plans were brought into effect. The major problem facing a military operation to re-take the islands was the distance from the UK base, thus a naval campaign would be needed, and the absence of airields from which to operate conventional aircraft — the nearest being Wideawake airfield on Ascension Island.

Within 24 hours the first air transport sorties were en route to Ascension and the build-up was underway. The air transport aspects of this, and almost every other, campaign are all too often ignored in favour of the more 'glamorous' sharp end but AT played an essential part in logistical support both within the UK and to the operational theatre. The same is true of the endless hours of maritime surveillance undertaken by the Nimrods in the shipping lanes between Britain-Ascension-Falklands. The only way to get the Vulcan to Port Stanley and back was by means of extensive and carefully planned air-to-air refuelling from Victor tankers, the vital role of AAR was to be one of the great lessons of this conflict and prompted the RAF to review its AAR assets.

While the naval Task Force commenced operations further Vulcan sorties were flown, the aircraft now specialising in a defence suppression role carrying Shrike anti-radiation missiles. On 3rd May Harrier GR.3s of No 1 Squadron left St Mawgan en route to Ascension where they deployed onto the container ship *Atlantic Conveyor* for the journey to the Falklands. The GR.3s were needed to supplement the limited ground attack capability of the already overworked Sea Harriers. The RAF Harriers flew their first operational missions on 30th May and from that point onwards were heavily involved in CAS missions, losing a number of aircraft to ground fire. The other RAF element was provided by a single Chinook of No 18 Squadron, three other aircraft having been lost when *Atlantic Conveyor* was sunk, this aircraft proving the value of its type by performing way beyond its design specification.

The conflict ended with the Argentinian surrender on 14th June. However, British forces have maintained a strong presence on the islands. The rather poor facilities at Port Stanley were duly replaced by a new airfield at Mount Pleasant from where the RAF keeps an eye on the South Atlantic.

GULF CONFLICT 1991

The Iraqi invasion of Kuwait on 1st August 1990 brought an immediate international response and UN condemnation. Within a matter of days the country was occupied and Iraqi forces appeared ready to move into Saudi Arabia. To counter this renewed threat the United States launched Operation DESERT SHIELD to move forces into the area to protect Saudi Arabia. Britain responded to a Saudi call for help and Tornado F.3 aircraft on detachment to Cyprus were deployed to Saudi Arabia to provide air cover, flying their first CAPs within hours of arrival. During the remainder of 1990 intense diplomatic efforts were made to persuade Iraq to withdraw from Kuwait but despite a plethora of UN resolutions applying increasing economic and

political pressure and isolation within the international community this they refused to do. Whilst this was continuing the Allied forces in Saudi and associated Gulf states continued to build up, partly to enforce the UN-sanctioned trade embargo, the maritime element of which involved RAF Nimrods working in conjunction with surface forces. The initial build-up was concerned with the prevention of an invasion of Saudi Arabia but it had become obvious by November that the Allies would need to build up an offensive option to demonstrate their intent to recover Kuwait. On 1st January the UN deadline for an Iraqi withdrawal passed and the Allies were authorised to use military force.

In the early hours of 17th January 1991 the first Allied air strikes went into action intent on crippling the Iraqi air defence, command and control, and nuclear/chemical warfare systems. Included in this first series of attacks were the Tornado GR.1s on long-range missions to hit Iraqi airfields. As the air offensive increased in tempo Tornado GR.1 made day and night attacks on targets in Iraq, Jaguars carried out interdiction missions in Kuwait and anti-shipping sorties in the northern Gulf, and Tornado GR.1A recce aircraft flew night missions along lines of communications and other targets. Most of the offensive missions were air-refuelled by Victor or VC.10 tankers and the Nimrods continued their maritime work as well as carrying out a number of special missions. Strategic and tactical transport was provided by Tristar, VC.10 and Hercules, the latter performing its usual wide range of tasks. Helicopter support was provided by Chinook and Puma detachments.

AAR was essential to ops in the Gulf region — VC10 to Tornado.

With the collapse of the Iraqi air defence network and the consequent reduction in SAM threat it was no longer essential for attack missions to operate at low level and so Tornado attack missions moved to medium level. Losses to this point had been less than expected overall although a number of Tornado GR.1s had failed to return. The change to medium level also required a change of weapon and tactic and so LGBs were employed for attacks against bridges, airfield targets (primarily aircraft shelters) and industrial installations. The use of LGBs also required a laser designator and in the absence of such for the Tornado, other than the two in-theatre trial TIALD pods, brought the Buccaneers into the war. These aircraft provided designation for Tornado missions as well as self-designating for their own bombs.

Throughout the conflict the Tornado F.3s flew CAP missions around the border areas.

Whilst the air victory in Operation DESERT STORM was very much an American one, based on the sheer scale of the American effort, the RAF contribution was significant, especially in the field of specialist weapons such as the JP233 anti-airfield weapon.

Tornado GR.1 'Foxy Killer' flew numerous Gulf War missions.

IRAQ 1991-1992

The end of the conflict did not mean the end of RAF involvement in the area. Despite his humiliating defeat Sadam Hussein continued to wield strong control within Iraq. A Kurdish rebellion launched in March 1991 was met with fierce opposition by the Iraqi army. As a result a multi-national force was assembled to give humanitarian assistance in support of UN Security Council Resolution 688 — and Iraqi forces were warned to step aside or face military action. Under Operation PROVIDE COMFORT, RAF Hercules, Puma and Chinook detachments undertook air supply to the Kurds. The first air drop of supplies by Hercules was 8th April 1991, following a proposal by the Prime Minister to establish temporary safe havens. All sorties being escorted by tactical aircraft in case of Iraqi intervention. Helicopter operations commenced in mid April using a forward base at Silopi with a main detachment base at Diyarbakir. Intensive operations were flown in hazardous terrain and in appalling weather. The air supply task was terminated in July when a no-fly zone was established banning Iraqi aircraft from flying above the 36th parallel. Operation WARDEN, the RAF name for this mission, began in September 1991. Since that date, RAF Jaguars and Harriers have flown routine recce sorties to monitor Iraqi activity in line with UN resolutions.

The revolt of the the 'Marsh' Arabs in southern Iraq was largely prompted by the Iraqi defeat in the Gulf War, these people sought independence from the repressive Baghdad regime. Unfortunately the Iraqi military had rapidly recovered from their defeat at the hands of the coalition and so took offensive action, destroying villages in the marsh area. This use of air power was considered to be contrary to the terms of the UN resolutions and as a result a second a no-fly zone was imposed south of the 32nd parallel. The RAF have participated in this operation since its inception and have contributed Tornado aircraft under the name Operation JURAL.

FORMER YUGOSLAVIA 1993

The requirement to support the United Nations operations in the former Yugoslavia led to a C-130 Hercules aircraft flying humanitarian relief supplies into Sarajevo, under the threat of gunfire. Nimrod Maritime Patrol Aircraft have been flying missions over the Adriatic in support of the UN trade sanctions in place against Serbia and Montenegro and the arms embargo in force against the whole of former Yugoslavia. Tornado F3 aircraft and their air-to-air refuelling support are taking part in operations to enforce a No-Fly Zone (NFZ) over Bosnia, imposed to prevent the use of air power by the warring parties. Sentry E-3D aircraft continue to participate in the monitoring of the NFZ. All of these operations, as with the Gulf commitment, are ongoing tasks. Most recently, 12 Jaguar aircraft have deployed to the region to take part in a NATO-led operation to provide close air support to the UN Protection Force.

BELIZE

The return of No 1417 Flight's Harriers from Belize in 1993 saw the first major easing of tension in this area since the original threat from Guatemala over 30 years ago. Over this period the RAF maintained a standing force, usually fixed wing and helicopter, to support the ground forces.

II(AC) Squadron GR.1As on the ramp at Dhahran for Op JURAL.